HEALTH CARE SYSTEMS AROUND THE WORLD

HEALTH CARE SYSTEMS AROUND THE WORLD

Characteristics, Issues, Reforms

MARIE L. LASSEY
University of Idaho

WILLIAM R. LASSEY
Washington State University

MARTIN J. JINKS
Washington State University

PRENTICE HALL
Upper Saddle River, New Jersey 07458

Library of Congress Cataloging-in-Publication Data

LASSEY, MARIE L.
    Health care systems around the world : characteristics, issues,
reforms / Marie L. Lassey, William R. Lassey, Martin J. Jinks.
        p. cm.
    Includes bibliographical references and index.
    ISBN 0-13-104233-5
    1. Medical policy—Cross-cultural studies.   2. Medical care—Cross
-cultural studies.   I. Lassey, William R.   II. Jinks,
Martin J.   III. Title.
    RA393.L328   1997
    362.1—dc20
                                                96–10745
                                                CIP

Editorial director: *Charlyce Jones Owen*
Editor in chief: *Nancy Roberts*
Acquisitions editor: *Fred Whittingham*
Marketing manager: *Chaunfayta Hightower*
Editorial/production supervision and interior design: *Joan Stone*
Copy editor: *Peter Zurita*
Buyer: *Mary Ann Gloriande*
Editorial assistant: *Pat Naturale*

This book was set in 10/11 Baskerville by
DM Cradle Associates and was printed and
bound by Hamilton Printing Company. The
cover was printed by Phoenix Color Corp.

Prentice-Hall International (UK) Limited, *London*
Prentice-Hall of Australia Pty. Limited, *Sydney*
Prentice-Hall Canada Inc., *Toronto*
Prentice-Hall Hispanoamericana, S.A., *Mexico*
Prentice-Hall of India Private Limited, *New Delhi*
Prentice-Hall of Japan, Inc., *Tokyo*
Pearson Education Asia Pte. Ltd., *Singapore*
Editora Prentice-Hall do Brasil, Ltda., *Rio de Janeiro*

To our wonderful families

Parents
William and Grace Lassey
Edward and Maxine Jones

Children and spouses
Sherry and Wes Hassard
Dione and Saul Greenberg
Derek Sellars
Maureen and Mat Rude
Dara Sellars
David Jinks
Sara Jinks

Grandchildren
Dustin Hassard
Chandra Edwards
Alyssa Sellars
Nicole Hassard

CONTENTS

PREFACE

Health care has become a major focus of international concern and a primary political, social, and economic issue in nearly every country. The resources required to meet public demand for high-quality and high-technology services are substantial, especially since the average length of life is increasing in most countries with consequent higher per capita expenditures.

Some countries rely on government-sponsored and managed health care, whereas at the other extreme, private enterprise provides the care. Most countries are located somewhere on a continuum between these extremes. In each case, income taxes, payroll taxes, or insurance systems are used to generate the needed revenue. The costs to governments, with accompanying tax increases, have grown steadily, as have insurance costs. When employers finance the insurance, the proportion of business expenditures to support health insurance has expanded to the point that the costs are threatening profits and international competitiveness.

As the proportion of the total economy required for health care in a country increases, other important services may be crowded out or endangered, such as education, environmental protection, and long-term social security. Overall economic growth may be jeopardized as well. When governments assume all or a major part of the responsibility for health care, the potential problem is even greater.

Reforms of one kind or another are therefore underway in all countries, driven in part by necessity but also by citizen and special interest group dissatisfaction with the current state of affairs. Inequity and lack of access to services remain a problem for many countries, most notably the United States. Even in countries with relatively universal access to care, coupled with comprehensive services, citizens are demanding changes that improve efficiency, increase quality of services, expand the use of technology, and improve primary care. Governments are faced with the need to satisfy these demands *and* constrain or lower costs at the same time that increasing proportions of the population are retired, aged, and in need of more health care as well as expanded long-term care. Some countries appear to be meeting these challenges much more effectively than others, as we shall see in the chapters that follow.

There is thus good reason to explore implications of these major issues through an examination of health care over a wide range of countries. Better understanding of how health care works on a number of dimensions can increase appreciation of both the underlying basis for the current "crisis" and the options available.

The following primary goals are pursued:

- Development of a general framework that describes the components of health care and the factors that influence its effective delivery (Chapter 1)
- Description and summary comparison of the demographic, political, economic, social, and health status characteristics of selected countries in North America, Western and Central Europe, and Asia (Chapter 2)
- Detailed summaries of health care in each country, including special features of the health care system, history, demography, political factors, social organization of health care, economic characteristics and problems, and recent or planned reforms (Chapters 3–15)
- Comparisons of some of the cultural, political, social, economic, and other factors that contribute to effective health care organization and service delivery (Chapters 16–17)
- Conclusions about what we have learned and what this might imply for the future (Chapter 18)

Our interest in this topic arises from considerable firsthand experience over many years. One or more of the primary authors has had professional experience in each of the countries examined in these pages. Marie L. Lassey, Ph.D., Department of Sociology and Anthropology, University of Idaho, is an associate professor and a medical sociologist, and has had professional experience in Canada, Japan, Germany, France, The Netherlands, Czech Republic, and Hungary, as well as the United States. William R. Lassey, Ph.D., Graduate Program in Health Policy and Administration, Washington State University, is an economist and professor of health policy and administration. He has had

professional experience in each of the countries noted previously, as well as in Mexico and the United Kingdom. Martin J. Jinks, Pharm.D., Department of Pharmacy Practice, Washington State University, was a professor of pharmacy and had professional experience in the United Kingdom, Russia, China, Japan, and other countries of Asia.

Other coauthors of selected chapters include Vaclav Benes, M.D., professor, Postgraduate Medical School, Prague, Czech Republic; Miklos Fodor, M.D., director, Postgraduate Education Program in Family Practice, Budapest, Hungary; Vlastik Martinu, Ph.D., director, ECOLAB, Znojmo, Czech Republic; and Sam Salek, Ph.D., Department of Clinical Pharmacy, Welsh School of Pharmacy, University of Wales, Cardiff, Wales, United Kingdom.

ACKNOWLEDGMENTS

We enjoyed outstanding assistance and support from a number of our colleagues. From the University of Idaho: Donald Tyler, chair, Department of Sociology/Anthropology; Roderick Sprague, professor and director, Laboratory of Anthropology; and Kurt Olsson, dean, College of Letters and Science. From Washington State University: Mahmoud Abdel-Monem, dean, College of Pharmacy; and William H. Gray, campus dean, Washington State University at Spokane. From the University of Wales, Cardiff: David Luscombe, chair, Department of Clinical Pharmacy.

A large number of other individuals have contributed to the formation of this volume. First and foremost, we are indebted to Vicki Croft, health sciences librarian, Washington State University, who guided the search for literature and produced an excellent and wide-ranging list of references that formed the basis for most of the chapters. Laura Larsson, head librarian, University of Washington Health Services library, was also very helpful in identifying important bibliographies and references. Lydia McNulty at the

Cooperative Academic Library in Spokane searched for and discovered many of the needed articles and books. We are thankful to the support staff who helped in assorted ways to complete the work, especially Cindy Beaty and Julie Estes.

Our students made important suggestions based on critical reading of drafts of many of the chapters. From the University of Idaho: Heather Albers, Gayle Anderson, Andy Ashla, A. Brooke Bennett, Jacqueline Bicandi, Justine Ely, Lori Everingham, Eric A. Gural, Justin Harvey, April Johnson-Berry, Mindy Krasselet, Jennifer Lajeunesse, Gregory Lawrence, Mary Theresa Luke, Rochelle Mendoza, Marigay Munn, Mike Myhre, Megan Patten, Scott Phillips, Monte Russell, and Debbie Shrum. From Washington State University: Steve Anderson, Nanette Dowling, Cynthia Haffner, Ryan Jacobsen, Tom Lienhard, Stephen Reichard, Kelly Rochelle Stanford, and Dianne Venzon.

Grants for travel and research from the University of Idaho and Washington State University were most helpful in enabling us to collaborate with colleagues and collect data in several countries.

Several colleagues were generous in providing critical reviews of earlier versions of selected chapters: Katerina Ciharova, M.D., director, Department of International Relations, Ministry of Health of the Czech Republic; Frantisek Osanec, consultant, Advisor to the Ministry of Health of the Czech Republic; Mort Doran, M.D., surgeon and professor of medicine, University of Calgary, Alberta, Canada; John Larson, M.D., surgeon, Spokane, Washington; and Burt Larson, M.D., retired surgeon, Alberta, Canada.

Preparation of this book ended on a very sad note with the untimely death of our co-author and good friend, Martin J. Jinks. He suffered a heart attack just before page proofs were to be reviewed for his chapter (with Sam Selak) on the United Kingdom.

Marie L. Lassey
William R. Lassey

1

Introduction: Basic Issues and Concepts

Accessibility of health care at reasonable quality and cost is among the great challenges of the day in all nations. Major progress has been made during recent years in expanding health care delivery, advancing the use of technology, improving quality, and raising the health status of populations. Policy makers and health professionals in each country are struggling, however, to implement additional reforms that will further improve health status while containing the growth in expenditures (Frenk, 1994: 30).

A number of major issues demand attention:

- Health status is at the core of life quality for individuals in every country. Citizens place great value on having access to the kind of services that will diminish illness and pain, while curing disease and trauma, as these conditions occur in themselves, their relatives, friends, and public heroes. Access to quality health care is probably among the core values in all societies (Blendon et al., 1993: 1011).
- Health care is among the largest economic activities in every advanced country and is among the most visible social enterprises. It consumes between 6 and 15 percent of national income (Gross Domestic Product, or

GDP) in all industrialized countries. Expenditures continue to rise steadily everywhere. Health care providers—hospitals, physicians, pharmacists, long-term care institutions, mental health care professionals, and others—are collectively among the largest employment sectors in most communities and nationally, representing approximately 10 percent of national employment in several countries. It is thus little wonder that health care is the subject of vigorous debate (Aaron and Schwartz, 1990; Peet, 1991).

- Health care is of broad international concern because all nations increasingly compete in the same market. Health care is financed largely through payroll deductions, which are a substantial segment of the overall cost of goods and services. The cost and financing of health care clearly have substantial influence on productivity and product costs (Steslicke, 1989).
- Numerous health care–related social challenges are demanding international attention. The issues include the question of how to meet the needs of the growing elderly population and provide services to low-income citizens. Increasing demand from aging populations is forcing major adjustments in other social services. All of the industrialized nations face the issue of increased length of life and consequent health care demands. Fifteen percent or more of the

population is over age 65 in several European countries, and an increasing proportion is over age 85. This older population consumes 30 to 40 percent of health care resources in most countries—three to four times as much cost per capita as the younger population. Chronic and expensive health conditions become more predominant in older people. The aging of populations thus offers major long-term care challenges in most countries (Rosenthal and Frenkel, 1992).

- Technological problems include the question of how to incorporate appropriate technology that will improve care and increase efficiency. There is greater demand for advanced technology than available resources can supply—a universal problem that is forcing many countries to limit use of some valuable medical procedures. Deliberate rationing is underway or under consideration in many countries. The *overuse* of technology to the detriment of patients may be an emerging problem in some countries (Aaron and Schwartz, 1990; McPherson, 1990; Graig, 1993).

- Nearly all countries are presently engaged in major health care reform processes that have enormous social and economic implications. Cost-cutting reforms are advocated everywhere—especially in the most advanced nations with the most universal and comprehensive systems of care. Health care is under sharp examination and critique by governments, the mass media, and individual citizens.

These issues are causing public priorities in a high proportion of countries to change. A level and quality of services that were viewed as relatively satisfactory at one point in time are now defined as quite inadequate (particularly in the former communist countries). Because of rapid communication and information exchange, these reform processes are contributing to convergence among nations in forms of health care organization, financing, and delivery. We are learning from each other on a daily basis (Anderson, 1989b; Field, 1989; Roemer, 1991, 1993; Graig, 1993).

This short list of important reasons for examining international health care is by no means exhaustive. Table 1-1 summarizes several additional specific issues (also not

exhaustive) that must be addressed by most countries during the immediate future—if citizens, health care providers, and governments are to be satisfied with provision of health care.

Apart from dealing with these major issues, the study of reform and change in health care provides an opportunity to learn important features about other countries as well as one's own in the course of examining evolution of new social and economic institutions to meet a highly important societal need.

Table 1-1 Common Challenges to National Health Care Systems

- What are the cost-related and ethical limits on technological growth and innovation in health care? How do we identify the diagnostic and treatment choices that are affordable and improve the human condition?

- How do we control overspecialization in physician services while overcoming shortages of primary care specialists? How do we appropriately revise training and incentives for health service professionals?

- How do we deal with the changing composition of delivery systems, including consolidations and mergers of current institutions? How do we appropriately evaluate the potential for linking or integrating primary with secondary and tertiary care?

- What are the long-term impacts of high-technology information management systems with their vast potential for increased productivity, accountability, clinical applications, and improved management?

- How do we deal with the changing ethnic composition of populations in many countries as cross-border migration increases, including value shifts and cultural implications for health care?

- How do we interpret the problems of serving rural and urban-center populations, including the challenges of balancing cost and quality for remotely located and low-income citizens?

- What are the implications of globalization in the world economy and the challenges of maintaining national competitiveness, with associated challenges of cost control?

- How do we manage citizen concurrent demands for greater clinical effectiveness, improved quality, fiscal control, and greater value for the resources expended?

Source: Based on Shortell and Reinhardt, 1992: 5.

HEALTH CARE SYSTEM COMPONENTS

A health care system may be defined as *the combination of health care institutions, supporting human resources, financing mechanisms, information systems, organizational structures that link institutions and resources, and management structures that collectively culminate in the delivery of health services to patients.* This definition captures the main points to be dealt with in the following chapters. Several basic concepts in the definition are critical to the discussion that follows (Anderson, 1989a; Frenk, 1994: 23–27).

Institutions include local, state, and federal public health departments; public and private providers of health care services, such as hospitals, clinics, health maintenance organizations, and nursing homes; educational enterprises that provide training for health professionals; environmental health departments; and other types of organizations responsible for some dimension of health promotion, illness prevention, or health care.

Supporting human resources include public health professionals, physicians, dentists, health services administrators, nurses, pharmacists, psychologists, public health workers, social workers, allied health personnel such as medical technicians, and other professionals directly involved in health promotion, prevention of disease, or health care.

Financing mechanisms include direct government financing of services, national health insurance plans, private health insurance (including employer paid plans), managed care financing arrangements, payroll and other taxing systems that generate revenue for health care, private out-of-pocket expenditures, and any other sources that pay for the cost of care.

Information systems include computer networks within and between institutions, including electronic mail (e-mail); printed media such as journals, magazines, and newsletters; telephone systems including voice mail and data transmission; interactive television and other video systems; and any other information media or technology that facilitates sharing or exchange of information, summarizes and collates data, or generally contributes to greater understanding of health and health care. Information systems are obviously the key element in measuring the expenditures and outcomes for health promotion, illness prevention, and health care procedures, as well as for cost control.

Linking organizational mechanisms include local, state, and national associations of public health professionals, hospitals, physicians, nurses, health care administrators, pharmacists or pharmaceutical producers, rural health, health professions schools, and a great variety of other organizations that deliberately attempt to link together the organizational units related to health care.

Management structures include public health system administrative systems at federal, state, and local levels; administrative systems within provider institutions; management systems that link multiinstitutional organizations such as hospital chains; financing administration such as the U.S. Health Care Financing Administration and European sickness funds; and other management mechanisms that enable organizations to function effectively and efficiently. Health system components are summarized in Table 1-2.

Each of the major categories and subcategories plays a crucial role in operation of a health care system. However, there is wide variation between countries in the design and functioning of the subcategories—as the following chapters will indicate. For example, use of high-technology information systems is much more advanced in some countries than others. The use of "medical informatics" and computer systems for collecting, storing, and analyzing information is well developed in Western European and North American countries but is much less used in Eastern Europe or China.

Using computers for "technology assessment" has become a basic tool in analyzing data on services, costs, and outcomes. Managers and other health professionals use the

Table 1-2   Basic Components of Health
Promotion, Illness Prevention,
and Health Care Systems

Institutions	*Supporting Human Resources*
Public health departments:	Public health workers
Local, state, federal	Physicians
Hospitals	Dentists
Clinics	Health services
Practitioner offices	administrators
Health maintenance	Nurses
organizations	Pharmacists
Long-term care facilities	Psychologists
Mental health clinics	Social workers
University or college	Therapists: physical,
health profession	occupational, speech
schools	Nutritionists, dietitians
Technology units	Medical technologists
Financing Mechanisms	*Information Systems*
Government health finance	Interpersonal
units	communication
National health insurance	Computer networks,
Regional insurance	including e-mail
(sickness) funds	Journals, magazines,
Private health insurance	newsletters
Managed care organizations	Telephone systems,
Specialized insurance such	including voice mail
as Medicare and Medicaid	Interactive and other
Payroll and other taxes	video systems
Private out-of-pocket	
payment	
Gifts and endowments	
Linking Organizations	*Management Structures*
Public health associations	Public health
Medical associations	administrative systems
Hospital associations	Primary, secondary, tertiary
Nursing associations	care administration
Pharmacy associations	Institutional provider
Rural health associations	administration
Mental health associations	Multiinstitutional
Managed care associations	administrative systems
	Financing systems
	administration
	Government

Source: Based on Anderson, 1989a; Frenk, 1994: 25.

results for decisions about the value of certain technologies. Computers are also a basic tool in quality assurance measurements and outcomes in some countries, but are barely used at all in other countries for these purposes. Nations without advanced understanding of computer technology may be increasingly disadvantaged in offering effective health care (Van Gennip and Gremy, 1993: 179).

The purpose of examining the detailed components of a health care system is to facilitate understanding of the key interrelationships and their significance for health outcomes. The health care *institutions* and *supporting health professionals* usually will be ineffective without a close and effective linkage to a functional and efficient *financing system*, appropriate *linkage mechanisms*, technologically advanced *information systems*, and effective organizational and resource *management*. In other words, health care is less effective in some countries because the components and relationships among components of the system are not adequately developed (Frenk, 1994: 24).

MAJOR INFLUENCES ON HEALTH CARE SYSTEMS

Historical and cultural influences pervade and define social organization, the political system, and the economic structure of a country. Fiscal realities have a profound influence on the kind of health care system a country can afford. But politics and culture have at least as much impact. Collectively, these interacting forces produce the structure and operational form of the health care system, whatever its adequacies or inadequacies in terms of good health status outcomes for the population.

The primary influences on overall health status of a population include a combination of the following:

- The general physical environment, including housing
- The political, cultural, community, and family environment
- Individual factors such as personality characteristics, genetic makeup, life-style, diet, tobacco or alcohol use, and exercise
- Encounters with the public or private health care system

Public health measures aimed at prevention of disease, illness, disability, and lowering death rates are increasingly understood as more important in the determination of overall population health status than is the nature or quality of the health *care* system (Smith and Giggs, 1988; Frenk, 1994: 21–22). Estimates suggest that 90 percent of the contributions to health status arise from these factors, whereas only 10 percent are a function of health care. The health care system is clearly not the major factor in creation of healthy populations. Nonetheless, there is value in maximizing the positive impact of the fraction that health care contributes to health status (Basch, 1990).

Environmental Influences

The physical environment is clearly a major contributor to health status. This has become painfully evident in locations with major pollution problems. Water pollution has been a major killer in many countries when unsanitary supplies are not available. Impure water has the potential to carry many types of waterborne diseases and continues to be a problem in some parts of most countries, but especially in less developed nations.

The recent shortening of life expectancy in Russia and other Eastern European countries is in part a direct result of severe air pollution from radiation and industrial production. The lengthening of life in Western European countries, on the other hand, is clearly due in part to environmental cleanup of air and water.

Quality of housing is also a major factor in the health of families and individuals. Good housing protects from the elements, insects, disease, and provides a locale for preparation of pure food and drink. Poor housing can contribute directly to exposures that can severely damage health.

The Historical Record

The historical development of a health care system may explain a lot about the cur-

rent system. For example, Germany initiated a national health care program in the late nineteenth century. Although not originally intended to serve all citizens, the system has evolved to nearly full coverage over more than 100 years. The earlier experience is reflected in the current commitment of German health professionals and citizens to universal and comprehensive care (Light and Schuller, 1986; Roemer, 1991).

Features that were refined over time include the following:

- Development of highly structured "sickness funds" as sponsors and payers for health care
- The relatively limited responsibility of government, which makes the rules but is not involved in direct operation of health care
- National cultural commitment to universal access and comprehensiveness
- Willingness until recently to commit an increasing proportion of national resources to health care and other social services

Public health, ambulatory care, hospital care, long-term care, and mental health care all have important roots in Germany's historical experience.

Common threads are often evident across several countries with some similarity of historical experience. The Western European countries, for example, are characterized by strong governmental intervention in health care and government rules for assuring universal access of citizens through a defined benefit package. Although health care is relatively comprehensive in each case, the availability of many types of technology is dependent on the economic advancement and cultural preferences of each country. The relative priority given to each type of technology varies widely (McPherson, 1990).

The form of financing and how it developed over time is a key ingredient in any system. The United Kingdom, for example, for fifty years has financed a national health care system through direct taxation of citizens. Primary care physicians ("general practitioners" in British parlance) were usually paid on the basis of *capitation* (a flat rate per enrolled individual, regardless of services provided), whereas specialists were largely paid *salaries.* In Canada, the system is national, but financing is under provincial control and physician payment has been on the basis of *fee for service* (payment for each service performed rather than per patient). In both countries, a tradition has evolved in support of public financing through taxation.

Demographic Influences

The characteristics of a country's population have a strong impact on the nature of the health care system. For example, the United States and Canada have vast rural areas with low-density population and many small jurisdictions. This makes delivery of health care much more difficult than in more densely populated and largely urban countries. On the other hand, the dense and low-income segments of the population in inner cities are also difficult to serve because practitioners are hesitant to live and work in these areas (Office of Technology Assessment, 1991).

Physicians have difficulty making an adequate living (from their viewpoint) in either sparsely populated rural areas or densely populated lower-income urban areas. Population-related issues, such as low incidence of private insurance, high incidence of elderly patients, lower average incomes, and lower average education create health financing problems. These issues are of much less significance in most European countries than in North America.

Culture Influences

Culture experience is clearly a key factor in the formation of health care systems. Traditions, values, beliefs, attitudes, and family structure significantly affect what kind of health care system will evolve. For example, citizens of European countries tend to believe that national and community responsibility are of great importance, whereas

Americans hold a deeper respect for individual autonomy, pluralism, and family responsibility. This explains in part why the Canadian and British systems of health care are unacceptable to many Americans, despite the higher satisfaction expressed by citizens of these countries toward their health care (Woolhandler and Himmelstein, 1991).

A Japanese hospital may look much like an American hospital. However, American hospitals place much more dependence on surgical procedures, whereas Japanese hospitals emphasize personal care, a pleasant atmosphere, and use of surgery only when absolutely essential. Medical technology is viewed as alienating and depersonalizing (Field, 1989: 19).

Most European countries, Canada, and Japan tend to have a strong sense of cultural and social "solidarity." That is, citizens feel mutual responsibility for each other. For example, citizens widely support use of tax or payroll deduction revenues to provide health care and social security for everyone, regardless of income. The sense of solidarity appears to be much lower in Russia, Central Europe, and the United States.

Political Influences

The political system in any country reflects its history, culture, and demography. Major decisions about organization and financing are determined politically in all national health care systems.

Public policy development guides the evolution of health care policies but varies considerably among countries. The following phases usually characterize health policy formation in democratic societies:

- Major efforts are made by public and/or private organizations to bring the issues of concern to the attention of politicians, who then propose new laws.
- Legislation is passed at the national or political subdivision level.
- Government units and interest groups responsible for the required actions enter a process to

legitimize the new policies with providers of health care and the public.

- Policies are transformed into regulations to be implemented by public and private agencies.
- Policies are eventually validated through public and provider acceptance.

Authoritarian political systems usually shorten this process somewhat, especially the first and last phases.

The interests of economically deprived groups are often represented in political decisions by public advocacy citizen groups who bring political power to bear on national health care issues. This led, for example, to initiation of a major national health program in Canada during the 1960s. Organizations of health care providers and insurers actively lobbied to protect their interests, but failed to counteract the public interest in universal health care under a tax-supported system.

Such interest groups as the American Association of Retired Persons (AARP) in the United States, with 35 million members, have gained immense influence on federal health care policy, particularly related to design and financing of such major programs as Medicare and Medicaid. Nonetheless, it was unable to secure the passage of major reforms in 1993 in the face of strong resistance by private insurers and major provider organizations that stood to lose influence and resources.

Social Influences

Characteristics of health organizational units tend to be somewhat unique from one country to another. For example, the public "polyclinic" as a delivery mechanism for ambulatory care characterized much of Eastern Europe under communism. It is difficult for health care professionals who were trained and worked under this system to visualize other alternatives.

Role of the family and community. As much as 90 percent of all health care episodes occur in the family. Most minor injuries and short-term illnesses—which constitute the great majority of needed care—are dealt with at this level. Methods of treating common diseases and injuries are taught by parents and grandparents to children and become the first dimension of any care system. Families may provide the only care in less developed countries and in low-income or isolated families where professional health care is not accessible. The formal health care system is largely uninvolved in these episodes in most countries (Kleinman, 1995).

Most *formal* health care occurs in the community where the family resides. Primary care providers do their work there, in physician offices or clinics, in hospitals, and in the wide range of settings noted in Table 1-2. It is in the family and community where culture, values, and ideology related to health care are formed and enforced.

Incentive and reward systems. Health care professionals are influenced by numerous incentives or rewards that attract and retain them in the health care professions. Such incentives have enormous influence on quality and effectiveness of the system. For example, adequate numbers of physicians were trained and available in most of the formerly communist countries. However, the incentive structure emphasized specialized training and provision of care in prestigious "institutes." Primary care provided in community "polyclinics" and public health programs was much less prestigious and greatly underfunded. Consequently, preventive care, primary services, and basic diagnostic technology were neglected, leading to poor health outcomes. Effective incentives in the organization and management of health care systems are crucial to efficient delivery of health services (Albert et al., 1992).

The social incentives that encourage young people to enter training for health careers are basic ingredients in medical education. Incentives, as well as attitudes and preferences, lead to choice of specialty and location of medical practice for physicians, nurses, pharmacists, and other health professionals. The type of incentives may result in high dedication and highly sophisticated primary care, or the opposite (Rosenblatt, 1992).

Sweden has had a modern high-technology system in place for many years, within a national and decentralized system, and with active citizen involvement at the local level. Good health outcomes are evident. The Czech Republic has a similarly long history of a national and socialized system, but a centralized and inefficient management system and weak incentives for quality care have led to less technology and considerably poorer outcomes. In both cases, social and behavioral characteristics, as well as incentive systems, have played a major role in determining results (Erikson, 1992; Janeckova and Hnilicova, 1992).

Structure of the health care system. Structural comparisons focus primarily on the organizational system for

- Implementing health policies and delivering health services
- Assuring and securing citizen access to services
- Providing universal insurance coverage for citizens
- Training professionals

For example, "regionalization" of health care services has become the organizational norm in most economically advanced countries. Day-to-day administration of health care is delegated by national governments to regions and communities. Nationally mandated organizational procedures are implemented through political subdivisions with responsibility for overseeing local services.

A major feature of the Swedish system, for example, is the powerful role played by the county councils (somewhat equivalent to state governments), which have primary responsibility for health care financing, management, and delivery. Counties also do health planning and regulation, provide ambulatory care, and finance most hospitals (Lindgren, 1990).

In the United Kingdom, regions of the country are divided into districts responsible for providing local health services. District health authorities directly manage primary care. Public hospitals are governed at the regional level. However, regional and district authorities make decisions based on national rules (Fearn, 1987).

In Germany, federal and state governments provide general oversight and generate needed resources through payroll taxes, while avoiding direct involvement in management of local health care. Decentralization is clearly the norm (Henke, 1990; Iglehart, 1991).

In Canada, the provinces are largely responsible for providing health care under general guidelines from the national level requiring basic benefits. Only limited financial assistance comes from the federal level. Management of services and insurance administration are handled by provincial governments.

Economic Factors

The level of expenditures on health care generally rises as per capita income grows and Gross Domestic Product (GDP) increases. That is, wealthier countries such as the United States, Canada, and Germany spend more on health care per capita than somewhat poorer countries such as the United Kingdom, the Czech Republic, Hungary, and Russia. Japan is to some degree an exception, with high incomes but somewhat lower per capita spending (Schieber and Poullier, 1990).

Those countries with a higher GDP per individual (higher per capita income) also tend to have better overall health status. The economic level of a country is thus closely related to the breadth and quality of the health care system and the health of citizens. For example, there is a close relationship between life expectancy at birth and GDP (Illsley, 1992).

The nature of the financing system, out-of-pocket cost to patients, and the overall costs to the society are all important to explain health care system operation. The specific mechanisms for financing health care vary considerably from one country to another, ranging from entirely private payment by individuals, to full financing through national taxes or payroll deductions. No two countries have exactly the same kind of system, although most European nations rely primarily on payroll deductions through employers (Graig, 1993).

Administration of health care in Sweden, the United Kingdom, Germany, and Canada is considerably more efficient from an economic standpoint, and somewhat less costly, than in the United States. The efficiencies are achieved in each case through nationally organized financing systems and a common insurance mechanism for primary, secondary, and tertiary care (Levin, Wolfson, and Akiyama, 1987; Woolhandler, Himmelstein, and Lewontin, 1993).

Interrelationships Among Influences

The following relationships illustrate the interactions among concepts and influences:

1. The physical environment, such as climate, altitude, precipitation, and particularly degree of purity, strongly affects health conditions. It is much more difficult to stay healthy in proximity to a polluted air or water supply, or in an environment where vegetation has been destroyed by mismanagement.
2. The history, cultural characteristics, customs, family structure, values, and attitudes lead to unique ways of defining health, health care provision, and priorities for use of resources.
3. The political or policy formation process forms the basis for organization, financing, cost control, and outcomes of health care.
4. Universality of access and benefits provided, via public or private insurance, public provision of health care, or other measures to provide services, affects health status and satisfaction of consumers.
5. Economic features of the system, such as the financing and reimbursement procedures, directly affect the proportion of national income expended and the universality of health care access.

THE VALUE OF INTERNATIONAL COMPARISONS

The process of health care development benefits enormously from comparing informa-

tion across national boundaries. Features of each system can be examined and evaluated—thus illuminating the common and contrasting patterns. Careful examination can determine which elements of organization, financing, cost control, or other variables seem to work well. Systems that fail to produce good results can be more adequately evaluated if they are compared with the workings of one or more other systems (Field, 1989: 5).

Moreover, comparisons among countries provide the basis for interesting scientific challenges—because of differences in types of health care activities measured and varied measurement techniques. The value of comparisons is improving rapidly as vigorous efforts are made to collect and standardize information through the initiatives of the World Health Organization (WHO), the World Bank, the Organization for Economic Cooperation and Development (OECD), and individual scientists. The challenge is to identify universal and measurable dimensions of health care experience that have the most impact on effective services (Parkin, McGuire, and Yule, 1989; Roemer, 1991).

Examination of the similarities and differences among countries can help us judge the features associated with high quality, universal access, and reasonable cost, as well as a number of other specific issues (Anderson, 1989b; Field, 1989; Roemer, 1991: 5; Illsley, 1992):

- Understanding and appreciating common health care problems and opportunities facing two or more countries.
- The relationship between the specific characteristics of health care delivery systems and health status outcomes for populations.
- Impact of mental illness in different cultures. Mental disorder is often unrecognized. Its importance is not always taken into account as a source of health-related economic loss, social stress, and individual disability. Comparisons can help sort this out.
- Comparative strategies can be examined for reforming and enhancing organizational and management structures, increasing quality of

health care, controlling costs, and improving other dimensions of the health care system.

Problems of Comparability

Health care statistics are not always comparable between countries. Information may not be reported in a standardized format from one country to another despite the efforts of WHO and OECD to create common formats. The data are clearly less adequate in countries with poorly developed health research traditions. Even the more advanced countries do not always collect the same kinds of data based on the same criteria. The challenge is especially troublesome when attempting to compare less developed countries with advanced industrialized nations (Roemer, 1991; Rosenthal and Frenkel, 1992).

Financial comparisons are often questionable because exchange rates among national currencies are used to convert each cost or expenditure to a common set of numbers. In fact, there is strong evidence that "purchasing power parities"—the resources required to purchase specified health care services—may be a much better method for measuring expenditures because it takes into account differences in prices for services between countries (Parkin et al., 1989).

Comparisons thus may be somewhat unreliable or misleading. It is particularly difficult to relate performance of health care systems to health status outcomes. Common outcome measures such as infant mortality rates and life expectancy are insufficient for precise comparisons, and yet they are the best indicators available across national boundaries. It is thus very difficult to fully account for historical, cultural, political, social, demographic, and economic differences between countries (Schieber and Poullier, 1990).

Gaps or inadequacies of data are noted regularly in the following pages when comparisons could be particularly misleading or when misunderstanding could result.

The Ongoing Process of Reform

Many of the features of health care systems discussed in these chapters will be out of date almost immediately because of the ongoing reform efforts in every country. Restructuring and redesign are underway everywhere—in the interest of lowering costs, increasing equity, improving quality, or for other worthwhile reasons. Insurance programs and patient services are being changed to improve cost effectiveness. Organizational and information structures are in process of alteration to increase efficiency and enhance productivity. New incentive structures for health professionals are being created to promote primary and preventive care. We can expect some very different forms of health care in the near future (Frenk, 1994: 30–31).

SUMMARY AND CONCLUSIONS

Patterns of health care in a diverse group of nations is an important area of study. As reforms proceed, each country can learn from the experience of other countries. Because health care has great significance for the economic status of countries, as costs increase and international competition for markets proceeds, the sharing of information and experience becomes especially relevant.

If growth in understanding of the common and varying features of health care is to proceed, it is important to understand the essential components of health care systems and the kinds of influences that caused each system to evolve to its present state. Specific influences on health status include the environmental conditions in each country, historical background, demography of the population, cultural influences, the political system, the social organization of health care, and the economics of how the system operates.

The quest for improvement of services in each country is in substantial part a direct consequence of evidence that some countries appear to be doing considerably better than others. This is not to say that any country has devised the best and most effective solutions for every health care challenge. Rather, there is much to be learned from the rich international experience available to us from many countries.

Vigorous economic competition between nations is undoubtedly having major influence on the evolution of attitudes about health care and, consequently, on national health care policies. Improvements in efficiency, and lowering of costs, may be critical to long-term economic well-being. There may be some danger that unnecessarily high health care costs may "crowd out" resources for other important purposes such as education, transportation, and other services critical to societal and international development.

Comparisons of health care systems can help sort out policies and practices that work best to resolve issues in individual countries and can serve as a basis for international collaboration in the solution of key problems.

REFERENCES

AARON, HENRY, and WILLIAM B. SCHWARTZ (1990). Rationing Health Care: The Choice Before Us, *Science*, 247 (5): 418–422.

ALBERT, A., C. BENNETT, and M. BOJAR (1992). Health Care in the Czech Republic: A system in transition, *Journal of the American Medical Association*, 267: 2461–2466.

ANDERSON, OLIN W. (1989a). *The Health Service Continuum in Democratic States: An Inquiry into Solvable Problems.* Ann Arbor, Mich.: Health Administration Press.

ANDERSON, OLIN W. (1989b). Issues in the Health Services of the United States, in Mark G. Field, (ed.), *Success and Crisis in National Health Systems: A Comparative Approach.* New York: Routledge, pp. 49–71.

BASCH, PAUL F. (1990). *Textbook of International Health.* New York: Oxford University Press.

BLENDON, ROBERT J., KAREN DONELAN, ROBERT LEITMAN, ARNOLD EPSTEIN, JOEL CANTOR, ALAN COHEN, IAN MORRISON, THOMAS MOLONEY, CHRISTIAN KOECK, and SAMUEL LEVITT (1993). Physician Perspectives on Caring for Patients in the United States, Canada and West Germany, *New England Journal of Medicine*, 328 (14): 1011–1016.

ERIKSON, ROBERT (1992). Social Policy and Inequality in Health: Considerations from the Swedish Experience, *International Journal of Health Sciences*, 3 (3/4): 215–223.

FEARN, R. (1987). Rural Health Care: A British Success or a Tale of Unmet Need?, *Social Science and Medicine*, 24: 263–274.

FIELD, MARK G. (ed.) (1989). *Success and Crisis in National Health Care Systems: A Comparative Approach.* New York: Routledge.

FRENK, JULIO (1994). Dimensions of Health System Reform, *Health Policy*, 27 (1): 19–34.

GRAIG, LAURENE A. (1993). *Health of Nations: An International Perspective on U.S. Health Care Reform*, 2nd ed. Washington, D.C.: Congressional Quarterly.

HENKE, L. D. (1990). What Can Americans Learn from Europeans?, in OECD, *Health Care Systems in Transition.* Paris: OECD, pp. 101–104.

IGLEHART, J. (1991). Germany's Health Care System, *New England Journal of Medicine*, 324: 503–508.

ILLSLEY, RAYMOND (1992). Equity, Health and Policy, *International Journal of Health Sciences*, 3 (3/4): 117–126.

JANECKOVA, HANA, and HELENA HNILICOVA (1992). The Health Status of the Czechoslovak Population: Its Social and Ecological Determinants, *International Journal of Health Sciences*, 3 (3/4): 143–156.

KLEINMAN, ARTHUR (1995). Incorporating Cultural Distinctions in Health Care Delivery and Education, paper presented at the conference on *Building the Workforce for a Diverse Society*, Congress of Health Professions Educators, Association of Academic Health Centers, Washington, D.C., June 19–20.

LEVIN, P. J., J. WOLFSON, and H. AKIYAMA (1987). The Role of Management in Japanese Hospitals, *Hospital and Health Services Administration*, 34 (3): 249–261.

LIGHT, DONALD W., and ALEXANDER SCHULLER (eds.) (1986). *Political Values and Health Care: The German Experience.* Cambridge, Mass.: The MIT Press, 1986.

LINDGREN, B. (1990). What Can Europeans Learn from Americans? Health Care Systems in Transition. Paris: OECD, pp. 74–79.

McPHERSON, K. (1990). International Differences in Medical Care Practices, in OECD, *Health Care Systems in Transition.* Paris: OECD, pp. 17–28.

OFFICE OF TECHNOLOGY ASSESSMENT, U.S. CONGRESS (1991). *Health Care in Rural America.* Washington, D.C.: U.S. Government Printing Office.

PARKIN, D. W., A. J. McGUIRE, B. F. YULE (1989). What Do International Comparisons of Health Care Expenditures Really Show? *Community Medicine*, 11: 116–123.

PEET, J. (1991). Health Care: The Spreading Sickness, *The Economist* (July 6): 3–18.

ROEMER, MILTON I. (1991). *National Health Systems of the World: The Countries*, Vol. I. New York: Oxford University Press.

ROEMER, MILTON I. (1993). *National Health Systems of the World: The Issues*, Vol. 2. New York: Oxford University Press.

ROSENBLATT, ROGER A. (1992). Specialists or Generalists—On Whom Should We Base the American

Health Care System?, *Journal of the American Medical Association*, 267 (12): 1665–1666.

ROSENTHAL, MARILYNN M., and MARCEL FRENKEL (1992). *Health Care Systems and Their Patients: An International Perspective.* Boulder, Col.: Westview Press, 1992.

RUGGIE, M. (1992). The Paradox of Liberal Intervention: Health Policy and the American Welfare State, *American Journal of Sociology*, 97 (4): 919–943.

SCHIEBER, GEORGE J., and JEAN-PIERRE POULLIER (1990). Overview of International Comparisons of Health Care Expenditures, in *Health Care Systems in Transition.* Paris: OECD, pp. 9–15.

SHORTELL, STEPHEN M., and EWE REINHARDT (1992). Creating and Executing Health Policy in the 1990s, in Stephen M. Shortell and Ewe Reinhardt (eds.), *Improving Health Policy and Management: Nine Critical Issues for the 1990s.* Ann Arbor, Mich.: Health Administration Press, pp. 3–36.

SMITH, CHRISTOPHER J., and JOHN A. GIGGS (eds.) (1988). *Location and Stigma: Contemporary Perspectives on Mental Health and Mental Health Care.* Boston: Unwin Hyman, 1988.

STESLICKE, WILLIAM E. (1989). Health Care and the Japanese State, in Mark G. Field (ed.), *Success and Crisis in National Health Systems: A Comparative Approach.* New York: Routledge, pp. 101–127.

VAN GENNIP, E. M. S. J., and F. GREMY (1993). Challenges and Opportunities for Technology Assessment in Medical Informatics, *Medical Informatics*, 18 (1): 179–184.

WOOLHANDLER, S., and D. U. HIMMELSTEIN (1991). The Deteriorating Administrative Efficiency of the U.S. Health Care System, *New England Journal of Medicine*, 324 (18): 1253–1258.

WOOLHANDLER, S., D. U. HIMMELSTEIN, and J. P. LEWONTIN. (1993). Administrative Costs in U.S. Hospitals, *New England Journal of Medicine*, 329 (6): 400–403.

2

The Countries and Their Characteristics

The countries were selected in part because they represent a broad range of political, social, and economic characteristics. The following selection criteria were also important:

- Geographic dispersion
- Diversity of the health care systems
- Range of economic development levels
- Availability of relatively comparable data
- Direct experience of the authors in the countries

Europe, North America, and North Asia are well represented, but no countries are included from South Asia, the Middle East, Africa, and South America. Health care systems of the countries range from largely decentralized and private to highly centralized and government-operated. Per capita incomes range from about $490 in China to more than $29,000 in Japan. Data on the countries are available from the World Bank and the World Health Organization, and for many nations, from the Organization for Economic Cooperation and Development and a great variety of researchers. The regions, countries, and populations are listed in Table 2-1.

It is important to emphasize that all of the countries described and compared here fall into the World Bank's most "advanced" health status category (1980 data), with the

Table 2-1 Geographic Distribution and Population of Countries

Region	Country	Approximate Population in 1993 (millions)
North America	Canada	28
	United States	258
	Mexico	90
Northern Europe	France	57
	Germany	81
	The Netherlands	15
	Sweden	9
	United Kingdom	58
Central Europe	Czech Republic	10.5
	Hungary	10.5
Eastern Europe/ North Asia	Russian Federation	149
North Asia	China	1,185
	Japan	125

Source: Based on data from World Bank, 1993: 200–201.

exception of Mexico. China shifted from the second (of five levels of health development) to the first rank between 1960 and 1980. The World Bank rankings use a series of outcome measures including infant mortality, male and female life expectancy, and other health outcome status indicators (Hunter, 1990: 435–438).

China is the least developed and has the only currently communist government among these countries. It has the largest population of any country and has a unique and relatively effective approach to health care. It is moving swiftly (as of 1995) toward a more advanced and free enterprise economic system and partially privatized health care. China has among the world's highest overall economic growth rates at present; per capita income is rising rapidly. Mexico is also relatively underdeveloped, but has been steadily advancing economically and as a democratic society.

Russia, Hungary, and the Czech Republic are in process of transition from communism to capitalism and democracy. All of the other countries except China have a relatively long tradition of democracy and free enterprise.

COMPARATIVE COUNTRY CHARACTERISTICS

Economic Advancement and Health Care Expenditures

Economic advancement is defined for our purposes as GDP per capita. Expenditure levels for health care include the proportion of GDP spent and per capita expenditures (in U.S. dollars). We focus on level of expenditures because improvement in health conditions is generally difficult to separate from economic progress. For example, general public health measures such as clean drinking water and improvement in general sanitation, coupled with specific health care measures such as good nutrition and access to primary care, are nearly always closely related to level of economic development (Hunter, 1990: 434–442).

Although the correlation between level of economic development and expenditures for health is not perfect, per capita income level is nonetheless the single best predictor of overall health status in a country. The relative average wealth and health expenditures in each country are summarized in Figure 2-1.

The Western and Northern European and North American countries (except Mexico) and Japan have higher per capita incomes and spend much higher proportions of GDP for health care than do Eastern and Central European countries, China, and Mexico. As per capita incomes drop sharply, so does the proportion of GDP devoted to health care and per capita health spending.

Availability of Basic Health Services

Availability of physicians and hospitals as well as public health services such as immunizations are important measures of access to health care. As indicated in Figure 2-2, relatively wide variation is evident even among the most advanced countries. The highest density of physicians is in the former communist countries: the Czech Republic, Hungary, and particularly Russia (with 4.69 per 1,000 people), whereas Mexico, the United Kingdom, China, and Japan have the lowest density. Many countries have an overall surplus in the cities and a shortage in the countryside.

The range of hospital bed density is enormous, from 15.9 per 1,000 population in Japan to 1.3 in Mexico, with a full distribution within this range. Japan has by far the greatest density of hospital beds among the most advanced countries—many of which serve effectively for long-term care. Among the less affluent nations, Russia and Hungary are well above the average. The density of hospital beds is very different than the density of physicians, with little overall correlation.

The public health indicators, immunization for diphtheria/whooping cough/tetanus (DPT) and measles, are entirely different than density of physicians or hospital beds, with the best records in Hungary, the Czech

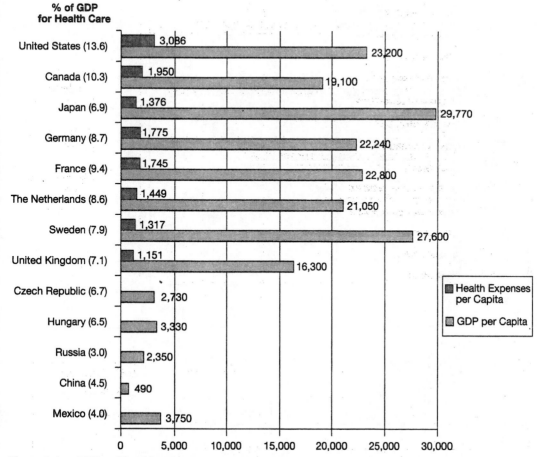

% of GDP for Health Care

Country	Health Expenses per Capita	GDP per Capita
United States (13.6)	3,086	23,200
Canada (10.3)	1,950	19,100
Japan (6.9)	1,376	29,770
Germany (8.7)	1,775	22,240
France (9.4)	1,745	22,800
The Netherlands (8.6)	1,449	21,050
Sweden (7.9)	1,317	27,600
United Kingdom (7.1)	1,151	16,300
Czech Republic (6.7)	2,730	
Hungary (6.5)	3,330	
Russia (3.0)	2,350	
China (4.5)	490	
Mexico (4.0)	3,750	

Figure 2-1.   GDP and health expenses per capita (1994).

Sources: Based on data from Wolfe and Moran, 1993: 55; Hakansson, 1994: 108; Organization for Economic Cooperation and Development, 1994: 37–38; Weil, 1994: 47; *The Europa World Yearbook*, 1995: 64, 65, 91; Memmott, 1995: 4B; National Center for Health Statistics, 1995: 220.

Republic, the Netherlands, and Sweden. The United States and Russia have among the poorest records, along with Mexico. Japan has the poorest measles immunization record.

It should be emphasized that immunization is not necessarily a good overall measure of public health effort, nor are physician and hospital bed density the best measures of health care access. Rather, these indicators emphasize the diversity of emphasis in allocation of health service resources. Some countries do better at child health protection, in the form of immunizations, even

with relatively modest overall health expenditures, and others provide lots of access to physicians and hospital beds at modest per capita cost. The results of these relatively different investments in health will be examined later.

Technology and Cultural Differences

Another indicator of health care development is access to high-technology and tertiary care. Level of technological development can be illustrated by a variety of measures such as incidence of complex surgi-

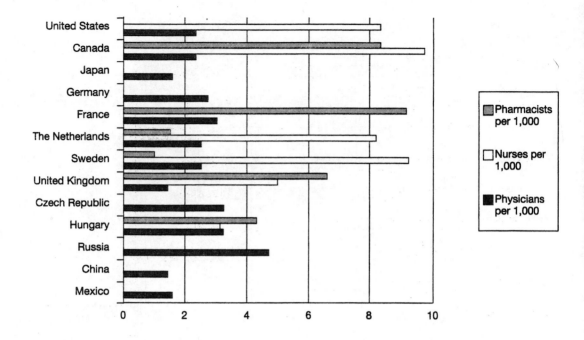

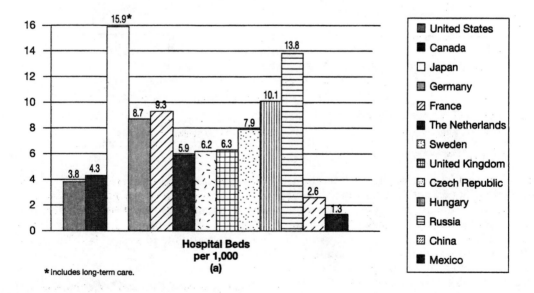

Figure 2-2. (a) Availability of basic health services (1991–1992); (b) children immunized (1991–1992).

Sources: Based on data from Organization for Economic Cooperation and Development, 1992; World Bank, 1993: 208–209; Organization for Economic Cooperation and Development, 1994: 41. Some discrepancies between these sources were evident.

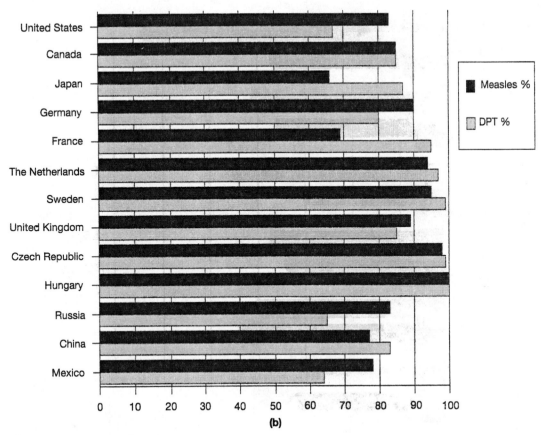

Figure 2-2. (*continued*)

cal procedures—which of course requires advanced physician training and high degrees of hospital technology. Figure 2-3 displays the use of such procedures for several countries with high per capita well-being. The countries are ranked according to the per capita GDP displayed in Figure 2-1. Figure 2-3 illustrates two major points:

1. *High-technology procedures become more possible as the per capita wealth of the country increases.* However, the highest investor in health care—the United States—implements only one of the four procedures at the greatest rate, kidney dialysis, and France is the heaviest user of both heart/lung and liver transplants.

2. *Cultural preferences appear to be more important as determinants of medical practice than strict national wealth.* Germany is the fourth most wealthy among these countries but is lowest in three of the high-technology categories. Transplantation surgery is clearly given lower priority in Germany. France gives greater priority to transplants as compared to the other countries, but kidney dialysis is less emphasized. Sweden gives greater emphasis to kidney transplants and less emphasis to liver transplants and dialysis.

Another illustration of the same type of cultural tendency is the use of pharmaceuticals, as summarized in Figure 2-4 for selected countries. Japan spends nearly twice as much per capita on drugs as any other country, with Germany second. The United States and Canada spend less than one-half of the Japanese total, the United Kingdom spends less than a quarter, and Mexico uses

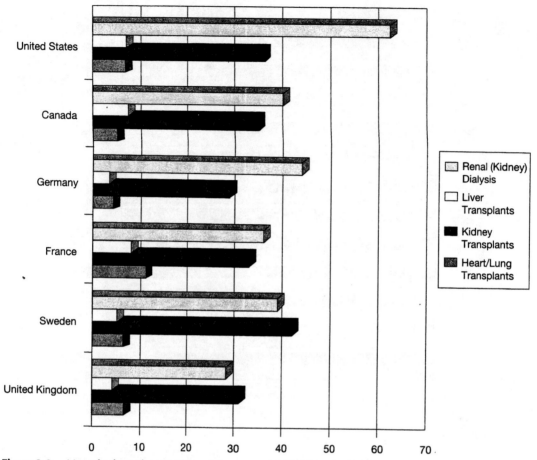

Figure 2-3. Use of selected surgical procedures per 1,000,000 population (1988).
Source: Based on data from Nair and Karim, 1993: 270.

only a fraction as much as any of the other countries listed. Yet, a range of drugs are fully available in all of these countries (except possibly in Mexico). It is thus clear that drug consumption is substantially a cultural preference (World Bank, 1993: 145).

The use of both high-technology procedures and pharmaceuticals is clearly affected by historical experience and value preferences, as well as national wealth. It is thus difficult to draw conclusions about which countries exhibit the best performance on all measures of access to health care, because the practices used are not directly related to any clear set of objective and technical crite-

ria. Outcome measures are needed that trace the use of practices directly to health status of the population.

Measures of Health System Outcome

Measurements of health system outcomes often include several major categories. Results from the first group of measures are *system outcomes* and from the second are *patient/population outcomes*.

Health System Outcomes

1. Proportion of the population covered by insurance

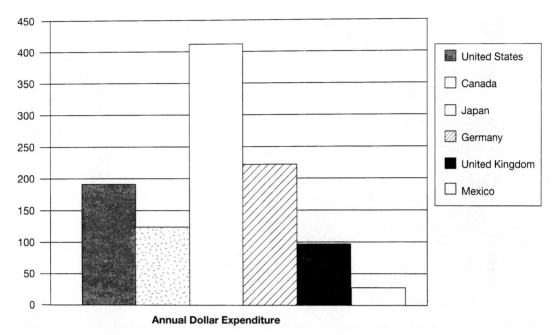

Figure 2-4.   Drug expenditure per capita (1990).

Source: Based on data from World Bank, 1993: 145.

2. Kinds of benefits available to those who have insurance

3. Ease of accessing the insurance coverage and benefits

4. Organizational features of the health care delivery system in terms of effectiveness, efficiency, and products delivered

5. Level and kinds of technology applied in the course of delivering preventive or health care services

Patient/Population Outcomes

1. Results for citizens based on measures such as
   a. Infant mortality
   b. Life expectancy
   c. Disease or illness patterns (morbidity)
   d. Overall functional health status
   e. Major causes of death
   f. Death rates from all causes
   g. Patient satisfaction with health care
   h. Degree of choice in the selection of physicians and hospitals
   i. Perception of access to services
   j. Acceptability of the payment system

The primary focus of much of the material in succeeding chapters will be on system outcomes, largely because patient or population outcome data are less available—except for infant mortality and life expectancy. However, other outcomes will be reported when available (Parkin, McGuire, and Yule, 1989).

The last four population outcome indicators focus on "dissatisfaction," or the manner in which patients perceive they are treated by the health service system. International surveys using satisfaction measures indicate much higher dissatisfaction with services in the United States and the United Kingdom than in Canada and continental Western Europe, as indicated in Figure 2-5. However, there is considerable evidence of unhappiness, and possible need for reform, in all these countries. Comparable data are not available for the other countries.

Technology assessment is a form of system outcome measurement that attempts to determine the effects, safety, feasibility, cost, cost effectiveness, and ethical appropriateness of

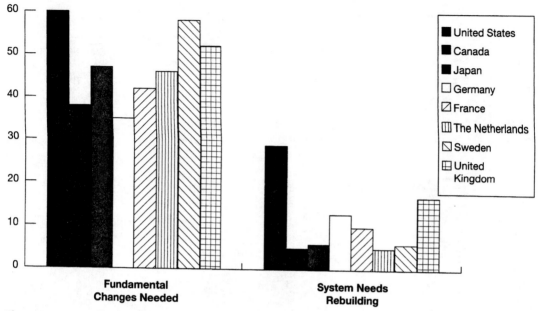

Figure 2-5. Satisfaction with health care (percent of population).

Source: Based on data from Blendon et al., 1990: 188.

new drugs, medical devices, surgical procedures, diagnostic practices, information units (such as computer systems), and other forms of technology. Such evaluations can be done at the local or hospital level, or at the national or international level, as a means of documenting the overall contribution of a form of technology to patient and societal well-being (Littenberg, 1992: 425; Franklin, 1993: 117).

Overall health status assessment has become a prominent method of determining clinical outcomes in the United States and some European countries, but is not widely used internationally. The long-term medical outcomes study in the United States provides highly useful data on a range of health care practices. The measures include such status measures as physiological status, cardiac functional capacity, ability to perform activities of daily living, satisfaction with current ability to perform physical activities, and many other physical and psychological indicators (Clinton, 1991; Bergner, Bowman, and Guess, 1992; Golden, 1992).

Outcome measures collected for individuals, such as physical health status, functional

capacity, complications in hospitals, and hospital readmission rates, have been devised and tested in the United Kingdom and in the United States but have not been used in most other countries. The Quality Adjusted Life Years (QALYs) concept has been used with small samples and may have potential as an international measure of outcomes—at some point in the future (Birch and Maynard, 1986; Vayda, 1989; Clinton, 1991).

Comparable statistics on most of these measures are simply not yet available for most countries. More cross-national research is needed using a wider range of variables if we are to more fully understand the comparative consequences of both public and private health care practices. In the meantime, the available measures will have to suffice (Rosenblatt, 1992; Anderson et al., 1994: 526–527).

Population Outcomes: Infant Mortality and Life Expectancy

The two most widely used international measures—infant mortality and life expectancy—are available in some form for nearly all countries but have slightly different meanings. The most common general definitions may be summarized as follows:

- *Infant mortality* is the death rate of children before the age of 1 year and is a crude measure of health conditions for mothers and children.
- *Adult life expectancy* at birth is the length of life projected for current adults. It is a crude measure of general health conditions, with separate measures for males and females because of the wide divergence in outcomes.

We generally expect that countries with the "best" health conditions will have lower infant mortality rates and higher adult life expectancy than countries with "poorer" overall conditions. These measures in no sense capture only health *care* results, but rather a wide range of contributors to individual and community health. Data on infant mortality and general life expectancy are summarized in Figure 2-6 and Table 2-2.

Japan has the best overall record, followed at some distance by Sweden, the Nether-

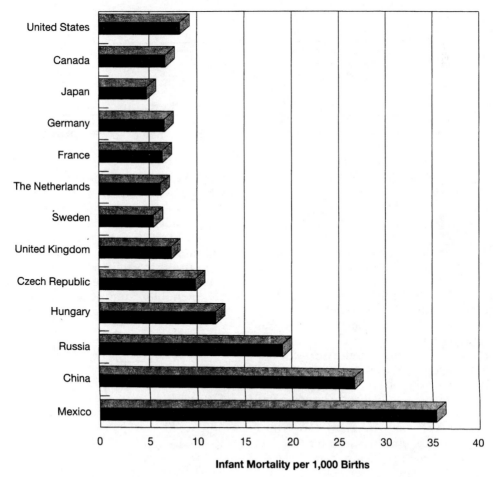

Figure 2-6.   Comparative infant mortality rates (1993 or later).

Sources: Based on data from World Bank, 1993: 200; Organization for Economic Cooperation and Development, 1994: 43; World Health Organization, 1994: table C-2; National Center for Health Statistics, 1995: 93.

Table 2-2   Life Expectancy and Proportion of Elderly in the Population (1991 or Year Indicated)

Country	Life Expectancy		Proportion of Elderly over Age 65
	Males	Females	
United States	72.3 ('92)	79.1 ('92)	12.6 ('90)
Canada	74.4	81.0	11.5 ('90)
Japan	76.4	82.8	11.2 ('88)
Germany	72.7 ('92)	79.2 ('92)	15.5 ('94)
France	73.5	82.0	13.5 ('89)
Sweden	74.9	80.6	17.8 ('88)
The Netherlands	74.1	81.1	12.8 ('90)
United Kingdom	73.5	79.0	15.7 ('90)
Czech Republic	69.3 ('93)	76.9 ('93)	
Hungary	65.1 ('92)	73.7 ('92)	
Russia	59.0 ('94)	74.3	
China	68.0	70.0	
Mexico	66.0	72.1	

Sources: Based on data from Nair and Karim, 1993: 272; World Bank, 1993: 200–201; Kirkman-Liff, 1994: 7; OECD, 1994: 43; National Center for Health Statistics, 1995: 94.

lands, Canada, Germany, France, and the United Kingdom. The United States and the Czech Republic have infant mortality rates near ten but do much less well than the leaders. Mothers and children appear to have the poorest health conditions in Mexico, China, Russia, and Hungary.

Life Expectancy and Aging of Populations

The proportion of population in younger and older age categories is a major indicator of general health conditions but also a significant factor in health care costs. Life expectancy is usually related closely to the proportion of elderly in the population, but not always. Japan and Canada have high longevity but somewhat lower proportions of older population than European countries, as indicated in Table 2-2.

Japan, Sweden, the Netherlands, and Canada have the greatest longevity for both men (over 74) and women (over 80), although France also does well for females. The United States, United Kingdom, and Germany are in the next tier for both males and females. The Czech Republic and Hungary follow. China and Mexico do relatively less well, but both have made considerable progress in

the past decade. Russia's life expectancy for males has substantially declined in recent years, from a high of 65 in 1970 to 59 in 1994.

TENTATIVE RANKINGS BASED ON POPULATION OUTCOME MEASURES

Japan, Canada, Sweden, and the Netherlands clearly achieve the best results for both infant mortality and life expectancy on the basis of the crude "outcome" measures summarized earlier. Mexico, China, Hungary, the Czech Republic, and Russia achieve the poorest results. The United Kingdom is low-

Table 2-3   Rankings Based on Health Outcomes

1. Japan
2. Sweden
3. Canada
4. The Netherlands
5. France
6. Germany
7. United Kingdom
8. United States
9. Czech Republic
10. Hungary
11. Russia
12. China
13. Mexico

est on female life expectancy among more advanced countries. The outcome measures, as rough indicators of overall health status, lead to the rough ranking in Table 2-3, from *most adequate* to *least adequate health* outcomes.

Other outcome measures and comparisons of course would be desirable in clarifying country status—if the data were available. For example, Canada was rated by the World Health Organization as having the best overall quality of life, based on a variety of social well-being measures; health care was only one of the indicators (Graig, 1993).

Overall Level of Health System Development: A Tentative Categorization

The health systems of these countries fall largely toward the middle and advanced part of the health services development continuum, as defined by the World Bank. Level of advancement in this case is defined to include the following:

- Use of *high-technology* medicine (magnetic resonance imaging, organ transplants, laser surgery, and so on)
- Level of *resources* allocated to health care (percent of GDP)

- *Accessibility of public and private health services* to members of the population (proportion covered by some form of insurance or who have direct access to preventive, primary, secondary, and tertiary care)

The rough ranking in Table 2-4 could easily follow a somewhat different order depending on the specific variables used. For example, *access* might be given greater weight if overall health of the population is considered of highest importance, as seems to be more the case in Western European countries and Japan than in the United States and Eastern Europe. If outcomes are given the greatest weight, a somewhat different order may be appropriate, as suggested in the previous section.

The order of the countries in each general category (Most Advanced, Somewhat Advanced, and Less Advanced) is only an approximation. The most advanced systems are listed first.

THE PRIMARY ISSUES TO BE ADDRESSED

These initial comparisons raise several important questions:

Table 2-4   Approximate Level of Health Care System Advancement

Degree of Advancement	Country	Technology	Resources	Access
Most advanced	Canada	Hi	Hi	Hi
	The Netherlands	Hi	Hi	Hi
	Sweden	Hi	Hi	Hi
	Germany	Hi	Hi	Hi
	France	Hi	Hi	Hi
	Japan	Hi	Mod	Hi
	United Kingdom	Hi	Mod	Hi
	United States	Hi	Hi	Mod
Somewhat advanced	Hungary	Low	Low	Hi
	Czech Republic	Low	Low	Hi
Less advanced	Russia	Low	Low	Mod
	China	Low	Low	Mod
	Mexico	Low	Low	Mod

Hi = high or advanced; Mod = moderate; Low = lower level of advancement.

- Why do some countries have lower infant mortality, higher life expectancy, and other indicators of good health status?

- What are the primary patterns of health care organization among major countries of the world, and which seem to be effective?

- What role does the health care system play in producing good individual and community health outcomes, as compared to historical, demographic, cultural, political, environmental, social, and economic factors?

- What difference does universal insurance coverage make in the health status of populations?

- What are the primary roles and responsibilities of health care professionals and health care institutions in each country, and how do roles and responsibilities vary between countries?

- What characteristics of a health care system count most in measuring the *quality* of a health care system?

- What reforms have proven successful in improving the health care systems in a country, and what measures of reform outcomes best indicate good results?

These are among the issues to be considered in the chapters that follow.

SUMMARY AND CONCLUSIONS

The countries considered here represent a broad spectrum of experience with health care at the relatively advanced end of the economic development continuum. No attempt is made to deal with the problems of underdeveloped countries, except to the degree that Mexico, Russia, and China continue to have relatively low average per capita incomes and certainly contain regions with very limited health care services. These countries are nonetheless relatively advanced compared to many of the countries of Africa, Asia, and South America.

The countries represent a substantial range of health care experience, ranging from the relatively centralized and publicly operated programs of the United Kingdom, Russia, and Sweden to the more private practice systems of Japan, Germany, and the United States.

The range of resources devoted to health care is similarly broad, from less than 6 percent in China, Russia, and Mexico to more than 9 percent in France, Canada, and the United States.

The availability of physician services, hospitals, and high technology is also highly diverse. Russia and the Czech Republic have more than three physicians per 1,000 people, whereas Japan, the United Kingdom, China, and Mexico have less than two. Japan, Hungary, and Russia have more than ten hospital beds per 1,000 people, whereas China and Mexico have less than three. Vaccination rates are over 90 percent for children in Hungary, the Czech Republic, Sweden, and the Netherlands, whereas they are less than 75 percent in Mexico, Japan, Russia, and the United States. The range is large on all these variables and generally not closely related to national wealth or general technological advancement.

Finally, tentative efforts to evaluate outcomes suggest that Japan, Canada, the Netherlands, and Sweden do best on care for mothers and children, with less than 7 infant mortality rate, whereas Mexico, China, Russia, and Hungary do less well with rates greater than 10. Similarly, Japan, Sweden, the Netherlands, and the United Kingdom extend male life expectancy to more than 74 years, whereas Mexico, China, Russia, the Czech Republic, and Hungary are at less than 70 years. All do much better on female life expectancy. We suggest that Japan, Sweden, Canada, and the Netherlands have the best overall health conditions.

REFERENCES

ANDERSON, GERARD F., JORDI ALONSO, LINDA T. KOHN, and CHARLYN BLACK (1994). Analyzing Health Outcomes Through International Comparisons, *Medical Care*, 32 (5): 526–534.

BERGNER, MARILYN, MARJORIE A. BOWMAN, and HARRY A. GUESS (1992). Where Do We Go from Here: Opportunities for Applying Health Status Measurement in Clinical Settings, *Medical Care*, 30 (5) (Sup.): 219–230.

BIRCH, S., and A. MAYNARD (1986). Performance Indicators and Performance Assessment in the U.K.

National Health Service: Implications for Management and Planning, *International Journal of Health Planning and Management*, 1: 143–156.

BLENDON, ROBERT J., ROBERT LEITMAN, IAN MORRISON, and KAREN DONELAN (1990). Satisfaction with Health Systems in Ten Nations, *Health Affairs* (Summer): 185–192.

CLINTON, J. J. (1991). Outcomes Research—A Way to Improve Medical Practice, *Journal of the American Medical Association*, 266 (15): 2057.

The Europa World Yearbook (1995). London: Europa Publications, Ltd.

FRANKLIN, C. (1993). Basic Concepts and Fundamental Issues in Technology Assessment, *Intensive Care Medicine*, 19 (2): 117–121.

GOLDEN, WILLIAM E. (1992). Health Status Measurement: Implementation Strategies, *Medical Care*, 30 (5) (Sup.): 187–195.

GRAIG, LAURENE A. (1993). *Health of Nations: An International Perspective on U.S. Health Care Reform*, 2nd ed. Washington D.C.: Congressional Quarterly.

HAKANSSON, STEFAN (1994). New Ways of Financing and Organizing Health Care in Sweden, *International Journal of Health Planning and Management*, 9 (1): 103–124.

HUNTER, SUSAN (1990). Levels of Health Development: A New Tool for Comparative Research and Policy Formation, *Social Science and Medicine*, 31 (4): 433–444.

KIRKMAN-LIFF, BRADFORD L. (1994). Management Without Frontiers: Health System Convergence Leads to Health Care Management Convergence, *Frontiers of Health Services Management*, 11 (1): 3–48.

LITTENBERG, BENJAMIN (1992). Technology Assessment in Medicine, *Academic Medicine*, 67 (7): 424–428.

MEMMOTT, MARK (1995). Redefining the Wealth of Nations, *USA Today*, September 18, p. 4B.

NAIR, CYRIL, and REZAUL KARIM (1993). An Overview of Health Care Systems: Canada and Selected OECD Countries, *Health Reports*, 5 (3): 259–279.

NATIONAL CENTER FOR HEALTH STATISTICS (1995). *Health, United States, 1994*. Hyattsville, Md.: United States Public Health Service.

ORGANIZATION FOR ECONOMIC COOPERATION AND DEVELOPMENT (OECD) (1992). *The Reform of Health Care: A Comparative Analysis of Seven OECD Countries*. Paris: OECD.

ORGANIZATION FOR ECONOMIC COOPERATION AND DEVELOPMENT (OECD) (1994). *The Reform of Health Care Systems: A Review of Seventeen OECD Countries*. Paris: OECD.

PARKIN, D. W., A. J. MCGUIRE, and B. F. YULE (1989). What Do International Comparisons of Health Care Expenditures Really Show? *Community Medicine*, 11: 116–123.

ROSENBLATT, ROGER A. (1992). Specialists or Generalists—On Whom Should We Base the American Health Care System?, *Journal of the American Medical Association*, 267 (12): 1665–1666.

VAYDA, EUGENE (1989). Private Practice in the United Kingdom: A Growing Concern, *Journal of Public Health Policies* (Autumn): 359–376.

WEIL, THOMAS P. (1994). An American Micromanaged Health Care System?, *Health Services Management Review*, 7 (1): 43–55.

WOLFE, PATRICE R., and DONALD W. MORAN (1993). Global Budgeting in OECD Countries, *Health Care Financing Review*, 14 (3): 55–76.

WORLD BANK (1993). *World Development Report 1993: Investing in Health*. New York: Oxford University Press.

WORLD HEALTH ORGANIZATION (1994). *World Health Statistics Annual, 1993*. Geneva: World Health Organization.

3

THE UNITED STATES

High-Technology and Limited Access

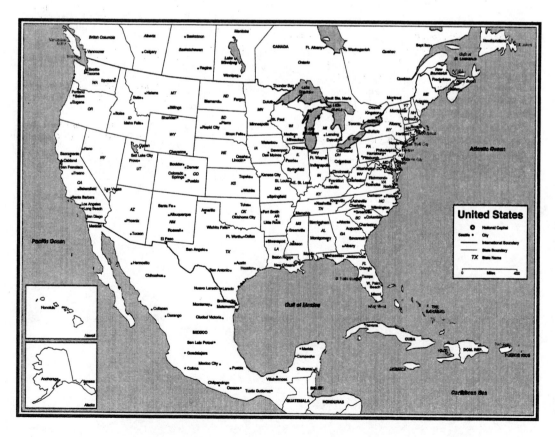

United States

- ⊙ National Capital
- Seattle ● City
- —— International Boundary
- —— State Boundary
- TX State Name

0   Miles   400

The American health care system has been called a "paradox of excess and deprivation" because it is characterized by both very high costs and inaccessibility to health care of good quality for a substantial segment of the population. This is difficult to understand because the United States is the most powerful country in the world, with a population of 258 million and a per capita income in 1995 of $23,260 (Graig, 1993: 20; Memmott, 1995: 4B).

Per capita health care costs, at about $3,300 in 1993, were nearly twice the average for twenty-four nations in the Organization for Economic Cooperation and Development (OECD). Health care absorbs nearly 14 percent (in 1995) of Gross Domestic Product (GDP)—far more than any other country. High expenditures mean that citizens with good insurance, who are fortunate enough to be located near good medical centers, probably secure the "best" health care in the world. Physicians and other health professionals receive the finest and most specialized training available anywhere, and they have access to a full array of diagnostic and treatment possibilities. Some parts of the U.S. system, such as medical research, are clearly outstanding because of high investments and high-quality medical institutions (Enthoven and Kronick, 1989: 29; Organization for Economic Cooperation and Development, 1992: 7).

However, serious questions have been raised about American standing with respect to adequacy and quality of care for some segments of the population. As noted in Chapter 2, the United States ranked far from the top on basic measures of health outcomes in 1990, among the twenty-four economically advanced countries of the OECD (Schieber, 1990: 159): twenty-first for infant mortality, and seventeenth in male life expectancy at birth and sixteenth in female life expectancy.

These statistics are to a significant degree indicative of inadequate health conditions for lower-income mothers and children, and inadequate quality of life for many minority and lower-income citizens in large city ghet-

tos, rural regions, and in particularly the southern states. This relatively poor performance is among the primary challenges to U.S. health policy (National Center for Health Statistics, 1995: 89). Other features of the U.S. system are summarized in Table 3-1.

Americans are demanding change, but have so far been unsuccessful in defining policies that are likely to resolve the major issues in the near future. The changes in 1995 were being driven more by private initiatives than by government policy. One commentator on the recent circumstances in U.S. health care suggests:

> Hospitals and payers today are . . . constructing a utilization-control structure that reviews physicians' clinical decisions in minute detail, with questionable dividends, but that adds

Table 3–1 Characteristics of American Health Care

- The greatest density of high-technology services of any country.
- More health workers are employed per hospital bed than in any other country.
- Medical education and medical research productivity are among the world's best.
- Roughly 15 percent of the population (40 to 45 million people) who are uninsured have uncertain access to basic services and even less opportunity for high-technology health care.
- Additional large numbers, estimated at 50 million, are underinsured; they do not have enough insurance to cover serious illnesses or must pay very high deductibles.
- The largest number of citizens are uninsured since the initiation of Medicare and Medicaid in 1965.
- Long-term-care costs are growing as the population ages, and consumed 7.9 percent of all health care spending in 1995.
- Hospitals and insurers regularly shift uninsured patients' hospital costs to paying clients and deliberately avoid high-risk patients altogether if possible.
- National opinion polls indicate that 75 percent of Americans support health care reform and want some form of national health care program—even if it means an increase in taxes.

Sources: Based on data from Schieber, 1990: 159; Himmelstein, Woolhandler, and Wolfe, 1992: 382; Graig, 1993: 3–20.

greatly to administrative costs, and (with physician and business investors) are engaging in a variety of entrepreneurial ventures that are changing the nature and image of medicine. (Iglehart, 1992a: 963)

DEMOGRAPHIC CHARACTERISTICS

The average life expectancy at birth in the United States was 75.8 years in 1992. Females could expect to live 79.1 years as compared to only 72.3 years for men. The overall infant mortality rate was 8.3 in 1992 and has been decreasing steadily since 1980 at a rate of 3.2 percent per year. However, American health status outcomes are much poorer, and even alarming, for low-income and some minority members of the population (U.S. Public Health Service, 1991: 8; National Center for Health Statistics, 1995: 16, 65):

- Twelve percent of the U.S. population are African-American; 33 percent are below the official poverty line.
- Eight percent are Hispanic (20 million); 31 percent are in poverty.
- One percent is American Indian (1.7 million); 28 percent are in poverty.
- Three percent are Asian or Pacific Islander (6.5 million); 13 percent are in poverty.
- Eighty-four percent are white and largely of European extraction; 12.2 percent are in poverty.

Huge variations exist between these racial and ethnic groups in health status and use of health care services. For example, in 1993, African-Americans had 2.4 times the rate of infant mortality (17.5) as whites (7.3), and had a life expectancy of nearly 8.3 *fewer* years for men (age 64.7 as compared to 73 for white males) and 5.8 *fewer* years for women (73.7 as compared to 79.5) (National Center for Health Statistics, 1995: 85, 97).

Despite these disadvantages, life expectancy for African-Americans has increased more for both males (by 0.6 year) and females (4.4 years) since 1950 than for the white population. However, infant mortality for African-Americans actually increased dur-

ing the 1980s, whereas white infant mortality declined. Only about 60 percent of Hispanic and African-American mothers receive prenatal care, as compared to about 80 percent for whites. The consequence is a much higher rate of low-birthweight babies with associated high neonatal and postneonatal death rates and health problems (Rice, 1991: 638; U.S. Public Health Service, 1991: 9).

African-American men under age 45 suffer a 45 percent higher rate of lung cancer and are ten times more likely to die from hypertension than white men of comparable age. This is among the reasons for a life expectancy statistics noted earlier. African-Americans are more likely to require health care and are less likely to receive it (Council on Ethical and Judicial Affairs, 1990: 2344; Rice, 1991: 638–640).

In addition to higher levels of poverty, African-Americans, Hispanics, and American Indians have lower levels of educational attainment—which is directly related to health status. Generally, individuals with more than 12 years of education have much better health status than those with fewer years (U.S. Public Health Service, 1991: 32).

Another consequence of poverty and lower education is lower levels of health insurance for African-Americans and Hispanics: only 58 percent of African-Americans and 54 percent of Hispanics had insurance in 1990—compared to 81 percent for whites—among the under-age-65 population. Fewer older members of minority groups (about one-third) had private insurance as a supplement to Medicare, compared to whites—about three-fourths (U.S. Public Health Service, 1991: 34).

American Indians who live in locations with Indian Health Service (IHS) facilities have access to a special form of publicly provided care. However, only about 60 percent of the population live in accessible locations. Roughly 55 percent have access to IHS facilities only, 28 percent had other insurance, and 11 percent had Medicaid coverage (U.S. Public Health Service, 1991: 34).

Social deprivation has clear adverse effects on the health status of children. African-

American children, for example, are much more likely to live in high-risk social environments—that is, single-parent families with low incomes and poor housing—which leads to poorer health. Asian parents, on the other hand, tend to exhibit health care practices and health status characteristics equal to or better than their white counterparts (McGauhey and Starfield, 1993: 867).

Variations Between States

Populations and health care practices are highly varied from state to state. The neighboring states of Utah and Nevada are quite different, for example. Utah had lower health care costs in 1992, greater longevity by 3 years, and lower infant mortality (6.5 vs. 8.1) than Nevada. The variation is largely because of life-style and value differences. Utah is heavily Mormon and has a strong emphasis against smoking and alcohol consumption, which is much less the case in Nevada. Health maintenance is not emphasized to the same degree in Nevada. However, both states exhibit generally better outcome statistics for infant mortality and life expectancy than the U.S. average because poverty is relatively low in each case (Mitchell, 1991: 14–16).

The regions of the country that are heavily populated by low-income and minority populations, in the Southern states particularly, have generally poorer health outcomes. These more deprived regions and populations drive down the national average indicators of health status, suggesting (somewhat inaccurately) that the overall health care system is performing poorly (Graig, 1993: 20).

Special Problems of Rural Regions

Rural areas have about 25 percent of the U.S. population. However, 38 percent of rural residents live in poverty (based on the U.S. Census definition of poverty). The proportion of elderly residents is also much higher than in urban areas at roughly 39 percent, compared to 12.6 percent nationally. A similarly high proportion of children live in rural communities, because birthrates tend to be considerably higher. Consequently, the proportion of working age citizens is lower—which is part of the explanation for higher poverty (Holden, 1990: 534; Barger, 1991: 290).

Many rural regions are consistently short of good-quality health care, depending on the location. For example, in 1990, there was only one primary care physician for every 2,850 residents in rural counties, as compared to one physician for each 614 residents nationally. Many of the physicians in urban areas are specialists, administrators, or medical educators, which distorts the situation somewhat. Nonetheless, there is clear evidence that physician shortages deprive rural citizens of access to primary care in areas that are remote from major population centers (unless they are resort or retirement communities)—despite a national surplus of some medical specialties. Rural family physician income is 15 percent below urban levels. Yet, rural physicians see 20 percent more patients per week and work longer hours (Lutz, 1991: 27).

Hospitals in rural regions have difficulty surviving financially because of the generally lower incidence of health insurance, inability to provide the full range of technology expected by patients, and a high proportion of patients who are elderly or poor. Reimbursement from Medicare or Medicaid tends to be lower than the cost of care, which is particularly troublesome for institutions with a patient population that relies on these public insurance programs. Of course, many rural residents travel to nearby urban places for health services—if distances are not too great. They often perceive urban services to be of better quality and more complete, and do not always have full confidence in rural providers (Lutz, 1991: 27).

HISTORICAL PERSPECTIVE

Private health care in the United States has been largely an entrepreneurial activity since the founding of the country. Public health activities, on the other hand, have been supported with federal, state, and local resources since 1798 when the U.S. Public Health Service was established. Control of effluents in the water supply and immunizations were the primary early activities, followed by the first federal effort to control quality of drugs after passage of the Import Drugs Act of 1848. Congress passed the Pure Food and Drug Act in 1906, initiating the first major drug regulation effort (Anderson, 1989a: 110).

Development of the American Hospital System

The first general hospitals were modest enterprises occupied largely by lower-income and destitute individuals, whereas the upper classes were cared for in their homes. Mental hospitals were developed first to house individuals who could not function in the community. The first major inpatient hospital facility, Pennsylvania Hospital, was built in Philadelphia in 1752, and became something of a prototype for facilities in other eastern and southern cities (Anderson, 1989a: 109; Larsson, 1994).

By 1900, some 4,000 hospitals were serving patients, heavily under the sponsorship of communities and churches, with much of the required capital coming from donations by wealthy individuals. Operational funds were paid with fees from patients. The hospital became the "workshop" for physicians, especially surgeons (Anderson, 1989a: 109).

The U.S. Congress passed the Hill-Burton Hospital Survey and Construction Act in 1946, which led to the proliferation of voluntary nonprofit hospitals in rural areas and smaller communities; a one-time federal government contribution of about 25 percent of costs served as an incentive for widespread efforts by every community to have a hospital. Communities throughout the country were thus enabled to establish a locally controlled health facility that could attract, and hopefully retain, physicians (Anderson, 1989b: 113).

Emergence of the Insurance Industry

The first health insurance company was founded in 1847 as the Massachusetts Health Insurance Company, initially offering sickness insurance. The first effort to create a national insurance system dates from the early twentieth century when proposals for such a system were supported by President Theodore Roosevelt. Although the American Medical Association advocated a national health insurance plan in 1917, it reversed course before any legislation was enacted, and joined with other powerful interest groups to vigorously oppose all efforts to provide universal health insurance (Iglehart, 1992a: 963; Numbers, 1992: 20).

Blue Cross insurance was initiated in 1933 by the Hospital Association of New Jersey as a prepayment experiment. It was sponsored by hospitals to help pay expenses at a time when patients were otherwise having difficulty with out-of-pocket payments. Blue Shield was initiated 2 years later by the American Medical Association in cooperation with the American Hospital Association. Medical societies in Michigan and California were the first to provide prepayment for physician care in 1937 (Larsson, 1994).

These plans, referred to as "The Blues," were eventually created in all states and have more recently merged into a single organization in many states—offering coverage of both hospital and physician expenditures. They originally used a system of "community rating" to calculate premiums, allowing everyone in a group or community to pay the same rate regardless of health status. They later began to use an "experience" rating, the pattern preferred by private indemnity plans to minimize risks associated with policyholders who have high-risk health conditions. Premiums are calculated on the basis of individual health status, and high-risk individuals were often excluded from coverage (Anderson, 1989b: 111; Iglehart, 1992b: 1718).

Private insurance evolved rapidly during the 1940s. The government allowed health insurance to be tax exempt if sponsored by businesses. The Blue plans and other forms of private insurance became institutionalized and gained major influence over the health care industry during this period. By 1952, nearly half of the population had some type of·health insurance coverage (Anderson, 1989a: 112).

Public efforts toward universal insurance were boosted in 1945 when President Harry Truman supported a campaign for compulsory health insurance. However, the American Medical Association opposed the idea, labeling it socialized medicine. When the bill came to a vote in 1950, it was soundly defeated, as were many of the congressmen who supported the legislation. The only type of legislation that the AMA would support was for grants to the states for the "medically indigent," eventually passed as the Kerr-Mills amendment to the Social Security Act in 1960 (Numbers, 1992: 20–21; Larsson, 1994).

Major Developments in the 1960s

President John F. Kennedy supported a health insurance program that would include everyone eligible for Social Security. This initiative set the stage for a period of major change in health care programs, as summarized in Table 3-2. Much of this activity became part of President Johnson's "war on poverty" after Kennedy was assassinated. These programs were designed to provide income and services to poor citizens.

Medicare covers all older and some disabled citizens; Medicaid provides for grants to the states for insuring selected lower-income individuals who qualify—largely single mothers with dependent children and elderly individuals without resources to pay for nursing home care. Medicare and Medicaid have become the largest federal programs by far. Medicaid is the principal financing mechanism for the private for-profit and nonprofit nursing home industry (Anderson, 1989a: 114).

Both programs were originally designed to function much like private insurance, with a

Table 3-2 Major Health Care Legislation of the 1960s

- The Migrant Health Act was passed in 1962, providing federal funding of health programs for migratory workers.
- Mental retardation assistance and mental health care were supported through creation of Community Mental Health Centers in 1963.
- The Social Security Amendments of 1963–1967 provided funds for state activities in maternal and child health.
- The Economic Opportunity Act of 1964 funded neighborhood health centers.
- Medicare and Medicaid were approved in 1965.
- The Comprehensive Health Planning Act of 1966 provided for integration of federal, state, and local planning for health facilities, personnel, and services.

Sources: Based on Anderson, 1989b: 60; Larsson, 1994.

"cost-based" reimbursement system that paid physicians and hospitals on the basis of "reasonable and necessary expenses." The founding legislation prohibited federal interference in operation of the program. Much of the power to provide the care was delegated to providers. However, this provision soon became difficult, as costs for the program grew very rapidly. Hospital costs were growing at the rate of 15 percent annually during the late 1960s and 1970s (Anderson, 1989a: 115).

The Migrant Health Act led to creation of rural clinics in communities around the country where migrant workers moved from community to community to engage in agricultural production of various kinds. Many migrant families were enabled to secure health care for the first time. The scope of many clinics has since been broadened to serve other low-income citizens in these communities. This program, in combination with the neighborhood health centers created under the Economic Opportunity Act and Maternal and Child Health programs, has provided increased access to many additional low-income families throughout the nation (Barger, 1991: 290).

Similarly, the Community Mental Health Centers Act initiated the expansion of mental health services throughout the country, vastly increasing the publicly funded accessibility of care for a wide range of mental disorders—particularly for people who could not afford the fees of private psychiatrists, psychologists, or psychiatric social workers.

The Comprehensive Health Planning Act was intended to bring order to the large number of health-related programs at the federal, state, and local levels. It met with some success, but was widely criticized as overly bureaucratic and ineffective at integrating public and private care. Most of the provisions of this Act were later discontinued.

Developments and Refinements of the 1970s

The 1970s was also a period of new initiatives as well as adaptation to the major changes of the 1960s. Some of the new initiatives have had profound implications for the 1990s, such as the emergence of "managed care" as the dominant form of health care delivery.

Cost saving was one of the prime goals associated with the passage of the Health Maintenance Organization Act of 1973—with a specific goal of subsidizing the formation of prepaid insurance groups. Grants from a $375 million appropriation were disseminated to prepaid group practices around the nation. The HMO concept was also intended to offer comprehensive services, greater efficiency, and improved convenience for consumers. Employers were encouraged to select an HMO option as one of the available insurance plans for employees. Medicare later began to offer annual capitation rates for HMOs enrolling older people (Anderson, 1989a: 115).

The Kaiser-Permanente prepaid plan was established in the Western United States and other plans were developed in the East and Midwest, sometimes as group health cooperatives (in Minnesota and Washington) owned by consumers. However, HMOs had enrolled only 5.3 percent of the population by 1989. Only recently with the threat of federally sponsored universal insurance have the cost-saving advantages begun to encourage many businesses to enroll their employees.

Independent practice associations (IPAs) and preferred provider organizations (PPOs) were initiated as other forms of managed care. Both are more flexible than HMOs and more popular with physicians who can maintain private practice. Both arrangements offer discounted fees to insured patients who use physician-members of the IPA or PPO. Forty-three percent of physicians had contracted with PPOs by 1987, but only 12 percent of their income came from these sources (Glaser, 1989: 129–146).

Refinement of Comprehensive Health Planning Efforts

As noted earlier, comprehensive health planning was introduced in the late 1960s as a vehicle to increase local coordination, facilities planning, and presumably more efficient use of available services. Regional medical programs were also created linking medical schools with practitioners—to improve integration of services for specific problems such as heart disease, cancer, stroke, and diabetes. The National Health Planning and Resources Development Act of 1974 mandated the implementation of 200 health planning areas with wide responsibilities to guide hospital construction, initiate new technology, and develop master plans for health services (Anderson, 1989b: 116).

Three types of activity were initiated through this planning effort: (1) control of hospital bed supply; (2) control of hospital charges; and (3) monitoring of physician decisions related to hospital costs. The federal government initiated certificate of need (CON) regulations for introduction of new technology in hospitals, hospital rate setting, and professional standards review organizations (PSROs) to monitor physicians, all of which introduced complex review procedures, but, unfortunately, did not significantly constrain costs (Ruggie, 1992: 925).

The CON requirements and other health planning responsibilities were delegated to the states but were often not implemented because there was little effective control. However, the PSROs (later PROs, or peer review organizations) became a significant factor in monitoring costs and quality of Medicare services even though the cost-control goal was not achieved. The planning agencies did not have sufficient support to withstand the effort by the Reagan Administration to eliminate them; funding was thus withdrawn in 1983 (Ruggie, 1992: 925).

Health Care Technology and Cost-Control Efforts

The federal Office of Technology Assessment (OTA) was created in 1974 as an agency to evaluate the role and effectiveness of technology in health care and other fields. Studies were conducted to determine if the costs of various technologies were both valuable and cost-effective. Results were to be used, among other things, to determine the level of federal funding that should be committed to additional technological development (Larsson, 1994).

Emphasis on Rural Health

The Rural Health Clinic Services Act of 1977 expanded resources for rural clinics and emphasized the role of midlevel nurse-practitioners and physician assistants in providing rural primary care. Rural Health Initiative grants increased the number of rural health centers staffed by nurse-practitioners and physician assistants (PAs) and with minimal physician support. As of 1991, rural health centers staffed primarily by nurses were made eligible for Medicare reimbursement (Barger, 1991: 290).

At the national level, the federal Office of Rural Health Policy was created and has become a major force in supporting research and advocating policies of benefit to rural areas. Rural health research centers were created in several regions of the United States and have been responsible for expanding knowledge about rural health while identify-

ing characteristics of health care in rural areas that need further attention.

Cost Control in the 1980s: The Advent of DRGs

Failure to control costs eventually led, in 1983, to prospective payment for services as an alternative to increasingly high retrospective costs for Medicare patients. Diagnosis-Related Groups (DRGs) were created as the first major national effort to specifically identify, describe, and specify costs for categories of disease and illness. The clear goal of the DRG system is hospital cost containment and greater efficiency in delivering services. A preestablished schedule of payments for each category of illness was developed for 383 (later increased to more than 470) groupings of diseases and illnesses. Payment levels are based on statistical averaging of past costs for treatment of each diagnosis category. Amounts to be paid are adjusted as new information is gathered (Ruggie, 1992: 929).

Resource-Based Relative-Value Scales (RBRVSs)

Congress established the Physician Payment Review Commission to investigate application of the DRG principles to physician payment. This eventually led to development of the "Resource-Based Relative-Value Scale," a device to measure and control costs of physician services. Implementation was authorized by the Omnibus Budget Reconciliation Act of 1989, with startup during 1992 under supervision of the Health Care Financing Administration (HCFA) (Iglehart, 1992a: 966).

Specific limits were placed on fee increases and constraints were placed on "balance billing." The relative rates of reimbursement were changed to give greater weight to primary care evaluation and patient management and somewhat less reward for specialist procedures. Private insurers have been hesitant to adopt the new approach, partially because it has the potential to substantially reduce physician income (Glaser, 1991a: 129; Iglehart, 1992a: 966).

Passage and Repeal of the Catastrophic Coverage Act of 1988

Inadequacy of long-term care and prescription drug coverage has been a major complaint of the older population. Medicaid as the principal funding source for nursing home care is not considered satisfactory because it requires a means test and provides only minimal coverage. Individuals who may have been relatively well-off financially are forced to "spend down" any resources they had accumulated until reaching the poverty level. Huge variations in coverage exist between states.

Consequently, Congress enacted a "catastrophic coverage act" in 1988 that would have alleviated this problem and provided prescription drug coverage as well. Part of the financing was to come from increased premiums from more affluent older individuals. However, the financing scheme was bitterly opposed by senior citizens groups, leading to repeal of most provisions of the Act in 1989 (Anderson, 1989b: 57).

Declining Insurance Coverage

Access to health insurance actually declined in the 1980s, with an accompanying steady rise in the number of uninsured. Rural and inner city areas have the highest increases in the proportion of uninsured. This problem continues to cause a high level of uncompensated and highly inefficient care and is one of the contributors to high costs for providers (Anderson, 1989b: 59).

Managed Competition in the 1990s

Continuing failure to control costs has led to a substantial shift to various forms of *managed competition* as an integrative mechanism and cost-control device. Managed competition uses the managed care concept to integrate financing and delivery in one organization. It reorders relationships between patients and providers and directly restricts the autonomy of physicians and hospitals. The concept further controls patient access and utilization of services by requiring prior approval of services and referrals. Financial incentives and penalties are used to control patients and providers (Iglehart, 1992b: 1715).

The Clinton Administration proposed to use this approach to solve many of the major problems of access and cost through legislative reforms in 1993. However, Congress was not prepared to make the changes and declined to seriously consider a significant reform proposal. The Clinton Plan was labeled as too bureaucratic and too expensive.

CULTURAL FACTORS

The difficulty in securing passage of major reforms is in substantial part a consequence of the dominant American value orientation that favors individual independence and self-reliance. Government-sponsored or -managed insurance is widely viewed as antagonistic to private initiative and responsibility. Those citizens who earn lower incomes and cannot afford health insurance, according to this value orientation, are judged to be of inferior status and undeserving. Everyone is expected to "lift themselves up by their bootstraps," regardless of any impediments that might interfere.

A related high-priority value favors private charity: the inclination to provide for those in need through voluntary assistance and "charity care." American communities are well populated with a wide range of voluntary organizations of many kinds, including nonprofit hospitals and charity care clinics. Many of these are supported largely by donations from individuals, businesses, foundations, and other types of organizations. Some of the proposals for reform of the U.S. health care system would place even greater emphasis on voluntary actions while diminishing the contributions of government.

As a result, these informal and formal activities provide some level of access to health care for many uninsured individuals. For example, Shriners Children's hospitals throughout the nation provide free care for children with many kinds of serious illnesses. Ronald McDonald houses, sponsored by the McDonald Restaurant chain, provide low-priced or free housing for families of children who are receiving hospital care.

Physicians and hospitals in most communities have voluntarily devoted a proportion of their services to "charity care." Public hospital emergency rooms have become an access point for many uninsured people. This value orientation was codified in law through a formal requirement passed by Congress in 1986, and strengthened in 1990, requiring publicly funded (through federal or state programs such as Medicare and Medicaid) health care facilities to provide some level of free care to those who cannot pay. Patients cannot be refused treatment or transferred to another facility if their condition is unstable. However, because of the very high cost of these services, hospitals in some locations have terminated emergency services (McMurray, 1991: 18).

The emphasis on pragmatic problem solving is another feature of American culture that strongly affects health care delivery. Americans tend to believe that any health care problem can be solved and are willing to invest heavily in finding the solutions. This leads physicians and other providers to take an aggressive attitude toward provision of health care. The consequence is many more diagnostic tests and surgeries than in most other countries. A particularly aggressive approach is taken in dealing with mental illness through strong doses of drugs as a primary means to solve both mild and severe psychiatric problems (Peters, 1991: 44–45).

POLITICAL INFLUENCES

Responsibility for public contributions to health care is divided among the four primary levels of government: federal, state, county, and municipalities. The federal government is responsible for overall policy, with the U.S. Congress, the executive branch, and the court system all having roles to play. This system of "checks and balances" works well for many governmental functions, but has been notably unsuccessful in developing a coherent national health care policy. Nonetheless, the federal government makes a wide range of focused contributions to public health and health care.

The federal Department of Health and Human Services has overall responsibility for development of health policy proposals, under the leadership of the Secretary and Surgeon General. Within this department, the Public Health Service is the lead agency. The Environmental Protection Agency has responsibility for maintaining the general quality of the physical environment and engages in a wide range of preventive health activities.

Both the House of Representatives and the Senate, the two bodies of the U.S. Congress, must of course pass the legislation supporting and financing federal activities. All approved bills must then be signed by the President. The complex committee structure of the Congress evaluates proposals and drafts legislation that is then presented to each body for approval.

If there is a challenge to any of the legislation, the federal court system passes on its constitutionality or legality, with the Supreme Court as the final arbiter. The court system has been highly influential in establishing the acceptability of many public health and environmental measures that have been challenged by businesses, states, or special interest groups. Key activities of several federal government units in the Executive Branch are summarized in Table 3-3.

These and many other direct federal contributions to health care services and supplies collectively added up to about 18.4 percent of the total health care budget in 1991. State and local contributions totaled about 16.6 percent. The total direct government funds reached 35 percent. If all national

Table 3-3   Examples of Federal Government
Health Programs

- Public health rules and programs, implemented
  primarily through the U.S. Public Health Service and
  the Environmental Protection Agency
- Research and development through the National
  Institutes of Health and the National Institutes for
  Mental Health
- Medicare for the elderly, and Medicaid (shared with
  the states) for segments of the low-income
  population, with supervision by the federal Health
  Care Financing Administration (HCFA)
- Health care insurance for the military services, war
  veterans, and all federal employees, including
  members of Congress, through a variety of publicly
  funded insurance plans
- Support for health professions education and
  research, through many programs that provide
  grants and contracts to universities throughout the
  nation
- Support for public community clinics in low-income
  rural and urban areas throughout the country,
  serving migrant workers and other low-income
  subgroups of the population
- Environmental monitoring and cleanup, through the
  Environmental Protection Agency

health care expenditures are totaled, including the contributions of Medicare beneficiaries and contributions of employers to federal programs, the proportion of public expenditures reached 43.9 percent in 1993, and direct private expenditures were 56.1 percent (National Center for Health Statistics, 1995: 223, 226).

In addition to part of the costs for Medicaid, the states support departments of health (often combined with other social services) that directly pay for many public health and private health care activities. Most long-term-care regulation and quality control is a state responsibility, although most facilities are privately operated.

Many states have taken initiatives on their own to reform health care. For example, Hawaii has for many years had a health insurance requirement covering most citizens with financing through payroll tax deductions. Oregon has developed a highly visible program to insure most of the low-income people by expanding Medicaid coverage—while limiting the range of procedures to be covered through a rationing process. Washington and Massachusetts legislatures passed major reforms increasing state responsibility for insurance provision only to have them reversed in later legislative sessions. Many other states have taken some steps to improve insurance coverage.

SOCIAL ORGANIZATION OF HEALTH CARE

Public Health Services

The public health care system in the United States is available to all citizens but is restricted to a specific range of activities. The U.S. Public Health Service provides prevention-oriented resources to states, gathers national epidemiological information on health status, distributes information about public health needs, and provides selected direct services to American Indian reservations. However, most of the actual delivery of public health services is managed by units of state and local government. Local public health departments focus primarily on preventive programs such as education, immunizations for infectious diseases, AIDs prevention and treatment, maternal and child health, occupational health, laboratory services, food and drug safety, and protection of public health through sanitation regulations and environmental health activities (Larsson, 1994).

Local departments are usually headed by a physician who in smaller jurisdictions serves part-time whereas programs are operated by a staff of public health nurses and other support personnel. The Indian Health Service is now operated by the U.S. Public Health Service in cooperation with tribal governments. Health care for Indian tribal groups has traditionally been a federal responsibility, although tribes in some locations have taken over full administrative responsibility. Other agencies of the Public Health Service and their primary functions are summarized in Table 3-4.

Table 3-4   Major Units and Functions of the U.S. Public Health Service

- Centers for Disease Control and Prevention: protection of health through leadership in prevention and control of major diseases
- Food and Drug Administration: protection against impure and unsafe food, drugs, cosmetics, and other potential hazards
- Health Resources and Services Administration: improvement of the health care system and overall health status, through health professions training, community health centers, maternal and child health, migrant health, AIDS prevention, and the National Health Service Corps.
- National Institutes of Health: biomedical research, including the National Cancer Institute; the National Heart, Lung and Blood Institute; the National Library of Medicine; and other research institutes
- Agency for Health Care Policy and Research: research on problems related to quality and delivery of health services
- Substance Abuse and Mental Health Services Administration: research and support for prevention and control of substance abuse and mental disorder
- Agency for Toxic Substance and Disease Registry: keeps track of use and distribution of all major forms of toxic substances and the incidence of use

Source: Based on *National Health Directory,* 1994.

The U.S. Public Health Service published a report in 1990, *Healthy People 2000: National Health Promotion and Disease Prevention Objectives*, a benchmark and milestone in public health activity. It was intended to increase the uniformity and intensity of prevention and promotion efforts throughout the country. It provides a summary of the health status for American citizens, and outlines the goals and methods that could (1) further improve healthy life-styles, (2) reduce health disparities among citizens, and (3) improve preventive services. Specific measures were developed to measure outcomes achieved over time (Stoto, 1992: 59).

Physicians and Primary Care

Primary health care refers to basic ambulatory health services that become the usual entry point to the larger health care system. Primary care is most often undertaken by physicians in family practice, general internal medicine, pediatrics, and obstetrics/gynecology. Some pharmacists, nurse-practitioners, physician assistants, and dentists are also providers of primary care. Hospitals are increasingly providers of outpatient primary care as a supplement to secondary inpatient care services (Koska, 1990: 24–25).

Independent private practices were the primary mechanism for delivering primary care until the post–World War II period. Some form of group practice or partnership, consisting of single or multiple specialties, has now become the norm.

The trend toward greater specialization by physicians in nonprimary care fields has been underway since 1930, when the ratio of general practitioners to specialists was 80 to 20 percent; in 1993, this ratio had shifted to 34 percent primary care to 66 percent specialists. The major growth in physician supply has been in nonprimary care specialties with most of the specialty concentration in metropolitan areas. By 1993 about 20 percent of M.D.s worked on salary in hospitals, medical schools, public health, for other organizations, or as part of capitated systems; the remainder were independent fee-for-service practitioners (Cockerham, 1995: 270; National Center for Health Statistics, 1995: 202).

Private practice physicians in group practice share some of their fees with the group to support the cost of the practice. Many of the insurance and organizational details are handled by hired professional administrative staff. Economies of scale are achieved through cooperative management and joint use of support equipment and personnel. Group practice is much more the norm for specialists than for primary care providers and is more prevalent in some parts of the country than in others. For example, the South and East have a lower proportion of physicians in group practice than the West and Midwest (Goldsmith, 1993: 168).

Prepaid managed care. Prepaid group practices are a mix of insurance and service delivery. Under the health maintenance organization (HMO) arrangement, a *closed panel of salaried staff physicians* serves clients who pay a per capita premium for which they receive a defined set of benefits without copayments. *Open physician panel* prepaid groups include independent practice associations (IPAs) and preferred provider organizations (PPOs). Physicians have more freedom under the open arrangements. Each physician may contract with one or more IPAs or PPOs. Physicians stand to gain additional patients although at lower fees than normally charged (Glaser, 1991a: 247).

A new and more flexible form of mixed plan, with both closed panel physicians and open panels, began to evolve in 1991 and has become the most rapidly growing type of insuring organization with about 12.5 million members in 1994—as compared to 13.6 million in group or closed panel plans and 16.1 million in open panel plans. Many of the mixed plans are sponsored by major private health provider organizations such as hospitals or physician hospital organizations. Some are voluntary nonprofit, and others are entrepreneurial private companies with high profit potential (National Center for Health Statistics, 1995: 39, 242). The primary features of managed care are summarized in Table 3-5.

Table 3-5 Characteristics of Managed Care Organizations

- A clearly differentiated and carefully examined member population
- A central management structure that controls and directs resource allocation for the entire enterprise
- A known group of physicians on fixed salaries (in HMO types) or discounted fee schedule, with family practice or generalist physicians having an equal role with specialists and serving as gatekeepers to specialist care
- Designated group of other professional and support staff
- Specific set of services or benefits
- An identified and limited supply of accessible hospital beds
- An annual budget based on subscription fees

Source: Based on Anderson, 1989b: 64.

The Kaiser Permanente group in the western United States, the Mayo Clinic Plan in Rochester, Minnesota, the Harvard Medical Plan in Massachusetts, and Group Health in the Twin Cities of Minnesota and in the Northwest are among successful and relatively low-cost examples of prepaid plans.

Prepaid managed care organizations attempt to achieve lower-cost and higher-quality health care by directly managing the full range of prevention, health maintenance, and care. The goal in each organizational form is to solve patient problems at minimum cost. Physicians are rewarded for making the correct diagnosis and treating patients to minimize complications and hospitalization. The organization discourages the use of any medical procedures that are not clearly indicated for patient well-being. A determined effort is made to employ only the number of physicians needed in each specialty, so that each physician has a full schedule and deals only with problems in their interest and skill area. Less control can be exercised under the open-panel arrangements as compared to the closed-panel HMO (Enthoven, 1990: 65).

Under ideal conditions, regular interaction occurs between specialists and generalists as they jointly attempt to solve problems while measuring and controlling quality of care. Both groups can make a good income at a relatively efficient cost per case. The organizations offer a major role for physicians in the design and management of care delivery, but professional administrators are generally in charge of financial and organizational management (Enthoven, 1990: 65–66).

The various forms of managed care have been widely adopted by government and private industry; studies indicate it is the least-cost health care delivery method currently available. Growth was high in the early 1980s (24 percent between 1983 and 1987), but slowed to about 7 percent annually during the early 1990s. By the end of 1994, approximately 16.1 percent of Americans (41.4 million people) were enrolled. So far the plans are more popular in the west where 26 percent of the population are enrolled, compared to 20 percent in the Northeast, 14 percent in the Midwest, and 9 percent in the South. In California, fully one-third of the population are members (Hilzenrath, 1994; Vincenzino, 1994: 32; National Center for Health Statistics, 1995: 39, 242).

The research evidence indicates clearly that managed care physicians hospitalize patients at a lower rate than fee-for-service physicians—for both diagnosis and treatment. Managed care physicians do more diagnostic testing and preventive care in their office practice. They see more patients and talk to them more. They also work fewer hours and earn less (Glaser, 1991a: 249).

Both private insurance companies and larger private businesses are actively developing their own prepaid health care organizations. They employ a staff of physicians and other health care professionals who must abide by company rules with respect to hospitalization and use of high-cost specialty services. Hospitals become a part of the service but are not the center of health care activity—as has usually been the case in the past (Goldsmith, 1993: 166).

Physician-hospital organizations. Physician-hospital organizations (PHOs) are sometimes formed with joint control by physician groups and hospital trustees—partially as a means of competing with the several forms of managed care noted earlier. In other cases, hospitals have purchased physician practices to create vertically integrated organizations with better control over costs. Physicians become salaried employees of the hospital (Goldsmith, 1993: 162–165).

Community, migrant, and Indian health centers. Indian, community, and/or migrant health centers were organized in many communities around the nation with federal support as authorized by the legislation noted earlier. They were designed to provide services in locations, and for populations, that otherwise lacked adequate health care. (Holden, 1990: S34; Wasem, 1990: 85).

Even with federal subsidies, it remains difficult to recruit health professionals to isolated and rural locations that often have modest facilities. The working environment is viewed by providers of care as generally undesirable because of isolation, bureaucratic requirements, and the perceived difficulty of working with many low-income and minority patients. Families who have become accustomed to urban services are often unhappy in rural locations and aspire to better schools and a wider array of high-quality services (Holden, 1990: S34).

Physician dissatisfaction. The "hassle factor" has become a major issue as physicians find their roles changing from patient advocate to cost-containment watchdogs. One visit to a physician's office is estimated to generate an average of ten pieces of paper, partially to document payment requests to Medicare and insurance companies (Meharg, 1992).

A 1992 survey of U.S., German, and Canadian physicians indicated that 77 percent of American physicians were dissatisfied with the health care system, as compared to 48 percent in Germany and 33 percent in Canada. Sixty-eight percent of American physicians feel that fundamental changes in the health care system are needed, compared with 46 percent in Germany and 63 percent in Canada. U.S. physicians are troubled by several major problems (Iglehart, 1992a: 963; Blendon et al., 1993: 1012–1013):

- Lack of access to care for many citizens
- High cost of care
- Close oversight of their professional work by third-party external reviewers (Medicare and other insurance organizations) attempting to control costs
- Intrusiveness of government
- Regulations, forms, arbitrary requirements, and other procedural hoops
- Delay in receiving payment for services provided
- Uncertainty of their personal status in a changing system

Continuing efforts to limit fees or force physicians onto salaries are likely to cause continuing stress. An example is the Resource-Based Relative-Value Scale (discussed earlier) for determining fee payments under Medicare. The new payment system attempts to place a cap on fees for services and procedures. Relative values are calculated for each type of physician service, office expenses, and malpractice insurance costs. Final details of the system were negotiated with physicians but the requirement was basically imposed by the Health Care Financing Administration as a vehicle to control Medicare costs (Evans, 1990: 101–128; Iglehart, 1991: 825).

The constant pressure from administrators to minimize hospitalization through conformance to the prospective payment system, and the consequent emphasis on outpatient rather than inpatient treatment, have changed the practice mode substantially. Many physicians feel they have been forced to increase clerical staff (now 47 percent of employed personnel) to adequately complete billing and administrative requirements. Increasing amounts of physician time are required for administrative detail. This generates anger at government insurance programs and private companies, while infringing on time for patient care (Meharg, 1992: 797).

Physician frustration is apparently having the effect of lowering interest in primary care specialties (family practice, internal medicine, pediatrics, obstetrics/gynecology) in medical schools. Fee income has been lower for these primary care fields (although the RBRVS system is supposed to correct part of the problem), whereas intensity of involvement with patients and difficulty of collecting fees was higher (Meharg, 1992: 797).

The private practice of medicine appears to many physicians to be "unraveling," without a clear and satisfying alternative available. Although physician income has continued to rise, on average, through 1992, take-home pay has begun to decline significantly in some regions of the country as a direct consequence of (1) implementation of RBRVS scale for Medicare patients, and (2) emer-

gence of "managed care" as the primary insurance mode in many markets. Tax rates for higher-income physicians have also increased. Some categories of specialist physicians have been most negatively affected, while primary care practitioners have benefited to some degree from the changes (Goldsmith, 1993: 161).

Medical education. Graduate medical education has become the primary path to professional practice. Very few physicians begin serving patients full-time immediately upon receiving an M.D. Some degree of specialization has become the rule even in primary care and general practice. Family practice now requires 3 or 4 years of postgraduate study, as do general internal medicine and general pediatrics (Foreman, 1990: 78).

Academic medical centers have been slow to adapt teaching programs to meet national needs, and have been unsuccessful in encouraging or forcing academic programs to produce an adequate number of primary care physicians. The federal government has provided incentives through scholarships and special programs such as the National Health Service Corps, but these have not been sufficient to increase the numbers of primary care practitioners (Foreman, 1990: 79; Holden, 1990: S32).

A number of regional programs have been initiated to help deal with the problem. For example, the so-called WAMI (Washington, Alaska, Montana, Idaho, and recently Wyoming) in the Northwest is operated through the University of Washington Medical School, which trains students from each of these states. Only Washington has a medical school. Medical students receive an initial year or two of preparation at collaborating universities in their home states, and then complete their studies at the UW. After completing their M.D. and specialty training, they are encouraged to return to their home states to practice in areas of need. Although the program has been reasonably successful, it by no means fills all of the needs in any of the states.

The shift to managed care is beginning to have an impact on education. Much of the demand for primary care practitioners is now coming from HMOs. Yet, most postgraduate medical education continues to be centered in hospitals. Residents-in-training provide a high proportion of patient care in teaching hospitals rather than in the new practice settings. Efforts are underway by some academic medical centers to shift some of their graduate training to managed care residencies (Moore, 1990: 427).

Minority and female enrollment in U.S. medical schools has increased substantially in recent decades, rising from 4 percent in 1968 to 30 percent in 1993. Seven percent were African-American, 5.8 percent Hispanics, and 15 percent Asian-Americans. Only 0.5 percent were American Indian. Enrollment increases for women have been dramatic, rising from 14 percent in 1972 to 42 percent of all beginning students in 1993. More than 60 percent of all African-American students were female, and more than 40 percent of Hispanic, American Indian, and Asians were female (National Center for Health Statistics, 1995: 208–210).

Nurses and Nursing

Most nurses have traditionally worked in hospitals. However, a major change is underway. Increasing numbers now also play a highly critical role in ambulatory care, long-term care, home health care, schools, industrial settings, and public community health. Smaller numbers work in education, utilization review, or as special representatives in professional organizations such as the National League for Nursing or the American Nurses Association. They are in many respects the operational core of the health care system. The distribution of nurses is summarized in Table 3-6.

The several levels of nursing—registered nurses, licensed practical nurses, and nurses aides—do most of the direct patient care in each of the roles noted earlier, while also serving as integrators of the various dimensions of health care within ambulatory and

Table 3-6   Distribution of Nurses by Employment Category (1993)

Employment Category	Percentage
Hospitals	68
Ambulatory care	7
Long-term care	8
Home health, schools, industrial	10
Public health	7
	100

Source: Based on data from Weiss and Lonnquist, 1994: 201.

hospital settings. Their numbers and level of training have increased sharply during recent decades as managed care, long-term care, home health care, and nurse-practitioner roles have expanded. Training of nurses has evolved to a highly specialized status. Nurse administrators and nurse-practitioners are now generally required to have graduate degrees (Weiss and Lonnquist, 1994: 201).

Most registered nurses come from working and lower-middle-class backgrounds and considerably increase their status and incomes by entering what has now become a largely middle-class occupation. The field of nursing remains dominated by women, although increasing numbers of men have entered the field—particularly in hospitals and long-term-care institutions (Weiss and Lonnquist, 1994: 203).

As the status of nursing and salaries have increased, the cost of well-trained nurses has also caused the overall cost of health care to increase. This has led hospitals and other providers to limit employment of highly trained nurses, replacing them with less-trained practical nurses or nurse aides who can undertake patient care and unit management activities at lower cost. At the same time, well-trained nurses are undertaking some of the primary care tasks formerly reserved for physicians, also at lower cost than physician services (Weiss and Lonnquist, 1994: 208).

Nursing education. Nursing education has shifted from historic hospital-based training offering diplomas programs to college or university preparation. Two-year junior colleges offering Associate Degrees (ADN) graduated 56,800 students in 1993, whereas Bachelor of Science in Nursing (BSN) programs had 24,440 graduates. An increasing proportion of nurses are seeking Masters of Science (MSN) degrees. The number of BSN programs has increased from 377 in 1980 to 501 in 1993. Growth in graduate degree programs has increased to 212 MSN programs and 47 doctoral programs. Specialization has increased with many graduates now entering nurse-anesthetist, nurse-midwife, clinical nurse, nurse-practitioner, and other advanced practice roles. Graduate education is the fast growing segment of nursing education (Morey-Pedersen, 1994: 76; National Center for Health Statistics, 1995: 207).

An increasing number of nurses are entering administration, in hospitals, visiting nurses organizations, long-term care, managed care, home health care, in community clinics, and in nursing education, as noted earlier. Others are engaging in research to measure outcomes of care, determine patient care needs, and a variety of other topics. Despite the cutbacks in hospital nursing positions, opportunities for well-prepared nurses in other health fields such as managed care appear to be relatively abundant (Morey-Pedersen, 1994: 77).

Pharmacists and Pharmaceuticals

The role of pharmacists is also changing rapidly, toward more advanced education and a greater role as pharmaceutical care specialists. As the number of prescription drugs proliferate, it is increasingly difficult for physicians to maintain an adequate knowledge of appropriate drugs for various ailments. Better trained pharmacists are assuming a stronger role as consultants to physicians in better use of available medications.

Pharmaceutical costs are increasing. More appropriate use of medications also can play a crucial role in lowering health care costs. Many mistakes are currently made in use of drugs. For example between 30 to 50 percent of patients deviate from appropriate use of prescription medications, and up to 55 percent of the elderly do not comply with medication regimens (Kessler, 1991: 1651).

This happens in part because of failure to understand the proper procedure. Either no instructions were provided, patients did not understand directions, or patients simply did not abide by what they understood as the correct procedure. Pharmacists and/or physicians may have failed to properly counsel patients and need better preparation in how to assist with compliance.

Pharmaceutical care can help alleviate these problems by providing much more intensive attention to education of patients in best uses of medications, while helping physicians make better prescription decisions. New federal and state rules require more counseling and improved instructions, but these new requirements may not resolve the problem without greater focus on patient education about the use of drugs (Kessler, 1991: 1651).

Medicare did not pay for prescription pharmaceutical costs as of 1995. This is a notable inadequacy of the program from the elderly patient perspective, and has created severe problems for many of the lower-income elderly who have their hospital and physician costs largely covered. Estimates indicate that about 80 percent of the cost for over-the-counter and prescription medications are paid for out-of-pocket. Some patients are covered by private insurance pharmaceutical care plans or through state-sponsored plans (Barer et al., 1992: 772).

Pharmacy education. The training of pharmacists is in transition. Decisions were made by the professional association of colleges of pharmacy to require a Doctor of Pharmacy as the entry-level degree by the year 2000. Most pharmacists have heretofore earned only B.S. degrees. The social status of pharmacists therefore has been viewed as less prestigious than physicians (especially by physicians!)—largely because of less stringent educational requirements and the perception of pharmacists as primarily dispensers of pills.

Colleges of pharmacy around the country are now quickly converting their curricula to eliminate B.S. programs and offer only the Pharm.D., or Ph.D., in pharmaceutical sciences. The expectation is that this change generally will enhance the status and role of the pharmacist as a member of the health care team, while increasing competency in the pharmaceutical care role discussed earlier.

The role of retail pharmacy is also changing. Corner drug stores are being replaced by large chain stores. Forty percent of new pharmacy graduates now begin their professions in chain pharmacies; fully 30 percent of practicing pharmacists now work in corporate chains (Hartzema and Perfetto, 1991: 678).

Health Services Administration

Professional health administration has become a highly critical professional field in health care. Most hospitals, managed care organizations, larger physician groups, and other provider organizations are now managed by individuals with graduate degrees in health services administration. The field draws from professional management research results and applies the findings to the specific issues and problems in health care. More than seventy colleges and universities, located in nearly every state, now offer graduate degrees in the field, often in Schools of Public Health, Schools of Business Administration, or in other health science colleges. Most programs are 2 years in duration. A high proportion of students have prior experience in health care, as physicians, nurses, or in other health fields.

Midlevel Practitioners

Nurse-practitioners, physician assistants, certified nurse-midwives, and certified nurse-anesthetists are often referred to as "midlevel practitioners." There were about 20,650 nurse-practitioners, 22,000 physician assistants, 22,500 nurse-anesthetists, and 4,000 nurse midwives at work in 1991. Approxi-

mately 16 percent of nurse-practitioners and 13 percent of physician assistants work in rural areas. They obviously do not have all the knowledge or skills of physicians but are prepared to function as independent practitioners in circumstances where they can be supervised by physicians while providing otherwise unavailable services. Many nurse-practitioners have graduate-level degrees in advance practice nursing, but the requirement is not standardized across the country (Lutz, 1991: 24–28; Geyman and Hart, 1993: 44).

Duke University established the first 2-year training program for physician assistants (PAs) in 1965. Since that time, many other programs have been established, supported in part by the Health Manpower Act of 1972. PAs usually have 2 years of specialized training but in most states are not required to have university degrees. Many of them work in managed care organizations as lower-cost primary care professionals. They are qualified to perform up to about 80 percent of the tasks usually performed by primary care physicians (Lutz, 1991: 24).

As noted earlier, federally certified rural health clinics and migrant worker clinics rely heavily on midlevels to serve primary care needs. However, there is a shortage of candidates for most positions; many managed care organizations and rural clinics are unable to recruit as many midlevels as they would prefer. Training programs are thus expanding to meet increased demand. The curriculum usually includes 1 year of basic medical sciences and a second year of clinical residency under physician supervision (Lutz, 1991: 24–28; Geyman and Hart, 1993: 44; Weiss and Lonnquist, 1994: 209).

Allied Health Workers

In addition to the roles described earlier, a wide range of other health care professions are critical to high-quality health care. These include the range of fields listed in Table 3-7 as well as others.

Training programs for these occupations are available in colleges of allied health

Table 3-7   Allied Health Care Fields

Medical laboratory technology	Emergency medical technician
Medical record administration	Radiographer .
Occupational therapy	Radiation therapy technologist
Respiratory therapy	Surgical technologist
Physical therapy .	Blood bank technologist
Speech therapy	

throughout the country. The demand for allied health staff has been growing rapidly, especially in such fields as physical therapy and speech therapy. Shortages are sufficiently evident in many fields to compromise quality of available care (Weiss and Lonnquist, 1994: 213).

Hospitals

Hospitals have long been the focal point of health care, using nearly 50 percent of all health resources. They represent one of the primary services and employment fields in most communities. It is here that high-technology medicine is most likely to be available. Physicians have traditionally demanded access to a good hospital as a prerequisite to establishing a practice within a community. However, the high cost and possible overuse of advanced technology has made hospitals a major target for cost savings. The number of acute-care hospitals has declined by 11 percent since 1975 and further declines are reported annually (Evans, 1990: 101–128; Hilzenrath, 1994).

Hospitals are subject to a wide range of detailed and costly regulations. Yet they retain considerable freedom to expand facilities and technology. Boards of trustees and administrators of private nonprofit and for-profit hospitals deliberately try to acquire the latest technology and high-quality facilities as the basis for attracting both physicians and patients—whether or not the technology duplicates what is already available in another nearby hospital (Glaser, 1991b: 396).

Many community hospitals therefore have been experiencing major financial problems

and have been forced to downsize to survive. Bad debt and required cost shifting to cover nonpaying patients have created a widespread sense of crisis. High administrative costs have forced cuts in organizational units. This has led to overall "flattening" of the organizational structure. The number of administrators and other employees, including professional nurses, has been declining steadily in the early 1990s.

Collaboration between hospitals and other providers (such as physician groups as noted earlier) is increasingly a vehicle for purchase of new technology or provision of common services such as rehabilitation. Many hospitals are creating their own managed care insurance programs or are collaborating with managed care providers in provision of controlled-cost hospital services (Glaser, 1991b: 393–394).

Increasing outpatient services. Outpatient surgery more than tripled between 1980 and 1992, going from 16 percent of all surgeries to 54 percent. Smaller hospitals with less than 100 beds emphasized outpatient surgery more (61 percent) than larger hospitals (46 to 58 percent). Outpatient visits nearly doubled during the same period, whereas total admissions declined. Average length of stay for inpatients declined gradually from 8.4 days in 1960 to 7.4 days in 1992. It is quite clear that the role of the hospital is shifting to less inpatient care and greater emphasis on outpatient services (National Center for Health Statistics, 1995: 190).

If only short-stay hospitals are considered, the change is even more pronounced. Days of inpatient care declined by nearly one-half between 1964 and 1993. Average length of stay declined from 8.9 days to 6.1. The number of smaller hospitals (less than 100 beds) declined by 25 percent between 1975 and 1992, while numbers of larger hospitals stayed approximately the same. Occupancy rates for smaller hospitals were 50 percent in 1992, down from 60 percent in 1980; the rate was down from 77 to about 67 percent for hospitals from 100 to 400 beds, and from 82 to 76 percent for larger hospitals with 500 beds or more. Again, less use of hospitals of all sizes is clearly indicated (National Center for Health Statistics, 1995: 178, 211).

Many hospitals have created specialty units for treatment of specific high-incidence diseases such as arthritis—which affects 37 million people (one in every seven), and costs approximately $37 billion (1 percent of GNP) annually. Arthritis is responsible for 10 percent of all hospital procedures and 9 percent of physician visits. It is thus a prime target for specialized services, providing better patient care while generating higher hospital revenues (Hinz, 1991: 19–22).

Distribution of costs.   Hospitals have been accused of overspecialization and undue bureaucratization, with accompanying inefficiencies leading to higher and higher costs. For example, in a study of one typical large hospital, the following distribution of expenditures was noted (Lathrop, 1991: 18):

- documentation (29 percent)
- standby time while waiting for the next work to be performed (20 percent)
- scheduling and coordination (14 percent)
- hotel and patient services (8 percent)
- transportation (6 percent)
- management and supervision (7 percent)
- patient care (16 percent)

In this case, it is clear that support activities heavily outweigh direct patient care as costs of doing business.

Reorganization and integration for greater efficiency.   Consequently, many hospitals are now drastically altering their operations, by flattening the hierarchy, training staff to undertake multiple roles, diminishing the training and salary requirements for support service roles, and focusing on "patient-centered care." Nurses, medical technicians, and laboratory technicians are cross-trained to provide more services, including respiratory care, EKGs, laboratory analyses, and other functions that can be done in the patient room. Nurse-extenders are widely used for routine tasks, thus lowering the need for higher-cost professional nurses. These and other changes are resulting in major staff reductions—which is the primary factor in lowering costs (Lathrop, 1991: 20; Coile, 1992: 5).

Many of the larger hospitals are now parts of multihospital systems with regional or national markets. Some are voluntary and nonprofit, whereas others are profit-making enterprises. Many have become units in managed care systems. In most cases, multiunit systems have been formed through mergers or acquisitions and have aggressively expanded geographically. They are developing new services and are acquiring advanced technology at the forefront of medical practice. A major goal is always to attract the most competent and prestigious physicians to their hospitals (Goldsmith, 1993: 161).

These developments are a part of a movement throughout the country to create integrated managed care health care organizations that can compete with HMOs and other forms of insurance-sponsored health service organization. The hospital chain operations are predicated on the ability of physicians and hospitals to cooperate, which may not always be a workable assumption because of long-standing mutual suspicion and conflicting goals, as noted earlier. Physicians are trained to be relatively autonomous and have great difficulty submitting to the authority of the new organizational structures. Lack of training in interpersonal skills and organizational behavior can become a serious problem. The adjustment is not easy for either hospital administrators or physicians (Goldsmith, 1993: 163–165).

"Joint-venturing" is one manifestation of integrative efforts between physicians and hospitals. Hospitals join with physician groups in ownership and management of diagnostic or office facilities (for example, MRI centers), and sometimes in co-ownership of hospitals. The ventures offer advantages to both physicians and hospitals in terms of efficiencies, greater income, and joint use of otherwise underutilized facilities.

Physicians may be fully or partially involved with hospital administrators in management decisions. Hospitals assume, for example, such management responsibilities as billing, patient records, and other routine functions—freeing physicians from responsibility for details that do not interest them. The physician/hospital organizations discussed earlier are one example of this trend (Hudson, 1991: 22).

The advantages may be greater for providers of care than patients. Evidence from Florida suggests that joint-venturing between hospitals and physicians in radiation therapy units may lead to higher cost and overuse of procedures. Less access is provided to poorly served populations in Florida. The joint-venturing appears to "skim the cream" by serving primarily well-insured individuals, whereas public community hospitals continue to serve the broader population of inner-city and rural people (Mitchell and Sunshine, 1992: 1492).

Special hospital issues in rural health care. Nearly half of the community hospitals in the United States are in rural regions. They tend to be smaller than average, often with fewer than fifty beds. The small size of service areas means that physicians are difficult to recruit. Without good-quality physicians, rural hospitals cannot survive financially (Lutz, 1990: 30).

The incidence of uninsured or underinsured families is somewhat higher than in urban areas, as noted earlier. Medicare has traditionally not reimbursed rural hospitals at the same rate as urban facilities. From the inception of Medicare until 1989, rural hospitals were reimbursed at a rate of nearly 40 percent less than the average for urban hospitals. That gap has since narrowed to less than 7 percent, greatly improving the situation. Rural hospitals nearly always serve a high proportion of elderly patients and therefore depend on Medicare for much of their financial well-being (Gay, 1990: 13).

Overall conditions for rural hospitals have improved in many states—because of special efforts by legislatures to remove some of the disadvantages. However, rural communities continue to have trouble recruiting enough physicians to serve hospital needs. Many hospitals have moved heavily into outpatient services, as noted earlier, but this has not always offset the loss of inpatient revenue.

Rural hospitals are sometimes located too close together for economic viability. In these cases, one regional hospital might adequately serve the need and have a large enough patient base for financial viability and better quality of services. Despite the inadequacies of rural hospitals, patients from rural communities are generally more satisfied in their community hospital than in urban facilities. Individualized attention and greater attention to the specific needs of patients are apparently more appealing than access to higher technology (Lutz, 1990: 30; Reamy, 1991: 219).

Medical Technology

The United States uses vastly more medical technology than most other countries. For example, the rate of use for magnetic resonance imaging (MRI) is nearly eight times more than in Canada and four times more than in Germany. Open-heart surgery and cardiac catheterization are also much more available in the United States (Rublee, 1989: 178–181).

Technology is credited with 33 to 75 percent of health care cost increases, depending on the mode of cost calculation. If both the equipment cost and the training and time of the personnel who do the procedures are included, the total proportion of cost increases is of course higher. Construction of new space may also often be required to house new equipment or services. The cost of new technologies may cause them to be "overused" to recapture the investment, causing still higher costs (Misener, 1990: 210).

However, new technology can often decrease costs as well, as is certainly the case with computerized management information and communication systems. Readily accessible information and communication systems can save administrative and clinical time while improving the quality of care to patients. Electronic technology is increasingly used to process insurance claims, maintain patient records, and manage health care enterprises—leading gradually to decreased need for the blizzard of paperwork that frustrates insurers, patients, and providers alike (Iglehart, 1992b: 1715).

Technology assessment. Health care technology assessment has existed in the United States since about 1977, but has come fully into practice only recently. The federal Office of Technology Assessment is responsible for evaluating the risks, benefits, and clinical effectiveness of new or current technologies. In addition, Blue Cross/Blue Shield supports a Technology Evaluation and Coverage program to assist in evaluating appropriate technologies for insurance coverage. The American College of Physicians has a Clinical Efficacy Assessment Project, which helps physicians evaluate new or existing technology. The American Medical Association supports a Diagnostic and Therapeutic Technology Assessment program, which encourages physician involvement in technology assessment activities. Collectively, these organizations maintain a constant review of technology to determine its appropriate use—through published reports and recommendations for "practice guidelines" (Kalousdian and Schneider, 1992: 10).

The federal Agency for Health Care Policy and Research has primary responsibility for determining the patient outcomes resulting from assorted uses of technology. Patient Outcomes Research Teams (PORTs) examine outcomes of treatments and offer recommendations based on results. Outcomes can include physiological status of patients after treatment, assessments of functional capacity, and use of health care resources (Clinton, 1991: 2057).

Quality Assessment and Management

Quality *assurance* systems have been established throughout the health care system. "Efficacy" (what a procedure can accomplish when appropriately used) and "effectiveness" (outcome results) are the major criteria for evaluation. Quality *assessment* is the primary tool for evaluating the effectiveness of hospital and other health care services. The Physician Payment Review Commission emphasizes more adequate assessments as the key factor in controlling the costs of health care. If all parties in the health care decision arena—practitioners, government agencies, third-party payers, academic groups, and professional organizations—are incorporated in quality assessment, it becomes a focal point for development of practice guidelines to achieve the best patient outcomes at acceptable cost levels. Clinical trials are used as the scientific method for measuring the effectiveness of procedures, medications, or clinical approaches to care (Salive, Mayfield, and Weissman, 1990: 700; Kalousdian and Schneider, 1992: 8).

Peer review organizations (PROs) are private nonprofit organizations that contract with the federal Health Care Financing Administration (HCFA) to evaluate the quality of health care services for Medicare and Medicaid clients. Each state has an organization for this purpose, although in several states, the process is administered by the same contractor (Washington, Alaska, and Idaho, for example). Physicians serve as advisors and reviewers of Medicare and Medicaid providers to ensure that care is medically necessary and is provided in an appropriate setting (McCully, 1995: 25).

Administrative uses of quality management. "Total quality management" is an expansion of the assessment procedure and has become a significant tool for improving hospitals and other health providing organizations. The process has led to major improvements in patient care services. Three primary components are usually measured (Mehlman, 1990: 371; Dunbar, 1992: 66):

1. *Structure:* Such factors as credentials of the providers, nurse-to-bed ratios in hospitals or other institutions, whether a formal system exists to measure quality of care, and so on.

2. *Process:* Procedures through which care is provided such as bedside care, physician/nurse

relationships, and the manner in which diagnosis, treatment, and therapy are conducted.

3. *Outcome:* Consequences of the structure and process for the patient's health, including physical condition and emotional status or satisfaction with care.

Consumers tend to focus on structure in hospitals, according to a nationwide study conducted in 1990. Priority is given to (*Healthcare Bottom Line*, 1990: 4)

1. Good physicians (37 percent)
2. Modern equipment (21 percent)
3. Modern facility (7 percent)
4. Reputation (4 percent)
5. Other factors (30 percent)

These findings are consistent with studies defining the primary components of health care quality. Bedside nursing care is the number one priority in hospitals and long-term care facilities, followed by clinical skills of the medical staff. Other major factors identified by health care administrators as top-quality components are identified in Table 3-8 (Omachonu, 1990: 47).

Physicians suggest a slightly different set of priorities, with greater emphasis given to nursing competence and quality of physician/patient relationships.

Consumers rate physician quality according to the following priorities (*Healthcare Bottom Line*, 1990: 4):

1. Up-to-date skills and training (24 percent)
2. Positive attitude toward patients (20 percent)

Table 3-8 Quality Factors in Hospital Care

Nursing care	Adequacy of performance
Clinical skills of	by support staff
medical staff	Public appearance
Employee	of the facility
attitudes	Convenience of access
State-of-the-art	to the facility
technology	Quality of the food service
Quality of hospital	Involvement of the trustees
administration	in quality assurance

Source: Based on Omachonu, 1990: 47.

3. Dignified treatment of patients (9 percent)
4. Good reputation as a physician (9 percent)
5. Keeps patients informed (9 percent)
6. Other factors (29 percent)

Patient satisfaction is an increasingly relevant part of quality studies, as competition between providers increases. A recent national survey of patients served by sixty-two hospitals indicated that most patients were quite satisfied overall and complained primarily about inadequate communication from hospital staff. As many as 45 percent of patients from some hospitals indicated they were not sufficiently told about the daily routine. A smaller segment did not feel staff adequately attempted to meet patient needs (20 percent). Patients were more concerned with how they were treated at the interpersonal level than with the technical or clinical dimensions of their care (Cleary et al., 1991: 258).

Outcome assessment and *practice standards* are now the primary formal tools for determining quality of health care. Outcome assessment is an evaluation method that uses objective and fair measurement tools in determining the physical condition and emotional status of patients after an episode of health care. Practice standards are the specific processes for diagnostic and therapeutic management of patient care, including the facilities, equipment, and staff required. Responsibility for development of practice guidelines based on the assessments has been delegated primarily to the federal Agency for Health Care Policy and Research with strong support from the Physician Payment Review Commission (Mehlman, 1990: 375; McNeil, 1993: 6).

An example of an early assessment study indicated that the Prospective Payment System (PPS) for paying hospitals, introduced in 1984, did not have a negative effect on the quality of care. A long-term trend toward improved hospital quality for older as well as younger people has been demonstrated, resulting in lower death rates. However, there is some evidence that older patients are being discharged in less stable condition, as a cost-saving measure, with occasionally negative outcomes. Other evidence suggests some discrimination against the oldest patients, possibly in part because elderly Medicare patients are more costly to care for than younger patients, but reimbursement under PPS guidelines is the same regardless of age (Rogers et al., 1990: 1993; Rosenthal and Landefeld, 1993: 89).

Long-Term Care

Long-term care is an expanding industry, absorbing 7.9 percent of the health care budget in 1995, and is expected to grow steadily as the population of older people increases. Facilities are of at least three types (National Center for Health Statistics, 1995: 234; Samuelson, 1995: 5): (1) skilled nursing, (2) combination of skilled nursing and intermediate care, and (3) intermediate care.

Skilled nursing facilities employ a larger number of nurses and offer more intensive health care than the other categories. Intermediate facilities are primarily custodial and serve residents who are not able to manage the activities of daily living, such as preparing food or toileting, but may be otherwise in reasonably good health. Long-term care facilities have fewer trained staff per patient than hospitals—which makes costs per resident lower (Kane et al., 1990: 359).

Long-term care is among the larger health care industries, with expenditures of about $70 billion in 1993. About 75 percent of the facilities are owned by private entrepreneurs; the remainder are nonprofit and may be owned by churches, local governments, hospitals, or other public organizations. The majority of residents are elderly (approximately 88 percent, mostly over age 75), but significant numbers of disabled younger people require nursing care (12 percent of residents) (Feinleib, Cunningham, and Short, 1994; National Center for Health Statistics, 1995: 234).

Roughly 6 percent of the over-age-65 population are nursing home residents for some part of the year. Residents tend to have lower incomes than the average elderly population and are disproportionately widowed women whose expenses are paid by Medicaid. The advent of Medicaid payment for nursing homes has had major influence on the contemporary nursing home industry as a stable source of revenue. Medicaid allocated about 40 percent of funds for long-term care at a cost of roughly $27 billion in 1993 (Feinleib et al., 1994; Morgan, 1994).

Unfortunately, nursing homes do not have a very positive reputation as places to live. Residents or families generally choose them only as a last resort. Most health care professionals tend not to be interested in working in long-term care if other choices are available, although there are certainly many exceptions. Physicians are less well reimbursed for nursing home care, as compared to ambulatory care or hospital practice, under both Medicare and Medicaid. They are thus often less than enthusiastic about attending to the needs of nursing home residents whose expenses are paid by one of these programs. Midlevel practitioners—physician assistants and nurse-practitioners—appear to be more attentive to such medical needs when they are allowed to provide primary care. They have generated somewhat better outcomes in experimental situations (Kane et al., 1990: 359).

Long-term care is provided in some smaller rural hospitals through "swing beds" in which long-term care patients are cared for in the hospital by skilled nurses. Hospitals can designate certain beds for this purpose and be reimbursed by Medicare, Medicaid, and long-term care insurance. This may be the only source of long-term care in communities with a shortage of, or inadequate, long-term care facilities. It also increases the financial viability of small hospitals. More than 50 percent of all rural hospitals offered swing bed services in 1989 (Grim, 1990: 32–34).

Home Health Care

Home health care has also become a growth industry during the 1980s and early 1990s. Patients usually prefer home care if available, according to several studies. Home care began primarily through "visiting nurses associations," which provided home support for daily living needs, physical therapy, and speech therapy. Services have expanded to include a huge array of options, including the following:

- Provision of durable medical equipment, such as hospital beds
- Respiratory therapy
- Nutrition services
- Infusion therapy
- Retail pharmacy
- Home self-diagnosis
- Health education
- Hospice care

Medicare has gradually increased coverage for many of these services, because costs are as a rule no greater, or may be lower, than institutional care for the same services. Services are usually provided by for-profit and nonprofit home health agencies, although hospitals have entered the home health care market as well (Miller and Dudek, 1991: 63).

Services can be short-term, intermittent, or long-term for chronic conditions. The staff of professionals providing service includes nurses (about 60 percent), social workers, health care aides, physical, occupation, and speech therapists, dietitians, and physicians. Home health care is often directly linked to homemaker and custodial services, which make living at home possible for disabled patients (Miller and Dudek, 1991: 66).

Mental Health Care

Mental health care has expanded considerably in recent decades and is now a major segment of the U.S. health care system ($28 billion in expenditures during 1990). In 1993, some form of mental disorder accounted for one-fifth of all hospital beds and affected about seven million Americans.

Care is provided through many types of providers (Geller, 1991: 150; National Center for Health Statistics, 1995: 236):

- Private general medical practitioners, such as family M.D.s (costs are not usually attributed to mental disorder)
- Private specialized mental health practitioners (psychiatrists, clinical psychologists, psychiatric social workers, and so on) (2.5 percent of costs)
- Private psychiatric and general hospitals (22 percent of costs)
- General hospitals with psychiatric services (16 percent of costs)
- City, county, and state government mental hospitals (27 percent of costs)
- Department of Veterans Affairs medical centers (5 percent of costs)
- Community or public mental health centers or clinics and other facilities (20 percent of costs)

Seventy percent of all costs are thus expended for some form of hospitalization, although primary care practitioners are often the first point of professional contact for individuals with disorders. Milder cases may be handled adequately at this point through counseling or medication. If specialized care is needed, referrals are made to appropriate specialists or hospitals.

Specialized care is provided primarily by psychiatrists and clinical psychologists in community settings where these specialists are accessible. Psychiatric social workers, psychiatric nurses, and counseling psychologists also provide private services. The costs may be paid by private insurance, usually with strict limitations, or through private out-of-pocket payment.

Community mental health centers were created to provide services to individuals without insurance or other ability to pay. Federal, state, and some local funds (depending on the locale) support salaried mental health professionals and other staff. The intent of the centers is to provide a community alternative to the often impersonal and bureaucratic state mental institutions. State hospital services have been greatly diminished in most states, with patients instead referred to the local mental health centers. Alcohol and drug treatment services were originally included in the centers but have since become more specialized and largely separated (Geller, 1991: 150).

The availability of public mental health services varies widely between states and communities, depending upon local willingness to provide resources. The widespread decrease in state hospital capacity has meant increased pressure on local and private services, often with serious consequences for those without ability to pay for care (Geller, 1991: 151).

State mental health hospitals were for many years the primary provider of mental health services to individuals without insurance or private resources. Curtailment of funds now allows state institutions to take only the most severe cases that cannot be cared for in the community. The quality and professional training of state hospital staff have been upgraded considerably, much improving the quality and image of services in most states (Geller, 1991: 148–149).

Private psychiatric hospitals generally serve patients with private resources or good insurance, as referrals from private practitioners. Costs of services tend to be much higher because no subsidization is available (Scallet, 1990: 123).

The mental health care system is highly fragmented. It is often difficult for potential clients to identify the part of the system that can most appropriately serve their needs. Federal funding was cut back substantially beginning in 1981, after the Community Mental Health Centers were well-established and somewhat self-supported. State and private funding has also declined in many states. Consequently, many patients without resources have been unable to secure care.

Although many of the most severe cases are kept in state institutions, others are among the homeless and destitute street people in large cities and small towns. Many individuals with severe problems "fall through the cracks" so to speak, and become a bur-den on the community through criminal or otherwise destructive behavior. The number of individuals involved, or the cost to society, is difficult to precisely determine (Drolen, 1990: 191; Scallet, 1990: 123–124).

ECONOMIC CHARACTERISTICS AND ISSUES

The health care sector is among the most vigorous parts of the U.S. economy, employing over nine million people in 1994 and representing about one-seventh ($884 billion in 1993) of the total U.S. economy—about $3,300 per capita and 13.9 percent of GDP. Health care costs increased at a rate of 8.3 percent annually between 1990 and 1993 (2.5 times faster than the overall Consumer Price Index), which was actually slower by 1.6 percent than during the 1985–1990 period when growth was 9.9 percent annually. Growth slowed significantly to 4.8 percent in the 1993–1994 period, a rate still nearly double the increase in the CPI (National Center for Health Statistics, 1995: 222–224).

Health care–related businesses are growing rapidly and contribute to the increasing proportion of health services in the GDP. The rate of health care spending increase has exceeded the rate of economic growth in the United States for three decades. Moreover, the health care segment of government spending—for Medicare, Medicaid, veterans programs, insurance for government employees, and other programs—is a rapidly increasing component of federal and state government budgets with increases from 12 percent in 1980 to 18.6 percent of federal expenditures, and 12.4 percent of state expenditures, in 1993 (Iglehart, 1992a: 964; National Center for Health Statistics, 1995: 219).

Health services added about 3.6 million jobs between 1980 and 1994, more than one in six of all new jobs. Employment in health services increased at the rate of 3.6 percent per year between 1985 and early 1994. Nearly 48 percent are employed in hospitals, 17 percent in nursing care and personal health care facilities, 14 percent in physicians' offices, 6.5 percent in dental and chiropractic offices, and about 16 percent in other health services (National Center for Health Statistics, 1995: 197).

The proportion of state or federal government budgets specifically designated for health care does not include other government supported health-related activities, such as health research through the National Institutes of Health and the National Institutes of Mental Health; the Food and Drug Administration; the Centers for Disease Control; the Alcohol, Drug Abuse, and Mental Health Administration; undergraduate and graduate medical and other health professional education; and many other health service support programs such as environmental health, preventive maternal and child health programs, nutrition programs, and other state or locally operated public programs. If these programs were added to the health care budget, it would be substantially higher by a minimum of $12 billion (Iglehart, 1992a: 964; National Center for Health Statistics, 1995: 235).

Despite increases in government spending for health care and other programs, the proportion of American income going to taxes remains among the lowest in the major industrial countries: 30 percent in the United States, as compared to 31 percent in Japan, 34 percent in Canada, 37 percent in Germany, 37 percent in the United Kingdom, 44 percent in France, and over 50 percent in Sweden. This is the case in part because the public share of health care costs is lowest in the United States among advanced countries, at 44 percent in 1993. The OECD average is 76 percent (Iglehart, 1992a: 963–964; National Center for Health Statistics, 1995: 223).

Expenditure Growth

Nursing home costs increased the most between 1980 and 1990 (11 percent annually), followed by physician services (nearly

11 percent), hospital costs (10 percent), and pharmaceuticals (9.6 percent). The costs of administration and insurance expenses rose by well over 11 percent. These cost increases slowed considerably in the early 1990s, except for home health care (approximately 25 percent annual growth) and administration (21 percent growth in 1992–1993), lowering overall health care cost increases to the 8.3 percent average noted earlier. Figure 3–1 summarizes the 1990s changes (Iglehardt, 1992a: 963–964; Organization for Economic Cooperation and Development, 1992: 9; Vincenzino, 1994: 34).

Prescription drug price increases have slowed to nearly the rate of inflation, but hospital costs generally, and outpatient services especially, have continued to grow at nearly three times the general inflation rate. Physician cost growth has slowed but is still rising at nearly twice general inflation (Vincenzino, 1994: 34). Overall expenditures for various types of health care or administration were divided roughly as indicated in Figure 3–2 for 1993.

The proportion of costs for hospital care (37 percent) and physician services (19 percent) have stayed reasonably level during the period since 1960. Nursing home and home health care costs have increased as a proportion of the total, whereas dental services have declined (National Center for Health Statistics, 1995: 224).

Approximately 66 percent of the annual increase in health care costs between 1990 and 1993 was for increases in the relative prices for health care. The remainder was for volume increases (14 percent), including 1 percent for population growth and 20 percent for increased medical services delivered. Medicare increased 14.3 percent annually (including general inflation) between 1970 and 1990. Medicaid has grown even more rapidly. The Congressional Budget Office estimates that Medicaid costs are about to exceed the costs of Medicare. Medicare and Medicaid together totaled 28 percent of all health care expenditures in 1990 (Organization for Economic Coopera-

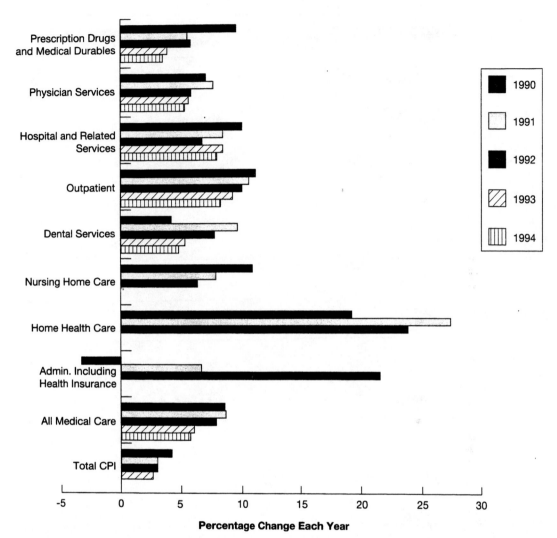

Figure 3-1.   Changes in health care expenditures (1990–1994).

Sources: Based on data from Vincenzino, 1994: 34; National Center for Health Statistics, 1995: 222–224.

tion and Development, 1992: 14; Graig, 1993: 22).

Federal expenditures would be even higher if the employer tax deductions for health insurance premiums were factored into the overall costs. The Office of Management and Budget estimates that the federal revenue lost equaled approximately $36 billion in 1991 (Organization for Eco-

nomic Cooperation and Development, 1992: 17).

State and local costs for Medicaid and other programs have also risen rapidly, but at a somewhat slower rate than federal expenditures. These costly increases have caused many states to shift much of Medicaid service delivery to managed care programs as a means of controlling costs (Organization for

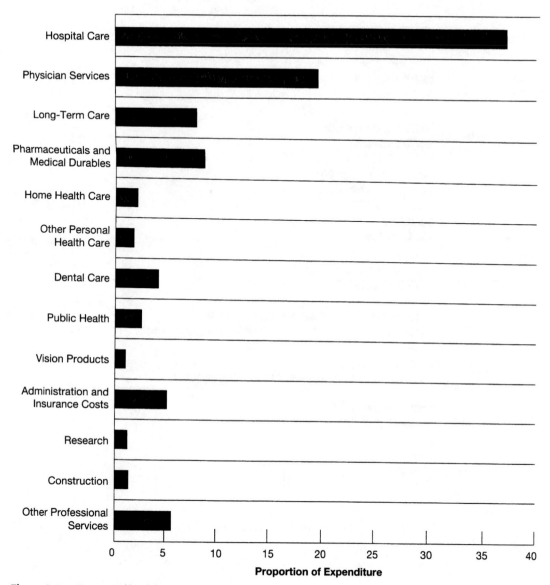

Figure 3-2. Percent of health care expenditure by type of service (1993).

Sources: Based on data from National Center for Health Statistics, 1995: 224.

Economic Cooperation and Development, 1992: 14; McNeil, 1993: 4).

Summary of factors causing expenditure growth. Other primary factors so far identified as contributing to increases in expenditures over the past decade are summarized in Table 3-9. Malpractice insurance premium

costs are a factor in the high cost of care, but are relatively small compared to other expenditures (approximately 2 percent). Physicians and hospitals practice "defensive medicine" in part to avoid the possibility of malpractice litigation. This leads to a large number of medically unnecessary tests and procedures, estimated at 15 to 30 percent of

Table 3-9 Causes of Health Care Cost Increases Since 1980 (Not in Priority Order)

- General inflation in the economy and in health care
- Expanding technology, oversupply in selected categories, and underutilization, requiring increased capital investment and higher operating costs
- Expanded insurance coverage for greater numbers of the population, through Medicare, Medicaid, state insurance programs, and private insurance
- Increased benefits within insurance packages
- Demographic change, particularly the increase in numbers of older citizens
- Increases in the number of physicians, dentists, and other professionals who deliver more care and a wider range of services
- Higher salaries for health professionals and oversupply in selected physician specialties as well as in some other personnel categories
- Increases in the quantity and comprehensiveness of hospital services
- Increased administrative costs for insurance provision and management of health services
- Medicalization of social services such as long-term care
- Malpractice litigation and threat or fear of law suits

Source: Based on Pfaff, 1990: 7.

all such activities. The additional procedures add substantially to costs but do not contribute to the quality of care (Organization for Economic Cooperation and Development, 1992: 32; Graig, 1993: 20).

The United States has by far the largest incidence of AIDS and illegal drug use among advanced nations. Although precise estimates remain to be calculated, the rise in HIV and the use of illegal drugs are adding substantially to the health care cost burden. The use of AZT to treat AIDS is a major cost, and long-term care required for patients who gradually lose their capacity is an additional major impact (Graig, 1993: 22).

Physician compensation in the United States is substantially higher than in most other countries, and has been growing more rapidly. Within the physician cost category, cardiology (38 percent growth annually) and radiology (20 percent annually) grew with greatest rapidity in part because of increased application of relatively new technologies

such as magnetic resonance imaging (MRI—which grew annually at a rate of more than 400 percent between 1985 and 1988), computed tomography (CT), and cardiac catheterization (McNeil, 1993: 4).

Financing

Financing is provided through some 1,250 private insurance schemes, including 73 Blue Cross and Blue Shield plans, managed care plans, self-insured companies (more than 44 percent of all benefits covered by employers), and a variety of state and federal public programs. Employer-financed insurance is the dominant mode for 73 percent of families, especially when employment is in large companies, government, and in all levels of public and private education. Larger businesses with 100 or more employees nearly always (98 percent) provide some level of insurance. However, only 27 percent of smaller businesses with fewer than ten employees offered insurance in 1991. Benefits are as varied as the range of insurance plans. The cost to businesses of health insurance is exempt from taxation (Iglehart, 1992a: 965).

Employer-sponsored health care insurance is thus a major American enterprise, paying for about 28 percent of all health care expenditures. Individual purchases of insurance or out-of-pocket payments for health care represented 34 percent. Federal, state, and local governments' expenditures were 35 percent of the total $884 billion health care bill in 1993. The distribution of financing sources is summarized in Table 3-10 (Iglehart, 1992b: 1716).

Increasing costs of health care to employers have caused a high proportion of them to shift from indemnity plans to self-insurance or managed care. The average monthly cost per individual worker for a managed care plan ranged between $100 and $150, or $150 to $250 for a family, in 1993, which is considerably less than the cost of indemnity insurance. The proportion of total compensation going to health benefits rose from 6 percent

Table 3-10   Sources of U.S. Health Care Funds
(1991)

Source	Percentage
All private sources	65
Private health insurance payments	(14)
Business-sponsored insurance	(28)
Out-of-pocket payments	(20)
Nonpatient revenue	(3)
Government sources	35
Federal	(18.4)
State and local government	(16.6)
Total	100

Source: Based on data from National Center for Health Statistics, 1995: 225.

in 1991 to 6.7 percent in 1994 for private industry, and 6.9 to 8.2 percent in state and local governments—up from 3.5 percent in 1970. Annual costs per worker had risen above $3,000 by 1991. Workers have been forced to increase their contributions toward insurance by accepting higher insurance benefits in place of higher salary increases (Graig, 1993: 22; National Center for Health Statistics, 1995: 227).

Self-insurance enables large companies to create their own insurance package and manage it directly. They do not pay commissions or contribute to insurance company profits. The Employee Retirement Income Security Act (ERISA) allows self-insured companies an exemption from medical benefits requirements established by many state legislatures (Iglehart, 1992b: 1719; Cockerham, 1995: 271).

Meanwhile, the rapid price increases mean that indemnity insurance companies are no longer as profitable as they once were. Nearly all of the top companies suffered losses in recent years because of their inability to increase rates rapidly enough to cover increased claims. The most notable illustration is the collapse of Blue Cross/Blue Shield of West Virginia in 1991. Blue Shield and Blue Cross plans have generally diminished in importance in recent years, losing more than

11 million customers during the 1986–1992 period. Approximately 112 small carriers also failed between 1986 and 1990. Managed care plans have been picking up the slack (Iglehart, 1992b: 1716; Graig, 1993: 23).

Paying physicians.   As noted earlier, physicians have traditionally been paid on a fee-for-service basis. This pattern is changing gradually with the advent of managed care, which usually pays physicians as employees on salary under the closed-panel group arrangement; the open-panel plans continue to pay on the basis of discounted fee for service. Slightly less than half (49 percent) of payments to physicians were from private insurance by 1993; 20 percent from Medicare; 7 percent from Medicaid; about 15 percent from patients out of pocket; 6 percent from some form of government payment other than Medicaid or Medicare; and 2 percent from some other form of private payment such as consulting (National Center for Health Statistics, 1995: 34, 224).

Financing hospitals.   Hospitals were generally reimbursed on a fee-for-service basis until the advent of Medicare DRGs; non-Medicare or nonmanaged care patients continue to pay fees, but often at negotiated and discounted prices. Physicians and administrators were forced to moderate their pattern of hospital care to stay within the DRG price guidelines. The nationwide shift to managed care has been a major factor in diminished hospital revenue from the under-age-65 population (Evans, 1990: 101–128; Iglehart, 1992a: 966).

U.S. hospitals generally cost more than in other countries, particularly for personnel, with 6.1 employees per occupied bed in 1992, up from 3 per bed in 1970. The average per capita cost of hospital care is nearly double the average cost in Western Europe, although Sweden and Canada are within $200 of the U.S. cost (Glaser, 1991b: 395; National Center for Health Statistics, 1995: 216).

Financing mental health care.   States provide the bulk of mental health care funding, as summarized in Table 3-11 for 1986 (Scal-

Table 3-11 Mental Health Care Funding

Sources of Mental Health Funds	Percentage
State sources	52
Federal sources	18
Local government	8
Client fees	17
Other sources	5
Total	100

Source. Based on data from Scallet, 1990: 119.

let, 1990: 119). The majority of state funding continues to be for state hospital inpatient services, despite a substantial decrease in hospitalization since 1964. States also contribute funds for disability payments, supplemental income benefits, special education, rehabilitation, corrections, and housing subsidies for individuals disabled by mental illness (Scallet, 1990: 122).

Major federal financing programs: Medicare. Medicare is unique among health care financing programs: It serves a clearly identified population of individuals who are over age 65, permanently disabled, or who have end-stage renal disease. It is the largest and most expensive publicly sponsored program (although Medicaid is surpassing Medicare in growth). Insurance coverage is divided in two parts: a compulsory hospital component (Part A) and a voluntary component for medical care, other outpatient care, and laboratory fees (Part B). Part A is financed by a payroll tax on employees and employers. Recipients pay a monthly premium for Part B that covers 25 percent of the costs; the balance is paid from federal tax revenues (Iglehart, 1992a: 966; Ruggie, 1992: 926).

Part A covers 90 days of hospitalization per year, plus a lifetime supplement of 60 days. Up to 100 days of nursing home care is covered, following hospitalization, as are 100 home health care visits. There was an annual deductible of $696 in 1993. Part B covers 80 percent of physicians services, diagnostic costs, ambulance services, outpatient hospital visits, home health care, and speech or physical therapy, with a deductible of $100 per

year, and at a cost of $46.10 per month in 1995 (Cockerham, 1995: 274).

Medicare has been very successful in helping to meet the health insurance needs of the elderly, but the elderly must pay a higher proportion of the income out of pocket for prescriptions and supplementary insurance than before the advent of Medicare. Rising costs caused Congress to reexamine the extent of coverage in 1995. The hospital insurance trust fund (Part A) is projected to be exhausted by the year 2002 unless the Medicare payroll tax is greatly increased. Supplementary insurance for physician and outpatient services (Part B) was costing $380 per individual in 1992, and is projected to nearly double to $700 per person by 2000. This will consume a considerably higher proportion of national health care expenditures, projected to grow to 19 percent of the federal budget in 2000 (Burner, Waldo, and McKusick, 1992: 1–6).

The Health Care Financing Administration (HCFA) is the agency responsible for rulemaking, management, and allocating payments for both Medicare and Medicaid—giving the agency enormous national influence. Most health facilities serve patients receiving payments from one of these sources and are thus subject to HCFA rules and mandates. To achieve adequate monitoring and quality control, HCFA operates an elaborate regulatory, control, and management mechanism. The actions of this agency are much more intrusive in the work of health care providers generally, and in treatment of patients, than is the case of financing agencies in other countries (Rettig, 1991: 16; Ruggie, 1992: 930).

However, vigorous regulation was deemed necessary because, for example, providers responded to the advent of Diagnosis Related Groups (DRGs) by choosing the diagnosis with the highest reimbursement whenever this was possible, thus maximizing revenue from Medicare payments. "DRG Creep" is the label given to this practice. The role of peer review organizations (PROs)—operating under the control of

HCFA—is to evaluate and control misuse of revenue maximization efforts (Ruggie, 1992: 930).

Physician diagnosis of an illness at the time of admission, coupled with input from hospital administration, determines the payment to be received by the hospital. If the hospital treats the patient for less than the designated payment, cost savings occur and the hospital keeps the difference. If costs are greater than the set payment, the hospital absorbs the additional cost. A strong incentive thus exists to choose a DRG with higher payment (Ruggie, 1992: 930–931).

Physicians generally have been unhappy with the inadequacies and constraints of the DRG system, even though they have served as consultants to HCFA in developing the system. They feel it does not allow for all the variations and alternative courses that illnesses and diseases can take. Their recommendations have led to a gradual refinement and increase in the number of classifications. Nonetheless, HCFA has been accused of "micromanaging" the health care system for elderly citizens, at the expense of provider and patient freedom (Ruggie, 1992: 933).

The consequences have, however, been positive from a cost-saving standpoint. Hospital stays for patients have become shorter, particularly for the elderly, and the general pattern of treatment processes for inpatient care has resulted in lower average costs. This is one of the factors that has led to a substantial increase in outpatient surgery and other forms of outpatient care. It has also contributed to the major shift toward "managed care," which tends to minimize hospitalization (Ruggie, 1992: 938).

Medicaid.   Medicaid is intended to provide care for selected segments of the lower-income population—largely families receiving "Aid to Families with Dependent Children" (AFDC) and elderly or disabled individuals. Most recipients are the institutionalized aged, blind, and disabled (66 per-

cent of costs) rather than low-income women and children (34 percent of costs). Recipients include children in working families, illegal immigrants, AIDS patients, and women delivering babies (four in ten U.S. births were covered by Medicaid in 1991). Because physician and hospital reimbursement rates under Medicaid are relatively low (often 50 percent or less of usual charges), many providers refuse to accept Medicaid clients (Burner et al., 1992: 7).

Coverage of lower-income individuals by Medicaid has dropped substantially since the mid-1970s, from 70 percent in the mid-1970s to about 42 percent in the early 1990s. It is the fastest growing publicly sponsored health care program in the nation—largely because of increases in long-term care and "disproportionate share" costs. The "disproportionate share" segment was created in 1987 by the U.S. Congress as a vehicle to subsidize health care facilities with a high proportion of low-income patients. Disproportionate share subsidies had grown to one-sixth of Medicaid costs by 1992 (Bodenheimer, 1992: 198).

As noted earlier, Medicaid has become the principal financing mechanism for long-term care, representing 40 percent of program costs. Eligibility for Medicaid subsidy of long-term care is directly linked to welfare status. Individuals must prove they have assets of no more than $2,500. However, a 1988 federal law allows spouses of long-term care residents to retain assets of up to $71,000 and a monthly income of $1,770 per month. The costs for low-income subsidies of older people are projected to grow substantially over the next 40 years as the number of elderly needing long-term care grows (Iglehart, 1992a: 966; Bodenheimer, 1992: 198; Morgan, 1994).

Funding of Medicaid in each state from federal tax revenues varies from 50 to 80 percent, depending on per capita income in the states. States pay an average of 43 percent of costs, but are fully responsible for program operation, management, and determination of eligibility. Consequently, there are wide differences among states in level of benefits and access to care, as noted earlier. The state-funded costs of the program have grown at five times the rate of inflation since 1989 and have become the single highest cost program in many states (Ruggie, 1992: 926; Morgan, 1994).

Many states have therefore adopted regulatory measures to control entry to the program and constrain costs. Regional and state health planning agencies have been formed to strengthen state control of providers. The 1981 Omnibus Budget Reconciliation Act (OBRA) allowed states to limit choice of providers and create or encourage creation of health maintenance organizations (HMOs) that Medicaid recipients must then use. Since each state devised its own procedures, great variations in definitions of appropriate provider behavior and patient eligibility evolved. Prevention activities were generally ignored in favor of treatment for illness. Quality and adequacy of care delivery were not particularly emphasized (Ruggie, 1992: 927).

The federal Prospective Payment Commission estimated in 1993 that Medicaid payment rates were about 80 percent of actual hospital inpatient costs, and private insurance payment rates averaged 128 percent of costs. The Physician Payment Review Commission indicates that Medicare rates are equal to about 65 percent of private rates. Medicare pays only 91 percent of costs, and Medicaid pays only 74 percent. Thus, private payment heavily subsidizes both Medicaid and Medicare on a national basis as a result of cost shifting within hospitals and in ambulatory care settings (Graig, 1993: 26; McNeil, 1993: 4; Sheils, Lewin and Haught, 1993: 232).

Military programs. The military services operate health care programs for members. Service men and women receive care through medical and hospital branches at each military base. Families of service members are insured through the Civil Health and Medical Plan of the Uniformed Services (CHAMPUS) with most costs paid directly by the U.S. government.

The Department of Veterans Affairs operates a health care program to serve the health care needs of retired military veterans, including 171 hospitals, 127 nursing homes, and 93 clinics. The programs employ more than 12,000 full-time physicians, 990 dentists, 34,000 nurses, and numerous other health professionals. Many of the hospitals and other facilities are directly associated with medical schools, and serve as locations for research and teaching as well as health care (Iglehard, 1992a: 966).

Insurance for government employees. An interesting commentary on the American system is the near universality of publicly financed health insurance for local, state, and federal employees. Federal employees, including those in the military services, have in the past had comprehensive coverage with low or no deductibles, although this is changing. State-financed coverage varies among states and local governments, but nearly all have comprehensive coverage that is equal to or better than Medicare or Medicaid.

The special case of Hawaii. Hawaii is the only state with near universal insurance coverage, largely because of employer-provided insurance mandated in 1974. Nearly 90 percent of workers were already covered by employers before the mandate. In addition, the State subsidizes insurance for unemployed, part-time employed, and farm workers. Individuals below the poverty line pay no premiums. Those defined as "near-poor" pay subsidized premiums on a sliding-scale (Bodenheimer, 1992: 203).

Financing Issues

The burden on employers. The escalating costs have become a major burden for American business. For example (Himmelstein, Woolhandler, and Wolfe, 1992: 395; Graig, 1993: 13–14):

- Health care costs are forcing up overall production costs and are absorbing a high proportion of corporate profit.
- Benefits are absorbing potential take-home wage increases, causing negotiation problems with labor.
- Business costs increase as a direct result of cost shifting by health providers to pay for uncompensated care.
- Postretirement health care benefits are becoming a major burden because companies are now required to budget for these costs.
- Health care costs have the potential to make U.S. firms somewhat less competitive internationally.

Risk avoidance by insurers. Private insurers are attempting to minimize risk by avoiding groups or individuals with high potential for claims. About 6 percent of applicants for insurance were denied coverage in 1991 because of preexisting conditions. This is justified by insurers because roughly 4 percent of the insured individuals incur 50 percent of claims costs; 20 percent of patients generate 80 percent of costs. Insurers therefore attempt to identify individuals in the "very high-risk" categories and exclude them from coverage, while minimizing the possibility of insuring the 20 percent of "relatively high-risk" individuals. In the case of large-group plans, this exclusion may not apply, but the exclusionary policy generally has the effect of making insurance costs prohibitive for individuals and small businesses engaging in high-risk work (Iglehart, 1992b: 1718; Organization for Economic Cooperation and Development, 1992: 36).

Health care for the uninsured. Both uninsured and underinsured must depend upon the willingness of health care providers and government agencies to serve their needs, often without compensation. In the case of serious illness or accident, their needs may not be fully met. This is the major contrast of the U.S. system with the more universal and comprehensive systems of other advanced countries (Graig, 1993: 1).

Financing for uninsured individuals who need health care but do not qualify for Medicaid or other public programs are expected to pay out of pocket or receive "charity" in one form or another in hospital emergency rooms, physician offices, and private or public clinics. When they are not paid, they shift all or part of the costs to other sources of revenue by increasing rates to insurance payers. The disadvantage for those seeking primary care is that emergency room care is possibly of lower quality than other forms of primary care, despite its higher cost. Emergency departments are not generally equipped to provide primary care, and staff are not trained for that purpose (Organization for Economic Cooperation and Development, 1992: 39).

Public community clinics or migrant worker clinics receive federal grants to cover part of their costs. But, these facilities are widely dispersed and overburdened, and are thus inaccessible to most uninsured families (Organization for Economic Cooperation and Development, 1992: 40).

Uninsured patients generally do not receive preventive care or prenatal and postnatal care. Consequently, their health care costs are often higher overall because illnesses become severe or chronic before treatment is provided. Furthermore, uninsured individuals appear to receive generally inferior care as compared with those who are covered by insurance (Iglehart, 1992a: 967). The uninsured fall into several major categories, as summarized in Figure 3–3.

Children and young adults tend to be uninsured at much higher rates than older people. About one-third of low-income families and individuals are uninsured. Roughly 80 percent of the uninsured individuals are members of families of an employed person who works for an employer without employee health insurance coverage (Organization for Economic Cooperation and Development, 1992: 38).

A number of states have initiated insurance programs that provide coverage for a substantial proportion of these families. For example, Oregon has expanded Medicaid to increase coverage while limiting the range of

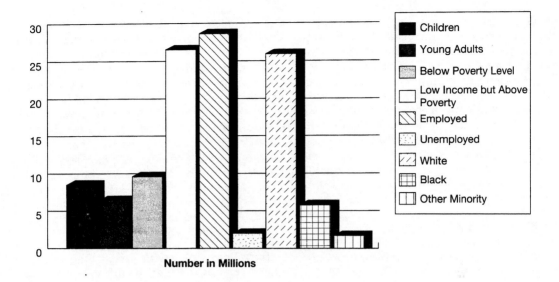

Number in Millions

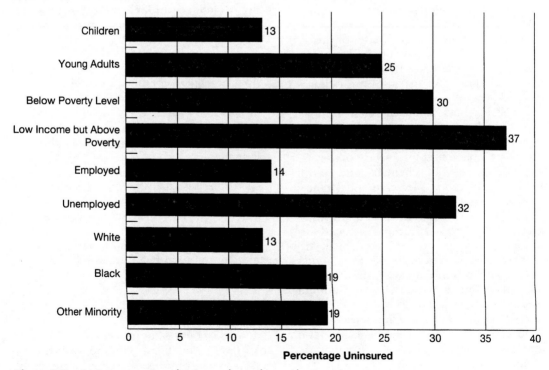

Percentage Uninsured

Figure 3-3. Major categories of uninsured: number and proportions.

Sources: Based on data from Organization for Economic Cooperation and Development, 1992: 37.

benefits. Maine and Delaware have expanded Medicaid with special financing through cigarette and alcohol taxes. Hawaii subsidizes coverage for lower-income families that are not covered under their employer-supported program, as noted earlier. Washington initiated a "Basic Health Plan" for lower-income families not covered by Medicaid. Participants purchase insurance from one of five health plans with premiums based on a sliding scale related to income. The state pays up to 90 percent of the premium for those least able to pay. Providers are paid on a capitation basis and are largely managed care organizations (Bodenheimer, 1992: 200).

Administrative costs.   Administrative costs for the private sector of health care in the United States are far higher than in other countries—more than twice as high as in countries with single-payer systems such as Canada, the United Kingdom, and Sweden. (It should be noted that estimates of this sort do not include the cost of collecting and administering the taxes that support health care.) Administrative expenses are estimated to be 25 percent of costs when all components are included, such as management of health care provider firms and insurer's costs for determining eligibility, verifying and processing claims, marketing insurance policies, selling policies, managing benefits, and complying with regulations. Medicare and Medicaid have costs somewhat comparable to public programs in other countries. Administration averaged 25 percent of hospital expenditures in 1990, ranging from 20.5 percent in Minnesota to 30.6 percent in Hawaii. Even in states with high HMO enrollments (California, Massachusetts, Minnesota, and Oregon), administrative costs were just as high (up to 25.6 percent) (Woolhandler and Himmelstein, 1991: 1256; Organization for Economic Cooperation and Development, 1992: 33; Woolhandler, Himmelstein, and Lewontin, 1993: 401).

Insurers' cost was estimated by HCFA to be 14.2 percent of private insurance claims in 1990, with a range from 5.5 percent for large firms with 10,000 or more employees to

40 percent for individuals and small groups. The General Accounting Office estimate was 5.3 percent in 1990. Medicare insurance was much more economical, at 2.1 percent of total expenditures in 1991—in substantial part because 89 percent of hospital bills and 47 percent of physician claims are processed electronically, eliminating much of the paper flow. Private health insurers have been very slow to adopt electronic processing with only 5 to 10 percent of claims handled this way in 1991. The major impediment has been the inability to agree on a common format for electronic processing (Iglehart, 1992b: 1719; Sheils et al., 1993: 232).

Social costs of health care.   One of the major reasons for high health care costs is the inclusion of many items or services in the health care bill that might more appropriately be lodged under other categories of expense. Examples include the following (Nix, 1990: 379):

- Professional liability insurance for physicians, hospitals, and other health professionals
- Legal costs and lawyer services associated with malpractice suits
- Advertising of health care services
- Administrative costs of supplying health care insurance
- Medical goods such as crutches and wheel chairs that ease the problems of dealing with disabilities
- Exercise equipment in health care facilities

If many of these nonhealth *care* costs were excluded, the total health care bill might be considerably smaller.

The Cost-Control Dilemma

Efforts by businesses to control health care costs have so far been only moderately successful. Small businesses have a particularly difficult time because of the high administrative costs for small groups. The problem is exacerbated by retiree health insurance costs that were "guaranteed" by many companies at a time when employees outnumbered retirees by 12 to 1 (20 years ago). That ratio had changed in 1993 to 3 to 1, putting great pressure on health insurance at a time when the Financial Accounting Standards Board decided to require that companies record retiree health costs on their balance sheets as liabilities (Graig, 1993: 28).

As noted earlier, the average cost to private employers per employee was 6.7 percent of total compensation in 1994 for private industry and 8.2 percent for state and local governments. The total cost per employee was $3,217 in 1990, up 17 percent from the previous year. These problems have also become an issue with unionized labor because the increasing health benefit costs have displaced much of take-home wage increases. Conflict over health benefits thus has become a major issue in labor-management negotiations. Workers have, however, been willing so far to accept lower wage increases to maintain health benefits (Rineberg, 1991: 377; Graig, 1993: 30; National Center for Health Statistics, 1995: 227).

Part of the problem is the lack of incentives for cost control. Patients who are insured have little incentive because they pay relatively little out of pocket for care. Physicians feel they have an "ethical obligation" to provide the best possible treatment and know that insured patients can afford expensive procedures. Physician behavior has a direct influence on overall costs, in part because physicians control the use of many forms of high-cost technology and in some instances (group or hospital practices, for example) have a financial incentive to maximize use. Physicians are often both owners and users of technology such as CAT and MRI scanners. Physicians also often demand that hospitals obtain the latest technology. Because hospitals are dependent on physicians for their economic viability, they are pressured to secure advanced technology even though it may be underutilized and comparable technology may be available nearby (Organization for Economic Cooperation and Development, 1992: 32).

In the absence of provider incentives, insurance payers have instituted mechanisms to hold down costs through preapproval for hospitalization, physician practice review, second opinion requirements, limitation on payments for preexisting conditions, or waiting periods before insurance takes effect (Organization for Economic Cooperation and Development, 1992: 28).

Some health economists argue that controls on providers are the most efficient and effective means of keeping costs under control. The optimal payment system, they suggest, uses financial incentives that cause providers to limit services. The reimbursement system must reward providers for limiting costs and involve them in a bargaining process with payers to determine their level of reimbursement (Ellis and McGuire, 1990: 393).

Health maintenance organizations that pay physicians on a salaried rather than fee-for-service basis use a bargaining process to set salaries. Lower costs are also due in part to decreased hospitalization that results from healthier patients who receive more adequate primary care and wellness education (Organization for Economic Cooperation and Development, 1992: 31).

Several individual businesses and groups of businesses have been quite effective at moderating costs. For example, businesses and other organizations in Rochester, Minnesota, have joined together in sponsoring a community plan that has demonstrated high-quality care and cost savings. The Kaiser Permanente Health Maintenance Organization has demonstrated similar success in lowering costs while providing high-quality care. These are tightly managed programs and operate only in limited areas of the nation (Graig, 1993: 27).

PROBLEMS AND REFORMS

National health care financing reform has been proposed several times in the period since 1946. Comprehensive reform proposals have become more numerous in recent years, as costs began to absorb higher and higher proportions of individual, corporate, federal, and state budgets in the 1980s and early 1990s. More than forty comprehensive health care reform bills were submitted to the 102nd Congress during the 1990–1992 period. As noted earlier, a number of states have approved health care reform of substantial scope (Organization for Economic Cooperation and Development, 1992: 41).

The serious shortcomings in the U.S. system noted earlier have been the basis for the current demand for change. Nearly all players in the health care system believe that major reforms should be instituted soon, before health care costs become entirely unmanageable. A 1993 *New York Times*/CBS News poll indicated that 74 percent of Americans were dissatisfied with the quality of their health care and 72 percent wanted some form of government intervention to improve the situation (Cockerham, 1995: 277).

However, major change has been stymied because each sector attempts to protect its interests while pointing to the need for change elsewhere. Although there is general agreement that health care costs must be controlled and access must be increased for uninsured families, there is little consensus on the procedure for achieving either goal.

The Clinton Administration effort to reform the system in 1993–1994 involved hundreds of consultants and substantial investment of public and private resources. It proposed to build on the current system by requiring employers to provide insurance coverage. Subsidies were to be available for small employers whose insurance would have a higher cost per employee. Insurers were to be required to provide coverage at the same rate to all applicants regardless of previous conditions or employment status. States were to assume major responsibility for implementation. Cost control was to be achieved in part through managed competition, coordinated care, malpractice reform, administrative savings, and prevention or wellness programs.

However, several major elements were particularly objectionable to one or more powerful interests:

- The proposal to require employers to provide insurance aroused the anger of small business, especially.
- Reform of the insurance industry was a direct attack on the viability of a major segment of American enterprise.
- The increasing role proposed for federal and state governments aroused the opposition of small business, much of the insurance industry, provider organizations, and conservative politicians.

The Clinton effort therefore was frustrated by the unwillingness of the U.S. Congress to counter pressure from special-interest groups and agree on any substantial reform proposal.

Primary cost-control strategies.   A limited number of choices are available. Many of these have been experimentally attempted in various communities and states, as summarized in Table 3-12. A study of results from managed care programs in California indicated major savings were achieved through selective contracting with hospitals by HMOs and PPOs. Hospital costs were reduced by 13 percent between 1980 and 1990. Price competition forced hospitals to become more efficient, which led to rate reductions over the 9-year period (Zwanziger, Melnick, and Bamezai, 1994: 118).

If major reforms as outlined in Table 3-12 do not occur for political reasons, surveys of the American population indicate a consensus in favor of selected insurance reforms. Insurance reforms are proposed in three primary categories, for example (Bodenheimer, 1992: 202):

1. Eliminate policy cancellations when policy holders incur major health care costs.
2. Prohibit huge premium increases for people with serious illness.
3. Require insurers to accept applicants with pre-existing conditions.

Table 3-12   Available Cost-Control Alternatives

Primary Alternatives	Major Program Types	Major Features	Illustrations
Managed competition	Health maintenance organizations	Competition for members based on price and quality	Kaiser-Permanente
	Independent practice associations	Pooled purchasing power	Public employee health benefit plans
	Preferred provider organizations	Potential limits on rate growth and employer contributions	Germany
Government limits on provider prices and volume	Hospitals	Global budgets	Rochester, Minn., Health Plan
		Diagnosis Related Groups with prospective budgets	Medicare
	Physicians	Capitation	HMOs
		Uniform fee schedule	Medicare, Canada
		Salaried payment	Sweden
	Pharmaceuticals	Reimbursement limits	Germany
		Global budgets	
	New technology	Co-payments	
		Budgets that exclude selected services	Canada/Germany
		Community pooling of technology	Rochester, Minn.
		Outright rationing of procedures	United Kingdom

Source: Based on Kilbreth and Cohen, 1993: 374.

Insurance companies indicate they are forced into these practices to make insurance affordable for policyholders without severe health problems. The Health Insurance Association of America takes the viewpoint that state or federal government must assume responsibility for high-cost or low-income citizens (Bodenheimer, 1992: 202).

State initiatives. Several states have altered regulations to allow insurance benefit packages with high deductibles and high copayments. This has allowed premiums to go as low as $60 per month—still a relatively high price for small employers and low-income individuals, but quite affordable for middle-income families who are satisfied with protection only from high-cost illnesses (Bodenheimer, 1992: 202).

The following general categories summarize the major state-level efforts at reform (Read, 1990: 28; Bodenheimer, 1992: 199–200; Kent and Havighurst, 1992):

- Expansion of Medicaid to larger numbers of low-income families has support from the private insurance industry and the American Medical Association. The state of Oregon is pioneering an approach to insurance for most lower-income citizens—but with a limited benefit package that does not cover some procedures. Rationing is thus a feature of the plan.

- Subsidized insurance through state government for low-income residents, as exemplified by Washington State's Basic Health Plan. The state created an insurance system on an experimental basis that has since been expanded to cover significant numbers of uninsured low-income residents. Premiums are charged on a sliding scale depending on income level. Capitated managed care is the delivery mechanism that helps limit costs.

- Minimal insurance benefit requirements are encouraged by the Health Insurance Association of America and Blue Cross/Blue Shield. As noted earlier, these plans have high deductibles, high copayments, and reduced benefits. Such changes do not necessarily increase access for poorer residents.

- Various forms of employer mandates have been tried in several states, notably Hawaii, which has had such a requirement since 1974. Hawaii also provides subsidies to cover the unemployed. Most residents (65 percent) are covered by a Blue Shield Plan, part of a long tradition of employer insurance provision prior to the 1974 mandate. Other states such as Washington, Massachusetts, New York, and Oregon passed legislation requiring employer provision of insurance, but have not been granted a waiver from federal prohibitions against employer mandates for health insurance. Small businesses have generally and successfully fought mandates because of the high costs involved.

- Rate setting for hospitals has been implemented in Maryland. The requirement puts a limit on how much hospitals can charge for specific services, which has had the effect of lowering average hospital costs in the state from 25 percent above the national average to 10 percent below the average.

Some commentators argue that some form of rationing is the only means of controlling health care costs and increasing access. Widespread advances in technology and the increasing range and cost of services will otherwise drive up costs without compensating increases in efficiency. Medicare creates a form of rationing by insuring wealthy 65-year-old individuals while failing to adequately cover poor 64-year-olds (Aaron and Schwartz, 1990: 418–422; Dougherty, 1991: 34).

A form of rationing occurs simply because low-income earners are unable to pay for insurance or pay direct costs of care. Under Medicaid eligibility requirements, income, marital status, and dependency of children serve as a basis for excluding many low-income people from coverage. Previous medical condition serves as a basis for rationing by

private insurance providers. Geography serves as the basis for rationing in many rural locations and inner cities (Dougherty, 1991: 35).

SUMMARY AND CONCLUSIONS

The U.S. health care system is the most expensive in the world in terms of per capita cost and proportion of GDP expended for health care. These high expenditures finance an abundance of high-technology hospitals, medical schools, and primary care facilities. Yet, access is limited and outcomes such as the infant mortality rate and life expectancy are far from the top rank of countries. Roughly 15 percent of the population had no health insurance coverage in 1995.

The public health system is decentralized and varies in comprehensiveness and quality from state to state and among communities. Smaller rural counties and communities tend to have much more limited services than larger and wealthier urban communities. The U.S. Public Health Service supports a wide range of programs of very high quality and establishes national requirements for food safety, drugs, and other health-related products. Several major research programs generate extensive new knowledge about technology and improved methods of treating diseases such as AIDS and cancer.

The United States has an excellent health care system for those with resources to purchase private insurance, who are employed in firms that provide insurance benefits, or who fit into a complex web of special public insurance programs to serve identified population categories. Wealthy individuals from throughout the world travel to the United States for the most advanced treatment procedures available. A second level with uncertain quality serves lower-income people, through charity care, special programs such as Medicaid, and publicly funded health clinics. Accessibility for families in the second track is clearly inferior to those in the private system. Quality and completeness of services varies widely among states and among communities within states. Remote rural regions generally have fewer services and shortages of health professionals.

The public/private mix of services is financed by a complex variety of insurance schemes, ranging from private fee-for-service plans available to those who work for employers with insurance coverage, or who can afford to purchase insurance out of pocket, to government-funded programs such as Medicare and Medicaid. Managed care insurance has been growing rapidly and has largely replaced fee for service as the insurance of choice for large businesses.

Efforts to reform the system, in the interest of creating universal coverage and comprehensive services, and lowering costs, have been slow and piecemeal. Cost increases have slowed, largely on the basis of private enterprise reforms, but expenditures are by no means under control. Some states have increased access for low-income families through various special programs that provide subsidies, but no state except Hawaii has a universal insurance system in place. The paradox of "excess and deprivation" therefore continues with no clear prospect for a permanent solution.

REFERENCES

AARON, HENRY, and WILLIAM B. SCHWARTZ (1990). Rationing Health Care: The Choice Before Us, *Science*, 247 (5): 418–422.

ANDERSON, OLIN W. (1989a). *The Health Service Continuum in Democratic States: An Inquiry into Solvable Problems.* Ann Arbor, Mich.: Health Administration Press.

ANDERSON, OLIN W. (1989b). Issues in the Health Services of the United States, in Mark G. Field (ed.), *Success and Crisis in National Health Systems: A Comparative Approach.* New York: Routledge, pp. 49–71.

BARER, MORRIS L., CLYDE HERTZMAN, ROBERT MILLER, and MARINA V. PASCALI (1992). On Being Old and Sick: The Burden of Health Care for the Elderly in Canada and the United States, *Journal of Health Politics, Policy, and Law*, 17 (4): 763–782.

BARGER, SARA E. (1991). Nursing Center: A Model for Rural Nursing Practice, *Nursing and Health Care*, 12 (6): 290–294.

BLENDON, ROBERT J., KAREN DONELAN, ROBERT LEITMAN, ARNOLD EPSTEIN, JOEL CANTOR, ALAN COHEN, IAN

MORRISON, THOMAS MOLONEY, CHRISTIAN KOECK, and SAMUEL LEVITT (1993). Physician Perspectives on Caring for Patients in the United States, Canada, and West Germany, *New England Journal of Medicine*, 328 (14): 1011–1016.

BODENHEIMER, THOMAS (1992). Private Insurance Reform in the 1990s: Can It Solve the Health Care Crisis?, *International Journal of Health Services*, 22 (2): 197–215.

BURNER, SALLY T., DANIEL R. WALDO, and DAVID R. McKUSICK (1992). National Health Expenditure Projections Through 2030, *Health Care Financing Review*, 14 (1): 1–29.

CLEARY, PAUL D., SUSAN EDGMAN-LEVITAN, MARC ROBERTS, THOMAS W. MOLONEY, WILLIAM McMULLEN, JANICE D. WALKER, and THOMAS L. DELBANCO (1991). Patients Evaluate Their Hospital Care: A National Survey, *Health Affairs (Millwood)*, 10 (4): 254–267.

CLINTON, J. JARRETT (1991). Outcomes Research—A Way to Improve Medical Practice, *Journal of the American Medical Association*, 266 (15): 2057.

COCKERHAM, WILLIAM C. (1995). *Medical Sociology*, 6th ed. Englewood Cliffs, N.J.: Prentice Hall.

COILE, RUSSELL C., JR. (1992). Patient-Centered Care: Reinventing the Hospital for the 21st Century, *Hospital Strategy Report*, 4 (10): 1–8.

COUNCIL ON ETHICAL AND JUDICIAL AFFAIRS, AMERICAN MEDICAL ASSOCIATION (1990). Black-White Disparities in Health Care, *Journal of the American Medical Association*, 263 (17): 2344–2346.

DOUGHERTY, CHARLES J. (1991). Ethical Problems in Healthcare Rationing, *Health Progress* (October): 32–39.

DROLEN, CAROL S. (1990). Community Mental Health: Who Is Being Served? What Is Being Offered? *Journal of Mental Health Administration*, 17 (2): 191–199.

DUNBAR, CAROLYN (1992). Four Countries Studied on Quality, *Computers in Healthcare*, 13 (1): 65–66.

ELLIS, RANDALL P., and THOMAS G. McGUIRE (1990). Optimal Payment Systems and Health Services, *Journal of Health Economics*, 9: 375–396.

ENTHOVEN, ALAIN C. (1990). What Can Europeans Learn from Americans, *Health Care Systems in Transition.* Paris: OECD, pp. 57–71.

ENTHOVEN, ALAIN, and RICHARD KRONICK (1989). A Consumer-Choice Health Plan for the 1990s, *New England Journal of Medicine*, 320 (2): 29.

EVANS, ROBERT C. (1990). Tension, Compression, and Shear: Directions, Stresses, and Outcomes of Health Care Cost Control, *Journal of Health Policy, Politics and Law*, 15 (1): 101–128.

FEINLEIB, STEVEN E., PETER J. CUNNINGHAM, and PAMELA FARLEY SHORT (1994). *Use of Nursing and Personal Care Homes by the Civilian Population, 1987.* Center for General Health Services Research, Agency for Health Care Policy and Research. Washington, D.C.: U.S. Government Printing Office.

FOREMAN, SPENCER (1990). Graduate Medical Education: Focus for Change, *Academic Medicine*, 65 (February): 77–84.

FUCHS, VICTOR R. (1992). The Best Health Care System in the World?, *Journal of the American Medical Association*, 268 (7): 916–917.

GAY, E. GREER (1990). The Rural Health Care Market: Strategies for Survival, *HealthSpan*, 7 (2): 11–15.

GELLER, JEFFREY L. (1991). "Any Place But the State Hospital": Examining Assumptions About the Benefits of Admission Diversion, *Hospital and Community Psychiatry*, 42 (2): 145–151.

GEYMAN, JOHN P., and L. GARY HART (1993). Primary Care at the Crossroads: Progress, Problems, and Policy Options. Seattle, Wash.: WAMI Rural Health Research Center, University of Washington, Working Paper #22, May.

GLASER, WILLIAM A. (1989). The Politics of Paying American Physicians, *Health Affairs*, 8 (4): 129–146.

GLASER, WILLIAM A. (1991a). *Health Insurance in Practice: International Variations in Financing, Benefits, and Problems*. San Francisco: Jossey-Bass, Inc.

GLASER, WILLIAM A. (1991b). Paying the Hospital: American Problems and Foreign Solutions, *International Journal of Health Services*, 21 (3): 389–399.

GOLDSMITH, JEFF (1993). Hospital/Physician Relationships: A Constraint to Health Care Reform, *Health Affairs* (Fall): 160–169.

GRAIG, LAURENE (1993). *Health of Nations*, 2nd ed. Washington, D.C.: Congressional Quarterly.

GRIM, SARAH A. (1990). Swing Beds: A Strategy in Rural Hospitals' Fight to Survive, *Healthcare Financial Management*, 44 (4): 32–37.

HARTZEMA, ABRAHAM G., and ELEANOR PERFETTO (1991). Pharmaceutical Sciences' Manpower Supply and Internal Rate of Return, *Pharmaceutical Research*, 8 (6): 676–682.

HEALTH CARE BOTTOM LINE (1990). Quality of Care Defined, *Health Care Bottom Line*, 6 (12): 3–4.

HILZENRATH, DAVID S. (1994). The Medical Business Says It's Taking Care of Itself, *Washington Post National Weekly Edition*, February 7–13.

HIMMELSTEIN, DAVID U., SIEFFIE WOOLHANDLER, and SIDNEY M. WOLFE (1992). The Vanishing Health Care Safety Net: New Data on Uninsured Americans, *International Journal of Health Services*, 22 (3): 381–396.

HINZ, CHRISTINE (1991). Aging Population Gives Hospitals Potential Focus, *Health Care Strategic Management* (April): 18–22.

HOLDEN, DAVID M. (1990). Rural Practice Modes, *Academic Medicine*, 65 (12) (Sup.): S32–S40.

HUDSON, TERESE (1991). Hospital-MD Joint Ventures Move Forward Despite Hurdles, *Hospitals* (May 5): 22–28.

IGLEHART, JOHN K. (1991). The Struggle Over Physician Payment Reform, *New England Journal of Medicine*, 325 (11): 823–828.

IGLEHART, JOHN K. (1992a). The American Health Care System: Introduction, *New England Journal of Medicine*, 326 (14): 962–967.

IGLEHART, JOHN K. (1992b). The American Health Care System: Private Insurance, *New England Journal of Medicine*, 326 (25): 1715–1720.

KALOUSDIAN, SONA, and ANDREA L. SCHNEIDER (1992). Health Care Technology Assessment, *The Internist*, 33 (9): 8–11.

KANE, ROBERT L., JUDITH BARRARD, JOAN L. BUCHANAN, ALAN ROSENFELD, CAROL SKAY, and SUSAN McDERMOTT (1990). Improving Primary Care in Nursing Homes, *Journal of the American Geriatric Society*, 39: 359–367.

KENT, CHRISTINA, and CRAIG HAVIGHURST (1992). Global Budgets: Medicine with Side Effects, *Medicine and Health* (Sept. 28) (Sup.): 1–4.

KESSLER, DAVID A. (1991). Communicating with Patients About Medications, *New England Journal of Medicine*, 325 (5): 1650–1652.

KILBRETH, ELIZABETH, and ALAN B. COHEN (1993). Strategic Choices for Cost Containment Under a Reformed U.S. Health Care System, *Inquiry*, 30 (4): 372–388.

KOSKA, MARY T. (1990). Primary Care: Hospitals Begin to Target Community Needs, *Hospitals*, 64 (7): 24–28.

LARSSON, LAURA (1994). Personal communication.

LATHROP, J. PHILIP (1991). The Patient-Focused Hospital, *Healthcare Forum Journal*, (July/August): 17–20.

LUTZ, SANDY (1990). Rural Hospitals Still Traveling Bumpy Road, *Modern Healthcare* (May 7): 28–36.

LUTZ, SANDY (1991). Practitioners Are Filling in for Scarce Physicians, *Modern Healthcare*, 2 (19): 24–30.

McCULLY, ANNETTE DENNIS (1995). Peer Review Organizations, *Northwest Physician* (Summer): 25–28.

McGAUHEY, PEGGY J., and BARBARA STARFIELD (1993). Child Health and the Social Environment of White and Black Children, *Social Science and Medicine*, 36 (7): 867–874.

McMURRAY, RICHARD J. (1991). Cost Containment and the Physicians' Ethical Obligations, *The Internist*, 32 (6): 16–18.

McNEIL, BARBARA J. (1993). Socioeconomic Forces Affecting Medicine: Times of Increased Retrenchment and Accountability, *Seminars in Nuclear Medicine*, 23 (1): 3–8.

MEHARG, J. G. JR., (1992). The Hassle Factor, *Annals of Internal Medicine*, 117 (9): 797.

MEHLMAN, MAXWELL J. (1990). Assuring the Quality of Medical Care: The Impact of Outcome Measurement and Practice Standards, *Law, Medicine, and Health Care*, 18 (4): 368–384.

MEMMOTT, MARK (1995). Redefining the Wealth of Nations, *USA Today*, September 18, p. 4B.

MILLER, THOMAS R., and RICHARD M. DUDEK (1991). Hospital Affiliated Home Health Care Programs: Successful Responses to Unique Environments, *Top Health Care Finance*, 17 (4): 62–72.

MISENER, JOHN H. (1990). The Impact of Technology on the Quality of Health Care, *Quality Review Bulletin*, 16 (6): 209–213.

MITCHELL, JEAN M., and JONATHAN H. SUNSHINE (1992). Consequences of Physicians' Ownership of Health Care Facilities—Joint Ventures in Radiation Therapy, *New England Journal of Medicine*, 327 (21): 1492–1501.

MITCHELL, SAMUEL A. (1991). Demographics and Health Spending, *Health Systems Review* (Sept./Oct.): 14–16.

MOORE, GORDON T. (1990). Health Maintenance Organizations and Medical Education: Breaking the Barriers, *Academic Medicine*, 65 (7): 427–432.

MOREY-PEDERSEN, JANICE (1994). Education Is the Key to Survival, *AORN Journal*, 60 (1): 76–80.

MORGAN, DAN (1994). The Medicaid Time Bomb, the Medicaid Gravy Train, the Nursing Homes: The "Sleeping Giant," the Middle Class and Medicaid: A Right or a Rip-Off, *The Washington Post National Weekly Edition*, February 7–13.

NATIONAL CENTER FOR HEALTH STATISTICS (1995). *Health, United States, 1994*. Hyattsville, Md.: U.S. Public Health Service.

National Health Directory (1994). Gaithersburg, Md.: Aspen Publishers.

NIX, J. ELMER (1990). Thoughts on Quality, Access, and Expenditures, *Journal of the Mississippi Medical Association* (November): 376, 379.

NUMBERS, RONALD L. (1992). The Specter of Socialized Medicine: American Physicians and Compulsory Health Insurance (1982), in David A. Kindig and Robert B. Sullivan (eds.), *Understanding Universal Health Programs*. Ann Arbor, Mich.: Health Administration Press, pp. 18–25.

OMACHONU, VINCENT K. (1990). Quality of Care and the Patient: New Criteria for Evaluation, *Health Care Management Review*, 15 (4): 43–50.

ORGANIZATION FOR ECONOMIC COOPERATION AND DEVELOPMENT (OECD) (1992). *U.S. Health Care at the Crossroads*, Health Policy Studies No. 1. Paris: OECD.

PETERS, TOM (1991). Medicine and Management—So Much for "Science," *Healthcare Forum Journal*, (May/June): 43–46.

PFAFF, MARTIN (1990). Differences in Health Care Spending Across Countries: Statistical Evidence, *Journal of Health Politics, Policy and Law*, 15 (1): 1–67.

READ, SUSAN D. (1990). A Hospital—Community Health Center Joint Venture in Utah, *Journal of Ambulatory Care Management*, 13 (4): 28–32.

REAMY, JACK (1991). Health Care in Canada: Lessons for the United States, *Journal of Rural Health*, 7 (3): 210–220.

RETTIG, RICHARD (1991). History, Development, and Importance to Nursing of Outcomes Research, *Journal of Nursing Quality Assurance*, 5 (2): 13–17.

RICE, DOROTHY P. (1991). Ethics and Equity in U.S. Health Care: The Data, *International Journal of Health Services*, 21 (4): 637–651.

RINEBERG, BERNARD A. (1991). The Economics of Health Care, *Orthopedics*, 14 (3): 377.

ROGERS, WILLIAM H., DAVID DRAPER, KATHERINE L. KAHN, EMMETT B. KEELER, LISA V. RUBENSTEIN, JACQUELINE KOSECOFF, and ROBERT H. BROOK (1990). Quality of Care Before and After Implementation of the DRG-Based Prospective Payment System, *Journal of the American Medical Association*, 264 (15): 1989–1994.

ROSENTHAL, GARY L., and C. SETH LANDEFELD (1993). Do Older Medicare Patients Cost Hospitals More? *Archives of Internal Medicine*, 153 (4): 89–96.

RUBLEE, DALE A. (1989). Medical Technology in Canada, Germany, and the United States, *Health Affairs*, Fall: 178–181.

RUGGIE, MARY (1992). The Paradox of Liberal Intervention: Health Policy and the American Welfare State, *American Journal of Sociology*, 97 (4): 919–944.

SALIVE, MARCEL, JENNIFER A. MAYFIELD, and NORMAN W. WEISSMAN (1990). Patient Outcomes Research Teams and the Agency for Health Care Policy and Research, *Health Services Research*, 25 (5): 697–708.

SAMUELSON, ROBERT J. (1995). The Cost of Compassion, *The Washington Post National Weekly Edition*, July 24–30, p. 5.

SCALLET, LESLIE (1990). Paying for Public Mental Health Care: Crucial Questions, *Health Affairs* (Millwood), 9 (1): 117–124.

SCHIEBER, GEORGE J. (1990). Health Expenditures in Major Industrialized Countries, 1960-1987, *Health Care Financing Review*, 11 (4): 159–167.

SHEILS, JOHN F., LAWRENCE S. LEWIN, and RANDALL A. HAUGHT (1993). Potential Public Expenditures Under Managed Competition, *Health Affairs* (Millwood), 12 (Sup.): 229–242.

STOTO, MICHAEL (1992). Public Health Assessment in the 1990s, *Annual Review of Public Health*, 13: 59–78.

U.S. PUBLIC HEALTH SERVICE, NATIONAL CENTER FOR HEALTH STATISTICS (1991). *Health, United States, 1990*, Hyattsville, Md.: U.S. Public Health Service.

VINCENZINO, JOSEPH V. (1994). Developments in Health Care Costs—An Update, *Statistical Bulletin* (Metropolitan Insurance Company), 75 (1): 30–35.

WASEM, CATHY (1990). The Rural Health Clinic Services Act: A Sleeping Giant of Reimbursement, *Journal of the American Academy of Nurse Practitioners*, 2 (2): 85–87.

WEISS, GREGORY L., and LYNN E. LONNQUIST (1994). *The Sociology of Health, Healing, and Illness*. Englewood Cliffs, N.J.: Prentice Hall.

WOOLHANDLER, STEFFIE, and DAVID U. HIMMELSTEIN (1991). The Deteriorating Administrative Efficiency of the U.S. Health Care System, *New England Journal of Medicine*, 324 (18): 1253–1258.

WOOLHANDLER, STEFFIE, DAVID U. HIMMELSTEIN, and JAMES P. LEWONTIN (1993). Administrative Costs in U.S. Hospitals, *New England Journal of Medicine*, 329 (6): 400–403.

ZWANZIGER, JACK, GLENN A. MELNICK, and ANIL BAMEZAI (1994). Costs and Price Competition in California Hospitals, *Health Affairs*, Fall: 118–126.

4

CANADA

Challenges to Public Payment for Universal Care

The 1992 U.N. Human Development Report ranked Canada first in the world with respect to health status, overall quality of life, and socioeconomic status. A recent World Bank report placed Canada second in national wealth per resident; only Australia rated higher. Canada also has the largest land mass in the Western Hemisphere and is the second largest country in the world. Providing health care to citizens in remoter parts of this huge expanse has always been a major challenge (Graig, 1993: 38; Memmott, 1995: 4B).

The total population was only 29.2 million in 1994, with one-third in the relatively dense province of Ontario. The three most populous provinces (of ten)—Quebec, British Columbia, and Ontario—contain 74 percent of the population. Other provinces are sparsely settled except for a few major urban centers. Most of the population (87 percent) lives within 200 miles of the southern border, where most of the health care resources are located (Hughes, 1991: 2348; Reamy, 1991: 212; Bagley, 1994: 1749; Desjardins, 1994: 42).

A national and universal health care system was approved in 1968 and fully implemented by 1971. Responsibility for management was delegated largely to the provinces. The national government initially provided about half of the financing, but has since decreased this proportion to less than 25 percent. Because each province is relatively autonomous within general federal requirements, there is considerable variation in specific health care system characteristics from one part of the country to another. Table 4-1 summarizes the noteworthy features generally characteristic of all provinces.

DEMOGRAPHIC CHARACTERISTICS

The average life expectancy at birth was 74.4 years for men and 81 for women in 1991. Infant mortality was 6.8 per 1,000 population (1991). Canada is ahead of the United States

Table 4-1 Primary Features of the Canadian Health Care System

- Hospital and physician services are covered by provincial health insurance—without significant co-payments at the point of service after a deductible amount.
- The provincial health plan is the only payer for "core" services. Funds are derived from personal, sales, and corporate taxes. Seventy-five percent of all health care costs are paid from public sources. Private insurance is not allowed for basic services.
- Citizens are free to choose their doctor and hospital.
- Physician practices are largely private and independent, with a fee-for-service payment system based on rates negotiated by physician organizations and provincial governments. A standard billing form is used by all physicians.
- Hospitals are largely public and nonprofit, with financing based on an annual global budget. Virtually all major surgery and high-technology diagnostic tests are provided in hospitals, with only a few recent exceptions.
- Essentially all high-technology available in other advanced countries is also accessible in Canada. However, a provincial planning process limits the distribution of high-cost technologies, such as CT scans and MRIs, to regional hospitals.

Sources: Based on Health Insurance Association of America, 1990: 1; Grogan, 1992: 217; Graig, 1993: 41.

and most industrialized European countries on these measures. Although the indicators are insufficient by themselves as measures of health care system effectiveness, the relative healthiness of Canadian citizens as compared to other countries is clear (Nair, Karim, and Nyers, 1992: 181; Graig, 1993: 38).

Canada has a relatively young population compared to other advanced industrialized countries. The high rate of younger-age immigrants is part of the explanation. The proportion of citizens over age 65 was 12 percent in 1991 and is projected to reach approximately 13 percent by the year 2001. This is a considerably lower proportion than in Western Europe, the United States, and Japan. The potential impact on health care of a rapidly aging population is nonetheless gaining increased attention here as elsewhere (Taylor, 1990: 19; Masi and Disman, 1994: 498).

The number and proportion of the elderly of advanced age (75 years of age or older) are increasingly rapidly. This will put particular pressure on health resources because it is these older individuals who use hospitals and other health services at an especially high rate compared to the younger population. Projections indicate that many additional nursing home beds will be needed to satisfy demand in the twenty-first century. An increased emphasis on home care as a less expensive alternative to hospitalization and institutional long-term care is among the alternatives being emphasized (Taylor, 1990: 194).

The potential long-term impact is illustrated by hospital admissions. General admissions for the population over age 65 were 13 percent of the total in 1960. The proportion rose to 29 percent by 1989. The older population accounted for only 29 percent of "days of total hospital care" in 1960, but the proportion was 55 percent by 1989 (Nair et al., 1992: 176).

Although urban areas generally have more than an adequate number of physicians and other health care professionals, the vast rural regions in the northern and central parts of the country have difficulty attracting sufficient providers to adequately provide ambulatory care and operate hospitals. Incentives are offered to new medical graduates to practice in rural areas by restricting their ability to secure billing numbers in oversupplied urban areas. Despite such efforts, only a few decide to move to rural regions on a permanent basis (Freeman, 1994: 11).

Native populations of the northern regions present a serious challenge for health professionals, especially in provision of prenatal and maternal care. The native cultures have their own traditions of health care and find modern methods of childbirth in hospitals somewhat contrary to tradition. Health professionals attempt to work with native healers and midwives to find ways of blending the traditional with the modern

without seriously disrupting native culture (Robinson, 1991: 600).

HISTORICAL PERSPECTIVE

The Early Period: 1867–1946

The original concept of universal health care can be traced to the British North American Act of 1867, which placed responsibility for health care at the provincial level. The idea of a publicly financed system was first introduced in 1919, but the more modern design developed gradually during and after World War II. Formal proposals for a federal system were first presented to the House of Commons in 1943 and were discussed in detail over 2 years. Gaining national consensus was difficult because of the relatively strong political power of provinces—which have distinctly different value orientations. Some prefer a strong federal involvement, whereas others (notably Quebec) prefer provincial autonomy. There was considerable concern in the wealthier provinces that the federal government was acquiring too much authority in the funding and control of health care (Health Insurance Association of America, 1990: 9; Graig, 1993: 42)

Post–World War II

Individual provinces, starting with Saskatchewan, began to proceed on their own in 1947. Initially, the emphasis was to increase universality of hospital insurance—already achieved in part through Canadian "Blue Cross" plans. The National Health Grants program was approved at the federal level in 1948, offering matching grants to provinces for planning, hospital construction, and demonstration/training funds for current services. British Columbia went further, approving a universal plan in 1949; Alberta followed in 1950. Another federal law, the Hospital Insurance and Diagnostic Services Act, was passed in 1957—offering 50 percent federal funding for medically necessary hospital care—as well as outpatient, diagnostic, chronic, rehabilitative, and acute services (Crichton, 1994: 150).

Under the 1957 Act, provinces were authorized to provide

- Universal and comprehensive coverage
- Public financing and administration by an accountable provincial government agency
- Uniform terms and conditions in benefit plans
- Portability of benefits so that citizens traveling or moving to another province would be covered

These conditions became part of the later broadened health plans.

Implementation of the single-payer system. Provincial hospital insurance was made available by 1961 in all provinces. A nationwide insurance standard was thus firmly established. Comparable coverage from one province to another was achieved despite differences in wealth between provinces (Graig, 1993: 43; Cockerham, 1995: 291).

Insurance for physician services was slower in coming. The first effort, the Medical Care Insurance Act, was implemented by the Saskatchewan government in 1962—provoking a 23-day physician strike. After intense negotiation, and concessions on both sides, the physicians grudgingly accepted the new approach. The actions of physicians in the Saskatchewan situation tarnished the image of the medical profession in the eyes of politicians and many citizens; they were viewed as self-serving in the face of strong public sentiment for the new system. Nonetheless, the agreement served to establish the continuation of the fee-for-service payment system and permitted physicians to bill through established insurance carriers. Physicians were to maintain autonomy of private practice (Crichton, 1994: 151).

The Canadian Medical Association, the private insurance industry (many companies were controlled by physicians), and several provincial governments continued their opposition to national ambulatory care insurance. A Royal Commission was appointed to study the issue at the request of the Canadian Medical Association. To the chagrin of many physicians, the Commission Report (1964) recommended provincially administered ambulatory care insurance—with subsidies to be provided by the federal government (Wedge, 1994: 273).

The recommendations were implemented through the National Medical Care Insurance Act (Medicare), enacted in 1966 and initiated in 1968. The program provided for 50 percent federal matching for provincial insurance, and required universal coverage, comprehensive services, portability, public management, and reasonable access to services (the same four criteria noted earlier). A number of concessions were made to physicians to secure their cooperation, including continuation of the fee-for-service system. All ten provinces had established Medicare by 1971. The legislation creating this program was among the most widely supported parliamentary decisions ever undertaken in Canada (Health Insurance Association of America, 1990: 10; Graig, 1993: 44–45).

The key provisions generating the strong support from the public were as follows:

- Elimination of financial barriers to care
- Maintaining the freedom of patients to select their own physicians and hospitals

Physician support was achieved by

- Maintaining physician freedom to choose their practice location and work schedules
- Allowing fee schedules to be negotiated between medical associations and provincial health plan representatives

Despite the last provision, physicians felt somewhat coerced in the negotiation process and were not convinced they had any real input. Many physicians feel the freedom to choose practice location has also been removed in several provinces. Legislators and health care leaders expected that costs would increase until everyone was brought into the system, causing health status to improve, and leading to a leveling of expenditures. Unfortunately, this was a miscalculation; expenditures have continued to increase as in other countries (Health Insurance Association of America, 1990; Larson, 1995).

A continuing series of national studies led to new legislation aimed at cost control through increases in preventive health care. Inadequacies of the "biomedical disease model," with its emphasis on curing disease rather than preventing illness, were becoming evident. Greater emphasis was given to public health as well as environmental and life-style factors in the next phase of legislation (Taylor, 1990: 201).

The Established Programs Financing Act was passed in 1977 and ended the open-ended formula through which the federal government matched provincial funding. Federal funding was converted to per capita block grants, with allocations to each province based on population. This caused the federal contribution to fall from 44.5 percent of provincial health expenditures in 1979, to 38.6 percent in 1987, and to 24.4 percent by 1991 (Health Insurance Association of America, 1990: 11; Rathwell, 1994: 7).

Expansion of benefits. The 1977 legislation also created the Extended Health Care Services Program, which provided support to provinces for services such as nursing home care, adult residential care, home care, and ambulatory health services. A federal contribution of $20 (Canadian) per capita was established, with annual increases based on GNP growth.

Further expansion of national oversight was implemented in 1984 through the Canadian Health Act—which amended and replaced several of the separate laws noted earlier. The Act provided for additional federal monitoring, including limitations on user fees and extra billing by physicians. By 1987, all user fees and extra billing were prohibited.

A single-payer health plan in each province, with essentially comparable features throughout the country, was now established. All residents were eligible regardless of employment status. Private insurance was

prohibited for any services covered under provincial plans. However, supplemental private insurance for noncovered services was allowed, and was often provided through employers. Private plans cover prescription drugs, dental and vision care, additional coverage for private or semiprivate hospital rooms, ambulance services, special nursing care, medical devices, podiatry, and chiropractic services. By 1985, 65 percent of Canadians had some form of private insurance, which accounts for 25 percent of national health care expenditures when combined with other out-of-pocket costs. This raises important questions about the "comprehensiveness" of provincial insurance benefits (Health Insurance Association of America, 1990: 15; Larson, 1995).

CULTURAL FACTORS

Canada is both multicultural and multilingual. Approximately 63 percent of the population are primarily speakers of English, whereas 25 percent are primarily French-speaking (largely in Quebec). Smaller numbers are native speakers of Italian, Chinese, German, Spanish, and Native American languages. High immigration from many countries has been characteristic of Canada through most of its history (Heidemann, 1994: 169).

Emphasis on social equity is a primary cultural value. Societal responsibility for individuals and families who are the most vulnerable is deemed especially important—which translates to government responsibility for a social "safety net." Citizens have continued to support social programs such as health care even in times of economic downturn (as in the early 1990s) and despite a relatively high overall tax rate. Furthermore, profit making related to health care is widely considered inappropriate. A service orientation among health professionals is expected (Evans, 1988: 162; Graig, 1993: 47; Health Insurance Association of America, 1990: 4; Loeppky, 1994: 12).

The Canadian heritage is broadly European, but the British have been the most influential. "Tory" conservatism, combined with many socialist traditions, is a primary ideological orientation. Nonetheless, the health care system incorporates a mix of conservative and socialist features. For example, general taxation is acceptable as the primary financing source, whereas fee for service is maintained for family practitioners who are the primary source of basic health services. Canadians have adopted a relatively clear set of national priorities related to health care that serve as the underlying rationale for the current system (Taylor, 1990: 214):

- Health care services should be available to all Canadians on equal terms and conditions. There should be no direct financial barrier to access.
- Health programs should be administered by public agencies accountable to legislators and, ultimately, to voters.
- The costs of health insurance should be borne by all income earners, roughly in accordance with ability to pay.
- Equalization of health care costs to patients is borne by the tax system, rather than through a sliding scale of fees.
- No means test should be imposed on the medically indigent. Costs of health services for the indigent should be assumed by the provinces and federal government.

These values have been supported steadily by Canadians since the creation of the national health care system and despite difficulties in financing services during the early 1990s (Evans, 1988: 164).

POLITICAL INFLUENCES

Governments at the provincial and national level are based on the parliamentary system, with upper and lower chambers having legislative responsibility. Administrative duties are lodged with the cabinet, which is appointed by the Prime Minister from elected members of parliament. The ten provinces are relatively autonomous within federal guidelines. Territories are governed more directly from the federal level. The political system and accompanying economic organization have been characterized as "capitalism with social responsibility." Collaboration is encouraged between corporate and government leaders. Voters do not appear to be distrustful of concentrated power, although many Western Canadians feel that government control is heavily controlled by the more populous eastern provinces (Graig, 1993: 47–48; Desjardins, 1994: 42).

The parliamentary system focuses on consensus building among all major parties and interest groups. There are no checks and balances, or "vetoes" of the kind that characterize the U.S. system. The "Liberals" and "Progressive Conservative" political parties are both interested in a collective approach to health care, despite their other ideological differences (Graig, 1993: 48).

Private special-interest influences, therefore, have limited power in political decisions. As a result, Canadians are not fearful of misuse of government power—because the parliamentary system allows for elections whenever the citizens generally conclude that government is ineffectively achieving their goals (Iglehart, 1989: 1770).

Political power and responsibility are delegated primarily to provincial governments, which have considerable economic power and are viewed as both closer to citizens and more responsive than the federal government. Provinces play a much more significant role in the lives of citizens than does the federal government (Health Insurance Association of America, 1990: 69–71).

SOCIAL ORGANIZATION OF HEALTH CARE

The federal Health Canada department is responsible for national health programs. Four branches include Occupational and Environmental Health Services, Health Promotion, Indian Health Services, and Health

Protection. There is considerable organizational variation at the provincial level, but each has a ministry responsible for health affairs—often combined with other social responsibilities. Each province also has a health insurance section and a medical services section with responsibility for overseeing provincial health plans (Freeman, 1994: 12).

In addition, several other national organizations have responsibility for important dimensions of health care (Heidemann, 1994: 173):

- The Canadian Council on Health Facilities is responsible for accreditation of health care organizations, including institutions for acute care, long-term care, mental health, rehabilitation, and cancer treatment. Continuous quality improvement techniques have been used to establish an effective accreditation process.
- The Canadian Hospital Association represents the nation's hospitals. The Association has recently taken leadership in implementing a mission- and goal-setting process to identify needed reforms and to construct a more effective framework for evaluating policy needs.
- The Canadian Medical Association represents most physicians and has been working vigorously in recent years on quality improvement, practice guidelines, and improved coordination/communication with other provider groups and organizations.
- The Canadian Association for Quality Health Care serves as a forum for health professionals and provider organizations to consider quality improvement issues.
- The Canadian Public Health Association represents public health issues.

These groups are providing much of the national leadership for improving effectiveness of public health and health care programs.

Canadian physicians and consumers have in the past thought highly of their system. A 1992 survey of 1,500 physicians and the same number of consumers indicated most physicians and consumers express general satisfaction, as summarized in Table 4-2. A relatively low response rate (29 percent for physicians and 35 percent for consumers) somewhat limited

Table 4-2   Satisfaction with Health Care: Physicians and Consumers (1992)

Item	Satisfaction Level (%)
Physicians	
Satisfied or very satisfied with quality of the system	79
Access to specialized care is adequate	82
Access to medical technology is adequate to excellent	75
Availability of elective surgery was good to excellent	63
Incomes are about right	56
Compensation is too low	44
Consumers	
Good to excellent relationship with my physician	93
Quality of care is good to excellent	93
Specialist care is readily accessible	85

Source: Based on data from Sullivan, 1992: 1219.

its confidence in results. Both physicians and consumers were worried about the future. There were strong concerns about financial viability of the system and potential deterioration of health care (Sullivan, 1992: 1222).

Public Health

Public health is a major focus. Many kinds of health promotion and disease prevention programs are supported, with responsibility resting primarily at the provincial level. Public health training is a medical school emphasis and is a major focus of the National Center for Health Promotion at the University of Toronto. Physicians and others with a public health orientation may choose to specialize in public health at the Universities of British Columbia and Alberta. Much of the responsibility for public health rests with primary care practitioners, hospitals, and other health care units in communities (Green, 1994: 133).

Attention to environment and life-style issues has increased throughout Canada. Antipollution requirements have been implemented nationally, particularly to improve water quality and reduce acid rain. National campaigns have been implemented to diminish smoking. Preventive actions at the community level are emphasized (Taylor, 1990: 203).

In the last 20 years, deaths from heart disease have dropped 40 percent among men and 30 percent among women. Death from stroke has declined by 50 percent overall. Nonetheless, expenditures on public health are only about 5 percent of the total health care budget (Fulton, 1993b: S60; Heidemann, 1994: 170).

Physicians

Fifty percent of active physicians are general or family practitioners, up slightly from 48 percent in 1982. If pediatricians, general internists, and obstetrician/gynecologists are included, the proportion of primary care providers increases to 67 percent. The annual rate of growth in physician numbers was 1.8 percent between 1980 and 1990, greater proportionally than population growth over the past 20 years. Canada had 1 physician for every 510 people in 1992 (53,800 total), which is roughly in the middle of the range for industrialized countries (Coyte, 1990: 172; Heidemann, 1994: 172; Rathwell, 1994: 7; Freund and McGuire, 1995: 312).

A 1990 survey conducted by the Canadian Medical Association provided a profile of physician characteristics. Women physician numbers are up from 14 percent in 1986 to 16.6 percent in 1990. Because many women are relatively new practitioners, they tend to be younger on average than men. About 32 percent practice part-time, as compared to 19.5 percent of men. Nearly 70 percent of physicians under age 35 are general or family practitioners, a radical change from earlier years, and possibly a direct result of a national policy emphasizing primary care training in medical schools. Younger physicians are also more likely to practice in rural areas than their older colleagues, although substantial numbers of older semiretired physicians also work in rural settings. Twenty-seven percent of physicians are graduates of foreign medical schools, a considerably higher proportion than in most other countries (Sanmartin and Snidal, 1993: 977–980).

Although about 50 percent of physicians identify themselves as solo practitioners, very few function independently of other physicians. They may bill for services as solo providers and have private offices, but in fact much of their work is collaborative with colleagues—through consultations, sharing calls, and referrals. The most common form of practice involves two or more physicians sharing a common office arrangement, practice support costs, and patient services. Off-time patient responsibilities are jointly managed. Formal legal arrangements are common to assure understanding of the group practice (Vayda, 1994: 1586).

Essentially, all Canadian physicians (99 percent) participate in provincial health plans. They have no other major source of payment for most medical procedures. Only about 10 percent of patients are served by Community Health Centers that employ physicians on salary or in capitated Health Service Organizations (similar to health maintenance organizations—mostly in Quebec and Ontario, but increasingly in other provinces). Some physician groups contract with the provincial health plan (mostly in Ontario) to provide services to one or the other of these organizations. In these instances, a capitated payment is made by the provincial health plan for each patient enrolled, regardless of number of services provided (Vayda, 1994: 1587).

Community Health Centers are operated by nonprofit community organizations and generally function through an interdisciplinary team of health professionals who provide health care and a range of other services for underserved groups. These centers include social workers and other nonmedical staff, as well as physicians (Health Insurance Association of America, 1990: 25; Vayda, 1994: 1587).

In Quebec, the community health service centers (French acronym: CLSC) serve more than 10 percent of residents and have legal status under provincial law, with boards of directors governing their activity. They are funded by global budgets and all staff members are paid salaries. As of 1994, 159 centers had been organized to serve all regions of the province (Crichton, 1994: 160–161).

Emergency departments of hospitals in several provinces are staffed by physician groups organized to provide 24-hour coverage. They are paid in a variety of modes depending on the local preference, including direct salaries from the hospital or percentage of the fees generated (Vayda, 1994: 1587).

Ontario is experimenting with "comprehensive health organizations." Physician groups and hospitals organize as nonprofit corporations to provide the full range of integrated health care services for a defined region. The organization receives a capitation payment from the provincial health plan for each member of the region's population, and it contracts with physicians and other providers for the needed range of services under a fixed budget (Vayda, 1994: 1587).

Private ambulatory and surgery clinics have appeared in some locations to serve patients who can afford to pay and do not want to wait for public hospital attention. Walk-in clinics have also appeared in larger cities. They provide quick service and collect the full consultation fee of $21 (minimum in 1995) or more (Doran, 1995).

Outmigration of physicians. Increasing outmigration of physicians to the United States has been underway for the past several years. In 1988, permanent U.S. residence status was chosen by 91 Canadian physicians. This rose to 119 in 1989, 157 in 1990, 192 in 1991, 689 in 1992, and 635 in 1993, as reported by the Canadian Medical Association and Health Canada's Health Information Division. Most are family practitioners and are recruited by U.S. managed care programs or rural communities. Advertisements by U.S. health care firms in the Canadian Medical Association Journal have increased dramatically (Fulton, 1993a: 31; Korcok, 1994: 1849; Sullivan, 1994: 1855).

The trend is in part a response to the surplus of physicians and the capping of incomes, as well as the failure of U.S. medical schools to produce enough primary care practitioners. The demand in the United States is unlikely to ease in the short run because medical schools would need to drastically alter their orientation toward specialty training if primary care practitioner needs are to be met. Easing of immigration restrictions, and reciprocal licensing agreements with more than forty U.S. states, makes it possible for physicians to be at work across the border within 3 months after an H-1B visa application is submitted. All Canadian medical schools are fully accredited by the U.S. Department of Education, and graduates are not considered foreign medical graduates, thus enabling them to forego residency training in the United States (Merritt and Shusterman, 1993: 48; Korcok, 1994: 1849).

Medical education. Canada has sixteen medical schools with a graduating class each year of approximately 1,650, down from 1,800 in the early 1980s. Quality standards in the schools are fully comparable to other developed countries. The focus of Canadian medical education is somewhat unique. Primary emphasis is given to training generalists and family practitioners, with comparatively less investment in specialist training. Physicians are trained to practice in a less aggressive style than in other countries. Fewer high-technology procedures are used and surgery is undertaken only with very good reasons. Intensive care is not emphasized by physicians in hospitals if less costly procedures will suffice (Zwanziger et al., 1993: 138; Gray, 1994: 1476; Kendel and Dauphinee, 1994: 1579).

Despite these training characteristics, outcomes for heart disease (myocardial infarction) appear to be comparable to other countries. A comparative study of patient outcomes in university hospitals at McGill (Montreal) and Stanford (California) indicated that mortality and recurrence of disease were basically similar, except that McGill

A Case in Point: Fort Francis and Vicinity

One example is Riverside Health Care Facilities, a Community Health Organization headquartered in Fort Francis, Ontario, a town of about 10,000 population near the U.S. border with Minnesota. The Organization serves the nearby smaller communities of Emo and Rainy River—adding an additional population of 8,000.

Riverside's mission is to provide primary and secondary care while integrating and coordinating health programs under one administration. The units do not attempt to duplicate highly specialized and low-volume services available in other locations, but instead refer patients as needed, principally to Winnipeg, Manitoba, or Thunder Bay, Ontario, via air ambulance or surface vehicle (4 hours travel time) and without jeopardizing the safety or welfare of clients. In emergency situations, services can also be obtained from International Falls, Minnesota, immediately across the border. For example, no CT or MRI services are available in Fort Francis and must be secured elsewhere (Riverside Health Care Facilities, 1994).

A ninety-three-bed hospital (La Verendrye Health Centre) in Fort Francis has the capacity for emergency services, general medicine, anesthesia and surgery, intensive care, obstetrics and gynecology, pediatrics, long-term care, rehabilitation, laboratory, counseling, and other services. The hospital was nearly fully occupied (Summer 1994), largely by elderly patients. The Emo (twenty-three beds, largely long-term care) and Rainy River (fifteen beds) health centers provide primary care, urgent care, diagnostic imaging, physiotherapy, pediatrics, health education, long-term care, home health care, and community public health services.

Eleven physicians serve the region and are employed directly by Riverside on a salaried basis or through contracts with Riverside for their services at a fixed rate. Three specialists, in surgery, urology, and obstetrics/gynecology, are located in Fort Francis. The pharmacy service is privately operated but with controlled prices and fixed payments to pharmacists. A serious shortage of specialists is among the primary problems of the Organization. A high-quality videotaped recruitment effort was used to inform potential applicants but had not yet been successful in May 1994.

We detected considerable uncertainty about the future. Physicians clearly felt deterioration of the Ontario health plan had taken place, and was likely to get worse as it impacts their region. Nonetheless, they were well aware that overall Provincial costs were out of hand and had to be controlled. They did not seem particularly disturbed by the recent change from fee-for-service compensation to salary, because their income had been determined fairly. The senior physicians, one a surgeon and the other a GP, were about to retire and replacements had not been found—despite a surplus of physicians in other parts of Ontario.

Nurses and pharmacists also expressed considerable unhappiness with the changes that were occurring. No pay increases had been provided for the 2 years prior to our visit, which was clearly an issue of major concern. Physicians, nurses, and pharmacists seemed satisfied that the Ontario health care system was of high quality overall—if the short-term problems could be satisfactorily resolved.

Source: The authors visited the region in May 1994 and interviewed administrators, physicians, pharmacists, and nurses.

patients felt somewhat more pain and American patients had a somewhat better functional status. These results are, of course, from teaching hospitals and might be quite different in provincial or local hospitals (Pilote, Racine, and Hlatky, 1994: 1095).

Some critics argue that there are more medical schools and graduates than needed to fulfill national needs, and others argue that a shortage may be evident shortly after the year 2000. Funding for academic medical centers has been decreasing, although public expectations for high-quality education and research continues. This places medical education in an unstable situation compared with earlier years when support was on the increase (Valberg et al., 1994: 1582).

Recommendations were offered by a Federal-Provincial Committee on Health Manpower in the early 1990s to

- Reduce the licensing of physicians who are trained abroad and are allowed to practice in Canada
- Lower postgraduate training in general practice and specialties
- Lower medical school enrollments
- Require that new physician practice opportunities be limited to geographic areas of demonstrated need

British Columbia has implemented the recommendations most forcefully by limiting new physician billing numbers to locations of demonstrated medical need, particularly rural and northern areas of the province. This was done in part because of the estimated $150,000 to $250,000 additional annual cost for each new physician—including fee income, overhead, diagnostic tests, hospital admissions, prescriptions, and other costs of physician practice. However, legal challenges have limited the effectiveness of the provincial right to restrict medical practice (Taylor, 1990: 198–199).

Because all medical school funds are from government sources, the federal and provincial governments have control over access to medical school and practice (through billing number allocations). However, errors were apparently made in the 1960s and 1970s in projected health care needs. More new medical schools were constructed than needed, thus increasing the number of graduates. As noted earlier, foreign physician immigration adds to the physician oversupply. A law passed in 1994 greatly decreases the possibility of foreign graduates securing licenses to practice in locations with surpluses (Taylor, 1990: 198).

The decrease in numbers of medical students, and outmigration to the United States, has caused the growth rate in physicians numbers to fall from 4 percent annually prior to 1989 to about 2 percent since 1990—roughly the population growth rate. An increasing number of medical school students are women, who represented 44 percent of all graduates in 1991. A higher proportion choose general or family practice than do their male counterparts (Sanmartin and Snidal, 1993: 984; Watanabe, 1994: 256).

Nurses

Careers in nursing have been constrained by limited opportunities for advancement. Differential pay for advanced education has been minimal—attributable in part to the continuing subsidiary status of the nursing profession. An attempt was made to overcome this problem as part of the Canada Health Reform Act of 1984, allowing nurses to collect fees through the insurance system. However, provinces have been very slow to implement the federal legislation, in part because of resistance from the medical profession. Nurses have not gained sufficient political power to fully overcome physician resistance (Shea, 1991: 332).

Nurses tend to have a low degree of job satisfaction. Working conditions (especially in hospitals) often involve long hours, evening and night responsibilities, and high stress. Most nurses (98 percent) are female and generally work under male administrators and physicians. Despite salary improvements and somewhat higher status, many women choose to leave the profession because of the difficult working conditions, and many have migrated to the United States in search of higher pay and better work settings. The situation has been made worse by the recent cutbacks in hospital services with wholesale dismissal of many nurses (Armstrong-Stassen et al., 1994: 416).

To help alleviate this problem, the Canadian Nurses Association (CNA) is encouraging the addition of a new requirement (by the year 2000) that nurses be required to have a university degree to enter practice. The CNA has gained influence as an active player in the national debate about improving the quality of health care services (Baumgart, 1993: 170).

British Columbia has made more progress than most other provinces in encouraging the training and professional work of nurse-practitioners. They have begun to assume, at considerably lower cost, some of the responsibilities formerly reserved for family physicians. Nurse-midwives are allowed to practice independently, for example. In other cases, nurse-practitioners and family physicians collaborate in practices that take best advantage of the training and skills of both. The nurse-practitioner gives greater attention to counseling, health promotion, and disease prevention, whereas the family physician concentrates on primary care. This combination has been particularly effective in Ontario where use of nurse-practitioners has been emphasized in enhancing health promotion and disease prevention (Birenbaum, 1994: 76–78).

Graduate programs in nursing have been established in most provinces, including four Ph.D. programs (in Alberta, British Columbia, Ontario, and Quebec). Certification programs have been established to conduct reviews and to validate qualifications in specialty areas of training. *The Canadian Journal of Nursing Research* is the only periodical that specializes in peer-reviewed nursing research. The National Nursing Research Conference publishes annual proceedings that supplement the journal. Some research articles are published in the *Canadian Nurse*, official journal of the Canadian Nurses Association—which has worked steadily over the years to increase the status and rewards in the field (Stinson, Lamb, and Thibaudeau, 1990: 108; Clark, 1994: 86–87).

Nurses have thus made some gains in both status and salaries. Compensation for the highest-paid nurses increased 30 percent between 1974 and 1988 ($20,573 to $29,307 Canadian), which may not mean much more than keeping up with inflation. Starting salaries of hospital nurses moved up somewhat more rapidly, from $16,380 in 1974 to $24,624 in 1988. Salaries and benefits are included in hospital budgets for hospital nurses and are negotiated between nurses unions and hospital associations, but hospitals and health plan officials clearly have the upper hand (Shea, 1991: 329–330).

Salary compression has become a major problem for experienced nurses because of the relatively small salary range and modest average increments per year. The difference between starting and maximum salaries was only about $10,000 in 1988. Specialization as a nurse-practitioner improves the situation somewhat, but salary growth has not been comparable to other professions (Shea, 1991: 330).

The effort to control costs in recent years has been problematic. On the negative side, as noted earlier, hospitals have cut back on nursing jobs. On the positive side, well-trained nurses have been given additional responsibilities formerly reserved for physicians. Community nursing has become more important with expanded opportunities for educational, home health care, and health promotion roles (Clark, 1994: 88; Heidemann, 1994: 172).

Pharmacists and Pharmaceuticals

Pharmacists are regarded as key members of the health care team. Clinical pharmacists are part of the staff in hospitals and in a few medical residency programs. They have contributed directly to improved prescribing, better patient outcomes, and more efficient use of pharmaceuticals. They supervise the pharmaceutical training of medical, nursing, and pharmacy students, provide drug consultations, offer patient education, and maintain drug-use profiles of patients. The current practice emphasis is on "pharmaceutical care" in which pharmacists assume greater responsibility for patient care than formerly, working directly on medication management in cooperation with physicians. It is their task to assure insofar as possible that adverse drug reactions are avoided, dosage is appropriate, and compliance education is undertaken (Robinson, 1994: 1132; Whelan, Burge, and Munroe, 1994: 469–470).

The high cost of drugs within the larger health care budget has led to vigorous efforts to cut pharmaceutical expenditures. Formularies of drugs covered by provincial health plans have been reexamined and the number of acceptable drugs has been cut. Most pharmaceuticals are not covered under health care plans, except in a few provinces, where they are part of the insurance coverage. The elderly continue to be subsidized but must pay some proportion of the cost (30 percent in 1995). Cutbacks have occurred in the dispensing fees paid to pharmacists and lower-cost, mail-order dispensing has been encouraged as has greater use of generic drugs (Freeman, 1994: 18; Robinson, 1994: 1132).

The Canadian government has been concerned about inadequate research funding to develop new and better pharmaceutical products. Consequently, a new law (C-22) was passed in 1987 requiring the industry to spend 10 percent of total sales on research and development. In 1993, another law (C-91) changed the rules so that pharmaceutical companies must disperse research-and-development expenditures more widely throughout the country (90 percent had been spent in Quebec and Ontario). However as a trade-off, they will no longer be required to license their products for a specified time period. In effect, the patent protection period for drugs is extended (Ellenberger, 1994: 1140).

Administrators and Health Care Management

Efficient and effective health care administration has been a key element in federal and provincial programs. Administrators have gained major policy and decision responsibility, sometimes at the expense of physicians and other clinicians. However, physicians are increasingly assuming formal managerial roles. In the past, they have tended to focus only on medical issues. Medical directors were part of a "dual" leadership structure in hospitals and other health care units, and competed with the formal administration. The current trend is to directly involve physicians in decisions within the formal structure. Administrative medicine has become a new medical specialty (Leatt, 1994: 174).

Health care organizations are generally very complex and thus difficult to manage. This has been particularly true of hospitals, in part because of the combination of functions and the great variety of skilled workers. The effort to streamline health care has caused the "flattening" of these organizations to fewer administrative levels, accompanied by an increase in flexible, team-oriented, and patient-centered management approaches. To be successful in this changing environment, administrators are expected to have several basic leadership competencies that will facilitate effective organizational functioning. For example (Leatt, 1994: 176; Steffan, 1994: 25):

- Understanding health policy and the political process
- Creating and sustaining a vision and a mission related to future needs
- Developing communication and conceptual skills to support institutionalization of the vision
- Understanding and using information systems and scientific data in the achievement of quality outcomes
- Developing and sustaining strategies to achieve desired results
- Building and managing effective health care teams and community alliances

- Developing creative thinking and systems development skills
- Having a capacity for life-long learning

The successful adaptation of health care organizations to future needs is challenging all members of the health care team, and is heavily dependent on the effective application of these competencies by federal, provincial and institutional administrators as they attempt to manage the transition (Brooks, 1994: 482–485).

Midlevel Practitioners

The roles of nurse-practitioners and nurse-midwives are increasing in the health care system. However, physician assistants do not exist as a formal discipline. Physicians discourage training and employment of midlevels except in circumstances where M.D.s do not wish to practice—such as in isolated rural locations and on native reserves. Midlevel practitioners are required to work under the supervision of a physician if they are to receive reimbursement under provincial health plans. This was changed in 1993 for licensed midwives who can now practice independently (Health Insurance Association of America, 1990: 26; Fulton, 1993b: S61).

Hospitals

All provinces have gone through a formal planning process to ensure that hospital facilities are in the right place as needed. Provincial authorities attempt to prevent duplication of facilities, or technology, or other secondary or tertiary hospital activities. However, as a consequence of changing health needs, new modes of treatment, improved transportation, and other changes, targets established through rigorous early planning have required adjustment to fit changing realities. The number of hospital beds grew steadily after hospital insurance was initiated in 1961, greatly exceeding the rate of population growth. Early estimates of bed needs were too high, forcing major cut-

backs in recent years (Coyte, 1990: 174; Taylor, 1990: 209).

The Canadian Council on Hospital Accreditation was established in 1952 with responsibility for inspecting and accrediting public hospitals. The name was changed to the Canadian Council on Health Facilities Accreditation in 1987, with nursing homes and ambulatory care centers also included. As of 1987, 92 percent of all hospital beds were located in accredited hospitals. Most hospitals also have quality assurance programs in place (Taylor, 1990: 210).

About 875 of approximately 1,240 hospitals (in 1990) were owned and managed as public institutions, with their sources of funds coming largely from provincial health plans. Nearly half (46 percent) were earlier owned by voluntary organizations, 30 percent by municipal or county corporations, 14 percent by provincial authorities, and 11 percent by church organizations. The majority of private hospitals are for long-term care, and collect fees from patients for services provided (Health Insurance Association of America, 1990: 18; Reamy, 1991: 214).

There were 6.1 hospital beds per 1,000 population in 1992. The occupancy rate (in 1987) was 82 percent (as compared to 64 percent in the United States). Admission rates were 142 annually per 1,000 population. Average length of stay was 11.2 days, a much higher figure than in many other countries. The evidence from surveys in the early 1990s suggests that all of these numbers have recently decreased, whereas the average wait for hospitalization and the number of people waiting have increased dramatically. Many procedures require at least 3 months waiting time, and some require a much longer wait (Health Insurance Association of America, 1990; Danzon, 1992: 34; Doran, 1995).

Much of the outpatient care is provided in hospitals, often in emergency departments but also through other forms of ambulatory care such as diagnostic and therapeutic procedures, day surgery, and many other forms of specialty clinic services. Estimates indicate that about 40 percent of hospital costs are for outpatient and nonpatient services. However, hospitals provide relatively few nonclinical services or "hotel-type" amenities as compared to some other countries (Redelmeier and Fuchs, 1993: 777; Jacobs et al., 1994: 21–22).

Hospital governance is the responsibility of regional boards of directors for groups of hospitals. This is a major change from the earlier circumstance where each hospital had its own governing board. Many small hospitals are being closed as regionalization of services proceeds. Decisions about priority programs and allocation of funds take place as part of a consultative process involving hospital administrators, boards of directors, medical school faculty, and representatives of provincial health plans. Some observers suggest that the real power rests with provincial governments and health plan administrators who control the funds (Fulton, 1993a: 30; Larson, 1995).

Because medical and surgical costs are substantially lower in Canada than in the United States, some HMOs are contracting with Canadian facilities for surgery with patients who arrive by charter flights for short-term stays. The practice is just beginning and data are not yet available on results of the scheme and how it will proceed in the future (Doran, 1995).

Use of advanced technology. Hospitals are generally the centers for high-technology and undertake nearly all major medical procedures. However, medical technology is somewhat less available than in some other advanced countries. For example, as indicated in Table 4-3, there were 0.46 magnetic resonance imaging (MRI) units per one million population in 1987, compared to 3.69 in the United States and 0.94 in Germany. Comparable differences in the use of advanced technologies occurred for open-heart surgery, cardiac care, lithotripsy, and radiation therapy. Canada was nearly equal to the U.S. in organ transplants in 1987, and was considerably more active than Germany in transplantation and open-heart surgery.

Table 4-3 Use of Advanced Technologies (1987)

Technology	Uses per Million Population		
	Canada	United States	Germany
Magnetic resonance imaging	.46	3.69	.94
Open-heart surgery	1.23	3.26	.74
Cardiac catheterization	1.50	5.06	2.64
Organ transplant	1.08	1.31	.46
Radiation therapy	.54	3.97	3.13
Extracorporeal shock wave lithotripsy	.16	.94	.34

Source: Based on data from Rublee, 1989: 179.

MRI units are located primarily in larger regional hospitals where they are heavily utilized. The public Foothills Hospital MRI unit in Calgary, Alberta, operated 16 hours per day, did up to 28 scans daily, and had a waiting list of 1,000 patients in 1994. The backlog led to initiation of a private MRI clinic in the same city, with approval of the Alberta health care authority (Brooks, 1993: 1155; Redelmeier and Fuchs, 1993: 777).

Another private initiative in Calgary has captured attention because it is unusual under the current system. An eye clinic was established in the late 1980s specializing in cataract surgery. It is a self-contained facility that charges a $2,500 fee for "use" of the facility and bills the health authority for the cost of surgery—to avoid the prohibition against extra billing for the surgery itself. The Foothills Hospital contracts with the facility for eye surgery because the clinic can function more cost-effectively and with higher quality than is possible at the hospital (Doran, 1995).

Advanced information systems. Although direct billing of the provincial health plans via computer is commonplace, hospitals have been slower to develop information systems that assist in comprehensive measurement of the allocation and outcome of services provided. It is thus very difficult to measure efficiency and to evaluate the global budgeting process (Rathwell, 1994: 14).

Emergency Medical Services

Emergency medical care is available to all citizens and foreign visitors, with only modest charges for some types of service. Quebec charges a $5 fee if an emergency room visit is judged not to be an emergency. A comprehensive radio-dispatched emergency medical system serves all communities and transports trauma victims to the nearest hospital via surface or fixed-wing aircraft. Helicopters are not widely used (Fulton, 1993a: 30).

Long-Term Care

Provincial insurance provides coverage for long-term care, but with variations. When an institutional setting becomes the principal place of residence, residents are required to pay some proportion of social security or disability income for room and board, with amounts varying by province. Manitoba has the highest requirement, insisting that 85 percent of social security income be used for care. Patients are assured a cash living allowance of $110 to $130 per month in most provinces, but the amount has declined considerably in the 1990s (Barer et al., 1992: 765; Larson, 1995).

Significant numbers of elderly patients reside in hospitals for extended periods, generally with low-service-intensity requirements. This explains the relatively high number of beds available and high occupancy rates. Twenty-three percent of public hospital beds were specifically designated for long-term care, but this number has declined recently. Alternative long-term-care options are limited although efforts are underway to alleviate the shortage. The long-term-care beds are not separated statistically from general short-term hospital beds—which is among the explanations for relatively low hospital costs as compared to other industrialized countries (Danzon, 1992: 34).

Some proportion of the waiting time for hospital procedures is a deliberate result of cost-containment and long-term-care policy. It is less costly to keep long-term but low-service-need patients for greater periods of time, as compared to admitting new acute care patients for surgery or other intensive procedures.

Special Services for the Elderly

The diversity of the elderly represents a challenge to the health care system, especially in primary care and geriatric medicine. For example, roughly 20 percent are not native speakers of either French or English (Masi and Disman, 1994: 498).

Older citizens face relatively few financial risks from health problems, however, because they have had full access to health care services covered by provincial insurance. They are generally not required to make the same level of co-payments for pharmaceuticals as are younger citizens. All provinces greatly diminish deductibles and co-payments by the elderly for other services as well. Furthermore, concerted public programs play a major role in preventing poverty among the elderly. This combination of services may explain why older people in Canada indicate high satisfaction with their health care. Sixty-six percent believe the system works well for them. However, as funds have been cut back recently, attitudes appear to be increasingly uncertain about the adequacy of health protection (Barer et al., 1992: 764; Larson, 1995).

Some variation between provinces does exist. For example, two-thirds of the older population has complete coverage for hospital, ambulatory care, and pharmaceutical products (those living in Ontario, Quebec, the Yukon, and the Northwest Territories). British Columbia, on the other hand, requires a medical care premium of $35 per month per older person, or $62 for a couple (1991). Even so, the maximum cost for medical premium and out-of-pocket pharmaceutical costs was $545 in 1991. This figure could range slightly higher in Manitoba and Prince Edward Island, largely because pharmaceutical costs for ongoing medications are not fully covered (Barer et al., 1992: 769–770).

A Regional Geriatric Assessment Program was created in Ontario to assist frail older people who want to live independently and avoid institutionalization. They can be referred to the Program by physicians, hospitals, long-term-care institutions, or fellow citizens. A multidimensional screening process examines the individual needs and requirements for home support. Referrals are then made to other agencies that can provide some of the needed support. New Brunswick has a somewhat different approach with a greater focus on delivering the full range of needed services directly to the home. However, neither program has been fully evaluated in terms of cost effectiveness or reduction of institutionalization (Pickles, Topping, and Woods, 1994: 183–184).

Geriatrics as a medical specialty has not been particularly emphasized until the relatively recent period. Medical schools in several provinces are now beginning to focus on geriatric medicine, with specific curricula dealing with care for the older population. However, funding cutbacks noted elsewhere may limit the effectiveness of these efforts (Pickles et al., 1994: 187–188).

Mental Health Care

Mental health care is integrated with the general health care system and is funded through provincial insurance plans. A mental health section is located in Health Canada at the federal level. Each provincial health ministry includes a community mental health branch that operates mental hospitals and is responsible for assuring availability of general mental health services in communities. Treatment requirements for severely ill mental patients are mandated by law in each province (Bachrach, 1993: 932; Freeman, 1994: 14).

General hospitals usually include psychiatric units. When these were established, they were intended to gradually replace provincial mental hospitals. However, general hospitals are not prepared to manage the most severe and chronic cases that continue to populate the less well-staffed provincial institutions. The result is a "two-tier" hospital system in which general hospitals serve the less severely ill and provincial specialized hospitals house the most difficult cases with fewer resources per patient (Freeman, 1994: 14; Wasylenki, Goering, and Macnaughton, 1994: 21).

A deinstitutionalized effort was initiated during the 1960s with the goal of moving most patients to community settings. Community mental health programs were established throughout the country during the period after 1976. In Ontario, for example, 350 such programs have been established with funding from the Adult Community Mental Health Program sponsored by the Provincial Ministry of Health. However, relatively little investment went toward creating community capacity for care, such as case management, housing, vocational and educational rehabilitation, and appropriate recreation. Provincial mental hospitals and general hospital psychiatric units continue to use most available funding (87 percent), whereas communities receive relatively little (13 percent)—although there is a wide variation between provinces. Saskatchewan allocates 23 percent to communities, whereas Manitoba provides only 3 percent (Freeman, 1994: 19).

Furthermore, there is little coordination between community programs, general hospital psychiatric units, and provincial mental hospitals in any of the provinces. The three types of programs are referred by mental health professionals as the "three solitudes" because they work independently on similar and overlapping issues. New Brunswick has begun to resolve this problem through creation of a Mental Health Commission with responsibility for developing coordination and integration of services (Goering, Wasylenki, and Macnaughton, 1994: 37; Wasylenki et al., 1994: 22).

British Columbia is credited with having the most advanced community-based system. The Greater Vancouver Mental Health Services Society has overcome many of the coordination problems noted earlier. It is fully funded by the Provincial Ministry of Health to provide coordination and service delivery in the metropolitan region, including operation of a Mental Health Emergency Service to respond to crisis mental disorder situations (Bigelow, Sladen-Drew, and Russell, 1994: 53–62).

Primary care physicians who often encounter mentally ill individuals are not linked directly to the three components of care noted earlier. An overall mechanism for organizing and managing mental health services at the community level remains to be developed. Research programs have been initiated at some universities (University of Toronto, for example) to help alleviate this problem (Wasylenki et al., 1994: 28).

Despite the mandate that care be provided to all needy patients, problems occur in providing for unemployment and homelessness of chronic mental patients. They are noticeable on the streets of large and small cities as in other countries, despite major efforts to reach and treat them. Many can only be managed in the mental hospital system. Several provincial health plans have recently increased their emphasis on treatment for the severely ill patients. The emphasis continues to be focused on comprehensive psychosocial rehabilitation in community treatment programs (Bachrach, 1994: 91; Freeman, 1994: 14).

Quality of Care

A renewed national effort to improve quality of health care was initiated in 1992 by the top national and provincial health officials. A strategy was adopted to prepare an improved vision of quality needs for the country—while also undertaking an inventory of quality improvement efforts already underway. Specific goals were to (Heidemann, 1994: 173; Rowan, Walters, and Morgan, 1994: 464)

• Advance effectiveness of health care institutions
• Develop greater efficiency
• Increase appropriateness of care
• Increase patient satisfaction

Clinical practice guidelines are under development as a vehicle to help achieve these goals. Scientific evidence is collected to determine appropriate and high-quality practices. Outcomes research is underway to help measure results. The quality of care efforts are closely linked to efforts by the Canadian Medical Association Working Group on Core and Comprehensive Services to further refine the list of core services to be paid for through provincial health plans (Rowan et al., 1994: 464).

Outcome studies of discharged patients indicate that satisfaction with physician care is relatively high (90 percent), but patients are more critical of hospital care. For example, in one large study, between 20 percent and 41 percent of patients were unhappy with failure to explain hospital routines, insufficiently explain medication side effects or possible pain from treatment, and failure to explain appropriate activities (given their condition) upon returning home. In general, they were seeking greater involvement in decisions about their care and wanted more information about treatment (Charles et al., 1994: 1813).

ECONOMIC CHARACTERISTICS AND ISSUES

The national economy suffered a major setback in the late 1980s and early 1990s, when the world economy took a downturn. However, the continuing effects appear to be profound, probably in part because of the relatively higher proportion of the total economy that depends on public spending. Government expenditures make up about 40 percent of GNP. Health expenditures represented an average of 35 percent of provincial budgets in 1993. Growth in health care and other social costs were well ahead of economic growth or population increases during the period from 1960 to 1990, but have leveled off considerably in the early 1990s as the recession forced cuts (Taylor, 1990: 188; Asmonga, 1994: 41).

The downturn led to the Government Expenditure Restraint Act in 1991, severely reducing the federal contributions to health care (down to 25 percent or less from nearly 50 percent earlier). This forced the provinces to increase their spending but also forced cuts in health care services. As national and provincial budgets tightened, provincial health ministries could provide very little budget flexibility. Hospitals were, for example, required to take beds out of service, limit services, and close hospitals entirely to remain within allocated budgets. Alberta and Ontario have lowered pay for government employees (including health care) by 5 percent (Barnett and Shustack, 1994: 333; Rathwell, 1994: 8).

Expenditures

Health care costs were absorbing 10.3 percent of GDP in 1994. The total was about $72 billion in 1993, or about $1,950 per capita. Health care spending grew much faster (83.3 percent) than the population (12.3 percent growth) between 1975 and 1987 (in constant Canadian dollars). Per capita spending for health care grew at a rate of 4.3 percent during the same period. After adjusting for inflation, the average annual growth rate for the longer period from 1960 to 1990 was 1.66 percent (Bagley, 1994: 1746; Rachlis and Kushner, 1994: 45; Janigan, 1995: 11; National Center for Health Statistics, 1995: 220).

Growth in costs is attributable in part to the following:

- Increases in numbers of physicians (23 percent growth between 1981 and 1987)
- Increases in other health practitioners, such as chiropractors, who have been allowed to receive payment from provincial health funds
- Advances in pharmaceutical costs (12.7 percent annual growth between 1980 and 1989)
- Increases in hospital costs, with more hospitals and beds than needed (annual growth of 4.6 percent between 1980 and 1989, controlled for inflation)

- Advances in high-cost technology for diagnosis and surgery

Similar increases have occurred in all Canadian provinces since 1980. Expansion in health expenditures after inflation has been nearly twice the rate of Gross Provincial Product increases. In Ontario, health expenditures grew at an average annual rate of 12.6 percent between 1980 and 1990 (5.7 percent after controlling for inflation). However, provinces have managed to keep administrative costs much lower (estimated at 8 to 11 percent) than in some other countries (Coyte, 1990: 174; Asmonga, 1994: 41).

If expenditures are expressed in "Purchasing Power Parities" (a term developed by the OECD to express ability to purchase a given quantity of goods with a given amount of national currency), growth in per capita health expenditures accelerated considerably after 1970 when the national and provincial health systems were fully implemented. The proportion of GDP for health care leveled off, but public expenditures per capita for health increased significantly. Per capita expenditures increased much more than in Germany and other European countries, for example, and were comparable to the United States. Use of "Purchasing Power Parities" to adjust prices thus reveals that spending increased faster than unadjusted prices would suggest (Pfaff, 1990: 5).

As a consequence of economic decline, health expenditure growth, and the growing national debt, it was necessary to cut back drastically—especially hospitals. Annual budget increases have since declined from about 9 to 1 percent. Employees (especially nurses) have been laid off as noted earlier, and the rationing process has been increased for non-emergency procedures. Projections indicate cutbacks will need to continue until near the year 2000. Alberta, for example, proposes to cut health care by 30 percent in the urban centers of Calgary and Edmonton over 4 years (Bagley, 1994: 1746; Barnett and Shustack, 1994: 335). The distribution of health expenditures in 1993 is summarized in Table 4-4.

Table 4-4   Distribution of Health Expenditures (1993)

Provider	Percentage of Expenditures
Hospitals	43.0
Physicians	15.0
Pharmaceuticals	13.8
Dentists and other health professionals	6.9
Capital spending	3.6
Other health institutions	10.0
Other expenditures	11.4

Sources: Based on Bagley, 1994: 1746; Rathwell, 1994: 9.

There is some difference of opinion about the data on distribution of health expenditures. For example, a well-known publication in Canada reports that physicians use 21.6 percent of costs vs. the 15 percent listed in Table 4-4; drugs are estimated to cost 5.3 percent vs. 13.8 percent; and hospital, other health care institutions, and capital expenditures total 60 percent vs. 56.6 percent. The totals for each category evidently depend on how each is computed and the source of data (Rachlis and Kushner, 1994: 48).

The physician proportion is somewhat lower than in other countries, attributable in substantial part to deliberate government payment caps, lower administrative costs, the single-payer system, and computerized billing. Malpractice insurance costs are also relatively low because Canada is not subject to high litigation rates (Taylor, 1990: 212).

The distribution of expenditures noted above may vary by province. For example, in Ontario, the distribution in 1993 according to one authority, was (Fulton, 1993a: 31)

Hospitals	44%
Physicians	30
Emergency services	6
Mental health	5
Pharmaceuticals	6
Community care	4
Administration	1

Financing

Funds for federal and provincial health care come largely from personal income taxes; excise taxes on commodities, such as alcohol, tobacco, and gasoline; and from lottery revenue. Some provinces have begun to charge a payroll tax or premium to consumers. Alberta and British Columbia now require approximately $36 per month for a single person, for example, paid by employers (Fulton, 1993a: 29; Janigan, 1995: 11). The sources of funding for health expenditures in 1991 are summarized in Table 4-5.

Payment for Physicians and Primary Care Services

Most physicians are paid on a fee-for-service basis, except in university hospitals and in community clinics or capitated programs. Fee schedules for each procedure are negotiated between organizations of provincial physicians (medical associations) and health ministries and thus vary by province. Medical associations decide independently after negotiations are complete how to reallocate resources among specialists and general practitioners. Extra billing for basic benefits has been prohibited by federal law. The negotiation process has also served to limit fee increases, which fell 18 percent behind inflation during the period from 1971 to 1985. Fees for both surgical and nonsurgical procedures are relatively lower than in many other advanced countries, as are fees for evaluation and management of patients during hospital visits (Fuchs and Hahn, 1990: 886).

Physicians willing to practice in underserved locations, especially in rural and northern communities, can receive 10 percent above the normal billing fee. Other subsidies are also sometimes provided, such as

Table 4-5   Health Care Funding Sources (1991)

Source	Percentage
Federal	24.4
Provincial	46.0
Local	1.1
Workmen's compensation	.9
Private	27.8

Source: Based on data from Rathwell, 1994: 7–8.

housing and transportation. On the other hand, new physicians moving to an over-served community are allowed to bill at only half the going rate in British Columbia (Doran, 1995).

Ambulatory care costs are limited to a set budget under each provincial plan—which means there is a limit to the fees that physicians can collect. Only a few organizations (largely in Ontario) provided services through a capitated payment system until the 1990s. This is changing radically in the mid-1990s as managed care and capitated payments are being imposed in several provinces to cut costs. Provincial health plans continue to be the primary payers, but the private insurance market is expanding as cutbacks occur in public insurance (Health Insurance Association of America, 1990: 30; Larson, 1995).

The efforts to "cap" overall physician costs have been a subject of considerable political controversy. For example, Quebec limited the amount payable to individual physicians in any one quarter. Billings beyond the limit were reimbursed at only 25 percent of the established fee schedule. Global caps for all physician fees have also been set in Ontario. If exceeded, a fee reduction is implemented in subsequent years to meet the overall target. Attempts by other provinces to cap payments to physicians have led to vigorous protests by medical associations, coupled with legal actions and binding arbitration between medical associations and provincial health plans (Health Insurance Association of America, 1990: 35).

Limits on physician fees per unit of service have caused individual providers who can attract additional patients to increase the number of services delivered—as the only means to increase income. More patients are seen and offered more services (known by economists as "physician-induced" demand). Per capita utilization of physician services in Canada has continued to grow, with increased work load for those who could attract the patients. Only recently has any effort been made to control physician utilization through cost accountability. In British Columbia, for example, physician visits have been limited to 44 per day with prorated fees (Hughes, 1991: 2349–2351; Health Insurance Association of America, 1990: 22; Doran, 1995).

Electronic billing and record keeping have been widely instituted, and help to control administrative costs. Major concerns have arisen about patient confidentiality, leading to several parliamentary acts limiting and defining access (the Access to Information Act, and the Privacy Act). Quebec has gone further than the federal government—requiring that patients have the right to review and correct their records. However, patient records are still largely done by hand on paper. Much greater efficiencies appear possible through use of "smart-card" technology (in experimental use in one province) and other electronic methods (Asmonga, 1994: 42).

The fee-for-service system has been criticized for a number of inadequacies (Bigelow and McFarland, 1994: 69; Freeman, 1994: 15):

- No fee is paid for telephone consultation—an efficient method for solving many health care problems.
- Procedures receive higher reimbursement than face-to-face consultation.
- Newly trained practitioners are paid at the same rate as experienced individuals (although this is changing in some provinces such as Ontario).
- No payment is allowed for supervising other nonmedical personnel.
- Unnecessary procedures, consultations, diagnoses, and new appointments are rewarded, whether or not they are appropriate—as a means for physicians to increase their income.
- Psychiatrists and physicians who serve mental health patients are constrained by a defined list of diagnoses for which they can get paid on the fee schedule.

Despite these shortcomings, the system continues to get strong support from physicians and the public, largely because the other primary alternatives also have serious drawbacks. Because the payment system has a single source and established fee rates, health professionals are able to concentrate their attention on patients without being distracted by problems of fee collection or bad debts.

Average gross income of physicians was $115,000 (Canadian) in 1993. Overhead averages about one-third of gross income. This may reflect a modest level of office amenities as well as the relatively efficient costs for billing and low malpractice insurance rates. There is some disagreement about the appropriate method for total net compensation calculations because expenses vary considerably depending on the type of practice (Merritt and Shusterman, 1993: 48; Bigelow and McFarland, 1994: 69).

Paying Hospitals

Funding for operations comes largely from provincial health plans through negotiated annual "global" budgets. Operating budgets are based on the ratio of beds and staff needed for the population served. Efficiency of the hospital operation and projected changes in volume or mix of services are also a part of the negotiations. Provinces have attempted to include incentives for economical operation by allowing hospitals to retain savings and use the funds to increase flexibility of operations. Capital improvements are negotiated separately, with improvements often funded through a combination of philanthropy, municipal funds, and provincial resources (Health Insurance Association of America, 1990: 28).

Provincial approval is needed for hospital expansion or renovation. Most funding for capital projects comes from provinces, with local contributions of between 10 and 40 percent. Any increase in staff or other resources needed to operate an expanded facility must have provincial approval as well. These limits often make it difficult to replace obsolete or worn equipment or purchase new advanced technology. New technology thus tends not to be available except in selected regional hospitals (Rublee, 1989: 179–181).

In Ontario, hospitals negotiate for a base budget, including an inflation increase. This includes a "life-support" component to pay for high costs associated with services like kidney dialysis or cardiovascular surgery and a growth component to pay for any increased volume. The base budget is derived from the costs during the previous year. Negotiations also include possible funding of new and expanded programs. Hospitals earn about 20 percent of their revenues from added fees for room upgrades, co-payments for chronic care, workers compensation payments, and veterans benefits, as well as such nonhealth services as parking, telephone, and television rental (Reamy, 1991: 214).

Ontario has attempted to create incentives for hospitals to stay within budgets by allowing them to keep any savings to spend for priority activities defined by the hospital. More recently, hospitals have been allowed to initiate revenue-generating activities through joint ventures with physicians (Rathwell, 1994: 10).

Both Ontario and Alberta have attempted to modify the global budgeting approach to expand outpatient ambulatory services. The idea is to create incentives for more efficient delivery of outpatient care. This was considered necessary to expand outpatient surgery when appropriate and to encourage lower-cost and high-volume ambulatory care. The approach is meeting with some success on the surgery side and with other day procedures. It is apparently less workable for emergency care and specialty clinics (Jacobs et al., 1994: 27).

Hospital workers are relatively well paid. Staff physicians are paid directly from the hospital budget, as are interns, residents, physician administrators, and emergency room staff. Unionization is clearly a factor, especially for nurses, 92 percent of whom belong to unions. Canada has made more progress than most other countries in creating female equity with males in health care (Evans, 1988: 160; Haber et al., 1992: 463; Nair et al., 1992: 178).

Despite the high use of hospitals in Canada, hospital expenditures per capita are relatively less costly than in other countries. For example, costs per patient are about one-third lower in Canada than in the United States, attributable to generally lower daily costs. Fewer personnel are used per occupied bed (Redelmeier and Fuchs, 1993: 772; Zwanziger et al., 1993: 138–147; Barnett and Shustack, 1994: 334; Newhouse, 1995: 1–38).

Summary of Cost-Control Measures

A three-part strategy serves as the primary basis for cost control, as noted earlier (White, 1993: 11):

1. Limits have been placed on the physical capacity of the system.
2. Price caps or controls have been placed on fees for physicians and hospitals.
3. "Global" budgets have been implemented to constrain growth of the system.

Within these constraints, providers and patients are left with considerable freedom—without day-to-day micromanagement and oversight by government. Some provinces (Ontario and British Columbia, for example) have taken the further step of insisting on certain cost-saving measures such as computerized electronic billing by physicians and hospitals (Forster et al., 1994: 1526).

Cutting back on hospitals and beds. Nearly all provinces have closed some hospitals and cut the number of available beds. The most drastic measures have been taken in Alberta and Saskatchewan where large numbers of hospitals have been closed since 1992, with more cuts anticipated. As noted earlier, governance was shifted to regional boards rather than local districts. Because most were owned by the provinces, it was possible to override the wishes of community residents. Overlapping services in close proximity were closed down (Corelli, 1995: 16).

Control of new procedures and technologies. Serious constraints have been placed on growth in use of new procedures or tech-

nologies. As Table 4-3 indicates, as compared with Germany and the United States, Canada makes considerably less use of magnetic resonance imaging (MRI), organ transplants, and cardiac catheterization. "Core medical services"—those that are medically necessary as determined by a qualified physician—have been defined as having priority. A number of other procedures have been specifically excluded in some provinces, such as cosmetic surgery, adult dental services, chiropody, optometry, osteopathy, psychology, hearing aids, and pharmaceuticals (except for the nonelderly or poor) (Rublee, 1989: 179; Rowan et al., 1994: 463).

Community health centers with salaried physicians. Quebec has introduced community-based health centers (as noted earlier) with salaried physicians—as one means of limiting expenditures. Ontario established Comprehensive Health Organizations that operate much like a health maintenance organization. Similar measures are in the process of implementation in other provinces. For example, in some Alberta locations physicians are being assigned lists of patients to be served, with payment on a capitated basis. Patients have the option to change physicians every 3 months if they so choose (Terris, 1991: 62; Rathwell, 1994: 11).

Limitations on payments for cross-border care. Some provinces have attempted to limit use by Canadians of medical care outside the country. The funds were paid for diagnostic and treatment services not available in Ontario and for travelers and/or "snowbirds" who spent long periods south of the border (an estimated 600,000 affluent Canadians spend the colder months in the southern United States). As of January 1, 1992, coverage for emergency hospitalization in the United States was cut from $400 per day to $100. Annual costs for overseas services dropped from $310 million in 1992 to $106 million in 1993, and to $71 million in 1994 (Warson, 1994: 72).

Across-border inpatient treatment of drug or alcohol abuse was also costly. Limitations on health plan payments were therefore imposed. Payment for the services has been shifted to the growing private health insurance domain or is provided within Ontario at alternative locations that have the capacity to provide care. Legitimate cross-border travelers are still able to secure payment through the provincial health plan for needed basic services (Korcok, 1993: 425–426).

Rationing of medical procedures. Explicit rationing is clearly one consequence of the budget constraints at the federal and provincial levels. The most obvious form is through increased waiting lists for selected medical procedures. Managers are controlling expenditures for new or additional technologies in hospitals—which serves to limit access without regard to patient needs (Rathwell, 1994: 12).

Quebec introduced the $5 charge for non-emergency use of hospital emergency rooms (as noted earlier). Other provinces have removed some marginally useful procedures from the "approved list" for insurance (Rathwell, 1994: 13).

New management techniques. Hospitals have begun to adopt new management techniques that may drastically alter the way they do business. One of these concepts is referred to as "human reengineering," which involves rethinking, redesigning, and reshaping the health care organization. Among the changes: assigning many nursing tasks to lower-skilled and lower-paid workers, while assigning nurses many of the less technical tasks formerly performed by physicians (Bagley, 1994: 1749).

Attempts to control physician supply. The physician-to-population ratio was 210 per 100,000 in 1990. Continuing increases in physician costs can be attributed in part to the substantial increases in the physician supply described earlier. Deliberate efforts have therefore been imposed in every province to limit entry of new physicians to practice. Because of the long lead time required, limitations on medical school enrollment have had only limited success to date. The British Columbia attempt to constrain the number of physicians with permission to bill the provincial health plans was challenged in court and at least temporarily overturned (Health Insurance Association of America, 1990: 36; Hughes, 1991: 2351).

Many rural communities have been served by foreign medical graduates, who continue to be allowed entry if they will serve in areas of need. A dramatic decline has been observed in obstetrics, anesthesia, general surgery, and emergency care in rural areas. The proportion of family physicians providing obstetric service declined from 85 percent in 1983 to 40 percent in 1988, in part because of litigation concerns. A Society of Rural Physicians has been formed with the goal of trying to improve the emphasis on, and training for, rural practice—but with relatively limited success to date (O'Reilly, 1994: 571–573; Rosser, 1994: 646).

PROBLEMS AND REFORMS

Several unresolved problems are noteworthy (Taylor, 1990: 187; Freeman, 1994: 20; Rathwell, 1994: 13–15):

- Administrative requirements of the Canadian Health Act may place inappropriate and destructive limits on needed innovation.
- The decision process for initiating uses of new medical technology may be too slow for introduction of appropriate and potentially cost-saving techniques; this frustrates health care professionals who continue to want access to the newest technology.
- Waiting lists have increased for many high-technology procedures such as coronary bypass surgery and hip replacement.
- Incentives may be inadequate to promote increases in hospital efficiency despite effective use of global budgeting to slow growth, increased use of outpatient surgery, and home care.
- Emergency rooms are often full to overflowing, with many ER patients seeking primary rather than emergency care. Few incentives have been developed to limit this expensive alternative.

- Payment for pharmaceuticals continues to be a high-cost item for consumers, particularly the lower-income population who have no coverage.
- Mental health services for the chronically mentally ill are not adequately supported through provincial health plans, despite legal requirements to do so.

Contracts have been negotiated with U.S. hospitals in Seattle, Detroit, and other U.S. cities to undertake urgent surgeries that cannot be adequately handled in Canadian hospitals. Access thus appears to be a major problem for some complex procedures (Health Insurance Association of America, 1990: 45–50).

Private surgery and MRI scanning clinics in Alberta and elsewhere have been allowed in defiance of national policy. These changes are viewed in the provinces as necessary to serve the needs of patients who would otherwise have to wait. But it is clearly contrary to what has been traditional for some time under the Canadian Health Act (Janigan, 1995: 11).

The public financing system in Canada generates certain "hidden" overhead costs, such as lost value of patient time while waiting for service, or costs in personal time of patients who must make unnecessary multiple appointments generated by physicians under the capped fee-for-service system. Studies indicate that time spent per office visit has declined substantially and the number of office visits has risen steadily as physician fees per visit have been constrained. This will quite likely change as capitated payment arrangements increase (Danzon, 1992: 32; Larson, 1995).

The cost of collecting additional required taxes is not fully considered in the calculation of savings from the single-payer system. The tax system may also cause people to change their work, saving, and consumption patterns to avoid payment of additional tax (Danzon, 1992: 37).

The United States may to some degree be subsidizing Canadian health care through diffusion northward of results from research and development. Pharmaceuticals are the most obvious example. Prices of drugs are considerably lower in Canada because of public constraints on costs. Research-and-development funds are reduced for manufacturers. Costs of research and development are shifted to the United States or other countries (Danzon, 1992: 38).

SUMMARY AND CONCLUSIONS

The severe economic turndown of the early 1990s has put great pressure on health care. Resources have been drastically reduced because of limited tax revenues. The number of acute-care hospital beds is being reduced and the number of health care workers is decreasing.

It remains uncertain as this is written what the ultimate effects of these problems will be on individual health and well-being. However, there is considerable evidence that the budget reduction requirements are changing the focus of the health care system more toward primary care, health promotion, home care, and community-based services—along with development of a coexisting privately funded system to supplement the underfunded public system (Sawatzky and MacDonald, 1994: 27; Doran, 1995).

Increasing attention is being directed to the *causes* of ill health and less focus is placed on curative medicine. A community-focused public health orientation is replacing the emphasis on health care institutions and treatment of disease or illness. The consumer is getting more attention. Physicians play a less influential role, whereas policymakers, nurses, and public health professionals who deal with the causes of good health are more influential. Multidisciplinary teams are being formed to bring a fuller range of knowledge and skills to bear on key problems (Walters, Toombs, and Rabuka, 1994: 839; Wedge, 1994: 275).

The effort to control costs has caused the government to reduce medical school enrollments, reduce physician immigration from other countries, and limit the billing numbers allowed for physicians to secure payment from provincial insurance plans.

Expensive technology and high-cost services are being explicitly rationed, with government approval required for purchase of magnetic resonance imagers (MRIs), computed tomographer (CT) scanners, lithotripters, open-heart units, and dialysis machines, as well as selected other equipment. Outpatient surgery has increased dramatically and inpatient hospital days have declined substantially. These cost-saving measures have not caused waiting times for elective surgery to be viewed as unreasonable by health professionals. Emergency surgery requires no waiting (Wedge, 1994: 275).

The judgments about overall effectiveness of the Canadian system vary depending on the kind of measurements and perspectives brought to the analysis. Some economists conclude that Canada has been more effective at expenditure control than the United States, and others insist this is not the case if all costs (such as those for collecting taxes) are considered (Chernomas and Sepehri, 1991: 803; Bernard, 1994: 27).

Nonetheless, it seems quite clear that major cost categories have been controlled—for hospitals through global budgeting, for physicians through negotiated fees, and for administration through a single-payer system. This has been achieved while also providing universal access to primary care, reasonably high quality, and improved outcome indicators for infant mortality, life expectancy, and general health status. Recent cutbacks are, however, raising major questions about the ongoing level of access to health care. A so-called "two-tier" system may be emerging.

REFERENCES

Armstrong-Stassen, Marjorie, Rowaida Al-Ma'Aitah, Sheila Cameron, and Martha Horsburgh (1994). Determinants and Consequences of Burnout: A Cross-Cultural Comparison of Canadian and Jordanian Nurses, *Health Care for Women International*, 15 (5): 413–421.

Asmonga, Donald D. (1994). The Canadian Healthcare System, *Journal of American Health Information Management Association*, 65 (7): 41–43.

Bachrach, Leona L. (1993). Spotlight on Canada, *Hospital and Community Psychiatry*, 44 (10): 931–933.

Bachrach, Leona L. (1994). Reflections on Mental Health Service Delivery in Canada: One American's View, *New Directions for Mental Health Services*, 61 (Spring): 87–95.

Bagley, Gordon (1994). Reorganization of Canada's Hospitals Likely to Have Major Impact on MDs, Consultant Says, *Canadian Medical Association Journal*, 151 (12): 1746–1752.

Barer, Morris, Clyde Hertzman, Robert Miller, and Marina V. Pascali (1992). On Being Old and Sick: The Burden of Health Care for the Elderly in Canada and the United States, *Journal of Health Politics, Policy and Law*, 17 (4): 763–782.

Barnett, Robert, and Allan Shustack (1994). Cost Containment: The Americas, *New Horizons*, 2 (3): 332–335.

Baumgart, Alice J. (1993). Quality Through Health Policy: The Canadian Example, *International Review of Nursing*, 40 (6): 167–170.

Bernard, Elaine (1994). Why Single Payer Is Still Our Best Bet, *Social Policy*, 3 (Spring): 24–31.

Bigelow, Douglas A., and Bentson H. McFarland (1994). Financing Canada's Mental Health Services, *New Directions for Mental Health Services*, 61 (Spring): 63–72.

Bigelow, Douglas A., Nicholas Sladen-Drew, and John S. Russell (1994). Serving Severely Mentally Ill People in a Major Canadian City, *New Directions in Mental Health Services*, 61 (Spring): 53–62.

Birenbaum, Rhonda (1994). Nurse Practitioners and Physicians: Competition or Collaboration?, *Canadian Medical Association Journal*, 151 (1): 1994, 76–78.

Brooks, Janet (1993). Canada's First Private MRI Clinic: Does It Signal a Shift to Two-Tiered Medicine?, *Canadian Medical Association Journal*, 149 (8): 1155–1158.

Brooks, Kathryn Ann (1994). The Hospital CEO: Meeting the Conflicting Demands of the Board and Physicians, *Hospital and Health Services Administration*, 39 (4): 471–485.

Charles, Cathy, Mary Gauld, Larry Chambers, Bernie O'Brien, R. Brian Haynes, and Roberta Labelle (1994). How Was Your Hospital Stay? Patients Report About Their Care in Canadian Hospitals, *Canadian Medical Association Journal*, 150 (11): 1813–1829.

Chernomas, Robert, and Ardeshir Sepehri (1991). Is the Canadian Health Care System More Effective at Expenditure Control Than Previously Thought? A Reply to Peter Coyte, *International Journal of Health Services*, 21 (4): 793–804.

Clark, Kathleen M. (1994). Nursing Specialization in Canada: Achievements and Challenges, *International Nursing Review*, 41 (3): 85–88.

COCKERHAM, WILLIAM C. (1995). *Medical Sociology*, 6th ed. Englewood Cliffs, N.J.: Prentice Hall.

CORELLI, RAE (1995). Saskatchewan's New Idea, *Maclean's* (July): 16–18.

COYTE, PETER C. (1990). Current Trends in Canadian Health Care: Myths and Misconceptions in Health Economics, *Journal of Public Health Policy*, 9 (2): 169–188.

CRICHTON, ANNE (1994). Health Insurance and Medical Practice Organization in Canada: Findings from a Literature Review, *Medical Care Review*, 51 (2): 149–177.

DANZON, PATRICIA (1992). Hidden Overhead Costs: Is Canada's System Really Less Expensive?, *Health Affairs*, 11 (1): 21–43.

DESJARDINS, PAUL R. (1994). The Canadian Health Care System, *Journal of the International Federation of Clinical Chemistry*, 6 (2): 42–43.

DORAN, MORTON (1995). Canadian physician and medical school faculty member, University of Calgary. Personal communication.

ELLENBERGER, BETH (1994). Medical Researchers Strut Their Stuff at Atlantic Canada's First Pharmaceutical Showcase, *Canadian Medical Association Journal*, 150 (7): 1140–1141.

EVANS, ROBERT G. (1988). "We'll Take Care of It for You," Health Care in the Canadian Community, *Daedalus*, 117 (4): 159–172.

FORSTER, JOHN, WALTER ROSSER, BRIAN HENNEN, RON MCAULEY, RUTH WILSON, and MAGGIE GROGAN (1994). New Approach to Primary Medical Care, *Canadian Family Physician*, 40 (September): 1523–1530.

FREEMAN, STANLEY J. (1994). An Overview of Canada's Mental Health System, *New Directions in Mental Health Services*, 61 (Spring): 11–20.

FREUND, PETER E. S., and MEREDITH B. MCGUIRE (1995). *Health, Illness, and the Social Body*, 2nd ed. Englewood Cliffs, N.J.: Prentice Hall.

FUCHS, VICTOR R., and JAMES S. HAHN (1990). A Comparison of Expenditures for Physicians' Services in the United States and Canada, *New England Journal of Medicine*, 323 (13): 884–890.

FULTON, JANE (1993a). Bordering on the Possible: Can U.S. Health Care Reform Learn from Canada?, *Administrative Radiology*, 12 (12): 26–31.

FULTON, JANE (1993b). Public Policy and Funding Issues, *Investigative Radiology*, 28 (4) (Supp.): S59–S62.

GOERING, PAULA, DONALD WASYLENKI, and ERIC MACNAUGHTON (1994). Planning Mental Health Services: Current Canadian Initiatives, *New Directions for Mental Health Services*, 61 (Spring): 31–40.

GRAIG, LAURENE A. (1993). *Health of Nations: An International Perspective on U.S. Health Care Reform*, 2nd ed. Washington, D.C.: Congressional Quarterly.

GRAY, CHARLOTTE (1994). Managing the Supply of MDs: Opinion Divided on Ministers' Proposal to Develop a National Plan, *Canadian Medical Association Journal*, 151 (10): 1476–1478.

GREEN, LAWRENCE W. (1994). Refocusing Health Care Systems to Address Both Individual Care and Population Health, *Clinical Investigations in Medicine*, 17 (2): 133–144.

GROGAN, COLLEEN (1992). Deciding on Access and Levels of Care: A Comparison of Canada, Britain, Germany, and the United States, *Journal of Health Politics*, 17 (2): 213–232.

HABER, SUSAN G., JACK ZWANZIGER, JACK GEOFFREY, M. ANDERSON, KENNETH E. THORPE, and JOSEPH P. NEWHOUSE (1992). Hospital Expenditures in the United States and Canada: Do Hospital Worker Wages Explain the Differences?, *Journal of Health Economics*, 11: 453–465.

HEALTH INSURANCE ASSOCIATION OF AMERICA (HIAA) (1990). Canadian Health Care: Implications of Public Health Insurance, *Research Bulletin*, June.

HEIDEMANN, ELMA (1994). The Canadian Health Care System: Cost and Quality, *Bulletin of the Pan American Health Organization*, 28 (2): 169–176.

HUGHES, JOHN S. (1991). How Well Has Canada Contained the Costs of Doctoring?, *Journal of the American Medical Association*, 265 (18): 2347–2351.

IGLEHART, JOHN (1989). The United States Looks at Canadian Health Care, *New England Journal of Medicine*, 321 (25): 1770.

JACOBS, PHILIP, JUDITH R. LAVE, EDWARD HALL, and CHARLES BOTZ (1994). Ambulatory Case Mix Funding, *Health Management Forum*, 7 (2): 21–28.

JANIGAN, MARY (1995). A Prescription for Medicare, *Maclean's*, 108 (31): 10–15.

KENDEL, DENNIS A., and W. DALE DAUPHINEE (1994). Barriers to Interprovincial Physician Mobility, *Canadian Medical Association Journal*, 151 (11): 1579–1580.

KORCOK, MILAN (1993). Ontario's Move to Limit Out-of-Province Health Care Spending Pays Off in a Big Way, *Canadian Medical Association Journal*, 148 (3): 425–426.

KORCOK, MILAN (1994). U.S. Health Care Reforms May Create Heavy Demand for Canada's Primary Care MDs, *Canadian Medical Association Journal*, 150 (11): 1849–1854.

LARSON, JOHN (1995). Physician educated in Canada and currently practicing in the United States. Personal communication.

LEATT, PEGGY (1994). Physicians in Health Care Management: 1. Physicians as Managers: Roles and Future Challenges, *Canadian Medical Association Journal*, 150 (2): 171–176.

LOEPPKY, BERNIE (1994). Made in Canada Health Care Reform, *Leadership Health Services*, 3 (2): 12–13.

MASI, RALPH, and MILADA DISMAN (1994). Health Care and Seniors, *Canadian Family Physician*, 40 (March): 498–504.

MEMMOTT, MARK (1995). Redefining the Wealth of Nations, *USA Today*, September 18, p. 4B.

MERRITT, JAMES, and CARL SHUSTERMAN (1993). Look North for Primary-Care Docs, *Modern Healthcare*, 23 (48): 48.

NAIR, CYRIL, REZAUL KARIM, and CHRISTINA NYERS (1992). Health Care and Health Status: A Canada–United States Statistical Comparison, *Health Reports*, 4 (2): 175–183.

NATIONAL CENTER FOR HEALTH STATISTICS (1995). *Health, United States, 1994.* Hyattsville, Md.: U.S. Public Health Service.

NEWHOUSE, JOSEPH P. (1995). *Costs in United States and Canadian Hospitals*, Abstract and Final Report, PB 95-148375. Washington, D.C.: Agency for Health Care Policy and Research,

O'REILLY, MICHAEL (1994). Bitter Physicians React Angrily to Uncertain Future Facing Rural Medicine, *Canadian Medical Association Journal*, 150 (4): 571–573.

PFAFF, MARTIN (1990). Differences in Health Care Spending Across Countries: Statistical Evidence, *Journal of Health Politics, Policy, and Law*, 15 (1): 1–67.

PICKLES, B., A. U. TOPPING, and K. A. WOODS (1994). Community Care for Canadian Seniors: An Exercise in Educational Planning, *Disability and Rehabilitation*, 16 (3): 181–189.

PILOTE, LOUISE, NORMAN RACINE, and MARK A. HLATKY (1994). Differences in the Treatment of Miocardial Infarction in the United States and Canada, *Archives of Internal Medicine*, 154 (May 23): 1090–1096.

RACHLIS, MICHAEL, and CAROL KUSHNER (1994). *Strong Medicine.* Toronto: HarperCollins Publishers.

RATHWELL, TOM (1994). Health Care in Canada: A System in Turmoil, *Health Policy*, 24 (1): 5–17.

REAMY, JACK (1991). Health Care in Canada: Lessons for the United States, *Journal of Rural Health*, 7 (3): 210–221.

REDELMEIER, DONALD A., and VICTOR R. FUCHS (1993). Hospital Expenditures in the United States and Canada, *New England Journal of Medicine*, 328 (11): 772–778.

RIVERSIDE HEALTH CARE FACILITIES, INC. (1994). *Riverside Health Care Facilities* (Flyer), Fort Frances, Ontario.

ROBINSON, ALEX (1994). Canada's Community Pharmacists Feel Threatened from Several Directions, *Canadian Medical Association Journal*, 150 (7): 1131–1133.

ROBINSON, ELIZABETH (1991). Maternal Health and Obstetrical Services: Measuring Health Status and Quality of Care in Remote Areas, *Arctic Medical Research* (Supp.): 596–600.

ROSSER, WALTER W. (1994). Threat of Litigation, *Canadian Family Physician*, 40 (April): 645–648.

ROWAN, MARGO, DAVID J. WALTERS, and DON MORGAN (1994). On the Path to Health Care Reform: Making Choices in Core and Comprehensive Medical Services, *Canadian Medical Association Journal*, 151 (4): 463–464.

RUBLEE, DALE A. (1989). Medical Technology in Canada, Germany, and the United States, *Health Affairs*, 8 (3): 178–181.

SANMARTIN, CLAUDIA A., and LISA SNIDAL (1993). Profile of Canadian Physicians: Results of the 1990 Physician Resource Questionnaire, *Canadian Medical Association Journal*, 149 (7): 977–984.

SAWATZKY, JOAN E., and MARY M. MACDONALD (1994). Challenges to Achieving Quality Care: Efficiency, Effectiveness and Beneficence, *International Nursing Review*, 41 (1): 27–31.

SHEA, SUSAN IRELAND (1991). Canadian Nurses Under a Single-Payer System: Advantage or Disadvantage?, *Nursing Economics*, 9 (5): 329–333.

STEFFAN, RANDY (1994). Competencies: Your Edge in a Tough Job Market, *Leadership in Health Services*, 3 (2): 24–25.

STINSON, SHIRLEY, MARIANNE LAMB, and MARIE-FRANCE THIBAUDEAU (1990). Nursing Research: The Canadian Scene, *International Journal of Nursing Studies*, 27 (2): 105–122.

SULLIVAN, PATRICK (1992). Canadian MDs and Nonphysicians Rate Health Care System Highly, U.S. Survey Reveals, *Canadian Medical Association Journal*, 147 (8): 1219.

SULLIVAN, PATRICK (1994). Growth in Number of Advertisements Indicates Increased U.S. Interest in Canadian MDs, *Canadian Medical Association Journal*, 150 (11): 1855–1856.

TAYLOR, MALCOLM G. (1990). *Insuring National Health Care: The Canadian Experience.* Chapel Hill: University of North Carolina Press.

TERRIS, MILTON (1991). Global Budgeting and the Control of Hospital Costs, *Journal of Public Health Policy*, 12 (1): 61–67.

VALBERG, LESLIE S., MEREDITH A. GONYEA, DUNCAN G. SINCLAIR, and JOHN WADE (1994). Planning the Future Academic Medical Centre, *Canadian Medical Association Journal*, 151 (11): 1581–1587.

VAYDA, EUGENE (1994). Physicians in Health Care Management: 5. Payment of Physicians and Organizations of Medical Services, *Canadian Medical Association Journal*, 150 (10): 1583–1588.

WALTERS, DAVID J., MILLICENT TOOMBS, and LORNE A. RABUKA (1994). Strengthening the Foundation: The Physician's Vital Role in Primary Health Care in Canada, *Canadian Medical Association Journal*, 150 (6): 839–841.

WARSON, ALBERT (1994). "Snowbirds" Want Better U.S. Coverage, *Modern Healthcare*, 24 (45): 72.

WASYLENKI, DONALD, PAULA GOERING, and ERIC MACNAUGHTON (1994). Planning Mental Health Services, *New Directions in Mental Health Services*, 61 (Spring): 21–29.

WATANABE, MAMORU (1994) Physician Resource Planning: Quest for Answers, *Clinical Investigations in Medicine,* 17 (3): 256–267.

WEDGE, JOHN H. (1994). The Impact of Health Care Reform on Orthopedic Surgery in the United States and Canada, *Clinical Orthopedics and Related Research,* 308 (November): 271–280.

WHELAN, ANNE MARIE, FRED BURGE, and KIRK MUNROE (1994). Pharmacy Services in Family Medicine Residencies, *Canadian Family Physician,* 40 (March): 468–471.

WHITE, JANE H. (1993). Global Budgets: A Key to Clinton's Reform Strategy?, *Health Progress,* 74 (3): 10–14.

ZWANZIGER, JACK, GEOFFREY M. ANDERSON, SUSAN G. HABER, KENNETH E. THORPE, and JOSEPH P. NEWHOUSE (1993). Comparison of Hospital Costs in California, New York, and Canada, *Health Affairs (Millwood),* 12 (2): 130–139.

5

JAPAN

Preventive Health Care as Cultural Norm

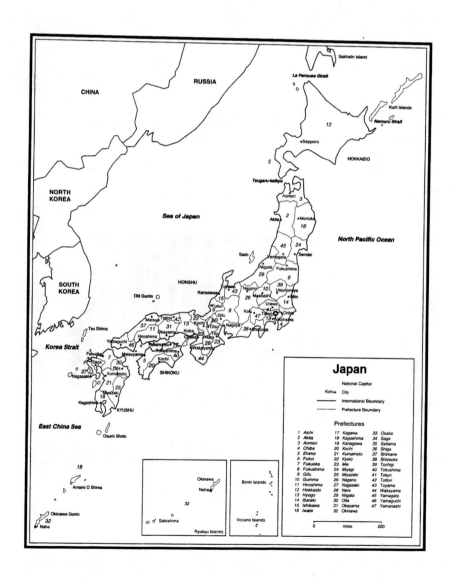

Japan is the third most densely populated country in the world, with 124.5 million people (1993) in a land area slightly smaller than California. Only one-fifth of the land area permits agriculture and urban habitation; the remainder is mountainous. The Tokyo metropolitan region is particularly dense, containing 26 percent of the population. The economy ranks second only to the United States in total size. Health care is financed by universal insurance largely through a government requirement that all employers offer coverage for employees and dependents (Iglehart, 1988a: 807; Reischauer, 1988: 3).

A public/private mix and a balance between prevention and care are somewhat unique to Japan. All levels of government are involved, as rule makers and sources of subsidies for public and private health services. However, 80 percent of hospitals and 94 percent of clinics (which can contain up to 20 beds) are privately owned. Within this overall framework, citizens have relatively free choice among private physicians and hospitals (Levin and Wolfson, 1989: 313). Some of the other distinctive and unique features of the system are summarized in Table 5-1.

The system has been characterized as follows (Levin and Wolfson, 1989: 312):

> Japanese health care is delivered, financed, and managed in a sociological environment in which excellence is expected, harmony cultivated, and conflict resolved through negotiations. Japan's government, insurance schemes, hospitals, physicians, and patients seek to carefully maneuver resources, politics, and culture to ensure a balance in the nation's health care system.

The Japanese government has an influential regulatory role. Although resources come largely from employer contributions, a national insurance program supplements these funds and guarantees universal coverage for anyone who is not fully employed. The government helps control costs by limiting prices for pharmaceuticals and discour-

Table 5-1   Features of Japanese Health Care

- A relatively healthy population that lives longer and is aging more rapidly than in any other nation
- The proportion of GDP devoted to health care is the lowest among the advanced industrial nations, at 6.9 percent (in 1992), with among the lowest per capita expenditures of $1,376
- An efficient and unusually powerful federal health services bureaucracy that oversees both public and private health care
- Most hospitals and clinics are owned by physicians, who also serve as both prescribers and dispensers of medications
- Leads the world in the per capita consumption of pharmaceuticals that represent approximately 19 percent of health care costs (1988)
- The highest number of hospital beds per capita of any nation
- The world's highest proportion of CT scanners and MRI machines per million population
- A proclivity toward self-care and health maintenance
- Special emphasis on preparing female physicians through Tokyo Women's Medical College, the only all-female medical school in Japan and possibly the world.

Sources: Based on data from Graig, 1993: 130; Cockerham, 1995: 300–304.

aging high-cost services—through consultation with the major provider groups: the medical association, hospital association, and pharmaceutical association (Levin and Wolfson, 1989: 315).

Physicians are highly influential because they not only provide individual ambulatory care but own and operate most hospitals and clinical practices. They generally have higher gross incomes than in any other country. Doctors are viewed by most patients with a sense of reverence and are seldom questioned. The idea of patient "rights" is not well-developed. There is a traditional high trust of, and dependence on, physicians (Fukami, 1992: 8; Graig, 1993: 130).

DEMOGRAPHIC CHARACTERISTICS

Japan leads the world in both life expectancy (82.8 years for women and 76.4 years for men in 1991) and has the lowest rate of infant mortality (4.3 per 1,000 live births). This represents a major leap forward in both categories since the end of World War II—when the situation was much less advanced in comparison to other countries. The quality of the health care system must be given some credit for these good outcomes but only as a supplement to cultural traditions and a public health system that have managed to create a generally healthier population than in most countries (Marmor, 1992: 10; Cockerham, 1995: 290).

The population is aging with particular rapidity. As of January 1991, 12.6 percent of the nation's population was 65 years of age or older. Projections indicate that this figure will reach 16 to 17 percent by the year 2000 and 24 percent by 2025. The birthrate (1.2 per family in 1992) has fallen well below replacement levels. The proportion of elderly varies widely between locations, with some towns averaging as high as 35 percent, and others have proportions as low as 6 percent (Kawakita, 1992: 14; Tokyo Metropolitan Government, 1993, 1994; Anbacken, 1994: 91).

HISTORICAL PERSPECTIVE

The Japanese have a reputation for selectively and successfully adopting and adapting the experience of other countries. This is no less true in the health care domain than elsewhere. The Chinese system of acupuncture and herbal medicines was widely adopted as early as the sixth century. More than 1,000 years later, Dutch and German medical care practices were highly influential in the development of the current system (Iglehart, 1988a).

The Shift Toward Modernization: Nineteenth and Early Twentieth Centuries

In the late nineteenth and early twentieth centuries, German health care programs were deemed the most advanced and therefore worthy of widespread adoption. Ger-

man instructors were employed to teach medical students, while helping to establish a westernized system of medical care. Medical education was considered a primary vehicle for modernization of the health care system. The policy was officially outlined in a 1925 government policy statement and was further enhanced by the collaboration between Germany and Japan during World War II (Powell and Anesaki, 1990: 27; Graig, 1993: 133).

Medical education was centered at Tokyo University—which remains the most prestigious imperial medical school. All schools in other regions of the country are subject to the strong influence of this national institution. Western-style hospitals were modeled on the German system, with research and training programs designed to increase the knowledge of medical specialists. The Japanese Medical Association was initiated during this period, adding major political strength to the medical profession. Health care was the province of entrepreneurial physicians who could charge what they pleased and serve only those with financial resources. Little attention was given to public health, in the form of clean water, sewage disposal, and other infrastructure to protect human health (Powell and Anesaki, 1990: 30–31, 87–88).

The basis for the contemporary insurance organization was provided by the Health Insurance Law of 1922. Coverage was provided to miners and factory workers in firms with more than 15 employees. Benefits were in the form of medical treatment and cash payments during illness. Other benefits in the form of social security payments result from occupational injuries. Dependents were not covered, and only about two million of the total population of 56 million were included at this stage. Insurance coverage was divided into two major categories: (1) private insurance for companies with more than 700 employees who could self-insure, and (2) government insurance that served smaller employers not covered by private insurance. The law was closely patterned after the German social legislation originated during the 1880s (Steslicke, 1982: 202).

Implementation of Insurance in the Modern Period: 1938 to 1980

The Ministry of Health and Welfare was established in 1938. The National Health Insurance Law (in 1938) extended coverage to farmers, fishermen, lumbermen, and other previously noncovered workers. The New Medical Service Law (1948) established the basis for development and regulation of health care facilities, notably hospitals and clinics. A Medical Care Council was created to review health care needs. It recommended a regional form of organization to coordinate hospital services and clinics, although the strong influence of physicians, who owned many of the medical facilities, eventually limited implementation of the recommendation (Steslicke, 1982: 206–207; Graig, 1993: 134).

The Constitution of 1947, initiated by the occupying American forces after World War II, was a substantial departure from earlier and traditional Japanese values. It further established state responsibility for promotion of social welfare, social security, and public health, and helped shape health policy up to the present period. A vital statistics system was initiated and has become an important part of the current record of medical care. However, many of the specific features were dropped when Japan recovered autonomy in 1952.

Further legislation in 1958 created universal coverage of all citizens through mandates requiring local governments to guarantee insurance programs for all nonemployed persons. Health care became universal in 1961. Essentially, everyone was covered by employers, trade associations, or some level of government (Iglehart, 1988a: 808; Sonoda, 1988: viii).

A number of new private medical schools were initiated with government support during the 1960s to overcome a physician shortage and to increase the distribution of clinics and hospitals in rural and remote parts of the

country. This effort has been generally successful, although some rural areas remain poorly served (Powell and Anesaki, 1990: 92–93).

However, there continued to be gross inequities in benefits and access to health services. The least affluent paid higher contributions and had the least access to care, whereas the more educated and affluent paid less and received more generous access and benefits. The period of the 1960s and 1970s was the "golden era" of health and welfare programs, greatly improving the organized systems for serving public needs. The general affluence of the country increased rapidly during this period (Iglehart, 1988a: 808; Powell and Anesaki, 1990: 89–92).

The health insurance system did not emphasize care for the mentally ill and handicapped, which have generally received only modest attention. Efforts were made, however, to establish widespread local clinics, mobile units, and transportation of patients to central medical facilities as needed. "Remote-area central hospitals" were initiated with staffing primarily by nurses and with linkages to urban medical information systems. It has been very difficult to attract physicians to remote rural areas; few incentives exist for maintaining a successful private rural practice—despite a student loan program in support of training for rural medical students (Powell and Anesaki, 1990: 176–177).

Public health programs and personal health institutions were not closely coordinated nor mutually supportive. The insurance systems were complicated, requiring considerable paper shuffling to secure reimbursement. Computers are now widely used by larger hospitals, but clinics and smaller facilities had not yet become automated by the late 1980s (Powell and Anesaki, 1990: 41, 92).

Increasing Costs and Other Stresses in the 1980s

Rapid increases in economic growth generally kept pace with the growth in health care costs during the 1960s and 1970s. The average annual increase in expenditures in the 1970s was 18 percent—with an accompanying increase in the proportion of GDP devoted to health care. The effects of rising demand and expectations were evident, in part because of the rapid demographic shift to an older population. This led to vigorous cost-control efforts in the 1980s, through new government policies to shift more costs to consumers, limitations on fee increases by providers, and a shift toward greater responsibility for local government (Powell and Anesaki, 1990: 95–96).

Stresses were created by the rapid social changes. One indicator is the high suicide rate, although this is not new and appears to be partially based on traditional cultural values. Drug-induced disorders have become a major problem since the 1960s. Pollution, inadequate housing, inadequate sewage and garbage disposal, traffic congestion and accidents have each caused serious health concerns (Iglehart, 1988a: 809).

Cancer and several other "adult" diseases are increasing rapidly. Cancer has become the leading cause of death. For example, the incidence of lung cancer increased by 85 percent between 1975 and 1985. Breast cancer was higher by 105 percent. This has led to a so-called "declaration of war" on cancer, supported by a 10-year cancer prevention project and undertaken cooperatively between the National Cancer Center of Japan and the National Cancer Center of the United States. Cerebrovascular disease, hypertension, neoplasms of several kinds, and cirrhosis of the liver have all risen dramatically in the recent period (Steslicke, 1989: 105; The Economist, 1990: 38–39).

CULTURAL FACTORS

Japan is ethnically homogeneous, with relatively few immigrants. The cultural context has major influence on the doctor and patient roles. Stability and continuity are very important to both physicians and their patients. Providers are expected to be both very scientific and very personal in giving recognition to patients and offering them a sense of belonging within the health care system (Gallagher and Subedi, 1995: 5).

Among the important traditions in Japanese society is the well-developed sense of group consciousness—including strong commitment to the family, community, and workplace. This is illustrated by the tendency for the elderly to live with their children (55 percent in a 1985 survey of metropolitan Tokyo) at a much higher rate than in most other countries. Dependency is the norm. Government hesitates to assume responsibilities that have traditionally been located with family and community (Anderson, Oscarson, and Yu, 1995: 33).

These traditions also operate in specific health care organizational arrangements. For example, most hospitals have a direct relationship with a medical school, usually the teaching institution from which senior physician managers or the hospital owner graduated. Hospital administrators (usually physicians) seek advice and support from medical school faculty in securing new staff or for clinical decisions in the hospital setting. Physicians maintain contacts and commitment to their university clinical department many years after completing medical school. Although these practices have some advantages in terms of continuity and stability, they are often disadvantageous to skilled younger physicians who are dominated by more senior but less well-trained practitioners— thus interfering with high-quality medical care. Traditional medicine continues to be widely practiced, based in part on the earlier Chinese traditions. Chiropractors and herbalists are widely sought after for specific ailments. Many people also self-medicate based on tradition or pharmaceutical advertising (Powell and Anesaki, 1990: 164–165).

Good health outcomes can be attributed in substantial part to such specific cultural characteristics as

• A generally low-fat and high-fiber diet
• Low crime rates that take very few lives

- High educational standards and achievement that lead to knowledge of healthy behavior
- Good basic housing with minimal sanitation problems
- Environmental protection that limits air and water pollution
- Relatively high incomes with little deprivation
- A highly successful, locally based, and prevention-oriented public health system

POLITICAL INFLUENCES

Japan is governed by a constitutional monarchy, modeled to some degree (following World War II) according to the British parliamentary system. Two tiers of government with some health care responsibility operate under the national parliament. Prefectures (47 in all) are comparable to states in other countries. Municipalities include cities, towns, and villages.

The national government deals with each prefecture and municipality on an equal basis, although municipalities fall within prefectures. The Tokyo metropolitan region is a special case in which the Tokyo Metropolitan Government has responsibility for coordinating services of public health, health insurance for nonemployed individuals, sanitary water supply, sewage disposal, other sanitation services, fire fighting, and law enforcement for four prefectures. A Metropolitan Assembly and the Governor of Tokyo have legislative and administrative responsibility for the region (Anbacken, 1994: 89; Tokyo Metropolitan Government, 1994).

The powerful Ministry of Health and Welfare (*Koseisho*) is responsible for the administration of public health, social welfare, and social security. This includes the bureaus that develop health policy, manage the national hospitals and sanitariums, operate programs for the elderly, and undertake environmental health, pharmaceutical monitoring, and regulation. Other units have responsibility for national health insurance, statistics and information, and other dimensions of health care. Despite the primary role of the Ministry

of Health and Welfare in administration of health affairs, several other national government units play a major role. For example, the Ministries of Finance, Education, Science, and Culture, Labor, Construction, Home Affairs, the Economic Planning Agency, the Environment Agency, and the National Land Agency all have specific health responsibilities (Steslicke, 1989: 112).

Much of the public health activity is delegated to the 47 prefectural governments and 26 larger municipalities. Each level of government is required to complete and implement a comprehensive health care plan, with specific targets and with a focus on building a system to promote good health (Roemer, 1991: 154).

Prefectural and municipal health activity are financed directly by the federal Ministry of Health and Welfare. Prefectures were required by the Health Center Law of 1947 to establish health and welfare departments, including public health departments. Local governments are required by the National Insurance Law of 1961 to establish and run insurance programs (Powell and Anesaki, 1990: 104).

The role of government in organization, financing, and even delivery of public health care is therefore pervasive and widely accepted, but not without vigorous debate and conflict. Health care policy in Japan has become highly politicized. Organized interest groups are very active. Nonphysician organizations have gained power at the expense of physicians. Citizen groups have taken an active role in pushing for improved access to care, quality care, and lower out-of-pocket costs (Steslicke, 1989: 107).

The Powerful Role of Physician-Bureaucrats

Physician-bureaucrats in these various levels of government play a leading role in policy making and implementation, and are considered to have much greater overall influence than elected politicians—who tend to be tran-

sitory under the fluid Japanese political system. The civil service is more prestigious and
powerful in Japan than in most countries and
attracts the graduates of leading universities.
Government research institutes associated
with the Ministry of Health and Welfare contain senior staff with major influence. These
institutes provide the statistical and research
basis for policy development and planning
(Powell and Anesaki, 1990: 106).

The higher-status civil servants effectively
control the administrative structures and
many specific policies. This means that
changes come slowly and only after a clear
consensus has been achieved that is agree-
able to the bureaucracy—which has massive
power to either constrain or implement
modernization of the health care system.
Civil servants are the source of most legislation related to health care and make a major
effort to befriend and work with leading
politicians. Many politicians in fact come
from positions in the bureaucracy. Civil servants also maintain careful relationships with
business and industrial leaders, who come
from similar educational and social backgrounds. Senior civil servants often "retire"
to high-ranking jobs in private industry or
quasi-government agencies (Powell and Anesaki, 1990: 107).

Although the bureaucracy has a very
strong voice at the national level, health care
organization is fragmented at the prefecture
and local levels. The Japanese reject a centralized health care delivery system that
imposes government preferences on individual providers or consumers. Implementation
of coordinated policies and cost-saving efficiencies is therefore difficult. The private sector maintains primary responsibility for the
largest cost activities such as hospitals and
primary care.

SOCIAL ORGANIZATION
OF HEALTH CARE

The health care delivery system operates
through four primary mechanisms—public

health centers, physician offices, clinics, and
hospitals. *Public health centers* focus particularly on prevention and health maintenance.
In smaller communities and neighborhoods,
the common pattern is for a solo-practice
physician to serve as the neighborhood
source of care from an *office* base. *Clinics* are
available in most large communities and
offer inpatient (up to 20 beds) as well as outpatient care. *Hospitals* also offer both inpatient and outpatient care, but have more
than 20 beds and tend to contain a higher
level of technology (Powell and Anesaki,
1990: 147).

The four subsystems are not always closely
coordinated and continually compete for
resources. Clinics and hospitals emphasize
"curative" rather than "preventive" care,
whereas public health and neighborhood
physicians concentrate more on preventive
measures. This arrangement is the basis for
the fragmentation described earlier (Tokyo
Metropolitan Government, 1994).

Traditional medicine is widely practiced,
although not usually by the medical profession. Training is offered in special schools
and is based on historical Chinese practices
of massage, acupuncture, moxibustion, bone
setting, use of herbal medicines, and other
practices. Herbal medicines are widely sold
at drug stores and are prescribed by some
physicians (Sonoda, 1988: 78–79).

Public Health

Prefectural and municipal health centers
are administered at the local level and are
financed by a mixture of federal and local
funds. The intent in the original law was to
have one large center for approximately
100,000 people. The health centers are
responsible for maternal and child health
in each community, supervise community
health services, and offer a range of other
public health programs. The physician-
administrators usually work only part-time
in public health and have private practice
responsibilities as well. They provide clinical
services, as well as coordinate clinical and

public health nursing. Other staff include allied health workers such as midwives; laboratory and X-ray technicians; nutritionists; health educators; food, sanitary, and meat inspectors; and statisticians who collect data and keep public health records. Specific responsibilities are summarized in Tables 5-2 and 5-3 (Graig, 1993). The completeness of these services varies widely among regions of the country. Rural regions generally have less complete services than urban areas. The Tokyo Metropolitan Region offers prenatal to elderly services, as illustrated in Table 5-3.

The effectiveness of the community health centers is reflected in the impressive statistics for infant mortality and longevity. The nation has been highly successful in improving maternal and child health as well as other public health activities. However, these services have not always been fully supported by office- or clinic-based private medical practitioners who perceive themselves as losing business to the public centers (Graig, 1993).

Contagious diseases have declined to a very low level as a consequence of improved public health and sanitation, antibiotics, and better nutrition, although AIDS is increasing gradually. At the same time, chronic diseases such as cancer, heart disease, and cerebrovascular diseases are increasing, as in other industrialized countries (Tokyo Metropolitan Government, 1993).

Physicians

The private practitioner usually offers a family or general practice focus while also claiming some level of specialization. Self-initiated identification with a subspecialty adds prestige. The claim is based more on personal choice than on completion of formal academic and clinical training requirements. Physicians comprised 17 percent of the health care workforce in 1990 (Powell and Anesaki, 1990: 173).

As noted earlier, physicians tend to dominate the physician–patient relationship. Patients have traditionally entrusted their health care to physician expertise and thus have little or no influence on medical decision making. However, this pattern is clearly changing with the younger generation of physicians and patients (Ishiwata and Sakai, 1994: 61).

Most solo-practice, office-based physicians do not have clerical help to process insurance forms and do not take appointments. Patients must sit in crowded waiting rooms for a short appointment. Communication between patient and doctor is usually brief and not necessarily informative to either party. The tendency is for the practitioner to soothe the patient's feelings, while offering impersonal diagnostic tests and medications for relief of symptoms. Nonetheless, a personal relationship with a physician is very important. The Japanese are socialized to be very conscious of the physical functioning of their bodies; the physician is likely to ask for descriptions of subjective feelings of tiredness, nervousness, or similar states (Anderson et al., 1995: 36).

The solitary practice pattern in smaller communities has led to some difficulty for physicians in maintaining their skills and specialized knowledge, and does not allow for much consultation with other physicians on

Table 5-2   Responsibilities of Public Health Centers

• Control of communicable disease	• Dental care and hygiene
• Control and prevention of TB, venereal and other such diseases	• Maintenance of environmental sanitation
	• Home nursing services
• Maternal and child health	• Advice and guidance on benefits
• Family planning	• Laboratory services
• Contraception and abortion	• Health education programs

Table 5-3 Public Health Center Activities at Various Life Stages in the Tokyo Region

Age	Procedure	Location
At birth	Congenital health screening	Clinic or hospital
	Home consultation	Visiting home health nurse
4 months	Health checkup	Public health center
	Guidance on diet	(formal notice to mother)
6 months	Health checkup	Public health center
9 months	Health checkup	Public health center
18 months	Dental checkup	Public health center
3 years	Health checkup: physical, mental development, vision, hearing	Public health center
	Vaccinations	
5 years	Health checkup for entry to school	Public health center
18 years	Blood test before marriage	Public health center
Pregnant	Maternal health exam	Public health center
women	Prenatal classes	4-day course in community
	Home consultation	Midwife visit
Postbirth	Health checkup	Public health center
Adults	Health checkups periodically	Public health center
	Blood pressure and test	
	Urine test	
	X-ray	
	Intestinal bacteria	
	Respiratory check	
	Tuberculosis	On-site at workplaces
	Health promotion classes	Community locations
	Mental health and alcoholism	Consultation with specialist
	Vaccination for influenza	Public health centers
	AIDS antibody test	Conducted anonymously
65 or older	Mental health consultation	Public health center with
	Classes and lectures on health maintenance	Community locations

Source: Based on Tokyo Metropolitan Government, 1993: 53.

problems of clinical care. Because no clear standards of practice or professional accountability have been developed, monitoring or evaluation is not the norm. Physicians are accountable only to themselves and their patients. The fee-for-service reimbursement system unfortunately reenforces these practices (Anderson et al., 1995: 36).

Solo and private-clinic practice have been declining, from 41 percent of practitioners in 1980 to 29 percent in 1990, whereas hospital practice has been increasing—especially for younger physicians. Roughly 33 percent worked in hospitals by 1985. The trend is a consequence of the major investment required for solo practice, including acquisi-

tion of expensive and necessary technology to maintain prestige and attract patient flow. Established physicians tend to see greater numbers of patients, increase diagnostic tests done by support staff, and increase prescriptions and dispensing of medications, all to justify installation of technology and generate revenue. The work load becomes severe, which is another reason that most younger physicians prefer salaried clinic or hospital practice. The average age of private practitioners increased from 56.4 to 59.7 between 1980 and 1990 (Powell and Anesaki, 1990: 173; Kobayashi and Takaki, 1992: 1393).

Private-practice physicians may see a very large number of patients per day, ranging up to more than 100. This is facilitated by the cultural readiness of the Japanese to recognize unhealthy characteristics in themselves and their inclination to consult their physician whenever something new occurs. Average annual patient visits to physicians are very high (15 per year) compared to other countries. The pattern is in part a function of the system of payment that rewards many short visits better than fewer long visits (Iglehart, 1988b; Garland, 1995: 258).

Physicians in Clinic and Hospital Practice

Physicians have traditionally been either private ambulatory care practitioners or hospital-based, but not both. Ambulatory care physicians cannot treat their patients in hospitals. The major distinction between hospitals and clinics is a matter of size and range of problems treated rather than basic function. Clinics are not supposed to keep patients for more than 48 hours, but the rule is not enforced. Roughly 37 percent of the clinics provide inpatient care (19 beds or less, with an average of 10 beds) and thus allow for many hospital-type services by ambulatory care specialists. Ninety percent of the clinics are staffed by only one physician. Group practice in clinics has not generally been viewed as desirable (Iglehart, 1988b: 1169; Powell and Anesaki, 1990: 149; Roemer, 1991: 160).

Clinics offer a varying range of outpatient as well as inpatient services. Nearly 39 percent of physicians owned private clinics in 1985 and 90 percent of the 80,000 or so clinics in the country were physician-owned and -operated. Nearly all hospitals are owned by physicians (Abe, 1985: 336).

Hospital-based physicians may be owners as well as administrators and may draw a salary as well as equity in the institution. Japanese law requires that all chief executive officers of hospitals and clinics be physicians. Other physicians are generally on salary as specialists or support medical staff. They have higher prestige and more specialized training than clinic or solo practitioners, but

earn significantly less and have fewer tax advantages. They earn 2.4 times the average Japanese wage as compared to 6.8 for private practitioners. The higher incomes of private practitioners are a result in part of both prescribing and dispensing medications. They earn a profit in both roles (Graig, 1993: 135).

Salaried specialists. Physicians in hospital practice function in a prestige hierarchy based on specialty and rank related to age and experience. They are supervised by a medical director who is often the owner. Advancement in rank may be associated with academic achievement (in teaching hospitals) or progression to department head. In the better hospitals, medical staff have excellent diagnostic and treatment facilities and enjoy a very high social status, including opportunities for additional advanced study and research (Powell and Anesaki, 1990: 205–206).

Problems with the centrality of the physician role. Physicians own much of the medical equipment and service units. One problem with this arrangement is the constraint it places on referrals to outside specialists. It also generates strong incentives to conduct many tests and tends to cause duplication of equipment among facilities in close proximity, as illustrated by the high density of CT (computerized tomography) scanners per million population (twice the United States rate and six times as many as Canada) (Graig, 1993: 144).

This circumstance has caused concerns about potential negative effects on quality of care due to use of unnecessary procedures and overmedication. Quality assurance is not well developed and few incentives have been created to encourage quality care. All providers are paid the same fee regardless of quality, and there is no direct relationship between training and salary level. The fee-for-service system, in the context of required limits on fees, has led to the same type of increases in volume of services per patient as noted earlier for the United States and Canada (Graig, 1993: 142; Garland, 1995: 257).

Physician organization. The physician community is not united. Major differences of viewpoint are obvious between hospital and private practice clinic physicians. Generational differences are also profound; younger physicians are more likely to take salaried positions and have a dim view of older and traditional medical practices. The Japanese Medical Association has in the past represented primarily the private practice clinic physicians. There were two classes of membership: a prestige class for private practitioners and a lower status class for hospital members. The clinic physicians thus had much greater influence on Japanese health care policy—a situation no longer acceptable to younger specialist physicians. The discord has seriously weakened the influence of the Association (Iglehart, 1988b: 1169; Wilsford, 1991: 285).

The status differences are therefore diminishing as more physicians are paid salaries and are based in hospitals. Private-practice physicians have been notably resistant to changes that would diminish their power and income. The overall standing of physicians has diminished in recent years as revealed by national surveys; 47 percent of the public believe the system needs fundamental change. Public information about overprescribing and use of unnecessary procedures, as well as reports of malpractice and corruption, have made the public uneasy about physician credibility (Levin and Wolfson, 1989: 317).

Medical education. Aspiring physicians may apply to one of 80 medical schools. Forty-three were federally operated in 1990. Another 8 were supported by prefectures and 29 were private. Acceptance is based upon successful completion of an entrance examination process. Costs are sufficiently high that only students from relatively well-off families can afford to attend. Academic qualification may be less important for entry to private schools than adequacy of resources—because tuition is extraordinarily high (Levin and Wolfson, 1989: 316; Powell and Anesaki, 1990).

Roughly 8,000 openings occur annually in both public and private schools. Approximately 30 percent of the applicants are children of medical practitioners who usually attempt to enter the institution from which their parent graduated. The Japanese medical student first completes 12 years of general education and takes the required entrance exam. If successful, the student takes 2 years of premedical training, followed by 4 years of clinical sciences and clinical practice with patients in hospital wards and outpatient clinics. After completion of this basic sequence, the students must then pass a national medical examination administered by the Ministry of Health and Welfare. Most physicians who successfully complete the examination proceed to 2 years of hospital residency training in their university teaching hospitals (Garland, 1995: 257).

Women comprised only 10 percent of the physician population in 1982, although their numbers in medical schools have increased steadily in recent years—especially in the fields of obstetrics, gynecology, and pediatrics. The most prestigious women physicians are often graduates of Tokyo Women's Medical College, the only all-female medical school in the country (Powell and Anesaki, 1990: 203, 213).

The supply of physicians is increasing faster than the population, especially hospital-based specialists. Heretofore, there has not been an established process for training or certifying specialists. Specialization has been poorly organized, without national standards and with considerable variation between universities. However, a reform movement in postgraduate medical education is underway. Many younger medical students are now choosing general or family practice with a focus on preventive care rather than curing disease (Iglehart, 1988b: 1171).

Medical schools are the center of power, prestige, influence, and patronage in Japanese health care. Professors are the single most influential individuals in Japanese medicine with the power to recommend physician placement or destroy opportunities. Physicians in each hospital tend to be graduates of the same medical school, with a single professor often the mentor for many of them. This means that rigorous and overt evaluation within hospitals is difficult, given the cultural tendency to avoid criticism of close associates. Outside evaluation must be informal and based on overall prestige of the hospital (Marmor, 1992: 11).

Medical research.   The disciplines of bio-statistics, medical economics, epidemiology, health services research, and medical care management have not been well-developed. Many kinds of medical research are thus neglected. A reform movement is attempting to alleviate these inadequacies, and substantial funds have been invested to increase quality and productivity of research in both medical schools and through research institutes. For example, Tokyo now has developed major centers for neurological research, psychiatric research, and clinical research (Tokyo Metropolitan Government, 1993: 57).

Field experiments have been undertaken in a number of communities. For example, the village of Sawauchi Mura in northern Japan initiated a comprehensive insurance, health screening, and prevention program in 1957—under the leadership of an energetic new mayor and with support of medical practitioners. They have since decreased infant mortality substantially, increased longevity, lowered health expenditures, and generally provided what appears to be a model for community health maintenance and care. Other communities in Japan are now examining the experience and are adopting some of the practices (Kiefer, 1987: 97).

Physician shortages in rural areas.   Rural communities tend not to have the amenities important to well-educated physicians and their families. Access to modern facilities and technology is difficult. Sparser populations provide less financial reward under a fee-for-service payment system. The average age of

practitioners in rural areas went up from 58.3 to 60.7 between 1980 and 1990, suggesting that inmigration of younger physicians has been very limited (Kobayashi and Takaki, 1992: 1393).

The current system of training and health care organization appears to discourage medical practice in remoter parts of the country. The problem has not yet been resolved by government efforts to encourage rural practice through various incentives such as scholarships and public financing of clinic facilities. A study of communities throughout Japan evaluated physician distribution between 1980 and 1990, revealing that towns of 10,000 or less gained only very modestly in physician services, and cities over 30,000 gained significantly. The least gain was in the communities with fewer than 5,000 people. The growth in total physician numbers in the country has therefore not yet solved the shortage problem in rural regions (Kobayashi and Takaki, 1992: 1392).

Nurses

Nurses provide a major part of public, primary, secondary, and tertiary health care. Their employment falls into four general categories related to training and responsibility: public health nurses, clinical nurses, nurse midwives, and assistant nurses (Powell and Anesaki, 1990: 217–222).

Public health nurses have the most advanced training, having completed clinical nurse training and a graduate program in public health nursing. They are smallest in number, but play a critical role in public health centers. They provide child health care, checkups, preventive care, and home nursing. Small numbers work in industrial or occupational nursing roles.

Clinical nurses have 3 years of training beyond high school and must pass a national examination. Eighty percent of clinical nurses work in hospitals, about 15 percent work in clinics, and the remainder in nursing education or research. Training is partially academic and partially supervised practical experience; both parts are completed in a hospital setting.

Nurse midwives play a very critical role throughout the country in prenatal care and delivery of babies. They must obtain a 3-year clinical nursing degree, followed by a year of midwife training. Roughly 50 percent of midwives work in hospitals and one-third own or practice in maternity clinics or obstetrics/gynecology clinics. This role has the longest tradition of any nursing occupation, dating from initiation of the first training program in 1876. They function largely under the supervision of physicians; in earlier historical periods, midwives had more independence of practice.

Assistant nurses provide support functions and are roughly comparable to practical nurses or nurses aides in the United States. They must be graduates of junior high school before they enter a 2-year training program through a school of nursing or junior college. They must pass a local government examination. Roughly 65 percent work in hospitals and the remainder in clinics.

The vast majority of nurses are female, although a small number of male nurses work in mental hospitals and general hospitals. A nursing shortage exists in many locations, in part because of relatively low status and pay, particularly as compared to physicians. This holds true even in metropolitan Tokyo, which is well supplied with physicians; projections indicate a shortage of 17,500 nurses in 1993 in the Tokyo region alone. The government is vigorously attempting to increase enrollment in nursing schools by providing loans, subsidizing private nursing schools, and providing services such as day care in hospitals to encourage trained nurses to continue working (Tokyo Metropolitan Government, 1993: 55).

Public hospitals have a considerably higher proportion of clinical nurses per 100 hospital beds than private hospitals; private hospitals serve more elderly patients and have a higher proportion of assistant nurses. Larger public facilities usually have a more developed administrative structure, with a director of nursing and departmental charge nurses. Nurses with advanced training are often in short supply and tend to be overworked. Private hospitals are usually owned and managed by physicians who give relatively little administrative responsibility or input to nurses (Imamura, 1993: 15).

Nursing education. Nursing education has advanced very little compared to other health fields. There is little opportunity for specialized training. The field has generally not yet achieved the level of status and pay accorded in Canada and the United States. Leaders of the Japanese Nursing Association aspire to a more uniform and modernized 4-year training program intended to enhance the general status of nursing. The move toward home care may provide greater independence of practice and greater leadership in the provision of care to the elderly. However, physicians continue to play the dominant role and expect nurses to be subservient (Imamura, 1993: 15).

Pharmacists and Pharmaceuticals

Because physicians are both prescribers and dispensers of medications, pharmacists have traditionally played a secondary role in dispensing medications. They have served as suppliers to physician pharmacies, worked as researchers in developing new drugs, operated pharmacies supplying medications in hospitals, and managed pharmacies that provide consumer medications or over-the-counter drugs not dispensed by physicians (Iglehart, 1988b: 1171).

However, efforts are underway here as elsewhere to increase the status and role of pharmacists. The Japanese Pharmacists Association strongly supported an effort in the early 1950s to limit the ability of physicians to both prescribe and dispense drugs. Their efforts—although supported by the Ministry of Health and Welfare as well as the Federation of Health Insurance Societies—were effectively overwhelmed by the political power of the Japanese Medical Association (Iglehart, 1988b: 1171).

Japan leads the world in the per capita consumption of pharmaceuticals that represented 18.4 percent of health expenditures in 1988 (down from 35 percent in 1984). Although official drug prices are set by the Ministry of Health and Welfare, physicians negotiate with drug companies to purchase supplies at discounted prices. They are then able to sell at the official price and keep the difference, with an average of 25 percent markup in 1991 (Powell and Anesaki, 1990: 182; Graig, 1993: 143).

The pharmaceutical industry.   Pharmaceuticals have clearly been a growth industry since World War II. Japan ranked as the second largest world market in 1983. Prior to the war, most drugs were imported, primarily from Germany. Huge increases in production and distribution occurred during the 1960s and 1970s, largely for domestic consumption and with strong encouragement from the government.

A major effort has been underway to advance innovation and production of pharmaceuticals. Most of the widely prescribed drugs are now manufactured in Japan, and considerable progress has been made in biotechnology as well (Benet, 1991: 427).

All pharmaceutical products sold are on the national health insurance reimbursement list and have a specified price. The list contained roughly 13,650 drugs in 1988. The government has been quite vigorously attempting to lower the overall cost of pharmaceuticals since 1981, with considerable success. Prices dropped 61 percent between 1981 and 1988, with the cuts largely to pharmaceutical companies rather than physician-dispensers. Physicians have tended to dispense more drugs at higher cost to replace price cuts on lower-cost drugs (Iglehart, 1988b: 1171).

Multinational pharmaceutical companies have begun to enter the market as a consequence of lowered import restrictions. However, approval of new drugs remains very tightly controlled by the Pharmaceutical Affairs Bureau of the Ministry of Health and Welfare. Tests of new drugs in Japan are required whether or not the item has been thoroughly tested in other countries. Estimates are that development and approval of a new drug costs a minimum of $20 million and requires a decade for full approval. Only about 1 in 10 of drugs submitted are in fact approved after the arduous testing and review process. In addition to the initial approval process, an ongoing monitoring system measures side effects on the basis of a testing procedure in selected hospitals and pharmacies throughout the country. Manufacturers must submit annual reviews of side effects for all newly approved drugs for at least 6 years (Powell and Anesaki, 1990: 184).

Problems of overprescribing.   Physicians have been accused of overprescribing of drugs and profiting unduly from high rates of pharmaceutical use. Pharmaceutical companies have also been suspect, since they joined with the medical profession to fight government efforts at controlling consumption. Patients have learned to expect long-term use of prescriptions. Over-the-counter drugs are also very popular with consumers, particularly vitamins, stomach remedies, and stress-reducing products (Powell and Anesaki, 1990: 179–182).

Pharmaceutical manufacturers are required to pay fees to an "adverse drug-reaction fund" that provides limited compensation and benefits to individuals who have suffered from taking drugs. The fund is designed to protect consumers, but also serves as protection for manufacturers. Initiation of the fund was inspired in part by the widely destructive use of a drug (chinoform) prescribed for stomach and intestinal upset during the 1960s—resulting in more than 11,000 serious illnesses and 500 or more deaths (Powell and Anesaki, 1990: 184).

Midlevel and Other Health Professionals

Training programs for allied health professionals are directly associated with medical schools but are of lower status. Modern health administration, mental health coun-seling, psychotherapy, speech therapy, and other allied fields have been slow to develop—largely because of physician domi-nance even in these specialized fields. "Mid-wifery homes" with a maximum of 10 beds can be licensed by prefectures, but must be operated by a fully qualified and registered midwife. These are commonplace in most parts of the country for normal deliveries not requiring the presence of a physician (Powell and Anesaki, 1990: 151, 223).

As noted earlier, Japan has a substantial focus on traditional therapy in the form of massage, acupuncture, chiropractics, and herbal medicines. Traditional practitioners are required to undergo formal training pro-grams and must pass prefectural examina-tions before obtaining a license to practice. Restrictions are placed on their scope of practice and their services are not usually covered by health care insurance plans (Pow-ell and Anesaki, 1990: 224).

Hospitals

Hospitals are classified into three primary categories based on specialization of patient care and ownership, as summarized in Table 5-4. The average size is relatively small (less than 100 beds). Patients with both acute and chronic diseases are treated in general hospi-tals. Because no formal distinction is made between acute and long-term or chronic care, national statistics place Japan at the top of the world in number of hospital beds per 1,000 population. Average length of stay is

Table 5-4 Types of Hospitals and Ownership

Type	Percentage of Total	Ownership
General acute and long-term care	88	80% private
Chronic, including	12	
Mental hospitals		95% private
Tuberculosis and communicable disease		60% private

Source: Based on data from Powell and Anesaki, 1990: 148.

similarly the longest. A study in 1987 revealed that 29 percent of all inpatients (not including those in mental hospitals or psychiatric wards) had been hospitalized more than 6 months. Sixty-nine percent were age 65 or older (Powell and Anesaki, 1990: 148; Anbacken, 1994: 91).

Distinction between ambulatory and hos-pital care. The referral system does not encourage return of hospitalized patients to the community and a local physician, largely because of the distinction between ambula-tory and hospital physicians. Rather, the hos-pital physician in charge of a patient is also responsible for monitoring the patient's progress after treatment in the hospital, whether for surgery or other less radical action. It may be more convenient for both patient and attending physician for hospital-ization to continue until full recovery. Fur-thermore, the insurance system provides no significant incentives for early discharge. The "point-fee" financing arrangement reim-burses hospitals at a standard rate per day and actually encourages the hospital and physician staff member to prolong inpatient care. Small housing units typical for most families also contribute to the problem because caring for a recovering patient is somewhat difficult, thus encouraging ill fam-ily members to remain in the hospital until recovery is relatively complete. Because pub-lic financing is involved, control over growth of public hospitals is much more effective than is the case with private hospitals. The surplus of hospital beds caused the federal government in 1986 to announce an inten-tion to diminish the number of public hospi-tal beds by 30 percent over 10 years (Powell and Anesaki, 1990: 150, 171).

National hospitals. The federal Ministry of Health and Welfare is responsible for national hospitals, most of which are spe-cialty centers focusing on research and train-ing in such fields as cancer or cardiovascular disease. Teaching hospitals are under the jurisdiction of the Ministry of Education and are attached to university medical schools.

Average bed size (approximately 486) for teaching hospitals is much larger than most private hospitals. Public hospitals also generally have higher prestige than private hospitals. A number of quasi-public, nonprofit hospitals are operated by the Red Cross, and are sponsored by social insurance associations, welfare associations, and industry groups (Powell and Anesaki, 1990: 152).

Private hospitals. Japanese law prohibits "investor-owned, for-profit hospitals" but allows any profits to be used for reinvestment or expansion of services to attract more patients. Owners can increase their equity and returns from their investment as long as revenues are not categorized as "profit." The consequence is duplication of both services and advanced technology between hospitals and between clinics and hospitals. The growth in size and number of private clinics with beds is attributable in substantial part to the exclusion of private medical practitioners from patient care in public hospitals. Referral to a hospital means giving up the patient. Physicians have preferred expanding their privately owned facilities rather than giving up patients needing hospital-type care (Powell and Anesaki, 1990: 156).

Outpatient services have become increasingly popular with many hospitals, to the considerable unhappiness of clinic physicians. Patients often prefer primary care in hospitals because they have greater levels of technology and more complete services for both diagnosis and treatment. Hospitals have particularly emphasized intensive periodic physical examinations for employees and executives of large companies—intended to prevent problems as well as treat any that are discovered. Many large companies run hospitals or clinics for employees and their dependents. Strong antagonisms between hospital and clinic physicians have been the result. The national government has attempted without much success to mediate the disputes by encouraging referrals from one to the other—to avoid expensive duplication of services (Levin and Wolfson, 1989: 318).

The living and service facilities such as nursing care in many smaller hospitals are limited—to hold down costs. Patients or their families hire their own nursing assistants to assure that care is available at night and on weekends. This is particularly a problem in remote rural areas where beds are in shorter supply than in urban settings (Powell and Anesaki, 1990:158).

Hospital conditions and procedures. If a private physician refers a patient for specialized care, reexamination is undertaken by the hospital staff. Waiting time is usually not required, but this obviously depends on the availability of space at the hospital. The more prestigious hospitals are often filled. Patients may share a ward with six to eight other patients, although private rooms are available in many facilities at an extra charge as are other extra services. The largest number of extra-charge rooms are in hospitals associated with private medical schools. The quality of nursing is generally judged by the public to be very good, although nurses may be in short supply and overworked. Individuals can obtain private insurance to cover these extra costs (which can be quite substantial) as well as co-payments required by the major public insurance programs (Powell and Anesaki, 1990: 167).

A relatively small proportion of the population is admitted to hospitals annually for acute care (6.7 percent) compared with other industrialized countries. The strong preference of the Japanese is for ambulatory care complemented by home nursing and family support. Nonetheless, there continues to be a steady increase in the number of private general hospitals, whereas specialty hospital beds have declined as the incidence of communicable and infectious diseases has diminished (Levin and Wolfson, 1989: 313).

Hospital organization and administration. Modern management practices in private hospitals and clinics have not been widely adopted, in part because of the ownership structure. Owner-physicians take personal responsibility for administration, business management, and clinical work. A business manager may be employed for billing and accounting duties. Nurses are responsible directly to the physician, with no one serving as director of nursing. This personal and untrained management structure is somewhat surprising given the worldwide effectiveness of Japanese industry. Although steps are underway to remedy this inadequacy, much progress remains to be achieved (Iglehart, 1988b: 1172).

Larger public and teaching hospitals tend to be organized much like those in the United States and Western Europe, with well-developed administrative and nursing staff management structures. Many hospital administrators are either former federal government civil servants or former medical school faculty. Very few have formal training in management, although health care administration programs have been initiated in a few prominent universities. Help is sought from senior faculty of medical schools in matters of staffing and clinical practice (Levin and Wolfson, 1989: 318; Anbacken, 1994: 96).

Multihospital chains have begun to form with professional management supplementing the required physician administrators for each facility. The "Tokushu-kai" hospital chain, for example, was organized by a surgeon and is well known for efficient management. It had the first 24-hour outpatient service in the country. Other firms are joining forces with U.S. health care management companies to organize multihospital and long-term-care facilities (Powell and Anesaki, 1990).

Medical Technology

Medical technology has become a major growth industry. Government policy officially encourages use of advanced technology and accompanying equipment that have been central to competitive advantage in the private health care marketplace. The entrepreneurial attitude among practitioners causes them to use technology as a means of attract-

ing and treating patients, whether or not the equipment always contributes to improved patient well-being (Powell and Anesaki, 1990: 187).

Automated laboratory testing has reached a high state of development, as has diagnostic and therapeutic radiology. The CT scanner and now MRI have become the measure of being modern and "up to date" for clinics and hospitals—with insurance programs providing resources to pay the costs. The government has begun to review and diminish reimbursement during the second half of the 1980s, thus causing purchases of the equipment to diminish somewhat. The government exercises no direct control over diffusion of the technology despite its very high cost (Anbacken, 1994: 97).

Similarly, the development and adoption of artificial kidneys and dialysis have proceeded rapidly since the 1950s, with full insurance reimbursement since 1972. Overall, production of medical equipment grew by 6 to 20 percent (depending on the year) annually after about 1965 and only began to slow down substantially in the late 1980s as government cost-control measures began to have substantial effect (Powell and Anesaki, 1990: 193).

Information Technology

Approximately 85 percent of all Japanese hospitals used computers in 1993, but only a few have complete information systems, including integrated patient records, drug records, and other facets of hospital business activity. Although Japan has been behind the United States and some European countries in the use of computers and information systems, a major effort is now underway to take advantage of the efficiencies to be gained through automation of communication and records. Much of the initial technology was originally adopted or adapted from other countries. Physicians want patient data, a medical information base, and computer consultation with specialists (Kaihara, 1994: 357).

Computerization and advanced communication systems have become central to the functioning of many parts of the health care system, including emergency medicine. The first large-scale information systems were established in university hospitals. Most teaching hospitals had health information systems (HISs) by 1990, although they were not standardized at the time. A network linking many of the major university hospitals has been initiated (called University Medical Information Network, or UMIN), headquartered at the University of Tokyo Hospital. Very few private facilities were this advanced in 1993, but evolution of integrated information systems is proceeding (Sasaki, 1993: S85; Kaihara, 1994: 360).

Emergency Medical Services

Modern emergency medical services have been slow to develop. Most hospitals and clinics do not operate 24-hour emergency departments. A standardized system for provision of coordinated care related to accidents or unanticipated illnesses did not exist until recently. These inadequacies generated enough concern among government officials and medical practitioners to cause formal action. The Japanese Association for Acute Medicine was formed in 1973 as a unit within the Japanese Medical Association and has been leading the effort to improve emergency services and training of both physicians and support personnel. An Emergency Medical Working Party was created in 1976, with recommendations offered in 1977. Gradual improvement has been underway since. Physicians with appropriate training and qualifications have been designated "certified emergency specialists" and practice primarily in tertiary emergency centers that get referrals from primary and secondary centers (Yoshioka and Sugimoto, 1985: 365).

The local fire department is the basic unit for emergency services. A toll-free number is available throughout Japan that connects directly to a computer-assisted, emergency dispatch system. The emergency dispatch operator immediately inputs the information to a command system that automatically assigns the nearest available ambulance to the emergency situation. A modern ambulance with basic life support (BLS) equipment is immediately dispatched from the nearest fire station. Firefighters are trained in basic life support but seldom have preparation in advanced life support (ALS). The patient can be stabilized, but will not likely have access to electronic monitors, IV fluids, and drug therapy (Hawks, 1989: 59).

Ambulance crews are largely professionals who remain in their jobs for life, and thus have considerable experience if not advanced training. They have access to detailed information about primary, secondary, and tertiary hospital facilities in the vicinity and transport the patient to the appropriate facility—given basic knowledge about the condition of the patient (Hawks, 1989: 59).

The problems with emergency response remain difficult in rural areas where clinics and hospitals have limited trauma capacity. A satisfactory solution remains to be implemented.

Long-Term Care

Specialized nursing home care has been slow to develop—because of the strong family orientation, the cultural expectation that families will care for the elderly at home, and the availability of clinic or hospital care for extended periods. Families have in the past faced severe criticism for placing a parent in a long-term-care facility. However, attitudes are clearly changing as younger generations become conscious of satisfactory alternatives that will lessen the burden. Significant growth of long-term-care facilities is therefore proceeding (Anderson et al., 1995: 41).

Frail elderly individuals can enter one of six institutional settings (Anbacken, 1994: 92):

1. General hospitals
2. Geriatric hospitals

3. Clinics with up to 20 beds
4. Geriatric health facilities
5. Special nursing homes for the aged
6. Rehabilitation facilities

As noted earlier, many of the *general hospital* beds are occupied by chronically ill patients who stay for extended periods. The standard hospital accommodation provided through insurance is a semiprivate room with 4 to 6 beds. Wards with 8 to 12 beds are not uncommon. Approximately one-third of patients admitted to general hospitals in 1984 were age 70 or older. Average length of stay was 81 days. This led the government to focus on regulating hospital capacity through a 1985 amendment to the national health insurance laws limiting the number of hospital beds (Powell and Anesaki, 1990: 153; Graig, 1993: 141).

Geriatric hospitals are simply general hospitals designated by the prefectural governor if more than 60 percent of inpatients are age 70 or older (initiated by the Aged Health Act of 1983). Care is provided with a smaller number of physicians (minimum of 3) and nurses (minimum of 17) than in general hospitals. Special care is taken in providing for elderly needs—such as daily bathing rituals (Maeda, 1989: 253).

Clinics serve a relatively small number of long-term-care patients, but fill a niche at the local community level when hospital or other facilities are full or not accessible. They are often very poorly equipped for high-quality long-term care. Substantial out-of-pocket payments by patients or their families may be required to cover private-duty nursing assistants (Ikegami et al., 1994: 629–630).

Geriatric health facilities or "health institutions for the aged" are similar to intermediate care facilities in the United States. Fewer physicians and nurses are available compared to geriatric hospitals, with reliance primarily on nurses aides. They are distinguished from nursing homes because of a greater "medical" orientation and are thus more culturally acceptable. These facilities are often located in proximity to a geriatric hospital, but are somewhat more homelike with a narrower range of services (Kobayaski and Reich, 1993: 345).

Publicly owned *nursing homes* are few in number (particularly in urban areas) and generally serve the economically impoverished who are at least 60 years old. Part of the resident's pension must be used to cover some of the expenses. Private nursing homes are more common and have lower requirements for physicians and nurses. Nurses aides are the primary staff members. Personal care is emphasized, with little priority given to rehabilitation. Intermediate-care facilities were initiated after 1987 (as a consequence of the Law of Health and Medical Services for the Elderly). As the number of facilities grew, hospital occupancy of older people was considerably lowered. The average 100-bed facility might employ 1 physician on a part-time basis, 3 nurses, and 22 nurses aides. Lower-income individuals may receive support from the local government welfare office if they are unable to pay the costs. Nursing home costs are shared by the national and local governments for low-income patients (Lawerence, 1985: 690–619; Maeda, 1989: 259; Kobayaski and Reich, 1993: 344–345).

The public and government expectation continues to be that the elderly will be cared for in the home if it is economically or physically possible. Caretakers are usually wives or daughters for older men, or daughters and daughters-in-law for women. Most of the caretakers are themselves over age 60. The rate of long-term institutionalization remains very small at 1.6 percent of those over age 65. However, increasing numbers of elderly patients with senile dementia are being admitted to mental hospitals and general hospitals, accompanied by additional home care programs sponsored by community health centers and hospitals (Kiefer, 1987: 100; Roemer, 1993: 278).

Major construction companies in Japan have begun to construct nursing homes and other types of long-term-care facilities in an effort to capitalize on a rapidly growing market for the care of the expanding elderly population. One large organization, Chugin Mansion Company, specializes in apartments for older people with varying levels of support services; the company has captured a major share of the market. An American company, Beverly Enterprises, has entered the market with a Japanese partner, and now has a chain of facilities that provides for independent elderly apartment living supplemented by health care services. They offer only minimal nursing services (Anderson, 1994).

Rehabilitation programs for the elderly have remained very limited, partially because of the predominant role of physicians who are focused on "cure" rather than care or rehabilitation. There has thus been a failure to develop specialists in rehabilitation. Many of the elderly are bedridden at home or in hospitals because they do not have access to rehabilitation services (Iglehart, 1988a: 1811; Maeda, 1989: 250).

Home Health Care

Home health services have begun to develop, in part as a cost-cutting measure in response to government incentives. Insurance reimbursement can be obtained for such home administered activities as diabetic insulin injection, coagulant injection for hemophiliacs, and dialysis for renal problems. Equipment for bedridden patients supplied at home is also an increasing activity. However, the costs of home care remain largely a family responsibility, with insurance plans paying less than 20 percent of the cost in 1990. As of 1992, 57 percent of those over aged 65 lived with their children (Kobayaski and Reich, 1993: 345).

A new program of Domiciliary Care Support Centers intended to greatly increase home health care provided by social workers and public health nurses was initiated in 1990 with public and private resources. Home visiting nursing centers were also expanded in 1992. As a consequence, home-based programs are developing rapidly to help bedridden or disabled older people remain in their homes as long as possible. All older citizens are given health handbooks, offered health examinations, and receive extensive health promotion education. Those who are disabled now have greater access to rehabilitation training and equipment, are offered bathing, meals, other home help, and social support in clubs for the elderly. Unfortunately, the severe shortage of nurses limits the potential value of these programs (Imamura, 1993: 6–10).

Moreover, the early evidence suggests that home health care is not less expensive than hospital care. Questions have also been raised about the relative quality of home health care as compared to hospital or other institutional care. In sum, it is not clear if home health is a solution to the problems of increasingly elderly population and dependence (Imamura, 1993: 14).

Mental Health Care

Mental illness has traditionally carried a stigma for the family and is often kept hidden. Patients will tend to report physical health symptoms rather than publicly admit to a mental condition. Entry to a mental hospital is considered an extreme measure and occurs only when the family is unable to assume the responsibility for care. The so-called *hogosha* system allows a family member or guardian to have total responsibility for a mentally ill person and sometimes results in abuse of rights. As a consequence, a law was passed in the 1950s prohibiting the forced confinement at home of mentally ill family members (Appelbaum, 1994: 635; Anderson et al., 1995: 39–40).

Publicly supported mental health centers for assessment of mental disorder and counseling of the mentally ill and their families are available in major cities and towns. Comprehensive community-based mental health treatment has received much more attention in recent years than previously. National and local governments are supporting psychiatric wards in general hospitals. Rehabilitation is being emphasized. Day care centers and group homes for residential care are securing greater support in urban locations (Tokyo Metropolitan Government, 1993: 32).

As knowledge of mental health treatment has increased, a powerful shift toward institutionalization of the chronically mentally ill has occurred. Most families no longer want to care for relatives who have been institutionalized. As of 1993, there were 2.8 psychiatric beds per 1,000 population and more than 50 percent of the patients had been institutionalized for 5 or more years. Costs are subsidized for patients not fully covered by national health insurance through a workplace (Phillips and Pearson, 1994: 132).

Nearly 90 percent of the available psychiatric beds are in private hospitals, because the government has preferred to subsidize private care rather than construct public hospitals. However, continuing abuses of patient's rights led to the passage of the Mental Health Law of 1988 that establishes a psychiatric review board in each prefecture to review mental health care and respond to complaints. A major focus is the protection of patient's rights through "informed consent" requirements (Appelbaum, 1994: 636).

ECONOMIC CHARACTERISTICS AND ISSUES

Dramatic improvements in living standards are evident in recent decades. The growth rate averaged 10.5 percent annually between 1955 and 1973, but slowed to 4.7 percent in the 1970s, and has been somewhat stagnated during the early 1990s. Health care costs have risen very rapidly, somewhat faster than growth in GDP throughout the period (Powell and Anesaki, 1990: 121–122; Wilsford, 1991: 285).

However, health care costs are the lowest as a proportion of GDP (6.9 percent in 1993) among advanced industrial nations. Provision of health care is among the most

equitable and efficient anywhere, despite the unresolved issues noted earlier. Health care insurance coverage is universal without significant rationing (Cockerham, 1995: 302).

Expenditures

Government-set targets for health spending are linked to growth in Gross Domestic Product. The targets are achieved in part though a national fee schedule—the "point-fee system"—which determines payment for both inpatient and outpatient services. Hospitals receive a standard per diem rate. Each of the insurance schemes pays the same rate for the same service, regardless of location or specialization of the provider. The rates are set through negotiations between representatives of the Ministry of Health and Welfare and a "Central Social Insurance Medical Council" representing providers, payers, and consumers (Graig, 1993: 141).

Expenditure increases are attributed to three major factors in addition to aging of the population:

1. Costly changes in the patterns of disease, with chronic diseases such as cancer and circulatory system treatment increasing with particular rapidity
2. Rises in use and costs of technology, new drugs, and other advanced therapies
3. Greater knowledge and expectations by the public, causing them to demand a higher quality and quantity of services

A significant pressure to increase expenditures comes from the nature of the delivery system. Use of new, expensive, and sophisticated technology has been one of the primary means for the private and highly competitive clinics and hospitals to attract patients, as noted earlier. Consequently, even small clinics and hospitals attempt to acquire the latest technology. The government's effort to restrict technology through limitations on payment through the point-fee system has been only partially successful because practitioners have tended to increase alternative diagnostic tests and examinations. Hospitals work hard to develop a large ambulatory case load that will help increase inpatient admissions (Powell and Anesaki, 1990: 127).

Steps to limit expenditures are considered necessary because of the steady rise in costs since 1960, from 2.9 percent of GDP to the current level. The slowdown in economic growth caused by the worldwide economic recession has diminished available resources (Powell and Anesaki, 1990: 96–97, 240–241).

The Financing System

Table 5-5 summarizes the types of insurance and the range of population covered. Roughly 35 percent of self-employed, unemployed, and the elderly are covered by national health insurance; 29 percent are covered by government-managed insurance funded by employers; 26 percent of all citizens are covered by privately managed insurance sponsored by employers; and 10 percent are covered through mutual-aid associations. As a general rule, those in the

first category are at higher risk, generate higher costs, and have more limited financial resources than those in the other three categories (Graig, 1993: 136).

A 20 percent co-pay applies for all services except Old Age Insurance, which requires 10 percent for individuals over age 70. Minimum benefits received under any of these arrangements are prescribed by law, including physician and hospital services, long-term care, dental care, and prescription drugs. Private insurers are encouraged to offer supplemental benefits for such amenities as private hospital rooms, supplemental nursing care, cancer care, and home care (Iglehart, 1988a: 811; Levin and Wolfson, 1989: 322).

The Social Insurance Medical Fee Payment Fund, a quasi-government agency, has branches in each prefecture and serves as the intermediary between the various insurance plans and providers. Its role is to serve as a central source to review claims and inform each insurance plan of the amounts owed to providers. One-third of the policy board are providers, one-third are insurers, and one-third are from medical schools or universities. There is relatively little formal

Table 5-5 Health Insurance Programs

Form of Insurance	Percent Insured	Insured Group	Insurer
National Health Insurance	35	Agricultural workers	Cities, towns, villages, and insurance societies
		Self-employed	
		Retirees with limited employee insurance	
		Dependent elderly	
		Unemployed	
Government-managed societies	29	Professional salaried workers	Federal government
		Small company employees	
		Sailors	
Privately managed insurance	26	Salaried workers of large enterprises	Voluntary societies
Mutual-aid associations	10	National and local public employees	Cooperatives

Source. Based on data from Tokyo Metropolitan Government, 1993: 10.

effort to review utilization or screen claims for accuracy (Levin and Wolfson, 1989: 322).

Preventive examinations and normal deliveries are not viewed as health "problems" and are not covered by insurance. If complications occur, such as the need for a cesarean section, insurance covers the necessary medical care (Iglehart, 1988a: 811).

Government insurance. *National* or community health insurance relies heavily on general tax revenue to provide coverage for the unemployed, low-income, elderly, and the self-employed—who contribute premiums. Health insurance tax rates vary by income and size of household. The program is administered at the local level through cities and towns or by trade associations, with about 50 percent direct government funding. Individuals must pay 30 percent of both inpatient and outpatient costs, with an out-of-pocket cost limit of $400 per month. Lower-income workers pay very little (Iglehart, 1988a: 810; Graig, 1993: 137).

Government-managed insurance programs act as the financial intermediary for smaller businesses and employees who contribute a proportion of salary—through the Social Insurance Agency. Contribution rates are fixed by government mandate for the benefit package prescribed by the government—with no extra amenities. The national government subsidizes the fund at about 16 percent of total costs (Iglehart, 1988a: 810).

Employer insurance. As noted earlier, one or more large companies can form a *privately managed* health insurance "society" to cover employees and dependents. These societies act as the financial intermediaries for the companies and must offer and finance the basic benefit package. Payroll deduction rates ranged between 3 and 9.5 percent in 1992. They are closely supervised by the Ministry of Health and Welfare (Graig, 1993: 137).

Their purpose is often broader than simple provision of health care; they also help implement the historical commitment of Japanese companies to encourage healthy, loyal, and long-term employees. The societies have considerable flexibility in setting rates and adding supplemental coverage. Coverage tends to be better if the employees are younger and healthier. As of 1984, employees paid 10 percent of out-of-pocket health care costs, and dependents pay 20 percent of inpatient costs and 30 percent of outpatient costs, with a limit of $350 to $580 per month, depending on their income. When the limit is reached, all remaining costs are paid by insurance (Iglehart, 1988a: 810; Cockerham, 1995: 301).

Employee insurance plans often include cash benefits to cover normal deliveries, injury and sickness allowances, maternity allowances while absent from work, a nursing allowance for women who nurse newborns, and partial coverage of patient cost sharing (Iglehart, 1988a: 810).

Mutual-aid associations. *Mutual-aid associations* offer coverage for other groups not associated with business, such as government employees, teachers, and other publicly employed people. Special insurance exists for groups not otherwise specifically included in the plans noted earlier, such as construction workers.

Generally speaking, individuals covered by mutual aid insurance and society (employer) insurance receive better benefits than those covered by government-managed plans. National Health Insurance provides the least-generous benefits (Powell and Anesaki, 1990: 135).

Commercial insurance and out-of-pocket costs. Because individuals covered by these various insurance programs do incur out-of-pocket costs for many services, a private insurance market provides coverage to offset personal costs, with particular focus on cancer coverage. Up to 60 percent of all households are estimated to have commercial insurance, often through special clauses in life insurance policies. Costs of these policies are relatively modest because the government requires that public insurance plans protect individuals against major costs from a serious illness (Iglehart, 1988a: 810).

Overall, out-of-pocket co-payments are roughly 12 percent of health expenditures. However, all administrative procedures and costs for the various insurance plans are at federal government expense. Mandatory coverage, uniform benefits, and a limited number of payers have helped to keep claims processing at a modest cost level. Marketing costs for insurance are largely nonexistent because consumers have no choice except for the addition of supplemental commercial insurance.

Physician payment. Physicians in private practice, whether alone or in clinics, are paid on a fee-for-service basis. The Ministry of Health and Welfare is responsible for establishing the fee rates through the *point-fee system*—a national schedule for payment of health care providers. The Ministry must consult first with the Central Social Insurance Medical Council, a 20-member advisory group representing the public, payers, and providers. Each medical service under the point-fee system is assigned a point. The number of points is based on the technical skill required to provide a unit of service and the cost of materials such as drugs or laboratory tests.

The same fee is then paid to all health care facilities regardless of location or specialization. This carefully structured fee schedule is the basis for reimbursement of nearly all health care and is thus highly influential in the allocation of resources (Iglehart, 1988b: 1168).

The fee schedule has been deliberately used to induce behavior change among physicians and hospitals. For example, by limiting the fees for surgical services, the schedule has kept surgery rates low, thus contributing to lower hospital costs. Organ transplantation is severely restricted, in part because of the cultural taboo on removal of organs from individuals who remain physically alive although brain dead. The schedule tends to favor private practitioners and clinic-based physicians over inpatient hospital care, in part because of the bias of the

Japanese Medical Association toward private practitioners. The Association has also been heavily responsible for winning favorable income tax status for ambulatory care physicians, which has meant that until recently, 72 percent of their income was exempt from taxation. This has now been lowered to a range of 52 to 72 percent depending on level of income (Iglehart, 1988b: 1169).

Hospital payment. Patients can go to any hospital or clinic simply by presenting their insurance card, allowing the hospital or clinic to collect from the appropriate insurance fund. Co-payments are made at the time of service by outpatients and at the end of stay for hospital inpatients. Medical facilities are reimbursed on a fee basis upon presentation of the patient bill to the intermediary organization for insurance payments—the Social Insurance Medical Care Fee Payment Fund or the Prefectural Federation of National Health Insurance Association offices. These intermediary organizations examine the bill for appropriateness of charges and reimburse the medical care providers (Powell and Anesaki, 1990: 138).

Facilities financing. The national government provides the funds for national hospitals, whereas prefectural or municipal governments finance local government facilities—often with some federal subsidy. The Medical Care Facilities Financing Corporation and the Pension Welfare Service Public Corporation provide low-interest, long-term loans for private facilities. Banks and loan companies provide financing for clinic and small-facility construction or expansion (Powell and Anesaki, 1990: 139).

Special financing provisions for the elderly. Free medical care for the elderly was introduced in 1973 at a time when Japan had been enjoying a 15-year continuous period of rapid economic growth. This led to a greatly increased incidence of elderly visits to clinics and longer stays in hospitals, rapidly boosting the cost of health care. Medical benefits to the elderly included physician consultation, hospitalization, surgery if needed, other therapy, nursing services, supply of medications and therapeutic materials, and transportation (Powell and Anesaki, 1990: 114).

These medical benefits are provided to everyone in Japan over age 65. Between ages 65 and 69, insurance subsidies are paid for anyone below a defined income level. Those with resources must provide a 10 percent co-pay. Nursing care is also subsidized for individuals who are unable to pay (Tokyo Metropolitan Government, 1993, 1994).

After a prolonged period of debate and negotiation among officials of the Ministry of Health and Welfare, the Finance Ministry, the Japanese Medical Association, and senior politicians, a 1982 law, Health and Medical Services for Aged, created a separate plan with specific funding within the national insurance program for the retirees and other elderly individuals (defined as over age 70, or between 65 and 70 but disabled) who shift from their company society or government managed plan to this new fund. The law provides for insurance and also attempts to be comprehensive. It focuses on prevention, treatment and rehabilitation, and integration of services that were formerly fragmented. This includes an annual health screening and checkup, use of a personal health notebook, and health education programs (Campbell, 1984: 53–64; Steslicke, 1989: 121).

Home care rather than lengthy hospitalization was encouraged by a decreasing reimbursement scale paid to hospitals for longer stays. Discharge planning, day care, and home health services were increased. These developments have caused the Japanese government to become much more supportive than in the past of nursing home and other housing or long-term-care alternatives (Kiefer, 1987: 93).

Twenty percent of the funding comes directly from the national government, and local governments provided 10 percent; the balance comes from employee insurance societies because the government views care of the elderly as part of an employer social obligation. Elderly citizens make minimal contributions of $6 per month and $3 per day for hospital care (Iglehart, 1988a: 811; Graig, 1993: 139).

Despite its inadequacies, the system provides a relatively uniform standard of medical care and is widely accepted by consumers and medical providers because it does allow freedom of choice among physicians and facilities while covering everyone with basic benefits.

PROBLEMS AND REFORMS

Since the beginning of the 1980s, cost control accompanied by efforts to improve equity of access to health care have been at the forefront of government health policy. Cost-control measures are partially aimed at creating the alternative institutions that can provide care at much lower cost. However, because private hospitals and physicians benefit from the current system, resources for lower-cost alternative arrangements such as long-term-care facilities have been difficult to secure (Powell and Anesaki, 1990: 126).

Increased levels of co-payment are now required. The 1995 target will mean 20 percent co-payment up to a prescribed ceiling. Attempts are underway to improved management of insurance programs through use of computer technology—to reduce administrative and clerical costs. A tighter monitoring system is intended to better control the fee-reimbursement system to limit overservicing and overprescribing. Use of high-cost technology will be reimbursed only in approved facilities, to cut down on the spread of such technology to unduly large numbers of providers (Powell and Anesaki, 1990: 98).

Issues Related to the Elderly

Government policies have not yet adequately responded to the rapid aging of the population, making payment for increasing health care costs difficult. The current cost-containment policy may not be adequate to deal with the major needs of an older society (Wilsford, 1991: 285).

Long-term care needs greater attention. The practice of caring for disabled or chronically ill older people in the hospital setting is difficult to justify because costs are clearly higher than in specialized long-term-care facilities with lower-intensity care and a more "homelike" setting. Definite progress is now evident, but the task is clearly incomplete (Powell and Anesaki, 1990: 230).

Differential Insurance Benefits

Although the various insurance schemes cover nearly every individual, the benefits vary considerably, depending on employment and status. Basic benefits are universal, but special benefits vary widely. "Extra" services are commonplace and are often covered by private insurance.

Inadequate Coordination between Public and Private Health Care

There is little formal cooperation and coordination between the private health care system on the one hand and the locally based public health care system on the other as noted earlier. Private health facilities are allowed to grow on the basis of individual entrepreneurship, leading often to overlap in services within one area and serious inadequacies in another. Very little formal planning for private facilities development has been evident until relatively recently.

Obsolete Physicians

Although physicians may be well-trained at the outset of their practice in "curative" medicine, there are no requirements for continuing education to keep them abreast of current developments and procedures. Consequently, many physicians practice outmoded methods, to the detriment of patients and at high cost to the insurance program.

Duplication and Overlap of Providers

The focus on "cost containment" in recent years has not been accompanied by full attention to priorities. No evidence of radical departure from the current structure is indi-cated. This is particularly true in the hospital realm, where oversupply, high average lengths of stay, and accompanying high costs are a continuing issue. There continues to be a large measure of costly duplication of facilities and services.

Inadequate Incentive Structure

The "point-fee" health care reimbursement system offers little incentive to hospitals or physicians to increase their efficiency or quality of operation. It does not actively encourage careful practice, because concrete services are rewarded regardless of quality or the skills of the provider.

Insufficient Attention to Modern Management

The relative lack of professional hospital administration has meant that modern knowledge of management and organization has not been applied to the same degree in health care as in other realms of enterprise in Japan. Hospitals lack formal systems to evaluate quality and appropriateness of care. Physicians without professional administration training continue to dominate decisions in most institutions. The current government policy of rigorous monitoring and auditing may eventually lead to much greater emphasis on efficient and high-quality service management (Powell and Anesaki, 1990: 235).

One example of inefficiency is the practice of not requiring appointments for physician visits. Patients go to the clinic when they are ill or need medical assistance and wait for their turn. Waiting for the short visit may consume much of the patient's day (Schlitt, 1993: 652–653).

SUMMARY AND CONCLUSIONS

The Japanese culture promotes many forms of good health. The diet is heavily vegetarian and low-fat, in part because of the high cost of meats and seafood. Exercise is widely practiced, at work and as enjoyment of nature and the outdoors. Consciousness of the body and its health has long been considered an important value. Avoidance of pollution and environmental degradation has been important because of high population density and general respect for nature. Thus, many of the important contributors to health arise from traditional culture and values.

Despite the list of problems identified earlier, the Japanese health care system is among the most advanced in the world, with better results than any other system in terms of low infant mortality, greater longevity, and wide access to high-technology care at lower cost than in any other industrialized country. Newly trained physicians are highly trained, very highly regarded, and quite prepared to practice the most advanced forms of medicine. The medical societies wield very strong influence in the councils of national power and in the national health bureaucracy, despite a loss of influence as compared to earlier periods (Wilsford, 1991: 285).

However, the same cannot be said for nurses, who continue to have relatively lower status than in many countries. Despite the fact that public hospitals and many private hospitals and clinics are equipped with the latest in advanced technology, skilled nurses get relatively little credit for their contribution to high-quality health care.

Preventive care and health promotion are given higher priority now than ever before, but the incidence of chronic illnesses such as cancer is increasing. The primary continuing challenge will be provision of adequate health care to a population that is aging more rapidly than any in the world while containing costs. Major restructuring of ambulatory care, hospital services, long-term care, use of pharmaceuticals, and home health care may be necessary to meet quality and cost-control requirements.

REFERENCES

ABE, MARATOSHI A. (1985). Japan's Clinic Physicians and Their Behavior, *Social Science and Medicine*, 30 (4): 335–340.

ANBACKEN, OWE (1994). Japanese Hospitals—Culture and Competition: A Study of Ten Hospitals, *International Journal of Health Planning and Management*, 9 (1): 87–101.

ANDERSON, JAMES G., RENEE OSCARSON, and YAN YU (1995). Japan's Health Care System: Western and East Asian Influences, in Eugene B. Gallagher and Janardan Subedi (eds.), *Global Perspectives on Health Care*. Englewood Cliffs, N.J.: Prentice Hall, pp. 32–44.

ANDERSON, STEVE (1994). Long-Term Care Services in Japan, student paper for international health care course.

APPELBAUM, PAUL S. (1994). Mental Health Law and Ethics in Transition: A Report from Japan, *Hospital and Community Psychiatry*, 45 (7): 635–636.

BENET, LESLIE Z. (1991). Ideals and Innovation: Drugs, Generics, the FDA, and Pharmacist, *DICP, The Annals of Pharmacotherapy*, 25 (April): 427–430.

CAMPBELL, JOHN C. (1984). Problems, Solutions, Nonsolutions, and Free Medical Care for the Elderly in Japan, *Pacific Affairs*, 57 (1): 53–64.

COCKERHAM, WILLIAM C. (1995). *Medical Sociology*, 6th ed. Englewood Cliffs, N.J.: Prentice Hall.

The Economist (1990). Japanese Health Care: Keeping Well in Their Own Way, *The Economist*, 316 (July 7): 38–39.

FUKAMI, AKIKO (1992). Informed Consent: Doctor Says Patients Have a Right to Know, *Japan Times Weekly International Edition*, August 17–23, p. 8.

GALLAGHER, EUGENE B., and JANARDAN SUBEDI (eds.) (1995). *Global Perspectives on Health Care*, Englewood Cliffs, N.J.: Prentice Hall.

GARLAND, T. NEAL (1995). Major Orientations in Japanese Health Care, in Eugene B. Gallagher and Janardan Subedi (eds.), *Global Perspectives on Health Care*. Englewood Cliffs, N.J.: Prentice Hall, pp. 255–267.

GRAIG, LAURENE (1993). *Health of Nations: An International Perspective on U.S. Health Care Reform*, 2nd ed. Washington, D.C.: Congressional Quarterly.

HAWKS, STEVEN R. (1989). Injured Abroad: How Would You Fare?, *Journal of Emergency Medical Services*, 14 (12): 55–59.

IGLEHART, JOHN K. (1988a). Japan's Medical Care System (Part One), *New England Journal of Medicine*, 319 (12): 807–812.

IGLEHART, JOHN K. (1988b). Japan's Medical Care System (Part Two), *New England Journal of Medicine*, 319 (17): 1166–1172.

IKEGAMI, NAOKI, BRANT E. FRIES, YASUO TAKAGI, SHUNYA IKEDA, and TOSHIKO IBE (1994). Applying RUG-III in Japanese Long-Term Care Facilities, *The Gerontologist*, 34 (5): 628–639.

IMAMURA, KYOKO (1993). Japan's Experience in Long-Term Home Health Care for the Elderly, *International Journal of Health Planning and Management*, 8 (3): 201–217.

ISHIWATA, RYUJI, and AKIO SAKAI (1994). The Physician-Patient Relationship and Medical Ethics in Japan, *Cambridge Quarterly of Healthcare Ethics,* 3 (1): 60–66.

KAIHARA, SHIGEKOTO (1994). Workstation Network System Which Enables International Exchange of Characters and Images at the University of Tokyo Hospital, *International Journal of Bio-Medical Computing,* 34 (1–4): 357–361.

KAWAKITA, HIROBUMI (1992). The Financial State of Japanese Health Care Institutions, *Japan Hospitals,* 11 (July): 11–22.

KIEFER, CHRISTIE (1987). Care for the Aged in Japan, in Edward Norbeck and Margaret Lock (eds.), *Health, Illness and Medical Care in Japan.* Honolulu: University of Hawaii Press, pp. 89–109.

KOBAYASHI, YASUKI, and HARUYOSHI TAKAKI (1992). Geographic Distribution of Physicians in Japan, *Lancet,* 340 (December 5): 1391–1393.

KOBAYASKI, Y., and M. R. REICH (1993). Health Care Financing for the Elderly in Japan, *Social Science and Medicine,* 37 (3): 343–353.

LAWERENCE, T. L. (1985). Health Care Facilities for the Elderly in Japan, *International Journal of Health Services,* 15: 677–697.

LEVIN, PETER J., and JAY WOLFSON (1989). Health Care in the Balance: Japanese Eurythmy, *Hospital and Health Services Administration,* 34 (3): 311–323.

MAEDA, NOBUO (1989). Long-Term Care for the Elderly in Japan, in Teresa Schwab (ed.), *Caring for an Aging World: International Models for Long-Term Care, Financing and Delivery.* New York: McGraw-Hill Information Services. pp. 246–264.

MARMOR, THEODORE R. (1992). Japan: A Sobering Lesson, *Health Management Quarterly,* 14 (3): 10–14.

PHILLIPS, MICHAEL R., and VERONICA PEARSON (1994). Future Opportunities and Challenges for the Development of Psychiatric Rehabilitation in China, *British Journal of Psychiatry,* 165 (24) (Supp.): 128–142.

POWELL, MARGARET, and MASAHIRA ANESAKI (1990). *Health Care in Japan.* New York: Routledge.

REISCHAUER, EDWIN O. (1988). *The Japanese Today.* Cambridge: Harvard University Press.

ROEMER, MILTON I. (1991). *National Health Systems of the World: The Countries,* Vol. I. New York: Oxford University Press.

ROEMER, MILTON I. (1993). *National Health Systems of the World: The Issues,* Vol. II. New York: Oxford University Press.

SASAKI, YASUHITO (1993). Status of Hospital Information and Image Transmission Systems in Japan, *Investigative Radiology,* 28 (7) (Supp.): S85–S86.

SCHLITT, MICHAEL (1993). Health Care Systems in Japan and Germany Provide Facts, Not Theories, *Journal of the Medical Association of Georgia,* 82 (December): 651–655.

SONODA, KYOICHI (1988). *Health and Illness in Changing Japanese Society.* Tokyo: University of Tokyo Press.

STESLICKE, WILLIAM E. (1982). Development of Health Insurance Policy in Japan, *Journal of Health Politics, Policy and Law,* 7 (1): 197–226.

STESLICKE, WILLIAM E. (1989). Health Care and the Japanese State, in Mark G. Field, (ed.), *Success and Crisis in National Health Care Systems: A Comparative Approach.* New York: Routledge, pp. 101–126.

TOKYO METROPOLITAN GOVERNMENT (1993). *Health Care for Tokyo Residents.* Tokyo: Tokyo Bureau of Public Health.

TOKYO METROPOLITAN GOVERNMENT (1994). *Social Welfare in Tokyo, 1994.* Tokyo: Tokyo Metropolitan Government.

WILSFORD, DAVID (1991). *Doctors and the State: The Politics of Health Care in France and the United States.* Durham, N.C.: Duke University Press.

YOSHIOKA, TOSHIHARU, and TSUYOSHI SUGIMOTO (1985). The Japanese Association for Acute Medicine (JAAM), *American Journal of Emergency Medicine,* 3 (4): 364–366.

6

GERMANY

A Tradition
of Universal Health Care

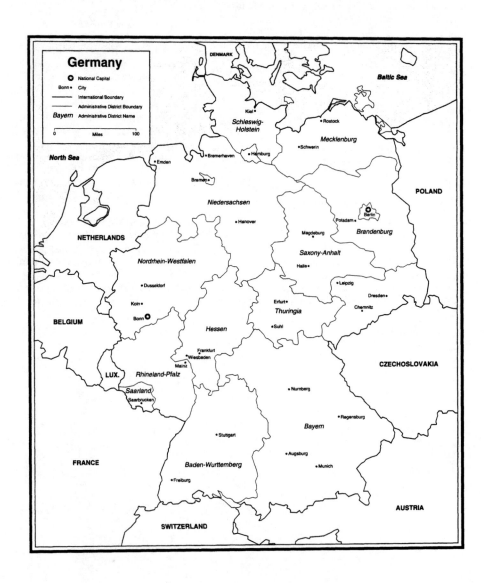

Germany has the greatest landmass, the most people, and the largest economy in Western Europe—as well as the longest tradition of universal health care among the advanced industrialized nations. The system of sickness insurance funds introduced in the nineteenth century has served as the model for health care systems in many other countries. Medical education is considered among the most prestigious for specialized training, which means it is preferred by physicians from other countries who seek the best preparation available. Other primary features of the German system are summarized in Table 6-1.

Formerly communist East Germany had much less technology than West Germany but a relatively good system of primary care provided by publicly owned polyclinics. East Germany has since been transformed to the West German pattern.

Table 6-1 Key Features of German Health Care

- Near-universal insurance coverage with access to services based on health care needs
- Private nonprofit public "sickness funds" governed by consumers and providers
- Mandated financing through payroll deductions from employers, with equal employee contributions, and based on ability to pay
- Benefits include medical, dental, eye, inpatient hospital, home health, rehabilitative treatment at health spas, and full maternity care as well as income replacement when sick
- Private-practice and relatively autonomous primary care by physicians who provide care under negotiated fee-for-service payment agreements with sickness funds, and no point-of-service charge to consumers
- Public and private nonprofit hospital care in which salaried physician specialists assume full responsibility for patients
- Government at national, state, and local levels does not directly manage any part of the system, but maintains considerable control over health care policy, regulations, and capital investment in hospitals
- Citizens have full access to comprehensive health care services with modest co-payments and with relatively free choice of both physicians and hospitals

Sources: Based on Iglehart, 1991a & b; Graig, 1993: 81–92; Pfaff, 1994: 30.

DEMOGRAPHIC CHARACTERISTICS

The population in 1993 was about 81 million, with an average per capita income of $22,240, among the highest in the world. Since Germany has been open to immigration, in part because of a shortage of unskilled labor, there is a substantial minority of residents from many other countries—especially in large industrial cities. Immigrants have come primarily from nearby countries (especially from the former Yugoslavia, Turkey, Greece, Italy, and Spain) seeking higher wages than can be secured in their country of origin. For example, the southern city of Munich has a minority population of 18 percent. Minorities have suffered from high rates of unemployment in the late 1980s and early 1990s during the economic downturn in much of Europe and have been subject to more health problems and higher rates of infant mortality than the general population (Shannon and Cutchin, 1994: 26).

Infant mortality was 6.9 per 1,000 in 1994, near the Western European average. Life expectancy was 72.7 for men and 79.2 for women in 1992—about average for Western Europe and slightly better than the United States. The proportion of the population over age 65 was 15.5 percent in 1994, also near the European average but somewhat higher than in the United States, Canada, or Japan (Reinhardt, 1994: 22; Weil, 1994: 26).

Because of the relatively high ratio of retirees to workers, increasing resources are needed to support retirement benefits, health insurance for the elderly, and other social benefits. In 1994, 39 cents went to such benefits for every dollar paid in wages. Estimates are that by the year 2030, there will be more people drawing retirement benefits than active workers (Weil, 1994: 29).

HISTORICAL PERSPECTIVE

The Early Period: 1854–1939

The origin of the current organization and financing system goes back to approximately 1854 when one region of present-day Germany (Prussia) passed a law making membership mandatory in mutual-aid societies that provided health care. Such societies were organized voluntarily by workers and employers prior to the government requirement. After Germany became a nation in 1870, Emperor Wilhelm recommended permanent status for sickness insurance funds in 1881 (Roemer, 1991: 131).

In 1883, the Sickness Insurance Act was approved by the new German federal Parliament at the behest of the first German Chancellor, Otto von Bismarck. The Act required that all low-wage workers be enrolled in an existing or new sickness benefit society. The purpose of the new legislation was in part to promote social stability by pacifying trade unions that were threatening an uprising. Coverage was soon extended to civil servants as well. Coal miners and other employee groups were included soon after. Sickness societies were required to provide a minimum set of benefits, report annually to the government, and use their funds prudently (Schulenburg, 1992: 85).

It might appear that German leaders of the day were benevolently looking out for the health care needs of their people. In fact, the health care benefit grew in part from a feudal tradition in which an employer had obligations to employees. The authoritarian and paternalistic government probably provided health care primarily to maintain control rather than to protect citizens in the case of illness (Light, 1986).

Nonetheless, this was the beginning of "social security" in Germany—a concept that has since been adopted to some degree in most countries of the world. Health care insurance and other social services gradually expanded to cover all workers and dependents as well as nonworkers. Coverage of unemployed and older citizens was provided through payments from federal welfare funds or pension funds (Roemer, 1991: 132).

The fundamental structure of health insurance coverage and other benefits has remained largely unchanged since its origin.

Other forms of social insurance, for disability (1884), old age (1889), public assistance (1924), and unemployment (1927), have followed a similar pattern (Iglehart, 1991a).

Originally, sickness funds were responsible for providing both health care *and* income continuation when ill. The funds financed hospitals in which physicians were employees. Physicians had relatively little power or influence at that point in history and were not recognized as full-fledged professionals. By 1926, professional recognition had been achieved in most states, but not at the national level. Physician groups were first allowed to contract for provision of their services during this period and were given the right to make decisions about how to allocate compensation to their members (Light, 1986: 7).

These associations have since become powerful collective-bargaining agents in negotiations with sickness funds. They gradually assumed responsibility for actually paying physician members with allocations from sickness funds and became the responsible organizations for provision of primary care beginning in 1931. Physicians were required to join the association if they were to treat members of sickness funds (Schulenburg, 1992: 85–90).

Post–World War II

After World War II, physicians attempted to consolidate the influence gained during the Nazi era. They were successful in prohibiting public health physicians from providing primary care and were able to entrench the private-practice physicians as the dominant role in primary care. Solo practitioners were the usual delivery unit. Group practices or clinics, and the use of midlevel practitioners such as physician assistants or nurse-practitioners, were strongly discouraged. Specialization of practice increased rapidly, as did a focus on technical procedures (Light, 1986: 21; Iglehart, 1991a).

Additional health-related enactments were implemented after World War II. The Federal Department of Health and Human Services was created in 1961 as the primary national administrator of health and social affairs. Statutory fee schedules for physicians and dentists were established in 1965 and revised in 1982. Employers were required to continue to pay wages during illness as of 1970. Laws to finance hospitals were approved in 1972. Cost-containment acts were approved in 1977 and revised in 1982, 1989, and 1993. The landmark Health Insurance Structural Reform Law was enacted in 1989, requiring that expenditure of the sickness funds increases no faster than wages. The fraction of national income to be spent for health care was clearly defined, the first time this had occurred in any country (Schulenburg, 1992: 85–95).

Sickness funds and regional associations of physicians have continued to be fully responsible for ongoing allocation of health care resources, although the arrangement was modified somewhat in the latest reforms, imposing greater government restrictions. The central government has traditionally played a modest role as a rule maker, but has recently intervened vigorously to control costs (Graig, 1993: 84; Henke, Murray, and Ade, 1994: 9–20).

CULTURAL FACTORS

The structure of the health care system is based in part on the widely accepted belief that the nation is obligated to offer a network of social benefits to all citizens. Cultural tradition emphasizes a "social contract" or "social solidarity" among citizens and with the government. The freedom of physicians and other health providers to practice as they wish is limited only by the requirement that they conform with the broader public interest (Iglehart, 1991b).

Citizens thus feel a strong sense of entitlement to health care, as well as to other social services. Individuals and families readily exercise these rights whenever there is any feeling of need. Consequently, annual physi-cian visits per family for basic care are among the highest in the world (Cockerham, 1995: 305).

Citizens and their leaders have a strong nationalistic attachment to Germany as a society and to the health care system as an expression of the commitment to look after each other. Citizens view themselves as an efficient and highly productive society, on the one hand, but consider themselves a romantic and emotional people, on the other; the health care system embodies each of these characteristics. High-tech medicine is of great importance, but so are the healing powers of nature and community, as illustrated by the strong emphasis on the *spa* as a curative institution (Payer, 1988).

The medical care system not only makes intense use of physicians services, but also uses pharmaceuticals at a higher rate than other European countries or the United States. Herbal drugs are very popular with physicians and patients. Physicians are trained to view health care somewhat holistically, with a variety of treatments considered appropriate, depending on the condition of the patient. "Balance" in the body is considered important. Treatment is applied for "low" blood pressure to bring pressure back into balance, even though low pressure is (unless very low) not usually viewed in other countries as a problem to be treated. The application of hydrotherapy (hot and cold water treatments and the use of the spa) is commonplace because it is viewed as helping to maintain body balance (Payer, 1988: 84, 91).

A common diagnosis is "cardiac insufficiency," a condition that would probably not be diagnosed as heart disease by physicians in other health care systems. The heart gets more attention here than in most health care systems. Six times more heart drugs are prescribed per capita as compared to France or the United States. Electrocardiograms are eight times more likely to be used, with heart abnormality diagnosed 40 percent of the time as compared to 5 percent in the United States (Payer, 1988: 84; Peters, 1991).

Cultural consensus is viewed as very important, whether with regard to health care or other matters. It is considered better to reach a compromise among competing interests than to allow a deadlock to occur. This undoubtedly serves as part of the basis for recent decisions to deliberately control costs in the face of rapidly increasing expenditures.

POLITICAL INFLUENCES

A federal system of government divides responsibilities between local, state, and federal levels. The 11 German states, 26 districts, and 328 counties manage public affairs with considerable autonomy. There is a mix of public/private financing and federal/state responsibility for health care. Providers and consumers have a major voice in the operation of the system, via advisory groups and sickness-fund management.

Citizens have historically supported strong governments, but public officials are not expected to directly administer social programs. Responsibility is instead placed with quasi-government institutions, a tradition sometimes referred to as "corporatism." These organizations of business and occupational groups take responsibility as intermediaries between government and other citizens. The role of the political system is to oversee and coordinate such organizations while assuring that the national interest is served (Light, 1986: 5; Graig, 1993: 87).

Health care is thus provided in the context of a federal legal framework that supports the balancing of interests. Power to make key decisions is balanced between the sickness funds, the medical profession, hospital professionals, and government. Budget caps negotiated with major stakeholders and imposed by government rules stringently limit the ability of hospitals and physicians to increase fees and services (Light, 1986: 21; Graig, 1993: 88–89).

These substantial changes were a direct result of citizen and business dissatisfaction with the increasing payroll deductions. Expenses were growing faster than revenues, which meant the payroll tax would have to be raised further if expenses were not curtailed. The unpopularity of such increases with employers, employees, and pensioners led to an agreement among the primary political parties to intervene forcefully by constraining the expansionary impulses of providers (Pfaff, 1994: 30).

Although sickness funds have a strong consumer orientation and worker control, physicians have achieved a very powerful political role. Regional associations of physicians not only have substantial influence over health policy, they also have major influence over their members. The payment system generates detailed knowledge of each ambulatory practice. The monitoring function means that physicians who deviate significantly from standards of practice may be disciplined by the association (Graig, 1993: 90).

Recommendations to government are formulated twice per year by a 90-member policy group referred to as "Concerted Action for Health Affairs." This national representative group includes sickness-fund members, providers, consumers, and a staff of seven medical and economic advisors. The organization develops guidelines and prepares an annual report summarizing the state of health care. Recommendations on needed policy changes are the major product (Henke et al., 1994: 259). Figure 6-1 summarizes the national and regional political organization for health care policy and management.

SOCIAL ORGANIZATION OF HEALTH CARE

The health care system in each region is managed primarily by sickness funds and physician associations, with a less prominent role for hospital administrators. Each fund serves specific employee groups or geographical regions and operates under an administrative structure controlled by a board of

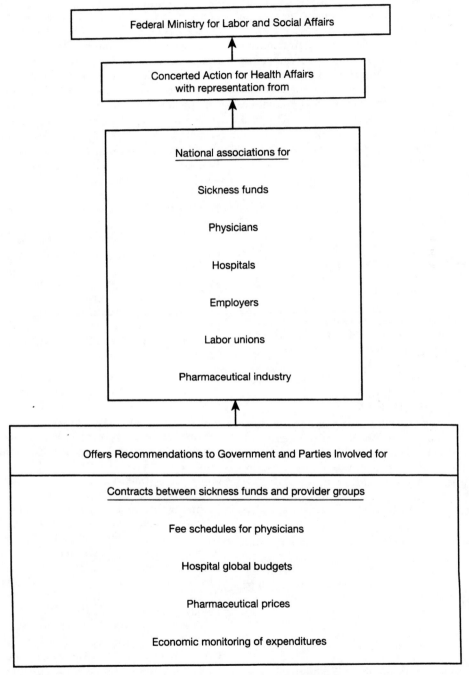

Figure 6-1. Political organization for health care policy and management.
Source: Based on Graig, 1993: 102.

employee–employer representatives who are fully responsible for the financial viability of the insurance program. Both the sickness funds and physician associations are compulsory membership organizations. Membership in any fund is based primarily on occupational status or location, although recent changes have greatly increased the competition between funds for members. The Federal Ministry for Labor and Social Affairs has responsibility for overseeing sickness-fund responsiveness to national policies (Iglehart, 1991a; Graig, 1993: 93).

Public Health

The public health system is decentralized to states and localities, although federal laws govern policies and priorities. The system is responsible for the basic protection of public health, including requirements for water systems, sewer systems, other forms of environmental protection, food safety, and health promotion. The environmental protection measures have been quite effective for cleaning up major rivers and other forms of water pollution. Air pollution has been cut drastically in the past 25 years.

Relatively less attention has been given to selected health promotion and disease prevention activities. Food labeling is minimal for calorie or salt content. Smoking cessation has not been particularly emphasized. Relatively little emphasis is given to prevention of cardiovascular disease. Water is not generally subject to fluoridation, which contributes to higher dental costs. However, the basic public health system is strong and is among the reasons for the relatively good health outcomes enjoyed by the population (Iglehart, 1991b:184; Roy, 1993: 1392).

Physicians

Germany has a relatively balanced distribution of office-based ambulatory care practitioners and hospital specialists. About 40 percent of the ambulatory care physicians

focused on primary care in 1990; the remainder were office-based specialists. Ambulatory care physicians serve as gatekeepers to specialty care and hospital referral, but are generally constrained from hospital practice. Hospital physicians are restricted from ambulatory care, but take full responsibility for patients referred by ambulatory care physicians. Each group has separate professional organizations to deal with the unique problems of ambulatory and hospital care. Female physicians make up 27 percent of the total physician population. Eight percent of physicians are foreign born, half from other European countries (Henke et al., 1994: 256).

Patients have free choice of an ambulatory care physician for primary care. Every member of a sickness fund receives a treatment voucher that is presented to the physician's office for recording of treatments. Primary care is usually provided by a solo general practitioner, although patients are also free to seek appointments directly with specialists (Jones, 1993: 59–60).

Medical associations.   Ambulatory physicians were required until recently to belong to 1 of 19 regional associations (State Medical Association of Insurance Doctors), and the associations were required to accept all applicants. Hospital doctors were required to belong to the Association of Hospital Physicians. Membership was also required for both groups in the "Medical Chamber"—for licensing, quality control, and continuing education. However, under the new Health Reform Act of 1993, membership in these associations can be restricted in oversupplied areas with more than a 10 percent surplus of physicians—based on negotiated physician-density standards (Rosenthal and Frankel, 1992: 98; Henke et al., 1994: 256).

The state medical associations guarantee services to people insured by the sickness funds. They receive sickness-fund allocations to pay member physicians according to the negotiated fee schedules. Associations are legally required to undertake a formal role in all dimensions of health policy making and are therefore somewhat more accountable to the national interest than is the case in other Western countries (Iglehart, 1991a: 507; Iglehart, 1991b: 184; Schulenburg, 1992: 88).

Problems of physician competition. The division of physicians into two major categories has placed some limitations on the efficiency of health care. Hospital physicians have been responsible for most surgeries and have strongly resisted the initiation of ambulatory surgery in outpatient clinics—even though considerable evidence demonstrates that appropriate outpatient surgery is cost-effective. The competition between ambulatory care physicians and hospital physicians has also led to duplication of equipment, repetitive diagnostic tests, and complicated referral patterns. Inpatient care is sometimes used as a mechanism for hospital physicians to provide primary care services, although at higher cost than ambulatory care (Iglehart, 1991b: 189).

Ambulatory care physician specialists make liberal use of diagnostic technology. Forty-two percent of all CT scanners are located in private offices. This leads to a relatively high proportion of gross income (averaging 25 percent) allocation to imaging and laboratory costs. The Uniform Evaluation Standard was revised in 1989 to counter this practice and give greater value to consultations, preventive care, and physical examinations, while lowering the value for technical diagnostic services. Incomes of technical specialists were lowered somewhat, while the income of primary care practitioners increased. Expenditures were monitored for basic primary care services, laboratory services, preventive services, and a separate category of special services—to allow for tracking and controlling each kind of service. Among other immediate consequences is the increase in formation of multispecialty group practices at the expense of the formerly predominant solo practice (Schicke, 1988: 401; Henke et al., 1994: 10).

Attempts have been made periodically to assure that primary care physicians are accessible to all members of sickness funds. For example, in 1955, a Health Guarantee Mandate was passed requiring an average of 500 families per physician. However, this rule was later rescinded because it restricted the freedom of physicians to choose their practice site, and limited competition (Shannon and Cutchin, 1994: 24).

Physician satisfaction. Physicians generally feel satisfied with the health care system—particularly as compared to Americans and Canadians. They feel their system is working well (48 percent, as compared to 23 percent for Americans and 33 percent for Canadian physicians). Only 15 percent detect an inability to provide necessary care for individuals because of limitations of insurance coverage, as compared to 73 percent in the United States and 25 percent in Canada. Moreover, only 20 percent are concerned about shortages of equipment in medical facilities, as compared to 54 percent of Canadian and 14 percent of American physicians. German citizens in general also feel a much higher sense of satisfaction than Americans, although Canadians were the most satisfied overall at the time of a survey in 1992 (Blendon et al., 1993: 1011; Graig, 1993: 109).

Medical education. The supply of physicians has been growing at a rate of about 3.2 percent annually (as of 1991)—far greater than in other Western countries. The increase has been particularly rapid in hospital physicians, who now exceed physicians in office-based practice. Medical schools are public institutions that must admit qualified applicants. Most student costs (except books and incidentals) are paid by the government. This complicates imposition of limits on medical school enrollment. Only recently have universities received a mandate to control the size of classes. A federal government decree now requires a longer period of residency training in hospital or ambulatory care before a physician can be certified for full practice (Iglehart, 1991b: 183; Weil, 1994: 27).

An influx of physicians from East Germany to West Germany occurred after the dismantling of the Berlin Wall. The number of foreign-born physicians has also increased substantially, further increasing the oversupply. An average of 40,000–45,000 physicians were unemployed in 1993, most in their first years of practice. Some accept jobs as nurses, receptionists, research subjects, taxi drivers, and other positions while waiting for a medical appointment. Others take further specialized training or go abroad to seek employment. Many jobs that formerly went to first-year physicians have been converted to 18-month internships at much lower pay. Unless entry into medical school is further restricted, unemployment could increase dramatically in the upcoming years (Morris, 1991: 1618–1619; Schulenburg, 1992: 87; Henke, Ade, and Murray, 1994: 256).

If medical school enrollments are further restricted, fewer graduates could mean increased inmigration of physicians from other European Union countries. Further restriction of migration has been proposed to avoid discriminating against German students who aspire to be physicians. Physician shortages have arisen in areas of some large cities inhabited largely by lower-income and minority workers—where many physicians prefer not to practice (Pfaff, 1994: 31).

Incorporating East German physicians.
The East German system was similar to other communist countries, with 626 polyclinics and 539 hospitals as the primary delivery system for 17 million people. The average GP salary was $18,280 for a 33-hour week, with a $3,000 bonus for staying in the country—far lower compensation than the average in the West. Most polyclinics and hospitals were overstaffed, often with former communists who were political appointees and not well qualified to practice. Reorganization of the polyclinic system resulted in loss of many positions for physicians. For example, in Berlin alone, an estimated 350 jobs were eliminated in the 1989–1991 period, with a cut of 2,500 more positions anticipated (Morris, 1991: 1619; Jones, 1993: 61).

The process of incorporating East German physicians into the private practitioner system of West Germany has been difficult. They were public employees in a highly socialized communist system and had no experience with private practice. Many had little interest in becoming private medical entrepreneurs, even though they were aware that physicians in West Germany have been much more highly compensated and specialized.

Nurses

Germany has a severe shortage of nurses, although considerable growth since 1960 increased numbers by 2.5 times by 1990 (physician numbers grew 4 times in the same period). Most are trained in hospital-based programs lasting 3 years, but very few receive university degrees. As in other countries, nurses have considerably lower pay and status than physicians (Kirchgassler, 1990: 254; Iglehart, 1991b: 183).

Health care traditions in Germany and other parts of Europe have not been particularly supportive of professional nursing. Early nurses were largely nuns. More recently, the profession was largely the domain of lower-class women willing to work for very low pay and with little professional status. They have always worked under the direction of physicians who retained the power and influence. Relatively few have graduate degrees or graduate training. Progress has certainly been made, but nursing as a profession has a long way to go to achieve the stature appropriate to the crucial role played in the health care system (Roemer, 1993: 20).

Pharmacists and Pharmaceuticals

The German pharmaceutical industry ranks first in exports among the nations of the world, with roughly 50 percent of all production sold outside the country. Approximately 19 percent of sickness-fund expenditures are for drugs and medical appliances, much higher than in most other countries. Physicians have the reputation of prescribing an average of 11 medicines per year for each patient, roughly three times the U.S. average. Surveys indicate that 60 percent of these prescriptions are at the request of patients. Furthermore, drugs have traditionally been very costly in Germany (Schulenburg, 1992: 92).

The 1989 Health Reform Act attempted to control costs by instituting a 15 percent co-payment on all prescriptions, while also creating incentives for use of generic drugs. A "blacklist" of inappropriate drugs was created. A Drug Transparency Commission was created to publish and distribute lists of comparative prices for drugs serving the same purpose. The medical associations and sickness funds were compelled to negotiate an annual overall ceiling on pharmaceutical expenditures (Schulenburg, 1992: 93).

The 1993 reforms went considerably further, in part because the 1989 rules were insufficient to control increases in costs. A pharmaceutical budget was introduced for ambulatory care physicians (general practitioners, general internists, and pediatricians)—who prescribe 80 percent of drugs for patients in sickness funds. A drug formulary was compiled of about 300 drugs. The new law was quite effective in cutting the number and costs of prescriptions (Kochen, Sandholzer, and Himmel, 1994: 400).

Midlevel Practitioners and Alternative Healing

In part because of the physician surplus and general shortage of nurses, midlevel practitioners have not been particularly encouraged. In fact, widespread use of midwives in East Germany before reunification has now been severely diminished. They had formerly visited homes of pregnant women and provided ongoing care. More recently, pregnant women have been *required* to secure care from physicians if sickness funds are to reimburse. Midwives work largely in support of physician-supervised hospital births and are replacing other nurses. Reimbursement from sickness funds for home delivery is allowed but at a relatively low rate (Davies, 1994: 199).

The "natural health" movement is relatively strong. An estimated 30 to 40 percent of patients consult homeopaths, naturopaths, and hydrotherapists and other natural healers. The use of nonbiomedical practitioners is generally acceptable as a complement to biomedicine (Freund and McGuire, 1995: 182).

Hospitals

More hospital beds are available per capita than in any other advanced industrial countries (11 beds per 1,000 people), except Japan and France. Many are in spa-type facilities offering physiotherapy, massage, and water and mud applications (15 percent of the total). Roughly one-third are publicly owned by cities, counties, or states. Another one-third are private nonprofit, usually operated by charitable institutions or churches. The remaining one-third are proprietary businesses operated for profit. The for-profit hospitals do not employ physicians directly, but instead use private practice physicians and are paid on a fee-for-service per diem basis. Approximately 50 percent of all hospital *beds* are public, because these tend to be the larger institutions. Thirty-five percent of beds are in nonprofit institutions, and only 16 percent are operated for profit (Organization for Economic Cooperation and Development, 1992: 61; Henke et al., 1994: 257).

Hospitals are represented in policy making by hospital associations, but bargain individually with sickness funds for operating costs. They negotiate with the state health care authorities for capital improvement and equipment costs. Accreditation is required for all hospitals (Schicke, 1988: 297).

Hospitals are largely regulated at the state or local government level. National planning efforts during the 1980s attempted to ensure equitable distribution of hospital facilities, while establishing regional balance. Diminishing the bed supply is thus difficult because of state-level efforts to maintain control in the face of federal government cost-cutting measures (Schicke, 1988: 397; Iglehart, 1991b; Schulenburg, 1992: 90).

Institutions are classified into nine categories based on their degree of specialization. University hospitals are usually in Category 1, with the broadest range of specialty services. Smaller rural hospitals with minimal specialty offerings are generally in Category 9.

The average length of stay is considerably greater than in many other countries (12.9 days in 1990). However, the number of employees per occupied bed (1.4) is considerably less than average. The occupancy rate in 1990 for larger public hospitals (400 beds) was 82 percent (Weil, 1994: 27).

The sharp differentiation between office and hospital physician practices means that the ambulatory care physician has traditionally referred patients needing hospitalization. Diagnostic findings have usually not been transmitted, thus requiring the hospital to repeat many of the same tests. This practice has begun to change in the early 1990s as incentives are introduced to decrease length of stay and diminish costs (Schulenburg, 1992: 90; Weil, 1994: 26).

As noted earlier, the sharp separation of hospital and outpatient services sometimes interferes with optimal patient care. Postoperative care needed for short-term minimally invasive surgery could be handled by ambulatory care physicians at lower cost. Current rules make this difficult, causing unnecessary hospital stays (Keuchel and Beske, 1993: 63).

Medical technology. Hospitals have been somewhat slow to adopt advanced technologies such as minimally invasive surgery (endoscopic appendectomies, for example). Equipment for such procedures is relatively expensive and both hospital owners and state authorities responsible for capital investment are reluctant to pay the costs—although many of the new procedures are both more cost-effective and more beneficial to patients than previous practices. Sickness funds are also hesitant to pay startup costs, and hospitals hesitate to invest in training of needed specialist personnel. The hospital financing

system thus appears to be something of a barrier to use of advanced technology (Keuchel and Beske, 1993: 50).

Furthermore, recent cost cutting has diminished access to some of the more expensive equipment. For example, the average 400-bed public or private nonprofit hospital is likely to have a CT Scanner, but probably not an MRI machine, a cardiac catheterization unit, an open-heart surgery facility, or a radiation therapy facility. These types of equipment are generally limited to university medical centers and teaching hospitals (Weil, 1994: 27).

Health Information Systems

Health information systems are evolving rapidly to include networks that provide patient information, general information, research data, education, and management information. The goal is to provide clinicians and administrators with desktop computer access to all needed information and data. For example, the university hospital in Gieben has 500 clinical workstations connected to a network, with 1,000 clinical users. The network includes a complete drug information system, a Medline library database, and an internal information system that replaces much of the paperwork. This type of system is not yet available throughout the country, but is being rapidly disseminated as the need for efficient information systems becomes more obvious (Prokosch et al., 1994: 115–119).

Emergency Medical Care

Only a few large hospitals have separate emergency departments. Emergency cases are handled instead in regular wards by the specialists most conversant with the patient's problems (Sefrin and Weidringer, 1991: 248).

Emergency medical services have a long history in Germany, with records of active Red Cross rescue services dating to 1863. The more modern system dates from the post–World War II era when local fire brigades were commissioned to undertake the responsibility. In the mid-1950s rolling clinics, or "Clinomobiles," were developed for treating accident victims. After 1967, these vehicles were replaced by smaller standardized ambulances supported by physicians, nurses, and ambulance specialists. During the 1970s, a regional system of rescue headquarters was established to focus more on provision of high-quality care from time of discovery to hospital entry. This arrangement serves as the basic infrastructure for the current system (Sefrin and Weidringer, 1991: 246–247).

Helicopter services are available in 90 percent of the country from 37 bases (prior to incorporation of East Germany). Surface ambulances cover the remaining areas. All emergency units are directly associated with trauma centers. The crew of an air ambulance with a physician member (usually a resident in training) is prepared to undertake initial evaluation, offer life-saving intervention, provide on-scene triage, and begin resuscitation if needed. Largely because of greater training and speedier transport, survival rate from air ambulance service is usually higher than with ground transportation (Schmidt et al., 1992: 548).

A much greater emphasis is given to having physicians on the scene of accidents than in most other countries, which may be a function in part of the physician surplus. EMTs have had relatively low status and were not until recently viewed as professional members of the health care team. The position of rescue assistant was created in 1989 to increase professionalization with a requirement of 2 years training. Special training for emergency physicians was also upgraded to a 1-year clinical residency requirement. Studies of emergency outcomes suggest strongly that the involvement of specially trained physicians and other personnel achieves very good survival rates (Arnold, 1988: 6; Sefrin and Weidringer, 1991: 247).

Long-Term Care

A sharp distinction is drawn between "health insurance" and "social welfare" services, with long-term care considered largely in the latter category. However, the scope of sickness funds has been extended partially to long-term care. The growth of resources has not been great enough to meet demand even though nursing homes are used primarily for the care of very frail older people (Iglehart, 1991b: 183).

Sickness funds have covered home health care for nonwelfare elderly only in conjunction with medical treatment. This was liberalized somewhat beginning in 1991, although guidelines for home care remain restrictive. Low-income individuals may receive home care services—such as nursing, home help, and homemaking—only if they can pass a strict means test. If one does not qualify for social welfare services, most of home care must usually be paid for by the elderly or their families. Families are considered to have the primary responsibility for providing care (Jamieson, 1992: 892).

Rehabilitation Services

A special emphasis is given to rehabilitation of injured or impaired workers. Medical assistance, preventive care, and income support (at 65 to 90 percent of previous pay) is provided while individuals undergo vocational training in preparation for appropriate new work (Burkhauser and Hirvonen, 1989: 173–176).

Mental Health Care

Progress in mental health care has been moving forward in West Germany since the 1970s. Until then most inpatient care was provided by large state mental hospitals. Few psychiatrists were available for ambulatory care. The situation was even worse in East Germany where the only care available was through polyclinics and in poorly financed and inadequately staffed long-term-care hospitals. Therapy was almost nonexistent (Rossler and Salize, 1994: 112).

A community-based system of outpatient care has been developing slowly. Sickness funds and other forms of insurance have begun paying for more psychiatric care and psychotherapy. The number of psychiatrists in office practices has risen considerably, as have the number of psychologists. By 1992, the ratio had grown to 1 therapist per 10,000 people. All western states have public social-psychiatric services, with social workers, psychiatric nurses, psychologists, and psychiatrists on staff. Their purpose is to assess patient needs and arrange assistance to treat any discovered conditions. Support is sometimes provided to families if needed. Social support networks are arranged. Training is offered to patients on skills for independent living. However, these services have not solved the problems of the chronically mentally ill who do not have the capacity for working and living independently. Most have continued to require residence in some form of institutional setting (Rossler and Salize, 1994: 115).

It is difficult to gain access to statistics on mental health because data collection is up to each German state. The methods of record keeping vary widely. Few statistics were available for the eastern states prior to unification, although a new system based on West German standards is under development (1994). Nonetheless, some estimates are possible based on data recently published by the German parliament and a committee of expert observers (Rossler and Salize, 1994: 113).

The number of long-term-care mental illness beds has been declining, whereas the number of beds in psychiatric departments of general and university hospitals has increased, to about 12 percent of all mental illness beds in 1990. These hospitals have also begun offering outpatient care. However, the proportion of patients served on this basis varies greatly between states, and large numbers of patients remain in long-term-care hospitals (Rossler and Salize, 1994: 113).

Most of the older and poorly equipped or serviced long-term-care hospitals continue to operate in the eastern states. Psychiatric departments have been initiated or are planned for general and university hospitals. Psychiatrists have initiated office practices, but the diffusion of other services has yet to reach western state standards. Sheltered homes or training workshops were unknown before unification and are slowly developing. Mental health care has continued to receive lower priority than improvement of the general health care system (Rossler and Salize, 1994: 116).

Despite evidence of progress, resources for mental health diagnosis and treatment remain limited, particularly for severe situations. Many mental health patients are on welfare (estimated at 43 percent) or are dependent on families (estimated at 20 percent). Funds for rehabilitation and training of mental patients remain severely limited (Rossler and Salize, 1994: 117).

ECONOMIC CHARACTERISTICS AND ISSUES

Roughly 8.7 percent of GDP was devoted to health care in 1994, down from 9 percent in 1988. Per capita costs were $1,775. The slight decrease from 1988 was a consequence in part of new and tighter cost-containment measures initiated in 1989, 1992, and 1993. As noted earlier, the 1989 law explicitly limits the growth of health care costs to the rate of wage increase—making Germany the first country to formally define the fraction of income to be spent for health care. The latest changes are a response in part to a growth rate of 10.9 percent in expenditures in 1991, compared to an income growth of only 4 percent, leading to a $5.5 billion deficit in 1992. Without further cuts, the projected deficit would have been $6.6 billion for 1993 (Muller, 1994: 1659; Weil, 1994: 25).

Benefits

Approximately 32 percent of sickness-fund expenditures went for hospital costs, 18 percent for ambulatory care, 16 percent for purchase of prescription drugs, 6 percent for purchase of medical appliances, 10 percent for dental care, 4 percent for preventive measures including spas, 2 percent for maternity benefits, and 1 percent for funeral benefits in 1990. In addition, 5 percent is spent for administration and 16 percent for offsetting income loss during illness (Iglehart, 1991a).

Benefits include cash payments for maternity leave (6 weeks before delivery and 8 weeks after). Women receive an amount equal to their current income—up to a fixed amount per day. People unable to work receive cash payments from their employer equal to current salary, for 6 weeks. The sickness fund will then pay 80 percent of salary for up to 78 weeks, at which time a disability or welfare pension begins (Henke et al., 1994: 255).

Financing

Health care is financed through a combination of local, state, and federal taxes (21 percent), payroll taxes (60 percent), co-payments and out-of-pocket costs (11 percent), and private insurance (7 percent). Workers and employers contribute equally to sickness funds through payroll deductions of a fixed proportion of gross income, one-half paid by the employer and the other half by the employee. The average was 13.4 percent for 1993. The deduction is calculated annually by each sickness fund and varies from 8.5 to 16.6 percent of gross employee earnings (Muller, 1994: 1658).

The net amount of the payroll deduction, as a proportion of income, is independent of the health status of the individual but increases with salary level. Sickness funds thus significantly redistribute income from the better-paid to the less well-paid. Employed individuals help pay the costs for the unemployed and retired. Single individuals and childless couples help pay for larger families. Males help pay for lower-paid or not-employed women (Iglehart, 1991a: 506; Graig, 1993: 89; Henke et al., 1994: 255).

Table 6-2 summarizes the types of insurance funds, membership, and proportion of the population served.

Primary funds include local and industrial groupings. About 46 percent of the population is covered by local funds serving specific geographic areas (working collaboratively through an organization referred to as the AOK, or Allgemeine Ortskrankenkassen). Industrial funds are generally formed by large employers (more than 450 employees) who sponsor a sickness fund for their employees; these account for about 11 percent of the population. Such "funds" have a distinct cost advantage over the local or regional funds because of a lower average employee health risk (Schneider, 1991: 87).

Roughly 9 percent of the population is covered by guild funds, agricultural funds, a seaman's fund, and a miners fund. Another 34 percent of the population is served by 15 "substitute" funds. These special funds are a matter of choice for those who qualify, such as the more highly educated professionals. The differential in cost has encouraged such people to opt out of higher-cost local funds in favor of these lower-cost "substitute" funds. Most blue-collar workers do not have a choice but are simply assigned to the fund related to their workplace (Henke et al., 1994: 253; Cockerham, 1995: 304).

Roughly 84 percent of all sickness-fund members and family dependents must belong to one of the primary or substitute funds because their incomes are not high enough to allow for a private insurance alternative. Children are covered until age 18, or age 25 if students. Beyond age 25, even students must contribute to the fund at a rate of $42 per month (in 1993). Spouses are covered by the husband's membership if they earn less than a designated income.

Recent changes. Sickness funds now compete against one another for members. However, various restrictions limit the competition because the primary funds must include individuals who do not qualify for industrial or lower-cost substitute funds. Sub-

Table 6-2   Types of Sickness Funds and Membership (1992)

Type of Fund	Number of Funds	Number of Members (thousands)	Percentage of Total Members
Primary funds			
Local	272	23,416	46
Industrial	829	5,470	11
Craft	179	2,575	5
Miners	1	1,296	2.5
Sailors	1	56	.1
Agricultural	21	708	1.4
Substitute			
White-Collar	7	16,680	32
Blue-Collar	8	821	2
Total	1,318	51,022	100

Source: Based on data from Henke et al., 1994: 254.

stitute funds have encouraged membership from lower-risk and higher-income groups, resulting in lower costs. Individuals with lower incomes (often blue-collar workers) and higher risk tend to pay higher payroll deductions than higher-income and lower-risk individuals (often white-collar workers). Funds serving higher-income individuals often pay higher payment rates to physicians and hospitals as an incentive for better-quality service (Henke et al., 1994: 260).

The 1993 Health Care Reform Act attempted to remove the inequities in this situation by increasing the choice (as of 1996) of all consumers to select the substitute fund they deem to be the best value. The other funds have the option of opening their membership beyond the traditional clientele or geographic groupings. In addition, a risk-equalization provision was implemented in 1994 mandating that low-risk and high-income funds subsidize the higher-risk and lower-income funds. If individual funds are able to keep their costs below the country-wide average, they can keep the surplus—creating an incentive for greater efficiency and tighter management (Henke et al., 1994: 260).

Private insurance. Individuals with an income greater than $3,253 per month (1993) have the option to buy private insur-

ance. About 16 percent of the population have sufficiently high incomes to choose this option, but half of these (8 percent) have opted to belong to a sickness fund instead. Married couples and families would have to pay higher premiums for private insurance than via the sickness funds. Single people with higher incomes pay less for private insurance (Schneider, 1991: 87; Henke et al., 1994: 254).

Private insurance usually includes the same benefits as the sickness funds, but often with additional amenities (such as private hospital rooms). Higher payments are allowed for physicians and hospitals than fees negotiated by sickness funds. The total costs for hospital care, including physician services, are roughly twice as high for private patients as for sickness-fund members. Families with sufficient income to purchase private insurance have the disadvantage of being excluded from later joining a lower-cost sickness fund (Schneider, 1991: 99).

Civil servants were treated somewhat differently than private employees until 1992. Those below a certain pay level were covered by sickness funds, with the full cost paid by the government. Others at high pay levels could opt for supplemental private insurance by paying the premium themselves—which many did. They submitted medical bills to their employer for 50 to 70 percent reimbursement and submitted the balance to their private insurance provider. Since the 1992 reform, self-employed people and civil servants who were not already enrolled in sickness funds must purchase private insurance (Schneider, 1991: 98; Henke et al., 1994: 254).

Private insurance and individual out-of-pocket expenditures accounted for about 25 percent of health spending in 1990. Many families enrolled in sickness funds have recently also purchased supplemental private insurance to increase benefits beyond the more restricted basic package approved in 1989. The numbers of people with private insurance have increased steadily since the mid-1970s. A higher inflation rate for private care (3.8 percent) than for sickness-fund reimbursements (2.3 percent) has made co-payments increase substantially. The lower increases for the sickness funds were largely due to caps on expenditures for physician services (Schneider, 1991: 99).

Extra private insurance benefits can include private rooms for hospitalization, medical coverage during overseas travel, and coverage for dentistry and vision care. Hospitals deliberately differentiate between sickness-fund members and the privately insured. Three "classes" are available. Sickness-fund accommodation is in the third class (three to six beds per room). By paying an extra $100 per month, it is possible to secure access to a semiprivate (second class) hospital room. For an additional $100 per month, first-class treatment by the hospital chief of staff and a daily financial allowance are provided (Greiner, 1992: 108).

The private insurance option is viewed critically by many Germans as a lower-cost alternative for single and higher-income individuals. It has the effect of diminishing funds available to support the larger health system for the less affluent, while decreasing the average cost to the more affluent citizens (Iglehart, 1991a: 506–507; 1991b: 179; Graig, 1993: 95).

Provisions for the unemployed and elderly. Unemployed workers remain in the sickness fund to which they belonged when employed. Their premiums are paid by the Federal Labor Administration or by local welfare agency. Premiums of retired workers are paid by their pension or social security fund at a level equivalent to worker contributions. Health care costs of older retired workers are of course considerably higher than the average. Premiums paid on behalf of retirees covered about 40 percent of costs in 1989. The balance comes from contributions of active workers as a subsidy for elderly health care (Graig, 1993: 95).

Paying Physicians

The mode of paying physicians is among the more interesting features of the German system. As noted earlier, ambulatory care practitioners work strictly on a fee-for-service basis whereas hospital-based physicians work strictly on a salaried basis (unless they are Chiefs of Service). Funds to pay hospital physicians come from the negotiated per diem schedules charged to the sickness funds by hospitals, whereas ambulatory care physicians receive their fees via physician organizations that secure resources from sickness funds. Hospital salaries are based on seniority and specialty. The physician component of sickness-fund expenditures accounted for 18 percent of the total in 1994 (Graig, 1993: 97; Henke et al., 1994: 260).

Sickness-fund and private insurance payments to physicians are governed by the Uniform Evaluation Standard (EBM) initiated in 1991. The EBM defines the schedule of charges and their relative "point" value. The schedule is updated regularly by a committee of seven physicians and seven representatives from sickness funds. Changes are made based on a majority vote. In the event of a tie, five members from each group are assigned to help settle the problem. Private insurance generally gives higher value to each point in the schedule than do sickness funds (Henke et al., 1994: 256).

Ambulatory care physicians submit a list of all patient treatments to their regional physician association every 3 months. The association calculates the amount earned and reimburses each physician accordingly. Patients pay nothing directly to the physician, and in most instances, do not learn what their treatment actually costs. One advantage of private insurance patients is the higher physician fee schedule, often twice as much as sickness-fund rates for the same service (Graig, 1993: 98).

Ambulatory care physicians have been subject to tighter national cost controls than hospital physicians, in part because states control hospitals and have protected their right to manage physician expenses. An expenditure cap was the primary control mechanism until the EBM system was initiated. Global budgets are negotiated for all ambulatory physician costs regardless of services rendered. Because payment is per unit of service, the caps have led to competition between physicians to provide more services as a way of securing a higher total compensation. Physician fees per unit of service were controlled, but the volume of services was not. Physicians continue to be relatively well compensated compared to other European countries (Schicke, 1988: 396; Henke et al., 1994: 256).

Physicians make roughly 3.5 times the average wage of an industrial worker, down from 6 times in 1970. However, considerable variation in compensation across physician specialties is evident. For example, radiologists make more than double the pay of generalist primary care physicians, and laboratory physicians make four times as much (Iglehart, 1991b: 181).

The 1993 reforms provide greater incentives for outpatient surgery and preventive care. Although overall expenditures are allowed to grow only as much as the growth in national income, an additional expenditure of 10 percent is allowed for outpatient surgery and an additional 6 percent is allowed for preventive care. In the eastern states, where costs were considerably lower, growth at a greater rate was allowed to encourage movement toward the western states average (Henke et al., 1994: 261).

Payment for Pharmaceuticals

Maximum reference prices for pharmaceuticals were established on a nationwide basis in 1989. A commission representing physicians and sickness funds (but not pharmaceutical companies) sets the rates. Manufacturers establish their price at or below this cap. Wholesalers are allowed a markup prior to retail or hospital pharmacy distribution. The government requires uniform retail prices throughout the country. The reference pricing system requires that sickness funds reimburse only at the rate established, usually the price of the generic product. If the retail pharmacist charges a higher price for a brand name drug, it must be absorbed by the consumer. Co-payments of 15 percent up to a maximum of $9 were required in the 1992 reforms, but were later changed to flat charges ranging from $1.80 to $4.00 depending on the total price of the drug (Henke et al., 1994: 258).

The 1993 reforms reduced prices by 5 percent for any drugs not under the reference pricing system; another 2 percent reduction was imposed for 1994. Additional monitoring of physician prescribing patterns was introduced to decrease overprescribing. Physicians promptly began to change their prescribing behavior so that very significant cost-saving effects were noticeable almost immediately. The potential negative or positive results for patients have not yet been determined (Henke et al., 1994: 262; Pfaff, 1994: 31).

Paying Hospitals

Hospitals are financed via two primary sources:

1. Current operating costs are paid by sickness funds or private insurance, based on per diem rates or special fees for high-cost procedures.
2. Capital costs are paid by states for construction and purchase of durable equipment.

Operating costs. Each hospital negotiates separately with the appropriate sickness fund. The per diem rates per patient were earlier intended to cover all operating costs regardless of the numbers of patients, length of stay, or cost of a particular illness. This was changed as part of the recent reforms so that justified high-cost procedures can be priced separately. Special per diem rates can also be negotiated for patients with expensive problems such as chronic illness, mental illness, neonatal care for infants, and burn victims. Cost-per-case payments are negotiated for very high-cost procedures such as organ transplants and other major surgical procedures. The total projected payments then become the basis for a "global" or annual budget. Substantial differences exist between hospitals in reimbursement rates because of historical variations in operating costs and specialized services (Schulenburg, 1992: 90; Graig, 1993: 98; Henke et al., 1994: 257).

Accurate estimation of costs for procedures is difficult because of inadequate measurement techniques for each hospital department and procedure. Efforts to increase efficiency through payment incentives are also a problem because there is often intense internal competition for resources between departments and physicians. The reimbursement system is thus somewhat antagonistic and makes planning for institutional growth and introduction of advanced technology difficult (Henke et al., 1994: 258).

The 1993 reforms began to remove the sharp distinction between ambulatory and hospital care. Hospitals are now allowed to do outpatient surgery in competition with ambulatory physicians. The intent is to increase efficiency by avoiding some of the overlap in services and equipment while also shortening hospital stays. After 1996, global budgets are to be replaced with prospective payments for defined groups of cases or services. Risk is to be shifted to the individual hospitals as an incentive to increase efficiency (Henke et al., 1994: 261).

Capital costs. A state health care planning process serves as the mechanism for allocation of funds for capital construction and equipment because states have primary authority over hospital capacity and technology. The federal government is providing additional financial incentives for the modernization of hospitals in the eastern states. The capital funding procedure has served to limit diffusion of technology when technological advances might have beneficial effects in terms of both patient care and more efficient services (Iglehart, 1991b: 180).

Administrative Costs

Estimates indicate that administrative costs to sickness funds are about 6.5 percent of total expenditures—which include administering payments to hospitals and providers, as well as regulatory and monitoring activities. Regional physicians associations spend about 2.5 percent of their revenues for administration of payments to physicians, monitoring, and regulatory functions (Roy, 1993: 1390).

PROBLEMS AND REFORMS

Dramatic cost increases for physician and hospital care occurred after 1970. Payments by sickness funds per member rose by five times between 1970 and 1990, from $518 to $2,350. Hospital costs rose most dramatically, from 25 to 35 percent of total health care expenditures. Pharmaceutical costs also rose substantially to 16.5 percent of total costs—despite efforts to limit physician prescriptions. Physician payments dropped from 23 to 18 percent of the total (Sewering, 1992: 14).

Although self-regulatory activities played a role in cost containment, they were not adequate. A "relative value scale" established in 1977 for some 2,000 medical treatments was insufficient for limiting cost increases (Schneider, 1991: 87–92; Graig, 1993: 103).

A further major effort in 1986 established overall expenditure "caps" for physicians (as compared to the expenditure "targets" in 1977—which were generally not met). When the cap was exceeded, the point value for medical procedures by ambulatory physicians was reduced. The intent was to prevent physicians from increasing the volume of their services to increase their incomes (Graig, 1993: 104).

Another major reform was enacted in 1988, becoming effective at the beginning of 1989. It essentially ended earlier cost-containment measures and initiated an alternative system. The Act attempted to stabilize the rate of payroll deduction requirements for employers and employees through several procedures (Iglehart, 1991b: 180–182; Graig, 1993: 105):

- Patient cost sharing was increased for hospital stays (up from $3.50 per day to $7.00), spa visits, dental prostheses, pharmaceutical products, and death benefits.
- Committees were created to develop methods for reduction of unnecessary duplication of hospitals and medical equipment.
- A controversial pricing limit was imposed on pharmaceuticals, requiring that prices be no higher than comparable generic drugs. Co-payments up to 15 percent were initiated.
- Measures were taken to decrease hospitalization, in the form of increased access to screening for disease and additional benefits for home care.
- Reimbursements for medically related travel costs were reduced to emergencies only.
- New benefits for home health care were introduced as an alternative to more expensive nursing home care.
- Lump-sum birth grants were eliminated.
- Death benefits were reduced for current members and eliminated as a benefit for new members of sickness funds.

Physician income declined in real terms as a consequence of the cost controls imposed during the 1980s. Despite increases in patient contacts, as noted earlier the physician proportion of total health costs also declined—whereas hospital costs continued to increase. The intent was to decrease total health care costs by about 10 percent—a target that was not fully achieved (Graig, 1993: 105; Roy, 1993: 1392).

Cost Control in the 1990s

Other cost-control efforts were initiated in 1992 and expanded considerably in 1993, along with a call for shared sacrifice by patients and providers. Physician and pharmaceutical expenditures will be controlled by global budgeting of the health service system and by direct limits on physician entry into practice, monitoring their productivity, and quantity-related co-payments on drugs. Other more specific changes include (Schneider, 1991: 98; Graig, 1993: 107; Henke et al., 1994: 8; Weil, 1994: 27–28):

- Out-of-pocket payments for prescription drugs were increased based on the volume of drugs purchased (3 Deutsche Marks [DM] for small quantities, up to 7 DM for larger quantities). Prices of prescription drugs not yet controlled under the earlier reference pricing system were reduced by 5 percent (1994); over-the-counter drug prices were reduced by 2 percent. "Negative lists" are established for drugs that will not be reimbursed, such as cold and flu remedies, laxatives, and travel sickness remedies.
- Global fixed budgets for drugs were introduced, with significant sanctions for exceeding budget and price. Physicians who prescribe at levels 15 percent above the average will be monitored. Prescribing 25 percent above average will mean automatic income reductions unless proof of patient need is provided. The pharmaceutical industry is to help pay for drug cost overruns as are physicians through fee reductions.
- Co-payments for hospitalization were raised from 5 DM per calendar day to 10 DM (roughly $6.60 in 1993), with the payment going to the sickness fund. Patients treated in spa clinics or rehabilitation clinics pay 15 DM per day.
- Hospitals are now to be paid prospectively. "Patient Management Categories" (similar to DRGs in the U.S.) were introduced and applied to about 70 percent of hospital admissions. By 1996, hospital operating costs are to be paid by sickness funds based on the annual volume of treatments, surgeries, and discharges, rather than on the basis of patient days.
- Hospital-based physicians will be allowed to offer outpatient counseling and treatment to patients who may be, or have been, admitted to the hospital. Ambulatory community-based surgeons

will be able to perform outpatient surgery in hospitals. These measures begin to break down the distinction between hospital and ambulatory care physicians, while increasing integration of the two forms of practice.

- Ambulatory physicians making referrals are expected to take into account the cost-effectiveness of each of the available hospitals—based on a comparative price list.

- Physicians, dentists, and hospitals face further limitation on fee increases to a maximum of 3 percent per year (for 1993–1995). Dentists were brought under price controls for the first time. Growth in dental costs went from 9.2 percent in 1992 to 2.2 percent in 1993.

- Limitations on numbers of new physicians who can practice within the sickness-fund system were imposed by constraining entry to medical schools. By 1999, physicians over age 68 must retire.

- Sickness funds will be required to compete with each other for patients and on the basis of premium cost—beginning in 1997. Patients will be allowed to select their preferred fund on an annual basis. Each fund is required to accept all applicants, except those in specific major industries.

- Limits were placed on the ability of physicians and dentists to strike for higher fees. Sickness funds would be allowed to take over provision of care if a strike occurs.

Despite the adjustments in 1992, physician expenditures continued to exceed growth in worker wages by 2.1 percent. Similarly, hospital, pharmaceutical, and dental costs were above estimates. The global health care budget, based on average wage increases, was exceeded by $5.7 billion. The 1993 law therefore attempted to control the volume of services, as well as the price, for the first time (Henke et al., 1994: 11; Kirkman-Liff, 1994: 22; Weil, 1994: 24).

Cost control is the primary focus of these changes, rather than integration or improvement in services. Reduction of the excessive supply of medical specialists, constraints on acquisition and use of selected medical technologies, and reduction of visits to physicians are all mechanisms to achieve that end (Weil, 1994: 24).

The actions have reduced price inflation. Overall, Germany appears to have been more successful at controlling costs than any other industrialized country—especially for pharmaceuticals. Pharmaceutical companies have vigorously objected to the reforms, indicating that research and development are suffering. There is also strong concern that the policy will lead to lower-quality health care or rationing if legitimate cost increases actually surpass the allowed reimbursement levels (Schneider, 1991: 100; Roy, 1993: 1389).

Integration of East and West Germany

Although physician numbers and hospital beds per capita were roughly the same in East and West Germany, the characteristics and quality of each were very different. For example, a high proportion of physicians in East Germany did not see patients but were a part of the administration of the publicly owned and operated national health service. Most of the available public hospital beds in East Germany were in obsolete old structures and in a serious state of disrepair. A major effort is underway to bring hospitals in East Germany to the standards of West Germany, at great effort and cost (estimated at $20 billion). It will take time to make the transition to the same level of quality as in the West German system even though sickness funds were created in each of the 14 districts of east Germany as of January 1, 1991 (Schulenburg, 1992: 94; Graig, 1993: 107).

Fee schedules set at 45 percent below the West Germany level were established—to account for differences in wages and sickness-fund revenues. The plan is to adjust the levels upward as wages in East Germany rise to levels in West Germany. However, the lower fee schedules have tended to impede investments in ambulatory care and hospital facilities in East Germany (Schneider, 1991: 100).

Rationing Care

Expenditures on health care are effectively limited to the revenue produced from the payroll deductions, constraining growth in overall health care costs by setting priorities and "rationing" access to lower-priority technology and services for consumers. However, growth in expenditures does occur because incomes are rising (Henke et al., 1994: 258).

Reform of the Sickness Funds

The number of sickness funds may be greater than needed for highest efficiency. Administrative costs would be lowered if the number of funds were decreased from the current level. Inequity exists between members of different funds because of varying risk and different costs to consumers and employers. The introduction of competition between funds is intended to help alleviate these problems.

Care for the Retired and Elderly

German physicians are very dissatisfied with the services available to the frail elderly, particularly in comparison to U.S. or Canadian physicians. Only 15 percent of German physicians rate such services as good or excellent, compared to 44 percent in the United States and 36 percent in Canada (Blendon et al., 1993: 1014).

Expenditures for long-term care in nursing facilities and at home are the fastest growing segment of health care costs. This dimension of the health care system has had a lower priority than other reforms and thus represents a major continuing challenge (Schneider, 1991: 100).

Because the funds are financed on an annual pay-as-you-go basis, reserves are not available for the higher costs of retired older patients—who make up an increasing proportion of the population. Long-term care is currently not fully covered by sickness funds. Consideration is being given to adding this sickness-fund responsibility with funding to come from increases in the payroll tax. These changes would further spread the cost of health care for the aged over the entire population (Graig, 1993).

Differences Between Ambulatory and Hospital Inpatient Care

Unnecessary duplication of tests and procedures occurs when ambulatory physicians refer patients for hospital care and cannot transfer patient data acceptable to hospital physicians. The 1993 reforms began to address this issue, but more integration of the two systems may be appropriate for better patient treatment and greater efficiency (Graig, 1993: 108; Henke et al., 1994).

Health Services Research

Germany has not placed as much emphasis on health services research as the United States, Sweden, The Netherlands, and some other advanced countries. Details on operation and outcomes of health care therefore are not readily available (Sullivan, 1992: 155).

SUMMARY AND CONCLUSIONS

Universal health care in Germany has a long and distinguished tradition. Despite major organizational adjustments, and limitations on expenditures in the last decade, the basic foundation remains firm. All citizens are guaranteed health care with relatively little out-of-pocket cost at the point of service. Health care is financed largely through payroll deductions, with equal contributions by employers and employees. Nonemployed individuals are subsidized by government allocations and/or contributions from sickness funds.

The sickness-fund system for financing and managing health care in collaboration with providers and government remains a durable and reasonably efficient form of organization. Nonetheless, inequities exist between sickness funds. Merging or integrating the funds may help make them more equitable and manageable. The more affluent members of the population who are not required to join sickness funds clearly have an advantage in range of benefits and (for younger people) cost through private insurance. Their required membership in sickness funds would increase revenue and public resources for services to the less affluent population.

Germany will be faced with increasing challenges in providing health services based on payroll deductions. The workforce is declining as a proportion of the total population, whereas the retired and older population is growing rapidly. The payroll tax funding of sickness funds may have to be changed to accommodate demographic changes.

It seems clear that providers at all levels, in ambulatory, secondary, and tertiary care, will have fewer resources available. Incomes of physicians have been squeezed substantially already, and hospitals have been forced to diminish inpatient services to accommodate global budgeting based on greater accountability. The pharmaceutical industry has been subjected to price limitations.

The German experience contains lessons that will be widely observed and assessed, as other nations search for effective tools to solve their own problems. We can observe a clear example of (1) effective cost-saving changes and (2) a system with new organizational approaches that may facilitate ongoing high-quality health care.

REFERENCES

ARNOLD, NORBERT (1988). We'll Call Your Roy! A German Perspective on EMS in the United States, *Journal of Emergency Medical Services*, 13 (4): 6–7.

BLENDON, ROBERT J., KAREN DONELAN, ROBERT LEITMAN, ARNOLD EPSTEIN, JOEL CANTOR, ALAN COHEN, IAN MORRISON, THOMAS MOLONEY, CHRISTIAN KOECK, and SAMUEL LEVITT (1993). Physician Perspectives on Caring for Patients in the United States, Canada and West Germany, *New England Journal of Medicine*, 328 (14): 1011–1016.

BURKHAUSER, RICHARD V., and PETRI HIRVONEN (1989). United States Disability Policy in a Time of Economic Crisis: A Comparison with Sweden and the Federal Republic of Germany, *The Milbank Quarterly*, 67 (Supp. 2, Pt. 2): 166–194.

COCKERHAM, WILLIAM C. (1995). *Medical Sociology*, 6th ed. Englewood Cliffs, N.J.: Prentice Hall.

DAVIES, BARBARA J. (1994). Germany: Healing the Wounds, *Midwives Chronicle*, 107 (May): 198–201.

FREUND, PETER E. S., and MEREDITH B. MCGUIRE (1995). *Health, Illness, and the Social Body*, 2nd ed. Englewood Cliffs, N.J.: Prentice Hall.

GRAIG, LAURENE A. (1993). *Health of Nations: An International Perspective on U.S. Health Care Reform*. Washington, D.C.: Congressional Quarterly.

GREINER, ANGELA (1992). German Health Care: A Patient's Perspective, in Marilynn M. Rosenthal and Marcel Frenkel (eds.), *Health Care Systems and Their Patients: An International Perspective*. Boulder, Col.: Westview Press, pp. 105–109.

HENKE, KLAUS-DIRK, CLAUDIA ADE, and MARGARET A. MURRAY (1994). The German Health Care System: Structure and Changes, *Journal of Clinical Anesthesiology*, 6 (3): 252–262.

HENKE, KLAUS-DIRK, MARGARET A. MURRAY, and CLAUDIA ADE (1994). Global Budgeting in Germany: Lessons for the United States, *Health Affairs (Millwood)*, 13 (4): 7–21.

IGLEHART, JOHN K. (1991a). Germany's Health Care System, Part One, *New England Journal of Medicine*, 324 (7): 503–508.

IGLEHART, JOHN K. (1991b). Germany's Health Care System: Part Two, *New England Journal of Medicine*, 324 (24): 1750–1756.

JAMIESON, ANNE (1992). Home Care in Old Age: A Lost Cause?, *Journal of Health Politics, Policy and Law*, 17 (4): 879–898.

JONES, FREDERIC G. (1993). Study Tour Examines Health Care Systems in Germany, Holland—Part II: The German System, *Physician Executive*, 19 (5): 58–62.

KEUCHEL, LEO, and FRITZ BESKE (1993). Minimally Invasive Surgery in the Federal Republic of Germany, *Health Policy*, 23: 49–65.

KIRCHGASSLER, K.-U. (1990). Health and Social Inequities in the Federal Republic of Germany, *Social Science and Medicine*, 31 (3): 249–256.

KIRKMAN-LIFF, BRADFORD L. (1994). Management Without Frontiers: Health System Convergence Leads to Health Care Management Convergence, *Frontiers of Health Services Management*, 11 (1): 3–48.

KOCHEN, M., H. SANDHOLZER, and W. HIMMEL (1994). Attitudes of Primary Care Physicians Towards the Use of a Drug Formulary—Preliminary Results of a Study in Germany, *Clinical Pharmacology and Therapeutics*, 32 (8): 400–402.

LIGHT, DONALD W. (1986). State, Profession, and Political Values, in Donald Light and Alexander Schuller (eds.), *Political Values and Health Care: The German Experience*. Cambridge, Mass.: The MIT Press, pp. 1–23.

MORRIS, NAOMI (1991). Canada's Medical Manpower Problems Pale in Comparison with Germany's, *Canadian Medical Association Journal*, 145 (12): 1618–1619.

MULLER, BERNARD (1994). Laboratory Diagnostics in Light of Massive Changes in Official Health Policies, *Clinical Chemistry*, 40 (8): 1658–1667.

ORGANIZATION FOR ECONOMIC COOPERATION AND DEVELOPMENT (1992). *The Reform of Health Care: A Comparative Analysis of Seven Countries.* Paris: OECD.

PAYER, LYNN (1988). *Medicine and Culture: Varieties of Treatment in the United States, England, West Germany, and France.* New York: Henry Holt.

PETERS, TOM (1991). Medicine and Management—So Much for "Science," *Healthcare Forum Journal,* (May/June): 43–46.

PFAFF, MARTIN (1994). German Reform: A Model for the U.S. (A Reply to Thomas Weil), *Health Progress,* 75 (7): 30–31.

PROKOSCH, H. U., B. PUHLE, M. MULLER, R. WAGNER, G. JUNGHANS, K. MARQUARDT, and J. DUDECK (1994). From HIS to IAIMS: Expanding the Scope of Information Processing Applications in a German University Hospital, *Computer Applications to Medical Care* (Annual Supp.): 115–119.

REINHARDT, UWE E. (1994). Germany's Health Care Systems: It's Not the American Way, *Health Affairs* (Fall): 22–24.

ROEMER, MILTON I. (1991). *National Health Systems of the World: The Countries,* Vol. I. New York: Oxford University Press.

ROEMER, MILTON I. (1993). *National Health Systems of the World: The Issues,* Vol. II. New York: Oxford University Press.

ROSENTHAL, MARILYNN M., and MARCEL FRENKEL (eds.) (1992). *Health Care Systems and Their Patients: An International Perspective.* Boulder, Col.: Westview Press.

ROSSLER, W., and H. J. SALIZE (1994). Longitudinal Statistics of Mental Health Care in Germany, *Social Psychiatry and Psychiatric Epidemiology,* 29 (3): 112–118.

ROY, MICHAEL J. (1993). The German Health Care System: Model or Mirage? *Southern Medical Journal,* 86 (12): 1389–1394.

SCHICKE, R. K. (1988). Trends in the Diffusion of Selected Medical Technology in the Federal Republic of Germany, *International Journal of Technology Assessment in Health Care,* 4: 395–405.

SCHMIDT, ULF, SCOTT B. FRAME, MICHAEL L. NERLICH, DENNIS W. ROWE, BLAINE L. ENDERSON, KIMBALL I. MAULL, and HARALD TSCHERNE (1992). On-Scene Helicopter Transport of Patients with Multiple Injuries—Comparison of a German and an American System, *Journal of Trauma,* 33 (4): 548–555.

SCHNEIDER, MARKUS (1991). Health Care Cost Containment in the Federal Republic of Germany, *Health Care Financing Review,* 12 (3): 87–101.

SCHULENBURG, J. MATTHIAS GRAF v.d. (1992). The German Health Care System: Concurrent Solidarity, Freedom of Choice, and Cost Control, in Marilynn M. Rosenthal and Marcel Frenkel (eds.), *Health Care Systems and Their Patients: An International Perspective.* Boulder, Col.: Westview Press, pp. 83–103.

SEFRIN, PETER, and JOHANN W. WEIDRINGER (1991). History of Emergency Medicine in Germany, *Journal of Clinical Anesthesiology,* 3 (13): 245–248.

SEWERING, H. J. (1992). Cost Control: Germany's Objective, *The Internist* (July/August): 13–14.

SHANNON, GARY W., and MALCOLM P. CUTCHIN (1994). General Practitioner Distribution and Population Dynamics: Munich, 1950–1990, *Social Science and Medicine,* 39 (1): 23–38.

SULLIVAN, ROBERT B. (1992). Introduction, in David A. Kindig and Robert B. Sullivan (eds.), *Understanding Universal Health Care Programs: Issues and Options.* Ann Arbor, Mich.: Health Administration Press, pp. 155–157.

Weil, Thomas P. (1994). Health Reform in Germany, *Health Progress,* 75 (7): 24–29.

7

FRANCE

Centrally Controlled and Locally Managed

France has achieved near universal insurance coverage but with diverse alternatives for consumers. The delivery system for health care has been characterized as the most complicated in the world. Major policy decisions are made at the national level, with direct responsibility emanating from the Ministry of Social Affairs—but with several other ministries involved in financing and supporting the system. However, health care delivery is through private providers who are paid largely fee-for-service. Payment of costs from insurance funds is delegated to Prefect (county) Social Security Committees who are responsible for local management and monitoring of providers (Fielding and Lancry, 1993: 748). Other special features of the system are summarized in Table 7-1.

DEMOGRAPHIC CHARACTERISTICS

France had a population of approximately 57 million in 1990. Infant mortality was 6.8 per 1,000 in 1991, similar to other European countries but lower than in the United States. Life expectancy was 82 for women (second highest in the world) and 73.5 for men in 1991. The differential between men and women is particularly notable. The proportion of the population over age 65 was approximately 13.5 percent in 1989 and is rising steadily as in other advanced countries. Nearly half of the individuals over age 65 in 1984 were 75 or older (Doty and Mizrahi, 1989: 85; Fielding and Lancry, 1993: 748–749; Cockerham, 1995: 288).

Approximately 28 percent of the French population live in smaller towns and rural areas. Rural–urban differences in health care have been observed in France as elsewhere. For example, one study found that diagnosis, treatment, and survival for cancer patients were less adequate in rural regions of Calvados province than in urban centers. Diagnosis tended to be at a later stage of symptoms in rural as compared to urban areas and survival rates were poorer, especially for women (Launoy et al., 1992: 365).

Despite the French reputation for high consumption of rich foods and wine, they have among the lowest cardiac death rates in the world. The explanation is unclear, although wine, fruits, and vegetables are given some credit for good health. A high-fiber and high-nutrient diet probably contributes. Studies indicate that red wine has some positive properties such as "resveratrol," which fights cholesterol. However, wine consumption undoubtedly contributes to one of the highest death rates in the world from cirrhosis of the liver (Foreman, 1994).

Table 7-1 Features of Health Care in France

- A highly sophisticated and professional federal bureaucracy manages national health care policy.
- The government is viewed by citizens as having the prime responsibility to assure health care at reasonable out-of-pocket cost.
- Benefits include the full range of health services, including preventive checkups at regular intervals; results of tests and procedures are inscribed on a health insurance "smart" card carried by the insured individual.
- Insurance coverage is not dependent on employment, although financing is primarily through employer payroll deductions.
- The working population is expected to subsidize older and dependent citizens.
- A comprehensive public/private mix of services is available but services are fragmented and complicated, with responsibility dispersed at local and national levels.
- Physicians have freedom of choice about location and mode of practice, with minimal hassle, but operate on tightly regulated fees negotiated by professional associations with national insurance funds.
- Fee-for-service physicians provide most ambulatory care, and salaried public or fee-for-service private hospital physicians provide varying types of competing outpatient services as well as specialized care.
- Public hospitals are financed under "global budgets"; private hospitals operate on a per diem fee basis and have considerably greater freedom to expand services.

Sources: Based on Roemer, 1991: 151; Richerson, 1992: 46; Schnieder et al., 1992: 159; Bach, 1993: 190; Fielding and Lancry, 1993: 748.

HISTORICAL PERSPECTIVE

France was among the first countries to develop a "rapid transit" system for trauma patients—beginning in 1792 during the French Revolutionary War. Carriages were invented to transport wounded soldiers from the battle lines. Emergency medical technicians and surgeons were trained specifically to care for the wounded and transport them to the nearest hospital. This early experience was not widely adopted in other countries until many decades later (Odom et al., 1990: 12).

Beginning of Voluntary Insurance

France's national health insurance system had its origins in the nineteenth century. Industrial workers and miners formed local sickness funds and voluntary mutual-aid societies for health protection. Only later did the government get involved in creating a relatively centralized national set of requirements (Roemer, 1993: 326).

The French medical profession was well organized by 1927 and did its best to protect its economic and professional interests. A Medical Charter was formulated on the basis of four principles (Anderson, 1989: 89):

1. Patients should be free to choose their physician.
2. Physicians should be paid fees for service.
3. Fees should be paid directly to physicians by the patients.
4. Physicians should be free to prescribe medications at their discretion.

These statements of principles were developed partially in response to the government effort at the time to create a capitated payment system based on contractual agreements between insurance funds and groups of physicians (a system that had been implemented earlier in neighboring Germany).

National Health Insurance: 1928

The first national law creating compulsory participation by lower-paid workers was initiated in 1928 and was soon followed by the social insurance act in 1930 that instituted compulsory payroll deductions as a funding mechanism. Only employees in lower-pay categories of major commercial establishments and manufacturing industries were included on a compulsory basis. Farmers, miners, other rural employees, workers in small enterprises, and lower-paid white-collar workers could participate voluntarily. Workers were free to choose their insurance scheme (Anderson, 1989: 89).

State subsidies supplemented payroll deductions to pay for insurance programs administered by sickness funds or mutual-aid societies such as labor unions and employer organizations. Governmental insurance units at the provincial level were created for individuals who were not included in voluntary insurance. Physicians had no set fee schedule and were reimbursed directly by patients who collected from the insurance funds (Anderson, 1989: 89).

A second major piece of legislation in 1945 led to a more universal insurance system covering all risks and with uniform benefits as well as workmen's compensation and retirement. Both employer and employee contributions were now required. However, implementation proved difficult (Pouvourville and Renaud, 1985: 161).

Medical Education Reform: 1958, 1981, and 1983

A 1958 hospital reform act (the "Debre reform") merged university medical schools with the most prestigious public hospitals, creating major academic medical complexes. Public hospitals were opened to all patients, with care to be provided by salaried physicians. This change was not strongly supported by the medical profession who had been free to treat their private patients in public hospitals on a fee basis. However, prestigious and highly paid faculty positions were offered to outstanding physicians who were provided with the latest technology and other amenities. More than 15,000 full-time salaried positions were created between 1965 and 1985, with dramatic positive effects on the quality of public hospitals (Lacronique, 1984: 261–283; Lacronique, 1988: 388).

The central university hospital (CHO) faculty became the elite of the medical profession. The faculty continues to have a highly influential role in planning and overseeing the health care system with major responsibility for naming individuals to fill vacancies in hospitals and medical schools. They were at that time able to engage in private fee-for-service practice and could admit their patients to public hospitals. This situation was later changed (1986); physicians agreed to a compromise that increased their social insurance and pension benefits in exchange for loss of private privileges in public hospitals (Pouvourville and Renaud, 1985: 157; Anderson, 1989: 91).

Medical education was changed in 1981 to bring French physician training more in tune with training in other European countries. This meant an additional year of clinical training for general practitioners. Educational requirements for various specialties were standardized. A 1984 reform attempted to abolish earlier status differences between university hospital physicians by instituting promotions based on seniority and merit. University hospital departments had become overspecialized "fiefdoms" with a lifetime appointed head physician with major authority over all patients and staff. The reform was intended to change the procedure so that chiefs of service are elected for specific time periods. Physician members of the department were to participate in developing a more comprehensive, less specialized view of patient care. However, the effort caused major negative reaction from hospital staff and was made voluntary rather than obligatory (Wilsford, 1991: 179).

Universal Coverage: 1967

The larger health care system began to approach universality in 1967 with creation of the National Health Insurance Fund for Salaried Workers, which covered 76 percent of the population and further centralized

health care funding and control. Agricultural workers and self-employed individuals were separately covered, adding 16 percent more population. Special welfare programs covered another 6 percent under the Ministry of Health. The final 2 percent of noncovered individuals were included under a 1978 law. Governance of the national funds was theoretically shared with representatives of workers and employers. However, employer groups tended to have greater influence (Anderson, 1989: 89; Roemer, 1991: 150).

In 1970, a health care "map" was created with the intent of better distributing resources throughout the country among 284 health districts. However, the regionalization effort was only partially successful. The medical establishment was not happy with the constraint on its freedom. Consequently, private hospitals and private practitioners continued to proliferate without regard to geography, although public hospitals were regionally dispersed (Pouvourville and Renaud, 1985: 158).

Initiation of Cost Controls: 1979

The first major effort to limit growth of the health care system occurred in 1979 when "block budgets" were introduced. A national limit was placed on the rate of increased cost for the public hospital system. Any increases over the limit were refused by the Ministry of Social Affairs. "Global budgets" were initiated in 1983 requiring a specific budget appropriated at the beginning of the year. Hospitals and the larger federal health care system had to operate within this limit. The procedure constrained growth in costs, but had the effect of keeping "rich" hospitals that way and forcing "poor" hospitals to remain poor (Sobczak, Fottler, and Chastagner, 1988: 26).

CULTURAL FACTORS

The French take pride in an intellectual approach to social issues. This has resulted in two primary and not entirely compatible ideological approaches in health care: egalitarianism and liberalism. Egalitarianism is a principle outlined in the national constitution emphasizing equal treatment of all citizens. Liberalism, or the freedom to pursue economic and personal interests with a minimum of government intrusion, is equally fundamental. Physicians have tended to put great emphasis on the second principle, whereas the government has emphasized equity—leading to limitations on physician freedom (Anderson, 1989: 88).

"Medical theorizing" is highly important to physicians; clinical trials using a more scientific approach are given relatively less importance. The "process" of health care is considered as important as "outcome." Treatment according to a refined process is more highly valued than whether or not a "cure" occurs. The physician's direct observation and perception of the patient is given greater importance in diagnosing a condition than scientifically-based diagnostic tests (Peters, 1991: 44; Giraud and Jolly, 1992: 19; Payer, 1988: 37–50).

Because of the relatively low birthrate in France, physicians are concerned about the potential for decreasing the rate even further. They are thus hesitant to perform hysterectomies. Only cancer and abnormal uterine bleeding are considered sufficient causes for surgery. French women place great value on retaining their uteruses and their breasts. French physicians thus perform less invasive surgery than in most advanced countries (Payer, 1988: 51).

Antibiotics are used far less on a per capita basis than in other countries. However, physicians prescribe vitamins in abundance to prevent the need for antibiotics. Many drugs are prescribed for digestive ailments. The French use much more radiotherapy for the treatment of cancer than other Western nations, in substantial part out of respect for Madame Marie and Pierre Curie, who were French pioneers in radiotherapy (Payer, 1988).

Temperatures are taken rectally or under the arm, but never orally. A routine checkup does not usually include urinalysis. Less attention is given to cleanliness of the body or in food and in use of the toilet than in most advanced countries. Living with grime is viewed as a way of building up resistance to disease (Peters, 1991: 44).

Discussion about money is viewed by many French people as a distasteful topic. The nationalized system of insurance has had the effect of removing the discussion of payment from the medical encounter, and is therefore appreciated. This contributes positively to the doctor–patient relationship. French physicians and their patients place great value on good social relationships, even when this involves withholding of information about the patient's condition (Feldman, 1992: 346).

These and other cultural features illustrate a certain distinctiveness of health care practice that places more value on relationships in the medical encounter and less value on the impersonal scientific diagnosis and cure of disease.

POLITICAL INFLUENCES

The national government bureaucracy exercises strong central control, with most health policy decisions made and implemented from Paris. The system of governance for health care has been described as a "fragile armistice" because of the many competing interests and compromises involved in the social security, health insurance, and health care delivery systems. An extensive effort is made to consult with all interested parties in the formation of policy. Commissions and boards are regularly formed to study issues and make recommendations (Wilsford, 1991: 223).

The political system has been characterized as "extremely pluralistic." A kind of revolutionary spirit, associated with regularized change and adaptation, remains strong. The high value placed on liberalism and relative freedom of both patients and providers (as noted earlier) pervades politics as well as medicine. Political party affiliation makes little difference in commitment to comprehensive health care with universal insurance coverage. For example, the almost autocratic leadership of Charles de Gaulle in the 1950s did not impede a series of liberalizing health care reforms noted earlier. The election of a Socialist president, François Mitterand in 1981, did not lead to a completely socialized health care system. This tradition seems to be continuing in the 1990s (Pouvourville and Renaud, 1985: 157; Wilsford, 1991: 118).

Central Role of the Health Care Bureaucracy

The political party in power has relatively little influence on health policy. The government bureaucracy is both highly professionalized and powerful. Influential officials manage the ongoing initiation of policy and implementation with little political interference. The professionals believe in the importance of equity and quality in provision of care, and have little cause to be unduly influenced by any one group, such as physician organizations. They tend to have a high commitment to fiscal restraint despite the interest of physicians and hospital administrators in expansion of the system and greater use of high-technology (Wilsford, 1991: 154).

The French National Assembly has substantial representation from the medical profession and other health fields. Physician organizations are not of one mind, but they have strong advocates for medicine in the government bureaucracy as well as in politics (Wilsford, 1991: 250).

The largest insurance fund (CNAMTS) is administered by one national board whose director is appointed by the Federal Council of Ministers (the President's Cabinet). Membership is representative of labor, management, the private insurance industry, the Ministry of Social Security, and other interests. The board manages policy formation, resource distribution, and budget balancing. It recommends changes in the level of payroll tax if the insurance fund runs a shortage or surplus (Pouvourville and Renaud, 1985: 157; Fielding and Lancry, 1993: 750).

Decentralization

Within each of the 95 departments (governmental subdivisions), the appointed federal representative, the Prefect, is responsible for coordinating social and health services within that political unit. Each of the six federal ministries with a health care function (Finance; Social Security; Social Affairs; Education; Research and Technology; Industry) acts somewhat independently with respect to Prefectures and local boards. However, no direct national authority exists over the local Social Security boards. All 129 boards remain autonomous in administering payments to private physicians and hospitals. Thus, despite central policy direction, the health care delivery system remains pluralistic, diverse, and somewhat uncoordinated (Pouvourville and Renaud, 1985: 157; Fielding and Lancry, 1993: 752).

National policy makers have attempted to maintain some degree of equity in allocation of resources among the various regions of the country. For example, each region has an organ transplant center—the highest total number of such centers per million inhabitants of any member of the European Community (Moatti, Chanut, and Benech, 1994: 1629).

Politics of Local Health Care

Five sets of players have major influence at the local level (Pouvourville and Renaud, 1985: 158–159): politicians who sit on hospital governing boards, doctors responsible for hospital care, administrators of health care units, civil servants in the health care bureaucracies, and local Social Security boards.

Politicians have general influence and often have specific capacity to help secure additional funds for the hospital. The hospital physicians are responsible for the units within hospitals and often hold lifetime positions as department heads; they have major influence on the specific treatments and services to be offered. The hospital administrator is officially responsible to the Ministry of Social Affairs rather than to local officials, but has direct ties to the hospital board and is a key coordinator of relationships among the other major players. Civil servants work at the local government "department level" and are responsible to the Prefect for effective administration of the Social Security insurance resources. "Physician-inspectors" from these units help assure compliance with rules and quality of care. Local Social Security boards are the payers for hospital services for insured individuals and assure that billed services have been delivered (Pouvourville and Renaud, 1985: 158–159).

Physicians have great power over hospital services in part because they have direct linkages to the physician administrators in the Ministry of Health. However, each player has a key role in resource allocation. There is a constant process of negotiation and compromise, as there is at the national level. Local interest groups have major influence because part of the health care system is financed at the local level—a requirement that is viewed as essential to the achievement of federal Ministry of Social Affairs goals (Pouvourville and Renaud, 1985: 159).

SOCIAL ORGANIZATION OF HEALTH CARE

The primary government agency for health care is the Ministry of Social Affairs (formerly the Ministry of Health). The Ministry regulates both health provision and the insurance funds. The Ministry of Education administers the schools of medicine and thus has major influence on university-affiliated hospitals (Lacronique, 1988: 385).

Public Health

The Ministry of Social Affairs has subdivisions for public health, hospitals, and phar-

maceuticals, and contains several national research programs (such as the Pasteur Institutes) as well as a school of public health. Regional offices are located in each of the 21 regions with supervisory responsibility for departments of health in each of the 95 provinces (departments) (Roemer, 1991: 151).

Responsibilities include control of communicable diseases and promotion of maternal and child health. Prevention and safety programs are offered in schools and workplaces. Occupational health programs have a long and respected tradition, as does environmental protection. Programs for the elderly are also emphasized, particularly those that deal with cancer and heart disease (Roemer, 1991: 152).

Physicians

Physicians remain relatively free to operate private medical practices if they so choose. They see an average of 10 to 12 patients per day, compared to much higher numbers in other countries, and earn an average of only $45,000 per year. The ratio of population to physicians was about 2.6 per 1,000 population in 1990. About 57 percent of private physicians are in solo practice. Thirty-five percent work on salary in hospitals. The other 8 percent work on salary in clinics, as academic faculty, in public health, with industry, or in government management or review roles. Thirty-one percent of physicians were women in 1990, with the proportion increasing steadily. Women fill about 43 percent of the salaried positions but only 21 percent of the private practice roles (DeLozier et al., 1989: 1–31; Wilsford, 1991: 119, 133; Schneider et al., 1992: 153; Fielding and Lancry, 1993: 749).

Many of the physicians in solo private practice secure some of their income from part-time work on salary. A private physician can only increase personal income by doing more procedures unless part of the income flows through salary for part-time consultation in publicly or privately funded facilities, because of the prescribed fee schedule. This pattern is the basis for greater length of consultation with patients than in most countries. However, establishing a private practice has become increasingly difficult because of a general surplus of physicians (Payer, 1988: 38; Wilsford, 1991: 137).

Despite the surplus, public hospitals had difficulty employing qualified surgeons in the late 1980s. Fifty percent of the positions for surgeons were not filled in 1988. The salaries were less than in the private sector and yet the work demands were substantial. As a consequence, private practitioners, who were often foreign-trained and sometimes not fully qualified according to official standards, were employed temporarily to perform the needed operations (Stevens, 1989: 125).

Malpractice claims are relatively uncommon. Physicians have a less harried life than in many other countries. Office-based physicians do not usually see patients in the hospital and are monitored only informally by one agency. Hospital-based practice is specialized and utilization review is relatively uncomplicated (Fielding and Lancry, 1993: 749).

Physician organization. French physicians have had difficulty over the years presenting a united stand in the face of government actions. Organized medicine has been splintered into two major interest groups or unions that do not always agree on appropriate policies. The divergence is largely between general medicine and specialists—who view their generalist colleagues as much less prestigious. Membership in the official organizations is relatively low.

When physicians are sufficiently upset by government action or inaction, they take to the streets in the French tradition. Protests, marches, and even occasionally strikes are means of capturing public attention for their views. The lack of effective organization may be part of the explanation for the relatively lower incomes and less physician influence as compared to most other industrialized countries (Wilsford, 1987: 497; Wilsford, 1991: 2, 85, 272).

Medical education. France supports 29 regional medical university and hospital centers, usually in regional capitals. Paris has nine medical schools. All but one are publicly managed and financed and are under the control of the Ministry of Education. This allows the government to mandate enrollments as well as resources (Wilsford, 1991: 110).

Aspiring physicians in France must take an entrance examination, referred to as the "baccalaureate," after completing high school. If successful, they apply to medical school and take 2 years of initial training focused primarily on the basic medical sciences. After the first year, they must successfully complete a comprehensive examination if they are to continue. About 3,000 of the initial 27,000 annual applicants (in 1990) proceed to the second phase—which lasts 4 years, including clinical, pathological, and professional skills. They must then take a qualifying examination. The less successful proceed to 2 years of general medicine based primarily in the hospital, and the more successful go on to the highly preferred postgraduate specialty training (Wilsford, 1991: 175; Fielding and Lancry, 1993: 753; Vogt, Smith, and Hendrickson, 1993: 293).

Enrollment in medical schools was relatively open for any qualified applicants until 1975. This caused the graduation rate to grow to approximately 8,000 per year—far higher than needed. Consequently, the Ministry of Education began reducing entry into the second year of medical school by 5 percent per year. This brought the annual graduation rate to 3,000 per year by 1990 (Lacronique, 1984: 273).

Nurses

Nurses experienced some deterioration in their status during the 1980s. They were not well represented in negotiations with hospital administration and felt they were suffering from inadequate rewards. The 1991 reforms created a board of nursing for each hospital comparable to the physician organization. These boards were to represent nursing, support training, and undertake evaluation of nursing needs (Bach, 1993: 197).

Most nurses work in hospitals, as is the case in other countries. However, roughly 33,000 are freelance nurse-practitioners. They are reimbursed from health insurance funds, but patients must make a co-payment of 35 percent (Schneider et al., 1992: 154).

Pharmacists and Pharmaceuticals

Hospital and private pharmacies are the only dispensers of pharmaceuticals; supermarkets and other commercial outlets are prohibited from entering the market for over-the-counter or prescription drugs. Midwives are allowed to prescribe certain drugs. Pharmacists can prescribe prepackaged drugs, but must have a prescription from a physician otherwise. Prices for retail pharmacies are negotiated between the pharmaceutical companies and the federal Ministries involved in regulation. Hospital pharmacies negotiate prices directly with the manufacturer (Schneider et al., 1992: 156; Fielding and Lancry, 1993: 755).

The French are the world record holders for tranquilizer usage and are high users of other drugs as well, with an average of 28 prescriptions per person in 1989. A rapid rise has been observed in both the number and cost of prescriptions, with growth at 10 percent per year in the recent period (Stevens, 1989: 225; Bach, 1993: 192).

Drug prices are under rigorous government control. The list of approved drugs is prepared by the Ministry for Social Security based on two primary criteria: (1) quality or improvement of therapy and (2) price or minimal treatment costs. A price commission monitors production and research-and-development costs, while assuring that prices are within government guidelines. The retail margin for pharmacists was 30 percent in 1988, and the wholesale markup was 7 percent (Schneider et al., 1992: 156).

Health Services Administration

Hospitals in France have generally employed professional administrators rather than physician clinicians. However, professional training in the field has been limited until recently. The National School of Public Health, in Rennes, Brittany, initiated a collaborative program of research and training in hospital management in 1962 involving the most prestigious business school in France (Ecole des Hautes Etudes Commerciales) with a focus on strategic management, regional planning, and optimal allocation of resources (Frossard, 1990: 61; Bach and Hyde-Price, 1994: 26).

The selection process is rigorous and competitive, requiring candidates to complete an entrance examination after completion of a university degree. The graduate program is 27 months in length, with seven phases of study, including extensive practical experience in the hospital setting with required reports (Bach and Hyde-Price, 1994: 26).

Graduation from the 3-year program has become the essential ingredient for a hospital administrative position. Administrators are civil servants within the Ministry of Social Affairs, if they work for a public hospital. The special training has clearly increased the professionalism and effectiveness of hospital administration (Nickson, 1988: 22).

Hospitals

The Ministry of Social Affairs is responsible for enforcing hospital rules for both public and private institutions. The Hospital Law of 1970 reorganized all institutions into a regional system designed to increase the efficiency and appropriate distribution of facilities (Lacronique, 1988: 388; Roemer, 1993: 226).

Public hospitals were given a mandate to provide a basic range of services, while sharing specialized services and personnel. Substantial new funding was provided for modernization. Private hospitals were incorporated into the system because they control one-third of the total beds. This has resulted in better sharing of costly resources among hospitals through cooperative arrangements within each region (Roemer, 1991: 152).

Types of hospitals. Hospitals were divided in four general levels (Sobczak et al., 1988: 21):

1. *Local hospitals* are usually private nonprofit, serve a primarily rural region, and have less than 50 beds.
2. *Second-level hospitals* are often private, are located in a small city, and provide mostly primary or secondary care with 50 to 200 beds.
3. *Hospital centers* are usually public, located in a regional city often in the capital of one of 95 prefects, and provide primary, secondary, and some tertiary care in from two to eight departments.
4. *Regional teaching hospitals* are associated with a medical school, provide primarily tertiary care, usually have more than 1,000 beds, and are located in a major regional city.

The regional hospitals must be prepared for all emergencies and are mandated to handle the most complicated cases, while also providing educational and research functions. A direct association among hospitals in a region is often developed in the form of a syndicate. Each public hospital has a governing board consisting of representatives of the Ministry of Social Affairs, local Social Security boards, and hospital personnel. The mayor of the host city often chairs the board and intervenes as deemed appropriate with the government in support of the hospital. The hospital administrator is a civil servant nominated by the Ministry of Social Affairs and approved by the governing board, and often has received training from the National School of Public Health (Pouvourville, 1986: 395).

Public hospitals are the most technologically advanced and serve as the training centers for physicians. They are not as highly regarded by the public, however, as private hospitals. Private hospitals are of smaller size

(averaging 200 beds), but tend to be both more modern and more abundant (70 percent of all hospitals). Public hospitals are much larger and collectively contain about 70 percent of all beds. Physicians in public facilities are largely salaried, as noted earlier, and physicians serving private facilities are usually paid on a fee-for-service basis (Anderson, 1989: 90).

Major issues. The initiation of "global budgeting" generated something of a crisis in the hospital system. The modernization of managerial methods and budgeting was difficult for the traditional medical staff to accept, and conflict within the hospitals between managers and medical staff was intense. The situation was exacerbated because medical chiefs of staff were appointed for life and many did not accept the need for cost limitations. The organization structure led to the formation of "medical empires" within the larger hospitals, which often meant duplication of some services, higher costs, and difficulty for professional senior administrators in the implementation of reforms (Pouvourville, 1986: 404; Bach, 1993: 193; Bach and Hyde-Price, 1994: 26).

Foreign investors began to enter the hospital market in the 1980s. This led to increased demand for high-technology in private hospitals and a general expansion in the private sector. The private system has grown more rapidly than the public system by offering desirable amenities through private clinics not available in public hospitals. A private health insurance system adds resources and benefits not available through the public insurance systems. This has led to complaints and strikes by nurses and physicians who have felt that staffing and salary increases were inadequate. The number of health care workers per hospital bed has remained very low compared to other industrialized countries. As of 1993, 65 percent of all hospital beds were public and 35 percent were private—up from 29 percent in 1987 (Anderson, 1989: 91–92; Schneider et al., 1992: 155; Bach, 1993: 190; Bach and Hyde-Price, 1994: 26).

Further national reforms were introduced in 1991, after widespread public debate that considerably affected the policy development process. Several major changes were implemented (Bach, 1993: 194):

- Public hospitals were given a new legal status but were required to establish a business plan and involve professional staff more fully in management decisions. Nonhospital care and outpatient services were encouraged for the first time. Hospital managers were allowed greater control over investment decisions and were given more flexibility in management of both human and financial resources.
- Private hospitals were placed under some of the same constraints as public hospitals. Both were required to provide patients with greater information about their condition. Technology was to be shared and greater public/private cooperation was required.
- Planning for public and private facilities was to be based more directly on the needs of the population through "population-based" services and greater attention to regional needs. Actual outcomes are to be evaluated in terms of both patient and community impact. Insurance funds are to be directly involved in the planning and will pay for some of the proposed new services.
- Professional management and greater institutional autonomy were emphasized, supplemented by a mandate to include medical and nursing staff in management decisions. Medical chiefs of service were to be appointed for 5-year terms rather than for life. Administrators were to be financially rewarded for cost savings and efficient operation.

The results of these changes are not yet clear. They focus primarily on the hospital and do not necessarily directly affect costs. Nonetheless, the changes bring a certain amount of additional orderliness and potential efficiency to the internal operation of the major consumer of health care resources (Bach, 1993: 198).

Quality Assurance

An emphasis on quality assurance was instituted in 1989, partially in response to some of the issues noted earlier. A new quality assurance agency was created and a law passed in 1991 made "evaluation" obligatory for hospital physicians. In France, this terminology includes quality assurance as well as technology assessment—both of which have financial as well as clinical implications. Medical school faculty tend to be very wary of the activity because it is viewed as primarily a cost-containment measure, which they dislike. It interferes with their focus on research and publication, which are viewed as of highest priority. However, many physicians have been supportive of the quality assurance and evaluation concepts in the hospital setting because they believe they do contribute to better clinical knowledge and better understanding of outcomes. A well-developed hospital information system that captures clinical as well as financial and other quantitative information can be one of the important outcomes (Giraud and Jolly, 1992: 20).

Medical Technology

The concern with costs has led to an emphasis on careful selection of new and expensive equipment in public hospitals. A regional committee for health equipment, composed of administrators of both public and private hospitals, was established to make recommendations to a national medical technology committee. Representatives of medical associations were asked to offer advice to the regional and national committees on needed equipment. The idea was to avoid unnecessary duplication, while improving the uneven distribution of technology. For example, CT scanners were limited to a standard of 1 per 1 million persons. This standard was later tripled, allowing for many additional machines (Lacronique, 1988: 389).

New forms of noninvasive surgery have been shown to markedly decrease the length of hospitalization, while increasing patient comfort. However, the system of review described earlier and costs of the new technologies have the effect of limiting the adoption of this technology in public hospitals—which have little incentive to constrain length of stay in any case. The present global budget financing system tends to support the existing allocation of resources. It is easier for a hospital to receive an annual budget for maintenance of ongoing activities, but very problematic to secure funds for new and higher levels of equipment, institutional innovation, and improvements in quality of care. The consequence is a relatively slow diffusion process for new technology (Rodwin, 1989: 269; Fielding and Lancry, 1993: 754).

The private sector has the advantage of moving somewhat faster in adopting the new technologies, especially for outpatient surgery. New technology gives prestige to innovative private institutions, whether or not the equipment is cost-effective. However, even here the Ministry of Social Affairs has obstructed change somewhat by limiting payments for short-term or outpatient surgery. A further constraint is the limited manufacturing capacity in France for new medical technologies. More than 90 percent of these advanced technologies must be imported (Weill, 1993: 34–45).

The consequence is a relatively modest level of technological advancement, particularly for imaging. Physician specialists argue that much of the equipment needed is in fact cost-effective because it contributes to better diagnosis and higher-quality medical care (Lamarque and Pujol, 1993: S52).

The French are ahead of other industrialized countries in the adoption of "smart cards" for medical record keeping. More than one-half million were in use in 1994. They are slated to be fully integrated with the Social Security card—which is the computer chip smart card called VITALE. The plan is to replace all paper Social Security cards with the plastic card that contains basic social and medical information—replacing a huge quantity of paper records and saving an estimated $17 billion over a 10-year period (Skolnick, 1994: 189).

Emergency Medical Services

The emergency medical system is operated by fire departments and managed by physicians who are usually anesthesiologists. Reception and dispatch centers take emergency calls and are directly connected to fire and police stations. Legal status was given to the system in 1986. It operates at three levels (Barrier, 1989: 1062):

1. At the community level, civil service firemen have responsibility for organization and management, although military personnel assume these responsibilities in Paris and Marseilles.
2. In provinces, emergencies that exceed local capability are dealt with through a regional disaster plan, under responsibility of the prefect (governor) in charge.
3. The Ministry of the Interior is responsible for emergencies that affect more than one province or a region of the country.

Ambulances are driven by firemen who are trained as Emergency Medical Technicians. Dispatchers are trained in anesthesia and emergency medicine and have the authority to channel emergency calls to the appropriate emergency unit. The ambulances are managed by a physician who is assisted by a nurse technician. This team is prepared to administer advanced life support (ALS) at the emergency scene and in transit as needed. They are directly linked by communication and computer dispatch systems with hospitals having intensive and/or critical care units. Emergency physicians have 7 years of medical training, including 3 years in operative anesthesia, on-scene resuscitation, and critical care medicine. The nurse technician has 3 years of nurses training, including 2 years of specialized anesthesia and emergency care training. An emergency physician and nurse are always on duty with immediate access to a unit equipped with intensive care (ICU) equipment in each of 255 regions designated as part of the national emergency plan (Nordberg, 1989: 35).

A crisis staff is available in each regional hospital consisting of an emergency medical consultant, a representative from hospital administration, and a representative from the Ministry of Social Affairs. It is their responsibility to coordinate with emergency units in the region, including the Red Cross, which operates nonmedical ambulances (Barrier, 1989: 1064).

Paris has been subject to terrorist attacks on a number of occasions and thus has special emergency "Red Plans," for first aid and advanced life support, and a "White Plan," for ALS as well as medical transport and hospitalization. These protocols attempt to coordinate all emergency services and facilities in the region. They were severely tested in 1986 when there were 9 terrorist bombings and 166 casualties (Barrier, 1989: 1066).

Long-Term Care

The French long-term-care system is progressive by contemporary standards, having been transformed through a deliberate process of reform beginning in the 1970s. Nursing homes and home health care services are the predominant mode of care for dependent elderly individuals. Prior to 1975, general hospital wards and/or hospices were the primary centers of long-term care. They continue to serve in that role for psychiatric and chronically ill patients. The elderly suffering from dementia were formerly placed in mental hospitals (Doty and Mizrahi, 1989: 58–59).

Retirement homes were partially converted to nursing care for residents who had become more functionally dependent or chronically ill. The idea was to enable long-term residents to remain in the residential facilities with which they were familiar. Homemaker chore services were considerably expanded to increase the potential for elderly individuals to remain in their homes. Insurance for home health care and institutional care became generally available in 1981 although not all costs were covered. Room and board are separated from medical and nursing costs, and are considered the patients' responsibility—to be deducted from pension payments or drawn from welfare funds for low-income patients. Home health care costs of four visits per day for 30 minutes or two visits per day up to 6 hours are fully covered by health insurance for medical and nursing care. Homemaker and chore services are funded through local health and social service agencies—with an income-based sliding scale of costs (Doty and Mizrahi, 1989: 62).

Long-term-care facilities have a formal policy (1986 law) of involving residents in the governance of the unit through resident councils. Most facilities are publicly sponsored or nonprofit and thus have more of a basis for democratic procedure than may be the case with largely private proprietary systems. The facilities have a reputation among the public for offering comfort, security, and companionship for frail elderly individuals, despite the loss of independence associated with long-term care (Doty and Mizrahi, 1989: 91).

For example, in St. Malo in northern France, a home for 90 men and women is operated by a religious order (Little Sisters of the Poor)—one of many similar homes operated by the same order in other parts of the country. The home is situated near the seashore and makes every effort to provide a comfortable environment, with good food and wine, for the residents (Ludvigsen, 1993: 42–43).

Approximately 50 percent of all long-term-care beds are occupied by individuals with senile dementia. Patients tend to be age 80 and older and live an average of 8 years after diagnosis of the disease. The expectation is that the proportion of individuals with the condition will increase as the proportion of elderly increase (Ritchie et al., 1994: 232).

Special Services for the Elderly

A National Committee of Pensioners and Elderly Persons was created in 1981 as an advisory group on policy and programs for the elderly, with the mandate to help alleviate aging problems, and with special responsibility to the federal Ministries of Health and Social Affairs. A Directorate for Social Services has specific responsibility for elderly health care and other elderly services. However, the unit has relatively limited resources and power as compared to the Social Security Directorate in the Ministry of Social Affairs, which allocates the majority of resources to the elderly (Henrard, Cassou, and Le Disert, 1990: 137).

The system of services for the elderly has been characterized as extremely fragmented. Health and social services are provided by a wide variety of agencies, both government and voluntary, at national, department, and local levels. Municipalities are responsible for most direct public services to supplement the support provided through nonprofit and commercial organizations. Basic funding for all health-related problems is provided through the health insurance system. The Social Security system provides for domestic home help for disabled elderly, as well as home nursing care and allowances for renovation of housing to accommodate incapacities. The allowances available for health care and other services are often inadequate and must be supplemented by personal resources or through the welfare system. Individuals over age 75 receive preventive checkups for cancer and influenza inoculations (Henrard et al., 1990: 127).

A study of noninstitutionalized elderly with some level of dependency reported (in 1987) that only 43 percent received assistance from family members. The remainder must depend on institutional support of some type. The family support system is diminishing in France as in other Western countries. Much remains to be accomplished in France as elsewhere in providing for the needs of older citizens, given the rapid increase in numbers and problems associated with advanced older age (Doty and Mizrahi, 1989: 86).

Mental Health Care

Mental health legislation in France dates from 1838 when a statute was approved creat-

ing treatment requirements for mentally ill individuals. Each province was to have an inpatient treatment facility. For the first time, mentally ill people were considered deserving of medical treatment rather than confinement as lunatics. The legislation was modernized only in 1990 (Laffont and Priest, 1992: 843).

The 1990 statute was designed primarily to protect the civil liberties of psychiatric patients. Two forms of required inpatient hospitalization were defined. The first could be initiated by a relative or a third party when immediate treatment and monitoring are called for. A medical certificate must be prepared by a physician (not necessarily a psychiatrist) and verified by the admitting physician. The second form is based on evidence presented to the police that the mental state of the individual endangers public order and safety of others. A medical certification is required for retention in this case as well, which then must be supported by public authorities. An elaborate process is defined through which decisions can be made to hold or discharge a patient. Patients have the right to appeal if they disagree with the requirements. Patients rights are thus protected from the potential arbitrary decisions of police, family, or the political authorities (Laffont and Priest, 1992: 847).

Mental health care has shifted considerably to the community level, as in other Western European countries. The movement toward decentralization and deinstitutionalization of mental patient care has been especially vigorous (Roemer, 1993: 278).

ECONOMIC CHARACTERISTICS AND ISSUES

Health care costs grew from 4.2 percent of GDP in 1960 to 9.4 percent in 1994, moving from eighth among OECD countries to first. This represents the highest annual rate of growth in health expenditures among the OECD countries during the 1980s, averaging 2.15 percent per year. Cost increases have continued into the 1990s largely because of rising volume and intensity of services. This has led to major cost-control efforts (Bach, 1993: 189; Fielding and Lancry, 1993: 752; Moatti et al., 1994: 1626).

Although coverage of the population is nearly complete, the proportion of costs covered by public insurance is incomplete. Approximately 71 percent of costs are paid from publicly sponsored resources. In 1990, about 74 percent of costs were paid through the major sickness insurance funds. Supplemental insurance paid 6.2 percent, local government 1.1 percent, and 19 percent was paid out of pocket (Fielding and Lancry, 1993: 750).

Benefits

Each of several insurance schemes has its own special features, but all provide a basic package of benefits. Most plans have a waiting period after enrollment before benefits apply, but benefits are unlimited thereafter. Under each plan, as noted earlier, the patient must pay the physician directly and seek reimbursement from the insurance fund for 75 percent of the cost—with the balance serving as a co-payment. Each insurance arrangement also requires co-payments of 20 percent for hospitalization. Co-payments are waived for the elderly and indigent. Most people (more than 80 percent of the population in 1993) carry private insurance through mutual-aid societies, employers, or commercial companies to cover the cost of co-payments or additional benefits (Roemer, 1991: 151; Richerson, 1992: 46; Schneider et al., 1992: 159).

In addition to medical and hospital benefits, glasses and hearing aids are covered but with a required 30 percent co-payment for the least-cost product; if a higher-priced product is preferred, the individual must pay the difference. Again, private insurance often makes up much of the difference, because actual public insurance reimbursement for glasses and hearing aids averages only 5 to 10 percent. Children in need of hearing aids are reimbursed 100 percent.

Major prostheses and appliances are fully covered (Schneider et al., 1992: 152–156).

All citizens are entitled to several cash benefits through Social Security. After 3 days of illness, workers can receive 50 percent of their normal salary for up to 12 months over 3 years, and up to 48 months for long-term illnesses or rehabilitation. Maternity benefits are paid at 84 percent of salary for 6 weeks before and 10 weeks after delivery (and may be extended to 34 weeks if special problems occur). Death benefits of 3 months of workers wages are paid to the surviving family (Schneider et al., 1992: 158).

Financing

Ninety-nine percent of the population has been covered since 1978 by the three primary national sickness insurance funds. The dominant group is the general wage earners' fund with 81 percent of the coverage, followed by the agricultural fund with 9 percent, and the professional worker and self-employed fund with 5 percent. Several smaller funds cover other working groups. Private insurers pay a 9 percent tax on their revenues to help support public insurance. In addition, the government traditionally has contributed relative small sums to make up deficits in the national insurance plans; this practice has changed recently under the cost-control schemes to be described later (Fielding and Lancry, 1993: 749).

Although the great majority of the funding is provided from worker payroll deductions allocated to the primary insurance schemes, consumer co-payments amounted to roughly 25 percent of the average health service expenditures. Co-payment variations depend on the type of service: 20 percent for hospitalization, 25 percent for ambulatory care visits, 25 percent for dentures, 39 percent for transport, and a varying rate for drugs from zero for essential drugs up to 60 percent for "comfort" drugs such as tranquilizers (Lacronique, 1988: 387; Sobczak et al., 1988: 20; Schneider et al., 1992: 151; Bach, 1993: 191).

As noted, much of the co-payment is in fact covered by private insurance.

All co-payments are exempted for people with extensive surgery requirements, those who must remain hospitalized over 30 days, pregnant women from the sixth month onward, severely disabled individuals, people injured at work, and disabled veterans. The average out-of-pocket cost for health care in 1989 was $260 per individual (Schneider, 1992: 150).

Salary level is the basis for assessing the payroll contribution of each employed person, which means the funding mechanism has an income-redistribution consequence. The total proportion of salary in 1993 was 19.6 percent, with 6.8 percent paid by the employee and 12.8 percent paid by the employer for industrial workers. Salary continuation benefits absorb 4 percent, so that only 15.6 percent are directly for health care. A small proportion also goes for cross-subsidization of the other smaller funds (Fielding and Lancry, 1993: 750).

Several insurance funds operate under similar arrangements but with different allocations. For example, civil servants rates are 14.85 percent (with salary continuation funded separately); electric and gas board staff rates are 14.8 percent. The self-employed must pay the employer rate of 12.8 percent, and the voluntarily insured pay their own premiums at the rate of 15.5 to 18.25 percent. A special additional assessment of 1.1 percent of income or profit was levied in 1991 to cover a shortfall in the insurance funds. Shortages have in the past been covered from government subsidies that until recently were only 1.4 percent or less of costs. Taxes have been imposed on alcohol and tobacco with revenues targeted for health care (Schneider et al., 1992: 150; Fielding and Lancry, 1993: 750).

The commitment to subsidized assistance to the dependent population means that local government contributes directly for costs of health care to the unemployed or indigent. The principle of "intergenerational solidarity" is the basis for relatively low contributions by the elderly: 1.4 percent on Social Security income and 2.4 percent on pensions (Fielding and Lancry, 1993: 750).

This system of financing suffers from fluctuation in employment levels. The high level of unemployment in the late 1980s and early 1990s (averaging 10.3 percent in 1992) has thus heavily impacted insurance funds and is partially the basis for substantial deficits. A new national tax was passed in 1990 mandating a 1.1 percent increase in personal income tax specifically for health care. The purpose of the new resources is to increase equality among income groups in the provision of primary care (Bach, 1993: 192; Fielding and Lancry, 1993: 752).

Physician payment. The physician fee schedule is based on a relative value scale, which is updated regularly by a national committee of physicians, Social Security staff, and other Ministry of Social Affairs representatives. The specific fees are then negotiated between the medical associations and Social Security insurance organizations. Physicians receive tax and Social Security incentives and can secure permission under some circumstances to bill patients directly for special services or if they have special academic expertise. Approximately 42 percent of specialists and 23 percent of GPs were able to bill extra in 1990. As noted earlier, the average net income of physicians remains considerably lower than in most other industrialized countries (Schneider et al., 1992: 153; Glaser, 1993: 103).

Ambulatory physicians receive full payment from patients at the time of the visit, based on the negotiated rate. The average fixed consultation fee was about $20 in 1993 for general practitioners and $28 for specialists. Physicians must accept the negotiated rate unless they qualify to bill patients directly for the extra amount negotiated (using "tact and restraint") with the patient. There is also a disincentive to bill extra. Those who qualify receive lower reimbursement levels from the public funds and must pay more for their own insurance coverage.

However, good physicians who work in affluent neighborhoods have patients who are willing to pay more for extra service or perceived higher-quality care. Inequality of income among physicians because of this procedure caused the government to suspend the practice in 1990 for new physicians, but those already designated were allowed to continue (Fielding and Lancry, 1993: 751).

Hospital payment. As noted earlier, public hospitals were subjected to global budgets beginning in 1983. They receive an allocation each month that must be sufficient for all expenditures. The goals of the global budgeting system were to (Thayer, 1986: 254)

- Simplify the payment structure from insurance organizations, while stabilizing and regularizing income to the hospitals
- Increase the clarity of the link between the purpose of a hospital service and its funding, through clinician involvement in the budgetary process
- Increase the incentive for administrators to be economical, because any savings could be used to finance projects of interest to the hospital

Administrators were quite favorable to the changes, but were critical of basing the global budget on past years; this procedure did not take account of changing circumstances or seasonal variations in hospital business (Thayer, 1986: 255).

Expenditure-cap rules require submission of retrospective cost reports and a proposed budget to the local government rate regulator who screens and approves it based on the financial guidelines from the federal level. The federal government can then place a cap on expenditures of all hospitals in a region. However, the local regulator can award individual hospitals more or less than the standard amount as long as the regional cap is not exceeded. The Social Security funds in a region pay the budget for each hospital based on its share of admissions in the past year (Bach, 1993: 189; Glaser, 1993: 106).

The new method of budgeting forced major attitudinal and behavioral changes in the hospital system. Managers heretofore had been able to request additional funds if they had exhausted their resources before the end of the budget year. Now the only basis on which extra funds could be obtained was a higher patient load than projected. Priorities therefore had to be established. Purchases could only be made based on priority needs. Personnel increases were severely restricted. Decisions to purchase new technology were thus undertaken with great care (Pouvourville, 1986: 404).

Reimbursement for private hospitals remained on a fee-for-service basis and was generally higher than for public hospitals. The difference was partially in recognition that private facilities must pay for capital requirements, whereas capital needs of public facilities are provided separately through special appropriations from the Ministry of Health and from local government. Capital funds are also sought from philanthropic and church sources for nonprofit hospitals. Private investment is the primary source for proprietary units (Lacronique, 1988: 390; Roemer, 1991: 153).

Public and private hospitals secure operating costs largely from insurance funds. Only about 8 percent comes from private payment or private supplemental insurance. Supporting services such as laboratory, radiology, and a proportion of food and lodging are paid on the basis of a fee schedule (Roemer, 1991: 153; Fielding and Lancry, 1993: 751).

Global budgets for public hospitals (70 percent of total beds) severely limited growth. However, private hospitals were not under any substantial limits and began to expand rapidly to meet the demand for services, securing the needed funds from per diem charges. The increased costs associated with rapid growth eventually led to inclusion of the private hospitals in global budgeting beginning in 1991 (Wilsford, 1991: 167; Fielding and Lancry, 1993: 751).

The 1991 hospital law also initiated a form of "diagnosis-related groups" as a basis for categorizing and paying for hospital services as an alternative to per diem charges. Implementation of the law was opposed by both administrators and physicians largely because they did not believe that adequate information could be assembled to appropriately group cases (Fielding and Lancry, 1993: 754).

Costs for each type of hospital vary considerably. In 1990, the average cost per day in a regional teaching hospital was $307; in a public general hospital, it was $199; and in a private hospital, it was $58. However, services provided in each case vary. For example, the public teaching hospital deals primarily with specialized and expensive problems; general hospital costs are for less difficult problems. Private hospital costs on the other hand include only nursing care, accommodation, and equipment; medical care costs are paid separately to a private physician. Public hospitals tend to get the sicker patients because costs are largely reimbursed by public insurance. Private hospitals are less able to absorb extra costs for the sicker patients (Schraub et al., 1991: 221).

Payment for pharmaceuticals. Drugs on the approved list are covered by health insurance funds. Patient co-payment depends on the type of therapy. Essential drugs, such as those for cancer, require no co-payment but are only about 1.5 percent of sales; 30 percent co-payment is required for normal prescriptions such as antibiotics, which account for 75 percent of all prescriptions; and 60 percent co-payment must be paid for so-called "comfort" drugs such as tranquilizers, which are about 24 percent of total sales. These co-payments are often covered by private insurance. Elderly individuals with a need for multiple drugs are reimbursed for all costs (Schneider et al., 1992: 156).

Long-term care. As noted earlier, the medical care part of long-term care is covered 100 percent by insurance, but lodging and food must be paid from Social Security income or from personal or family sources. Local governments pay these costs for indigent or unemployed individuals (Fielding and Lancry, 1993: 752).

Administrative Costs

Administrative cost estimates for the various components of health care vary considerably. The general insurance fund estimates that about 6 percent of payroll tax receipts go for administration, mostly to pay employees for processing bills and conducting utilization reviews. Hospitals estimated administrative costs range from 10 to 15 percent (Fielding and Lancry, 1993: 752).

PROBLEMS AND REFORMS

A summary of specific measures taken to control costs includes

- Increased co-payments for services
- Expenditure limits on hospitals through global budgets
- Efforts to reduce the excess number of practicing physicians, and modify physician behavior to less costly patterns
- Cooperative negotiations with medical associations to lower fees
- Requirement of "certificates of need" for major hospital investments
- Decreases in reimbursement for some categories of drugs
- Regionalization and coordination of ambulatory and hospital services

These efforts, however, have failed to entirely stem growth. Increased co-payments were not sufficient to offset larger costs. The expansion of private hospitals operating on a fee-for-service basis has increased competition for personnel *and* resources. Global budget limits on public hospitals have had the direct effect of allowing private hospitals to expand, and even flourish. The result overall has increased expenditures and has been characterized as "chaotic" (Bach, 1993: 191–192).

Physician numbers increased by 250 percent between 1960 and 1991, or an average of 3.4 percent per year. Beginning in 1971, entry into medical schools has been restricted but not sufficiently to reduce the oversupply of physicians—many of whom are underemployed. There is at least a 9-year lag in impact, and several decades are required to substantially decrease the number of practicing physicians. Monitoring of physician behavior was introduced in an effort to reduce overuse of costly technology, medication, and other forms of physician-ordered ambulatory care (Fielding and Lancry, 1993: 753; Glaser, 1993: 118).

The medical associations have agreed to help implement target budgets, after years of resistance. In 1992, negotiations between the associations and Social Security insurance officials led to an average 7 percent increase for physicians, with some variation between specialty areas. Approximately two-thirds of this is based on increases in patient utilization and one-third on an increase in physician income. These results contribute to local cost-control plans, which then go to the federal level for incorporation in a national plan. Any disputes that cannot be resolved by bargaining are referred to an arbitration commission (Glaser, 1993: 118).

Introduction of new technology in public hospitals has been subjected to a detailed evaluation to determine need and appropriateness. Regionalization efforts limit the adoption of certain technologies within given regions to a defined number of institutions.

Drug prices have been regulated and reimbursement for nonessential prescribed drugs has been reduced. Direct efforts are underway to reduce public insurance reimbursement for overused drugs that may have limited therapeutic value.

The regionalization effort is viewed as an important mechanism for cost control through more efficient distribution of expensive and high-technology health care resources. More vigorous regional health planning has been implemented. Deconcentration and decentralization, as well as more equitable distribution of services, are a primary part of the current planning process.

The 1971 efforts to decrease the number of physicians was not fully successful. The physician population grew by 43 percent between 1983 and 1993. Physicians have strongly resisted limits on entry or income growth. Their political influence has made government bureaucrats hesitant to further constrain their freedom (Bach, 1993: 193).

The government has not been very successful in promoting manufacture of medical technology. Roughly 80 percent of all high-technology equipment is imported. The tightly regulated environment for hospitals, accompanied by increasing cost controls, appears to severely constrain innovation and locally implemented efficiencies. Greater freedom for hospital administrators and/or improved incentive systems for productive innovation may be necessary if quality and productivity are to be maintained or improved (Sobczak et al., 1988: 31; Lacronique, 1988: 392).

The health care system in France has been characterized as "organized anarchy" and continues to be fragmented. Responsibility is divided at the local and national levels. This leads to lack of coordination and considerable waste and inefficiency. The system is complicated, which limits easy access by unemployed, homeless, and single individuals with low incomes, especially women. For example, pregnant, lower-income women often have difficulty securing full maternity benefits simply because of system complexity (Pouvourville and Renaud, 1985: 162; Stevens, 1989: 126; Blondel and Saurel-Cuizolles, 1991: 214).

Accurate accounting of resource allocation is difficult because of limited information systems. This also complicates adequate communication between fee-for-service physicians in the private clinics and salaried full-time physicians in public hospitals. Problems have been identified in continuity of care, disease prevention, health promotion, and especially posthospital followup care (Rodwin, 1989: 265–285).

The incidence of AIDS is increasing but is not yet a major problem. Although care of AIDS patients is an issue, comparative studies indicate that younger French physicians are less inclined to fear treating AIDS patients than are young physicians in the United States and Canada (Shapiro et al., 1992: 510).

SUMMARY AND CONCLUSIONS

National health insurance was initiated in the 1920s and became universal in 1967. Well-trained professionals in federal and local government bureaucracies are in charge of health care policy and overall management of health care programs. There is considerable local diversity, substantial provider freedom, but fragmentation and lack of service integration. Government does not severely limit freedom of choice for either patients or providers.

The health care system provides relatively comprehensive benefits but is complicated and expensive—with the highest proportion of GDP allocated to health care among European countries. Much of the increasing cost is associated with growth in private hospitals through expanding services and beds, heavy use of pharmaceuticals, and a surplus of physicians. Measures to curb costs, such as global budgeting for hospitals, have had the effect of limiting use of high-technology medicine more than in some other countries.

Physicians earn considerably less per capita income than in other countries because of limited bargaining power, a government-imposed fee schedule, and excess numbers, but they see fewer patients and suffer considerably less hassle than elsewhere. They are able to concentrate on patient care with little requirement for defensive medicine and do not have to deal directly with cost-containment issues, because public authorities and hospital administrators have this responsibility. Nor do they have to worry about billing or collection of fees, since they collect at the time of service (ambulatory physicians) or are paid a salary (hospitals).

Long-term care is supported through the insurance system and is relatively well developed throughout the country. Facilities are largely public and designed to provide comfortable environments for dependent older and disabled residents. The system of services for the elderly is also fragmented but appears to treat older people with respect.

A continuing series of reforms have helped modernize the health care system but have so far not fully allowed for introduction of needed cost-effective technology. Much remains to be accomplished on the financial management, modernization, and cost-control agendas.

REFERENCES

ANDERSON, ODIN W. (1989). *The Health Service Continuum in Democratic States: An Inquiry into Solvable Problems.* Ann Arbor, Mich.: Health Administration Press.

BACH, STEPHEN (1993). Health Care Reforms in the French Hospital System, *International Journal of Health Planning and Management,* 8 (3): 189–200.

BACH, STEPHEN, and CAROLINE HYDE-PRICE (1994). French Lessons, *Health Service Journal,* 104 (April 14): 26–27.

BARRIER, GENEVIEVE (1989). Emergency Medical Services for Treatment of Mass Casualties, *Critical Care Medicine,* 17 (10): 1062–1067.

BLONDEL, BEATRICE, and MARIE-JOSEPHE SAUREL-CUIZOLLES (1991). An Indicator of Adverse Pregnancy Outcome in France: Not Receiving Maternity Benefits, *Journal of Epidemiology and Community Health,* 45: 211–215.

COCKERHAM, WILLIAM C. (1995). *Medical Sociology,* 6th ed. Englewood Cliffs, N.J.: Prentice Hall.

DE LOZIER, J., H. E. KEREK-BODDEN, T. LECOMTE, A. MIZRAHI, S. SANDIER, and E. SCHACH (1989). Ambulatory Care: France, Federal Republic of Germany, and the United States, *Vital Health Statistics* (Series 5), 5 (5): 1–31.

DOTY, PAMELA, and ANDREE MIZRAHI (1989). Long-Term Care for the Elderly in France, in Teresa Schwab, *Caring for an Aging World.* New York: McGraw-Hill, pp. 58–94.

FELDMAN, JAMIE (1992). The French Are Different: French and American Medicine in the Context of AIDS, *Western Journal of Medicine,* 157 (3): 345–349.

FIELDING, JONATHAN E., and PIERRE-JEAN LANCRY (1993). Lessons from France—"Vive la Difference," *Journal of the American Medical Association,* 270 (6): 748–756.

FOREMAN, F. (1994). Those Hearty French, *Boston Globe.*

FROSSARD, MICHAEL (1990). Hospital Strategy and Regional Planning in France, *International Journal of Health Planning and Management,* 5: 59–63.

GIRAUD, ALEXANDRA, and DOMINIQUE JOLLY (1992). How to Induce Physicians to Engage in Quality Assurance Activities in a University Hospital: A Policy, *Quality Assurance in Health Care,* 4 (1): 19–24.

GLASER, WILLIAM A. (1993). How Expenditure Caps and Expenditure Targets Really Work, *Milbank Quarterly,* 71 (1): 97–127.

HENRARD, JEAN-CLAUDE, BERNARD CASSOU, and DOMINIQUE LE DISERT (1990). The Effects of System Characteristics on Policy Implementation and Functioning of Care for the Elderly in France, *International Journal of Health Services*, 20 (1): 125–139.

LACRONIQUE, J. F. (1984). Health Services in France, in Marshall Raffel (ed.), *Comparative Health Systems: Descriptive Analysis of 14 National Health Systems*. University Park: Pennsylvania State University Press, pp. 261–283.

LACRONIQUE, J. F. (1988). Technology in France, *International Journal of Technology Assessment in Health Care*, 4: 385–394.

LAFFONT, I., and R. G. PRIEST (1992). A Comparison of French and British Mental Health Legislation, *Psychological Medicine*, 22: 843–850.

LAMARQUE, JEAN LOUIS, and JOSEPH PUJOL (1993). The Impact of New Imaging Techniques on Health Care and Its Costs in France, *Investigative Radiology*, 28 (Supp. 3): S51–S54.

LAUNOY, G., X. Le LOUTOUR, M. GIGNOUX, D. POTTIER, and G. DUGLEUX (1992). Influence of Rural Environment on Diagnosis, Treatment, and Prognosis of Colorectal Cancer, *Journal of Epidemiology and Community Health*, 46: 365–367.

LUDVIGSEN, CAROL (1993). Positively French, *Nursing Times*, 89 (3): 42–43.

MOATTI, J. P., C. CHANUT, and J. M. BENECH (1994). Researcher-Driven Versus Policy-Driven Economic Appraisal of Health Technologies: The Case of France, *Social Science and Medicine*, 38 (12): 1625–1633.

NICKSON, KEITH (1988). Hospital CEOs: Management French-Style, *Health Care*, 30 (7): 22.

NORDBERG, MARIE (1989). EMS in China and France, *Emergency Medical Services*, 18 (3): 32–36.

ODOM, JOHN W., RONALD W. JARL, CARL R. BOYD, and KENNETH G. SWAN (1990). The First Flying Ambulance, *Journal of Air Medical Transport*, 9 (12): 11–13.

PAYER, LYNN (1988). *Medicine and Culture: Varieties of Treatment in the United States, England, West Germany, and France*. New York: Henry Holt.

PETERS, TOM (1991). Medicine and Management—So Much for "Science," *Health Care Forum Journal* (May/June): 43–46.

DE POUVOURVILLE, GERARD (1986). Hospital Reforms in France Under a Socialist Government, *The Milbank Quarterly*, 64 (3): 392–413.

DE POUVOURVILLE, GERARD, and M. RENAUD (1985). Hospital System Management in France and Canada: National Pluralism and Provincial Centralism. *Social Science and Medicine*, 20 (2): 153–167.

RICHERSON, MICHAEL (1992). Managing International Medical Costs, *Benefits Quarterly*, 8 (4): 45–49.

RITCHIE, KAREN, JEAN-MARIE ROBINE, LUC LETENNEUR, and JEAN-FRANCOIS DARTIGUES (1994). Dementia-Free Life Expectancy in France, *American Journal of Public Health*, 84 (2): 232–236.

RODWIN, VICTOR G. (1989). New Ideas for Health Policy in France, Canada, and Britain, in M. Field (ed.), *Success and Crisis in National Health Systems*. London: Routledge, pp. 265–285.

ROEMER, MILTON I. (1991). *National Health Systems of the World: The Countries*, Vol. I. New York: Oxford University Press.

ROEMER, MILTON I. (1993). *National Health Systems of the World: The Issues*, Vol. II. New York: Oxford University Press.

SCHNEIDER, MARKUS, RUDOLF K.-H. DENNERLEIN, AYNUR KOSE, and LEA SCHOLTES (1992). *Health Care in the EC Member States*. Amsterdam: Elsevier.

SCHRAUB, SIMON, MICHEL MOUGEOT, MARIETTE MERCIER, and PIERRE BOURGEOIS (1991). Evaluation from Population Registry Data of Health Care Expenditure During the Six Months after Cancer Diagnosis, *Health Policy*, 18: 219–229.

SHAPIRO, MARTIN F., RODNEY A. HAYWARD, DIDIER GUILLEMOT, and DIDIER JAYLE (1992). Residents' Experiences in, and Attitudes Toward, the Care of Persons with AIDS in Canada, France, and the United States, *Journal of the American Medical Association*, 268 (4): 510–515.

SKOLNICK, ANDREW A. (1994). Protecting Privacy of Computerized Patient Information May Lie in the Cards, *Journal of the American Medical Association*, 272 (3): 187–189.

SOBCZAK, PATRICK M., MYRON D. FOTTLER, and DANIEL CHASTAGNER (1988). Managing Retrenchment in French Public Hospitals: Philosophical and Regulatory Constraints, *International Journal of Health Planning and Management*, 3: 19–34.

STEVENS, J. B. (1989). Some Lessons from France, *Health Services Management* (October): 124–127.

THAYER, CHRISTINE (1986). New Approaches to Budgetary Control in the Health Service in France, *Hospital and Health Service Administration* (November): 254–257.

VOGT, H. BRUCE, DAVID A. SMITH, and ROMAN M. HENDRICKSON (1993). Family Practice—World Perspective, *Journal of the American Board of Family Practice*, 6 (3): 293–295.

WEILL, CAROLINE (1993). Minimally Invasive Therapy, *Health Policy*, 23: 31–47.

WILSFORD, DAVID (1987). The Cohesion and Fragmentation of Organized Medicine in France and the United States, *Journal of Health Politics, Policy, and Law*, 12 (3): 481–503.

WILSFORD, DAVID (1991). *Doctors and the State: The Politics of Health Care in France and the United States*. Durham, N.C.: Duke University Press.

8

THE NETHERLANDS

Gradual Adaptation

The Netherlands is highly urbanized and densely populated although much of the country is rural agricultural land (the "polders") reclaimed from the sea. The Dutch have a long history of industrious attention to expansion of opportunities within a relatively small landmass, including one of the most comprehensive, universal, and well-funded health care systems in the world. They take great pride in their ability to constantly adjust and upgrade services in keeping with medical advancements in other countries of Europe and North America. Key features of the health care system are summarized in Table 8-1.

Widespread evaluation and debate have been underway for some time about growth in costs as the population ages. These concerns formed part of the basis for a reform movement initiated in 1987 to introduce more market-based approaches to cost control. Costs are to be market-driven through incentives for providers and private insurers to limit expenditures, with somewhat less direct government oversight and regulatory control than before (Graig, 1993: 117).

The Netherlands scores consistently near the top on measures of life expectancy, infant mortality, access to primary care, and public satisfaction with health care, suggesting an overall high rate of effectiveness for the health care system.

DEMOGRAPHIC CHARACTERISTICS

The Netherlands had 15 million people as of 1993, with an age 65 or greater population of 12.8 percent. This is a somewhat lower proportion than in nearby European countries. Life expectancy is among the highest of the industrialized nations (81.1 for females in 1991; 74.1 for males), and infant mortality is among the lowest (6.5 in 1991). Poverty is minimal as a direct result of a widely accepted social support system. The government deliberately redistributes income through the tax system to minimize social class distinctions (Cockerham, 1995: 288–290).

A high proportion of the population lives in the four major cities: Amsterdam, Rotterdam, the Hague, and Utrecht. These cities are also the locations for many of the principal health problems, such as AIDS (75 percent of all patients live, or were treated in, Amsterdam), mental disorder, and hard drug abuse (75 percent of cases are in the four major cities). A small proportion of the population of ethnic minority status (5 percent) have a higher incidence of health problems than the dominant group. The big cities generally seem to be less healthy as places of residence than smaller cities and the countryside (Garretsen and Raat, 1991: 160–163; Visser, 1993: 252).

The overall mortality rate is somewhat lower in rural areas than in cities. However, mortality rates are higher in the less urbanized region of the south than in the northern region. A higher incidence of lower-income residents live in this region and are more prone to smoke, drink, and live a generally

Table 8-1 Features of Dutch Health Care

- The government is expected to assume responsibility for organizing and regulating health care and is deeply involved in directing and regulating the delivery system.
- A very conscious health promotion policy has been in place since 1984 when the World Health Organization health targets were formally adopted by the government.
- A public health system with local offices distributed throughout the country promotes health education and healthy living.
- Financing and services are implemented through a mix of public and private initiatives, with a recent emphasis on greater use of the private market.
- A global budgeting system for hospitals and fee regulation for physicians have enabled the government to stabilize costs at about 8.6 percent of GDP.
- General practitioner physicians are paid on a capitated basis for 62 percent of the population in sickness funds, and on a fee-for-service basis for 38 percent (the more affluent) of the population who are privately insured; specialist physicians, largely hospital-based, are paid on a fee-for-service basis.

Sources: Based on data from ten Have and Keasberry, 1992: 466; Graig, 1993: 115.

less healthy life-style than the larger population. Consequently, they contract a greater number of high-risk illnesses such as cardiovascular problems (Mackenbach, Kunst, and Looman, 1991: 231).

The long-term government policy of creating new and modern cities and towns in other formerly rural regions has meant that rural–urban differences in access to health care have been largely erased. Recent surveys also indicate few differences in health status and health care between elderly residents of rural and urban areas. Similarly, differences in access to health care between the poor and affluent have been largely eliminated (Perenboom, Lako, and Schouten, 1989: 127).

HISTORICAL PERSPECTIVE

The health care system has a history somewhat comparable to its German neighbor. The system grew from mutual-aid societies associated with medieval guilds. Employment-based insurance was expanded over time until approximately 40 percent of the population was covered in 1933. National health insurance was introduced for the first time during the German occupation of World War II, and has evolved since to a distinctive Dutch system. For example, somewhat more compassion and provision for the elderly and disabled seem evident in the Netherlands as compared to Germany (ten Have and Keasberry, 1992: 465).

Health care policy has shifted from an emphasis on growth of services toward cost containment and cutbacks after 1980. This has led to serious conflicts at the political level and between major stakeholders in the system: hospitals, the medical profession, and insurance providers, both public and private (Maarse, 1989: 257–258).

The Dekker Commission Recommendations

The Dekker Commission on Structure and Financing of the Health Care System pub-

lished its report, *Willingness to Change*, in 1987, with recommendations for improvements in ambulatory care, more cost-effective hospital services, greater coordination of services, and privatization. The recommendations were largely adopted by the government, beginning the shift toward creation of incentives for cost control rather than direct government regulation. A series of studies indicated that approximately 15 percent of health care costs could be saved through greater efficiencies and more financial responsibility by consumers (Schneider et al., 1992: 73).

The first steps toward implementation were undertaken in 1989. A formal legislative reform proposal was introduced for parliamentary consideration with emphasis on restructuring the insurance system and increased reliance on market forces. The recommendations for cost control aroused great controversy among public interest groups; the Ministries of Welfare, Health, and Cultural Affairs; and other interested parties (Schneider et al., 1992: 73; Graig, 1993: 122).

The revised package of benefits included (Schneider et al., 1992: 73) the following:

- Preventive care
- Obstetric and maternity care
- Nursing, treatment, and care of the chronically ill including home care
- Rehabilitation for the physically handicapped
- Medical and surgical treatment and recovery
- Psychological care
- Nursing, treatment, and care of the physically handicapped, mentally ill, and psychiatric patients
- Care of the elderly, including home health care and support

A Reformulated Plan Simons

Before the package could be fully implemented, national elections led to a change in government with a more liberal persuasion. Some modifications were made to emphasize equity and increased quality of care. Public insurance had been primarily for lower-income and high-risk consumers; private insurance was purchased by higher-income and lower-risk individuals. This approach was viewed by the new government as inappropriate. The distinction between private and public insurance was therefore decreased. Basic coverage was to be provided to all members of the population through the publicly defined package of benefits. Sickness funds and private insurers would be required to offer the basic plan, but could offer supplemental coverage for such things as private hospital rooms, artificial appliances, outpatient therapies, plastic surgery, abortion, sterilization, and full prescription drug coverage. Competitive rates could be charged (Schneider et al., 1992: 79; Graig, 1993: 123–124).

The reformulated *Plan Simons* thus gave greater emphasis to payroll taxes for public insurance (82 percent of costs) supplemented by flat rate premiums (18 percent) paid by consumers. Ninety-seven percent of health care expenses would be covered by public insurance, and the remaining 3 percent could be covered by private insurance. Hospital bed capacity was to be substantially reduced as a cost-cutting measure, and even greater emphasis was given to ambulatory care and outpatient treatment (Graig, 1993: 126).

The government-initiated changes had the effect of creating greater incentives for efficiency in the sickness funds. For example, new information systems have been developed by the sickness funds to capture utilization and cost data. Financial incentives have been created for GPs as rewards for lower referral rates. Home health care has been emphasized as a more cost-effective method than institutionalization for care of the chronically ill (Schneider et al., 1992: 82).

CULTURAL FACTORS

The government-initiated social support system demonstrates an ideological commitment to social solidarity on the one hand and an emphasis on self-help and individual-

ism on the other. Private initiative is encouraged but in the context of rather strict public expectations of behavior. Equity and universality in basic health care are widely supported by all citizens regardless of income or circumstances. However, a certain skepticism toward scientific medicine is also an important part of the public value system (ten Have and Keasberry, 1992: 467).

The cultural tendency is to approach major problems from an objective and rational standpoint, which means careful study and extensive discussion are undertaken prior to major changes in health care policy. For example, rationing is widely viewed as necessary, given the ongoing growth in health care costs. However, systematic study of various forms of rationing is required to create a rational basis for the choices to be made.

The Dutch heart transplant evaluation study is an illustration. It generated information on the economic, ethical, legal and social, as well as medical issues associated with heart transplantation after 1984. Although the study suggested it was not economically efficient to transplant hearts for people over age 55, because of limited benefits in additional years of life, ethical considerations predominated and no limit was placed on age of surgery. Equity won out over efficiency in the public debate (van Hout et al., 1993: 90).

A second example was the appointment of the Dekker Commission. The report of this committee served as the rational basis for a redirection of health care investments toward, among other things, more and better primary care while constraining secondary care and high-technology medicine (ten Have and Keasberry, 1992: 468).

The Dutch have long been an experimental and entrepreneurial society, causing them to reach overseas to colonize new territories in earlier historical periods. More recently, they have focused on developing new communities and social experiments in the polder lands reclaimed from the sea. These communities have provided a rich basis for testing new approaches to health care, through creation, for example, of a U.S. style health maintenance organization in the new town of Almere (Kirkman-Liff, 1989: 35; Sixma et al., 1993: 2567).

Dutch citizens feel a sense of entitlement to health care. They are willing to tolerate cost-saving measures, but continue to demand the basic benefits. A survey eliciting opinions from consumers, physicians, and nurses found the overall level of satisfaction to be quite high, although with some variation between groups, as indicated in Table 8-2. Nurses are considerably less satisfied than consumers or physicians (explained at least in part by the high workload in nursing), but the overall level of satisfaction is very high (Starfield, 1991; Graig, 1993: 126; Tymstra and Andela, 1993: 2996).

POLITICAL INFLUENCES

Substantial differences in liberal and conservative ideology among political parties requires a major emphasis on consensus building prior to major national decisions—always accompanied by vigorous and confrontational debate. Assorted national organizations, such as the sickness funds, the Central Authority for Health Care Tariffs, the National Health Council, the National Hospital Facilities Board, and the National Council for Public Health, as well as numerous other special interest groups contribute to the debate (Saltman and de Roo, 1989: 776).

Although government takes a significant role in guiding the policy debate, much of the immediate control and responsibility for implementation are delegated to the local and individual level. Study groups or commissions appointed to examine major issues play a critical role in securing input from interested groups. Their recommendations for action are very carefully considered by the parliament before new programs are implemented.

SOCIAL ORGANIZATION OF HEALTH CARE

Public health, primary care, and hospital care are very separate enterprises. Basic health care is provided through a public health system with local offices throughout the country. Primary health care is provided by general practitioners who maintain independent and largely solo practices in each community. Each patient is supposed to be on a GP patient list and must be referred by the GP to specialist physicians or hospitals. Secondary and tertiary care in hospitals is largely in private nonprofit institutions (Sixma et al., 1993: 2567).

Public Health

A public health planning report was issued in 1988 based on World Health Organization guidelines: *Health for All by the Year 2000*. The plan enumerated national goals and policies to improve health status. Particular attention was given to the physical and social environment as well as life-style factors

Table 8-2 Consumer, Physician, and Nurse Judgments About Adequacy of the Dutch Health Care System

Question		Consumers	Physicians	Nurses
How do you rate the quality of health care?	Adequate or very adequate	84%	91.6%	68%
	Fair	14	8	29
	Poor or very poor	2	0.4	3

Source: Based on data from Tymstra and Andela, 1993: 2996.

that contribute to health. The plan focused on involving the public in health education and promotion of healthy living. This included, for example, efforts to reduce alcohol and tobacco consumption (especially among young people) while promoting good nutrition, exercise, and stress reduction. The health status of the elderly is also emphasized. These efforts have resulted in substantial declines in smoking, among other achievements, as indicated by periodic national Health Interview Survey results (Swenkels, 1989: 74).

Physicians

The general practitioner is the central gatekeeper and dominant figure in the primary health care system. Few people see a specialist without first visiting a GP. Referrals are made to a specialist only if the GP cannot complete the diagnosis or treatment. Approximately 85 percent of patient visits end without further referral. However, the GP generally has limited access to diagnostic and treatment technology. The GP has an average of 2,300 patients, with five visits annually per patient as the norm. Fifteen percent of the contacts are house calls. General practitioners outnumber specialists 2 to 1. The overall physician/patient ratio is 2.4 to 1,000 (ten Have and Keasberry, 1992: 463–464).

General practitioners have been working vigorously to establish national standards for quality of care. Most physicians are supportive of such standards. A careful procedure has been implemented to assure that the standards are sound and contribute to better patient care. However, many physicians do not necessarily abide by the standards in their personal practice of medicine because there is little financial reward for doing so (Grol, 1990: 361).

Both GPs and specialists are represented in fee and capitation negotiations by their professional units (National General Practitioners Association and the National Specialists Association) of the Dutch Medical Association. Negotiations include representatives from Ministries of Social Affairs, Welfare, Health Care and Culture, the Association of Dutch Sickness Funds, and private insurers—as required by the law. More than 90 percent of all physicians are members of the professional associations (Kirkman-Liff, 1989: 472).

Patient choice of primary and specialist physicians is very limited. Patients must register with a GP in the area of residence. In some rural areas, the GP also acts as pharmacist, dispensing drugs as well as primary care (Schneider et al., 1992: 202).

A comparative study of attitudes toward medical decisions in the Netherlands, the United Kingdom, and Belgium indicates that Dutch physicians may be more willing to take risks in trying new procedures than their counterparts in the other two countries. They also appear to have more patient-centered attitudes (as contrasted to a disease-centered or impersonal attitude) than their counterparts in the United Kingdom, and especially Belgium. They appear to take greater interest in patients and give them more autonomy and responsibility in self-care (Grol et al., 1990a: 100–103; 1990b: 135).

Hospital-based specialists. Physician specialists have traditionally worked as private entrepreneurs—except in university teaching and other specialized hospitals where they are on salary. They are usually members of group practices or partnerships in which decisions are made on the basis of unanimous consent. Responsibilities are defined by internal contracts between physicians. New members of a partnership are expected to "buy in" at substantial cost, because membership is conceived as a type of property ownership. Specialists are contractually related to the hospital with stipulations regarding use of facilities and responsibilities. Nearly all specialists practice in hospital polyclinics. The exceptions are ophthalmologists, dermatologists, and psychiatrists, who generally maintain ambulatory practices as well as polyclinic practices (Kirkman-Liff, 1989: 471; Saltman and de Roo, 1989: 776–777).

A rapid increase in the supply of specialists has kept incomes from rising significantly. The negotiation process among physicians, sickness funds, and private insurers has limited fees and income, as have increases in GP numbers. Here, as elsewhere, deliberate increases in services provided to patients is used as a vehicle for increasing income. General practitioner income in the Netherlands is less than half the U.S. average. Specialist income is only modestly greater than for GPs (Kirkman-Liff, 1989: 476; Graig, 1993: 121).

Pediatrics has been growing as a specialty with consequent growth in children's health services. Four children's hospitals serve as specialized centers. Most pediatricians are on salary with these hospitals or with general hospitals having pediatric departments. Children's health services are heavily focused on preventive care, with a high incidence of vaccination and regular examinations to detect problems early (Visser, 1993: 251).

Sickness funds maintain detailed records on physician practice patterns as a condition for payment of fees. Submission of data is required on referrals; use of laboratory, radiology, and physical therapy; hospital admissions; lengths of stay; and pharmaceutical prescriptions. Consequently, an extensive database exists to monitor practice patterns, including physician-specific profiles that can be summarized to provide regional and national profiles. The data are used by medical advisors (usually physicians themselves) in the sickness funds as social pressure to encourage improvement of quality and cost control (Kirkman-Liff, 1989: 477).

Physicians in the Netherlands have gone on national strikes in an effort to maintain or improve their position in the health care system, but not necessarily with satisfactory results. The sickness funds, private insurers, and government appear to have the upper hand (Kirkman-Liff, 1989: 479).

Women physicians. Although only 13 percent of physicians were female in 1992, increased numbers are enrolling in medical schools; student bodies are now more than 50 percent women. Practices consist heavily of female patients (71 percent in one study) and pediatrics. Research indicates that female physicians spend more time than men in patient encounters, as counselors and in diagnostic testing. However, female physicians are less inclined to perform surgery. They appear more interested in continuity of care rather than single appointments with patients (Bensing, van den Brink-Munen, and de Bakker, 1993: 225–227; Visser, 1993: 253).

Alternative medicine. Alternative medical procedures such as homeopathy, acupuncture, and manipulative therapy are covered in part by sickness funds and are included in most private insurance packages. More than half of all GPs either support such approaches through referrals or include alternatives in their practice—especially homeopathy and manual or hot bath therapy. However, GPs believe that alternative practitioners should be fully trained and certified in their specialized fields, as is required of physicians (Knipschild, Kleijnen, and ter Riet, 1990: 625; Visser and Peters, 1990, 227–228).

Medical education. Nine medical schools are supported by the national university system and are funded fully by the federal department of education. The Netherlands has eight university teaching hospitals that offer basic medical residencies and specialization training. Funding comes directly from the Ministry of Health. Basic medical training is a 6-year process, followed by advanced training in one of the 28 official specialties (Lapre and de Roo, 1990: 173).

Physicians were free until 1983 to specialize as they chose within the space limitations of training institutions. Under the existing law, insurance companies were required to offer a contract to new specialists without restriction. Enrollments had increased steadily before the hospital global budget process diminished opportunities. As the economy slowed between 1975 and 1985, revenue declined, requiring a policy change. University budgets were cut back drastically. A lower physician supply was deemed critical to cutting health care costs, because specialist services were growing more rapidly than any other health care sector (Lapre and de Roo, 1990: 92).

A general agreement on limitation of new specialist training was concluded between the government and the specialists association in 1984. Medical school enrollments were cut to 1,400 new students per year, a decrease of 30 percent from the prior years. In 1989, the graduation rate was down to 1,150 new physicians. The enrollment change did not solve the oversupply problem because of certain defects in the agreement that allowed new specialists to continue contracting with insurers (Lapre and de Roo, 1990: 181).

The policy changes led to serious tensions within training programs and among members of the medical community. However, specialist organizations eventually agreed to cutbacks in specialty training to make the supply fit more appropriately with available positions and health service needs (Lapre and de Roo, 1990: 92, 181; Stevens, Diederiks, and Philipsen, 1992: 301).

Nurses

Nursing developed long ago into a full-fledged profession but without achieving a status comparable to physicians. Particularly strong efforts have been underway since the mid-1970s to improve both education and prestige (Dassen, Nijhuis, and Philipsen, 1989: 389).

One consequence of global budgeting for hospitals was an increase in the workload for nurses. Although the number of operational beds and patient-days have declined, patients are generally older and sicker, requiring more intense nursing care. As noted earlier, a survey in 1991 revealed that nurses were considerably less satisfied with the health care system than the general public or physicians (see Table 8-2). The attractiveness of

nursing as a profession has appeared to decline. Widespread dissatisfaction led to unrest and a strengthened union (in 1989) to undertake collective bargaining with employers (Pool, 1991: 197; Tymstra and Andela, 1993: 2996).

Increased emphasis on primary care is strongly supported by consumers (90 percent), physicians (89 percent), and nurses (98 percent), as is home or community nursing. The changing emphasis has caused major changes in nursing responsibilities and is leading to increased status. The district nurse now serves as the coordinator or case manager for home care—in consultation with GPs, physical therapists, dietitians, social workers, and home help workers. Consultation and education at child health centers are also major responsibilities—in keeping with the national emphasis on maternal and child health. Nurses are assigned to specific geographic areas and have primary responsibility for public health education as well as public nursing care—often under the sponsorship of Cross Associations that have networks throughout the country. Even so, community nurses are not yet compensated sufficiently to attract adequate numbers into the profession. Their role is overshadowed by the generally higher status and much higher salaries of physicians in district centers (Jonkergouw, Kruyt, and Hanrahan, 1990: 211–213; van der Zwaard, 1992: 1137; Tymstra and Andela, 1993: 2999).

Male nurses. The Netherlands has a relatively higher proportion of male nurses, who make up 18 percent of the total number. They are more inclined than females to undertake highly technical roles, such as in intensive care units, and are more involved in managerial positions. They also appear to be more professionally oriented. Many function somewhat more like physician assistants or nurse-practitioners. However, no formal designation of "midlevel practitioner" has been initiated (Dassen et al., 1989: 387).

Nursing education. Formal nurse-training programs were initiated in the 1870s by hospitals. This continued to be the tradition until 1972 when the first undergraduate programs were initiated at institutions of higher education. The 18 university schools of nursing offer baccalaureate degrees to about 1,200 graduates per year (in 1991). Hospital-based training continues to dominate nonetheless. Each hospital-trained nurse now receives a basic theoretical foundation and then specializes in a chosen field (Diepeveen-Speekenbrink, 1992b: 395).

Secondary schools offer vocational training programs for junior nursing positions. Even this level of training continues to be primarily in hospitals. Most larger hospitals have their own educational programs with a curriculum based on national statutory requirements (Dassen et al., 1989: 389; Diepeveen-Speekenbrink, 1992a: 101; O'Sullivan, 1992: 34).

Graduate education and research have been very slow to develop. The Netherlands is behind some other advanced countries in this respect. Part-time graduate programs were started at universities in Limburg, Utrecht, and Groningen in the 1988–1990 period. However, very little nursing research is yet underway. The field of nursing is thus continuing to undergo appraisal and evolution (Diepeveen-Speekenbrink, 1992a: 109; 1992b: 408).

Pharmacists and Pharmaceuticals

Drugs were fully covered by insurance funds as of 1992, but with tight government controls through negotiations with manufacturers, wholesalers, and pharmacists to establish prices. Pharmacists receive a fixed markup for dispensing, but receive an incentive bonus for promoting lower-cost generic drugs. Fewer pharmacies per 100,000 population exist here than in other European countries, in part because of the tight price controls (Schneider, 1992: 205).

Pharmacists have developed a computer-based drug surveillance and information system that encourages close cooperation between pharmacists and physicians. Nearly every pharmacy uses a computer to provide the information base for evaluating the medical and drug history of a patient before issuing medication. This is possible in part because of the manner in which pharmacy services are organized (van Gruting and de Geir, 1992: 1008).

Each pharmacy serves a population of 6,000 to 7,000 people and has a registered list of clients for whom it has nearly complete automated records or histories of prescriptions and nonprescriptive medications. Most families secure their prescriptions from the same pharmacy over a period of many years. They are also hospitalized as needed in the same location and receive medications that are also recorded. Hospital pharmacists in particular have played a leading role as part of the patient care team in implementing clinical pharmacy, including a beneficial role in developing new drug therapy and increased emphasis on home medication. As the population becomes more mobile, a linked national system has become necessary with less dependence on local records (Vree, 1990: 26–29; van Gruting and de Gier, 1992: 1008).

Pharmacists receive more extensive education than is required in most other countries, often reaching a knowledge and skill level comparable to physicians. Physicians therefore treat pharmacists as full colleagues. If evidence suggests an error, immediate consultation between pharmacist and physician is initiated. Pharmacists feel relatively free to suggest an alternative drug that might be more appropriate, given the patient's record and condition. They exchange detailed information about patients via computer so as to improve the management of patient care and drug usage while diminishing the potential for harming people through misuse of medications. The physician retains legal responsibility for prescribing drugs, but the pharmacist is a close consultant and advisor (van Gruting and de Gier, 1992: 1008).

Pharmacists also advise physicians on available new drugs—rather than relying on salespersons from drug manufacturers. Formal discussions between pharmacists and physicians have led to cooperation in developing standard drug treatments, or "formularies," for use with specific problems. Studies indicate that negative drug interactions have been relatively common and can be largely avoided through careful record keeping and consultation (van Gruting and de Gier, 1992: 1009).

The interaction between physicians and pharmacists is more difficult in community pharmacies than in hospitals because GPs are more hesitant than specialists to share their records with pharmacists—for reasons of local confidentiality. However, pharmacists have adopted a strict confidentiality code to guard against misuse of the information (van Gruting and de Geir, 1992: 1010).

Increased effort has been undertaken to directly involve the patient in drug management through education and understanding of the role of drugs in health care. Because patients tend to forget much of the advice given by physicians about medications, the pharmacist plays a very important role in further assuring that patients understand the nature of their medications and how to best use them (van Gruting and de Gier, 1992: 1011).

Health Care Administration

Professional training in health care administration has a long tradition. Several universities offer undergraduate and graduate degrees in the field. Faculty have exhibited considerable interest in improving education for administrators. For example, in 1982, Erasmus University in Rotterdam initiated a multidisciplinary and problem-oriented curriculum in health care policy and management. The idea was to develop an educational approach that would focus on development of the problem-solving capacities of students while giving them a broad exposure to the several disciplines associated with management: social science, policy and organizational theory, health care law, health care economics, and research methods. Although the effort had some positive out-

comes, many of the innovative elements were lost because of increasing emphasis on faculty and student research (Moen and Moll, 1993: 105–106).

Hospitals

Ninety percent of the hospitals are private and nonprofit. Most have a church affiliation, although a few are municipally owned. Nearly all hospitals have outpatient as well as inpatient facilities. Outpatient services are provided primarily by specialists who do preadmission diagnostic examinations as well as outpatient treatment. Most patients are referred to the hospital by general practitioners who do not have hospital privileges. As of 1990, there were 400 hospitals in the country, varying in size from 60 to 900 beds, with a total bed capacity of 122,350 (Schneider, 1992: 204).

Many smaller hospitals are trying to survive by shifting to outpatient primary care as a partial alternative to inpatient care. Arrangements with primary care providers allow the hospital to provide services complementary to GP primary care—often in the form of home care by GPs, nurses, home health workers, and others associated with the hospital. The intent is to provide comprehensive health care through a combination of hospital and home services (Maarse, Mur-Veeman, and Tijssen, 1990: 53).

This approach requires a level of cooperation and integration not heretofore widely achieved. Hospital administrators must collaborate with primary care providers, and specialists must collaborate with GPs and community nurses. The payment mechanism must be designed to compensate the collaborating providers, often requiring special arrangements with insurance funds. It has proven a challenge to bridge the cultural and experience gap between the various health care professionals involved (Maarse et al., 1990: 57).

Hospitals have increased their capacity through mergers or expansion despite the required decrease in beds within each region under global budgeting. Management has been streamlined with middle management gaining responsibility for departmental functions at the expense of central managers. A greater integration of physician specialists into the hospital administrative structure has also occurred, somewhat at the expense of physician influence as a distinct group within the hospital. Directors of nursing have been replaced by administrators with broader roles (Pool, 1991: 202).

Top management has gained overall power and professionalism (compared to physicians) as a result of the changes. The specialist medical staff continues to have great influence on hospital operations but is more dependent on executive leadership than formerly. Hospital trustees now play more of a supporting role in decisions, with major policy responsibility delegated to administrators (Pool, 1991: 202–206).

Medical Technology

The Dutch Health Council is responsible for decisions about adoption and diffusion of new technology. This influential group decides which technologies are to be reimbursed through public insurance programs. Most of the evaluations are based on investigations by medical school faculty and university hospitals, often with assistance from the Institute for Medical Technology Assessment at Rotterdam University (Borst-Eilers, 1993: 226).

The formal process of technology assessment includes several stages (Gelijns and Rigter, 1990: 157–158):

- Identifies technologies in need of assessment
- Collects needed data to conduct the evaluation
- Synthesizes relevant clinical outcomes and cost data
- Disseminates findings to decision makers
- Takes needed action

Each of these steps requires assurance that findings are scientifically and financially valid. The emphasis in the past has been on conducting clinical trials—particularly in

determining appropriateness and efficacy of new drugs, medical and surgical procedures, and vaccines or blood products. Technical and clinic appropriateness were particularly emphasized. Greater emphasis has recently been given to economic, social, ethical, and legal issues as well (Gelijns and Rigter, 1990: 157–158).

Regulation of technology was initiated by the Hospital Provisions Act, which required licensing permits for major new items. Hospitals have been quite ingenious in finding avenues for expansion within the regulatory environment—sometimes getting ahead of the government through installation of new technology prior to formal approval. The national authorities have rarely forced withdrawal of technology once it is in place (Saltman and de Roo, 1989: 784).

Physician specialists often insist on acquisition of new technology. They are directly responsible for up to 80 percent of all hospital revenues and expenditures and thus exert major influence on these decisions. They are given most of what they request if at all possible within global budget constraints. In fact, informal understandings essentially prohibit hospital administrators from interfering with activities that generate fee-for-service income to hospital specialists. Despite the administrative restructuring noted earlier, physician specialists continue to wield enormous influence on clinical dimensions of hospital operation (Saltman and de Roo, 1989: 784; Vondeling et al., 1993: 69).

Nonetheless, some types of technology, such as minimally invasive therapies, have been relatively slow to spread because of regulatory constraints. Physician conservatism also plays a role. For example, endoscopic treatment of colon cancer has been limited because of a strong taboo against open discussion of cancer with patients. Consequently, there is hesitation to recommend advanced treatments. Appropriate payment methods and sufficient funds for new therapies are slow in coming from the health care regulatory authorities (Vondeling et al., 1993: 76).

Information Systems

Much greater need for management information systems is evident—to increase understanding of costs for specific services as well as productivity data for hospitals and other providers. More medical decision-making data are also needed, such as the relationship between the mix of patients and costs for treatment. Greater use of computers is the most obvious solution for incorporation and management of such data. Hospitals are generally well-advanced in adopting computer information networks (Maarse, 1989: 272).

As of 1992, 38 percent of general practitioners had also introduced computer-based patient records, largely replacing paper records. The government is encouraging automation by providing an incentive (beginning in 1991) through payment for 60 percent of the expenses, up to $3,600 annually per physician. In exchange, the practitioners must provide their data to the government for analysis (van der Lei et al., 1993: 1936–1941).

Quality of Care

Quality assurance procedures and overall improved quality of care have become major priorities. The National Organization for Quality Assurance in Hospitals (CBO) was established in 1979 as a resource center to assist with the quality improvement process. It provides technical assistance, education, research, and development, while serving as a clearinghouse for information. Physicians, hospital medical directors, nurses, and other health professionals trained in the quality concepts support and supervise center activities. A professional staff works with hospitals and other providers throughout the country to develop quality assurance programs (Reerink, 1990: 16).

Studies have been initiated to assess the level of quality in hospital departments. Widespread involvement of medical and nursing staff is emphasized, under the assumption that key personnel must accept the needed changes or they are not likely to happen. A national policy on quality assurance was formally adopted in 1989, with responsibility for implementation left to health care practitioners (Reerink, 1991: 1445).

Emergency Medical Services

General practitioners are required to offer 24-hour service, and thus have the first-line responsibility for emergency care of their listed patients. A nationwide emergency number was initiated in 1990 to facilitate rapid response, bypassing general practitioners for the first time. Ambulances can be dispatched or the caller can be referred to a general practice physician. Ambulances are staffed by a driver trained in first aid and a nurse with emergency training. This team decides whether a patient should go to the hospital or can be helped adequately at the site. A GP is often consulted by phone in the process. Part of the purpose is to avoid unnecessary trips to hospital facilities (Sramek, Post, and Koster, 1994: 440–445).

Emergency departments are distinguished in large hospitals from *accident units* to which ambulances deliver victims of auto and other trauma situations. The emergency department only receives (1) referrals from GPs or specialists for quick entry to hospital care and (2) self-referred patients who do not first consult a physician. A substantial proportion of emergency room patients are seeking some type of primary care. Many are of low socioeconomic status, members of ethnic minority groups, elderly, or (the largest group) young people without a regular GP or health insurance coverage (Kooiman, van de Wetering, and van der Mast, 1989: 632–635).

Long-Term Care

Institutional settings served as the primary residence for 9.3 percent of the population aged 65 or older in 1990. Another 23 percent were served by some form of home care. The distribution of services is summarized in Table 8-3.

More than 90 percent of all nursing home beds were occupied by elderly residents in 1990. In addition, 44 percent of all hospital beds were occupied by individuals over age 65. Projections indicate the increase in demand for these services will grow at 1.5 to 2 percent per year through the year 2000. Several experiments are underway with case management of home care and residential care in an effort to find the combination that will provide high quality and yet minimize costs (van den Berg Jeths and Thorslund, 1994: 9).

Home Health Care

As noted earlier, home health care is receiving increased emphasis. Attempts are underway to make primary care more integrated with home care, adding to the continuity while replacing hospital services with more extensive, efficient, and less expensive home care. Any home care provided must be certified by a general practitioner who determines if there is sufficient need. Sickness fund insurance will then cover visits by physicians. Community nursing services are covered through the Exceptional Medical Expenses Act, allowing for 3 visits per day for 2.5 hours. Drugs and durable equipment used at home are also covered (Schneider, 1992: 206).

Table 8-3 Distribution of Elderly Citizens in Specialized Forms of Care (1990)

Facility Type	Number	Proportion of Elderly
Homes for the elderly	129,300	6.7
Nursing homes	45,000	2.4
Home health care	160,700	8.4
District nursing	306,500	14.6

Source. Based on data from van den Berg Jeths and Thorslund, 1994: 8.

Home care is predominately for the elderly, with only 28 percent for nonelderly (based on a study in one region). Several experiments have tested provision of home care for geriatric patients—yielding psychiatric problems with positive results. Household assistance as well as technical nursing care are provided at home for other physical problems (Kerkstra and Vorst-Thijssen, 1991: 47).

Other Special Services for the Elderly

Services for the elderly are generally well developed. Housing especially designed for older citizens is widely available with local home support services in addition to home health care. The Social Security system provides basic income for essentially all retired individuals. Even so, the family continues to play a very important role in caring for and generally supporting elderly members.

Mental Health Care

Mental health care is covered largely by private insurance or the Exceptional Medical Expenses Act. Mental health funding has gone largely to hospitals, which continued to consume 70 percent of available resources in 1990. Nonetheless, the number of hospital beds for mental disorders is declining, replaced by government efforts to forge a policy of regionalized community mental health services (Dekker and van den Langenberg, 1994: 494).

A residential component offers supported housing or halfway housing for former hospital patients, under the management responsibility of psychiatric and social service agencies. Day hospitals and outpatient clinics provide group, occupational, and psychotherapies. Crisis intervention centers are prepared to deal with individuals who need immediate assistance in the form of intensive short-term treatment. These centers serve primarily outpatients and have a small inpatient capacity—for short stays of 1 day to 1 week. Staffing consists of psychologists, psychiatrists, psychiatric nurses, and social workers. Clients can refer themselves to these units without entering the primary care system through GP referrals. Typical clients include individuals with depression, schizophrenia, or victims of spousal, child, and incest abuse (O'Sullivan, 1992: 34).

The Regional Institute for Ambulatory Mental Health Care provides psychiatric care to clients before and after hospital treatment. Each of the 58 regions of the country has a unit that attempts to integrate social, psychiatric, and psychotherapeutic care. Institutes work closely with Crisis Centers in provision of 24-hour services. Service centers also provide staff support for 275 patient support organizations located throughout the country. Seven asylums house individuals who have escaped from psychiatric confinement. Substance abuse victims are also served through this system (O'Sullivan, 1992: 35).

The city of Amsterdam is experimenting with an outreach program providing part-time residential treatment, continuity of care, and monitoring to provide ongoing support from teams of professionals. Early evidence suggests results are positive and could lead to less need for hospital treatment (Dekker and van den Langenberg, 1994: 495).

The mental health care system is not adequately prepared to deal with the serious mental disorder cases that result in criminal activity. This is particularly a problem with drug addicts. Problems of drug abuse are increasing, causing pressure on both the mental health system and the criminal justice system (Kat, 1991: 305).

ECONOMIC CHARACTERISTICS AND ISSUES

Although the health care system is relatively prosperous and is widely supported by the population, cost pressures have been a continuing problem here as elsewhere. The implementation of market-oriented policies in the early 1990s to increase efficiency and control costs was still in process of development in 1995, but several significant results were already evident. Competition between insurers was in place and consumers were given greater choice of insurance alternatives. Physician and hospital costs appeared to be contained. The types of care included in the insurance package were broadened to include 95 percent of current health services (Tymstra and Andela, 1993: 2995; Kirkman-Liff, 1994: 19).

Benefits

All Dutch citizens are entitled to a basic package of benefits. A Committee on Choices in Health Care was formed in the early 1990s to examine the required benefit package and possible adjustments. It recommended new methods for defining and assessing (1) necessary care, (2) clinical effectiveness, and (3) economic efficiency of alternative assessments. The new procedure and benefits were to apply to all citizens, regardless of income or age (Kirkman-Liff, 1994: 20).

A cash benefit is available for individuals who are unable to work because of illness. Full wages extend for the first 6 weeks. Then sickness benefits are available for 1 year at 70 percent of normal wages. Maternity leave extends for 16 weeks, with up to 6 weeks taken before delivery; full wages are paid for the entire period (Schneider et al., 1992: 207).

Financing

Basic support of sickness funds is from payroll taxes and general taxation. Employers contribute an average of 4.95 percent of salaries and employees contribute 3.15 percent, for a total of 8.1 percent of gross wages. The unemployed, elderly, and poorer members of the population are covered through premiums paid by national unemployment funds, retirement funds, or federal government contributions from tax revenues. Widows and orphans pay no premiums (Graig, 1993: 119).

Sickness funds are organized on a geographic basis and vary considerably in size, ranging from 4,000 to 250,000 members. Everyone in the middle- to lower-income categories (under $32,000 in 1992) within a region must be a member, regardless of employment status or health condition (62 percent of the population). Higher-income individuals must have private insurance. Most are covered under group plans sponsored by employers. Public employees are covered under a special public insurance fund. The Exceptional Medical Expenses Act (AWBZ) covers several types of medical expenses not insured by sickness funds, including child health problems, long-term care, medical devices, mental health care, and care for the physically disabled or mentally retarded (Schneider et al., 1992: 199).

A co-payment is charged for medical aids and appliances such as glasses, hearing aids, and physiotherapeutic treatments. Public health activities, research programs, subsidies to hospitals, institutional care, and management of the public insurance system are directly supported by the national government from tax revenues (Schneider et al., 1992: 200; ten Have and Keasberry, 1992: 464).

Catastrophic coverage (AWBZ) is also financed through payroll taxes, which were 5.8 percent of wages in 1992. Total health insurance costs were thus 13.9 percent of average wages. The share of financing by each program is summarized in Table 8-4.

Table 8-4 Sources of Funds for Health Care (1990)

Source	Percentage
Basic public insurance	39
Exceptional Medical Expenses Act (AWBZ)	24
Private health insurance	17
Co-payments and employer payments	11
Income and other nonpayroll taxes	8

Source: Based on data from Schneider et al., 1992: 200.

Self-employed individuals and students are insured privately but must pay full premiums. About 90 percent of the publicly insured population also have supplemental private coverage for dentures and other benefits not provided (Schneider et al., 1992: 208).

Payments to physicians. General practitioners are paid on a capitation basis for 62 percent of the population insured under the Sick Fund Act. Private insurance pays physicians on a fee-for-service basis for the remaining privately insured population. Negotiated fee rates are based on national "norms" for physician income, patient list size, and practice costs. The capitation payment rate is computed by adding average income to average practice costs, and dividing by the norm practice size. Most GPs also see privately insured patients and are paid fixed prices for routine office visits, phone consultation, and home visits (Graig, 1993: 120).

Specialists are paid on the basis of a separate fee-for-service schedule also based on norms or averages. However, payment for publicly insured patients is a fixed fee per month for all patients treated. Patients referred by a GP must choose a specialist who has a contract with their sickness fund or insurance company. The system is regressive in the sense that specialists who exceed the norm income are supposed to pay back between one-third and two-thirds of the extra income—depending on how much they exceed the norm (Graig, 1993: 120).

Many physicians refused initially to cooperate. They did not want to submit income records or pay required refunds. The perception of government interference particularly angered leaders of the specialist physician organization, leading to a 1-day national strike (1986) to protest the government policy. When the government retaliated by issuing an order to reduce all physician fees, further strikes and lawsuits were initiated. Negotiations with the sickness funds were undertaken in an attempt to reach an acceptable agreement—finally achieved in 1990. An expenditure target was established with fees frozen at 1989 levels until indicators established by the National Bureau of Statistics reveal whether spending was continuing to increase (Glaser, 1993: 114).

Payments to hospitals.   As noted earlier, a global budgeting process for hospitals was initiated in 1983. For the first 2 years, the budget was set for each hospital at the spending level of the previous year. After 1985, the payment process was adapted to account for increases or changes based upon fixed costs, such as number of beds, types of specialist units in the hospital, and variable costs such as the number of admissions and patient-days. The final budget is negotiated between the hospital and the primary local sickness fund that pays the hospital (Casparie and Hoojendoorn, 1991: 1442).

The national planning process systematically controls the supply of hospital beds and technology through licensing requirements. All hospitals, public and private, are subject to a planning and budgeting system. Within the overall plan, allocations to each hospital are negotiated with the sickness funds and private insurers. These two procedures have enabled the government to maintain relatively tight cost controls (Graig, 1993: 121).

Analysis of hospital "outcomes" since global budgeting began indicates that admission rates, length of stay, patient-days, and surgery rates have all declined—except for patients over age 65 for which increases continue as the elderly population grows. This is of course part of a national and international trend that began well before 1983. Nonetheless, the pattern may have been reinforced by limitations on hospital care imposed under global budgeting. Overall efficiencies were achieved largely with patients under age 65 (Casparie and Hoojendoorn, 1991: 1444–1446).

Hospitals have been able to treat a larger number of elderly patients at a higher average cost per day but without overall cost increases because of improved diagnostic and therapeutic methods. Hospital mortality rates and general mortality rates have declined over the same period, suggesting that decreased inpatient hospitalization has not had negative effects on longevity. There is thus clear evidence that greater efficiencies in the operation of hospitals have been achieved (Casparie and Hoojendoorn, 1991: 1444–1446).

The consequences of global budgeting have been much more significant than simple containment of costs. Controls have led to polarization within the health care system as the government, insurers, and administrators imposed the budget requirements on physicians, staff, and patients. Decision making was a result of a political process in which charge rates for hospital services and overall budget levels were established by a national committee rather than by hospital managers and boards of directors.

The convergence of interests between physicians and hospital managers was partially lost as hospital managers were required to limit the freedom of physicians to admit and treat patients. On the other hand, physicians were forced to shift from their primary focus on clinical patient management to a much more integrative and shared responsibility with management to achieve budget goals. Negotiations between insurers and hospital management over budget levels also became a more antagonistic process; insurers were forced to support limitations on hospital growth potential (Maarse, 1989: 264–270).

On the positive side, detailed public regulation of hospital financing was relaxed, leading to somewhat greater autonomy to plan and allocate resources within the constraints of a limited budget. Thus, the global budgeting policy has become a combination of both centralizing tendencies on the one hand and decentralization of decision responsibility on the other. Problems have nonetheless arisen because of difficulty in predicting the inflationary rate variations and the costs of new high-technology (Maarse, 1989: 2674–275).

PROBLEMS AND REFORMS

The financing system has, to some degree, had the effect of rewarding inefficient delivery of care. For example (Kirkman-Liff and van de Ven, 1989: 38):

- Hospitalization is often ordered when lower-cost day surgery would suffice.
- The fee-for-service system sometimes rewards unnecessary and expensive treatments.
- The capitation system for paying GPs encourages referrals when treatment could be adequately provided by the GP.
- Sickness funds have limited incentives for efficiency; reimbursement is provided for all medical expenses for members, regardless of whether efficiencies are achieved.
- A comparison of costs among sickness funds indicates a 69 percent difference in per capita expenses.

The government attempts to control the introduction of expensive new health care technology through licensing requirements. However, the individuals or groups responsible for these decisions are not always in the best position to understand and appreciate the advantages of the new technology and may thus slow down the adoption of efficiency-increasing investments. This appeared to be the case with heart transplantation and the lithotripter technology for treatment of kidney stones. In both cases, extraordinary means were used by advocates and hospitals to circumvent government regulators. Government planning policies were judged to be ineffective and not necessarily cost-effective in these cases, leading to a shift toward more market-based competition as the best mode for health care resource allocation decisions (de Roo and Maarse, 1990: 15–25).

The capitation system used by insurers for payments to providers is intended to create efficiency incentives. However, the system overpays for relatively healthy individuals and underpays for less healthy individuals. This causes providers to make choices detrimental to those who are less healthy. A broader capitation formula is viewed as unfair because illness is not equally distributed in the populations served by each insurance fund and would thus lead to inequity in service access (van Vliet and van de Ven, 1992: 1045–1046).

The hospital and physician partnerships play a powerful role as entrepreneurs in expanding services despite attempts by government to implement cost-containment strategies. This could very well interfere with the positive effects of the market-oriented privatization programs now underway. The national government appears to be somewhat helpless at reining in the fiercely independent locally controlled hospitals and their specialist physician allies (Saltman and de Roo, 1989: 791–793).

Recent Financing Reforms

Sickness funds are allowed under the new legislation of 1993–1994 to compete nationally on the basis of premium costs and convenience of services. Mergers between private insurance companies and sickness funds are now possible. Both sickness funds and private insurers are allowed to contract for services with hospitals, ambulatory care centers, nursing homes, and home health agencies, at negotiated prices (Kirkman-Liff, 1994: 20).

So-called "risk-adjusted capitation payments" were implemented in 1993 and were to be fully in place by the end of 1994. The goal is to provide universal coverage without disadvantaging individuals who have high health risks, such as the older population or those with preexisting conditions. Consumers are free to choose the insurer they prefer every 2 years during open enrollment and may choose a high-option (greater benefits without deductibles) plan with higher premiums or a low-option plan with lower premiums. Insurers are required to quote the same premium to all individuals who inquire about their plan. Each insurer has the freedom to establish its premiums but must offer the publicly defined set of required benefits. Premiums will vary depending on the efficiency and cost-control effectiveness of the insurer (van de Ven et al., 1994: 126).

SUMMARY AND CONCLUSIONS

The Dutch health care system is undergoing a gradual change toward a more equitable and comprehensive national system while controlling costs at about 8.6 percent of GDP. Outcomes have generally been very good in terms of infant mortality, life expectancy, and overall health status. Citizens appear to be generally satisfied with the quality and accessibility of health care.

Public health programs provide for environmental protection, excellent maternal and child health care, and a range of services supportive of health promotion and disease prevention. The country is moving effectively to achieve the World Health Organization goals for the year 2000.

Competition among physicians and hospitals is regulated but is also encouraged. The shift toward greater market orientation (Dekker Commission reforms) occurred because the regulatory approach of the 1980s appeared to be only partially successful in providing good service and containing costs. It remains to be seen whether this shift toward "managed competition" will continue containing costs while increasing equity and maintaining quality.

The Dutch have a highly sophisticated system of medical education and research, and make notable international contributions to medicine. Training of health administrators is also notable and is evident in the efficiency of health care management. Nurses are making progress, but as elsewhere professional progress is somewhat thwarted by the tradition of subservience to the more influential physicians. Hospitals are modern but the high cost of technology limits their ability to offer the latest diagnostic and surgical services to all patients. Nonetheless, health care services are clearly of high overall quality.

Services for the elderly and long-term care are among the most impressive anywhere, despite some inadequacies. Mental health services are similarly well developed and widely available to individuals with mental illness or problems of drug or alcohol abuse.

The financing system for health care is in a state of transition, but remains dependent on payroll deductions from employers as the primary funding tool. Publicly sponsored insurance has expanded as the basic tool for insuring health care, although private insurance for additional coverage continues to be available to families with the resources to pay the costs. Inequities and inefficiencies in the financing and payment systems continue to be a challenge to policy makers.

REFERENCES

BENSING, JOZIEN M., ATIE VAN BEN BRINK-MUNEN, and DINNY H. DE BAKKER (1993). Gender Differences in Practice Style: A Dutch Study of General Practitioners, *Medical Care*, 31 (3): 219–229.

BORST-EILERS, E. (1993). Assessing Hospital Technology in the Netherlands, *British Medical Journal*, 306 (January 23): 226.

CASPARIE, ANTON, and DICK HOOJENDOORN (1991). Effects of Budgeting on Health Care Services in Dutch Hospitals, *American Journal of Public Health*, 81 (1): 1442–1447.

COCKERHAM, WILLIAM C. (1995). *Medical Sociology*, 6th ed., Engelwood Cliffs, N.J.: Prentice Hall.

DASSEN, THEO W. N., HANS J. N. NIJHUIS, and HANS PHILIPSEN (1989). Male and Female Nurses in Intensive-Care Wards in the Netherlands, *Journal of Advanced Nursing*, 15: 387–393.

DE ROO, AAD A., and HANS A. M. MAARSE (1990). Understanding the Central-Local Relationship in Health Care: A New Approach, *International Journal of Health Planning and Management*, 5: 15–25.

DEKKER, J. J. M., and S. J. A. M. VAN DEN LANGENBERG (1994). Trends in Mental Health Care in Amsterdam, *Hospital and Community Psychiatry*, 45 (5): 494–496.

DIEPEVEEN-SPEEKENBRINK, J. C. M. H. (1992a). The Developing Discipline of Nursing from a Dutch Perspective, *International Journal of Nursing Studies*, 29 (2): 99–111.

DIEPEVEEN-SPEEKENBRINK, J. C. M. H. (1992b). The Need for Graduate Nursing Education and Nursing Research in the Netherlands: An Exploratory Study, *International Journal of Nursing Studies*, 29 (4): 393–410.

GARRETSEN, H. F. L., and H. RAAT (1991). Urban Health in the Netherlands: Health Situation, Health Care Facilities and Public Health Policy, *Health Policy*, 18: 159–168.

GELIJNS, ANNETINE C., and HENK RIGTER (1990). Health Care Technology Assessment in the Netherlands, *International Journal of Technology Assessment in Health Care*, 6: 157–174.

GLASER, WILLIAM A. (1993). How Expenditure Caps and Expenditure Targets Really Work, *Milbank Quarterly*, 71 (1): 97–127.

GRAIG, LAUREEN A. (1993). *Health of Nations: An International Perspective on U.S. Health Care Reform,* 2nd ed. Washington, D.C.: Congressional Quarterly.

GROL, RICHARD (1990). National Standard Setting for Quality of Care in General Practice: Attitudes of General Practitioners in Response to a Set of Standards, *British Journal of General Practice,* 40 (September): 361–364.

GROL, R., J. DE MAESENEER, M. WHITFIELD, and H. MOKKINK (1990a). Disease-Centered Versus Patient-Centered Attitudes: Comparisons of General Practitioners in Belgium, Britain and the Netherlands, *Family Practice—An International Journal,* 7 (2): 100–103.

GROL, R., M. WHITFIELD, J. DE MAESENEER, and H. MOKKINK (1990b). Attitudes to Risk-Taking in Medical Decision-Making Among British, Dutch, and Belgian General Practitioners, *British Journal of General Practice,* 40 (April): 134–136.

JONKERGOUW, P. H., J. E. KRUYT, and M. H. HANRAHAN (1990). Community Nursing in the Netherlands, *International Nursing Review,* 37 (1): 211–213.

KAT, C. F. A. M. (1991). Planning and the Mental Health System, *Medicine and Law,* 10 (4): 305–310.

KERKSTRA, ADA, and TREES VORST-THIJSSEN (1991). Factors Related to the Use of Community Nursing Services in the Netherlands, *Journal of Advanced Nursing,* 16: 47–54.

KIRKMAN-LIFF, BRADFORD L. (1989). Cost Containment and Physician Payment Methods in the Netherlands, *Inquiry,* 26 (Winter): 468–482.

KIRKMAN-LIFF, BRADFORD L. (1994). Management Without Frontiers: Health System Convergence Leads to Health Care Management Convergence, *Frontiers of Health Services Management,* 11 (1): 3–48.

KIRKMAN-LIFF, BRADFORD L., and WYNAND P. M. VAN DE VEN (1989). Improving Efficiency in the Dutch Health Care System: Current Innovations and Future Options, *Health Policy,* 13: 35–53.

KNIPSCHILD, PAUL, JOS KLEIJNEN, and GERBEN TER RIET (1990). Belief in the Efficacy of Alternative Medicine Among General Practitioners in the Netherlands, *Social Science and Medicine,* 31 (5): 625–626.

KOOIMAN, CORNELIUS G., BEN J. M. VAN DE WETERING, and ROSE C. VAN DER MAST (1989). Clinical and Demographic Characteristics of Emergency Department Patients in the Netherlands, *American Journal of Emergency Medicine,* 7 (6): 632–635.

LAPRE, RUUD M., and AAD A. DE ROO (1990). Medical Specialist Manpower Planning in the Netherlands, *Health Policy,* 15: 163–187.

MAARSE, J. A. M. (1989). Hospital Budgeting in Holland: Aspects, Trends and Effects, *Health Policy,* 11: 257–276.

MAARSE, J. A. M., I. M. MUR-VEEMAN, and I. M. J. G. TIJSSEN (1990). Changing Relations Between Hospitals and Primary Health Care: New Challenges for Hospital Management, *International Journal of Health Planning and Management,* 5: 53–57.

MACKENBACH, JOHAN P., ANTON E. KUNST, and CASPTER W. N. LOOMAN (1991). Cultural and Economic Determinants of Geographical Mortality Patterns in the Netherlands, *Journal of Epidemiology and Community Health,* 45: 231–237.

MOEN, JAN, and HAN MOLL (1993). Erasmus University: An Innovative Program in Health Policy and Management, *Journal of Health Administration Education,* 11 (1): 95–107.

O'SULLIVAN, MICHAEL (1992). An Enviable System, *Nursing Times,* 88 (6): 34–35.

PERENBOOM, R. J. M., C. J. LAKO, and E. G. SCHOUTEN (1989). Health Status and Medical Consumption of Rural and Urban Elderly, *Comprehensive Gerontology (B),* 3: 124–128.

POOL, JERGEN (1991). Hospital Management: Integrating the Dual Hierarchy, *International Journal of Health Planning and Management,* 6: 193–207.

REERINK, EVERT (1990). Improving the Quality of Hospital Services in the Netherlands, *Quality Assurance in Health Care,* 2 (1): 13–19.

REERINK, EVERT (1991). Arcadia Revisited: Quality Assurance in Hospitals in the Netherlands, *British Medical Journal,* 302 (June): 1443–1445.

SALTMAN, RICHARD B., and ADRIAN A. DE ROO (1989). Hospital Policy in the Netherlands: The Parameters of Structural Stalemate, *Journal of Health Politics, Policy and Law,* 14 (4): 773–795.

SCHNEIDER, MARKUS, RUDOF K.-H. DENNERLEIN, AYNUR KOSE, and LEA SCHOLTES (1992). *Health Care in EC Member States.* Amsterdam: Elsevier.

SIXMA, HERMAN J., ELLEN H. LANGERAK, GUUS J. P. SCHRIJVERS, and JAAP VAN DER BENT (1993). Attempting to Reduce Hospital Costs by Strengthening Primary Care Institutions: The Dutch Health Care Demonstration Project in the New Town of Almere, *Journal of the American Medical Association,* 269 (19): 2567–2572.

SRAMEK, MICHAEL, WILFRIED POST, and RUDOLPH W. KOSTER (1994). Telephone Triage of Cardiac Emergency Calls by Dispatchers: A Prospective Study of 1386 Emergency Calls, *British Heart Journal,* 71 (5): 440–445.

STARFIELD, BARBARA (1991). Primary Care and Health: A Cross-National Comparison, *Journal of the American Medical Association,* 266(16): 2268–2271.

STEVENS, FRED, JOSEPH DIEDERIKS, and HANS PHILIPSEN (1992). Physician Satisfaction, Professional Characteristics, and Behavior Formalization in Hospitals, *Social Science and Medicine,* 35 (3): 295–303.

SWENKELS, HENK (1989). Statistics on Health Promotion and Disease Prevention in the Netherlands, *Netherlands Central Bureau of Health Statistics.* The Hague: Department of Health Statistics.

TEN HAVE, HENK, and HELEN KEASBERRY (1992). Equity and Solidarity: The Context of Health Care in the

Netherlands, *Journal of Medicine and Philosophy*, 17: 463–477.

TYMSTRA, TJEERD, and MARGRIET ANDELA (1993). Opinions of Dutch Physicians, Nurses, and Citizens on Health Care Policy, Rationing, and Technology, *Journal of the American Medical Association*, 270 (24): 2995–2999.

VAN DE VEN, WYNAND P. M. M., RENE C. J. A. VAN VLIET, ERIK M. VAN BARNEVELD, and LEIDA M. LAMERS (1994). Risk-Adjusted Capitation: Recent Experiences in the Netherlands, *Health Affairs* (Winter): 120–135.

VAN DEN BERG JETHS, ANNEKE, and MATS THORSLUND (1994). Will Resources for Elder Care Be Scarce, *Hastings Center Report*, 24 (5): 6–10.

VAN DER LEI, JOHAN, JOOP S. DUISTERHOUT, HENK P. WESTERHOF, EMIEL VAN DER DOES, PAUL V. M. CROMME, WILFRIED M. BOON, and JAN H. VAN BEMMEL (1993). The Introduction of Computer-Based Patient Records in the Netherlands, *Annals of Internal Medicine*, 119 (10): 1036–1041.

VAN DER ZWAARD, JOKE (1992). Dutch Training Nurses and Their Views on Migrant Women, *Social Science and Medicine*, 35 (9): 1137–1144.

VAN GRUTING, CORNELIS W. D., and JOHAN J. DE GIER (1992). Medication Assistance: The Development of Drug Surveillance and Drug Information in the Netherlands, *Annals of Pharmacotherapy*, 26 (July/August): 1008–1012.

VAN HOUT, BEN, GOUKE BONSEL, DIK HABBEMA, PAUL VAN DER MAAS, and FRANK DE CHARRO (1993). Heart Transplantation in the Netherlands; Costs, Effects and Scenarios, *Journal of Health Economics*, 12: 73–93.

VAN VLIET, RENE C. J. A., and WYNAND P. M. M. VAN DE VEN (1992). Towards a Capitation Formula for Competing Health Insurers: An Empirical Analysis, *Social Science and Medicine*, 34 (9): 1035–1048.

VISSER, G. J., and L. PETERS (1990). Alternative Medicine and General Practitioners in the Netherlands: Towards Acceptance and Integration, *Family Practice*, 7 (3): 227–232.

VISSER, HENK K. A. (1993). Paediatrics in the Netherlands: Challenges for Today and Tomorrow, *Archives of Disease in Childhood*, 69 (2): 251–255.

VONDELING, HINDRIK, ENRIA HAERKENS, ARDINE DE WIT, MICHAEL BOS, and H. DAVID BANTA (1993). Diffusion of Minimally Invasive Therapy in the Netherlands, *Health Policy*, 23: 67–81.

VREE, P. H. (1990). The Challenge of Health Developments in Hospital Pharmacy, *Pharmaceutisch Weekblad, Scientific Edition*, 12 (1): 26–29.

SWEDEN

Decentralized
Comprehensive Care

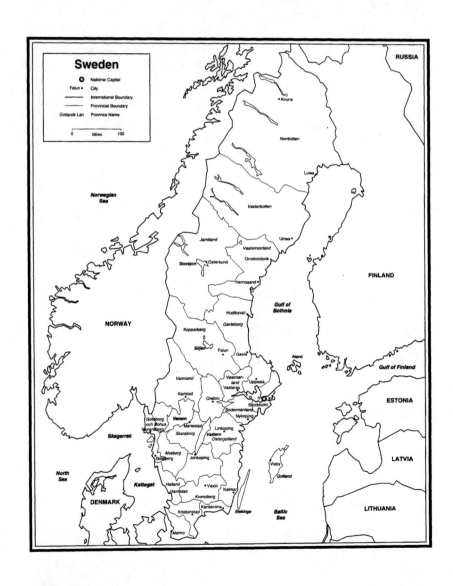

Sweden has the largest government-financed social sector, as well as the highest taxes, among modern industrial nations. It is also a highly egalitarian democracy and implements this ideology through widespread programs of income redistribution. The country has been referred to as a "prototype welfare state," because it has one of the most comprehensive and universal social welfare systems anywhere. Technological development is well-advanced and citizens have access to one of the best job-training programs in the world (Navarro, 1990: 236; Ostman, 1992).

Roughly 67 percent of the total gross domestic product is spent in the public sector. Social service costs were 33 percent of GDP in 1990, including unemployment benefits, pensions, family allowances, and public assistance, as well as health care. About 8 percent of government spending and 7.9 percent of GDP went for health care in 1994 (Zappolo and Sundstrom, 1989: 22; Thorslund, 1991: 456; Roemer, 1993: 327; National Center for Health Statistics, 1995: 220).

The publicly supported health care system directly finances 93 percent of all hospital beds and 87 percent of physician office visits. The share of health care that is publicly funded has grown from 60 percent in 1960 to roughly 91 percent in 1991. The health care system employs between 10 and 11 percent of all employed individuals in the country (approximately 400,000 people), up from 3 percent in 1960 (Thorslund, 1991: 456). Other features of Swedish health care are summarized in Table 9-1.

DEMOGRAPHIC CHARACTERISTICS

Sweden has among the highest GDPs per capita in the world, at $27,600 in 1994, and is also among the most urbanized of countries, with 83 percent of the population of 8.7 million residing in cities. The good incomes and high standard of living are a result of advanced industrialization and high productivity, as well as high rates of advanced educa-

Table 9-1 Features of the Swedish Health Care System

- A long history of public and decentralized primary health care. Counties (comparable to states or provinces in other countries) are responsible for financing and providing most services. Seventy-five to eighty percent of county budgets are for health care

- A pioneer in comprehensive public health promotion and prevention, environmental protection, and other measures to protect health

- Full participation by all major players in designing and managing local health care: physicians, health service administrators, other health professionals, and political leaders

- A strong emphasis on democratic control of services through decisions by elected county council officials

- Very high value is placed on specialist care in hospitals; 53 percent of physician visits are to hospital outpatient departments, whereas only 30 percent are to local public health and primary care centers

- Tertiary care services are regionally planned and coordinated among groups of hospitals and counties

- The highest ratio of nurses to the population of any country. Nurses have relatively high status, major responsibility for primary care, and relatively good compensation

- The highest proportion of elderly in the population of any country (18 percent) and a very low infant mortality rate.

Sources: Based on data from Saltman and von Otter, 1987: 22; Wennstrom, 1992: 180; Bjork and Rosen, 1993: 144.

tion. About 80 percent of the female population of working age is employed (Kohler, 1991: 185; Slunge, 1991: 12).

The southern urban regions tend to have a rich array of services, whereas the northern rural areas have fewer services and shortages of personnel and facilities. Mail carriers and taxi drivers sometimes deliver groceries and look after the needs of isolated rural people.

Five percent of the population are foreign nationals and another 5 percent have become naturalized citizens. More than 150 nationalities live in Sweden, and now number 1 million. Immigration contributed 45 percent of the population growth between 1944 and 1980. Immigrants are generally less educated than the native Swedes and occupy lower-status occupations. However, average income is close to the national average.

Health surveys indicate that immigrants have more health problems and are overrepresented in hospital and outpatient visits, thus contributing more than their share to health care costs (Kohler, 1991: 185).

The elderly population has been increasing rapidly, whereas overall population growth is very low at 0.1 percent annually. The proportion of elderly population (18 percent over age 65) is the highest among advanced countries. Life expectancies are also among the highest at 74.9 for men and 80.6 for women in 1991 (Hakansson, 1994: 103; Cockerham, 1995: 287–289).

Approximately 55 percent of all health care resources are consumed by individuals aged 65 or older. Per capita expenditures for health care are five times greater for individuals over age 65 as compared to those under 65. The situation is more serious here than in other countries because the proportion of elderly over age 85 is particularly high (Andersson, 1991: 496).

Adult mortality has thus been decreasing steadily, at a faster rate than in most other countries. The total number of elderly individuals is now leveling off, however, although the proportion in the oldest-age categories will continue to increase. At the same time, fewer children are available to provide family care. Only 4 percent of the elderly live in the same home with children (Zappolo and Sundstrom, 1989: 24; P. C. Globe, 1991).

The aged dependency ratio has been increasing steadily (a measure of the proportion of elderly individuals compared to the working population age 15 to 64 years old) and is expected to rise from 25 in 1980 to 34 by 2030, which means a much lower number of working people will have to support a larger number of older people (Cates, 1993: 275).

The infant mortality rate is among the lowest in the world at 5.5 in 1994. Infant mortality has been declining steadily as a consequence in part of several key factors: excellent housing, good nutrition, good hygiene, and good education of mothers. Sweden's relatively high overall standard of living is certainly a primary factor, although maternal and child health and other preventive measures emphasized in Sweden also make definite contributions. For example, hospitals are well equipped to handle high-risk deliveries. These factors apparently counteracted the rapid growth in out-of-wedlock births, which increased from 8 percent in 1950 to 50 percent in 1988. The average Swedish woman gives birth to two children. The incidence of families with four or more children has diminished drastically (Diderichsen, 1990: 360; Kohler, 1991: 177–182; National Center for Health Statistics, 1995: 93).

Despite the egalitarian emphasis, some social class differences in health status continue to exist within counties and from one part of the country to another. Although overall mortality rates have fallen steadily, a considerable divergence remains between blue-collar workers and white-collar workers. Nonetheless, Sweden has among the lowest variations in income level of any country (Zappolo and Sundstrom, 1989: 23; Diderichsen, 1990: 365; Ostberg, 1992: 480).

Social class differences are especially evident among the elderly population. When specific measurements of physical capacity were undertaken among a random sample of older individuals, former blue-collar workers, both skilled and unskilled, performed considerably less well than white-collar workers and professionals. Similarly, when mortality rates are controlled by socioeconomic status for children, there are differences. The universal health care system and social equity policies have not fully eliminated divergencies (Diderichsen, 1990: 363; Kohler, 1991: 181; Parker, Thorslund, and Lundberg, 1994: 196; Thorslund and Lundberg, 1994: 66–67).

HISTORICAL PERSPECTIVE

Sweden has a very long tradition of publicly sponsored health care. A "Collegium Medicum" was established in 1660 under parliamentary sponsorship, serving as the forerunner to the current National Board of Health and Welfare. State-sponsored medical appointments were initiated on a regional basis for "provincial physicians." The first general hospital was established in Stockholm in 1752. The public welfare orientation began during this period—when district physicians delivered free medical services financed by the local government (Wennstrom, 1986: 70).

Gustavus Adolphus, King of Sweden during the early nineteenth century, created a system of crown hospitals in selected parishes around the country. Their specific purpose was to fight syphilis contracted by soldiers during the Thirty Years War. However, they were financed by a head tax on all citizens. Beginning in 1864, 20 percent of the tax on liquor was allocated for health, to be replaced by personal income taxes and property taxes around 1900. Citizens have had essentially free access to medical care from this point onward. One historian suggests this was the first example of a sickness insurance fund, enduring until 1873 as the primary source of public health care financing. The surcharge was then changed to a general tax for health care (Anderson, 1989: 47; Johannisson, 1994: 169).

The county government system was created during the 1870s, replacing the parish organization that preceded it. The primary county role from the beginning was to operate hospitals. Publicly employed priests were active in managing basic medical care, distributing general health information, and determining causes of death (Anderson, 1989: 47).

Public health was institutionalized in 1867 with the creation of a professorship in public health at the Karolinska Institute, the medical school of Stockholm. The Public Health Act of 1874 created local Boards of Health with responsibility for sanitation, sewage, water supply, and other public health activities. Enforcement was provided by sanitary inspectors and health officers. Sweden was clearly a pioneer country in promoting public health (Johannisson, 1994: 172).

Hospital specialization began about 1900 and has continued to the present. University hospitals support 40 to 50 specializations (Hessler and Twaddle, 1986: 137).

Focus on Mothers and Children: 1930 and Later

Beginning in the 1930s, the government focused on the health needs of mothers and young children. Legislation was passed providing for free mother and child health examinations, screening for both physical and psychological conditions, provision of medications and vaccinations, as well as health education. Visiting nurses would go to the homes of those mothers who did not appear at public clinics. This is obviously one explanation for the low infant mortality rate (Rosenthal and Frenkel, 1992: 342).

The National Institute for Public Health was created in 1938 with support from the Rockefeller Foundation, and with responsibility for occupational health, supervision of hygiene in food and housing, and health education. This strengthened the public health tradition under national sponsorship and was the predecessor to the Institute for Public Health created in 1992 (Johannisson, 1994: 179).

Universal Insurance and Regionalization of Services: 1947–1960

The first insurance scheme for universal coverage of physician and pharmacy services was enacted in 1947 and implemented in 1955. Financing came from payroll deductions with contributions from employers and employees. Primary care and specialist physicians services were provided through some 600 federal government sickness insurance agencies (Anderson, 1989: 50).

Regionalization of hospitals was implemented in 1958, after a report and recommendations were prepared by the Swedish Planning and Rationalization Institute (a health services research agency). Seven regions were identified based on the service area of the medical schools and associated hospitals. The federal government assumed direct financial responsibility for medical education and teaching hospitals. Counties retained responsibility for other hospital services (Anderson, 1989: 52).

Decentralization: 1960 and Later

In 1961, outpatient and psychiatric mental health services were shifted from the central government to counties, effectively transferring full responsibility for service delivery to a regional level. Physicians in salaried public positions had been allowed to maintain private practice on a fee-for-service basis until 1969—when the rules were changed. They became fully salaried and were employed directly by hospitals or district health centers. They were still able to undertake off-duty private work until 1983 when even this option was essentially eliminated (Gaensler, Jonsson, and Neuhauser, 1982: 169; Wennstrom, 1992: 182).

Rising Costs

Health care costs were relatively small as a proportion of the national budget until after World War II; the proportion of GDP attributable to health care was only 1.8 percent. By 1960, it was 3.3 percent, rising to 6.6 percent in 1970. A rapid increase in expenditures was particularly notable during the 1970s, with the proportion of GDP rising to near 10 percent by 1980. This was moderated through a series of cost-control efforts, to 8.6 percent by 1988 and to 7.9 percent by 1994. The rate of economic growth did not keep pace with the rise in health care costs (Hessler and Twaddle, 1986: 138; National Center for Health Statistics, 1995: 220).

Sweden was heavily impacted by economic recession during the 1970s and 1980s (as were many other European countries), with deleterious effects on the health care of the population. This was among the factors that led to the election losses of the Social Democrats in 1976, when the government

shifted in a more conservative direction. The recession was associated with higher levels of mortality and morbidity, particularly from cardiovascular disease, cerebrovascular disease, malignancies, disorders of infancy, and psychopathological conditions (suicide, for example). Studies in Sweden and elsewhere suggest such problems increase during periods of economic recession and improve during periods of income growth (Brenner, 1987: 183).

Stability of Health Care Services

Throughout the stressful period of the 1970s and 1980s, continuity of health care and other services was maintained by the relative stability of the medical civil service. Sweden has a long tradition of highly professional bureaucrats who provide ongoing attention to public services despite political and economic changes. This is one of the factors that appears to cause citizens to cooperate with and respect the government (Gaensler et al., 1982: 170).

Although physicians dominated health care in earlier periods of Swedish history, as in other countries, they have lost power in recent years as a consequence of the effort to control costs. The Swedish Medical Association was almost alone in opposing the Dagmar reforms of the mid-1980s. The reform converted the fee-for-service payment system to capitation and gave greater emphasis to primary care, prevention, and health promotion, while diminishing the emphasis on specialized health care and inpatient care in hospitals. The role of counties in managing and financing health care was strengthened at the expense of physicians (Duffy, 1989: 191; Glennerster and Matsaganis, 1994: 245).

The Federation of County Councils initiated a study of future health care needs in 1989, in cooperation with the Ministry of Health and Social Affairs and the National Board of Health and Welfare. The *Crossroads Report* that resulted (1991) established the basis for major changes toward a more market-based system with increased consumer choice (Glennerster and Matsaganis, 1994: 246).

CULTURAL FACTORS

The Swedish population has long had a value orientation toward public responsibility for those who may be deprived, sick, or elderly and has been willing to pay the higher taxes required to provide the needed support. A 1993 survey revealed an inclination by the public to allocate even more resources to health care, as a third priority after education and pensions (Bjork and Rosen, 1993: 144–145).

The means of achieving these values are, however, hotly contested. For example, the following issues have been deliberated at length prior to the recent reforms (Duffy, 1989: 188):

- Whether outpatient care should be delivered from hospitals or local ambulatory care centers
- The degree of control to be exercised by the general practice physician gatekeeper, as compared to control by specialists and professional administrators
- The degree of emphasis and resources that should be devoted to acute care versus long-term care

The Swedish population firmly supports the belief that care for the elderly is a societal as well as a family responsibility. The public sector must provide support or benefits to undergird this obligation. Furthermore, the work of implementing the public obligation is to be undertaken by professionals who are especially trained and qualified for the service responsibility. Access to health care is viewed as a basic human right (Thorslund, 1991: 456).

Among the societal attributes of great concern is the relatively high suicide rate, especially among health professionals—who rank at the top in suicide among occupational groups. Female physicians and dentists have a particularly elevated suicide rate. Physician

rates in general are 2.5 times the national average (Stefanson and Wicks, 1991: 259–264).

POLITICAL INFLUENCES

Interest group participation in policy decisions is deeply ingrained in politics. A negotiation or bargaining process among interest groups is a built-in component of all major health policy decisions, with ample time allowed for assessment and reaction by all interested parties. Cooperation and consensus are part of the policy process (Calltorp, 1990: 113).

Government decisions in Sweden are made through a parliamentary democracy and implemented by a relatively small number of national ministries. The Social Democratic political party has dominated government in Sweden since the mid-1930s, except for a period in the mid-1970s, late 1980s, and early 1990s. At the national level, the Ministry of Health and Social Affairs and the semi-independent National Board of Health and Welfare are responsible for establishing the legal and developmental framework for county implementation of health care (Diderichsen, 1990: 359).

County health services planning and provision are largely the responsibility of county councils under the general oversight of the National Board of Health and Welfare. There are 23 counties somewhat comparable to states or provinces in other countries; three major municipalities have independent governments with the same responsibilities as counties (Zappolo and Sundstrom, 1989: 30–31; Glennerster and Matsaganis, 1994: 242).

Role of Royal Commissions

Special study of major issues is delegated to relatively independent and broadly representative "royal commissions." Their task is to facilitate the achievement of consensus on policy preferences and decision priorities.

The health care system as it functions today is a direct result of several royal commission initiatives (Hessler and Twaddle, 1986: 140).

For example, the *Hojer Commission* established after World War II provided the basic outline for the current health care system. The commission recommended widespread public regulation and public control of ambulatory care through county councils. Physicians were placed under contract to the county councils and a fixed fee schedule was established. A 1979 *Serner Commission* report focused on reduction of hospital and specialist physician responsibility for, and influence in, health care by transferring control directly to the county councils. The Swedish Medical Association generally opposed these changes, but because consensus had been achieved through commission actions, the physicians were overruled by parliamentary action (Hessler and Twaddle, 1982: 446–459).

The results of royal commission deliberations, with input from interest groups, are taken to the National Board of Health and Social Welfare. The Board transmits the recommendations to the Ministry of Health, which drafts the needed legislation for presentation to Parliament. The commission approach to implementation of a health policy process has led to effective health outcomes at the national level (Hessler and Twaddle, 1986: 135; Duffy, 1989: 133).

Major Players in Health Care

In addition to county councils, other major players in health policy include the National Board of Health, the employers association (SAF), the union of university graduates (SACO), the University Chancellors Office, the trade union federation (LO), white-collar unions (TCO), the County Councils Federation (CCF), the health professional bureaucracy, and the Swedish Medical Association (SMA). The SMA represents 92 percent of physicians and works through SACO, which is one of the so-called "peak" associations with major influence (Heidenheimer and Johansen, 1985: 366).

The CCF acts as the collective unit for county councils and has exceptional influence because of the major role of counties in financing and delivering health care. Counties employ 75 percent of all physicians (Duffy, 1989: 133; Calltorp, 1990: 114; Ham, 1992: 137).

Health Care Planning

Counties are required by the central government to develop five-year plans for health care, including recommendations for needed changes. Representative committees include politicians and health professionals who prepare study and planning documents. These are submitted to the county planning office and eventually move to the county assembly for debate and possible legislative action (Hessler and Twaddle, 1986: 142).

The boundaries between county and municipal responsibility have been recently diminished. Municipalities now take greater responsibility for health care of the elderly and handicapped, including nursing homes and home health care. Further decentralization is being considered that could lead to turning all primary care over to municipalities. Decentralization of decisions and budgets to hospitals and health centers is a part of current experiments to improve efficiency in several counties (Wennstrom, 1992: 187).

Counties suffer somewhat from a failure to use professional management techniques in the operation of health services. Greater management training may be needed, as well as a more distinct separation of functions between elected politicians and professional managers (Ham, 1992: 138).

SOCIAL ORGANIZATION OF HEALTH CARE

The National Board of Health and Welfare has responsibility for evaluating health services. It serves as the knowledge center for medical care. Another important unit is the Swedish Planning and Rationalization Institute of Health and Social Services (SPRI), a joint enterprise of the National Board and the County Councils Federation. It focuses on joint planning, increasing efficiency of health services, special investigations, and research and development in health care administration (Swedish Institute, 1992).

The national health insurance system is administered by regional social insurance offices under the general supervision of the National Social Insurance Board. It is responsible for payments to providers in health centers, hospital outpatient services, or private practitioners, and to the county councils for hospital inpatient care (Swedish Institute, 1992).

County council staff are directly responsible for the operation of insurance programs and primary care health centers, acute-care hospitals, long-term-care hospitals, nursing homes, and home nursing care. Each county contains primary care districts with populations ranging from 5,000 to 50,000 residents (Swedish Institute, 1991: 1). The general organization of health service delivery is summarized in Table 9-2.

Public Health

District health centers provide local primary care and are staffed by medical officers, district nurses, and midwives who provide minor surgery and preventive health services for pregnant women, babies, and children. They usually include a laboratory, physiotherapy, occupational therapy, dentistry, and pharmaceutical services. The centers also conduct mass screenings for cancer, mammography, and vaccinations. School health services under direction of municipalities undertake health promotion and prevention programs for school children. Industrial health services cover 70 percent of employees with health promotion and prevention programs. Environmental health and social welfare services are primarily a responsibility of municipalities. The focus of occupational health services is on preventive care in the workplace. Public health responsibility is

Table 9-2 Organization of Health Services

Local District Health Services
  Primary care services, public health, maternal and
    child health
  2,000 to 50,000 people served
  School health services
  Industrial health services

District County Hospitals
  500 beds
  Medicine, surgery, radiology, and anesthesiology
  60,000 to 90,000 people served
  Inpatient and outpatient services

Central County Hospitals (26)
  500 to 1,000 beds
  15 to 20 specialized wards and clinics
  200,000 to 300,000 people served
  Inpatient and outpatient services

Regional Hospitals (6 regions)
  1,200 to 2,300 beds
  Highly specialized tertiary care and high-technology
    equipment
  Medical school affiliation
  Research, neurosurgery, open-heart surgery, etc.
  1 million or more people served
  Inpatient and outpatient services

National Government Units
  Ministry of Health and Social Affairs
  National Board of Health and Welfare & Planning and
    Rationalization Institute (SPRI)
  County Councils Federation

Sources. Based on data from Hessler and Twaddle, 1986: 137; Swedish Institute, 1992.

more integrated with private health care than in most countries (Swedish Institute, 1991).

As noted earlier, maternal and child health services are a major emphasis of the local health centers, at no cost to clients. They promote the physical, mental, and social development of women and children and maintain a very high participation rate. Nearly 99 percent of pregnant women and 97 percent of children up to 4 years of age secure regular checkups and screening for disease. Psychosocial family support, family planning, and health education are also provided. Psychologists, dentists, dental hygienists, social workers, dietitians, physiotherapists, and speech therapists are available for assistance—depending somewhat on the location. Redistribution of health resources to geographic areas and groups in need is viewed as important to the public health responsibility (Duffy, 1989: 133; Saltman, 1989: 286; Kohler, 1991: 189).

Additional preventive public health activities are required by the Health and Medical Services Act. For example, the Stockholm Cancer Prevention Program is a community-based intervention effort that attempts to systematically change life-styles and bad habits by reducing tobacco consumption, reducing dietary fat, increasing fiber consumption, and reducing damaging sun-bathing, among other activities. Base-line measures have been established and a long-term monitoring process is underway (Holm, 1991: 455–457).

Physicians

The senior physician in district health centers is usually supported by assistant and temporary physicians who provide on-call services during evenings, weekends, and holidays, and who often deal with the majority of acute-illness episodes. The senior physician on permanent appointment tends to deal heavily with chronic illness in the older population. General practitioners in primary care centers do not act as gatekeepers to specialized services as in some other countries. Patients are free to go directly to specialists in hospital outpatient settings (Krakau, 1991b: 182; Hansagi, Calltorp, and Andreasson, 1993: 34).

Private health care clinics have been encouraged to increase and expand services as a deliberate government policy and as a possible means of cutting health care costs. Market competition is now viewed as a mechanism to increase efficiency and service quality. One alternative is for private physician entrepreneurs (or physician cooperatives) to contract with county councils to serve specific geographic regions with service shortages. The private centers are required to abide by the same principles that guide operation of the district health

centers. Income is derived from patient fees and a monthly grant from the county council based on patient numbers (Hansagi et al., 1993: 33).

Only 5 percent of all physicians were in private practice in 1991, but 17 percent of all patient visits were to these practitioners. Approximately 53 percent of patient visits were to hospital physicians, and 30 percent were to district health center physicians (Ham, 1992: 136; Swedish Institute, 1992; Wennstrom, 1992: 178).

Research in one suburb of Stockholm indicated that private practice health care was of comparable quality and at a lower cost than in three nearby district health centers. Satisfaction levels among patients of both public and private centers were generally high (85 percent or more), without significant differences. The private centers were able to operate with significantly lower costs (10 to 48 percent less, depending on the district center) largely because of a lower input of staff salaries and management expenses. However, the average physician workload and income at the private centers were considerably higher than in district centers (Hansagi et al., 1993: 37).

Physician characteristics. Physicians can be categorized into four main levels or ranks, from lowest to highest status:

1. M.D.s doing internships or specialist training
2. Specialist consultants in outpatient or inpatient services of hospitals
3. District physicians or a clinical unit head physician in a hospital
4. Administrators responsible for a facility

Appointments to these positions are publicly advertised and filled by the most qualified candidates who have the needed administrative or specialist credentials. Appointments to university hospitals or medical schools are similarly advertised, with appointments going to individuals most qualified in teaching and research—usually with joint appointments in a hospital (Wennstrom, 1986: 71).

Opportunities for practice are limited in areas of physician oversupply, forcing practitioners to move to areas of need, such as rural communities. A deliberate policy of reallocating medical school graduates was undertaken by the National Board of Health and Welfare but has been only partially successful because county councils have failed to cooperate (Duffy, 1989: 134; Rosenthal and Frenkel, 1992: 341; Wennstrom, 1992: 183).

Among 4,000 physician positions in 800 community health centers, 2,000 were not filled in 1993, with shortages of general practitioners particularly acute in rural regions of the north. In addition to rural shortages, maldistribution occurs in psychiatry, long-term or geriatric medical care, and in selected laboratory specialties. This has led to a relative open policy of foreign physician migration, at the rate of approximately 150 per year (Calltorp, 1990: 116; Glennerster and Matsaganis, 1994: 244).

A notable change has been observed in the work week of physicians. Average working hours went down from 48 per week in 1970 to 30 hours in 1985. This has not always been viewed as satisfactory to physicians, many of whom would like to work more and receive greater remuneration (Calltorp, 1990: 117; Wennstrom, 1992: 183).

The stress level among physicians in Sweden is relatively high, as in other countries—especially in a changing health care environment. They suffer from relatively high rates of heart disease and cardiovascular problems, despite their presumed greater knowledge of prevention possibilities. However, they still indicate the highest levels of work satisfaction among white-collar occupational groups in Sweden (Arnetz, 1991: 197–198).

Professional organization. Physicians are organized at two levels within the Swedish Medical Association. A "younger doctors association" consists of relatively new hospital physicians who are in process of establishing their specialist credentials and who are not as well paid as more senior doctors. They are "on call" and do much of the basic work in hospitals. Senior doctors tend to hold administrative and specialist positions and are well-established in the profession. The younger doctors, however, are tightly organized and negotiate directly with the government (principally the County Council Federation) to establish their incomes and working conditions. Physicians lost considerable power in the 1980s because of resentment of their higher incomes and better working hours by other professional groups such as psychologists, lawyers, and social workers (Heidenheimer and Johansen, 1985: 348).

Malpractice insurance. Treatment Injury Insurance was created in 1975 as a "no-fault" system. Insurance premiums are paid by county governments. Any patient who claims ill effects from medical treatment may submit the claim to the Patient Compensation Insurance Fund. A Medical Responsibility Board deals separately with any evidence of physician malpractice. No proof of medical negligence or incompetence is required for payment of compensation, however. If harmful effects are shown, the patient is compensated. The system has essentially removed the threat of malpractice from physicians and other providers. The cost to counties is roughly $2.38 per capita or a total of .16 percent of health care costs (Roemer, 1991: 210; Danzon, 1994: 200).

Medical education. Planning for physician manpower began systematically in the 1950s. During these years, the primary goal was to increase the number of physicians. At that time, the ratio of population to physicians was considered too high (1440:1). The ratio is now becoming too small (390:1). In the late 1980s, the goal was to slow down the growth in numbers by limiting the entrants to medical schools (Calltorp, 1990: 108; Swedish Institute, 1992).

Postgraduate medical education for the specialties was reformed and expanded beginning in 1969, with full cooperation from county authorities and physicians as well as the central government. A national physician manpower plan was designed to train and distribute specialists as needed throughout the country—under the leadership of the National Board of Health and Social Welfare. About 25 percent of Swedish physicians earn postgraduate scientific degrees to do research and gain research experience—which they believe contributes to their clinical effectiveness (Wennstrom, 1986: 70).

Medical schools are supported fully by the national Department of Education. Each school is directly associated with regional universities and hospitals, at Uppsala, Stockholm, Lund, Linkoping, Gothenburg, and Umea—the latter three initiated in the 1960s. Approximately 865 new students are accepted annually under the new restrictive admission policy, down from 1,026 in 1980. More than half of the entering classes to medical schools are now women. The required study period is 5.5 years, including preclinical, preparatory, and clinical segments. A 21-month internship is required after graduation before a license to practice can be obtained. This is usually followed by a 4- or 5-year postgraduate residency to qualify as a specialist or general practitioner. A total of 10 to 12 years of training is thus required for a full practice opportunity (Sivik, 1992: 375; Wennstrom, 1992: 181).

During the training period, basic expenses are paid through government scholarships; salaries are very low despite a heavy workload. The training focus tends to be on the biomedical model, with relatively little preparation for social and psychological dimensions of human health (Sivik, 1992: 375; Wennstrom, 1992: 181; Totten, 1993: 137).

Further modernization of medical education has been initiated in some medical schools. For example, in 1981, Linkoping University created the new Health University of Ostergotland with six health disciplines included (medicine, nursing, physiotherapy, occupational therapy, laboratory technology, and community care management). Each curriculum is problem-focused, including early patient contact for each group of students and close coordination between pre-

clinical and clinical studies. The focus is heavily on primary and community care. Students from the six disciplines work together on common issues and problems, as a means of integrating the health care team. Early evaluations indicate the new educational design is producing better prepared health professionals (Areskog, 1992: 1–4).

A physician distribution program established by the Health Planning Committee of the Ministry of Health and Social Affairs serves as the basis for allocating slots for residency training. Counties have the power to limit the growth of private medical practice, in terms of numbers and who will be allowed to practice privately—through constraint on private contracts for payment. Encouragement of private practice has been implemented particularly in fields where there are public shortages of services, such as intraocular lens transplantation, hip replacement, and coronary-bypass surgery (Calltorp, 1990: 106; Wennstrom, 1992: 181).

Medical research.   Sweden has an internationally recognized medical research program. Research funds from the federal Department of Education support approximately 28 percent of the total research-and-development budget. Other units of the national government contribute roughly 22 percent, and the balance is from counties or outside grants. Despite a relatively abundant budget, shortages of resources for research and education create a competitive atmosphere between clinical departments in the teaching hospitals and between the counties that fund most of the hospital research (Erikson, 1993: S108).

Growth of geriatric medicine.   Emphasis on geriatric medicine has been increasing in response to growth in the elderly population. For example, Gothenburg University situated in Sweden's second largest city established a department of geriatric medicine in 1977. The university hospital (Vasa) devoted 475 beds to geriatric assessment and rehabilitation. Facilities for outpatient care and day care are also available. The program is interdisciplinary and maintains close ties with international collaborators. Advanced geriatrics training at the Ph.D. level is provided for physicians and other health professionals (Steen and Djurfeldt, 1993: 164).

Among the important research findings is evidence that chronological age is not necessarily the best independent predictor of ability to function. Of greater importance is the incidence of disease in older age. If health can be promoted, or illness avoided, excellent function can be maintained. Furthermore, the evidence indicates that increased longevity and ability to function are directly related to greater education, higher living standard, and higher participation in social activities. Intelligence and memory function do not decline significantly up to age 90 in the absence of major disease such as cardiovascular problems. However, cardiovascular disease rates increase rapidly after age 70 (Steen and Djurfeldt, 1993: 166).

Longitudinal study of individuals between age 70 and 85 indicates a high potential for "reactivation." It is possible to train older individuals to undertake many physical and mental activities that have been lost because of illness or lack of use, leading to a healthier and more satisfying life-style well into late older age. This can improve quality of life, but can also lower the risk of illness, thus lowering the need for health care (Svanborg, 1990: 407).

Finally, economic studies of the impact of aging on health care expenditure in Sweden suggest that the cost-increasing effects of larger numbers of elderly are not so much a function of age as the increased application of medical technology to the diseases and illnesses of the older population. Expenditure for individuals 75 and older increased by 54 percent between 1976 and 1985, whereas the increases for the under-75 population were quite modest (Gerdtham, 1993: 7–8).

Alternative Medicine

Alternative medicine refers to practices such as acupuncture, manipulation therapy, and vegetarian diet regimens that fall outside of standard scientific medicine. Use of such practices has become relatively widespread in Sweden as in other Western nations, with roughly one-third of all licensed physicians involved. Although a sizable proportion of this group have had a long-standing interest in these forms of medicine, others have become dissatisfied with the manner and outcomes of scientific medicine as it has been practiced. Alternative medicines are now being incorporated more actively into medicine as evidence of their proven effectiveness increases (Lynoe and Svensson, 1992: 55).

Nurses

Sweden has the highest ratio of trained nurses to patients of any country, with 1,000 per 100,000 population, or 123 people per nurse. Nonetheless, a nursing shortage has been reported largely because trained nurses leave practice to enter more satisfying occupations. Wages remain low relative to other jobs requiring equal preparation. The supply situation improved somewhat, however, after reforms were initiated in 1982 (Kohler, 1991: 188; Wennstrom, 1992: 180; Roemer, 1993: 22).

As noted earlier, the District Nurse is a key player in community health care. The nurses are directly responsible for a high proportion of patients, giving advice by telephone, managing home health care, doing health promotion and prevention education, and generally serving as "front-line" health care providers. They are part of a team with the District Physician and other staff. Reception nurses in the health centers perform similar functions for walk-in patients but have a somewhat narrower range of practice and responsibility (Marklund et al., 1991: 165).

All schools in Sweden are required to have one nurse on staff for each 800 students (although some schools have fewer than this number because of shortages). Most nurses work at more than one school, many on a part-time basis. The nurse does health screening, helps prepare for physician medical examinations, offers health and sex education classes, deals with psychosocial problems when a school psychologist is not available, and treats accidents and student illnesses (Katoda, W-Lindgren, and Mannerfeldt, 1990: 441–446).

Recent changes in hospital nursing have led to more focus on primary patient care for registered nurses—who were increasingly absorbed with administrative responsibilities. The result has been greater satisfaction for nurses, patients, and physicians. Each feels better served (Degerhammar and Wade, 1991: 330).

Nursing education and research. The 1982 reforms shifted nursing education to universities, replacing an advanced secondary education program. The study program leads to six nursing specialties:

1. General nursing
2. Psychiatric nursing
3. Ophthalmic technology and nursing
4. Operating room nursing
5. Diagnostic radiology
6. Oncology

Nurses must complete a 2-year postsecondary basic course prior to entering the field. Specialization requires 2 additional years or more. Completion of specialty curricula leads to a University Certificate in Nursing and registration as a nurse. Evidence from attitude studies suggests that the advanced education is causing the nursing role to become increasingly professionalized in the minds of experienced nurses (Olsson and Gullberg, 1991: 35).

Graduate study and research have been emphasized in recent years. There were 35 trained faculty-researchers with doctoral degrees in the country as of 1990. The professionalization of nursing as a science has now been generally accepted and supported by the other health professions. However, much remains to be done in the advancement of graduate study and research (Hamrin, 1990: 155; Ehnfors, 1993: 201).

Pharmacists and Pharmacies

All pharmacies are part of the National Corporation of Swedish Pharmacies and have the exclusive right to sell drugs. Here as elsewhere, only physicians are allowed to prescribe medications, with pharmacists serving as advisers (Tomson, 1991: 240).

Every hospital has a drug therapeutic committee that recommends approximately 200 to 300 drugs to be listed in a formulary for use in the hospital and in health centers within the service area. Decisions are based on scientific documentation, therapeutic tradition, and cost. GPs have developed their own "essential drug lists" for use in health centers (Tomson, 1991: 242).

Sweden also has a well-developed drug information system (Drugline) sponsored by the National Corporation and the national health care sector. It is operated by clinical pharmacologists and pharmacists. Drugline originated in 1974 and has been computerized since 1982. It is updated monthly from published literature or through questions raised by professionals via phone inquiries. Any questions received are investigated by the staff who respond to the inquiry. A network of Drug Information Centers at university hospitals serves the entire country. The system is now widely used by physicians, medical libraries, hospital pharmacies, university clinics, and the pharmaceutical industry (Ohman et al., 1992: 563–568).

Midlevel Practitioners

Physiotherapy has become a central part of health care practice. Since 1977, it has required university-level training and must be based on research knowledge. Physiotherapists are independently functioning health professionals who respond to physician prescriptions but are not considered subservient to medicine (Bergman, 1990: 83–84).

Nurse-midwives play an active role in district health centers in care of pregnant mothers and preparation for birthing. Normal deliveries in many hospitals are managed primarily by midwives (Kohler, 1991: 192)

Hospitals

Hospital beds are allocated to three major functions: general acute care (about 35 percent), psychiatric care (about 17 percent), and long-term care (about 48 percent). Approximately 53 percent of all physician outpatient visits are to outpatient departments attached to hospitals (Roemer, 1991: 209; Swedish Institute, 1992).

Although the county councils are responsible for public health, primary health care, and hospitals, the three types of service are not always closely integrated, nor does organized collaboration between health centers and hospitals generally occur in any systematic sense. For example, primary care center physicians who refer patients are not able to follow their patients to hospitals nor can they participate in care while their patients are hospitalized. This is the province of hospital or outpatient physicians (Roemer, 1991: 209).

Patients are encouraged to seek care at local health centers, but hospital emergency departments also provide such services at modest out-of-pocket cost—particularly during the hours when the health centers are closed. Surveys indicate many patients prefer primary care in hospital emergency rooms rather than district health centers if they have an urgent complaint (Hansagi, Carlsson, and Brismar, 1992: 72–74).

Nearly 99 percent of all births occur in hospitals, most of them with full access to obstetric and pediatric specialists. All high-risk cases identified by general practitioners or midwives are referred to obstetricians (Kohler, 1991: 192).

Physician staffs in hospitals have major influence on resource allocation and planning. Clinic chiefs responsible for each specialized service oversee outpatient and inpatient care, with support from nurses and unit managers. This divided management arrangement has not contributed to integra-

tion of primary care, social care, and hospital care because other units of county and municipal agencies operate social services with similar independence (Ham, 1992: 135).

Medical Technology

Technological development has a very high priority in Swedish society. The successful developer of new products is given high social status. The importance of advancing technology has been emphasized by citizen interest groups and politicians as well as physicians. Consequently, heavy investments have been made in most advanced forms of medical care (Hessler and Twaddle, 1982: 457).

The Swedish government created the Council for Technology Assessment in Health Care in 1987 for the specific purpose of evaluating appropriateness of new medical technology. The basis for evaluation includes (Ringertz, 1993: 44–45):

• Technologies already established but without careful examination
• Potentially underused technologies
• Potentially overused technologies
• New products

The goal is to make the best use of health care funding for technologies that serve the most useful purposes. Patient outcome data are used to establish cost-benefit ratios. For example, a study of preoperative examinations indicated that many were unnecessary and costly, with little evidence of positive impact on outcomes. Elimination of these procedures could save substantial resources. An educational program was launched to inform physicians and others about the findings (Werko, 1991: 3).

Medical technology tends to be allocated first to the major regional and university hospitals, with the county hospitals, district hospitals, and health centers following. The most widely used and cost-effective technologies are made available to all four types of hospitals (Gaensler et al., 1982: 178).

Advanced Information Systems

Use of computers for medical records and other purposes is well underway. However, most patient records are still in the form of paper files. Studies have indicated that physicians make efficient use of the paper records and may in fact find computer records slower to use. Research is underway to improve the potential for computer applications for all health professionals (Nygren and Henriksson, 1992: 1).

A computer-based patient record system and drug information system is in use at the Kronan Health Center in Stockholm. The system has three primary components:

1. A patient database (medical events)
2. A data dictionary with basic vocabulary (medical terms)
3. A knowledge base (medical facts and medical logic modules)

The medical record is accessible to district physicians, nurses, physiotherapists, the hospital, and the pharmacy. Data can be transferred electronically between units. The goal of the system is to support improved decisions regarding patients and to detect errors that might occur in drug prescription interactions (Linnarsson, 1993: 131–142).

Quality Assurance

A formal set of rules has been developed by the Medical Quality Council, a group created by professional physician organizations. The plan is for use by health care practitioners as a guideline for improved medical care and quality and as a formalized procedure for further developing quality practice. The system registers patient complaints and undertakes disciplinary actions through local complaint committees, chief health officers in the Public Health Service, and the National Board of Health and Welfare. The Medical Responsibility Board is the highest disciplinary authority, consisting of nine members and chaired by a qualified judge (Rene, Westesson, and Owall, 1993: 189).

Complaints lodged by patients are formally processed and investigated by these local, regional, or national units. Although legal malpractice recourse through the courts is possible, most problems are handled through the quality assurance system without legal action. If complaints are legitimate, patients can be compensated through a no-fault insurance program, as noted earlier, and practitioners can be formally disciplined or their licenses withdrawn. Generally speaking, the system attempts to be corrective, preventive, and compensatory (Rene et al., 1993: 196–198; Garpenby and Carlsson, 1994: 183).

External "medical audits" are conducted in health facilities throughout the country, based on a set of national guidelines published by the National Board of Health and Welfare in 1993. National registers have been developed to measure performance in hospital departments and to establish standards of practice, thus making it possible to compare any unit with the ongoing quality standard. Attention is given to (Garpenby and Carlsson, 1994: 186)

- Variations in practice procedures or methods used
- Differences in treatment outcomes
- Long-term effectiveness of varying treatment methods
- Followup treatment and its effects
- Detection of errors or deficiencies in procedures and correction of these through further treatment

The results of these studies are used primarily by the participating hospital units to improve the overall quality of outcomes and performance of staff. They have not so far been used to develop formal national standards or policies (Garpenby and Carlsson, 1994: 192).

Emergency Medical Care

Trauma care is decentralized. No formal trauma system exists, although hospitals are generally quite well equipped to handle most injuries. Emergency cases from accidental injuries are taken via ground transportation to the nearest hospital regardless of size or facilities, except in cases of severe head injuries or burns (Alberts, Brismar, and Nygren, 1993: 16–17).

A nurse triage system has been developed in some hospitals to channel nonemergency cases to another hospital unit or to outpatient primary care. Many of these cases can receive higher-quality care if they are immediately transferred to lower-cost options and to the care of physicians who are better trained to deal with the condition (Hansagi, Edhag, and Allebeck, 1991:59).

A central ambulance and emergency medical service is directly associated with the emergency hospitals and are financed by the county. Fire departments were responsible for this function until 1983. The alternative system is new enough that extensive advanced training for emergency medical technicians was not implemented until recently. A few EMTs are nurses and have advanced cardiac life support training, but they are the exception. Most have only 7 to 8 weeks of EMT training, including driving, extrication techniques, defibrillation, and basic cardiac pulmonary resuscitation. Trainees have advanced high school or junior college vocational nurse training (Totten, 1991:42).

Very few physicians are specifically trained in emergency medicine. Emergency cases are usually handled initially by GPs, many of whom are young and relatively inexperienced. They usually transfer responsibility to the acute care unit of the nearest emergency hospital when a patient is transported by ambulance (Totten, 1991: 43).

Physicians have begun to develop private-practice, street-front, emergency care centers. The income derived often supplements modest salaries received in public employment in a hospital or primary care center. Retired physicians often work in such settings to supplement retirement income. Nurses working in such centers are paid somewhat better than in public hospitals or clinics. Patients pay an initial modest fee upon entry. The balance of costs is billed to the national health insurance system (Totten, 1993: 132).

Long-Term Care

Long-term care in Sweden has a somewhat different meaning than in other countries. The term refers primarily to care in long-stay hospitals, even though other institutions also provide various forms of care over extended periods. The number of individuals residing in all types of institutions actually declined by 34 percent during the 1980s (Cates, 1993: 271).

The proportion of elderly under institutional care was 1 percent of individuals 64 to 75 years of age, and about 6 percent of those 75 to 84 in 1990. Among the 85 and older group, fully one-third lived in institutional settings. A high proportion of institutional residents are demented, have not been married, are single women, or are poor and have no alternative home (Johansson and Thorslund, 1992: 58).

Several parliamentary decisions have strongly impacted long-term care. The Health and Medical Services Act and the Social Services Act of 1982, the Housing Act of 1985, and the Caring Services for the Elderly in the 1990s Act of 1988, all emphasize home health care and services, as opposed to institutionalized care. The assumption is made that older and dependent individuals are happier and likely to be better served in the community, with services provided at lower cost. However, the cost of home care has not yet been fully documented (Zappolo and Sundstrom, 1989: 27, 45; Cates, 1993: 271).

The 1988 legislation emphasized coordination at the municipal level among long-term medical care, nursing home, home health care, and other home services. Although the great majority of older people continue to live in their own homes, institutional care still absorbs about 65 percent of all resources available for service to the elderly population (Thorslund, 1991: 456).

Wide variation in degrees of institutionalization are evident depending on the location. Among individuals over age 80, only 9 percent are dependent on institutionalized care in one municipality, but as many as 37 percent are dependent in other locations. Comparable variation exists in the availability of service houses for older people. A system of Municipal Tax Redistribution allows more rural and less affluent counties to offer more and better services to the elderly to make them somewhat comparable to more affluent urban regions (Berg et al., 1993: 182–183).

Geriatric rehabilitation units emphasize rehabilitation of physically and mentally impaired older people. Many severely impaired individuals, with dementia or other chronic problems, remain in these units indefinitely (Zappolo and Sundstrom, 1989: 31).

However, geriatrics as a subspecialty is not well-developed for many of the staff who work in these units, such as nurses, social workers, or other health professionals. A special emphasis on training for management of health problems in the older population has not taken hold in Sweden as it has in some other countries (Zappolo and Sundstrom, 1989: 47; Wennstrom, 1992: 180).

Old age homes are operated by municipalities for individuals who need 24-hour care. Two-thirds of residents are women who are widowed or were not married. These homes have much less privacy and personal attention than the "service" homes to be described. The national government is deliberately trying to phase them out in favor of subsidized private apartments or houses (Zappolo and Sundstrom, 1989: 55; Parker et al., 1994: 196).

Special Issues in Elderly Care

Despite the growth in numbers of the elderly, resources for their care and support

have grown relatively more slowly. The number of people receiving institutional care decreased, but home health services have not grown rapidly enough to replace the institutional services. The number of people living in service houses more than doubled between 1982 and 1987, which may partially explain how this was possible (Thorslund, 1991: 461).

Many of the current staff are women who work part-time; indications are that the proportion of their time given to staffing elderly services is increasing. However, increased time may not be sufficient to meet the rapidly increasing needs without also increasing compensation—which has lagged behind other competing professions (Thorslund, 1991: 461).

Older people not only have higher medical costs generally, they are also more prone to injury and trauma. A study in the Umea area of northern Sweden indicated that the cost of caring for injuries in the elderly was four times greater than for those under 65. Nearly 42 percent of the cost of inpatient and outpatient medical care for injuries in Umea Regional Hospital was for elderly patients. For more severe injuries, the cost attributed to the elderly was 70 percent (Sjogren and Bjornstig, 1991: 204–206).

The older population occupied 65 percent of hospital beds and consumed 40 percent of all dispensed prescription drugs according to a recent study. They were using drugs from four pharmacologic groups—leading to concerns about the potential for adverse drug reactions. The extent of adverse reactions is not currently known (Jorgensen, Isacson, and Thorslund, 1993: 1123).

Home Health Care

Home care may be provided in a private home, a group home, or service houses. A very high proportion of the elderly (90 percent) live in their own homes rather than with children or other relatives—in part because of the generous housing subsidies that have been characteristic of Sweden. *Ser-*

vice houses, a type of home somewhat unique to Sweden, are available throughout the country to house elderly and dependent individuals who do not otherwise have adequate housing. Apartments are equipped with an alarm, rails in bathrooms, and other amenities needed by residents to offset disabilities. Staff members are on duty 24 hours a day to assist residents as needed (Zappolo and Sundstrom, 1989: 45).

Home nursing services are operated by the district primary health care clinics, with the major responsibility delegated to district nurses and nursing assistants. Primary care physicians, physiotherapists, and geriatritions serve as supporting consultants. The service is offered to all retired older or dependent people who need domestic and personal support. The proportion of elderly over age 80 who receive home care varies between 17 percent in one municipality to 80 percent in another; the average is 43 percent. For all individuals over age 65, the range is between 8 and 33 percent. Informal caregivers may be employed to assist with activities of daily living. Retired individuals can also receive tax-free payment for assisting disabled relatives (Johansson, 1991: 235; Cates, 1993: 274; Melin, Hakansson, and Bygren, 1993: 356).

Nursing assistance is usually supplemented by other social support services such as day care, shopping, housekeeping, laundry, meals, transportation, bathing, dressing, snow removal, security alarms, and occasionally special housing for the disabled—all provided through the municipalities responsible for social services. One study indicated that 70 percent of home nursing is a permanent part of the support system for individuals served; the other 30 percent is temporary care for persons recovering from an acute illness who do not need indefinite care (Zappolo and Sundstrom, 1989: 32; Cates, 1993: 274).

"Night patrols" provided under the supervision of district nurses are a unique feature. Nurse aides are available on a 24-hour basis to visit homes, provide emergency services,

administer medications, sometimes prepare evening meals, help prepare dependent individuals for bed, and generally look after the welfare of home-based patients (Zappolo and Sundstrom, 1989: 31).

Individuals with severe impairments, such as dementia (estimated at 6 percent of the older population), nearly always receive professional home care. Many older and disabled people also take advantage of day centers. They provide a range of services in a multiservice setting. However, not all counties provide these facilities. Access to day centers, and other services, is provided by an extensive especially equipped transportation system for the frail elderly as a supplement to other forms of public transportation (Zappolo and Sundstrom, 1989: 36; Sjobeck and Isacsson, 1994: 35).

Home care versus institutional care.   A recent controlled experiment indicated that intensive home care, as an alternative to hospital care followed by less intense home care, produces healthier patients, fewer problems, fewer hospitalizations, and fewer drugs—with a more cost-effective result. Yet, most of the resources for care of older people continue to be focused on institutional care. The number of people served by home care actually decreased by 10 percent during the 1980s; the reasons for the decline are not entirely clear (Andersson, 1991: 496; Berg et al., 1993: 176; Melin et al., 1993: 362).

The principal obstacle to expanded home care appears to be the limited number of workers available to provide services. However, a high proportion work part-time (93 percent), and might presumably, with adequate tax adjustments and other incentives, be encouraged to work longer hours (Andersson, 1991: 496).

Home health care has become increasingly professionalized, with required special in-service professional training. However, severe shortages of staff and high personnel turnover of as much as 30 percent annually continue to be problems. Efforts are underway to increase the coordination of home care with other services, through direct and continuing consultation among professionals working with each patient (Johansson, 1991: 234–238; Cates, 1993: 274).

Most home care is provided by family members. Formal home health care is largely a supplement and allows many elderly to stay at home when the family would otherwise have great difficulty managing. Beginning in 1989, working family members were given the right to paid leave for up to 30 days to care for an elderly family member, primarily in acute or terminal illness cases—with reimbursement from the social insurance system (Johansson, 1991: 234–238).

Mental Health Care

Mental health services are regionalized, with responsibility resting with counties. Psychiatric clinics serve populations ranging in size from 30,000 to 120,000 inhabitants. These are either colocated with health care centers or are located in offices within communities. Physicians see about 15 percent of patients, but the majority are seen by clinical psychologists (15 percent), psychiatric social workers (30 percent) and nurses (40 percent). Inpatient care is provided by mental hospitals, general hospitals, nursing homes, or halfway houses (Westrin, 1991: 53).

The policy in Sweden, as elsewhere, has been to shift patients to community settings and decrease the emphasis on hospitalization. The number of inpatients in mental hospitals decreased from 26,000 in 1967 to 10,000 in 1987. However, the increase in patients between 1982 and 1988 in psychiatric wards of general hospitals approximately equaled the decrease in mental hospital patients. Inpatient care continued to use 90 percent of all direct costs for mental health services in 1990 (Borga et al., 1991: 223).

Community-based psychiatric facilities provide diagnosis and treatment. Severely ill patients are sometimes cared for in nursing homes. Studies suggest this policy is not entirely effective because individuals with appropriate psychiatric training may not be available in communities to provide adequate care. Wide variation exists in access to trained mental health professionals, between counties and between districts within counties. For example, availability of psychiatrists ranges from 5 to 18 per 100,000 population depending on location (Dencker and Gottfries, 1991: 325–327; Westrin, 1991: 54).

Sweden has gone farther than many countries in implementing U.N. guidelines for the protection of rights in cases of mental retardation or mental illness. The law on Guardianship and Trusteeship (1986) provides for a paid independent spokesman for severely mentally ill or handicapped people. A patient can appeal decisions requiring treatment. Every health care district must have a supervisory board to monitor compulsory care. The board must visit institutions, consult with staff and patients, and make judgments on the appropriateness of care (Bean, 1988: 32).

The quality and access to care is widely criticized by patients, their families, and by professional psychiatrists. However, further research that effectively measures effectiveness, quality, ethical appropriateness, or cost efficiency of mental health services is needed (Westrin, 1991: 55).

Patient and Physician Satisfaction with Health Care

Many surveys have been undertaken to determine consumer attitudes toward health care. These generally indicate a relatively high level of satisfaction with primary care services, especially from private physicians, but critical attitudes toward hospitals—because of waiting time and lack of readily available services. Results obtained from a 1988 mailed survey to a representative sample of the population (83 percent return rate) in a community near Stockholm (Sollentuna) are summarized in Table 9-3.

Table 9-3   Consumer Attitudes Toward Health Care in a Swedish Community*

	Attitude	
Institution	Positive	Negative
Public health center primary care	70%	36%
Private practice primary care	81	12
Hospital care	28	64
Health care in general	45	40

*The questions were open-ended and coded as positive or negative. Respondents could include both positive and negative comment about particular forms of health care. Thus, the totals for each category do not add to 100%.

Source: Based on data from Krakau, 1991a: 59–61.

Primary care was rated positively by most people, whether delivered in public health centers or through private physicians. Hospitals are viewed much less positively. Health care in general clearly gets mixed reviews from the public in this community (Krakau, 1991a: 59–61).

ECONOMIC CHARACTERISTICS AND ISSUES

Health care is a major component of the economy, employing about 10 percent of the work force. Sweden spends near the average proportion of GDP for health care among European countries, at about 7.9 percent (1992)—which was down from 8.5 percent in 1991 and 9.4 percent in 1980. The per capita cost was $1,317 in 1992. Some of the decline is attributable to accounting changes. Costs would have been about 0.6 percent higher in 1992 except for the transfer of care for the mentally retarded from the health care budget to the education and Social Security budgets (Gerdtham and Jonsson, 1991: 213–228; Swedish Institute, 1991; National Center for Health Statistics, 1995: 220).

The proportion of GDP expended for health care has included the nursing home costs that tend to be lodged with the Social Security budget in other countries. Proposals to make this change were under serious discussion in 1993. County Councils have been directed by national legislation to shift long-term-care responsibility to municipalities in the near future. If these costs and those for nonhealth home services are excluded, the proportion of GDP for health care drops to approximately 7.3 percent in 1993 (Swedish Institute, 1991; Glennerster and Matsaganis, 1994: 243; Cockerham, 1995: 298).

Fees for health services, salary levels of health care workers, and the number and distribution of health facilities are set at the national level in consultation with County Councils. Established procedures are in place to secure input from the "grass roots" as well (Duffy, 1989: 187).

As noted earlier, health care resources were relatively abundant during the 1960s and 1970s. This changed during the economic slowdown of the 1980s—meaning less available revenue for all services. A 1990 reform in the tax system limited the tax increases for 2 years. The consequence was serious constraint on services and the beginning of shortages for surgery and other procedures (Slunge, 1991: 12; Glennerster and Matsaganis, 1994: 243).

The following patient charges were therefore implemented to help fill the gap, but with a $200-per-year maximum (Glennerster and Matsaganis, 1994: 243):

Physician consultation	$12
Prescriptions	10
Physical therapy/other therapy	6
Hospital inpatient care/per day	8

Increases in charges was a rather substantial policy change in a country where health care has been available largely without direct out-of-pocket costs for many years.

Benefits

The benefit package is summarized in Table 9-4. Primary care outpatient services and hospitalization are available to all citizens with payment of the consultation fee and daily charges. Physiotherapy, convales-

Table 9-4 Health Insurance Benefits in Sweden

Benefit	Services
Medical expenses	Outpatient services Hospital treatment Paramedical treatment Pharmaceuticals Counseling on birth control Dental care Medical devices for rehabilitation Travel expenses
Sickness	Payments while ill Subsidization of salary while caring for a close relative
Maternity	Before and after birth
Parental benefit	For care of a child under age 8

Source: Based on Swedish Institute, 1991.

cent care, and care for the handicapped are available without charge. The cost for pharmaceuticals is paid for treatment of chronic diseases, but a co-payment is required for other prescribed medications. Counseling for birth control, abortion, or sterilization is available without charge, as is reimbursement for contraception costs. Nondurable medical goods and excess travel costs directly associated with health care are reimbursed as well (Wennstrom, 1992: 179; Glennerster and Matsaganis, 1994: 243).

Dental treatment and preventive dental care for adults are partially reimbursed; the patient must pay 60 percent of the costs up to 3,000 Swedish Kroner and 50 percent thereafter. Children age 19 and younger receive care without cost (Swedish Institute, 1991: 2).

Disabled individuals, young and older, can receive various kinds of devices without cost, to increase independence, mobility, self-care, and quality of life. The devices are prescribed by occupational therapists, physical therapists, and nurses, as well as physicians (Sonn and Grimby, 1994: 85–92).

Income replacement insurance during childbirth and early child care pays 90 percent of gross income for up to 450 days, with either parent eligible. Pregnant women can begin receiving the benefit 2 months before scheduled delivery. The benefit also can be used to take children for medical care or to look after them when ill (Swedish Institute, 1991: 2).

The sickness benefit payments to individuals who are ill is paid at the rate of 60 percent of normal income for the first three days, 80 percent from the fourth to ninetieth day, and 90 percent thereafter. This benefit represents nearly half of the total social insurance cost and is the single largest expense. If an expectant mother is unable to work prior to delivery, she can receive 90 percent of normal income for 50 days. Parental insurance is also available with benefits for 450 days during the first 8 years of a child's life. Either parent can use the benefit for care of a young child or to provide health care, but both parents cannot benefit at the same time (Swedish Institute, 1991).

Absenteeism from work due to illness increased by 30 percent during the 1980s, from 18 to 25 days per year per individual. A study in Malmo indicated that sickness benefit use rates (and absenteeism) was highest for single, female, older, lower-income, and/or immigrant workers. Older individuals tend to have longer periods of illness, and women tend to be sick more often and are higher consumers of health services (Isacsson et al., 1992: 234–239).

Financing Mechanisms

The primary source of funds for health services is county government income taxation of about 13.5 percent of income (in 1990), which covers about 70 percent of costs. Another 19 percent comes from the federal government as allocations to compensate for the substantial differences in wealth between counties. Federal funding includes allocations specifically for medical education, research, and psychiatry. Patient fees make up 2.2 percent and health insurance covers about 8 percent (these estimates may vary somewhat between counties and because of rapid changes in the early 1990s) (Swedish Institute, 1991; Hakansson, 1994: 105).

If direct health care expenses exceed $200 (in 1994), a consultation fee and hospital daily charge are not required. Patient costs vary somewhat from county to county and are established at the county level. Although private health insurance is available to cover extra expenses, only about 15,000 policies were in effect as of 1990 (Wennstrom, 1992: 180; Swedish Institute, 1992: 1; Calltorp, 1990: 106).

Sweden follows a "fixed-allocation" approach to distributing health care resources. That is, budgets of health care providing organizations for the following year are based on the previous year and adjusted for inflation, utilization, and possible new services provided. Performance indicators such as patient load, referral rates, operating efficiency, or health outcomes are not generally considered. Although some movement toward competition between facilities based on patient preference has been undertaken, counties largely control where patients receive care (Saltman and von Otter, 1990: 106).

Paying physicians. The counties employ most physicians on a salaried basis. Incomes are relatively less than in other industrialized nations at about two times the average personal income, which is of course quite high. This is a consequence in part of the political structure that has enabled other interest groups to gain power and influence at the expense of physicians (Anderson, 1989: 53).

Until 1969, laboratory physicians, surgeons, and radiologists were able to earn substantially more than their counterparts in other specialties or general practice—because they received fees for service in addition to their base salaries. The fee system was abolished by the national government and replaced by a standardized salary schedule—to promote greater equity among specialists and general practitioners. But the change was not achieved without a struggle. Negotiations were intense, with specialists threatening to withdraw services if forced to accept the government proposal. Agreements were successfully completed in 1970, and about 7,000 specialists had their income reduced; others stayed the same or received increases (Anderson, 1989).

Financing for health care facilities. Health care facilities are financed largely from county budgets, although the national government makes a contribution for special facilities such as university training institutions. Much of the growth in hospital costs is attributed to the high cost of technology. This has led to the recent emphasis on lower-cost primary and preventive care. Inpatient care as a share of health expenditures gradually fell during the 1980s, whereas outpatient care has steadily increased—especially for elderly patients (Gerdtham and Jonsson, 1991: 214). Allocation of the health care budget is summarized in Table 9-5.

Hospitals use 47 percent of the health care budget, and primary care services use 18 percent, drugs about 8 percent, and long-term as well as other care for the elderly 27 percent (1991). Hospitals are thus the major utilizers of health care resources in Sweden as elsewhere (Slunge, 1991: 11–12; Hakansson, 1994: 104).

PROBLEMS AND REFORMS

Productivity in the public sector generally, including health care, has been declining relative to other European countries. The DRG (Diagnosis-Related Group) approach is being studied as a possible method to further quantify and control the prices for diagnosed illnesses in both primary care and hospitalization (Wennstrom, 1992: 186).

Table 9-5   Allocation of Health Care Resources (1991)

Item	Percentage of Budget
Primary care	18
Hospitals	47
Pharmaceuticals	8
Long-term and elderly care	27

Sources: Based on data from Slunge, 1991: 11–12; Hakansson, 1994: 104.

Several other serious problems were evident in the early 1990s. Criticisms include the following (Slunge, 1991: 18; Ostman, 1992: 189–199; Ham, 1992: 136):

- Primary care, hospital care, and social care were not adequately integrated for efficiency.
- The strong emphasis on inpatient and outpatient hospital care has led to the relative neglect of locally based primary care.
- Rationing of elective surgical procedures, particularly for the elderly, is common. Waiting lists exist for hip replacements, coronary surgery, cataract surgery, and corneal lens transplants, among other procedures.
- Long waiting times for primary care are common despite scheduled appointments.
- The system has trouble accommodating legitimate individual patient preferences for treatment and may limit choice more than appropriate.
- The system appears to some observers as unduly rigid, and provider- rather than patient-oriented.
- Health care professionals, including some physician specialties, nurses, and physical therapists, were in short supply. Young people are less attracted to these professions than in the past—a serious problem given the relatively limited supply of workers.
- The sickness benefit system that allows for salary continuation while ill has grown substantially in the 1980s. Strong concerns have been expressed that this growth may need to be curtailed if unreasonable costs are to be avoided.

Recent Reforms

Reforms were introduced in Stockholm county during 1992, with full implementation scheduled for 1995. The "Stockholm Model" was based on several experiments in making the system more responsive to patient preferences. Patients were given greater choice of providers and services through a form of "public competition." Local health districts buy hospital services for patients within their boundaries. Hospitals are paid by the health districts using DRGs as the measure of output. Prices are established in advance through negotiation, along with other agreements on service volume and quality expectations (Hakansson, 1994: 115).

Hospital income is then determined entirely on the basis of sale of services to health districts rather than by the former global budgeting system—except for educational activities and research. Cooperative agreements between hospitals and health centers attempt to integrate primary and secondary care. The patient is free to choose a physician, health center, and hospital, locally or in some other district or county (Glennerster and Matsaganis, 1994: 247; Hakansson, 1994: 115).

The reform statement declares that no one should have to wait more than 3 months for surgical procedures. Greater emphasis was to be given to "medical audits" as a vehicle for improving quality. Patients were given the right to appeal to health administrators or local government officials for inadequacies they experience or observe. The revised system thus focuses more on the needs of the consumer in a competitive system requiring higher levels of performance from providers if they are to secure patients (von Otter and Saltman, 1991: 463; Caveney, 1994: 362).

Early evidence suggests that these reforms have had the effect of revitalizing the health care system while also improving productivity (estimated at 11 percent improvement for 1992) and reducing waiting times for selected procedures. However, any complete evaluation will have to await full implementation of the new approach and an adequate information system to measure results. Nonetheless, the Stockholm experiment clearly has implications for resolution of many of the problems noted (Caveney, 1994: 363; Hakansson, 1994: 121).

A second experiment was initiated in 1991 in Kopparberg County (referred to as the "Dala Model"). The county council agreed to decentralize health care delivery to 15 municipal districts, with responsibility lodged with appointed boards. The boards determine health needs of the population in their area and submit a plan to the county. Funds are allocated to each district based on population and health care needs. The county, however, retains ongoing responsibility for auditing allocation of health care funds (Glennerster and Matsaganis, 1994: 248).

Continuing economic constraints on growth of health care can be expected, requiring greater efficiency .and hard choices. County councils have been vigorously pursuing improvements in management, leadership, financing, and organization. Computer technology is serving as a primary mechanism to monitor costs and performance in health care units, such as hospital departments, laboratories, and primary care centers. Attempts are being made to increase patient choice of physicians and hospitals both within and across county boundaries (Slunge, 1991: 13).

The decentralized structure gives considerable responsibility to teams of health care providers at the department level in hospitals and clinics. This has led to a need for more executive management training at the county council and health departmental levels, as well as training programs for staff to improve use of their knowledge and skills at the local level (Ham, 1992: 134).

Private health care is evolving, but the vast majority of services remain public. Profiting from health care is viewed as inappropriate, whether in providing care for the general population or the elderly. This value orientation makes it difficult to provide financial incentives for potential private entrepreneurs (Zappolo and Sundstrom, 1989: 55).

SUMMARY AND CONCLUSIONS

Sweden has perhaps the most effective health care systems in the world. The long history of efforts to improve public health programs has resulted in one of the best records of outcome in terms of high life expectancy, low infant mortality, and ready access to health care as needed for all citizens. The elderly population is growing more rapidly than in most countries and their care absorbs an increasing proportion of health care resources.

Counties have primary responsibility for generating the needed resources and delivering health care; they operate within a national policy framework emanating from a cultural preference for equity and democratic decisions on resource allocation. Despite the equity emphasis, social class differences remain evident. Ethnic minorities have poorer outcomes than the mainstream population. Rural regions are less well served than urban regions.

Physicians are highly trained and have an international reputation for high-quality care as well as high productivity as university medical researchers. They are not as well compensated as physicians in some other industrialized countries, but nonetheless have high status and a major role in managing the health care system as part of a team with highly trained nurses and professional health care administrators. Nurses generally have higher status and greater responsibility than in most countries, but compensation rates are modest, and limited entry to the field is causing shortages.

High-technology hospitals are the preferred source of care for the majority of citizens. Specialty outpatient care is more popular with patients than district primary care services. However, surveys indicate that hospitals have become somewhat impersonal and do not provide the personal attention or choices that citizens prefer. Primary care providers in districts receive better ratings. Reform efforts are attempting to resolve this problem by increasing competition between hospitals and other providers, while offering patients greater choice among services.

Home health care is receiving increasing emphasis as an alternative to higher-cost hospital and nursing home care. The major focus is for the elderly population, who also receive a range of other benefits including high-quality housing. District health centers and district nurses assume much of the responsibility, with good success rates.

An economic downturn in the 1980s and early 1990s forced cutbacks in the health care budget. Patient charges were increased for physician services, hospitalization, and pharmaceuticals. Benefits were not generally diminished except for some decreases in the extensive sickness benefit system that pays generously for maternity and family leave, as well as income replacement for individuals who are ill. Resource shortages have led to waiting lists for elective surgery and waiting times for primary care.

As public resources for care of the elderly become more constrained, and as the numbers increase, families and the private sector have been forced to expand their roles in filling elderly care needs. Government policy is now encouraging this trend by providing tax incentives to families and encouragement to private initiative.

Despite these problems, the Swedish health care system remains among the most effective and complete among modern nations.

REFERENCES

ALBERTS, KARL AKKE, BO BRISMAR, and AKE NYGREN (1993). Major Differences in Trauma Care Between Hospitals in Sweden: A Preliminary Report, *Quality Assurance in Health Care*, 5 (1): 13–17.

ANDERSON, OLIN W. (1989). *The Health Services Continuum in Democratic States*. Ann Arbor, Mich.: Health Administration Press.

ANDERSSON, LARS (1991). The Service System at the Crossroad of Demography and Policy Making—Implications for the Elderly, *Social Science and Medicine*, 32 (4): 491–497.

ARESKOG, NILS-HOLGER (1992). The New Medical Education at the Faculty of Health Sciences, Linkoping University—A Challenge for Both Students and Teachers, *Scandinavian Journal of Social Medicine*, 20 (1): 1–4.

ARNETZ, BENGT B. (1991). White Collar Stress: What Studies of Physicians Can Teach Us, *Psychotherapy Psychosom*, 55 (2–4): 197–200.

BEAN, PHILIP (1988). Mental Health Care in Europe: Some Recent Trends, in Christopher J. Smith and John A. Griggs (eds.). *Location and Stigma*. London: Unwin Hyman, pp. 21–35.

BERG, STIG, LAURENCE G. BRANCH, ANNE DOYLE, and GERDT SUNDSTROM (1993). Local Variations in Old Age Care in the Welfare State: The Case of Sweden, *Health Policy*, 24 (2): 175–186.

BERGMAN, BIRGITTA (1990). Professional Role and Autonomy in Physiotherapy, *Scandinavian Journal of Rehabilitative Medicine*, 22: 79–84.

BJORK, STEFAN, and PER ROSEN (1993). Setting Health Care Priorities in Sweden: The Politician's Point of View, *Health Policy*, 26: 141–154.

BORGA, P., B. WIDERLOV, J. CULLBERG, and C.-G. STEFANSSON (1991). Patterns of Care Among People with Long-Term Functional Psychosis in Three Different Areas of Stockholm County, *Acta Psychiatric Scandinavia*, 83 (3): 223–233.

BRENNER, M. HARVEY (1987). Relation of Economic Change to Swedish Health and Social Well-Being, 1950–1980, *Social Science and Medicine*, 25 (2): 183–195.

CALLTORP, JOHAN (1990). Physician Manpower Politics in Sweden, *Health Policy*, 15: 105–118.

CATES, NORMAN (1993). Trends in Care and Services for Elderly Individuals in Denmark and Sweden, *International Journal of Aging and Human Development*, 37 (4): 271–276.

CAVENEY, BRIAN J. (1994). Lessons from the Swedish Health Care System, *The West Virginia Medical Journal*, 90 (9): 362–363.

COCKERHAM, WILLIAM C. (1995). *Medical Sociology*, 6th ed. Englewood Cliffs, N.J.: Prentice Hall.

DANZON, PATRICIA M. (1994). The Swedish Patient Compensation System, *Journal of Legal Medicine*, 15 (June): 199–247.

DEGERHAMMAR, MARI, and BARBARA WADE (1991). The Introduction of a New System of Care Delivery into a Surgical Ward in Sweden, *International Journal of Nursing Studies*, 28 (4): 325–336.

DENCKER, KARINA, and CARL-GERHARD GOTTFRIES (1991). The Closure of a Mental Hospital in Sweden: Characteristics of Patients in Long-Term Care Facing Relocation in the Community, *European Archives of Psychiatry: Clinical Neuroscience*, 240 (6): 325–330.

DIDERICHSEN, FINN (1990). Health and Social Inequities in Sweden, *Social Science and Medicine*, 31 (3): 359–367.

DUFFY, DIANE M. (1989). The Effect of Sweden's Corporatist Structure on Health Policy and Outcomes, *Scandinavian Studies*, 61 (2–3): 128–145.

EHNFORS, MARGARETA (1993). Nursing Documentation Practice on 153 Hospital Wards in Sweden as Described by Nurses, *Scandinavian Journal of Caring Sciences*, 7 (4): 201–207.

ERIKSON, UNO (1993). Function of a University Hospital and Its Relationship to Bureaucracy, *Investigative Radiology*, 28 (Supp. 3): S108–S109.

GAENSLER, ERIK H. L., EGON JONSSON, and DUNCAN vB. NEWHAUSER (1982). Controlling Medical Technology in Sweden, in David H. Banta and Kerry Britten Kemp (eds.), *The Management of Health Care Technology in Nine Countries*. New York: Springer Publishing.

GARPENBY, PETER, and PER CARLSSON (1994). The Role of National Quality Registers in the Swedish Health Service, *Health Policy*, 29 (3): 183–195.

GERDTHAM, ULF-G. (1993). The Impact of Aging on Health Care Expenditure in Sweden, *Health Policy*, 24 (1): 1–8.

GERDTHAM, ULF-G., and BENGT JONSSON (1991). Health Care Expenditure in Sweden—An International Comparison, *Health Policy*, 19: 211–228.

GLENNERSTER, HOWARD, and MANOS MATSAGANIS (1994). The English and Swedish Health Care Reforms, *International Journal of Health Services*, 24 (2): 231–251.

HAKANSSON, STEFAN (1994). New Ways of Financing and Organizing Health Care in Sweden, *International Journal of Health Planning and Management*, 9 (1): 103–124.

HAM, CHRIS (1992). Reforming the Swedish Health Services: The International Context, *Health Policy*, 21 (2): 129–141.

HAMRIN, ELISABETH K. F. (1990). Nursing Research in Sweden, *International Journal of Nursing Studies*, 27 (2): 149–157.

HANSAGI, HELEN, BARGRO CARLSSON, and BO BRISMAR (1992). The Urgency of Care Need and Patient Satisfaction at a Hospital Emergency Department, *Health Care Management Review*, 17 (2): 71–75.

HANSAGI, HELEN, JOHAN CALLTORP, and SVEN ANDREASSON (1993). Quality Comparisons Between Privately and Publicly Managed Health Care Centers in a Suburban Area of Stockholm, Sweden, *Quality Assurance in Health Care*, 5 (1): 33–40.

HANSAGI, HELEN, OLOF EDHAG, and PETER ALLEBECK (1991). High Consumers of Health Care in Emergency Units: How to Improve Their Quality of Care, *Quality Assurance in Health Care*, 3 (1): 51–62.

HEIDENHEIMER, ARNOLD J., and LARS NORBY JOHANSEN (1985). Organized Medicine and Scandinavian Professional Unionism: Hospital Policies and Exit Options in Denmark and Sweden, *Journal of Health Politics, Policy and Law*, 10 (2): 347–369.

HESSLER, RICHARD M., and ANDREW C. TWADDLE (1982). Sweden's Medical Care: Political and Legal Changes, *Journal of Health Politics, Policy, and Law*, 7 (2): 440–459.

HESSLER, RICHARD M., and ANDREW C. TWADDLE (1986). Power and Change: Primary Health Care at the Crossroads in Sweden, *Human Organization*, 45 (2): 134–147.

HOLM, L. -E. (1991). Community-Based Cancer Prevention—The Stockholm Cancer Prevention Program, *Cancer Detection and Prevention*, 15 (6): 455–457.

ISACSSON, AGNETA, BERTIL S. HANSON, LARS JANZON, and GUNEL KUGELBERG (1992). The Epidemiology of Sick Leave in an Urban Population in Malmo, Sweden, *Scandinavian Journal of Social Medicine*, 20 (4): 234–239.

JOHANNISSON, KARIN (1994). The People's Health: Public Health Policies in Sweden, *Clio Med*, 26: 165–182.

JOHANSSON, LENNARTH (1991). Elderly Care Policy, Formal and Informal Care: The Swedish Case, *Health Policy*, 18 (3): 231–242.

JOHANSSON, L., and M. THORSLUND (1992). Care Needs and Sources of Support in a Nationwide Sample of Elderly in Sweden, *Gerontologie*, 28 (1): 57–62.

JORGENSEN, TOVE M., DAG G. L. ISACSON, and MATS THORSLUND (1993). Prescription Drug Use Among Ambulatory Elderly in a Swedish Municipality, *The Annals of Pharmacotherapy*, 27 (9): 1120–1125.

KATODA, HIROSHI, GUNILLA W-LINDGREN, and RUTH MANNERFELDT (1990). School Nurses and Health Education for Pupils with and without Intellectual Handicaps: A Study Conducted in Japan and Sweden, *Nurse Education Today*, 10 (6): 437–447.

KOHLER, LENNART (1991). Infant Mortality: The Swedish Experience, *Annual Review of Public Health*, 12: 177–193.

KRAKAU, INGVAR (1991a). Satisfaction with Health Care in a Swedish Primary Care District, *Scandinavian Journal of Primary Health Care*, 9: 59–64.

KRAKAU, INGVAR (1991b). Trends in Diagnosis over a 10-Year Period in a Swedish Primary Care District, *Health Policy*, 19: 177–183.

LINNARSSON, R. (1993). Decision Support for Drug Prescription Integrated with Computer-Based Patient Records in Primary Care, *Medical Informatics*, 18 (2): 131–142.

LYNOE, NIELS, and TOMAS SVENSSON (1992). Physicians and Alternative Medicine—An Investigation of Attitudes and Practice, *Scandinavian Journal of Medicine*, 20 (1): 55–60.

MARKLUND, BERTIL, CALLE BENGTSSON, PETER BRYNTESSON, ROSE-MARIE FORSSELL, KERSTIN KJELLBERG, DORIS SEVERINSON, and ASTRID STARKE (1991). Telephone Advisory Service, Visits to District Nurses and Home Visits Made by District Nurses at a Swedish Primary Health Care District, *Scandinavian Journal of Primary Health Care*, 9: 161–166.

MELIN, ANNA-LISA, STEFAN HAKANSSON, and LARS OLOV BYGREN (1993). The Cost-Effectiveness of Rehabilitation in the Home: A Study of Swedish Elderly, *American Journal of Public Health*, 83 (3): 356–362.

NATIONAL CENTER FOR HEALTH STATISTICS (1995). Health, United States, 1994. Hyattsville, Md.: U.S. Public Health Service.

NAVARRO, VICENTE (1990). Public Sector Health Spending May Aid Competitiveness, *Health Affairs* (letter), 9 (2): 235–236.

NYGREN, E., and P. HENRIKSSON (1992). Analysis of Physicians' Ways of Reading the Medical Record, *Computer Methods and Programs in Biomedicine*, 39 (1–2): 1–12.

OHMAN, B., H. LYRVALL, E. TORNQVIST, G. ALVAN, and F. SJOQVIST (1992). Clinical Pharmacology and the Provision of Drug Information, *European Journal of Clinical Pharmacology*, 42: 563–568.

OLSSON, HENNY M., and MATS T. GULLBERG (1991). Nursing Education and Definition of the Professional Nurse Role: Expectations and Knowledge of the Nurse Role, *Nurse Education Today*, 11 (1): 30–36.

OSTBERG, VIVECA (1992). Social Class Differences in Child Mortality, Sweden, 1981–1986, *Journal of Epidemiology and Community Health,* 46 (5): 480–484.

OSTMAN, LARS (1992). A Swedish Patient's Experience of the Medical Care System: Ideal and Reality, Power and Dependence, in Marilynn M. Rosenthal and Marcel Frenkel (eds.), *Health Care Systems and Their Patients: An International Perspective.* Boulder, Col.: Westview Press, pp. 189–199.

PARKER, MARTI G., MATS THORSLUND, and OLLE LUNDBERG (1994). Physical Function and Social Class Among Swedish Oldest Old, *Journal of Gerontology: Social Sciences,* 49 (4): S196–S201.

P. C. GLOBE (1991). Tempe, Ariz.

RENE, NILES, PER-LENNART WESTESSON, and BENGT OWALL (1993). Complaint and Disciplinary Systems in Dentistry in Sweden: A Presentation and Discussion of Their Efficacy in Preventing Malpractice, *Quality Assurance in Health Care,* 5 (3): 187–199.

RINGERTZ, HANS G. (1993). Radiology and the Swedish Council of Technology Assessment in Health Care, *Investigative Radiology,* 28 (Supp. 3): 44–45.

ROEMER, MILTON I. (1991). *National Health Systems of the World: The Countries,* Vol. I. New York: Oxford University Press.

ROEMER, MILTON I. (1993). *National Health Systems of the World: The Issues,* Vol. II. New York: Oxford University Press.

ROSENTHAL, MARILYNN M., and MARCEL FRENKEL (1992). *Health Care Systems and Their Patients: An International Perspective.* Boulder, Col.: Westview Press.

SALTMAN, RICHARD B. (ed.) (1989). *The International Handbook of Health Care Systems.* Westport, Conn.: Greenwood Press.

SALTMAN, RICHARD B., and CASTEN VON OTTER (1987). Revitalizing Public Health Care Systems: A Proposal for Public Competition in Sweden, *Health Policy,* 7: 21–40.

SALTMAN, RICHARD B., and CASTEN VON OTTER (1990). Implementing Public Competition in Swedish County Councils: A Case Study, *International Journal of Health Planning and Management,* 5 (2): 105–116.

SIVIK, TATJANA (1992). Education of General Practitioners in Psychosomatic Medicine, *General Hospital Psychiatry,* 14: 375–379.

SJOBECK, BARBRO, and AKE ISACSSON (1994). Caring for Demented Elderly in Rural Primary Health Care, *Scandinavian Journal of Caring Sciences,* 8 (1): 29–37.

SJOGREN, HARMEET, and ULF BJORNSTIG (1991). Trauma in the Elderly: The Impact on the Health Care System, *Scandinavian Journal of Primary Care,* 9 (3): 203–207.

SLUNGE, WALTER (1991). New Approaches to Managing Health Services, *International Hospital Federation,* 27 (1): 11–20.

SONN, U., and G. GRIMBY (1994). Assistive Devices in an Elderly Populaton Studied at 70 and 76 Years of Age, *Disability and Rehabilitation,* 16 (2): 85–92.

STEEN, B., and H. DJURFELDT (1993). The Gerontological and Geriatric Population Studies in Gothenburg, Sweden, *Z. Gerontologie,* 26 (May–June): 163–169.

STEFANSSON, C.-G., and SUSANNE WICKS (1991). Health Care Occupations and Suicide in Sweden, 1961–1985, *Social Psychiatry and Psychiatric Epidemiology,* 26 (6): 259–264.

SVANBORG, ALVAR (1990). How Aging Related Frailty Will Influence the Quality of Care Results from a 15-Year Follow-Up of 70-Year-Old People in Gothenburg, Sweden, *Quality Assurance in Health Care,* 2 (3/4): 403–409.

THE SWEDISH INSTITUTE (1991). Social Insurance in Sweden, *Fact Sheets on Sweden.* Stockholm: The Swedish Institute.

THE SWEDISH INSTITUTE (1992). Health and Medical Care in Sweden, *Fact Sheets on Sweden.* Stockholm: The Swedish Institute.

THORSLUND, MATS (1991). The Increasing Number of Very Old People Will Change the Swedish Model of the Welfare State, *Social Science and Medicine,* 32 (4): 455–464.

THORSLUND, MATS, and OLLE LUNDBERG (1994). Health and Inequalities Among the Oldest Old, *Journal of Aging and Health,* 6 (1): 51–69.

TOMSON, G. (1991). Drug Utilization Studies and People: A Swedish Perspective, *Ann. 1st. Super. Sanita,* 27 (2): 239–245.

TOTTEN, VICKEN Y. (1991). Paramedic Run: Swede Talk, *Emergency Medical Services,* 20 (7): 40–46.

TOTTEN, VICKEN Y. (1993). Five Looks at the Swedish Medical Care System, *Annals of Emergency Medicine,* 22 (4): 131–138.

VON OTTER, C. V., and R. SALTMAN (1991). Towards a Swedish Health Policy for the 1990s, *Social Science and Medicine,* 32 (4): 455–464.

WENNSTROM, GUNNAR (1986). Health Care and Medical Care in Sweden, *Journal of Medical Practice Management,* 2 (1): 65–72.

WENNSTROM, GUNNAR (1992). New Ideological Winds Are Blowing in the Swedish Health Care System, in Marilynn Rosenthal and Marcel Frenkel (eds.), *Health Care Systems and Their Patients: An International Perspective.* Boulder, Col.: Westview Press, pp. 175–188.

WERKO, LARS (1991). Do We Know What We Are Doing? (Editorial), *Journal of Internal Medicine,* 230: 1–3.

WESTRIN, CLAES-GORAN (1991). Strategies Implemented but Goals Not Attained, *Scandinavian Journal of Social Medicine,* 19 (1): 53–56.

ZAPPOLO, AURORA A., and GERDT SUNDSTROM (1989). Long-Term Care for the Elderly in Sweden, in Teresa Schwab (ed.), *Caring for an Aging World: International Models for Long-Term Care Financing and Delivery.* New York: McGraw-Hill, pp. 22–57.

10

THE UNITED KINGDOM

The Economy Model

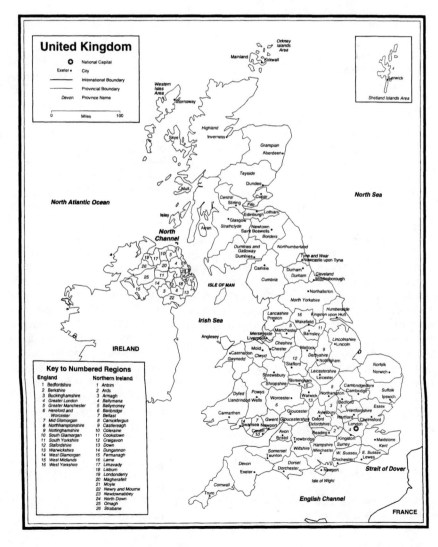

The United Kingdom was one of the first nations in Europe to implement a publicly funded National Health Service. The British NHS was established in 1919, shortly after the German chancellor, Prince Otto von Bismarck, implemented a compulsory, state-subsidized, sickness-insurance law in 1883. After World War II, the growth of national systems of health insurance in Europe was extensive, although the amount of benefits, conditions of eligibility, treatment of dependents, and provisions for maternity care varied widely.

In 1948, the U.K. National Health Service Act was enacted that espoused three principles for a publicly funded universal health care system:

1. Equal access to medical care
2. Availability of comprehensive preventive and curative care
3. Provide the service at no cost at the point of service

Health care in the NHS is free at the point of use and covers the whole resident population of 57 million citizens. It has been funded primarily through general taxation, with a small contribution from insurance (Levitt and Wall, 1992: 1).

Traditionally, the NHS has provided high-quality and cost-effective care relative to its European neighbors. In 1994, average health expenditure per person was $1,151, compared to an average of $1,735 for all other Western European nations, Japan, Canada, and the United States; expenditures expressed as percent of GDP was 7.1 percent, compared to an average of 9.1 (Memmott, 1995: 4B). In 1990, the NHS exhibited the highest estimated rate of public share of medical care billing, with the average percent of health bills paid at 90 percent, the average percent of hospital bills paid at 98 percent, and the average percent of prescriptions paid at 90 percent (Connah and Lancaster, 1989: 1; Nair and Karim, 1993: 259).

This chapter was co-authored by Martin J. Jinks, Pharm.D. and Sam Shayegan-Salek, Ph.D.

The NHS has thus been one of the strongest examples of a publicly funded low cost health service in Western Europe. However, since 1990, following passage of the NHS Community Care Act and the establishment of a system of market forces, the U.K. health care environment has been in a state of significant fluctuation. Another important factor contributing to change is the growing private insurance sector, which is projected to reach a coverage of 15 percent of the population by the year 2000 (Ham, 1994: 4).

DEMOGRAPHIC CHARACTERISTICS

The population of Great Britain (1993 estimate) was 57,970,200. The overall population density was 239 persons per square kilometer (619 per square mile). Individuals over age 65 number 8.7 million, or 15.7 percent of the population. Very few Britons live in rural areas; 92 percent are classified as urban dwellers. However, the concept of rurality is relative and considerably different from larger nations, particularly in comparison to the United States. The largest cities in the United Kingdom are London (population, 1991 estimate, 6,803,100), Birmingham (994,500), Leeds (706,300), and Glasgow (687,300). Most Britons (94 percent) are English, Irish, or Scottish. The remainder include Indians, West Indians, Pakistanis, Chinese, Africans, Bangladeshis, and Arabs. The country's official language is English (Funk & Wagnall's, 1994).

In 1994, the life expectancy for males was 73.5 years and for females 79.0 years. These figures compare favorably with other nations (Organization for Economic Cooperation and Development, 1994). The largest single category of patients served by the NHS is the over-65 age group, who occupy 46 percent of the acute hospital beds.

HISTORICAL PERSPECTIVE

The modern NHS is a proud British achievement, the expression of over 40 years of a sustained commitment to the ideal of providing "effective health care as a public service to all who need it." The strong concept of public responsibility for the health of individuals dates back to at least 1834 when the Poor Law Amendment Act was passed that gave legal mandates for workhouses to provide health care for inmates, and later for sick paupers. By the 1870s, an evolving network of workhouses, isolation hospitals, asylums, and volunteer hospitals formed a relatively official public service for the provision of health care. In 1919, the Ministry of Health was established, which provided a stimulus for radical change toward reorganization and combining medical services and the insurance system to be supported from general public funds. However, it was not until 1939 when, as part of Britain's wartime measures, the Minister of Health was officially empowered to direct the day-to-day services of hospital care, and, in return, the government took over the financial burden, which had been underwritten previously by patients' contributions, local authority rates, and voluntary hospital funds (Levitt and Wall, 1992: 1).

The advent of the modern NHS dates from the early 1940s. The landmark Beveridge Report of 1942 recommended radical changes in the delivery of health care in the United Kingdom (Beveridge, 1942). For the first time, a comprehensive system was envisioned, including access to both community-based care and hospital treatment. Three principles for a publicly funded universal health care system listed earlier were espoused. The National Health Service Act of 1948 established a firm government commitment to improving the nation's health care. The newly nationalized NHS was organized in a tiered system of central administration, regional hospital boards, local health authorities and executive councils, and a tripartite of providers: hospital, community, and family practitioner services (see Figure 10-1).

Although the system was to be comprehensive, it did not include the nationalization of commercially run hospitals or nursing homes, and there was no legal prohibition of the establishment of new voluntary or commercially run hospitals. GPs and consultant physicians were free to see private patients and admit them to NHS hospitals. Patients retained freedom of choice to use the NHS or go to doctors outside the service, and all previous restrictions on NHS services to the insured or those who could afford private treatment were removed.

Reforming the NHS

In 1974, the NHS began a series of reorganizations designed to combine and improve administration of the tripartite components. By the 1980s, the Regional Health Authorities (RHAs) and the District Health Authorities (DHAs) were legally empowered to improve integration of services and provide a greater public health planning role with regard to regional inequities associated with urban/rural differences, demographic differences, and so on. New RHA tasks included responsibility for overall planning of clinical services, allocating funding to the DHAs, setting and monitoring performance, and supervising the newly established Family Health Service Agencies (FHSAs) as an integrative mechanism for primary care.

Other functions included service planning, staff development, information management, legal affairs, public relations, setting medical standards, and administering disciplinary action. Very importantly, the RHAs were required to allocate funding, ensure that DHAs have cash management systems in place, ensure that quality assurance mechanisms are in place and working, and balancing the distribution of medical personnel in terms of numbers and specialties so that all districts can meet the needs of their patients in accordance with national health objectives.

At the local level, DHAs became responsible for planning the provision and integration of primary care, general hospital, maternity and child health, chronically mentally ill, and the elderly services. The majority of

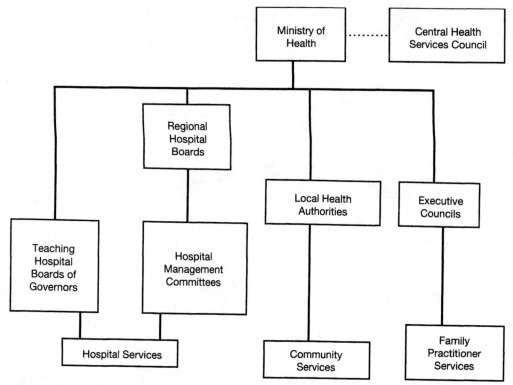

Figure 10-1. The National Health Service in 1948.

DHAs serve an average population of 250,000 to 350,000 and operate a District General Hospital of about 600 beds. However, despite attempts to integrate and consolidate NHS structure and planning, it was clear that unnecessary duplication of roles, unclear lines of authority, and a substantial increase in the number of administrators had evolved (Connah and Lancaster, 1989: 1; Levitt and Wall, 1992: 75).

The 1990 National Health Service and Community Care Act

After a relatively long period of political dominance by the national Labor Party, with its solid commitment to public ownership and central financing of services, the conservative Thatcher revolution in the early 1980s brought new thinking and a change in attitudes toward the public/private ownership debate. These successes increased potential public acceptance of change in the NHS, which was also spurred on by acute funding problems due to expensive new health technology, increased public expectations for health services, and an aging population. Some of the structural changes are summarized in Figure 10-2.

After a few successful privatization initiatives, notably British Airways, the petroleum industry, and British TeleCom, the conservative leadership launched a similar initiative to reorganize the NHS. A closed planning strategy of internal think tanks was established to explore theories and proposed solutions, and conceptual trial balloons were floated to assess public palatability. Eventually, the various deliberations were distilled into a series of government White Papers that articulated a philosophy of radical change in the delivery of health care.

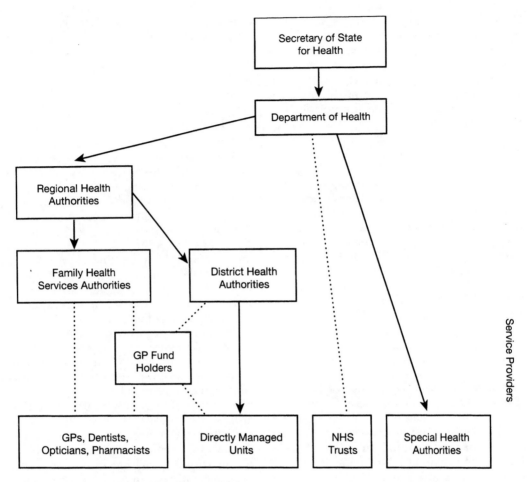

Figure 10-2. Structure of the NHS after the 1990 National Health Service and Community Care Act.

Whether or how these initiatives will be influenced by the future political climate in the United Kingdom is unclear, but fundamental and irreversible change has already occurred.

The first significant departure from the old NHS came with the Griffith report in 1983 recommending (1) that the NHS become more businesslike, (2) address the problem of growth of public expenditures, and (3) initiate internal market forces within the NHS. The main recommendations were to create competition between hospitals and providers through a separation of purchaser and provider role. Self-governing trusts would be created to run hospitals and other services, and DHAs would be transformed into purchasers for their local constituencies. GP practices would become fundholders, become purchasers of some hospital services, and establish contracts for other services. The fundamental idea was to assure that funding would follow the patient and this competition for patients would stimulate increased efficiency and greater response to patient needs (Ham, 1994: 2).

In 1989, public health and finance officials of England, Scotland and Wales released the document entitled *Caring for People* (1989).

Along with the Griffith Report, the principles outlined in this watershed document are embodied in the *1990 National Health Service and Community Care Act*, whose overall mission was to shift resources to primary care by introducing fundamental change in the management of hospital and family practitioner services. Another primary objective was to improve the health/social services interface. Interestingly, as early as 1963, the Gillie Report had suggested that the GP should function as the primary coordinator of hospital and community care in order to deal with problems encountered with the tripartite structure, which included a lack of public health planning and poor integration of services and primary care. The 1990 Act represents a major shift to community-based care, privatization, accountability, quality assurance, and cost containment that was envisioned over 30 years ago (Gillie, 1963).

CULTURAL FACTORS

As an island nation comprised of England, Wales, Scotland, and Northern Ireland, the United Kingdom has led an insular existence resulting in a relatively conservative attitude and reluctance to join fully in the rapid political and social unification of the European nations. The British people exhibit great resistance to altering their economic and political systems that stem from their historic isolation from the European mainland. Although significant change will eventually come, one can expect it to be vigorously debated with change slow to be implemented.

The United Kingdom has a strong tradition of labor political activism. The total British labor force in the late 1980s numbered about 27.9 million, of whom about 9.2 million were members of 87 unions affiliated with the Trades Union Congress. Collective bargaining is generally conducted on a national and industrywide basis, including industrial action among unions of health workers. In the prosperous postwar era, unemployment generally averaged between 1 and 2 percent of the total

workforce. In the mid-1960s, however, a persistent payments deficit and inflationary pressures caused unemployment rates to soar as high as 10 percent, although this figure has declined in recent years as new jobs have become available.

During the 1970s, successive British governments also faced internal difficulties in Ireland and Scotland. In conflicts with the Roman Catholic minority in Northern Ireland in 1969, the British government sent troops to keep order, and in 1972, it abolished Northern Ireland's autonomous parliament. This led to a campaign of terrorism by the Irish Republican Army (IRA) resulting in bombings and killings in Northern Ireland and England. However, in August 1994, the IRA declared an unconditional cease fire, promising to suspend all military operations in favor of peace; at this writing, a settlement is still under negotiation.

In Scotland, a Scottish Nationalist party scored impressive gains in the elections of 1974, and a semi-independent parliament in Edinburgh was proposed. When only 33 percent of the Scottish electorate supported the plan in a 1979 referendum, the project died, at least temporarily. However, Scotland consistently sends a large number of labor and Socialist Democrats to Parliament in defiance of the Tory majority in power, and a strong residual sentiment in favor of independence still remains (Funk & Wagnall's, 1994).

POLITICAL INFLUENCES

Great Britain is a parliamentary monarchy with an unwritten constitution consisting of historic documents such as the Magna Carta, the Petition of Right, a Bill of Rights (1689), and a system of statutes, judicial precedents (common law), and customs. The written law is flexible and may be changed by an act of Parliament.

The British monarch is head of state. Executive power, however, is wielded by a prime minister, who is head of government, and a committee of cabinet ministers. The cabinet, under the doctrine of collective responsibility, acts as a unit. The defeat of important legislation or a vote of no confidence usually brings about the resignation of the entire cabinet and a general election. The prime minister is usually the leader of the majority party in the House of Commons. By custom, cabinet ministers are selected from among members of the two houses of Parliament. Cabinet ministers are also among the members of the Privy Council, the traditional, but now largely ceremonial, advisory body to the Crown. Since the end of World War I (1914–1918), the Conservative party and the Labor party have been dominant in British leadership, and both parties have provided broad-based political support to the NHS, despite recent efforts to reform it so as to reduce costs.

In principle, the "Crown in Parliament" is supreme. This means that legislation passed by Parliament, which consists of the House of Commons (elected directly by the people) and the House of Lords (made up of hereditary peers and appointive members—archbishops, senior bishops, law lords, and life peers), becomes law upon royal assent. In practice, legislation is dominated by the prime minister and the cabinet, who initiate virtually all proposed bills and who are politically responsible for the administration of the law and the affairs of the nation. Fiscal legislation always, and other legislation usually, is initiated in the House of Commons. Bills from the House of Commons are passed to the House of Lords for discussion. Although no vote from the House of Lords is necessary to pass legislation, it often suggests revisions and provides a forum for debate free from party politics. The power of the Crown to veto legislation has not been exercised in over 280 years.

The election of April 1979 was a milestone in British politics with great implications for radical reform of the NHS. The Conservatives led by Margaret Thatcher emerged with a substantial majority of parliamentary seats and with the first woman prime minister in British or European history. The economic role of government declined as Thatcher promoted privatization—the turning over to private investors of government monopolies such as British Airways, the telephone service, and the distribution of gas and water. Following resounding success with these industries, the Conservatives turned their attention to the anchor of British society and its well-being, the NHS.

SOCIAL ORGANIZATION OF HEALTH CARE

The British system of national health insurance, comprising Social Security and the NHS, was thoroughly reorganized after World War II and is one of the most comprehensive systems in operation. The system is under the jurisdiction of the Department of Health and Social Security, which administers the payment of cash benefits for sickness and maternity. All employed and self-employed persons up to the age of 65 are eligible for benefits, and the funds for the program are derived from weekly tax contributions by employers and employees. Sickness benefits are payable up to pensionable age. Maternity benefits include weekly allowances, before and after confinement, to women who ordinarily work, as well as certain cash grants.

The cost of the program is met largely from public funds. Benefits, which are of unlimited duration, include hospital services, general medical services outside of hospitals, and local health services. Hospital services are provided in general and special hospitals, for inpatient, outpatient, and day-patient care, including the services of specialists. General medical services include those of general practitioners and dental, pharmaceutical, and ophthalmic services. The local health services include maternity and child-welfare services, domiciliary nursing care, aftercare, immunization, and some mental health services.

Persons may use all the facilities of the National Health Service or only a part of the service. They may, for example, make private arrangements with a practitioner for medical care and apply for free hospitalization. Practitioners are not required to participate in the program. Those who participate and work outside of hospitals receive a fee for each patient as well as a basic practice allowance. Participating physicians may also engage in private practice. Almost all of the hospitals in Great Britain are administered by the NHS.

Beginning in 1948, the modernized NHS was conceived as a tripartite structure of hospital services, community services, and family practitioners. The Minister of Health was responsible for the provision of all hospital and specialist services, for the quality of laboratory and blood products, major capital projects, and health research, and reported directly to the Parliament. Each tripartite component was funded separately from central and local government sources and was organizationally distinct. The divisions resulted in overlapping services in some cases and the predominance of the hospital component. Relegation of community services and family practice into the background, coupled with lack of coordination, soon led to calls for changes (Levitt and Wall, 1992; Schneider et al., 1992).

The NHS encountered many problems in the period 1948 to 1974 as a result of compromises with providers and hospitals, and the idea of free service was quickly breached with the introduction of compulsory fees for certain services, such as prescription drugs and optician services. More importantly, the demand for services increased and resources were stretched, which maintained and even exaggerated the uneven distribution of services between regions that existed before 1948. Because power was invested to greater extent in hospitals, services to the acutely ill were excellent, whereas needs of the chronically ill and disabled were relatively neglected.

Scotland, Wales, and Northern Ireland

Broadly speaking, the NHS is the same throughout the United Kingdom, and ministers responsible in the member countries normally adopt policies applied to England by the Secretary of State for Health. Some differences exist due to the different legal and political traditions of each country and also due to demographic and geographical difference.

Scotland has traditionally spent more on the NHS (504 pounds per person in 1989) compared to England and Wales (444 pounds per person). Staffing patterns probably account for this. Because the average GP patient list size is nearly 20 percent smaller, there is a considerably higher ratio of medical staff per 1,000 population (94 vs. 81 in England and Wales); of the total employees in 1987, half (49 percent of 128,000) were nurses and midwives, a significantly larger proportion than in England and Wales (Office of Health Economics, 1989).

Scotland maintains an independent legislature from England and Wales. As a result, the structure of health delivery in Scotland has some significant distinctions from the rest of the United Kingdom. First, there is a greater centralization of health services within the Scottish Health Services Planning Council. This Council advises the Scottish Secretary of State on health matters and coordinates local services through a Common Services Agency, a level of management not found in the English NHS. The Common Services Agency administers to 15 local Health Boards, which are responsible for planning and integration of local services, including GP services. As a result, there has never been a separate authority for GP services as in the English or Welsh NHS. Health centers are prominent in Scotland, and many GPs can hold hospital specialist appointments. Finally, even though the NHS Community Care Act of 1990 applied to the whole of the United Kingdom, Scotland has shown little enthusiasm for the introduction of market forces into their version of the NHS.

All English NHS acts apply in Wales, and the main differences relate to minor administrative structure based on the fact that Wales is a small country of only 2.85 million.

The Welsh Office Secretary of State answers to the British Parliament and is the NHS Director for Wales.

Health services in Northern Ireland are considerably different from England and Wales. Established by the Northern Ireland Parliament in 1948, the Northern Ireland NHS is modeled on, but not part of, British NHS. Ministerial responsibility lies with the Secretary of State for Northern Ireland. A distinctive feature, reflecting different local government arrangements, is that the Health Districts have fewer responsibilities than their counterparts in England. As in Scotland and Wales, many services are undertaken by a Central Services Agency, which does the work that in England is the responsibility of the Family Health Services Authorities.

Due to prolonged sectarian troubles and also a high number of professional health care workers, Northern Ireland spends 25 percent more on health and social services than does the rest of the United Kingdom (Connah and Lancaster, 1989; Levitt and Wall, 1992: 105).

Implementation of the 1990 Reforms

The 1990 Act has been called the most radical reform of health financing since the formation of the NHS in 1948. It fundamentally changed the relationship between the providers of health care (for example, hospitals, community units, and so on) and the purchaser, usually a health authority. An "internal market" was established to correct imprecise funding formulas and unequal distribution of resources across the country resulting from differences in patient catchment and based on the array of specialty services and providers within a DHA. In the new system, the concept of "catchment population" is replaced by "resident population," meaning that DHAs are responsible for those people who live within its boundaries. Thus, a district whose hospitals previously treated patients from a wide area experienced a drop in income, whereas a DHA whose patients travel in large numbers to other dis-

tricts will have an increase in income to pay for these "foreign units." Regional specialties continue to be funded by RHAs under separate contract (Gilby, 1991: 76).

Only 5 months after passage of the 1990 Act, NHS Trusts were given a legal mandate to begin operations. In April 1991, fifty-seven NHS Trusts came into existence, covering a range of services, including acute hospitals, community services, mental health, ambulance services, and a combination of all these services. Over the next 3 years, most of the remaining units achieved Trust status by 1994, at which point over 90 percent of NHS services were managed this way. The major impetus behind the NHS Trust initiative was massive problems in costly technology, increased public expectations, and an aging population, all of which stretched resources and produced rationing and access concerns (Ham, 1994: 14).

NHS Trusts are bodies established under statute as distinct legal entities within the NHS and separate from the health authorities. Each is run by a board of directors and a chairman appointed by the Secretary of Health. NHS Trusts hospitals have considerably more autonomy than NHS hospitals, which includes responsibility for acquisition, ownership, and disposal of assets, ability to borrow funds, retention of operating surpluses, determination of management structure and staffing control. However, NHS Trusts remain fully part of the NHS, because they are publicly funded and are subject to legislation that applies to NHS facilities. The rationale for establishing NHS Trusts is to stimulate a managed care system, with incentives to reward efficiency, quality, and cost effectiveness, and provide citizens with choices (Brookes, 1991: 47).

Critics have argued that there is no evidence that NHS Trusts provide better care; they suggest the initiative is the first step in the privatization of the NHS. The concern is that NHS Trusts, independent of the health authorities, may be less accountable to the planning process for the health care of the total population, and that NHS Trusts may concentrate on profitable services and leave less attractive services, for example, long-term care or community mental health, to the nontrust hospitals. The traditional role of the NHS in preventative medicine and public health may be threatened.

The NHS Trusts no doubt carry both risks and opportunities, with cost and quality being the key issues. Personnel issues are also important, with each trust responsible for setting up negotiating machinery for pay and work conditions, which is a major departure from the uniform NHS system. Because NHS Trusts must at least break even, staffing costs are a major discretionary variable, and skeptics fear lower skills and pay reductions, which may affect quality and access. Even though there is commitment to the NHS Trusts concept from top managers, the basic question of commitment and trust from the rank and file, and thus the question "will it work?" remains unanswered (Brookes, 1991: 47).

GP Fund Holders

In another significant change, the concept of general practitioner fund holders (GPFHs) was introduced. Because GPs originate most of the hospital work and referral to specialists, control of funds would be shifted from DHAs to GPFHs; the shift is on the order of 500,000 pounds per GPFH per annum. GPFHs must have a minimum of 7,000 patients enrolled and can purchase a number of provider services directly on behalf of their patients. These reforms are intended to apply market forces to GP referral habits and DHA provider practices based on the choice of quality and price available; GPFHs who obtain treatment more quickly for patients will attract and retain more patients and secure greater remuneration. End-of-year surpluses can be used for purchasing or upgrading office medical equipment and premises, thus further enhancing competitiveness. Reimbursement schemes in the reforms include experimentation with capitation and cost risking. To guard against

practitioners reducing quality to save costs, a comprehensive system of quality assurance through formal medical audit has been implemented.

Private medicine in the United Kingdom is a small but growing sector. Everyone has the option of taking out private health insurance with one of the few insurance companies. About 10 percent of the population have private health insurance, but often with limited coverage for benefits. Most private health insurance is a work-related benefit; premiums are usually age-, gender-, and risk-related, and are paid by employers. Private health care can also be financed by the individual patient; approximately 20 percent of the private sector is financed this way (McCarthy and Rees, 1992).

Like most modern health care systems coping with forces of new technology, an aging population, increasing patient demand for services, and diminishing resources, the NHS is a dynamic system characterized by experimentation and change.

Public Health

Of the three categories of doctors (hospital consultant, GP, and public health doctor in community medicine), the public health doctor is by far the smallest group and traditionally considered the least prestigious. However with the recent reforms and the 1990 Act in place, the emphasis on community medicine has started to attract more interest among medical graduates. With the institutionalization of medical audits, quality assurance requirements, and strategic planning for local health resources, the public health doctor assumes a vital role. Currently, each FHSA must have a Medical Audit Advisory Group that includes one public health doctor member. Public health doctors can advance to senior appointments as District or Regional Public Health Directors, or work in other consultant grade positions (Levitt and Wall, 1992: 102).

Because of the audit system and local reporting/planning data that are available, the NHS is very advanced in tracking health outcome indicators and developing prospective plans for resource allocation. For example, prenatal, maternal, infant care, and immunizations are comprehensively monitored at the local level and national compliance figures compare very favorably with other nations (Baxter, 1990: 267; Nutbeam, Farley, and Smith, 1990: 318; Burr, 1992: 299; Stocking, 1993: 497).

Regarding health promotion, only recently has the NHS demonstrated a commitment to the concept in a systematic way. Until the recent publication of two documents addressing the issue, health promotion was viewed as a fluffy, nonessential "extra service." In the documents, the components for a specific strategy were delineated for local health authorities, and included smoking cessation efforts, family planning programs, improvement in school health programs, immunization target goals, cardiovascular health, and more (Department of Health and Social Services, 1981; Department of Health, 1991).

Physicians

General practice and primary care in the NHS today have become recognized as a fulfilling alternative to hospital practice, and the GP can reach an optimal salary level much more quickly than a hospital consultant. About 50 percent of qualifying doctors enter the NHS as GPs. GP group practice is the norm, and a typical surgery (clinic) is comprised of two or more GPs and one or two part-time trainees. Attached to this practice are a district nurse; a health visitor, a specialist nurse who works with children, mothers, and the elderly; and an office nurse employed by the GPs. GPs act as gatekeepers to the NHS, seeing nearly 300 million patients yearly, many of whom in other countries would be dealt with by a specialist or referred to the hospital. All citizens register with a GP and are then eligible for comprehensive health care managed by the selected GP. The average number enrolled per GP is

2,000 (Office of Health Economics, 1989; Grumbach and Fry, 1993: 940).

The distribution of GPs is controlled by the NHS Medical Practices Committee (MPC). Approval for practice in any area is based on the number of persons per physician, or "list," and a list of over 1,800 is generally approved by the MPC. Under the 1990 Act, GPs wishing to practice must apply to the local FHSA for approval. In underserved or "designated areas" with a list over 2,500, FHSAs can offer financial incentives to attract GPs to their area (Levitt and Wall, 1992: 208). The GP then contracts with the FHSA. Larger practices are encouraged to become GPFHs and purchase services from any source to meet the needs and wishes of their patients. Because the RHAs shift money from the DHAs' budget to the GPFHs, the DHAs are motivated to improve and market their services to earn the money back. GPFHs are protected from catastrophic patient occurrences amounting to more than 5,000 pounds and from all emergency care patients who are covered by the DHA. In this new arrangement with the FHSA, GPs practices are now more closely scrutinized for prescribing, referral, and other patterns, and their targeted public health activities, such as vaccination rates, may be publicly disclosed.

Rural services. The adequate supply of GPs in the NHS is very amenable to quality rural services. For example, in Lincolnshire (population 600,000), rural GP practice is considered by many to be more desirable than the urban GP practice. Income is capitated at the same rates, except there are additional reimbursement opportunities for "rural practice patients." GP distribution in rural communities is excellent and even the smallest village will have group practices of two to four GPs. Villages of less than 2,000 without a GP are never more than 5 to 10 miles from a surgery. Thus, "rurality" in England is clearly different in magnitude than in the United States. The economic situation for rural GPs may also be superior to urban GPs, given the opportunity to augment income through GP dispensing of drugs, and with the advent of GPFHs. Rural GPs can set up branch surgeries and hold office hours in smaller villages.

Rural patients have little or no choice of GPs, and despite much better proxemics compared to the United States, rural access problems still exist. First, the idea of traveling 1 mile for health care may be as onerous to a Britisher as traveling 50 miles is to an American. Second, few alternatives to care are present in rural England. The NHS has experimented with mobile outreach facilities (for example, mobile cancer screening units), but this is rare. Rural GPs do make routine in-home visitations, and for home visits requiring more than 3 miles travel, the GP's expenses are supplemented with a "rural practice payment."

Ambulance service for acute illness is excellent in rural areas, with the average response time for a rural ambulance 19 minutes compared to 12 minutes average for urban response time. Unfortunately, public bus deregulation has greatly diminished bus services in rural areas, but volunteer transportation can be provided by the Department of Social Services. Seventy-five percent of individuals in Lincolnshire have personal access to cars (Gilmore, 1992).

Medical education.   As previously mentioned, there are three principal types of medical school tracks in the United Kingdom: (1) the hospital consultant, (2) the GP, and (3) the public health doctor in community medicine. All graduates receive 5 years of standardized training followed by an internship year working in a hospital. Once licensed, the graduate can select any branch of medicine for residency and practice. However, it is very difficult to attain acceptance to certain specialties, such as cardiology, infectious diseases, general surgery, and other specialties due to the large number of specialists already in practice in these areas. On the other hand, specialization in geriatrics or anesthesiology and some other specialties will assure a senior post. The time

line for the hospital consultant is 1 year as a house officer, 2 to 3 years as a senior house officer, 3 to 4 years as a registrar in the specialty, and up to 4 more years as a senior registrar.

GPs complete a 3-year postqualifying course of study that includes experiential rotations in general medicine, pediatrics, and obstetrics along with a supervised traineeship with a GP preceptor. Training of the public health doctor follows a similar pattern to the GP, with specialization in community health beginning at the registrar level (Levitt and Wall, 1992: 189).

Nurses

Nurses are the most numerous of the various NHS staff, and nurse salaries account for 40 percent of the NHS budget. Nursing was historically a fragmented profession until passage of the Nurses, Midwives and Health Visitors Act in 1979 that united the three groups into one profession. The impetus for this consolidation came from the Committee on Nursing, which set forth a plan whereby a basic entry-level course of study would be standardized, with specialization to follow. After an initial core course of study, the trainee would then select one of the branches of nursing, such as adult, children, mental health, and so on. Midwifery has not fully joined the organization, continuing to operate as a profession in its own right (Department of Health and Social Security, 1972).

The 1989 White Paper *Caring for People* served to promote the role of the nurse in community service and envisioned a more autonomous professional who works closely with the GP to provide continuity of care. Activities would include health visiting by nurse specialists, for example, community mental health nurses, midwives, pediatric nurses, and care of the physically disabled (*Caring for People*, 1989). The nursing profession has further elaborated this vision for the role of the community nurse in equal partnership with the GP, especially in meeting the needs of specialized, high-risk populations (Bowers, 1992: 739; Trobranski, 1994: 773).

Pharmacists and Pharmaceuticals

In the United Kingdom, a pharmacist wishing to establish a community practice must register the business premises with the Pharmaceutical Society of Great Britain, and then apply to the FHSA for a contract. Separate arrangements are made for hospital pharmacists, who are employed by the NHS Hospital Pharmaceutical Service and who serve hospital inpatients and outpatients receiving prescriptions from the hospital's doctors.

In community practice, the pharmacist supplies the drug on the receipt of a doctor's prescription and sends the forms to the regional Prescription Pricing Authority (PPA), which then calculates the cost of the ingredients and notifies the FHSA the amount to reimburse the pharmacist. In 1988, the PPA introduced its first detailed drug use review report called the Prescribing Analysis and Cost Report. PACT revealed that over 427 million prescriptions were filled in 1988 costing over 2.5 billion pounds, and representing a 13 percent increase in drug cost during the decade. PACT currently makes monthly reports to GPs so they can monitor their own prescribing patterns and compare them with peers. The NHS also maintains a restricted formulary of prescription drugs as a cost-containment measure (Office of Health Economics, 1989).

Incentives exist to encourage and support pharmacies in rural locations. In a plan supported by NHS, a rural pharmacy can be classified as an "essential small pharmacy" and receive a government subsidy of up to 18,000 pounds per year if the dispensing volume is at least 600 but not more than 16,000 prescriptions per year (Byrt, 1992).

In the United Kingdom, pharmacists are not the only legal dispensers of prescription medications. A major attraction for rural GP practice is the possibility to augment income through GP dispensing. For example, GP dispensing contributes to a major problem in Lincolnshire, which has the highest prescription volume of any DHA in England. Although the nondispensing rural GP makes as much money as any other nondispensing GP, the dispensing activity can provide very lucrative supplemental income. There are 80 community pharmacies in Lincolnshire, but based on the demographics, an estimated capacity of 120; the discrepancy is attributed to GP dispensing. Approval of one pharmacy in an area served by a dispensing GP would result in the loss of an average of 16,000 pounds per GP; many GPs augment their incomes by several times this amount by dispensing. The conflict of interest and the troubling incentive to overprescribe could become a moot point with the increasing formation of GPFHs and a capitated system of reimbursement. Interestingly, rural England has a much stronger tradition of dispensing GPs compared to Scotland and Wales (Baumber, 1992).

Despite the problems noted earlier, drug expenditures per capita in the United Kingdom is $97 per year, a relatively low figure compared to similar nations (World Bank, 1993: 145).

Midlevel and Other Practitioners

Opticians and other professions supplementary to medicine, including chiropody, dietetics, occupational therapists, and medical laboratory technicians, provide a critical rounding out of the comprehensive services of the NHS. These disciplines in particular are key supporters of the community-based services emphasized in the 1990 Act. Through needs assessment and planning, the NHS attempts to assure an adequate supply of ancillary health personnel.

Health Care Administration

Professional health care administration is highly developed in the United Kingdom. The complex tiered system of regional and local management requires considerable expertise in the planning and evaluation of services in the NHS. Health care administrators are present at all levels, including regional managers, district managers, and FHSA managers. With the advent of the 1990 Act, and the incorporation of an internal market system of cost containment, the needs for qualified health care administrators became even greater. A backlash to the large administrative component of the latest NHS reforms is a proposal to abolish RHAs, merge the DHAs and FHSAs and replace the RHAs with new NHS Management Executives operating through eight regional offices. This proposal is controversial and will not be resolved until 1996 or 1997, but the proposal further emphasizes the dynamic nature of the NHS (Ham, 1993: 1089).

Hospitals

The NHS hospital capacity is nearly 400,000 beds, and hospital care absorbs just over half of the NHS budget. The hospital network is widely distributed and accessible throughout the United Kingdom, and hospital sizes range from the small community facility, to the large District Hospital (400- to 800-bed capacity with full diagnostic treatment capability in all major specialties), to the large, comprehensive tertiary care facility that is normally associated with an academic health sciences center. The average length of stay for all ages was 8.8 days in 1991, compared to 12.5 days in 1981 (Murphy 1993: 65).

In addition to the NHS facilities, there are over 10,000 beds available in private and voluntary hospitals that also provide a wide range of acute care and surgical services. This private sector may grow rapidly in the future as purchasers of services, such as the GPFHs, decide they can derive better value for their patients or minimize the long waiting lists for certain services (that is, surgical procedures) associated with the traditional NHS hospitals (Levitt and Wall, 1992: 145; Harrison and Bruscini, 1994: 7).

Role of Information Systems and Technology

The NHS information and technology capability has good resources for the collection of population-based data related to the health of the nation. A strong tradition for this activity exists, sustained by providers who are interested in quality of care, health planners who are interested in evaluating services for resource allocation, and politicians and policy makers who are interested in cost-containment issues. As mentioned previously, GPs are required to undertake a systematic medical audit review of their practice patterns to assess patient outcomes, and each FHSA has a Medical Audit Advisory Group to assess GP adherence to local targeted care, such as childhood immunizations, and to other regional or national initiatives, such as quality improvement in diabetes care. Medical audit is now an accepted process across most major health disciplines. The main weakness at this point is the lack of computerized integration of health data with social services data, although several pilot projects exist in which GP practices are attempting to access social services care management data for comprehensive patient tracking capability (Miller and Britt, 1993: 471; Murphy, 1993: 74; Sonjsen, Harris, and Jarman, 1993: 80).

Quality Assurance

The 1989 White Paper *Caring for People* provides a blueprint for implementing quality assurance at the local level. Each health authority should be clear in advance how quality is specified and monitored, and how the authority would deal in a situation where a contractor does not meet predetermined standards for acceptable service. Based on the local assessments, the NHS Department of Health coordinates the QA process, working with local authorities. Using base lines established through initial QA activity, local authorities are then required to publish plans for community care against which performance can be measured. The result enables the Secretary of State to monitor plans and issue general directives based on population needs (*Caring for People*, 1989). Table 10-1 lists the scope of the QA activities.

Emergency Medical Services

The emergency medical system in the United Kingdom is well-developed. Dialing a three-digit emergency call code on any telephone will result in the dispatch of ambulance service with delivery of the patient to the nearest casualty department of the local GP hospital or the accident and emergency department of the District hospital, both of which are fully staffed. Ambulance service for acute illness or accidents is excellent, with the average response time for a rural ambu-

Table 10-1 Quality Assurance Expectations of Local Authorities

---

- Assessment of needs of population served
- Strategic objectives for community care in the next 3 years and how these relate to national policy objectives
- Method to identify and meet needs for information on which to base planning
- Arrangements for assessments of individual applicants for care and how they are integrated within the budgetary framework
- How purchasing tasks are organized and managed, including budgetary arrangements
- How services for people at home, including their caregivers, are to be improved
- Methods to coordinate plans and activities with those of health authorities, family practitioners committees, and housing authorities
- What arrangements are made for case management
- What information is to be provided to service users and their caregivers about services
- Training provided for relevant staff groups
- How contribution of the independent sector is to be stimulated
- Establishment of inspection and registration units
- What QA and systems for safeguarding service standards are to be established, including complaints procedures

---

Source: Based on data from Ham, 1993: 8.

lance 19 minutes compared to 12 minutes average for urban response time, as noted before.

Long-Term Care

Until recently, the emphasis for care of the elderly was to provide community support via home helpers, district nurse visitations, consultants in geriatric practice, physical therapists, day center, and meals on wheels to stabilize and maintain the elderly at home, and utilize NHS hospital beds designated as "long-stay care" beds when needed by elderly patients for acute illnesses (Department of Health and Social Security, 1978; Murphy, 1993: 65).

In keeping with this philosophy, the NHS established Geriatric Assessment Units in every District Hospital, and Social Security support services were increased to encourage older adults to remain in their homes. The concept of a NHS elderly nursing home was not seriously considered until the 1980s (Department of Health and Social Services, 1980), and even then virtually all long-term care was provided by the private sector and benefits were paid from Social Security funds. With recent changes in Social Security funding policies resulting from the 1990 Act, there has been a dramatic increase in private sector registered care homes and nursing homes in the past decade. In April 1993, the responsibility for payments currently made through Social Security for nursing home accommodation was transferred to local authorities, and this resulted in increased competition for long-term-care patients in the public sector as well (Murphy, 1993: 65).

At the present time, as measured by the number of available places per person over 65 and by the number of staff members per bed in nursing homes, the United Kingdom has the most highly developed standards when compared to the United States and to other European nations. This is arguably the result of the new funding system, in which local authorities were given the responsibility to manage and contract for services, whether for nursing home or residential care. From 1980 to 1990, core community service expenditures increased from 1.17 billion pounds to 3.44 billion, with nearly half spent on residential care for the elderly. Also during this time, the number of residential homes increased by 47 percent, private nursing home beds more than doubled, and the number of elderly treated by district nursing services increased by 24 percent (*Caring for People*, 1989; Alber, 1992: 929).

Special Programs for the Elderly: Palliative Care

A medical specialty unique to the United Kingdom that greatly improves the quality of care in elderly patients is palliative care. Palliative care is now recognized as a medical specialty that is concerned with relief of problems associated with advanced, incurable, and ultimately fatal disease. From its initial scope of caring for terminal cancer patients, hospice care has now broadened to include patients with many nonmalignant diseases, who may not be seen as imminently dying. Many victims falling within this definition are the frail elderly with chronic diseases (MacDonald, 1993: 11).

The main influence in the development of palliative care has been the hospice movement, which has traditionally been independent of the NHS, usually administered by charities, and with roots in Catholic nursing and medical initiatives in Ireland in the late 1800s. In the United Kingdom, Cicely Saunders pioneered the "modern" hospice growth by founding St. Christopher's Hospice in London. Later, St. Christopher's and other large cancer-based charities expanded into the home care area. The final contribution to development of palliative care was recognition in 1987 of palliative medicine as a distinct specialty of internal medicine by Royal Colleges of Physicians. In 1990, the NHS established a "Cooperative Palliative Care Minimum Data Set" to evaluate services. The ultimate result is that palliative care developed from a holistic model designed to meet

physical, emotional, social, and psychosocial needs of dying elderly patients and their families. Recognition as a medical specialty provides elderly patients in the United Kingdom a resource found in no other country in the world (Ahmedzai et al., 1995: 18).

ECONOMIC CHARACTERISTICS AND ISSUES

The United Kingdom provides one of the most cost-effective health care systems in the world. The publicly funded NHS accomplishes this at one of the lowest costs (7.1 percent of GDP or $1,151 per capita) in Western Europe (Organization for Economic Cooperation and Development, 1994). Nevertheless, the NHS faced serious funding shortages in the mid-1980s due to massive problems associated with the world recession, costly medical technology, increased public expectations for health care, and an aging population, all of which stretched resources while producing concerns over possible rationing and reduced access. As a result, the NHS implemented a number of reforms designed to contain costs. Culminating with the 1990 Act, several internal market strategies for the purchase and provision of services were implemented, including the establishment of NHS Trust and GPFH organizations, and a better coordination of health and social services, as noted earlier.

A key financial change of the 1990 Act was a switch of funding for nursing home and residential care from the Social Security budget to local authorities. Opinion regarding the impact of the change is mixed. A survey of GPs within the first year revealed criticism that access to home care and nursing homes had either not improved or deteriorated. On the other hand, the NHS Audit Commission concluded that although the changes in some community care services are slower to improve than others, the foundation being set in place will allow the new arrangements for community care to flourish in the future. Clearly, the financial impacts of the NHS reforms are yet to be quantified, and are thus controversial (Harrison and Bruscini, 1994).

The Financing System

In leading up to the reforms of the 1990s, the NHS review document *Working for Patients* examined the various systems for financing health care. After some study of the impact of switching to an insurance-based system, it concluded that the existing method of public funding through taxation should be retained. Certainly, the U.K. system is efficient as reflected in lower administrative costs (less than 5 percent) compared to the United States (25 percent) or France (10 percent) (Department of Health, 1989).

Patients pay no doctor's or hospital fees at the point of service, and pay a small co-payment on a few services, such as prescription drugs or optician services. However, about 80 percent of patients are exempt from these co-payments because they meet special criteria of need, including pregnant women, mothers, children, most elderly persons, and patients with some chronic diseases. Finally, there is a small but growing private insurance sector accounting for less than 10 percent of financing, as noted earlier, but which is estimated to reach a coverage of 15 percent of the population by the year 2000 (Ham, 1994: 4).

Payment of providers. As discussed earlier, GPs rapidly formed GPFHs to provide care and purchase services for their patients, which included hospital services, pharmaceutical care, health visiting and district nursing, dietetic, and chiropody services. The GPFH budget was based on the use and costs of services purchased in the past and set by a formula. However, the Department of Health is attempting to develop a capitation formula to replace the reimbursement based on historical use patterns.

GPFHs are insured against catastrophic care by being held liable for only the first 5,000 pounds for treatment of any one patient per year. As noted earlier, GPFHs with surpluses at the end of the year can use

the funds to improve their premises, enhance their staffing, or increase their range of services. Early research into the impact of fundholding demonstrated that GPs tended to employ a wider range of staff, negotiate shorter waiting times for hospital services by switching contracts, and reduced prescription drug utilization and costs. From the public's point of view, the greatest benefit of GPFHs was the quicker access to hospital care and consultants (Ham, 1994: 21).

A number of issues relating to contracts were revealed in the initial years of NHS Trust existence. In the absence of reliable information on case mix initially, "fixed" contracts were written that preempted increases in service activity from receiving concomitant increases in income. Providers who fulfilled their contracts early were forced to wait until a new contract period arrived before treating new patients, a classic case of mismatching resource allocation and service needs. To overcome this problem, the Department of Health has developed guidelines to assist authorities to develop more appropriate contracts to meet specific patient care needs and demands (Ham, 1994: 26).

Facilities financing. A similar reimbursement scheme was developed for hospital care, consultants, and ancillary services in the form of NHS Trusts. NHS Trust hospitals are the primary provider of specialty services to the GPFHs. They also have the freedom to develop capital schemes and have responsibility for acquisition, ownership, and disposal of assets, ability to borrow funds, retention of operating surpluses, and determination of management structure and staffing control.

Cost-Control Efforts

The NHS reforms described in this chapter were all directed at lowering the cost of health care in the United Kingdom. The main recommendations were to separate the purchaser and provider roles and create a competitive "internal market." The fundamental idea was to assure that funding would follow the patient and this competition for patients would stimulate increased efficiency and greater response to patient needs. The rationale for establishing NHS Trusts and GPFHs was to stimulate a managed care system, with incentives to reward efficiency, quality, and cost effectiveness, and provide citizens with choices. These initiatives, along with the Department of Health's strong commitment to effective medical audit practices, are direct cost-containment strategies.

To address fears that quality would be sacrificed by purchasers in order to increase activity and reduce costs, the Patient's Charter (Table 10-2) was developed to ensure that emphasis would continue to be placed on the quality and convenience of patient care. The ten rights of the Charter form the basis of

Table 10-2   The Patient's Charter (October 1991)

Ten rights are included in the Patient's Charter:

1. To receive health care on the basis of clinical need, regardless of ability to pay

2. To be registered with a GP

3. To receive emergency medical care at any time through a GP or through the emergency ambulance .service or hospital accident and emergency department

4. To be referred to a consultant, acceptable to the patient, when a GP thinks this is necessary, and to be referred for a second opinion if the patient and GP agree this is desirable

5. To be given a clear explanation of any treatment proposed, including any risks and alternatives

6. To have access to health records, and to know that those working for the NHS are under a legal duty to keep the contents confidential

7. To choose whether to take part in medical research or medical student training

8. To be given detailed information on local health services, including quality standards and maximum waiting times

9. To be guaranteed admission for treatment by a specific date no later than 2 years from the day when the patient is placed on a waiting list

10. To have any complaint about NHS services investigated and to receive a full and prompt written reply from the chief executive or general manager

medical audit indicators to assure the desired behavior of providers (Ham, 1994: 28).

PROBLEMS AND REFORMS

The years since the initiation of the NHS reforms have been characterized by unprecedented innovation and experimental change in the delivery of health care. The heart of the reforms has always been the attempt to introduce an "internal market" or managed care strategy to contain costs, along with the strong Conservative ideology espousing the value of the marketplace as a singular mechanism to improve performance. However, the implementation process involved a relatively closed planning strategy, which is unusual in British politics given the nature of the system for fostering consensus, assuring broad public support for changes, and leaving nothing to chance when deliberating issues of this magnitude. The resulting strategy was ambiguous and inconsistent to planners, with much of the detail missing, and the discovery by NHS Trust and GPFHs of the importance of separation of purchaser and provider roles have led to changing policy, and making up new policy, in the midst of implementing the reforms (Ham, 1994: 34).

At the end of the day, the success or failure of the reforms will be determined by their impact on patient care. There are many indicators that the 1990 Act is having its intended effect, and NHS Ministers have listed the following improvements in patient care:

- Overall, more patients are being treated in the same time period

- There is a 16 percent increase in hospital encounters, with NHS Trust hospitals outperforming nontrust hospitals

- Waiting lists have been shortened and waiting times decreased

- There has been an overall improvement in the quality of care

Although there is an element of truth to the Ministers' claims, they need to be treated with caution in view of the following perspectives (Ham, 1994: 43):

- The improvements in care could arguably be a function of the additional funding that was provided for the implementation of the NHS reforms
- Each GP joining a GPFH practice was given a 16,000-pound preparatory fee and a maintenance allowance of 34,000 pounds
- The improvement in activity rates could be the result of improved record keeping; the GPFH practices were provided with an additional allowance to upgrade their computer record-keeping capability
- The 1983 Griffiths report set a policy agenda for improvements in service and a stronger focus on the patient's perspective; the NHS reforms may have simply helped to continue what was already being done (Griffiths, 1983)

Nevertheless, a clear advantage of the reformed NHS is the elevation of the GP practice to a managerial role for services and patient care at the local level, and the overall shift of NHS resources to primary care and community-based care.

On the other hand, the increasing control of the GPFHs over resources has led to some legitimate concerns that GPs might engage in practices to maximize their budgets, such as excluding high-risk, high-cost patients or underreferring patients to hospitals. To date, there is evidence that these practices have occurred, but the magnitude is quite small.

Finally, there are other issues facing the NHS as it continues to explore and evaluate the effects of the NHS reforms:

- The NHS has become top-heavy with management. From 1990 to 1993, the number of managers increased from 6,091 to 20,478, and over the same period, administrative and clerical staff increased by 13 percent, figures far greater than any other sector of the NHS, including providers. This has prompted proposals for new rounds of reforms that would eliminate the RHAs, merge the DHAs and FHSAs, and create eight regional NHS Management Executives to administer the NHS programs. In keeping with previous practices, the "make it up as you go" approach to reform continues (Ham, 1993: 1089).

- Waiting lists are an epidemic problem that must be addressed. In 1990, there were nearly 1 million people waiting for admission to a hospital, and 20 percent were required to wait a year or more to receive services (Levitt and Wall, 1992: 316).
- The equity in access issue is unsolved. In common with all national health systems, the United Kingdom has the highest incidence of illness among its poorest and most deprived.
- One of the main reasons for the "success" of the NHS in terms of cost per capita and percent of GDP is that its health workers are paid considerably less than their counterparts in other countries. Is this fair or will it lead to conflict in the future?
- A primary impetus for the NHS reforms in the mid-1980s and early 1990s has been a Conservative government that has retained power during that entire era. In Britain today, the political winds appear to have shifted, and the question remains how committed will the British society continue to be to these significant changes when a national leadership with a different ideology assumes control?

SUMMARY AND CONCLUSIONS

The NHS is an excellent example of a publicly funded health service coping with modern problems. The NHS reforms have been characterized by unprecedented innovation and experimental changes in the delivery of health care, the heart of which is the introduction of an "internal market" or managed care strategy to contain costs. The NHS reforms of the 1990s provide more opportunities for entrepreneurship and management strategies but also for more quality control through accreditation, medical audit, and strategic planning.

A great benefit of reform has been the elevation of GP status, the emphasis on primary care, and the attempts to improve the interface between health and social services in the community. The increased emphasis on standards, quality of patient outcomes, and cost-effective care are all important challenges to the broad range of providers who make up one of the most innovative health care systems in the world.

REFERENCES

AHMEDZAI, S., D. J. E. CLEGG, R. A. CATTERALL, and K. MANN (1995). A Cooperative Palliative Care Database: Field Study of a Minimum Data-Set. The Second Conference in Palliative Medicine, Tronheim, January 19–21, 1995, *Clinical Oncology* 11: 18.

ALBER, J. (1992). Residential Care for the Elderly, *Journal of Health, Politics, and Policy Law*, 17: 929–957.

BAUMBER, N. (1992). Personal communication from the Secretary, Lincolnshire Local Pharmaceutical Committee, Grantham, Lincs.

BAXTER, D. N. (1990). Improving Immunization Uptake in the United Kingdom, *Public Health*, 104: 267–274.

BEVERIDGE, W. (1942). *Parliament, Social Insurance and Allied Services* [Cmnd. 6404]. London: His Majesty's Stationery Office.

BOWERS, L. (1992). A Preliminary Description of the United Kingdom Community Psychiatric Nursing Literature, *Journal of Advanced Nursing*, 17: 739–746.

BROOKES, W. T. (1991). Self-Governing Trusts, *Pharmaceutical Journal*, 47–48.

BURR, S. (1992). *Pediatric Nursing in the United Kingdom*, 7: 299–302.

BYRT, S. (1992). Personal communication from the Research Assistant, University of Wales at Lampeter, and Secretary, Dyffed Local Pharmaceutical Committee, University of Wales at Lampeter.

Caring for People: Community Care in the Next Decade and Beyond [Cmnd. 849] (1989). London: Her Majesty's Stationery Office.

CONNAH, B., and S. LANCASTER (eds.) (1989). *NHS Handbook, The National Association of Health Authorities*, 4th ed. London: MacMillan.

DEPARTMENT OF HEALTH AND SOCIAL SECURITY (1972). *Report of the Committee on Nursing* (Briggs Report) [Cmnd. 5115]. London: Her Majesty's Stationery Office.

DEPARTMENT OF HEALTH AND SOCIAL SECURITY (1978). *A Happier Old Age*. London: Her Majesty's Stationery Office.

DEPARTMENT OF HEALTH AND SOCIAL SECURITY (1980). *Hospital Services: The Future Pattern of Hospital Provision in England*. London: Her Majesty's Stationery Office..

DEPARTMENT OF HEALTH AND SOCIAL SECURITY (1981). *Care in Action—A Handbook of Policies and Priorities for the Health and Personal Social Services in England*. London: Her Majesty's Stationery Office.

DEPARTMENT OF HEALTH (1989). *Working for Patients* [Cmnd. 555]. London: Her Majesty's Stationery Office.

DEPARTMENT OF HEALTH (1991). *The Health of the Nation* [Cmnd. 1523]. London: Her Majesty's Stationery Office.

FUNK & WAGNALL'S CORPORATION (1994). *Great Britain, in Microsoft Encarta*™. Bellevue, Wash.: Microsoft Corporation.

GILBY, J. (1991). The Changing NHS—Purchaser and Provider, *Pharmaceutical Journal*, 76–77.

GILLIE, A. (1963). *The Field Work of the Family Doctor*. London: Her Majesty's Stationery Office.

GILMORE, J. I. (1992). Personal communication from the General Manager, Lincolnshire FHSA, Lincoln, Lincolnshire (Lincs).

GRIFFITHS, R. (1983). *The NHS Management Inquiry Report*. London: Her Majesty's Stationery Office.

GRUMBACH, K., and J. FRY (1993). Managing Primary Care in the United States and the United Kingdom, *New England Journal of Medicine*, 328: 940–945.

HAM, C. (1993). The Latest Reorganization of the NHS, *British Medical Journal*, 307: 1089–1090.

HAM, C. (1994). *Management and Competition in the New NHS*. Oxford: Radcliffe Medical Press.

HARRISON, A., and S. BRUSCINI (eds.) (1994). Main Events, Health Care UK 1993/1994, in *King's Trust Fund*. Bristol: J. W. Arrowsmith Limited.

LEVITT, R., and A. WALL (1992). *The Reorganized National Health Service*, 4th ed. London: Chapman and Hall.

MCCARTHY M., and S. REES (1992). *Health Systems and Public Health Medicine in the European Community*. London: Royal College of Physicians of London.

MACDONALD, N. (1993). In D. Doyle, G. Hanks, and N. MacDonald (eds.), *Oxford Textbook of Palliative Care*. Oxford: Oxford University Press, pp. 11–17.

MEMMOTT, M. (1995). Redefining the Wealth of Nations, *USA Today*, September 18, p. 4B.

MILLER, G,. and H. BRITT (1993). Data Collection and Changing Health Care Systems: I. United Kingdom, *Medical Journal of Australia*, 159: 471–476.

MURPHY, E. (1993). Services for Elderly People, Health Care UK 1992/1993, in *King's Trust Fund*. Glasgow: Bell & Bain Limited.

NAIR, C., and R. KARIM (1993). An Overview of Health Care Systems: Canada and Selected OECD Countries, *Health Reports*, 5: 259–279.

NATIONAL HEALTH SERVICE, ENGLAND AND WALES (1991). *The National Health Service Fund-Holding Practices, General Regulations*, Publication No. 582. London: NHS, pp. 1–13.

NUTBEAM, D., P. FARLEY, and C. SMITH (1990). England and Wales: Perspectives in School Health, *Journal of School Health*, 60: 318–323.

OFFICE OF HEALTH ECONOMICS (1989). *Compendium of Health Statistics*, 7th ed. London: OHE.

ORGANIZATION FOR ECONOMIC COOPERATION AND DEVELOPMENT (1994). *The Reform of Health Care Systems: A Review of Seventeen OECD Countries*. Paris: OECD.

SCHNEIDER, M., R. K. H. DENNERLEIN, and A. KOSE, et al. (1992). *Health Care in EC Member States*. Amsterdam: Elsevier.

SONJSEN, P., A. HARRIS, and B. JARMAN (1993). Perceived Strategic and Practical Problems in the Use of Information Technology for Quality Improvement in Diabetes in the United Kingdom, *Diabetes Metabology*, 19: 80–88.

STOCKING, B. (1993). Implementing the Findings of Effective Care in Pregnancy and Childbirth in the United Kingdom, *Milbank Quarterly*, 71: 497–521.

TROBRANSKI, P. H. (1994). Nurse Practitioner: Redefining the Role of the Community Nurse, *Journal of Advanced Nursing*, 19: 134–139.

WORLD BANK (1993). *World Development Report, 1993: Investing in Health*. New York: Oxford University Press, p. 145.

11

THE CZECH REPUBLIC

A New Mixture
of Public and Private Services

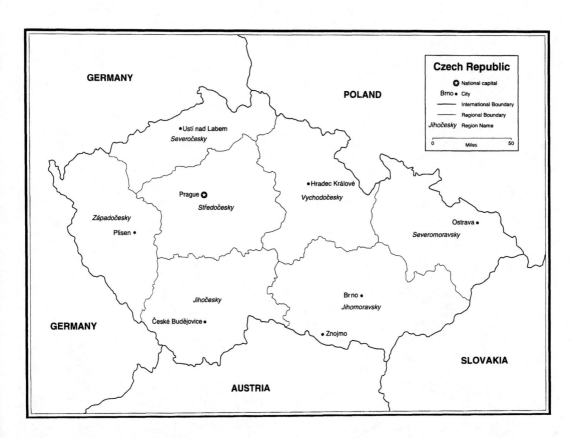

The Czech Republic has been in a state of very rapid and dramatic transition since the "velvet revolution" of 1989 shifted the country from communism to democracy. The more recent separation from Slovakia in 1993 has also resulted in substantial adjustments. Until the change to democracy, health care had been centrally managed and entirely controlled by the government. Patients had little choice of physicians or hospitals. Budgets were developed by government bureaucrats, with little relevance to the realities at the community and consumer levels. Health services were generally underfunded, averaging only approximately $127 per capita (Massaro et al., 1994: 1870).

An aggressive effort has now been implemented to decentralize the government role in health care, while encouraging free-market reform and competition. A compulsory employment-based health insurance program was initiated in 1992. A fee-for-service payment system was initiated and salaries for poorly paid health professionals were increased. As a consequence, health care spending rose by 50 percent in 2 years. Expenditures are currently approaching the average proportion of GDP allocated to health care in Western European countries (Massaro et al., 1994: 1870). Features of the new system are summarized in Table 11-1.

DEMOGRAPHIC CHARACTERISTICS

The Czech Republic had a population of 10,500,000 in 1993. The land mass after the separation from Slovakia is about the size of the U.S. state of South Carolina. Per capita income was about $2,730 in 1994 and the Gross Domestic Product was roughly $75 billion (USA Today, 1994: 4B; *Europa World Yearbook*, 1995: 65).

Life expectancy of males at birth in 1993 was 69.3 years, whereas females could expect to live 76.9 years. Infant mortality was 9.9 per 1,000 live births in 1993. Overall health status, life

---

This chapter was co-authored by William R. Lassey, Marie L. Lassey, Vaclav Benes, and Vlastik Martinu.

Table 11-1 Features of the Reformed Czech Health Care System

- All workers must participate in one of the employer-financed national insurance plans that are publicly sponsored but operate independently of government.
- The government subsidizes insurance for children, students, mothers on maternal leave, retirees, the unemployed, and individuals in the military services.
- Insured individuals receive a full range of benefits, including transportation and spa treatments, and have largely unrestricted choice of physicians, including specialists.
- Physicians now have a choice of practice mode; many are shifting to private practice, while others continue to work on salaries in public polyclinics and hospitals.
- Co-payments are required for some pharmaceuticals and some dental services. Cosmetic surgery is available only on a private pay fee-for-service basis.
- All permanent residents may participate in the system, regardless of nationality or citizenship, when they are employed by an organization operating in the Czech Republic.
- Increased emphasis has been given to the public health sector as a means of improving environmental conditions, improving health promotion and prevention of disease, and counteracting a decline in life expectancy.

---

expectancy, and infant mortality are improving rapidly but were well behind Western industrialized countries when the transition to democracy began (Ministry of Health, 1991a: 3; Albert, Bennett, and Bojar, 1992: 2462; Ciharova, 1995).

Health conditions improved gradually after the communist takeover in 1945 until 1960. At that point Czechoslovakia was tenth in longevity among the twenty-seven European countries, was thirteenth in the world, and was among the leaders in indices of overall health status. A dramatic reversal began in the 1960s. By 1970, the country had dropped to twenty-second, and in 1980 was in the twenty-seventh or last place in Europe and forty-first in the world. This trend continued to 1990. The state of public health was clearly on a downward spiral in the last years of the communist regime. The life expectancy had decreased considerably for men, whereas morbidity and disability increased nationwide (Ministry of Health, 1990: 3).

The two major causes of mortality are diseases of the circulatory system (55 percent) and cancer (21 percent), similar to Western European counties. Death rates from injuries, hypertension, and cerebrovascular diseases for men are higher than elsewhere in Europe. The high death rates for men were attributable at least in part to hazardous work in badly polluted environments, poor diet, alcoholism, and stress (Albert et al., 1992: 2461).

At least 57 percent of the population lived in hazardous environmental conditions in 1991, according to a Ministry of Health estimate. Nutritional characteristics were also unhealthy for many people, with fat consumption at least one-third higher than recommended by dietitians. Nearly half of the men and two-thirds of women were judged to be overweight. Alcohol and cigarette use was very high. Mortality from cardiovascular disease increased by 80 percent between 1950 and 1988 according to recently published statistics. Inadequacies of the health care system were thus only a small part of the problem (Bojan, Hajdu, and Belicza, 1991: 191; Ministry of Health, 1991b: 10).

The rate of abortion is about four times the average for Western Europe. Nearly 50 percent of all pregnancies were terminated in 1990; 90 percent of these were induced. In 1988, the rate of abortion was 94 per 100 live births; this had fallen to 69.2 by 1993. The use of contraceptives was relatively low—only 20 percent of women in childbearing ages in 1988, but up to 22.8 percent by 1993. Family planning and educational services to alter this trend have not been widely practiced, although gynecologists strongly support contraception as an alternative to abortion (Ministry of Health, 1991b: 27; Albert et al., 1992: 2461; Visser et al., 1993: 351; Ciharova, 1995).

Although depression, abuse of alcohol, and drug use were common under the previous communist government, little provision was made for treatment because of social prejudice and taboos. Consequently, the problems were not resolved. This has now changed dramatically (Ministry of Health, 1991b: 38).

Programs to prevent infectious disease are generally similar to Western European countries and are one of the bright spots in the health data. The regional "hygiene stations" were quite successful in implementing vaccination programs for childhood infectious diseases, achieving one of the highest coverage rates in the world. AIDS has been slow to spread. An increased risk is expected, however, as more interaction with other countries occurs (Ministry of Health, 1991b: 33).

HISTORICAL PERSPECTIVE

The Czech Republic was prepared for modernization in 1989 after a long history of industrial and cultural development prior to 1945. Education has been emphasized throughout, providing a large pool of well-educated professionals and a generally literate population (Roemer, 1991: 261).

Until 1989, the health care system was modeled after the Soviet design. The communist governments imposed a system that had evolved in other communist countries since the 1917 revolution in Russia. The Ministry of Health created and managed a centralized system of polyclinics and hospitals. Planning and budgets were the responsibility of civil servants acceptable to the communist government, with little attention to actual needs or costs at the local level. Health professionals were poorly paid, and few incentives existed for high-quality work. Patients were in large part assigned to primary care physicians. Referrals to specialists were controlled by the primary physician. Membership in the communist party was required for advanced specialist training and scientific degrees. Party membership often meant that incompetent physicians received privileges, whereas well-trained noncommunist physicians were not allowed in leadership positions because they refused to participate in party activities (Platinova, 1992; Subert and Martinu, 1992; Benes, 1995).

Physicians numbers were allowed to increase significantly after 1970, leading to an estimated oversupply of 6,000 to 8,000 specialists. In 1989, there were only 10,507 primary care practitioners (5,300 general practitioners, 3,500 pediatricians, 1,200 gynecologists), and 46,435 specialists. Approximately 55 percent were women. The average income was $191 per month for physicians and $102 for nurses (Albert et al., 1992: 2462; Benes, 1995).

Private sector physician practice was not legal but persisted nonetheless, largely with unregulated gratuities as payment. Patients offered these "under-the-table" payments in hopes of securing better care and benefits in the poorly equipped and inefficient health care system. The incomes of some participating physicians were substantially increased. Estimates place the illicit payment at more than $200 million per year, or as much as 25 percent in unrecorded health care costs (Albert et al., 1992: 2462; Benes, 1995; Ciharova, 1995).

When the new democratic government was formed, there was thus great unhappiness with health care. The following specific shortcomings were evident (Ministry of Health, 1990: 4–5; Benes, 1995):

- A rigid and hierarchic system of services
- Focus on treatment instead of prevention
- Lack of modern management techniques
- Little economic incentive for practitioners
- Poor quality control
- Deterioration of equipment and structures
- A surplus of specialists and restricted preparation of GPs
- No patient choice of physician, except among the privileged elite
- Long hospital stays and sometimes an insufficient linkage between ambulatory and hospital care.
- No consumer rights or influence in the system
- Insufficient and distorted information about health services

Reform was a high priority in the new democratic state. A group of specialist physicians and their colleagues formulated a widely circulated document entitled "Draft of the New System of Health Care." It was sup-

ported by 83 percent of health care workers who reviewed the draft and served as the basis for the new approach submitted to the National Council (parliament) in 1991. The changes were approved and implemented beginning in 1992, with the following emphases (Albert et al., 1992: 2461):

- Demonopolization of the health care system by government
- Decentralization of services and control
- Creation of a mixture of public and private financing sources
- Greater freedom of choice for patients
- Increased autonomy for health providers
- Greater emphasis on ambulatory care, prevention, and health promotion

A new insurance system was also initiated in 1992, 1 year before the separation from Slovakia. Several new organizations were created to increase representation of health professionals in formation of health policy. The Medical Chamber (founded in 1991), the Union of Czech Physicians (founded in 1990), and the Trade Union of Health Workers all had a role in redesigning and implementing the new system (Potucek, 1991: 291; Massaro et al., 1994: 1870; Benes, 1995).

Some features of the old system and the new system continued to coexist since the full process of reorganization could not be implemented instantly. The new insurance program led to substantial redistribution of health expenditures. The reallocation of resources has caused major stress for two groups: (1) primary care providers and hospitals with high demand but insufficient growth in resources, and (2) other institutions such as the national research institutes that had been well-supported but had to be cut back because their budgets could not be justified (Massaro et al., 1994: 1872).

CULTURAL FACTORS

The Czech population has a long and rich cultural experience, including a tradition of democracy and free enterprise prior to the communist takeover after World War II. The Czechs have historically viewed themselves as Western European in value orientation and preferences. Given the new freedom, they are returning to the European private enterprise mode as quickly as possible.

However, some of the European traditions have been partially lost. For example, the communist state emphasized an absolute government responsibility in providing for citizens. The tradition of volunteerism was discouraged and self-help groups were essentially prohibited. Since the advent of democracy, advocacy and self-help organizations have begun to emerge once again, but only very slowly. By 1994, about 100 self-help organizations were officially registered with the government. The idea that government should provide everything has been difficult to overcome (Albert et al., 1992: 2465; Ciharova, 1995).

Openness to Western ideas and values has meant a major influx of support and consultation from European and American experts. Resources and technical assistance have been offered and accepted, although sometimes without adequate attention to the indigenous cultural and economic ideology. The free flow of ideas and resources across borders is nonetheless highly valued in the Czech culture (Albert et al., 1992: 2466; Ciharova, 1995).

POLITICAL INFLUENCES

The current democratic structure has evolved rapidly since the 1989 revolution, but not without major turmoil. Differences in ideology and cultural traditions with Slovakia have long been a problem, in substantial part because the Czech Republic was dominant, wealthier, more democratically oriented, and generally much more progressive. Slovakian leaders wanted to be more influential and independent of control by their Czech neighbors (Musil, 1992: 11–13; Ciharova, 1995).

The national health insurance organization and private companies (27 initiated by 1995) are having major influence on health policy and performance as the primary payers of health costs. The Medical Chamber serves as the representative body for physicians and also plays a significant health policy role. As of 1995, the major changes in policy were largely completed, although many details remained to be worked through (Albert et al., 1992: 2465; Benes, 1995).

The central government has now been supplemented by a much stronger system of community and district governments where many of the local decisions are made about health care organization, policy, and services. The Ministry of Health continues to play a major role, but some health care units such as ambulatory care, hospitals, rehabilitation institutes, preventive medicine institutes, pharmaceutical services, and certain technical services are subject to greater local control. There is considerable concern that rural communities may have difficulty competing for resources and services under the new system; nonetheless, financing is equally distributed on a per capita basis and may be sufficient to cover basic costs in rural communities (Potucek, 1991: 292; Ciharova, 1995).

Despite major problems, democratic institutions are firmly in place. The political process is characterized by strong differences of opinion, but is able to reach consensus on priorities. Insufficient resources are available to move as rapidly to redistribute services as both health care professionals and consumers would prefer (Osanec, 1992; Benes, 1995).

SOCIAL ORGANIZATION OF HEALTH CARE

Responsibilities of the Ministry of Health include continued development of national policy, establishing and assuring public health care standards, definitions and distinctions in local and national roles, assuring availability of services, and professional education of providers. Public health services remain primarily a national responsibility, whereas personal health care has been considerably decentralized.

The new policies have led to wholesale personnel changes at all levels of the health care system, with personnel selection transformed from patronage to a merit system. About 80 percent of the top officials in the Ministry of Health have changed, as well as 40 percent of the staff. Approximately 90 percent of hospital administrators have been replaced, as have 60 percent or more of department heads. Efforts to cut costs have meant loss of jobs for many "surplus" personnel. Some medical scientists, scholars, and specialist physicians have chosen to emigrate to other countries where there is a demand for their services and they are able to earn greater income (Albert et al., 1992: 2464).

Public Health

The country had a relatively strong and effective public health system prior to 1945. Under the communist government, the system had become embedded in the political system and suffered from decisions that were not conducive to preventive health activities. Sulfur dioxide levels during temperature inversions in some industrial regions had reached twenty times the level considered harmful, and were often at harmful levels in other parts of the country. Much of the water did not meet safety standards. Incentives for both professional health care workers and citizens to pursue good health practices were particularly lacking (Ministry of Health, 1991b: 14; Benes, 1995).

The health reforms initiated in 1989 and continuing to the present have been systematically directed toward strengthening of a national public health system. The new plan emphasizes increased focus on public health in the training of physicians, establishment of disease registries to track effects of health problems, and reevaluation of environmental health safety standards (Albert et al., 1992: 2465).

Major responsibility is lodged with district Hygiene or Public Health Stations that undertake monitoring of health conditions, inspection of facilities for health hazards, offering of advice for improving conditions, and research on basic health issues. Larger stations have departments for environmental health, occupational health, nutrition and food, child and adolescent health, radiation hazards, epidemiological studies, and microbiological laboratories (Cikrt, Blaha, and Fuchs, 1993: 5–6).

Specific health problems associated with environmental pollution have been identified, including a high incidence of particularly severe respiratory diseases near coal-burning power plants and in heavy industrial areas. Information to fully document the problems has been slow to accumulate, but is now being systematically collected. A new project, "Monitoring of Environmental Pollution and Health Impact," was started in 1992 by the National Institute of Public Health in the Ministry of Health, in collaboration with the Ministries of Agriculture and the Environment. A Toxicological Information System was initiated to systematize and make available international information as well as results from studies within the country. The new Ministry of the Environment is playing a major role in the formulation and implementation of improved environmental policies and programs (Cikrt et al., 1993: 4–5).

Progress has already been clearly demonstrated. Life expectancy has begun to increase. Infant mortality is declining. Many polluting factories have been closed. Stream and water supply conditions are improving. The incentives for health professionals and citizens to practice health promotion and disease prevention have vastly improved.

Physicians

Until 1991, most physicians worked at very low salaries ($130 to $190 per month average) in state-operated polyclinics or hospitals. With the advent of the new national insurance and nonprofit insurance programs, they began a rapid shift to fee-for-service medicine—often paying rent to practice in the same facilities in which they were previously employed on salary. By the end of 1993, 14,000 physicians (one-third of general practitioners) had moved to private practice; only 900 private practices existed prior to 1992. The shift was slower in some specialties than in others. Because private practitioners have the potential to earn double or more income compared to state-salaried physicians, the incentives for changing are considerable. A 1992 survey indicated that 72 percent intended to enter part-time (37 percent) or full-time (35 percent) private practice (Albert et al., 1992: 2464; Massaro et al., 1994: 1873; Ciharova, 1995).

As noted earlier, roughly 55 percent of physicians are women—who serve primarily in primary care roles, often work part-time, and usually earn less than men. Strong pressure to increase parity of female and male physicians has been quite successful. A shortage of primary care practitioners had been somewhat alleviated by 1995, although a surplus of specialists was still evident in some of the larger cities. By 1994, 71 percent of non-government physicians were working in ambulatory care, up from 57 percent in 1992 (Ciharova, 1995).

The substantial oversupply of specialist physicians was a result of more advanced medical school training than population growth could absorb. Academically qualified medical students have not had to pay tuition and no limits were placed on entry. Limitations on medical school enrollments are now government policy (Massaro et al., 1994: 1873; Benes, 1995).

Geriatrics is in the early stages of development as a specialty; consequently, physicians trained in the care of older people are badly needed. An early 1990s effort to retrain specialists to serve in primary care and geriatric settings was generally not successful (Osanec, 1992).

Workers can often receive health care in clinics directly associated with their place of employment. Other workers, children, un-employed adults, and older people are served by general practitioners and pediatricians at clinics in residential communities. In rural communities, general practitioners provide care in community clinics, with about 2,000 clients each. Staffing of the clinics usually includes a GP, a dentist, a pediatrician, and a gynecologist as well as support staff. Private group practices have been encouraged by the Ministry of Health (Osanec, 1992; Benes, 1995).

Physician organization. The Czech Medical Chamber was recreated in 1991 (as noted earlier) after having been abolished by the communist government in the early 1950s. It has responsibility for development of training, licensing, monitoring of physicians, disciplinary actions, accreditation of facilities, creating ethical standards, generally assuring quality of physician care, and negotiations with insurance organizations. Membership is required of all physicians. The Association of General Practitioners was organized in 1991 to work toward increasing the status and quality of ambulatory care. The current emphasis is on creation of "family practice" with broader training for primary care and as gatekeeper to specialized services (U.S. Embassy, 1991: 5; Albert et al., 1992: 2465; Benes, 1995).

Review panels of physicians monitor practice patterns, particularly with respect to insurance billing, treatment protocols, and quality standards. Peer review is difficult, however, because few mechanisms are in place to enforce compliance when deviations from norms are discovered (Massaro et al., 1994: 1872).

Medical education and research. Medical education at the undergraduate level has remained a university responsibility, in contrast to Russia and other former communist countries where the ministries of health have had direct roles. Basic medical education at Charles University (the most prestigious) consists of 6 years of study after high school. Three to five years of preparatory secondary school study precedes entry. Undergraduate curricula includes: 2 years of didactic theory, 1 year of preclinical, 2 years of clinical, and 1 year of internship. The preclinical and clinical years include courses in medical sociology, medical psychology, ethics, and health care organization. Major emphasis, however, is given to the diagnostic/therapeutic procedures and less to prevention, communication, or research training. Successful completion of study leads to the University Medical Degree (MUDr, or Medicinae Universae Doctor, a traditional medieval Latin title) (Zvarova and Vacek, 1989: 246; Roemer, 1991: 262; Benes, 1995).

Undergraduate medical training has been criticized as too theoretical, without sufficient opportunity for contact with patients until the fourth year of study. Students have in the past been channeled toward the hospital specialties, rather than general or family practice. No training was provided in the organization and economics of private practice. This has made development of an effective and efficient primary care system difficult (Benes, 1995).

An additional 3 to 5 years of graduate residency training and successful completion of a specialist examination qualifies graduates for "Level One" certification—which is compulsory for all physicians. "Level Two" requires 3 to 4 years of specialized residency training and successful completion of an examination in the Postgraduate Medical School. Level One physicians are qualified to work in polyclinics, emergency departments in hospitals, general practice, pediatrics, or in hospital support positions. Level Two status is required for broader hospital practice and specialist polyclinic services (Valkova, 1991: 5; Elam and Harvey, 1992: 593; Benes, 1995; Ciharova, 1995).

A new 3.5-year curriculum for general practice has been developed by the Institute for Postgraduate Education in Medicine and Pharmacy. M.D.s with specialist degrees can complete the program in a shorter period. It has been difficult to secure the resources for retraining, even though this has become government policy. The new program emphasizes the following content in addition to basic biomedical education (Vysohlid, 1991: 452; Valkova, 1992):

- Specialized training for primary health care
- Knowledge and skills in humanities and psychosocial disciplines
- Modern management methods
- Appropriate use of information systems
- Use of international medical knowledge and experience

At Charles University special emphasis is also focused on communication with patients to improve diagnosis and treatment. Role playing, case studies, simulation, interview practice, and observation of communication in clinic situations are all used as training tools. This new emphasis is based on the need for effective patient/physician interaction in a health care environment in which patients have the right to choose their physicians. This was not viewed as particularly important in the centralized structure prior to 1989, in which neither patients or physicians had much choice. Those practitioners who are able to effectively relate to their patients are expected to be more successful in the new circumstances (Mares, 1992: 178).

Medical research. Medical research under the previous regime was largely undertaken by employees of the various research institutes, without competition for grants and with little emphasis on quality. The institutes have been largely abolished, and the research fund allocation process converted to a grant system under the general supervision of the Ministry of Health, universities, and the Academy of Sciences. Scientists must now submit research proposals that are reviewed by peers, with grant funds distributed on the basis of greatest scientific value or current priorities, the competence of the scientist, and the potential contribution to health care. The remaining research institutes are in process of reorganization to reflect a more productive approach to medical research (Pfeifer, 1991: 191–192; Benes, 1995).

Nurses

A serious shortage of nurses exists in some health care facilities, especially in the big cities. This is a direct result of low status and pay short-comings. The average monthly income of nurses was about two-thirds that of physicians in 1991, or $102 per month. Many nurses migrate across national borders to Austria and Germany, where they can earn up to ten times more income (Heginbotham and Maxwell, 1991: 39; Subert and Martinu, 1992).

A new Czech Nursing Association was organized in 1991 to promote professionalism and training, including exchanges with other countries. Under the new health care law, private nurses are allowed to provide independent home care and preventive care services. Community nursing is to receive emphasis, with greater attention to home care (Albert et al., 1992: 2464; Blazkova and Mullerova, 1992: 45; Benes, 1995).

Nursing education.   Prior to 1989, nursing education was a direct responsibility of the Ministry of Health. However, the training of nurses is now in the process of change (since 1992). The new requirement will mean aspiring nurses must complete secondary school before applying for university nurses training. A new college of nursing has been created at Charles University. The new curriculum includes undergraduate and postgraduate education in specialized fields. A substantial effort is thus underway to improve the competence and independence of nurses (Roemer, 1991: 262; Blazkova and Mullerova, 1992: 45; Benes, 1995).

Pharmacists and Pharmaceuticals

The initial insurance reform in 1992 allowed all pharmaceutical costs to be covered. However, drugs were consuming 25 percent of the health care budget. Several changes were therefore made. Drugs were divided into four classes: basic, necessary, supportive and avoidable. Those approved as basic and generic prescription drugs continue to be fully covered, but co-payments were introduced to control costs for supportive drugs. Other drugs deemed avoidable or not medically necessary require full out-of-pocket payment (Massaro et al., 1994: 1870; Benes, 1995).

Hospitals

Nearly all hospitals remain in state ownership. They are usually directly associated with an adjacent specialty polyclinic and contain the available advanced technology that is used by polyclinic physicians. Because of resource shortages, a high proportion of hospitals are in very poor physicial condition. Nonetheless, their services are in great demand. Utilization has increased considerably since 1992, with accompanying increases in costs (Massaro et al., 1994: 1874).

The case study on page 249 illustrates characteristics of a polyclinic and two hospitals in one medium-sized community.

Emergency Medical Services

Emergency services are reasonably well-developed. A system of ambulances, emergency clinics, and hospital departments throughout the country provide rapid response. A three-digit emergency telephone number can be used to seek assistance or secure dispatch of ambulance service. Ambulances are usually well-equipped and staffed by physicians (usually specialist anesthesiologists), sometimes nurses, and trained drivers with at least 100 hours of training in first aid and resuscitation. They are usually stationed at hospitals. First aid cars are operated by trained drivers and staffed by general practitioners, internists, and/or pediatricians. The cars are available in urban locations and serve patients at home in nonemergency situations (Elam and Harvey, 1992: 593).

A Case in Point: The Znojmo Hospitals and Clinics

The town of Znojmo is located in the southern region, near the border with Austria. It serves as the primary medical center for a sizable rural region. The one hospital and polyclinic are adjacent and a second hospital is located nearby; both hospitals and the polyclinic were under the direction of a prominent physician (Dr. P. Subert in 1992, who also had responsibility for twelve smaller clinics in the region). Both the hospital and clinic are relatively new, with modern construction and strong evidence of a dedicated and competent staff. About half of the staff physicians are female. All nurses are female, and are in short supply—because they can cross the border into Austria and earn much higher salaries. About forty nurses had left Znojmo for Austria during 1991–1992.

The central hospital has relatively modern and high-technology equipment such as a CT scanner and dialysis units. It provides services to the less modern smaller clinics and the other hospital, which do not have adequate resources for purchase of the latest equipment. Patients who need radiology, kidney dialysis, specialized laboratory work, or other high-technology diagnosis or treatment must secure those services at the central hospital.

Dr. Subert emphasized that the reformed system is separating social care from medical care, which means that health insurance is for medical purposes and hospitalization is for serious illness rather than for social needs such as long-term care. Under the former system, these two kinds of care were often mixed, making it difficult to separate the costs of each. Physicians and nurses want to concentrate their specialized training on the medical needs of patients. This has been difficult because there are not enough nonhospital nursing care beds available for the elderly who could function adequately with less specialized care (Ciharova, 1995).

Physicians in the hospital and clinic earned about $130 per month in 1992, and nurses earned about $65. All physicians were paid the same, regardless of competence or specialty training level. This was a major disincentive for the more competent and dedicated physicians who were more productive. The reformed health care system is supposed to change this by rewarding productivity through fee-for-service payment and patient choice of physician.

Znojmo is also the location of an ECO-LAB, a scientific private laboratory that does environmental measurement and monitoring, including the measurement and evaluation of important hygienic parameters of food (directed in 1992 by Dr. Vlastimil Martinu, a chemist). The focus is on improving environmental health in the region, in cooperation with the state authorities. Relatively little emphasis was given to this work prior to 1989. Staff members are anxious to receive further training based on scientific knowledge, standards, and experience in Western European and North American countries (Martinu, 1995).

The Znojmo region has relatively good environmental conditions, including clean lakes and streams. Few environmentally damaging industries are located here. This contrasts with the northern part of the country and other regions where the environment is seriously polluted. Much greater emphasis will be given to public and environmental health in the future.

Source: This case summary is based on direct observations and interviews by the senior authors in 1992, with later updates by Dr. Martinu.

Medical helicopters are also available at selected airports adjacent to major hospitals. They are staffed by a physician and a paramedic as well as a pilot and are designed to respond to calls from auto or other accidents in rural and remote areas. Few hospitals have helipads, but other locations for landing have been identified, such as nearby rooftops. Air transport is considerably more developed here than in other Central or Eastern European countries (Mika et al., 1990: 22–23).

Information Systems and Technology

The new general insurance system has developed an information system designed to provide a standardized claims reporting process throughout the country. The goal is to improve accuracy and timeliness of claims processing and management information components of health care (Massaro et al., 1994: 1872).

Health Care Administration

Professional health care administration has been slow to develop, largely because the communist system depended on non-professional communist bureaucrats to run things, with accompanying alienation, cynicism, and pessimism. Strengthening of management skills with assistance from other advanced nations has been among the highest priorities in the reformed health care system. The shortages of entrepreneurial and organizational skills are major barriers to successful privatization of health services (Heginbotham and Maxwell, 1991: 40).

Long-Term Care and Special Programs for the Elderly

Specialized care for the disabled and elderly is not well-developed. Homes for the elderly have in the past been generally underfunded and inadequately maintained. Improvement in long-term care is therefore another major goal of the reformed system (Osanec, 1992).

Departments of geriatric medicine are evolving in the medical schools, but the specialty is not a preferred choice for most physicians. Those physicians who do wish to specialize can secure financial support from the Ministry of Health for training in gerontology through Western institutions. The International Congress of Gerontology met in Budapest in 1993 and included representatives from the Czech Republic (Suri, 1991: 127; Ciharova, 1995).

Social services for the elderly are also poorly developed. Pensions are very low, and public programs are limited. The family retains primary responsibility for support of elderly members.

Mental Health Care

Mental health care has been heavily based on the biological model with relatively little emphasis on clinical practice. Psychiatrists were steeped in biology but had relatively little training in psychology until recently. Patients enter the mental health care system through local polyclinics where they are seen by a general practitioner who refers them to a psychiatrist if the initial diagnosis suggests serious problems. Some clinics also employ psychologists, but there has been little teamwork between psychologists and psychiatrists. Patients with serious problems are admitted to a psychiatric hospital, also with a biological emphasis and little psychotherapy (Peck and Kerr, 1990: 1774).

Psychiatrists are active in the effort to reform both mental health care and general medical care. They secretly practiced psychotherapy, established private day hospitals, and taught psychoanalysis to mental health workers "underground" under the communist regime. Mental health care is now in the process of modernization and is taking advantage of the knowledge and experience of Western methods in the treatment of mentally ill patients (Peck and Kerr, 1990: 1775; Trevelyan, 1990: 18).

Laboratory Services

Private laboratories have been established in some areas of the country to provide diagnostic testing for hospitals and physicians. For example, in the southern region, well-equipped facilities serve fifty physicians in Znojmo and thirty-five in Trebic with clinical biochemistry and hematological services. The laboratories are reimbursed by the health insurance companies (Martinu, 1995).

ECONOMIC CHARACTERISTICS AND ISSUES

The cost of health care rose from 5.3 percent of GDP in 1991 to 7.3 percent in 1993, and was 6.7 percent in 1994. The increased costs were largely to finance the new insurance program. Capital expenditures have actually decreased, however, because the needed facilities were largely in place albeit of modest quality. Shortages of medical technology in some hospitals continue to impair the potential for high-quality health care. Because of the high cost of drugs, as well as high usage rates, pharmaceuticals represented 25 percent of the health care bill in 1992 and were subjected to strict controls. As of 1994, the only out-of-pocket costs to consumers for health care were for selected prescription drugs, specialized dental care, and cosmetic surgery (Albert et al., 1992: 2462; Massaro et al., 1994: 1871; Ciharova, 1995).

Financing

The government created the General Health Insurance Company in 1992 as a publicly sponsored but nongovernmental company. By 1995, it was the primary insurance program for 73 percent of the population. The balance of the population is covered by twenty-seven insurance companies that function somewhat like German sickness funds. Additional companies are being created.

Each is approved by the government to cover special populations, such as government employees (police, army, teachers, and so on), miners, bank employees, and certain large private businesses that prefer to self-insure (Ciharova, 1995).

Individuals who work in one of the employment fields covered by sickness funds also have the option to join the General Health Insurance Company. Employee premiums are the same, but supplemental benefits may be better in the sickness funds. A limited private insurance market also operates, to cover dental care, cosmetic surgery, and certain other amenities (Massaro et al., 1994: 1871).

Premiums for health insurance equal 13.5 percent of salary, with 9 percent paid by the employer and 4.5 percent paid by the employee. Employee payments are capped at nine times the national average salary. Self-employed individuals and other persons not employed by an organization must pay their own premiums. The basis for payment by self-employed individuals is 35 percent of income rather than 100 percent, to encourage business initiative. Costs for the elderly, the military, all children, and other dependent individuals are paid through the insurance system, financed with direct contributions from the national treasury to the general insurance fund. Government contributions are about 34 percent of costs, and employer/employee premiums are 60 percent. Direct out-of-pocket payments of 6 percent make up the balance (Massaro et al., 1994: 1870).

The per person government payment for dependent individuals is not as high as the cost to employers and employees. Workers and employers subsidize those who are dependent or in the military. Health insurance premiums paid to any of the insurance plans are tax-deductible (Massaro et al., 1994: 1871).

The goal of the new financing system is to use market competition as the primary means to increase productivity, discourage waste, and increase quality. Financial incentives are to be used as the basis for attracting professionals to areas in need of additional service. Payment will follow the patient to the provider who offers the highest patient satisfaction, rather than via the former model in which the consumer was forced to use services regardless of their quality.

Physician payment. Physicians who have opted for private practice are reimbursed on a fee-for-service basis from the insurance programs. Payment is based on a list developed by the Ministry of Health of more than 4,000 reimbursable services. Each service has a "point value," based in part on the level of specialization and the material and supply costs required for various procedures (Massaro et al., 1994: 1871).

The point system is uniform throughout the country and is monitored for accuracy and controlled by the Ministry of Finance. The Schedule of Procedures catalogs, published by the Ministry of Health, identifies the points for each of the reimbursable procedures or services—using a "relative-value scale." An average service and procedure workload was calculated for each medical specialty. The point value varies somewhat, depending on the insuring unit. The general insurance points are valued somewhat lower than in the more generous sickness funds. Providers are better paid by these generous funds. The relative-value scale and point system are in constant process of reevaluation and adjustment based on claims data and other ongoing studies (Massaro et al., 1994: 1872).

Payments for hospitals. Hospital reimbursement is based on a per diem rate, calculated in points per day. Points are also calculated for any hospital services provided. Capital spending for building construction, equipment, technology, and other infrastructure is provided by municipalities and other local sources, with modest supplemental support from the government—particularly for university medical centers. Hospital reimbursements from the insurance systems include a depreciation allowance that pro-

vides part of the capital resources needed. As of 1994, there was no national effort to plan for, and coordinate, capital facilities. This is left to local authorities (Massaro et al., 1994: 1871).

PROBLEMS AND REFORMS

The new health insurance system provides the potential for incentives to improve service by providers on the one hand and greater utilization by consumers on the other. The response has been positive on both fronts, with the consequence that costs are rising more quickly than insurance revenues. The payroll tax, which provides the bulk of resources, is already about as high as politically feasible. As a result, some form of rationing may be necessary to keep costs within bounds (Massaro et al., 1994: 1873).

Increasing Costs

Limitations on costs through a capitated or prospective fee system are under consideration. Unrestricted fee-based payment is likely to cause expenditure increases at a greater rate than can be readily financed. Although private practice is clearly viewed as advantageous by both consumers and many providers, the first evaluations of relative costs indicate that private practitioners collect about 10 percent more from insurance funds than salaried practitioners in the remaining state-operated polyclinics. Private practitioners saw patients more often (ten times per year) than polyclinic physicians (six times per year) during the first year of operation (Massaro et al., 1994: 1873).

The fee-for-service payment systems with no required gate keeping by general practitioners has been identified as one basis for the higher than expected costs. Patients can go directly to specialists, and may receive unnecessary and overly expensive treatment. A shift to a partially capitated system may help resolve this problem (Benes, 1995).

Financial Stress of Providers

The financial situation of many health care institutions was precarious in 1995. Some firms are unable to pay for health insurance of employees because of severe financial problems. This means the insurance companies do not receive the needed premiums. Actual health care costs, especially for hospitals, were underestimated when the insurance program was planned. Some primary care physicians have been guilty of filing false claims to increase their income (Ciharova, 1995; Martinu, 1995).

Shortages of funds have made renovation, maintenance, and investment in facilities very difficult. The condition of many structures is substandard by any measure. Acquisition of new technology and quality equipment was postponed until other basic changes were achieved in many facilities throughout the country. The situation seems to be improving steadily and was much more optimistic in 1995 than in 1992 (Albert et al., 1992: 2466; Ciharova, 1995).

Health Promotion

The high incidence of cancer, heart disease, and obesity has caused health professionals and public authorities to begin a major emphasis on improved nutrition. The Central European Center for Health and Environment (based in Berlin) initiated a program to increase consumption of vegetables and fruits, while deemphasizing meat and dairy products. Schools have begun major educational programs on diet and health. The government stopped subsidizing such products in 1991, helping the mortality rate from heart disease to decline by 13 percent for men and 9 percent for women by 1995 (Kucera et al., 1993; Elliott, 1995: 42).

Environmental Preservation

Environmental pollution has been a major problem as is the case in other Central and East European countries. This has led to a relatively high incidence of cancer and cardiovascular disease and the shorter life spans noted earlier. Although the new government is committed to improving the situation, and has made substantial progress, many jobs are dependent on the polluting industries. Time and resources are required to make the necessary changes to cleaner forms of production (Dickman, 1990: 91).

SUMMARY AND CONCLUSIONS

Health conditions in the country were in a seriously declining state when the new democratic government assumed control in 1989. The previous communist government had emphasized industrial production ahead of improved conditions for the population, which meant serious pollution and low investments in public health or health care. Health professionals were disillusioned and poorly compensated for their efforts.

Consequently, improvement in the public health and personal health care systems was a high priority. Despite the serious shortage of resources, immediate steps were taken to dismantle the old system and rebuild with concepts borrowed from Western Europe and molded to fit the specific values and priorities of the Czech people.

Public health programs have helped to diminish environmental pollution, provide education to citizens on improved diet and life-styles, and lower the stressful conditions under which workers found themselves. The health care system is going through a process of privatization. A high proportion of physicians have shifted to private practice, although polyclinics and hospitals have remained largely controlled by the government with increased local influence on management and priorities.

The restructured health care system appears to be largely successful, despite the noted problems. Physicians are more highly motivated and are expanding their knowledge and skills through greater use of continuing medical education and international travel. Increased competency and improved performance seem to be an important result, particularly for general practitioners. Doctor–patient relationships appear to be improving.

Environmental health conditions are improving steadily, although major expense is involved in refitting factories and other polluting industries. Measurements of environmental conditions are underway and provide feedback to public officials on serious and unhealthy problems.

The general public appears to be responding positively to the educational efforts of the Ministry of Health and health professionals. There is evidence of healthier life-styles. Smoking, alcohol consumption, and overeating appear to have diminished, and greater interest in improved nutrition and exercise seems evident.

The Ministry of Health in the past was the dominant force in health care, and the source of many of the miscalculations. It has now relinquished much of its authority and has decentralized responsibility. Universities, working health professionals (especially physicians), insurance funds, and local authorities have taken on additional responsibility for designing, planning, and managing the health care system.

Despite the frustrations of health professionals with the slow pace of change, and shortage of resources to move as quickly as preferred, the country is on a much improved track. Progress is clearly being made toward a much higher-quality and more efficient health care system.

REFERENCES

ALBERT, ALEXA, CHARLES BENNETT, and MARTIN BOJAR (1992). Health Care in the Czech Republic, *Journal of the American Medical Association*, 267 (18): 2461–2466.

BENES, VACLAV (1995). Personal communication.

BLAZKOVA, JANA, and NINA MULLEROVA (1992). Come to Czechoslovakia, *Nursing Times*, 88 (22): 45.

BOJAN, FERENC, PIROSKA HAJDU, and EVA BELICZA (1991). Avoidable Mortality. Is It an Indicator of Quality of Medical Care in Eastern European Countries?, *Quality Assurance in Health Care*, 3 (3): 191–203.

CIHAROVA, KATERINA (1995). Personal communication with the Director, International Relations Department, Ministry of Health of the Czech Republic.

CIKRT, M., K. BLAHA, and A. FUCHS (1993). Chemical Risk Assessment and Management in Czech and Slovak Republics, *Central European Journal of Public Health*, 1 (1): 4–6.

DICKMAN, STEVEN (1990). Pollution as Czech Public Enemy Number One, *Nature*, 344 (8): 91.

ELAM, KENNETH, and RICHARD HARVEY (1992). Emergency Medical Systems in Czechoslovakia, *American Journal of Emergency Medicine*, 10 (6): 593–594.

ELLIOTT, DORINDA (1995). The Fat of the Land, *Newsweek*, March 20, p. 42.

Europa World Yearbook 1995 (1995). London: Europa Publications, Ltd., p. 65.

HEGINBOTHAM, CHRISTOPHER, and ROBERT MAXWELL (1991). Managing the Transitions: A Western European View of Health Care Development in Eastern Europe, *European Journal of Public Health*, 1: 36–44.

KUCERA, Z., A. STEFLOVA, J. JANOVSKA, J. LOTULAN, F. OSANEC, M. POTUCEK, Z. STEMBERA, B. TICHACEK, and J. WINTEROVA (1993). *National Project of Health Restoration and Promotion in the Czech Republic*. Prague: Ministry of Health.

MARES, JIRI (1992). *Communication with Patients as a Problem in Undergraduate Medical Education*. Prague: Department of Social Sciences Medical Faculty, Charles University.

MARTINU, VLASTIK (1995). Personal communication.

MASSARO, THOMAS A., JIRI NEMEC, and IVAN KALMAN (1994). Health System Reform in the Czech Republic, *Journal of the American Medical Association*, 271 (23): 1870–1874.

MIKA, LADISLAV, CHRISTIAN BUHLER, FRANK THOMAS, OLGA KRALOVA, RICK FRAZER, and DON STAMPER (1990). The Development of Air Medical Services in Czechoslovakia, *Journal of Air Medical Transport* (July): 22–26.

MINISTRY OF HEALTH (1990). *Reform of Health Care in the Czech Republic*, Version II. Prague: Ministry of Health.

MINISTRY OF HEALTH (1991a). *CSFR Health Statistics Yearbook*. Prague: Institute of Health Information and Statistics.

MINISTRY OF HEALTH (1991b). *National Program of Health Restoration and Promotion (Mid-Term Strategy)*. Prague: Government of the Czech Republic.

MUSIL, JIRI (1992). Czechoslovakia in the Middle of Transition, *Czechoslovak Sociological Review*, 28 (Special Issue): 5–21.

OSANEC, FRANTISEK (1992). Personal communication with the Consultant to Czech Ministry of Health.

PECK, EDWARD, and ALAN KERR (1990). Unpicking the Monolith, *Health Service Journal*, 100 (November 29): 1774–1775.

PFEIFER, I. (1991). Transformation of the Medical Research Organization in the Czech Republic, *Czech Medicine*, 14 (3): 191–192.

PLATINOVA, HELENA (1992). Personal communication, physician, Czech Republic.

POTUCEK, MARTIN (1991). The Health Care Reform in Czechoslovakia after 17 November 1989, *Journal of Public Health Medicine*, 13 (4): 290–294.

ROEMER, MILTON (1991). *Health of Nations: The Countries*, Vol. I. New York: Oxford University Press.

SUBERT, P., and VLASTIMIL MARTINU (1992). Personal communications with the Director of Znojmo Medical Center and the Director of ECOLAB, respectively.

SURI, Y. P. (1991). Czechoslovakia Revisited, *Journal of the Royal College of Physicians of London*, 25 (2): 124–127.

TREVELYAN, J. (1990). Health Czech, *Nursing Times*, 86 (36): 18.

USA TODAY (1994). Czech Leader Sees Higher Unemployment, *USA Today*, November 25, p. 4B.

U.S. EMBASSY (Prague) (1991). *Health Care Delivery and Financing Reforms in the Czech Republic: A Leap into the Unknown*. Prague: U.S. Embassy.

VALKOVA, LIBUSE (1991). Research in General Practice in Czechoslovakia, in *Health Care 2000*. Prague: Ministry of Health, pp. 5–6.

VALKOVA, LIBUSE (1992). Personal communication with the Chair of the Department of General Medicine, Postgraduate Medical and Pharmaceutical Institute.

VISSER, A. P., R. UZEL, E. KETTING, N. BUYNIKS, and B. J. ODDENS (1993). Attitudes of Czech and Slovak Gynecologists Toward Family Planning, *Advances in Contraception*, 9 (4): 351–362.

VYSOHLID, JOSEF (1991). Proposed Changes in Medical Education in Czechoslovakia, *Medical Education*, 25: 452–453.

ZVAROVA, JANA, and ZDENK VACEK (1989). Medical Education System in Czechoslovakia: Achievements and Perspectives of Medical Informatics Education, *Methods of Information in Medicine*, 28 (4): 246–249.

12

HUNGARY

Creating
a Remodeled System

The new democratic government of Hungary is vigorously reintroducing free-market institutions in health care and throughout the economy. The health care system had been centralized and managed by the Ministry of Health, based on the communist model. A new social welfare insurance system and more modern management have been reintroduced. The plan is to deliver health care nearly free of cost at the point of service, but under a competitive market system (Gulacsi, Kovacs, and Janeski, 1994: 551). Unique features of health care in Hungary are summarized in Table 12-1.

The country has already made considerable progress in dealing with the major health issues left over from the earlier period. Infant mortality has declined rapidly, and longevity has begun to increase. The reorganized health care system is raising both quality and access to care (Fodor, 1995).

DEMOGRAPHIC CHARACTERISTICS

Hungary had a population of about 10.5 million people in 1993—a decrease since 1980 because of a declining birthrate and an increasing death rate. Roughly 19 percent of the population lives in Budapest (with 2 million people); another 37 percent reside in other towns and cities; and about 44 percent are rural residents (Forgacs, 1989: 145).

Infant mortality was among the highest in Europe at 12 per 1,000 live births in 1992, but is down substantially from 15.5 in 1989. The infant mortality problem is particularly acute among the mobile gypsy population in rural areas. They tend not to secure regular prenatal or followup medical care, and generally have lower access to health care (Schuler, 1992; Fodor, 1995).

Life expectancy in 1992 was about age 65 for males (down from 66.8 in 1970) and 73.7 for females (up from 72.1 in 1970)—among the lowest in Europe for both males and

This chapter was co-authored by William R. Lassey, Marie L. Lassey, and Miklos Fodor, M.D.

Table 12-1   Features of Hungarian Health Care

- Longevity rates for males have been in a state of decline since the mid-1960s as a result of a high-fat diet, high rate of alcoholism, and environmental contamination, all leading to high rates of circulatory problems, cirrhosis, and cancer.
- An effort during the communist period to recruit medical students primarily from the working classes, to the near exclusion of students from upper classes, contributed to poor training and many unqualified physicians who remain in the system.
- The physician-to-population ratio is among the highest in Europe. Roughly 76 percent of physicians are specialists and in surplus; primary care providers are in short supply in small town and rural locations.
- Physicians in the Ministry of Health have major policy and administrative responsibility. Health care administrators in hospitals and polyclinics are nearly all physicians who have had very little management training.
- Major disparities exist between parts of the country in health outcomes and access to health services. Urban centers such as Budapest have an abundance of physicians with good training. Remote and rural regions have poorer outcomes and fewer health care resources.
- Despite their physical and technological inadequacies, hospitals are heavily used by patients who suffer from many acute and chronic illnesses. Hospitals have higher rates of admission than in most other European countries.
- The new health insurance and management system attempts to create incentives and structures to correct the major inadequacies inherited from the communists.

Sources: Based on Forgacs, 1989: 147; Wnuk-Lipinski and Illsley, 1990: 882; Raffel and Raffel, 1992: 274; Gulacsi et al., 1994: 554.

females. The mortality rate increased significantly between 1965 and 1990, particularly for males and especially among manual and agricultural workers. More than 40 percent of the population was overweight in 1989, and more than 10 percent under age 40 have hypertension. Major causes of death are heart diseases (74 per 10,000) and cancer (31 per 10,000). The country had the highest rates of cancer and cardiovascular disease in Europe in 1989. Hungary also has the highest incidence of suicide in the world, and cirrhosis of the liver is widely prevalent—reflecting high rates of depression and alcoholism

(Wnuk-Lipinski and Illsley, 1990: 882; Raffel and Raffel, 1992: 274; Gulacsi et al., 1994: 554).

A clear relationship appears to exist between access to physician services and mortality rates. In Budapest, for example, with 19 percent of the population, 36 percent of physicians, and 30 percent of hospital beds, mortality rates are lowest, whereas in the more remote counties with the fewest medical resources, mortality rates tend to be highest (Wnuk-Lipinski and Illsley, 1990: 885).

HISTORICAL PERSPECTIVE

Hungary has a long history of efforts to modernize health care, possibly beginning with the Pantokrator Monastary hospital in A.D. 1136, founded (the story goes) by a Hungarian princess. Historical records indicate the hospital had five specialized wards, for trauma, eye diseases, gynecology, and two wards for internal medicine. A surgical unit was available. The hospital was heated and had bathing facilities. The primary treatments were physical therapy, bath, and massage, supported by a staff of physicians and nurses. A long-term-care unit was available for invalids and incurable older patients. The hospital also served as a training institute for physicians and nurses, and had a polyclinic to serve outpatients (Jozsa, 1993: 153–155).

Prior to World War II, the health care system was oriented toward the West and was similar to the neighboring countries of Austria and Germany. However, only about 30 percent of the population was covered by health insurance of any kind. Physicians were primarily in private medical practice and were sometimes associated with health insurance companies. Hospitals compared favorably with those in Western Europe. A well-organized health insurance system was formed in the late 1930s, employing trained physicians who served patients in the home. The system was terminated when the com-

munists came to power after World War II (Raffel and Raffel, 1992: 273; Fodor, 1995).

The Communist Era

Major devastation and disruption characterized health care facilities and the medical system after the war. When the country became part of the Soviet sphere of influence, a highly centralized and government-operated health care bureaucracy was created to rebuild the system, employing all physicians and nurses, and operating all hospitals. A Uniform State Health Service Act was approved in 1950 and provided the basis for free and universal health care to all citizens. Industrial and mine workers had priority although the same services were theoretically available to everyone. A network of polyclinics was developed in all areas of the country, but hospital facilities were only modestly enhanced. Private insurance was eliminated (Raffel and Raffel, 1992: 275; Cockerham, 1995: 315).

The Health Act of 1972

The ideology of free health care was reaffirmed in the Health Act of 1972, which emphasized universal accessibility, equal treatment of everyone, and a priority for preventive and rehabilitative services. District general practice physicians, pediatricians, occupational health physicians, and nurses in various industrial settings were supposed to provide comprehensive care to workers and families. A school health service composed of one doctor and nurse for each 2,000 to 3,000 children was available to provide preventive services and screenings in all schools (Forgacs, 1989: 149).

Large polyclinics and hospitals in towns and cities provided specialist and acute care to populations of about 110,000 people each. Tertiary care was provided in large county hospitals, using more advanced equipment and services than smaller hospitals. National health "Institutes" of several kinds provided tertiary care at the most advanced level. They also conducted research, provided special services, and were the oversight units for national health care (Forgacs, 1989: 149).

Resources tended to flow most abundantly to the institutes and other specialized health care, and primary care was short-changed. A 1986 study sponsored by the Center for Regional Studies, Hungarian Academy of Sciences, indicated major disparity between regions of the country. This discrepancy had actually widened between 1960 and 1982 (Roemer, 1991: 261).

The stated intentions of the 1972 Act were not generally fulfilled. Individuals with special status and greater resources continued to have priority; the rigidity of the system and very limited resources restricted improvement in facilities—and severely limited quality of care. There was clearly inequitable access to medical services. Members of the communist officialdom, however, were provided with reasonably good services, modern equipment, and did not have to wait in line. Waiting time for surgery was sometimes as long as 3 years for procedures such as hip replacement, coronary bypass, or renal transplant. Only one MRI machine and two CT scanners were available in the country. Health care was defined as a "gift" from the state or the employing organization rather than a deserved service (Forgacs, 1989: 146–148; Bogdonoff et al., 1991: 14).

Resource Limitations Under Communism

Shortages of technology and inadequate facilities were a consequence of the modest resources allocated to health care, and the limited perspective of communist government bureaucrats. For a time, access required specific permission from a district physician who had to issue a permit before individuals could seek any form of specialized care. The very modest district health centers were not equipped for X-rays or laboratory tests, which meant that diagnosis for many illnesses only could be completed in specialized facilities. These constraints led larger industries to create independent health care

systems with greater resources and quality of care than was available in the state system (Csazi, 1990: 279).

Another consequence was the development of the system of "tipping" through which physicians and nurses could supplement their very poor incomes with gifts from their clients. This practice was widely regarded as both illegal and unethical, but was justified because it served to supplement the very low salaries. The additional payment was estimated to be 30 percent or more of total physician income. Medical ethics committees appointed by communist governments did little to enforce the law because a high proportion of physicians were involved. The practice allowed individuals with high status or sufficient resources to secure better quality of care and easier access to services, whereas those with marginal status and incomes had to accept limited access and poor-quality care. Good physicians were embarrassed; they would generally have much preferred higher salaries (Adam, 1989: 316; Csazi, 1990: 280; Blasszauer, 1991: 277–278).

Among the nuances of the communist approach was the effort to recruit medical students from the working classes, to the exclusion of those from the upper classes and somewhat regardless of intellectual ability. Sixty percent of the students were from the working classes at one point. This eventually resulted in many ill-prepared physicians. The effort to install an "equality of opportunity principle" led to ineffectiveness at the operational level. In the 1980s, this selection process was changed to a system based on entrance examinations (Csazi, 1990: 279).

The New Democracy After 1989

Plans were immediately prepared to revamp the health care system. A compulsory health insurance system was implemented with financing from payroll deductions. Patients were once again allowed to freely choose a general practitioner who served as gatekeeper for referrals to specialists. However, resource limitations continued to seriously constrain the rapid change preferred by both health professionals and consumers (Cockerham, 1995: 315).

Rural physicians were often overworked, with caseloads sometimes exceeding 2,400 patients. Their facilities had limited equipment and staff were poorly trained and poorly paid (Fodor, 1992a).

CULTURAL FACTORS

Hungary has historically been oriented more toward Western European culture than to the East. Austria and Hungary were very similar because they were once one country and both come from a "Magyar" ethnic background.

The communist period, and the Soviet imposition of economic and political organization, was therefore clearly an interruption of cultural preferences. Many attempts were made during the communist period to restore earlier and preferred forms of organization, often with painful and destructive outcomes for the participants.

Hungarian health professionals now take considerable pride in the health care institutions being created; they are based on the values and preferences of Western civilization.

POLITICAL INFLUENCES

The reorganized democratic political system is a parliamentary democracy with a Council of Ministers having administrative responsibility. The Ministry of Health oversees health planning and management, sets priorities, develops appropriate standards, and generally coordinates health care. The country is subdivided into nineteen counties and the capital district of Budapest. Each county is governed by an elected council. Municipal and village health departments are directly related to county departments, under the supervision of elected

bodies at the local level (Raffel and Raffel, 1992: 274).

A major effort is underway to increase capacity of local jurisdictions to help finance and manage health care facilities. The impersonal bureaucracy at the national level is gradually being replaced by professionals with a more democratic and local orientation. The county health authority is responsible to the executive committee of the county council, with a professional relationship to the Ministry of Health for implementation and maintenance of a national health program.

SOCIAL ORGANIZATION OF HEALTH CARE

Public health remains a national responsibility, with service and research units located throughout the country. Primary health care has been shifted away from central control and is increasingly delegated to municipal and village levels. Hospital support and inpatient care are principally a county responsibility (Raffel and Raffel, 1992: 274).

Public Health

A national organization of public health stations has branches throughout the country with responsibility for preventive services against infectious diseases and unsanitary conditions. Each station is administered by a physician trained in hygiene or public health. Regional units are supervised by a State Sanitary and Epidemiological Inspectorate in the Ministry of Health. The following regional responsibilities have priority (Lassey and Lassey, 1992):

- Inspecting public places such as restaurants, factories, and hospitals
- Public laboratory services
- Monitoring and controlling infectious diseases
- Monitoring workplace health and safety
- Control of environmental hazards

Research, education, and consultation with regional offices are the responsibility of four major national institutes: General Public Health, Labor and Industrial Hygiene, Nutrition and Food, and Radiation Health and Hygiene.

Research conducted by the institutes has demonstrated the link between respiratory problems of children and environmental pollution. Other studies indicate serious toxic problems of high nitrate, arsenic, and low iodine content in the drinking water in many small communities. The U.S. Centers for Disease Control have been working closely with the Institutes to improve capacity for epidemiological and other studies. One goal of the reformed system is to create a closer linkage between public health and the privatized health care system (Rudnai, 1992).

Physicians

Roughly 80 percent of all primary care is provided in polyclinics, industrial clinics, and hospitals. The remaining 20 percent of physicians provide primary care in district clinics. Only 24 percent of physicians were general practitioners in 1990, although that proportion has since been increasing. Forty-five percent of all physicians are women—who are more likely than men to focus on primary care. Railways, the police, and the army have separate facilities and services. The pediatric service for children also has separate service units, polyclinics, rehabilitation centers and hospitals. Prenatal, obstetrical, and postpartum care is provided by obstetricians and maternity nurses as part of the municipal or village health care system (Raffel and Raffel, 1992: 275–277; Gulacsi et al., 1994: 552).

Primary care has been integrated with hospitals since 1976. District physicians are usually part of a county hospital staff and work under the supervision of a regional medical director, even though they may not be located in a hospital or polyclinic. Normal staffing includes at least a general practice physician, a pediatrician, a nurse, an assistant physician, and one or more home health visi-

tors. Children and pregnant women are the primary clients of pediatricians and health visitors who have responsibility to follow the health condition of children until age 14. Health visitors also visit the homes of older individuals (Schuler, 1992).

District hospital staff and physicians are often unhappy with the inadequacies of their facilities, their isolation from professional contact and support, and their relative lack of resources. Although private practice is now encouraged, it is closely regulated by the government and relatively few physicians have had the resources to give up their salaries (Lassey and Lassey, 1992).

The senior authors visited several communities during the summer of 1992, including Eger and Ozd, as described in the case study on page 262.

Medical education and research. Four medical schools have graduated an abundance of physicians and pharmacists. In 1950, there were only 110 physicians per 100,000 population; by 1987, the number had tripled to 320 per 100,000. The emphasis until 1991 was on training of specialists, with relatively little focus on family or general medicine (Roemer, 1991: 260).

Prior to 1989, only one Postgraduate School of Medicine provided advanced training. The curriculum was designed for full-time students as well as a wide range of continuing education courses. The Postgraduate School is staffed in part by specialists from the several national research and training institutes—which provide 80 percent of the courses (Forgacs, 1991: 7–9).

A new postgraduate retraining program was implemented in 1992 to better prepare family physicians, with the intention of lowering the physician/patient ratio for primary care to 1,500:1. The training also prepares tutors and mentors who will then be responsible for supervising the residency training of approximately 250 physicians per year. Sixty residency sites had been implemented by 1995. The European Community has been directly supporting this effort (Fodor, 1995).

A Case in Point: Eger and Ozd in 1992

Eger serves as the regional medical center for a mountainous northern county and had 80,000 people in 1992. The historic old city is located 90 miles east of Budapest and is the center for the nation's wine production, most notably "Bulls Blood." The polyclinic and hospital serve as headquarters for the county medical director. Ozd is a small city in a nearby county and was the location of a massive closed industrial facility that had contributed to a very polluted local environment.

The hospital and clinic facilities in Eger were relatively modern although somewhat rundown. The hospital had a preventive health program, a medical library, and other regional services such as laboratories. Several of the physicians in Eger had just begun a private practice, although the great majority remained on salary in the polyclinic or hospital.

Both Eger and Ozd were experiencing a serious shortage of nurses but had sufficient numbers of physicians in both primary care and in the basic specialties. Many of the other staff were relatively young and only modestly trained. They took great pride in the health education resources available in their education center and library. The expanding emphasis on health promotion and disease prevention was clearly viewed as of great importance.

In addition to medical care, twenty-six dentists work in five clinics located in the city and smaller towns of the county. A dental laboratory provided crown and bridge work, but orthodontic appliances were made in Budapest.

The Ozd clinic and hospital were very old, severely limited in scope, and in a state of serious exterior physical decay. A high proportion of the physicians were foreign medical graduates. Some were in residency training and others were in permanent staff positions. None of the physicians was yet in private practice. All indicated their rate of pay was inadequate ($125 per month).

Physicians did not have private offices, but rather used examining rooms and a central lounge for their work. The per capita payment received for each patient was the same as in Eger, but the number of patients was much smaller—thus limiting revenue for the hospital and clinic. The hospital was spartan, with minimally furnished large wards. However, it appeared to be very clean and relatively well maintained inside, despite the external state of disrepair. Equipment and supplies were very limited.

They were quite dubious about the health care reform process, indicating it would not have a significant effect on their situation for some years into the future—because of the severe shortage of resources. They were also highly concerned about the severe shortage of technology for diagnosis and treatment of patients.

A major retraining program has been initiated to help physicians adapt to the rapidly changing priorities. As noted earlier, many physicians are poorly trained because of inadequate standards during the communist period; they would lose their patients under the new more competitive environment if they did not upgrade their skills and change their attitudes. The European Community has also provided resources for retraining.

Part of the focus is on preparing physicians, pharmacists, and other health professionals to function effectively as health care managers under a private enterprise system (Fodor, 1992b, 1995).

A Health College in the Postgraduate School of Medicine trains allied health professionals, including physiotherapists, dietitians, public health specialists, epidemiologists, nurse administrators, nursing faculty, and ambulance officers. However, health professions schools generally are very short of resources needed for high-quality training and research. They need modern textbooks, scientific journals, and up-to-date diagnostic and treatment equipment. Funds are needed to support scientists and the expenses of medical research. The shortage of resources has caused many scientists to leave the country at least temporarily to find better sources of work and income (Dickman, 1990: 573; Bogdonoff et al., 1991: 16).

Among the major changes is the shift to a competitive grants approach for research funding and away from allocation of funds to prominent researchers without competition. Most research in Hungary has been done in the past by government institutes rather than universities. Universities are shifting more to the Western model, and will produce Ph.D.s with more rigorous scientific training than in the past (Anderson, 1991: 745).

Advanced training of Hungarian faculty in Western countries would help speed the modernization process, and has been a high priority of technical assistance programs to date. Several U.S. medical schools have established formal associations and exchange programs with Hungarian universities. Several U.S. foundations, European organizations, and the World Bank have provided helpful if limited resources (Forgacs, 1989: 154; Bogdonoff et al., 1991: 16).

Nurses

A sufficient number of nurses are trained to provide the needed care, but they have low status compared to physicians, and receive such low pay that many do not remain in the profession. Consequently, there is a severe shortage of nurses for hospitals, long-term-care facilities, and other nursing services. Possibly the highest status role is "home visitor." The visitors have special responsibility, with pediatricians, for looking after the health of prenatal and postnatal mothers, children, and older adults in the community (Blasszauer, 1994: 15).

Nursing administrators in hospitals (referred to as "matrons") have not generally had much power or influence in the health care system. Rather, the matron takes her instructions from physician administrators who make the key decisions. Her primary role is to carry out orders by transmitting instructions to the nursing staff. The matron serves officially as the deputy to the general director or chief physician in a hospital. However, she does not usually serve as a member of the management team (Mucha et al., 1991a: 115–117).

A 1987 survey revealed that other nurses under the matron's direction think of her as their primary leader. She has status and responsibility among support staff, although the importance of the role has not been recognized by physician administrators. New programs have recently been initiated to train nurse administrators in professional management techniques. Nursing leaders have proposed major changes in the health system to give nurses greater status and responsibility (Mucha et al., 1991b: 147–149).

Nursing education. Nursing education is primarily given in health specialty secondary schools and in nursing professional schools. Specialty nursing preparation is offered in thirty-four specialties, including home nursing visitation. Three years of training are required beyond secondary school (Forgacs, 1989: 154; Charles, 1992: 37).

Graduate nurses training is offered through the College of Health Workers in the Postgraduate Medical University in Budapest. The focus is primarily on training nursing administrators, nursing faculty for other schools, and health visitors. Special courses are also available in research methods, psychology, sociology, statistics, management, and health care organization. The Hungarian Nurse Researchers Group is attempting to improve the knowledge and status of nurses through several research projects (Mucha, 1992: 37).

Midlevel Practitioners

Nurse midwives secure their initial training in nursing vocational schools or in professional programs. Prior to 1977, additional training of 3 years was required. Since 1977, this was shortened to 10 months in an effort to rapidly increase the supply of midwives. A recent survey indicated that their primary hospital responsibility is to help prepare for births, assist obstetricians at birth, and followup as immediate caretakers of babies and mothers. They have relative autonomy as compared to midwives in other European countries and have opportunity for independent practice (Charles, 1992: 38; Farrell et al., 1994: 67–72).

Hospitals

The country supported 166 hospitals (including nine long-term-care facilities) in 1990. Their combined capacity is equivalent to one bed for each 104 citizens. The most prestigious are the National Institute hospitals, followed in status by the regional medical schools, with county hospitals next and municipal facilities having lowest status. Eighteen of the major hospitals are operated directly by the Ministry of Health. Another five are a part of university medical schools. National Institute and regional medical school hospitals have access to the best technology and secure the greatest resources. They serve as tertiary care referral centers for municipal and county hospitals. Several are devoted to psychiatric patients, serve as sanitoria for recovering patients, or serve the special needs of mothers and children (Raffel and Raffel, 1992: 278).

County hospitals serve 400,000 to 600,000 people in facilities ranging in size from 1,000 to 2,000 beds. Most medical disciplines are available in these major hospitals or in adjacent polyclinics. However, they have somewhat less advanced technology than would be available in Institute or university hospitals. Municipal hospitals usually have four basic specialties in associated polyclinics: internal medicine, surgery, pediatrics, and gynecology/obstetrics (Forgacs, 1989: 149; Raffel and Raffel, 1992: 278; Gulacsi et al., 1994: 551).

Special pediatric hospitals serve the needs of children with difficult conditions such as cancer or heart disease. For example, the Second Department of Pediatrics, Semmelweis University of Medicine, Budapest, operates a children's hospital that provides a specialty center for children. In 1991, the hospital received 9,000 inpatients and 25,000 outpatients. It is the national center for diagnosis and treatment of malignant diseases and heart diseases in children, but provides a wide variety of other services as well (Bodanszky, 1991: 39–43).

Hospitals tend to be heavily used, with relatively higher rates of admission than the average for Europe. Most were built since 1960, but were often poorly maintained. Introduction of new technology is closely controlled by the Ministry of Health to conserve resources. Six to twenty patients are housed in a ward. Bathroom facilities are often in short supply. As noted earlier, there is a chronic shortage of qualified nurses. Given the relatively small geographic area of Hungary, most citizens are within 25 kilometers of one of these hospitals (Schiff, 1990: 314; Raffel and Raffel, 1992: 278).

Hospital administration. Central control is diminishing. Responsibility for hospital management has been largely transferred to municipal or county governments and federations of local governments. Health boards consisting of local leaders are responsible for governance (Raffel and Raffel, 1992: 286).

Hospital administrators are nearly all physicians, who are also in charge of the polyclinics associated with hospital care. They must operate within a specified budget based on number of beds; increases can be secured only under special circumstances. Vice administrators have responsibility for nursing and financial management (Raffel and Raffel, 1992: 278).

Quality Assurance/Quality Management

Quality assurance programs were first introduced in 1991 and were almost immediately institutionalized in many hospitals throughout the country based on the Quality Standards of the European Community. In 1992, a Department of Quality Assurance was established in the Ministry of Welfare. At about the same time, the Hungarian Society for Quality Assurance in Health Care was established. The Hungarian Institute for Quality Assurance was initiated by the Society in 1993. A National Education Program for quality assurance was created in 1994 for inservice training. Medical schools are adopting the concept as well (Gulacsi et al., 1994: 554).

The quality management approach is being used as a central tool for upgrading administrative, management, and teamwork skills. However, shortage of high-quality information systems limits the potential for gathering the needed information and monitoring results. Nonetheless, considerable progress seems to have been made (Gulacsi et al., 1994: 556).

Emergency Medical Services

Emergency services are provided by the National Ambulance Service from 165 ambulance stations throughout the country. Equipment is available for provision of first aid at the scene of an emergency. District and county hospitals provide trauma treatment in emergency outpatient units (Raffel and Raffel, 1992: 280).

Long-Term Care

Three levels of special care for the elderly are available (Raffel and Raffel, 1992: 282):

1. *Day homes* for those who cannot fully meet their own needs and have little family support. Meals, medical care, social activities, and entertainment are provided. Some payment is required of those with resources.
2. *Home care* is provided by visiting social workers or nurses for individuals who have limited mobility or are confined to bed. Services include personal care, meals, cleaning, medications and other support.
3. *Nursing homes* (also referred to as "social" or "welfare" homes) are supported by municipal

councils with professional supervision from counties. They are not intended to provide skilled nursing or around-the-clock care.

Nursing or social homes evolved from an older system of "poor" houses and carry a stigma associated with poverty. Most residents are permanent and most are males. Many are war veterans, and others are alcoholic, mentally ill, mentally retarded, or otherwise handicapped. Accommodations tend to be minimal, with several people to a room. The locations are generally in older buildings with inadequate restroom or bathing facilities. Few services or activities are available for rehabilitation or entertainment. Most homes suffer from a serious shortage of space and staff. Specialized staffs, such as dietitians to assure a balanced diet or physical therapy to maintain bodily function, are largely unknown (Blasszauer, 1994: 14).

Medications are used heavily, often to sedate patients as a means of keeping them under control. One survey indicated that 37 percent of patients took six or more drugs daily, and 18 percent took seven or more. The rate of suicide among the dependent elderly is among the highest in the world (Blasszauer, 1994: 16).

Families with sufficient resources place dependent older relatives in hospitals or sanatoria, rather than social homes. Even in this situation, however, there is little capacity to treat or rehabilitate patients. Hospital beds are often allocated for social care rather than medical care (Blasszauer, 1994: 15).

Efforts are now underway to improve the situation. Churches and private foundations have become interested in helping and are attempting to increase home care for the elderly. Private social homes are appearing as businesses that provide something closer to a home atmosphere while offering better treatment that includes more physician care. Geriatric health care and rehabilitation as practiced in most industrialized countries are only beginning to emerge (Blasszauer, 1994: 17).

Special Services for the Elderly

Retirement age has been 55 to 60, which means the number of retired people is substantial—estimated at about 2.5 million in 1994, or 22 percent of the population. Emergency income assistance was provided to about one-half million elderly, and about 43,000 received other forms of assistance. Some apartment complexes are designated for retirees (Blasszauer, 1994: 14).

As the free market has been implemented, inflationary costs have increased substantially for rent, transportation, utilities, food, drugs, and other cost-of-living items. Pensions and Social Security payments have not kept pace. Consequently, many older people have become relatively poorer and less able to afford basic necessities. They are even more dependent on social and financial support from relatives or the state than was the case under the communist regime. Many workers hold two or more jobs while they attempt to support a three-generation family (Pflanczer and Bognar, 1989; 546–550; Blasszauer, 1994: 16).

ECONOMIC CHARACTERISTICS AND ISSUES

Hungary persisted in developing a freer and more liberal economic system than most other communist countries. The standard of living was generally higher. However, living standards dropped considerably between 1979 and 1990 although per capita income ($3,330 in 1993) was higher than in any other Central European country. A high proportion of the population (estimated at 70 to 80 percent), including physicians and nurses, were forced to hold two or more jobs to support a family. The associated stress is one of the explanatory factors for the generally poor level of health, high alcoholism, and high mortality rates (Forgacs, 1989: 146; Csaszi, 1990: 282; *Europa World Yearbook*, 1995: 91).

The national GDP was about $20 billion in 1985 and grew only modestly until 1990.

Only about 3.2 percent of GDP was devoted to health care. Expenditures have since increased, estimated at 6.5 percent of GDP in 1991. However, payments to hospitals have actually been reduced. The difficult financial situation makes import of technology very limited because the needed currency has not been available. The low level of resource input makes high-quality health care very difficult even under the reformed and more equitable system (Raffel and Raffel, 1992: 273).

Financing

The Ministry of Health proposes the national health budget to the Parliament. It is then debated and eventually approved at a level acceptable to elected members. Appropriated funds are distributed to the national institutes, counties, and districts. Counties also tax their residents to support health care services and facilities. Patients pay out of pocket for part of spa treatments, long-term care if they have resources, and some medications (Raffel and Raffel, 1992: 280).

The National Health Insurance Fund is intended to be a self-sufficient, semi-independent agency. Its resources come from payroll deductions by employers and employees and from federal tax funds to cover individuals outside the employment system. Affluent individuals and families are free to purchase private health insurance and are not required to subscribe to the national fund (Raffel and Raffel, 1992: 285; Cockerham, 1995: 315).

Payment to Providers

The health insurance fund pays general practitioners on a capitated basis, whereas specialists are paid on a fee-for-service basis. Physicians in the municipally owned facilities are paid salaries; general practitioners are paid through a mixture of sources, including prepayment, fee for service, and insurance cards. Hospitals are paid through a fee schedule based on "diagnostic-related groups" of related illnesses (Cockerham, 1995: 315).

Financial incentives in the form of housing, an automobile, or salary supplement may be offered in locations that have difficulty attracting physicians. Those working at industrial or mining locations were formerly paid somewhat higher annual bonuses than community physicians. They were also provided with extra equipment not available elsewhere. Salary rates for nurses and other health professionals are very modest and vary depending on specialization, location, and longevity (Roemer, 1991: 260; Gulacsi et al., 1994: 552).

SUMMARY AND CONCLUSIONS

When democracy was reinstated, Hungary was enduring the unfortunate situation of declining health status, decreasing life expectancy, relatively high infant mortality, poor public health programs, and a diminishing health care system. The communist government initiated a centralized system after World War II, but it was rendered ineffective by the ineptness of communist bureaucrats and few resources. As a consequence, improvements in health care were among the highest priorities of the new government. The health system is emerging with features much like other countries in Europe.

Physicians are abundant and have greater influence and responsibility for the system at all levels than is the usual case elsewhere. They administer nearly all health activities, in the Ministry of Health and at the local level. However, they are poorly paid by international standards. Nurses and other health professionals have much lower status and are even more poorly compensated.

A national network of public health stations has been strengthened and given a new mandate to improve sanitation, protect the environment from toxins, conduct health promotion and prevention activities, improve workplace conditions, and undertake research

that will help to measure progress. Many of the highly toxic and inefficient industries have been closed.

The shortage of resources has made upgrading physical facilities and technology in hospitals very difficult and slow. Health care facilities are relatively old, with minimal technology. Cleaning and repairs have improved appearances and instilled a greater sense of pride, but health workers remain frustrated by their inability to make greater progress. Efforts to integrate primary and specialty care in polyclinics and hospitals have proceeded, however, with support from the Ministry of Health and the new National Health Insurance Fund. Counties and municipalities have primary responsibility for operating and managing local polyclinics and hospitals. The larger cities generally have much better facilities than are available in rural areas.

Medical education has focused on improving family medicine and primary care, somewhat at the expense of specialty care, which had received the major resources under the previous regime. Efforts are also underway to upgrade nursing education.

The primary problem confronting the health care system is resource constraints. Health care leaders have a clear idea of needed changes and would like to move much more quickly with development than is feasible. Major social-organizational changes have been made and progress is underway to reorient the formerly centralized and rigid system to a more locally based and flexible arrangement.

REFERENCES

ADAM, GYORGY (1989). Gratuity for Doctors and Medical Ethics, *Journal of Medicine and Philosophy*, 14: 315–322.

ANDERSON, CHRISTOPHER (1991). Hungarian Science Faces Sweeping Reforms, *Nature*, 352 (August 29): 745.

BLASSZAUER, BELA (1991). Medical Ethics Committees in Hungary, *HEC Forum*, 3 (5): 277–283.

BLASSZAUER, BELA (1994). Institutional Care of the Elderly, *Hastings Center Report*, 24 (5): 14–17.

BODANSZKY, HEDVIG (1991). Scientific, Teaching and Clinical Activity of the 2nd Department of Pediatrics, *Acta Biomedica de L'Ateneo Parmense*, 62 (1–2): 39–43.

BOGDONOFF, MORTON D., WILLIAM R. GRIFFO, JACK A. DEHOVITZ, HARVEY J. MAKADON, and VICTORIA SHARP (1991). Medical Education and Health Care in Central and Eastern Europe, *The Pharos*, 54 (2): 14–16.

CHARLES, JULIE (1992). Hungary for a Change, *Nursing Times*, February 26 to March 3, pp. 36–38.

COCKERHAM, WILLIAM C. (1995). *Medical Sociology*, 6th ed. Englewood Cliffs, N.J.: Prentice Hall.

CSASZI, LAJOS (1990). Interpreting Inequalities in the Hungarian Health Care System, *Social Science and Medicine*, 31 (3): 275–284.

DICKMAN, STEVE (1990). Luring Back the Exiles, *Nature*, 348 (December 13): 573.

Europa World Yearbook, 1995 (1995). London: Europa Publications, Ltd., 91.

FARRELL, MARIE, GENE HARKLESS, LOUIS H. ORZACK, SUSANNA HOUD, ANN OAKLEY, and CLARA SOVENYI (1994). Hungarian Midwives and Their Practice: A National Survey, *Midwifery*, 10 (2): 67–72.

FODOR, MIKLOS (1992a). Personal interview with the Director, Institute of Family Medicine, Budapest.

FODOR, MIKLOS (1992b). Professional Education Development (informal paper), Budapest.

FODOR, MIKLOS (1995). Personal communication.

FORGACS, IVAN (1989). Hungary, in Richard B. Saltman, *International Handbook of Health Care Systems*. New York: Greenwood Press.

FORGACS, IVAN (1991). Postgraduate and Continuing Education in Hungary, *Cahiers de Sociiologie et Demographia Medicales*, 31 (1): 5–14.

GULACSI, LASZLO, ATTILA KOVACS, and JAMES F. JANESKI (1994). Quality Assurance in Hungarian Hospitals: A New Focus for Management Development, *Journal of Health Administration Education*, 12 (4): 551–558.

JOZSA, L. (1993). Was the "Founder" of the First Modern Hospital in Europe a Hungarian Royal Princess? *Ther. Hungary*, 41 (4): 153–155.

LASSEY, WILLIAM R., and MARIE L. LASSEY (1992). Personal interviews and observations at several regional facilities.

MUCHA, KATALIN (1992). Hungarian Research, *Nursing Times*, 88 (2): 36–37.

MUCHA, KATALIN, B. SCHREINER, J. NYILASI, I. SZAB, and M. SZANT (1991a). The Status of Nursing Administrators in Hungary, *International Nursing Review*, 38 (4): 115–117.

MUCHA, KATALIN, M. FUSTOS, E. HOSCHKE, T. KESZLER, L. KISS, E. REISZ, and I. SZABO (1991b). Developing Nurse Managers in Hungary, *International Nursing Review*, 38 (5): 147–149.

PFLANCZER, STEVEN I., and BELA J. BOGNAR (1989). Care of Elderly People in Hungary, *The Gerontologist*, 29 (4): 546–550.

RAFFEL, NORMA K., and MARSHAL W. RAFFEL (1992). The Health System of Hungary, in Marilyn Rosenthal and Marcel Frenkel (eds.), *Health Care Systems and Their Patients: An International Perspective*, Boulder, Col.: Westview Press, pp. 273–286.

ROEMER, MILTON (1991). *Health of Nations: The Countries*, Vol. I. New York: Oxford University Press.

RUDNAI, PETER (1992). Interview with the Head, Department of Community Hygiene, National Institute of Hygiene, Budapest.

SCHIFF, ARTHUR F. (1990). Medicine in Budapest, *Southern Medical Journal*, 83 (3): 313–314.

SCHULER, DEZSO (1992). Interview with the Director, Department of Pediatrics, Semmelweis University Medical School.

WNUK-LIPINSKI, EDMUND, and RAYMOND ILLSLEY (1990). International Comparative Analysis: Main Findings and Conclusions, *Social Science and Medicine*, 31 (8): 879–889.

13

RUSSIA

Transition to Market and Consumer Orientation

The Russian Federation had a population of 149 million in 1993 and has the largest land area among the group of countries considered here. A country of great contrasts, it is rich in culture and history, with highly developed technology for space travel and military weaponry. However, governmental policies focusing on heavy industry and military production over many years have had a devastating effect on the standard of living for the general population and have resulted in major environmental deterioration in many regions (Gellert, 1992: 1023).

As a nation, Russia is at an economic level somewhere between the so-called underdeveloped or Third World and the developed nations of Europe, North America, and Asia. Housing is modest and social services such as health care are in some respects quite modest. Nearly half the population (71 million people) fall in the lower-income range, with incomes of less than $15 per month (World Bank, 1993: 201).

The revised constitution of the Russian Federation includes a proclamation that all citizens are entitled to free medical care, with the government responsible for organization and financing. Health care has therefore become one of the targets for reform, along with many other dimensions of the new Russian society. One of the primary goals is to increase responsiveness to consumers, while decreasing the dominance of impersonal bureaucratic providers (Gellert, 1992: 1021; Sheiman, 1994: 39).

Until the period of *Perestroika* (the opening of Russian society), relatively little information was available about the health care system. In recent years, it has become clear that major limitations in technology and funding exist, particularly in remote cities and rural areas. Moreover, public health care and primary care deteriorated significantly during the 1980s. Support for preventive services declined, and funds to support ambulatory and hospital care were not sufficient to maintain the quality of services. An unfortunate side effect of the economic changes of the early 1990s was severe shortages of staple goods, such as food, drugs, and medical supplies (Albrecht and Salmon, 1992: 247).

The system remains both unduly rigid and underfinanced, as well as very inefficiently managed. Russia spends a much lower proportion of GDP (estimated to be 3 percent in 1994) on health care than do most Western countries. Some improvement has taken place since the fall of communism, but economic problems and the continued existence of a ponderous bureaucracy have made progress very slow. Fortunately, the situation had begun to improve somewhat more rapidly in 1995 (Gellert, 1992: 1021; Sheiman, 1994: 50; McKeehan, 1995: 174). Special features of the Russian health care system are summarized in Table 13-1.

DEMOGRAPHIC CHARACTERISTICS

Russia achieved major progress in lowering infant mortality and increasing longevity between 1945 and the mid-1960s. The trends then began to reverse. Life expectancy at birth was about 59 years for males in 1995, down from 67 in 1964, 65 in 1987, and 64 in 1990. Female life expectancy was 72 years in 1995, slightly down from 73.9 in 1989. This downward shift is attributed to a variety of factors, including poor diet, environmental pollution, alcoholism, violence, stress, and a relatively high incidence of infectious diseases and accidents. More than 20 percent of all premature deaths were attributed to alcohol in 1980. Cardiovascular disease increased by 50 percent between 1960 and 1980, accounting for 57 percent of all deaths in 1988; cancer caused 18 percent of deaths; and trauma from injuries, accidents, homicide, suicide, and fatal alcohol poisoning contributed 10 percent. The rate of death from infectious and circulatory diseases, injury, and poisoning remains very high by world standards (Cockerham, 1995: 312; McKeehan, 1995: 179).

A high abortion rate contributes to maternal health problems and infant mortality. Women may have three to five abortions during their reproductive years. Infant mortality

Table 13-1   Characteristics of Russian Health Care

- The number of physicians per capita is the largest in the world, at about 350 people per physician. Approximately 77 percent of physicians are women.

- Essentially all administrators of health facilities are also physicians.

- Much of the health care in rural and remote areas is provided by *feldshers*, minimally trained providers who offer very basic services.

- Although hospitals are modest in their capacity to cure ailments, the rate of hospitalization is very high by world standards—in part because private housing is usually inadequate for care of illness.

- House calls are common in larger cities, by ambulatory care physicians or via ambulance services and emergency physicians who handle many nonemergencies.

- Nurses have relatively little patient contact and instead are responsible for the maintenance and cleaning functions usually performed by aides or support staff in other countries.

- Patients are expected to keep their own medical records, including X-rays. They must have these available if needed at ambulatory care visits or in the hospital.

- Physicians are poorly paid and have very limited technology and facilities, except in a few prestigious institutions.

- A chronic shortage of all medical supplies, including equipment and medications, is pervasive. Existing equipment is often inoperable for lack of spare parts.

- A system of more advanced medicine and relatively modern hospitals is available to the domestic and foreign elite; these institutions have priority for equipment and supplies.

Sources: Based on Albrecht and Salmon, 1992: 256; Sheiman, 1994.

has, however, been falling, from 24.7 deaths per 1,000 births in 1970, 27.3 in 1980, and 19.0 in 1993—but remains well above the international average for industrialized countries. Diets for mothers were inadequate, with high content of grains, potatoes, and fat, and a shortage of vegetables, fruits, and animal protein. Undernourished babies are at high risk for pneumonia, which is the basis for approximately half of all infant deaths. Rates of infectious diseases in children were also very high by world standards (Albrecht and Salmon, 1992: 258; Gellert, 1992: 1022; Cockerham, 1995: 313; McKeehan, 1995: 179).

The major urban areas tend to be more highly developed and have better access to health care than rural regions. On the other hand, many urban areas are heavily polluted. Wide differences in health status and quality of health services are evident among the eighty-eight regions of the Federation (Mezentseva and Rimachevskaya, 1992: 134–136).

Four categories of the population are particularly at risk for major health problems (Laumark, 1992: 810; Mezentseva and Rimachevskaya, 1992: 140–141):

1. Retired workers suffer a major loss of income when they stop working. Most of them join the poverty ranks because pensions are so low, often in the range of $3 to $10 per month. Nutrition, housing, and medical care all suffer. Most have some form of chronic disease.

2. Workers employed in industries with high pollution and other harmful working conditions often suffer high rates of cancer, cardiovascular problems, and injuries.

3. The rural and agricultural population are subject to very difficult working and housing conditions, and are exposed to fertilizers, herbicides, and pesticides. Access to public health services is very poor.

4. Children and teenagers are exposed to environmental contaminants, often do not secure adequate nutrition, and do not always secure preventive care. Maternity, pediatric, and obstetrical care, and pediatric hospitals are of poor quality.

AIDS has not become a major problem as yet. About half of the cases are a result of blood transfusions, rather than sexual contact. Efforts are underway to develop prevention programs (Swartzberg and Tichtchenko, 1994: 280).

HISTORICAL PERSPECTIVE

The Pre-*Perestroika* Period: 1912–1980

The first national health insurance act was approved in 1912. However, medical care did not begin to modernize until after the communist revolution of 1917. The Ministry of Health Protection was the responsible national agency and was directed by the Central Committee and Politburo of the Communist Party. All major officials were Party members. The communist ideology was the basis for organization and management of the system. The Union for Medical Workers for Health Planning represented doctors, nurses, and other health workers to the Party and Ministry, but had relatively little influence. They were merely salaried functionaries in the system (Field, 1975: 457; Albrecht and Salmon, 1992: 249; Cockerham, 1995: 286).

Women were the primary entrants into the medical profession from the beginning of the communist system. They comprised 45 percent of the physician population as early as 1928. By 1950, the proportion had reached 77 percent. Women and medicine in the Soviet Union have been compared to similar dominance of women in elementary and secondary education in the United States and other countries. Health care professions were accredited relatively lower prestige than industrial workers. Salaries were kept relatively low (Field, 1975: 462).

Health care personnel were not well trained in preventive and primary care. Facilities were usually of a very poor standard. For example, running water was not available in approximately 24 percent of hospitals and polyclinics, particularly in rural areas. No sewer systems were available in 27 percent of rural hospitals. Twenty-nine percent of all polyclinics and 49 percent of hospitals lacked hot water. Medical equipment was often not usable for lack of spare parts. Pharmaceuticals were not available or in short supply. A system of illegal private fee-for-service "under-the-table" payments evolved as a mechanism to secure services outside the public system. Medical necessities, such as drugs, bandages, sheets, and better food, could be purchased by inpatients through hospital administrators, physicians, nurses, or orderlies (Gellert, 1992: 1022; McKeehan, 1995: 181).

Perestroika: 1985 to the Present

The opening of Russian society under President Gorbachev in 1985 led to a reexamination of health care policy. More than one billion workdays per year (3 percent of the workforce) were lost because of absenteeism attributed to illness. Productivity of health care facilities was generally very low. Health problems were clearly becoming worse and were going untreated. Basic sanitation and hygiene deteriorated. Health care spending did not increase, but the government began to encourage fee-for-service medicine and physician-owned medical practices—with profits to be retained by the providers. This was reversed in 1988 to some degree, and many of the private efforts were curtailed until after reforms were proposed in the Health Insurance Act of 1991 (Davis, 1989: 244; McKeehan, 1995: 185–186).

Russian officials hosted conferences to examine alternative reforms, with experts invited from North America and Europe. The World Bank was invited to make recommendations based on studies by health economists. Russian legislators visited the United States, Japan, and other countries, seeking ideas and examples (McKeehan, 1995: 187).

The health care crisis led to strikes by physicians and other health care workers in 1992, who protested poor working conditions, low wages, scarce supplies, and generally inadequate resources for health care. This set the stage for the reform legislation finally approved in 1993 (McKeehan, 1995: 187).

CULTURAL FACTORS

Russian culture is a subject of great national pride, with widely respected literature, arts, architecture, and other attributes. However, these experiences were accessible only to a very small proportion of the elite population in the major cities. Most people have had relatively little opportunity to participate. The difficult experiences of Russian history have instilled a certain stoicism and an expectation that people will suffer regardless of promises from government (Davis, 1989: 241).

The prevailing value system under communism emulated manual work and denigrated those who did not toil with their hands. Many of these values continue to prevail and are the basis for much lower pay for physicians than for factory workers. Untrained healers are sometimes trusted more than physicians. In rural areas, there is great reluctance to seek help from the health care system until illness has reached an advanced state (Cassileth, Vlassov, and Chapman, 1995: 1570).

Many unhappy experiences have made the Russian people doubt the possibility of significant progress, whether in health care or other parts of the economy. However, the more educated elite seem to be more optimistic at the present. The underground economy (some of it run by criminals) has prospered since communist controls were withdrawn, suggesting the possibility of a transition to greater trust in the potential of free enterprise and progress toward a better life.

POLITICAL INFLUENCES

Political organization for health care management has changed substantially since the breakup of the Soviet Union and the fall of centralized communist control. Much of the basic structure remains, but regions are assuming greater local responsibility. Health departments have a mandate for improving health care in the provinces (*oblasts*). Provinces are divided into districts (*rayons*) averaging about 190,000 people. Each has subdivisions, or microdistricts (*uchastocks*), that are the delivery areas at the most local level (Albrecht and Salmon, 1992: 250).

Local officials associated with polyclinics are now supposed to take on greater responsibility for primary care in their regions, with fewer referrals to hospitals and greater responsiveness to consumers. Physicians are to have greater power to make decisions on appropriate care, as an incentive to increase quality and quantity of services provided. Medical care providers have increased freedom to allocate resources, select management organization, select staff, determine pay, and sell their services for direct payment. However, they must provide a designated range of services, must abide by established prices for services, and must obey norms or standards established by the health authorities (Sheiman, 1994: 45).

The reforms have not yet been implemented sufficiently for adequate measurement of results. In a few regions, such as St. Petersburg and Kemerovo, where reforms have been underway since 1985, there is evidence that increased local responsibility, with greater freedom of polyclinics to take initiative for improvement of primary care, has had positive results for providers and patients (Sheiman, 1994: 50).

In 1991, the national parliament passed a law ("On Local Self-Management") that was supposed to further decentralize government services and give full financing of health care to the 88 provinces. However, implementation of the law has been very slow. The health care system remains centralized, with little room for major decisions at the local level. Physicians are expected to abide by "practice guidelines," or norms, developed at the national level for diagnosis and treatment (Cohen, 1993: 12; Sheiman, 1994: 41).

SOCIAL ORGANIZATION OF HEALTH CARE

The central coordinating organization for the health care system is the Semaschko Institute on the Organization of Health Care in the Ministry of Health in Moscow. Under the communist regime, the professionals in the Institute determined the needs for medical equipment, hospital beds, personnel, and other resources. They developed reports that became the planning documents for the country. They also gave advice and technical assistance to the Republics; to the Medical Collegium, which has charge of medical education; and to the provinces. Decisions on medical practice and training programs were thus directly controlled by officials of one central Institute (Albrecht and Salmon, 1992: 249).

Several distinct systems provide primary care. Roughly 30 percent of the population receives health care at the workplace. The police, railroad employees, university employees, and high-level government officials each have their own clinics and hospitals. The balance of the population is served by polyclinics in the communities (Albrecht and Salmon, 1992: 248).

Most of the smaller polyclinics employ one or two physicians and one or two nurses. A separate unit at the same level employs pediatricians who have responsibility for the health of 800 to 1,000 children. These local provider units refer patients to ambulatory care polyclinics at the district level (Albrecht and Salmon, 1992: 250).

Patients have increasing freedom to seek care at a more distant and higher-status polyclinic or emergency hospital facility. Registration at a specific clinic has been eliminated. They must still wait in line to be seen by the first available physician. If the problem cannot be resolved at this stage, the patient is referred to secondary or tertiary care, but with little choice of provider. Experiments have recently been undertaken to give patients greater choice; physicians are reimbursed on the basis of patient load *and* satisfaction (Albrecht and Salmon, 1992: 249).

Experiments with other new delivery mechanisms have been initiated in fifteen of the eighty-eight Russian provinces. Territorial Medical Organizations (TMOs) have been formed as mechanisms that encompass all nonhospital providers, including polyclinics as well as pediatric clinics, obstetric/gynecology clinics, and other services (hospitals are not included because they are viewed as suppliers of services to the TMOs). The TMOs are financed by the regional health authority on a per capita basis, and will eventually be supported through the new insurance scheme. Polyclinics control the flow of funds to hospitals that contract for services at negotiated rates. The basic idea is similar to managed care as practiced in the United States through health maintenance organizations (World Bank, 1993: 164; Sheiman, 1994: 42).

Physicians

Physicians are abundant, roughly 4.7 per 1,000 people (1992), or more than twice the European average. Male physicians hold most of the prestigious positions in the Ministry of Health, academic centers, research institutes, and hospitals despite the numerical predominance of women. A highly structured status system characterizes relationships among physicians. Academic research scientists are at the top, followed by senior specialty physicians, hospital directors, and polyclinic directors. General practitioners and hospital staff physicians are of lower status (Cockerham, 1995: 312).

GPs and hospital staff physicians have well-developed diagnostic and clinical skills, even without access to advanced technology. This is particularly evident in the larger urban polyclinics and research institutes—but is also the case in rural areas and in smaller clinics (Albrecht and Salmon, 1992: 256).

The range of practice for specialist physicians tends to be quite narrow. A clinic gynecologist, for example, does only outpatient consultation. Deliveries and surgery are performed by a hospital staff gynecologist. Communication and coordination between general practitioners, specialized physicians, and specialized hospitals or institutes are limited (Cohen, 1993: 13).

The polyclinic. The polyclinic is the basic primary health care delivery unit. Clinics are usually associated directly with a hospital, and serve populations of 30,000 to 70,000 people, although the largest clinics serve populations up to about 200,000. They offer a wide range of services including diagnostic examinations, neurological care, ophthalmology, obstetrics, maternity, surgery, and rehabilitation. In the communist era, all citizens were required to register with a particular polyclinic. They had little choice of physician except through private payment. The registration requirement has now been dropped, as noted earlier (Albrecht and Salmon, 1992: 250).

Smaller polyclinics are located near residential complexes. In work settings, occupational clinics (*medsanchasts*) serve on-site employees and are often of higher quality than in communities because enterprises invest more in technology and often employ better physicians—as an incentive to attract workers and keep them healthy (Albrecht and Salmon, 1992: 250; Mezentseva and Rimachevskaya, 1993: 140; Sheiman, 1994: 40).

Patients access health services by going to the nearest polyclinic. Obstetrical and gynecology offices serve female patients. Psychiatric dispensaries serve mental health needs. Special pediatric clinics serve children. Pediatricians undertake regular examinations, do immunizations, and provide general child care (Cohen, 1993: 12; Sheiman, 1994: 43).

The primary care physician is likely to spend approximately half of each day seeing patients in the local clinic. The other half day is devoted to house calls for acutely ill patients. Full-time emergency physicians ride in ambulances and also make housecalls for nonemergencies (Cohen, 1993: 12; Sheiman, 1994: 41).

Record keeping requires extensive paperwork that must be completed in longhand by the physician or nurse. Physicians are required to certify illness for individuals who must be away from work. Records also must be kept of each type of diagnosis, each patient visit, and other details of health care, with records held by the patient (Cohen, 1993: 13).

Local physicians refer complicated cases to larger polyclinics or hospitals. Further referral of complicated cases may be made to tertiary care hospitals located in larger cities and usually associated with medical schools or research units (Albrecht and Salmon, 1992: 256).

Practice patterns vary considerably from those in the United States and Europe, based in part on tradition and in part on different knowledge bases. Because of poor sanitary conditions, there is great concern about infection—and a consequent strong effort to isolate infectious disease treatment to special clinics and separate hospitals (Cohen, 1993: 15).

Use of traditional medicine. Russian physicians have adopted forms of traditional medicine from China. For example, acupuncture is used in some clinics for the treatment of pain, digestive disorders, and pulmonary problems. Herbal medicines are used for many ailments. Mud baths and spas are prescribed for mental and physical illnesses and for rehabilitation after surgery. In fact, access to deluxe spas is one indication of status within the Russian hierarchy. Faith healing is very popular; it receives formal recognition among administrators of the health care system (Albrecht and Salmon, 1992: 259; Cassileth et al., 1995: 1571).

International contacts. Linkages between Russian physicians and the international medical community have been firmly established. Physicians seek outside scientific and health policy information and are now exposed to the international literature and conferences—although resources for this purpose continue to be very limited (Cassileth et al., 1995: 1569).

Medical education and research. Students aspiring to be physicians are required to complete 7 years of higher education after high school, plus additional time for specialization. They must score well on an entrance examination after having a record of high achievement at the secondary school level. Once entrance is approved, medical education is free, usually including a small stipend for living expenses (Albrecht and Salmon, 1992: 255).

Entrance requirements have recently been tightened, with higher test scores now required for entrance. The goal is to limit physician numbers while increasing quality. A quality assurance monitoring requirement was initiated in 1994 (Cassileth et al., 1995: 1571).

The Research Institutes referred to earlier investigate a range of medical problems, and are among the most advanced public enterprises in Russia. The most prestigious physicians work in the tertiary hospitals and Institute system, where they are able to pursue research, secure graduate specialty training, and undertake specialized patient care. The Institute of Cardiology, for example, is located on an attractive campus and has very modern equipment. The scientific work completed here is widely known internationally; a former director shared a Nobel Peace Prize for work on prevention of nuclear war. A few other institutes have similarly high international stature (Albrecht and Salmon, 1992: 254).

Most Institutes are affiliated with the prestigious Academy of Sciences in Moscow. Research and training opportunities are available for top physicians from outside of Moscow, although economic problems have drastically curtailed the options. A criticism leveled at Institutes is their tendency to attract limited resources unavailable to polyclinics and hospitals—which provide most of the services to individual citizens (Albrecht and Salmon, 1992: 254).

Nurses

Hospital nursing does not have much prestige. Compensation is very modest. Nurses play a supporting role at the direction of physicians and have relatively little patient contact. They are instead responsible for the maintenance and cleaning functions (Goehring, 1993: 69).

However, opportunities exist in specialized hospitals for nurses to administer medication, document intravenous solutions, administer respiratory therapy, and monitor vital signs in surgical intensive care. Keeping charts and physical assessment

remain the physician's responsibility. Consequently, there is a severe shortage of nurses (Fleischman and Lubamadrov, 1993: 135).

Nursing education. Nursing has not been part of the university curriculum. Training consists of 3.5 years at a medical technical college, following 8 years of elementary school. Alternatively, students may take 2 years of clinical training after 10 years of primary and secondary school. Since the opening of Russia to the West, efforts have been made to provide nurses with additional training and specialization. For example, special training has been provided in such fields as pediatric nursing at St. Petersburg Children's Hospital #1—the most prestigious such facility in the country. Nurses are given instruction in the specialized fields of pediatric cardiology and cardiac surgery—both badly in need of nursing support (Fleischman and Lubamadrov, 1993: 135).

Pharmacists and Pharmaceutical Services

Pharmacists function as the dispensers of medication in clinics and hospitals throughout the health care system. They serve under the general direction of the physician in charge of each unit and have relatively little autonomy. Their role is heavily affected by the extensive development of the so-called "second economy." The low wages and limited opportunity for pharmacists and physicians have led to widespread use of the black market as a vehicle for earning extra money by informal transactions in medications for individuals with the resources to pay. Formal drug distribution mechanisms have been notably inefficient. The black marketers have profited from the frustration generated by inability to secure supplies through regular channels (Davis, 1989: 252).

The most basic medications such as antibiotics are in short supply. This was a chronic problem through much of the communist period. Estimates indicate that no more than

75 percent of needed medications have been available because of inefficient and poorly managed production. Surgery is sometimes postponed because appropriate anesthetics are not available—except in the medical facilities for the elite citizens, which have first choice of available supplies. Many of the formerly monopolistic government pharmaceutical companies have gone bankrupt. Russia is more dependent on imported medications than in earlier times. Importation is, however, complicated by the severe shortage of foreign exchange. Shortages are likely to continue until the current economic difficulties are resolved (Davis, 1989: 248; Cassileth et al., 1995: 1570).

Herbal medicines make up approximately 30 percent of medications and may legitimately be prescribed in the absence of a more modern medication (Albrecht and Salmon, 1992: 258).

Health Services Administration

As noted earlier, essentially all administrators in the Ministry of Health and throughout the delivery system are male physicians. Modest training in health administration is offered at postgraduate medical institutes through 4- to 6-month courses. However, the level of training is not comparable in terms of modern management concepts or scientific sophistication to professional health administration in Western countries (Albrecht and Salmon, 1992: 251).

Midlevel Practitioners

The larger towns are likely to be served by general practitioner physicians, but smaller towns may have only midlevel practitioners such as an assistant doctor (*feldsher*) and/or a midwife. *Feldshers* have very modest training but respond to emergency situations and provide very basic primary care and refer patients with significant problems to the nearest city polyclinics or hospitals. They also assist physicians in larger towns and cities (Cohen, 1993: 14).

Hospitals

General hospitals are available in all large towns and cities but tend to be minimally equipped with modern technology or sanitary facilities. Buildings are usually old and poorly maintained—especially in outlying regions. As noted earlier, many hospitals in the outlying regions are without indoor plumbing, centralized heat, or hot water (Cassileth et al., 1995: 1570).

It is not uncommon in a regional city to have separate hospitals for emergencies, maternity, children, infectious diseases such as tuberculosis, railroad workers, one for each of the military services, one for the KGB, one for veterans, and a special more modern hospital for the elite officials of the region. Relatively little linkage exists between them and all are likely to have relatively modest technology and very limited supplies—except for the elite hospital, which gets first priority (Albrecht and Salmon, 1992: 251; Cohen, 1993: 13).

Electronic monitoring equipment is available only in the most prestigious hospitals. Computers are largely unavailable except in prestigious institutes and hospitals. Such items as syringes, needles, tubing, and gloves are saved, sterilized, and reused because they are in short supply. This can lead to serious sanitation problems, but does not directly hamper basic hospital services (Goehring, 1993: 69; Cassileth et al., 1995: 1570).

The average length of stay is 15 days. Admissions rates are generally greater than in other European countries. Approximately 13.8 beds are available per 1,000 population, with an annual admission rate of 22.8 per 1,000. Bed rest in the hospital is widely prescribed for an assortment of maladies, in part because crowded housing conditions make home recovery and isolation very difficult (Goehring, 1993: 73; Sheiman, 1994: 41).

Variations in quality. The Lenin Institute for Advanced Medical Studies, with 2,000 beds, operates the most prestigious hospital (*Botkin*) in the country. The level of modernization here and in a few other facilities is comparable to Western standards. However, entry is available only to those in high positions or with substantial financial resources. Important officials and affluent individuals also have access to Western technology and medications outside the country. The military services have special facilities with higher quality available to ranking officers (Albrecht and Salmon, 1992: 252).

Experiments with greater market incentives have been successful in a few locations, such as St. Petersburg. As a consequence, new quality standards have been established and are in process of implementation. Financial penalties are to be enforced when these quality standards are not met (Sheiman, 1994: 48).

Emergency Medical Care

The emergency medical system is relatively well-developed in urban locations. Dialing an emergency number in the larger cities connects callers with a central dispatching system. An ambulance is sent from the nearest substation to take care of the needs or transport the patient to the nearest hospital. Patients are examined at the first point of contact. The physician's judgment is then to leave them at home if they can be adequately treated. Transportation to the hospital occurs in only 17 to 20 percent of the cases. Even in these instances, patients must have their medical records, including X-rays, and produce them when needed by the physician. Hospitals do not have emergency departments as such, but simply place trauma patients in available beds (Goehring, 1993: 69–71).

Some rural areas are served by air ambulances that move patients to the nearest appropriate specialty hospital. Each is staffed by an emergency care physician, an assistant (*feldsher*), and a driver or pilot. Many of the vehicles are especially designed for the type of care needed and are equipped with two-way radios. A specialized critical care ambulance is available for the most serious cases. The intent is to reach any citizen living in a metropolitan area within 15 minutes. In rural areas, access within 25 minutes is the goal. The emergency system is supplemented by clinics at the workplace and first-aid stations in various locations around large cities—such as subways (Albrecht and Salmon, 1992: 252).

Home Health Services

Nonemergency home health services are provided by the nearest polyclinic and hospital complex. Home visiting by physicians and nurses is commonplace throughout the country, especially for the elderly and disabled. As noted earlier, emergency physicians visit homes in ambulances for many problems.

Mental Health Care

Mental health care received relatively little attention under the former Soviet regime. Although a network of outpatient psychoneurological clinics and psychiatric hospitals existed throughout the country, the science of mental health care was poorly developed and mental patients were often very badly treated in psychiatric hospitals. Special attention was given to children with psychiatric problems, through special clinics, hospitals and homes, and in close cooperation with pediatric health care professionals (Serzhpinskaja, 1994: 41).

A new mental health law was passed in 1990 to correct some of the inadequacies of earlier times. Consent of the patient is now required for hospitalization. Admission under duress requires an order by a psychiatrist who must file the document with the legal authorities. In the case of children under age 15, parental request is required. Psychiatrists must also inform the patient of diagnoses and proposed treatment. A formal record must be kept on file of the diagnosis and treatment process. These new rules may seem obvious, but were clearly not followed under the communist system, when many dissidents were detained against their will on the basis of fictitious mental illness problems (Serzhpinskaja, 1994: 41).

Access to Information

Russian citizens under the communist regime had little access to information about what was happening around them that might affect their health. For example, they were not told of radiation effects from nuclear accidents. The new laws give them the right to know about the ecological conditions where they live and in the workplace. They are also given the legal right to know about their medical condition, including diagnosis, prognosis, and treatment recommendations—which were often not available earlier (Swartzberg and Tichtechenko, 1994: 278).

ECONOMIC CHARACTERISTICS AND ISSUES

Overall economic conditions worsened during the 1989 to 1994 period. Real wages have fallen substantially to a per capita average of $2,350. Roughly 38 percent of wages go to payroll taxes for employee benefits, but even this level is inadequate to support industrial needs and social services, given the relatively low income levels of the population (World Bank, 1993: 164; *Europa World Yearbook*, 1995).

The proportion of GDP going to health care actually decreased between 1989 and 1994, falling from roughly 3.4 to 3 percent. The relatively low access to resources results in poor health professional salaries and low levels of medical technology compared to international standards. Despite the reform effort since 1985, health care still does not have a high priority at the national government level. Allocations to heavy industry, defense, and agriculture continue to be emphasized and health care in some sense gets what is left over (Sheiman, 1994: 50; Cockerham, 1995: 311).

Financing

Until very recently, nearly all financial support (95 percent) came directly from the national government and was derived from tax levies. Resources were channeled through the central government budget to regional and local institutions. The new health insurance scheme, initiated at the beginning of 1993, is supposed to change the pattern. Financing is to come from employer payroll deductions of 3.6 percent (3.4 percent for local health care and 0.2 percent for federal funding distributions). However, the old system is deteriorating more quickly than the new system is being implemented—causing major insecurity among many members of the population and among health care professionals (Vienonen and Wlodarczyk, 1993: 168–169; Sheiman, 1994: 39).

The Health Insurance Act of 1991 was approved by the Russian Parliament but put on hold in 1992. It was revised, and approved a second time. It was signed into law by President Yeltsin in April 1993. Administrative boards were to be formed at the regional level to develop regulations, manage the claims process, and disperse funds to providers. They were to function as intermediaries between providers and patients (McKeehan, 1995: 192).

In the short term, the financing arrangement was strongly opposed by the employing enterprises because it directly affects their ability to profit from industrial reform. The argument was that a payroll tax will cause labor costs to rise and prices for products to increase. Private insurance companies are encouraged to supplement the mandatory program, but have been slow to develop because of political and financial uncertainty as well as a lack of needed legal infrastructure for private enterprise (Sheiman, 1994: 54; McKeehan, 1995: 175).

The process of collecting employer contributions is difficult because one in seven enterprises is either bankrupt or in serious financial difficulty. New enterprises are short of resources and often are not able (or willing) to afford the extra costs. Furthermore, the administrative structure to collect the payroll tax, process claims, and make payments is slow to develop because of so little previous experience with such systems (Light, 1992: 236).

A Federal Fund of Mandatory Health Insurance was created as a national resource to subsidize and stabilize regional funds, which are responsible for collecting revenues from employers and dispensing to providers. Both are public nonprofit organizations responsible to government authorities. The insurance provides for basic benefits, but regions can supplement benefits and individuals can further supplement services with private payments or with supplemental private insurance. Cost sharing is required for some services (Sheiman, 1994: 55).

A further intention is to increase revenues from patient visits. Polyclinic contracts with hospitals are to make them discriminating payers, forcing the hospitals to become more efficient and provide higher-quality care. However, payments to the hospitals are made directly from the Technical Medical Organizations (TMOs) as the umbrella organization. Any savings remain with the TMOs and polyclinics for local use, for allocation to salaries or facilities. Bonuses to staff members for high productivity exceed their salaries in some cases (Sheiman, 1994: 42).

Payments to polyclinics and physicians. Until recently, allocations to polyclinics were entirely on the basis of numbers of registered patients and the number of staff. Physicians and staff were all on salaries. Decisions on payment were made by officials in the health care bureaucracy. Few adjustments were possible when inflation increased or numbers of patients went up. However, the reforms now underway may change the payment structure substantially, providing for greater incentives based on productivity and service quality (Sheiman, 1994: 40).

Physicians can now legitimately work in polyclinics and also engage in private practice. Individuals with private resources can secure services from the better physicians and at the higher-quality polyclinics. Special services can be purchased using a voucher system. Physicians who are prestigious enough to attract patients can organize a private clinic and charge fees. This allows the patient to avoid the queue in a polyclinic and

increases the income of the physician. In other cases, as noted earlier, physicians can receive a bonus from a polyclinic for increased performance if they attract larger numbers of patients (Albrecht and Salmon, 1992: 253–256).

New physicians were paid about $24 per month in 1995, roughly the same as starting teachers, and less than 70 percent of the average pay for factory workers or bus or ambulance drivers. Inflation has further eroded physician (as well as other) incomes. After threats and strikes in 1992, the government promised to double the salaries of physicians, but lack of resources has limited implementation of the promise (Cohen, 1993: 12).

Physician incomes, however, are not necessarily indicative of living standard. Higher-status practitioners have access to a variety of special benefits such as preferred apartments, cars, vacation benefits, homes (*dachas*), access to better schools for children, vouchers to shop in special stores, sporting event tickets, and other special amenities (Cohen, 1993: 12; Cassileth et al., 1995: 1570; Cockerham, 1995: 312).

People with private resources are increasingly able to secure health care from the best doctors and hospitals. The private system is growing rapidly in part because the public system is changing more slowly than the demand for better services (Cockerham, 1995: 311).

The effort to save money may be negatively impacting the quality of care in some instances. Polyclinics avoid appropriate referrals to specialists in hospitals because they want to save funds for bonuses and improved equipment. Results are thus clearly mixed at this early stage.

Financing hospitals. Roughly 70 percent of the health care budget continues to be spent on hospital costs. Hospital facilities are now largely financed from government budgets at the regional level. Operational budgets are based on the number of beds and number of staff. The regional Ministry of Health authorities allocate funds for hospitals, as well as to polyclinics, emergency centers, and other services (Zelkovich, Isakova, and Tsarik, 1989: 243; Albrecht and Salmon, 1992: 255; Sheiman, 1994: 41).

The recent reforms allow for experimentation with the use of Diagnosis-Related Groups or fixed rates of payment established for each diagnosis. This requires a level of management expertise that is not yet available in most locations. The more common method of payment is by a "global budget," which is close to the traditional payment method except for the addition of quality and volume standards (Sheiman, 1994: 47).

PROBLEMS AND REFORMS

Many significant problems have been noted in the previous pages. However, the deterioration of the Russian economy during the transition from communism to capitalism has probably been the most significant obstacle to change. The health care system has been seriously damaged, as have other segments of society. Public health and rehabilitation have been particularly hurt by the lack of resources. Basic support, such as wintertime heating of hospitals, laboratories, and clinic buildings, has become difficult. The research budget dropped by two-thirds between 1990 and 1993. Many health scientists are emigrating, at least temporarily, to other countries (Albrecht and Salmon, 1992: 261).

The polyclinics were the weakest link in the Soviet health care system. Despite an appreciation of the problems, it has not been possible to transform the delivery system to a private-practice market as rapidly as might be preferred. Observers indicate the "best" physicians continue to work in hospitals or Institute settings rather than in private health care. An OECD panel of experts recommended in 1993 that Russia diminish the number of research institutes and the size of staffs, while increasing support for a few of the most productive units—if complete collapse of the institute system is to be avoided (Aldhous, 1993: 1200–1202; Sheiman, 1994: 50).

The potential for rapid improvement remains, however, because of the relatively high level of literacy and education throughout the country. Human resources are available to initiate major improvements in health care, as well as other endeavors, if the political support and financial resources were available.

The Western nations and the World Bank are assisting development by providing some of the needed outside resources to support improvement of primary care and prevention programs. Major problems continue to be encountered with limitations in financial infrastructure. For example, several U.S. professional organizations have attempted to provide direct assistance to Russian medical scientists. Simply arranging transfer of funds from the United States to Russia has been very difficult. The banking system in Russia has not had the capacity to easily transfer funds for travel and other support to scientists. Even major private groups with vast resources, such as the Soros Foundation, have had difficulty undertaking their work without having to create a workable financial infrastructure (Gellert, 1992: 1023; Roberts, 1993: 1382; World Bank, 1993: 164; Cassileth et al., 1995: 1573).

SUMMARY AND CONCLUSIONS

The Russian Federation is in process of reforming a health care system that has an abundance of trained physicians (mostly women), polyclinics, and hospitals, but very limited resources for their support. Resources have not become available to improve public health, to significantly modernize polyclinics, hospitals, and other facilities, or to significantly increase the disposable income of physicians and nurses. The economic decline of the early 1990s has placed many health care institutions in jeopardy, and made implementation of major reforms extremely difficult. Privatization is well underway, however, and health care is available to those able to pay out of pocket.

The general public must continue to rely primarily on the deteriorating public system.

The health status of the population, especially men, declined significantly during the 1980s and early 1990s, as indicated by sharp increases in mortality, particularly among men. Infant mortality has been gradually declining during recent decades but improved very little during the early 1990s. The public health system was in a serious state of decline and has been unable to provide the needed level of maternal and child health care.

New laws have created a mandatory health insurance system that depends heavily on the eighty-eight regions of the Federation for implementation. The major goal was decentralization and localization of responsibility as well as financing. Physicians are encouraged to establish private practices and can collect payment from the new insurance organizations or fees for service from individuals with resources. Many rural communities continue to be served only by medical assistants (*feldshers*) who have minimal training and must refer patients with significant problems to polyclinics and hospitals in larger towns.

Public education in modern medicine will be necessary to counteract the many years of misinformation and blatant misrepresentation of the facts about the state of public health and health care. Massive shifts in attitudes and values, as well as resources, will quite likely be required.

Increasing collaboration with international colleagues, as well as gradual adoption of the most accessible procedures and technology, will help facilitate the transition to a more modern health care system. Interest in the needed changes is certainly clear among Russian physicians and health administrators. But the barriers of cultural tradition and short resources mean that many years will be required to make the full transition.

REFERENCES

ALBRECHT, GARY L., and J. WARREN SALMON (1992). Soviet Health Care in the Glastnost Era, in Marilynn M. Rosenthal and Marcel Frenkel (eds.), *Health Care Systems and Their Patients: An International Perspective.* Boulder, Col.: Westview Press, pp. 247–266.

ALDHOUS, PETER (1993). Can Russia Slim Down to Survive, *Science,* 262 (19): 1200–1202.

CASSILETH, BARRIE R., VASILY V. VLASSOV, and CHRISTOPHER C. CHAPMAN (1995). Health Care, Medical Practice and Medical Ethics in Russia Today, *Journal of the American Medical Association,* 273 (20): 1569–1573.

COCKERHAM, WILLIAM J. (1995). *Medical Sociology,* 6th ed. Englewood Cliffs, N.J.: Prentice Hall.

COHEN, LEE J. (1993). Another Face of Medicine: A Report from Russia, *Minnesota Medicine,* 76 (4): 11–15.

DAVIS, CHRISTOPHER M. (1989). The Soviet Health System: A National Health Service in a Socialist Society, in Mark G. Field (ed.), *Success and Crisis in National Health Care Systems: A Comparative Approach.* New York: Routledge, pp. 233–262.

Europa World Yearbook 1995 (1995). London: Europa Publications, Ltd.

FIELD, MARK G. (1975). American and Soviet Medical Manpower: Growth and Evolution, 1910–1970, *International Journal of Health Services,* 5 (3): 455–474.

FLEISCHMAN, CATHERINE, and VADIM LUBAMADROV (1993). Heart to Heart: Teaching Pediatric Cardiology and Cardiac Surgery to Nurses in St. Petersburg, Russia, *Journal of Pediatric Nursing,* 8 (2): 133–139.

GELLERT, GEORGE A. (1992). International Health Assistance to Eurasia, *New England Journal of Medicine,* 326 (13): 1021–1024.

GOEHRING, MAURINE (1993). From Russia with Love, *Emergency Medical Services,* 22 (5): 69–74.

LAUMARK, S. (1992). Nutritional Needs Surveys Among the Elderly—Russia and Armenia, 1992, *CDC Morbidity and Mortality Weekly Report,* 41 (43): 809–811.

LIGHT, DONALD (1992). Perestroika for Russian Health Care?, *Lancet,* 339 (January 25): 236.

MCKEEHAN, IRINA V. (1995). Planning of National Primary Health Care and Prevention Programs: The First Health Insurance Law of Russia, 1991–1993, in Eugene B. Gallagher and Janardan Subedi (eds.), *Global Perspective on Health Care.* Englewood Cliffs, N.J.: Prentice Hall, pp. 174–197.

MEZENTSEVA, ELENA, and NATALIA RIMACHEVSKAYA (1992). The Health of the Populations in the Republics of the Former Soviet Union, *International Journal of Health Sciences,* 3 (3/4): 127–142.

ROBERTS, LESLIE (1993). A Thin Lifeline to Genome Researchers, *Science,* 261 (5127): 1382.

SERZHPINSKAJA, S. V. (1994). The Organization of Child Psychiatric Treatment in Karelia, *Arctic Medical Research,* 53 (Sup. 1): 40–49.

SHEIMAN, IGOR (1994). The Development of Market Approaches in Russia, *International Journal of Health Planning and Management,* 9 (1): 39–56.

SWARTZBERG, DANA, and PAVEL TICHTCHENKO (1994). Interview with Rudolf S. Goon, *Cambridge Quarterly of Healthcare Ethics*, 3: 277–280.

VIENONEN, MIKKO A., and W. CEZARY WLODARCZYK (1993). Health Care Reforms on the European Scene: Evolution, Revolution, or Seesaw?, *World Health Statistical Quarterly*, 46 (3): 166–169.

WORLD BANK (1993). *World Development Report 1993: Investing in Health.* New York: Oxford University Press.

ZELKOVICH, R. M., L. E. ISAKOVA, and G. N. TSARIK (1989). Economic Approaches to Health Care Planning at the Regional Level, *La Sante Publique*, 32 (3): 243–246.

14

CHINA

Privatizing Socialist
Health Care

China

- ⊗ National Capital
- Xi'an • City
- —— International Boundary
- —— Provincial Boundary
- *Hunan* Province Name
- – – Disputed Boundary

0   Miles   500

China is the most populous country in the world with 1.2 billion people in 1994. It is the third largest geographically after Russia and Canada. Between 70 and 80 percent of the population (depending on the source of estimates) live in rural areas or small cities and towns, dispersed in twenty-two provinces, five autonomous regions, and three major municipalities (Shanghai with 12.5 million, Beijing with 11 million, and Tianjin). The provinces have an average population of 35 million, but range from 2 million (Tibet) to 100 million (Sichuan) (Liu and Wang, 1991: 104; Brand, 1992: 101).

China's health care system combines highly centralized control with increasingly decentralized responsibility. Control rests with the national Ministry of Public Health, but most responsibility is delegated to government health units in each province, county, municipality, township, and village. The military has its own system somewhat independent of the national health service, as does each major employment sector: factories, mining, railroads, postal service, public security, education, and civil administration, as well as a number of other organizational categories (Liu and Wang, 1991: 196).

The health status of the Chinese has improved greatly in recent decades, largely because of major national emphasis over a long period on preventive care and immunization for infectious disease. The fitness of the people is among the most striking features of modern China. People of all ages walk, bicycle, and work vigorously (Richmond, 1991: 707). Other unique features of the Chinese system are summarized in Table 14-1.

DEMOGRAPHIC CHARACTERISTICS

Infant mortality in 1990 was approximately 27 per 1,000 live births, a decline from 150 in 1960. This is three times greater than the OECD average, but substantially better than the average of 92 for developing countries.

Table 14-1   Characteristics of Chinese Health Care

- Centralized communist party control, coupled with modernization and decentralization of health care
- Mix of modern Western medicine and traditional Chinese medicine (herbal, acupuncture, and other forms)
- Awarding of the "doctor" designation for completion of a wide range of professional health care training and skill levels; women predominate in these roles
- Minimal status and salary differences between physicians, nurses, pharmacists, and other health professionals, but substantial public/private gaps
- Heavy reliance on mid- and lower-level practitioners, such as assistant doctors and health aides, for primary health care
- Major disparities between rural and urban regions in quality and access to care and insurance
- A very strong health and wellness emphasis in schools—as a socialization, education, and fitness process
- Lower heart disease than in most other countries, in part because of a low-fat diet, vigorous exercise, and otherwise healthy life-style—although widespread smoking is a problem

Sources: Based on Liu and Wang, 1991: 104; Richmond, 1991: 707; Brand, 1992: 101; Liu, Liu, and Meng, 1994: 161.

Similar improvements are evident in life expectancy—which increased from 32 years in 1949, to 47 years in 1960, and to 69 years in 1991. The variation between 68 years for men and 70 for women is lower than in most other countries. On the other hand, cancer and stroke have become the leading causes of death as in Western countries (Roemer, 1991: 606; Shi, 1993b: 723; Weiss and Lonnquist, 1994: 368; Cockerham, 1995: 330).

Substantial differences between rural and urban regions are evident. Efforts over many decades to alleviate these variations have been partially successful, but great discrepancies remain. Per capita income in rural areas is half the urban average. The urban population ranks considerably better on health status indicators than rural people. Life expectancy is 4 years greater in urban areas for both men and women (Shi, 1993b: 731).

This may be the case in part because per capita funding for health care is four times greater in urban areas and availability of physicians and hospital beds is three times greater. Only 43 percent of Chinese physicians are located in rural regions, where the great majority of the population is located. Newly trained physicians resist practice in rural communities, in part because of limited income potential. The discrepancy actually became worse during the 1980s, but is beginning to improve somewhat during the 1990s. An effort is being made to achieve World Health Organization goals under Health for All 2000 targets (Liu and Wang, 1991: 110; Umland et al., 1992: 307; Shi, 1993b: 730).

Rapid aging of the population is one of the major demographic realities. It is particularly a problem because the Social Security system may not be adequate to meet future needs. The urban elderly tend to have access to pension systems and health care, but 80 percent of the elderly who live in rural regions do not. Regional variations between provinces are also substantial. Older people continue to be dependent on their children and personal savings in older age, as has traditionally been the case. Additional medical care resources will be needed in rural China, particularly for treatment of chronic illnesses, to meet the needs of this expanding older population (Shi, 1993b: 723–730).

HISTORICAL PERSPECTIVE

Ancient Traditions

Ancient traditional medicine can be traced to the Chou Dynasty of 1121–1255 B.C. It was during this period that the doctrines of *yang* and *yin* and the Five Elements began, attributing disease to imbalances in the human body through the forces of nature, as described in the classic work called *Ching*. Health was viewed as a state of equilibrium between opposite but complementary forces. As early as 200 B.C., acupuncture and massage therapy were discussed in a document (as translated) called *The Yellow Emperor's Classic of Internal Medicine*. Medical schools to train traditional

healers were well established by the Song dynasty of A.D. 960 to 1279 (Chung-tung, 1991: 316; Roemer, 1991: 579).

Traditional nursing also developed very early in China, in part because strict segregation of the sexes required that women be treated by female medical practitioners. However, there is no precise historical record of the evolution of nursing prior to the nineteenth century. The tradition of families as providers of certain elements of nursing care in hospitals—food, bedding, and personal care—started very early and was reinforced during the introduction of Western medical practices (Chung-tung, 1991: 320).

Western medicine was first introduced in the seventeenth century by Jesuit priests who were missionary physicians. They began to challenge and replace some of the practices of traditional Chinese medicine. Vaccination against smallpox was introduced about 1805. The first surgeon of record opened a clinic in 1808. Other missionaries from Britain and the United States offered Western medical care to Chinese patients as early as 1820. The first formal medical training in Western medicine was introduced about 1837. A 3-year training program for medical apprentices was initiated in 1863. This was followed by the introduction of several Western medical schools beginning in 1881 and continuing into the twentieth century (Roemer, 1991: 579).

Public health programs were initiated in Shanghai in 1873, and later spread to other parts of the country, primarily to control epidemics. The first trained English nurse came to Shanghai in 1884 and became the predecessor for a succession of Western nurses who played a key role in development of the nursing profession, especially after the creation of the Chinese Republic in 1911 (Chung-tung, 1991: 320; Roemer, 1991: 579).

Formation of the Chinese Republic: 1912–1930

After the formation of the Republic in 1912, a parliamentary party known as the

Kuomintang led the country. It was largely dominated by merchants, professionals, and intellectuals dedicated to Chinese nationalism. During this period (1914), the Rockefeller Foundation began supporting the Union Medical College in Peking (now Beijing), helping to develop it into a modern medical center. It eventually served as a model for other medical colleges around the country. A school of nursing was added in 1920 and a department of public health was initiated in 1921 (Roemer, 1991: 580).

The Chinese Communist Party was also formed in 1921 and grew rapidly among the peasants and in opposition to the *Kuomintang*. European commercial interests played a major role in exploiting resources and even controlling some parts of the country (such as Hong Kong) in collaboration with the *Kuomintang*. The Nationalist government formed a Ministry of Public Health in 1927, but it was later disbanded during World War II. Nursing became officially recognized by the Ministry in 1930 and a director of nursing for China was appointed. By 1945, thirty medical colleges were operating in various parts of the country (Roemer, 1991: 500).

The Rise of Communism: 1931–1945

Chiang Kai-shek, leader of the *Kuomintang* military services, fought the Japanese after the invasion of 1931, and then turned his forces primarily against the communists in an effort to control their expanding power. Health care was included as part of the military services, involving, among other elements, a military nursing school beginning in 1943. However, after World War II, the power of the *Kuomintang* was overwhelmed, despite U.S. military support, and the remaining forces fled to the island of Taiwan—taking along the school of military nursing. The Communist Red Armies under Mao Zedong assumed control of the mainland and created the People's Republic of China (Chung-tung, 1991: 315; Roemer, 1991: 577).

County hospital systems were initiated in the early twentieth century but were slow to develop until the 1930s, when rural hospitals were established in several parts of the country. Physicians were still primarily practitioners of traditional medicine. Consequently, the country was greatly in need of more modern health care when the communists assumed control of the country (Weiss and Lonnquist, 1994: 366).

Transition to the Communist People's Republic: 1945–1965

The Chinese Republic under the *Kuomintang* had not successfully modernized public or private health care. Poverty was widespread, epidemics were rampant, and the economy was generally in a bad state. Hospitals and other health facilities were in short supply throughout the country, and particularly in rural areas. Public health efforts were thus an important part of initiatives after World War II (Rosenthal, 1992: 295).

Modern health services had been organized in the territories held by the communists. The Red Army provided health care and helped organize hospitals for treating soldiers and civilians, generally with a mixture of traditional and Western medicine. In rural areas, health care was provided largely by practitioners of traditional medicine (Roemer, 1991: 583).

In 1947, 60 percent of the hospitals were privately operated, as were most clinics. After the People's Republic was founded in 1949, the medical care system was gradually transformed from a private system to a largely socialized system. By 1956, all hospitals were public, generally following the traditions of the Soviet Union, which was befriending and assisting the communist government at the time (Roemer, 1991: 583).

Major efforts were made to increase the supply of health care providers, largely by expanding the size of existing medical universities. These medical centers trained both senior and assistant physicians, as well as other health care personnel such as nurses, midwives, and pharmacists. Health facilities were quickly expanded to serve additional areas of the country (Roemer, 1991: 584).

Expansion of Health Insurance

China initiated a Labor Medical Service in 1951 and a Free Medical Service based on the Russian model in 1952. The Labor Medical Service was to cover all individuals in publicly controlled industries, or roughly 10 percent of the population. Insurance premiums were paid largely by the government, although industries made contributions as well. Workers were not required to pay fees. Care was delivered at the employment site or in designated local facilities. However, dependents received reimbursement for only 50 percent of costs, and then only in the largest industrial organizations. Dependents of government workers were not insured (Roemer, 1991: 585).

The Free Medical Service was for selected segments of the population not employed in industry, such as public employees, college students, and retirees. Recipients had to secure their care in specified clinics and hospitals. Since 1984, a co-payment has been required (Liu and Wang, 1991: 113).

A Cooperative Medical Service for rural regions was initiated in 1955 and further expanded in the 1960s. Services were financed largely at township and village levels through "voluntary" payments by recipients. This was later altered to a system of taxation based on local production. Well-trained doctors were located in medical cooperatives or health centers at the township or county level; health centers increased very quickly, as did the total number of health care workers and hospital beds—expanding by twenty times between 1949 and 1975 (Liu, Liu, and Meng, 1994: 161).

The Cultural Revolution and "Barefoot Doctors": 1966–1977

The changes were made more dramatic in 1966 by the "Cultural Revolution," which

nearly eradicated private health care providers over a period of 10 years, while building up a centralized state-operated system. Doctors were rapidly shifted to public health care facilities. University faculty and senior doctors were required to do manual work in the countryside. Massive campaigns were used to eliminate venereal disease and other infectious diseases—with considerable success. New hospitals were constructed so that each county had a facility by 1966 (Roemer, 1991: 586).

It was during this period that the so-called "barefoot doctor" (like the Russian *feldsher* in some respects) was introduced to provide modestly trained auxiliary health care workers and services in rural communities. The strategy was based in part on the Maoist effort to meet the needs of rural people through local self-reliance while undercutting the power of the urban medical profession, which did not always subscribe to communist principles. More than 1.7 million (estimates vary from 1 to 3 million) of these local health practitioners provided primary health care in most villages until about 1977, when their numbers began to decline (Rosenthal, 1992: 299; Liu et al., 1994: 161).

Their task was to provide education on prevention of disease, participate as leaders of mass health promotion campaigns, and provide basic health care services—while also pursuing a role as agricultural workers. They were usually young people recruited from the community and trained for a month or more (up to 2 years) in a local health center or hospital. The content of training usually blended traditional herbal medicine with the elementary features of modern medicine. No formal credentials were required to practice as a barefoot doctor, although changes were later made to upgrade the role. Modest fees were assessed for services and to support purchase of modern and traditional drugs. Barefoot doctors were often assisted by health aides with even less training. In the cities, housewives were recruited as *red medical workers* and performed a similar function, although with less responsibility. These practitioners were later accused of widespread malpractice and poor quality care (Roemer, 1991: 587; Rosenthal, 1992: 296).

A strong effort was made during the 1960s and onward to gain the confidence of the rural population by continuing to support traditional medicine supplemented by more modern practices. Acupuncture clinics became widely available, but in the context of Western-style clinics and supervised by trained physicians. Applicants to traditional medical schools were required to pass the same national examination as was required of applicants to Western-style medical schools (Rosenthal, 1992: 297).

Modernization After Mao: 1977 to the Present

After 1977, new leadership took over the communist party. The private market was encouraged and the country gradually entered a period of modernization, with very rapid development in the late 1980s and early 1990s. As privatization began, both the Cooperative Medical System and the "barefoot doctors" began to disappear. The communal funding base was destroyed and confidence in the system declined. By 1985, much of the central government support was withdrawn (Chen, Hu, and Lin, 1993: 733).

"Barefoot practitioners" were now required to pass competency tests, which many of them failed. If they continued to practice, their status was redefined as "health aide" under the supervision of trained village doctors or assistant physicians. Many could in fact earn more income by other forms of work, and simply quit their local practice. Their replacements usually had 3-year post-high school medical degrees or higher-level medical school training (Chen et al., 1993: 733; Liu et al., 1994: 161–163).

The changes were demanded by rural residents. Average incomes were estimated to have doubled in the 3 years after the beginning of the reform in the late 1970s. Many chose to seek health care in county or city hospitals away from the villages. Meanwhile, private physicians—some retired from the public health service—were allowed to practice privately and leased or contracted with village clinics to provide local care. Fee-for-service payment and an evolving insurance system financed the new privatized system. The number of health care providers declined considerably in rural areas, whereas increased demand on urban and county hospitals and clinics created serious shortages of access to care. Longer waiting times for both primary and hospital services became the rule (Liu and Wang, 1991: 113; Liu et al., 1994: 161–163).

The result was even greater pressure to increase private health care opportunities. By 1990, nearly half of all village health care was provided through private practitioners. Similar changes were taking place in urban areas, but at a much slower pace. Only about 3.3 percent of physicians in urban areas were in private practice by 1990, many of them part-timers who also worked in public facilities on salary. Private hospitals also began to emerge in large urban areas such as Shanghai and Beijing (Liu et al., 1994: 165).

China's "barefoot doctor" system of the 1960s and early 1970s became an example of a health care solution to be replicated. It was advertised to the developing world by the World Health Organization and the United Nations in the quest for "Health for All by the Year 2000." Nonetheless, the drive toward economic and social development in the 1980s led to near dissolution of this idealized system. Deterioration in sanitation, immunization, and other public health practices has been reported for rural areas, although the situation in urban areas may have substantially improved. There apparently has been a substantial shift away from preventive care and toward curative care in recent years. Dramatic shifts in policies and programs related to health care have been characteristic of China during the twentieth century, and the current changes appear to be another stage in that process (Shi, 1993b: 731; Sidel, 1993: 1666).

CULTURAL FACTORS

China has great depth of cultural tradition based on 4,700 years of evolving civilization. Many traditional medical practices arose from ancient religious principles with roots in Confucian, Buddhist, Taoist, and other traditions. The patient has tended to be viewed holistically and treated as part of the cultural unit of which he or she is a part (Lee, Yen, and Chou, 1993: 292).

Family-oriented health care is particularly congruent with Chinese society. Assignment of status and expected behavioral differences between men and women are associated with family values, and directly affect care. Women tend to predominate both as physicians and nurses, because this is culturally defined as an appropriate role for women (Shi, 1993b: 731).

A recent epidemiological study of sixty-five Chinese counties indicates that people eat relatively little fat, but consume great quantities of high-energy foods, such as rice, wheat, and potatoes. One consequence is evidence of a much lower consumption of saturated fats, resulting in a lower average cholesterol level (158 milligrams per deciliter) than in the United States (216) (Junshi et al., 1990; Richmond, 1991: 707; Vartiainen et al, 1991: 41).

The strong cultural traditions have enabled the Chinese people to make the transition through a series of major twentieth-century political upheavals while maintaining family and community traditions. Modern Western medicine has been adopted while also maintaining the viability and use of traditional medicine.

POLITICAL INFLUENCES

The Chinese Communist Party continues to have major influence on all dimensions of the political and social services systems. Units of the party function in each political subdivision and directly influence local policy. The Party has, since 1977, supported the major shift to a market economy and privatization of much of the health care system under the leadership of Deng Xiaoping (Roemer, 1991: 596).

The State Council of the Republic is the central authority to which all units of government are subordinate. Within each province, there are city, county, township (formerly commune), and village (formerly production brigades) governments (Liu and Wang, 1991: 104; Brand, 1992: 101).

The political system was highly centralized prior to the takeover by the communists. This tradition has changed quite dramatically under Deng Xiaoping. Leadership remains controlled by the communist hierarchy in Beijing, but financing and decision making have been decentralized. The change has had the effect of encouraging diversity and innovation at the provincial, county, and township levels during the 1980s and early 1990s (Phillips and Pearson, 1994b: 129).

As a result of the Fourteenth National Congress of the Communist Party in 1992, health care was officially included as part of the change to a "socialist market" economy in which central planning was to be supplemented by market competition. This transition had in fact already been underway for a decade. Increasing incomes led to a demand for higher quality and more choice in health care as in other sectors of the economy (Liu et al., 1994: 158).

SOCIAL ORGANIZATION OF HEALTH CARE

The Ministry of Public Health under the State Council has direct responsibility for national health policy and management. Direct control is also lodged here for national hospitals, medical universities, drug control, and major health care publications. The Ministry has the following divisions:

- Health Promotion and Communicable Disease Prevention
- Medical Administration

- Science and Education
- Maternal and Child Health
- Pharmaceutical Administration
- Traditional Medicine
- Planning and Finance

Other federal ministries have responsibility for certain dimensions of health. For example, the Ministry of Labor issues regulations and manages occupational health programs, in cooperation with the Ministry of Health. The Ministry of Education has responsibility for health education and personal hygiene for students. As noted earlier, the Ministry of National Defense has its own health care system for military personnel. The Ministry of Finance manages the health insurance programs in cooperation with the Ministry of Labor (Roemer, 1991: 595).

Each of the twenty-one provinces, five autonomous regions, and three centrally administered municipalities has comparable departments. Each subdivision now has considerable autonomy for development of local health policies and management within national guidelines. Each province has responsibility for provincial hospitals, sanitariums, public health departments, and drug management units, as do counties and cities. Counties (approximately 2,300 of them) have a health department or bureau and responsibility for the operation of health activities at that level. The fifty-three larger cities, each with more than 100,000 population, have local responsibility for municipal health care (Roemer, 1991: 594).

Public Health

Public health has received major emphasis since 1950. Essentially, all health workers at the local level were assigned a major health promotion and prevention role. In fact, much of the success in improving longevity, lowering infant mortality, and enhancing overall health status was a direct result of massive emphasis on public health.

However, public health or prevention activities have gradually been separated from patient care services at the township or urban neighborhood level. This is part of the transformation toward decentralization and privatization in the last decade, in accord with comparable changes in overall administrative and industrial organization (Liu and Wang, 1991: 108).

School Health

School health programs are pervasive. Health professionals are employed in school clinics and have assigned responsibilities for preventive health programs, assessment of child health, and health education. A health record is created and maintained to monitor individual student health status, serve as the immunization record, and for general use in securing health care services. Students are trained as "little health workers" and as "Red Cross Adolescents," to assist with health promotion, health examinations, treatment of minor wounds, and immunizations (Xiangdong and Blum, 1990: 483–486).

Physicians

Physicians generally hold the key posts in all parts of the system. Consequently, they exercise great influence in the policy and management process as well as health care delivery (Roemer, 1991: 596).

Within counties, townships support health centers and hospitals that serve the villages within their jurisdiction. Each village has a clinic, staffed by one or more assistant doctors, nurses, and support staff. It is at this level that most citizens obtain their primary and preventive care. In urban areas, the comparable units are street hospitals and clinics in each district (Shi, 1993b: 726).

As noted earlier, township governments in rural areas are responsible for financing and management of health centers and local hospitals. Each village must support basic primary care, emergency care, maternal and child health care, and health promotion activities. As of 1989, 59 percent of all rural clinics were fee-for-service private practice operations. Eleven percent were groups of doctors and 49 percent were individual practitioners (Liu and Wang, 1991: 108).

Urban health care is organized somewhat differently. Only about 3.5 percent of urban medical practices are private. Each city over 100,000 is divided into districts. In the largest cities, these districts may include one-quarter to one-half million people. Districts are further subdivided into neighborhoods of 50,000 to 100,000, which are further divided into "lanes" of 2,500 to 12,000 people. The smallest subdivision is served by a clinic with physicians and support staff, whereas the districts will have a hospital and outpatient service for more complicated problems referred by the local clinics. Industrial and government organizations operate their own clinics at the workplace (Weiss and Lonnquist, 1994: 367).

Illnesses that require greater knowledge and skill than are available in the district or village are referred to the second tier: the township or municipal hospital, which is staffed by physicians trained in Western and traditional medicine, nurses, and support personnel. More difficult cases may be further referred to the third-tier township hospitals or the better-equipped and -staffed county hospitals. Relatively few rural patients are referred to provincial or national hospitals—which tend to largely serve the urban population (Cretin et al., 1990: 668).

Although this is the basic pattern, there is considerable variation around the country, depending on the relative resources and remoteness of the location. Rural areas generally have less developed health care systems than urban areas, depending on the affluence of the community (Rosenthal, 1992: 301; Shi, 1993b: 727).

As noted earlier, the supply of physicians has increased rapidly in recent decades. Senior specialist physicians are fully prepared in the science of Western medicine with 8 years of medical training. These better-trained physicians usually practice in urban centers or large towns. Most primary care is now provided in urban locations by physicians with 5 years of postsecondary school training. As in other countries, the quality of facility and health care professionals varies considerably, depending on the affluence of the community (Roemer, 1991: 593).

Roughly 70 percent of all physicians are females. The ratio is even higher in obstetrics (90 percent) and pediatrics (90 percent), in part because of the cultural preference for female patients to be examined only by other females. Women doctors and midwives also provide the bulk of primary care for maternal care, birthing, and child health at the village level. Maternal and child health continues to be one of the major thrusts of the health care system (Gupta, 1991: 1511; Jia-Zhen, 1994: 388).

Professional organizations. The Chinese Medical Association was founded soon after the formation of the Chinese Republic in about 1915. The Association supports continuing medical education and offers recommendations on health policy and medical education to the Ministry of Health. More recently, the Association has deliberately attempted to establish and maintain linkages with physician groups in other countries. Traditional medical practitioners have a separate association. Societies of General Practice were established in 1989 to promote further training for primary care physicians (Lee et al., 1993: 295).

A system of incentives, referred to as the "personal responsibility system," has greatly improved the professionalism and productivity of physicians as well as other health care workers—by rewarding them financially for good work (Liu and Wang, 1991: 115; Richmond, 1991: 707).

Medical education. China had 116 medical schools in 1990; 23 focused primarily on traditional medicine and 91 were primarily based on Western medicine. All but 13 were operated by provinces. The 13 federal universities were located in the 12 major cities and were directly managed by the Ministry of Public Health. Most provincial schools offered a 5-year or 7-year curriculum following secondary school (10 years are required for primary, middle, and secondary school). The curriculum included Western medicine, traditional medicine, public health, pediatrics, and dentistry (Butler and Ruma, 1990: 498).

The physician in China can have three levels of training and be referred to as "doctor" (wide variation in training is also true for nurses and other support personnel), as summarized in Table 14-2.

The focus in the past was on capability to do a certain health care task, rather than on formal credentials. The general adoption of Western medical education standards has formalized the requirements to the three higher skill levels requiring 3, 5, or 7 or 8 years of formal training (Roemer, 1991: 601; Stillman and Sawyer, 1992: 496).

The 3-year program condenses the basic sciences and clinical subjects in the first 2 years and offers hospital practice in the third year. It is particularly oriented toward training doctors for work in rural communities. Experiments have been undertaken to develop a new curriculum that better prepares students and promotes understanding of the unique needs in rural medicine. Considerable effort is made to recruit students from rural regions and offer them a practical program that is "problem-based and community-oriented." The hope is that this approach will help alleviate the disparities in health care between rural and urban regions (Umland et al., 1992: 307; Tu, Xia, and Cheng, 1994: 347).

The 5-year curriculum includes all of the basic sciences in the first 3 years. General medicine, surgery, and other clinical subjects are offered in the fourth year. The fifth year focuses on hospital experience.

A few prestigious schools (6 in 1990) offer a 7- or 8-year curriculum. They train the most advanced specialists and receive higher levels of funding. The faculty in these schools (such as Peking Union Medical College, mentioned earlier) has often received advanced training in Western countries. Medical education is largely free to students except for costs of food and some books (Butler and Ruma, 1990: 498; Rosenthal, 1992: 302).

China continues to train doctors in traditional medicine, often supplemented with training in Western medicine. They are required to learn (1) the basic theories and diagnostics of traditional medicine, (2) human anatomy and physiology, (3) knowledge of location (acupoints) for applications of acupuncture, (4) techniques of acupuncture and moxibustion (manipulative techniques), and (5) knowledge of diagnosis and treatment of common diseases. This curricu-

Table 14-2   Training Requirements of Physicians and Medical Assistants

	Assistant Doctor, Formerly "Barefoot Doctor" Certificate	Medical Doctor Degree: Level 1 and 2	Medical Degree as Specialist
Education	3–24 months	3 years/5 years post-jr./post-sr. high school	7–8 years post-sr. high school
Internship/ residency	None	Intern	Intern/resident
Work site	Village or township	Township or county	County, province, federal
Responsibility	Ambulatory care	Ambulatory, inpatient, and simple surgery	Ambulatory, inpatient, and complex surgery

Sources: Based on Lee et al., 1993: 294; Phillips and Pearson, 1994a: 103.

lum requires 5 years of study beyond high school, and additional years to learn Western medicine. Practitioners of traditional medicine vary widely in basic preparation, but generally fit the same range of educational levels noted earlier—although few would complete the most advanced degree without focusing primarily on Western medicine. (Buxiong, 1990: 6–8).

Medical education is largely controlled by the Ministry of Public Health or provincial ministries. Until 1991, enrollment and job assignments of medical students were entirely state-planned. The government paid all costs for student tuition and support. After 1992, medical schools were allowed to enroll additional students and charge tuition and fees. Graduates are then free to select their own jobs in private practice. At least 40 percent of medical students in Shangdong province, for example, were privately enrolled in 1992 (Liu et al., 1994: 166).

The primary shortcoming in medical education is at the advanced graduate and continuing medical education level, especially for primary care physicians in rural regions. The World Bank made loans to the Ministry of Health for purchase of modern medical equipment as teaching tools in medical universities to help alleviate this problem and to provide specialized services. Most of the equipment is imported from Japan, which also provides training for the technicians and professionals who maintain and operate the equipment (Hu and Meng, 1991: 559).

The recent initiation of the General Practice Training Center in Beijing (with funding from the Canadian International Development Agency in 1991) is intended to further advance medical education. Residencies in general practice are to be offered to qualified applicants. The new Chinese Society of General Practice will evaluate qualifications of members and offer a diploma in general practice. Some graduates will then become faculty for residencies at the provincial level. The intent is to upgrade the competence and status of general practice as a legitimate specialty (Lee et al., 1993: 298).

Experiments with a new curriculum at Jiujiang Medical College offer another option. This region has had serious problems with out-migration of doctors who were no longer required by law to serve in remote locations. Applicants to the new program (begun in 1986) are selected from rural areas and must agree to return upon graduation. Community-oriented education and problem-based learning are central to the 3-year curriculum, which offers four specialties: clinical medicine, pediatrics, orthopedics and trauma, and medical laboratory. Radiology is to be added later. The program is an attempt to develop innovative methods with a higher likelihood of preparing professionals who will be willing to serve rural communities (Yang and Zhang, 1991: 34–37; Stillman and Sawyer, 1992: 495–496).

Nurses

Although the Chinese Nursing Association was founded in 1909, and became the eleventh member of the International Council for Nurses in 1922, further development of professional nursing proceeded rather slowly. Although the number of nurses trained increased dramatically during the 1950s and early 1960s, the Cultural Revolution (1966–1976) caused the profession to suffer a loss of status, with strongly negative effects. A major shortage of nurses was evident beginning in the mid-1980s. One estimate suggests that only half enough nurses are available (Gay, Flowers, and Tu, 1990: 65–67).

Physicians generally make all decisions about patient needs and often perform nursing functions in the ambulatory care offices because of the nurse shortage. Nursing care is limited largely to the hospital setting. The relationship between nurses and physicians seems generally to be quite harmonious (Morales-Mann and Jiang, 1993: 739).

Nursing education. Nine college-level training programs were in operation in 1990. Textbooks and instruction space were in short supply, even at Peking Union Medical

College. Although greater emphasis on nursing education was initiated beginning in 1977, sufficient training programs are not available to fulfill national needs (Morales-Mann and Jiang, 1993: 737).

Pharmacists and Pharmaceuticals

Modern clinical pharmacy has developed rapidly since the emergence of a market economy in 1978, and is now fully available in urban hospitals. Most hospitals with more than 400 beds have a department of pharmacy and associated clinical laboratory services. Several of the larger hospitals have independent departments of clinical pharmacology that specialize in pharmacy and drug analysis—often serving other hospitals and ambulatory care clinics in the region. Smaller rural hospitals generally have no clinical pharmacy capability and no on-site pharmacists. Use of traditional herbal medicines continues to be predominant, although there is evidence of change (Cai et al., 1994: 695).

Most pharmacy schools offer only a 4-year degree, although M.S. and Ph.D. degrees are available in a few institutions. Masters degree programs comparable to Pharm.D. degrees have been initiated at Shanghai Medical University and Huaxi Medical University. Many students have traveled abroad for advanced study. A Society of Hospital Pharmacy has been organized to coordinate continuing education programs throughout the country (Cai et al., 1994: 696).

The Academy of Traditional Medicine in Beijing conducts scientific research on the pharmacology and clinical practice of herbs and traditional medicine. Engineers and pharmacists are employed in factories to refine and produce herbal medicines, which are then sold in large quantities throughout China and other parts of Asia, as well as in Chinatowns of foreign cities. Traditional medicines are an important export to eighty countries (Rosenthal, 1992: 297).

Pharmaceuticals, both modern and traditional, account for 58 percent of the Chinese health care budget, according to recent estimates. Although some prescriptions are used for inpatient hospital care, the great majority are dispensed for primary care. "Tonics" are used by millions of adults, particularly at older ages. Rural physicians serve as both prescribers and dispensers of drugs—for which they collect 10 to 15 percent markup over their purchase price. Many medications require no prescription and are freely dispensed by hospitals as well as local providers (Hu, 1984: 141; Roemer, 1991: 593; Fox, 1994: 1–4).

China has a very large number of pharmaceutical manufacturing plants (estimated at 1,300 in 1990) that produce sufficient quantities of modern and traditional pharmaceutical products to meet internal and export needs. Herbal medicines are produced in family plots and on large mechanized farms. Warehouses and distribution units are located in each province for both modern and traditional medicines. Independent pharmacies, health centers, and hospitals serve as the points of local distribution. Prior to the privatization process all of these enterprises were centrally managed, but have now been largely transferred to private enterprise (Roemer, 1991: 593).

Health Care Administration

Most physician-managers also practice medicine and cannot devote their full energies to administration. They are able to earn more money in clinical work than in administration. Hospitals tend to be governed by units of government, which means administrators do not have the freedom to undertake more effective new policies without securing permission from higher authorities (Brand, 1992: 104).

Six hospital management programs have been developed in major universities, mostly to prepare doctors for management roles. These are relatively new programs training entry-level graduates and have been somewhat limited in the use of modern management theory because little research on management development has been undertaken. High-quality teaching materials have not been developed. A few physicians have gone to the United States or other countries in order to secure advanced training. A Management Training Center was established in Nanjing in 1991 that offers a correspondence course for senior managers (Brand, 1992: 104).

A new Health Administrative Staff Training Center was created in 1989 near Beijing. Its purpose is to train administrative staff from all levels of the health care system. It has both academic facilities and guest rooms for visiting teaching staff and administrators in training, serving as a conference center for health administrators. The programs range from 3-week intensive training courses to short-term meetings. Although participants are primarily from the Beijing Bureau of Public Health, the activities of the Center should help to strengthen advanced administrative training (Brand and Juntian, 1992: 105).

Hospitals

Village and township hospitals have an average of eighteen beds for primary care. County, district, and city hospitals offer secondary care, and provincial and national hospitals offer tertiary care. At each level, ambulatory outpatient services, including family planning, maternal and child health, and preventive care, are provided in addition to inpatient care. Hospitals are usually owned by government units at each level. Rural township and county hospitals often have low occupancy rates of 50 percent or less because rural people with sufficient resources go to more sophisticated county or urban hospitals—which tend to have 85 to 90 percent occupancy (Roemer, 1991: 592; Shi, 1993b: 726).

Publicly owned hospitals were allowed to become joint-stock or partnership institutions with shared government and private ownership as a consequence of the changes in 1992. This is a direct result of the inability

of the government to meet the demand for high-quality health care facilities. The stockholders of privatized hospitals are often the medical staff of the hospital. However, the new arrangements allow for foreign-investment participation. The extent of this change has not yet been carefully studied because it is all very recent (Liu et al., 1994: 167).

Considerable progress has been made in the modernization of hospitals, but resource shortages have placed major limitations on technological advancement. Hospitals tend to be crowded, with large numbers of patients per room. Most reuse syringes, needles, rubber gloves, and other materials because disposable products are not available. Equipment tends to be old and in poor condition. Refrigeration for medication and food for patients is often not available. Infection control is a continuing problem. However, hospital administrators, physicians, nurses, and other staff appear eager to improve the conditions as rapidly as their expanding knowledge and resources will allow (Moscovich, 1991: 95–96).

The Ministry of Public Health has initiated a nationwide system of assessing hospitals—as an attempt to increase the standards of management. Three grades have been established (Zhi-kuan, 1994: 243):

1. Grade 1 refers to community hospitals at the local level that offer the most basic prevention, treatment, and rehabilitation.
2. Grade 2 refers to regional hospitals with more comprehensive services serving a range of communities, and with limited teaching and research responsibilities.
3. Grade 3 refers to highly specialized hospitals with major medical, educational, and research responsibilities.

Within each grade, institutions are classified as A, B, C, or S, depending on their technical level, service quality, facilities, and professionalization of management. The grading and evaluation are conducted by committees of experts from the national, provincial, and municipal offices (Zhi-kuan, 1994: 243).

Emergency Medical Care

Emergency Medical Centers have been created in the larger cities with emergency vehicles, a dispatching system, special telephone lines, and a rescue staff of physicians, nurses, and technicians. These Centers usually serve several hospitals (forty hospitals in Beijing, for example). Some larger hospitals have emergency departments or clinics with on-call physicians, nurses, and technicians with responsibility for resuscitation and monitoring of patients during transport (Ding, 1990: 62).

Emergency medicine as a formal part of health care is relatively new. Prehospital emergency care is generally not well developed except as practiced in the village or community clinics. Although county hospitals operate ambulances, the vehicles are usually not equipped with resuscitation equipment or trained emergency technicians (Ding, 1990: 62).

Medical Technology

China has been systematically attempting to learn from Western countries since 1977. Academicians from U.S. and European universities have been invited to lecture at conferences in China and at medical universities. Large numbers of Chinese students have been sent to study at Western medical and other health science schools. This has enabled health care to move forward much more quickly than would otherwise have been possible (Roemer, 1991: 594).

Modern medical technology is still in very short supply, however, particularly at the most local level. Advanced technology such as CT scanners is available only in major tertiary care centers. A forceful effort is underway to diffuse the most basic and affordable technology to local levels (Rosenthal, 1992: 303).

Major advances have been made in many specialized health care fields, such as diagnosis and treatment of heart disease. For example, the Cardiovascular Diseases Training Center at the Fu Wai Hospital in Beijing works with fifty-one other hospitals around the country to train professionals in cardiac surgery, use of hypothermia, anesthesia, bypass techniques, intensive care, and noninvasive cardiology. Fellowships are also provided to specialists for intensive training abroad, with an obligation to return to China and share their knowledge. This is only one of many efforts to improve application of advanced knowledge, skills, and technology (Sloman, 1990: 289–290).

Information Systems

Medical informatics (the use of computers as information and management tools in health care) began in 1973 with the formation of a Medical Computer Application Department in the Chinese Academy of Medical Sciences. Several applications in Chinese hospitals were initiated in the 1970s, but major development did not take place until the 1980s when the rapid introduction of microcomputers led to the formation of the Chinese Medical Informatics Association. By 1988, more than 8,000 computer systems had been installed. More elaborate hospital information systems were in process of installation but had not yet moved to the status of integrated networks by 1990. Medical universities have made the most widespread use of computers and offer training courses in medical informatics and computer applications. Several medical libraries have installed literature retrieval systems (De-xian, 1990: 95).

Computer-aided diagnosis and treatment have been advancing steadily. International exchange, including the Sixth World Congress of Medical Informatics held in Beijing in 1989, has greatly facilitated developments in the field. The primary obstacle to further development has been the shortage of resources to purchase the needed technology and software (Wang, 1993: 1–10).

Long-Term Care

The family serves as the primary unit for care of the elderly and disabled. Institutional long-term care has not been widely developed. A few sanitariums serve as rest homes for recovering patients as a supplement to hospitals. Physical therapy is particularly emphasized in these institutions for rehabilitation of elderly and other chronically ill patients (Roemer, 1991: 592).

Home Health Care

A system of household sickbeds was developed beginning in 1983, to serve the elderly, disabled, and chronically ill. Medical consultation is offered as are other forms of formal support. Although a formal system of home health care does not exist in the same form as in Western countries, it is commonly practiced at the village level (Rosenthal, 1992: 304).

Mental Health Care

Mental health care has made substantial progress since 1950, when a major mental health conference was held in Nanjing and served as the impetus to greatly expand services. In 1949, nine psychiatric hospitals and fifty psychiatrists were available to serve the entire country. By 1986, these numbers had grown to 348 hospitals and 6,000 psychiatrists. The official attitude toward rehabilitation of mentally ill people has changed profoundly since 1980—in substantial part because of the leadership of Deng Xiaoping's disabled son, Deng Pufang. He has been influential in starting a major emphasis on mental health services in the eighth Five-Year Work Program of the government during the 1991–1995 period. However, there is considerable doubt that full implementation will occur (Liberman, 1994: 68; Phillips and Pearson, 1994b: 128, 133).

Diagnostic criteria in mental health are similar to those in the West, as are the psychotropic drugs used for treatment. Chinese psychiatrists and other mental health workers are anxious to learn from the experience of other countries and are quick to apply what they learn (Liberman, 1994: 76).

The larger cities generally have much better mental health facilities than rural provinces. For example, the city of Shanghai (13 million population) has a Mental Health Center affiliated with the World Health Organization that performs several important functions (Hequin and Mingdao, 1990: 82):

- Inpatient and outpatient treatment, consultation, and education
- Training of medical personnel to provide mental health care in counties and townships
- Helping to establish policies and methods for improving and promoting mental health services
- Responsibility for gathering information and maintaining a registry of mental health patients

Comparable activities are performed through district and county psychiatric hospitals in the region around Shanghai. At the village or urban district level, psychiatric outpatient services, work therapy stations or clinics, home care, day hospitals, and rehabilitation centers are available. Much of the volunteer staff are retired workers who serve patients in community settings as part of "guardianship networks." County or district and township hospitals offer some level of psychiatric services, largely by medical practitioners with supplemental training in mental health care. The most chronic patients are cared for at rehabilitation centers. Shanghai is given credit by psychiatry professionals for having the best community mental health program in the country (Hequin and Mingdao, 1990: 82; Pearson, 1992: 168; Zhang, Yan, and Phillips, 1994: 71).

Although 90 percent of diagnosed mentally ill individuals live with their families, confinement in specialized mental hospitals is the primary treatment for severely ill patients. They are housed in large wards staffed by psychiatrists, nurses, and psychologists. Lengthy hospitalization is the rule, until symptoms have been largely eliminated. Rehabilitation activities include occupational therapy, music therapy, behavior therapy, pharmacotherapy, and physical exercise. Heavy emphasis is given to supervised work in the community as the primary means of reintegration after hospitalization. In a few instances, the hospitals have implemented "therapeutic communities" in which respect for the patients' rights is paramount and rehabilitation is emphasized, greatly improving the hospital atmosphere and recovery of patients (Liberman, 1994: 69; Phillips and Pearson, 1994a: 105; 1994b: 137).

Most workers in China have been guaranteed a lifetime job in state-run enterprises. The employing unit has an incentive to keep workers healthy and is usually responsible for paying the cost of physical and mental health care. A job is kept open until the mentally ill individual is able to return. In Nanjing (3.5 million people), for example, several large enterprises operate sheltered workshops (work therapy stations) to rehabilitate mentally ill employees who may have been treated in one of seven psychiatric hospitals in the city. Patients spend an average of about 4 months in the workshops before returning to full-time work. The success rate has been quite high (Luo and Yu, 1994: 89–95).

Work or therapy stations are designed for assistance to mentally handicapped people who need assistance at the local level. Patients are given work tasks to do and receive support in overcoming their disabilities. The stations are managed by a local committee consisting of representatives from the Civic Affairs Department, the Public Health Department, and the Public Security Department. Factories sometimes provide on-the-job mental health care for workers through psychiatric care units operated with the assistance of psychiatric hospitals (Pearson, 1992: 173).

Psychiatric services for nonchronic mental illness have been integrated with primary care medicine and dispersed throughout the country in local clinics and hospitals. In the Yantai region, local doctors are given basic psychiatric training by professional psychiatrists and deliver their services in the commu-

nity through outpatient clinics. They use traditional herbal medicines and acupuncture to supplement treatments. Family members are trained to assist patients, help them take appropriate medication, and report progress to the local doctor or a township psychiatrist. Local police and public officials are involved in supporting the efforts to rehabilitate patients (Liberman, 1994: 68; Phillips and Pearson, 1994a: 104).

Families often attempt to hide the mental illness of a family member. The stigma associated with mental illness is probably more prevalent in China than in Western countries. Considerable effort is therefore required to overcome the stigma when hospitalized patients are returned to their community (Liberman, 1994: 73).

ECONOMIC CHARACTERISTICS AND ISSUES

The World Bank estimated that health care expenditures represented about 4.5 percent of GDP in 1994. National statistics are not released by the government. More recent estimates suggest that actual spending, including military, industrial, construction, and village expenditures, may approach 6.5 percent. Growth in health care costs is a consequence in part of the very rapid overall growth of the Chinese economy, at a rate of 10 percent annually over the past decade, or about 8.7 percent after inflation. Incomes are increasing rapidly, but per capita income in 1994 was estimated at only about $490, making China a relatively poor country by international standards (Liu and Wang, 1991: 112; Lee et al., 1993: 294; *Europa World Yearbook*, 1995).

The World Bank estimated the allocation of funds for health care roughly as indicated in Table 14-3 (Roemer, 1991: 598).

This is a very different distribution of expenditures than in other countries. The hospitalization category excludes personnel salaries, medical equipment, and inpatient

Table 14-3 Estimated Allocation of Health Care Resources

Expenditure	Percentage of Costs
Salaried health personnel	20
Assistant doctors, aides, midwives	4
Hospitalization	13
Medical equipment	5
Modern pharmaceuticals	49
Traditional herbal medicines	9

Source: Based on Roemer, 1991: 598.

pharmaceutical costs. If these items were added, total hospital costs might rise to 35 or 40 percent. The percentage of resources going to pharmaceuticals is even higher in rural areas, estimated at 90 percent of costs. Most of the pharmaceuticals are manufactured in China, and, as noted earlier, are a major source of income to the nation (Roemer, 1991: 603; Chen et al., 1993: 733).

Public health programs provide for prepaid maternal and child health care and immunizations, as well as assistance with family planning. However, many rural residents may not be securing adequate access to such services. The employed urban population continues to be more adequately served. The inequity involved has been a subject of considerable debate and is a significant national policy problem. A system that was considered successful and socially equitable has apparently been transformed to a much less comprehensive and less egalitarian arrangement (Chen et al., 1993: 735).

Financing

National policy requires that each level of government, or each major enterprise, be responsible for financing health care within its domain. Only about 10 percent comes from the national level. The Ministry of Public Health maintains a modest reserve in the National Health Service Fund (NHSF) to assist poorer jurisdictions. The NHSF also supports national level health care activities, such as free medical service for Social Security recipients and the national medical universities (Liu and Wang, 1991: 111).

Medical services funded by national resources are provided for public employees (including university faculty) and college students—without co-payments. However, the services must be secured through health facilities maintained by the employing unit. Dependents are not included (Roemer, 1991: 599).

Administrators and workers in industrial, communication, and other enterprises receive insurance coverage through Labor Medical Services supported by enterprise clinics. A small registration fee is required for each visit. Services secured elsewhere must be privately paid and reimbursement sought from the organization. Dependents are covered for 50 percent of costs (Roemer, 1991: 599).

Despite the various financing schemes, the great majority (71 percent) of the population had to pay for health care out of pocket in 1994. Roughly 81 percent of villagers paid directly for their care, but only about 13 percent of urban residents pay directly because most are covered by one of the methods described earlier. Overall, the proportion of national public subsidy for health care declined from about 30 percent in 1980 to about 19 percent in 1988 as the share of total health spending; private payment increased during the same period from 14 to 36 percent and has continued to increase. The balance is covered by provincial, county, township, and village contributions, which vary considerably between regions (Liu et al., 1994: 168).

The earlier Cooperative Medical System (CMS) has been characterized as an early form of health maintenance organization. This worked relatively well for approximately 90 percent of the rural population until 1979. Since 1980, personal responsibility and private payment have been emphasized instead. By 1990, only 10 percent of the rural population were served by the CMS. An alternative national arrangement has not developed to replace the earlier family supported funding system under the CMS (Chen et al., 1993: 734).

Development of Private Insurance

More affluent regions, such as Shanghai, have begun to create local insurance schemes—usually excluding coverage of drugs. Recent estimates suggest that roughly 30 percent of the villages have developed some level of insurance service financed in part by profits from collective economic activities, village factories, or other traditional sources of village reserves. Villages that have retained the CMS or something comparable appear to have more complete health services with greater access than communities where fee-for-service private practice has become the norm. The Ministry of Public Health has begun to encourage formation of "rural health security systems" to deal with the lack of resources for health care (Liu and Wang, 1991: 112; Xingzhu and Huaijie, 1992: 506; Chen et al., 1993: 731).

The Shanghai Insurance Company was created in 1982 as a profit-making enterprise, and began to provide coverage for rural collective industries. Premiums were privately paid and 70 percent of expenses were covered. Other nonprofit private insurance schemes were initiated in 1985 in Sichuan province with somewhat lower benefits. Focused insurance programs were also initiated to cover infectious diseases in children, maternal and infant care, and surgery. Several other experiments have been conducted to test the value of insurance programs in rural regions where coverage is otherwise very low. Results suggest that insurance is a feasible alternative and within the ability of many rural families and communities to afford. These experiments have been very popular and results are being diffused throughout the country (Cretin et al., 1990: 684; Liu and Wang, 1991: 114).

Recent studies suggest strongly that lack of insurance and higher charges have become a strong deterrent to hospital care because one hospitalization can easily cost an entire year's income for rural families. The barriers do not appear to be as great for ambulatory care, in part because of the low charges by village physicians. The insurance schemes underway may alleviate the financing problem in the more affluent rural areas, but may not work as well in the poorer communities (Xingyuan et al., 1993: 390).

PROBLEMS AND REFORMS

China is clearly undergoing dramatic changes. Rapid economic development and privatization are leading to huge benefits for those with good preparation and an entrepreneurial spirit. But major difficulties have arisen for those unable to cope with the changes. The following problems are noteworthy (Shi, 1993: 479):

- Inadequate insurance coverage and services in rural areas where most of the population reside
- An insufficient supply of health professionals in rural regions
- Uncertain provision for the elderly population as family solidarity and family planning appear to be diminishing the family support capability, with no Social Security support system as an alternative
- Increasing demand for high-quality health services by more affluent citizens
- Severe shortage of modern health care technology.

The World Bank provided China with $100 million to train rural health workers during the 1993 to 1997 period. If this proves effective, rural services could improve substantially (Liu and Wang, 1991: 115; Phillips and Pearson, 1994b: 140).

Although the more affluent citizens want more modern health care, incorporation of health care technology has moved slowly because most is imported at relatively high cost. The capacity to maintain and repair equipment is not yet in place. Consequently, available modern equipment falls into disuse (Becker, 1990: 441).

The change to privatization has several additional potential dangers, often characteristic of market-based health care (Liu et al., 1994: 169; Phillips and Pearson, 1994b: 130):

- Inequality of access to health services
- Less emphasis on preventive care in favor of the more profitable curative care
- Continuing serious cost escalation as private practitioners and hospitals strive to make a profit
- Higher proportions of health care providers in pursuit of higher incomes are locating in more affluent urban areas with greater population density and near higher-technology hospitals. As in Western nations, most will avoid dispersed and lower-income rural areas because achievement of personal and professional goals is more difficult
- Decreased government subsidies to hospitals means that institutions must survive on fees and high-revenue services
- Increased regional inequities; poorer regions will be less prepared to self-finance services
- Potential decline in quality of care, because of lowered or insufficient government regulation
- Mentally and physically disabled individuals may suffer loss of services and support

Market-based health care has the potential to fill some of the gaps in the current system as trained providers congregate in more populated and affluent rural and urban areas. Increased competition from trained physicians will replace poorly trained traditional providers, providing potential for better-quality service to patients and increased application of technology. However, lower-income citizens, the elderly, and the chronically ill with mental or physical disabilities will be at a severe disadvantage. If fee for service is the norm, only those with insurance and higher incomes will benefit (Liu et al., 1994: 172; Phillips and Pearson, 1994b: 131).

The World Bank in a 1992 report offered a series of recommendations, based on experience elsewhere, suggesting appropriate measures to deal with privatization and shortage of public resources:

- Greater emphasis on primary care
- Decreased hospitalization

- Improvement in quality of personnel
- More focus on cost effectiveness
- Greater quality of health care management

The report warns that cost increases at the rate evident in the early 1990s could seriously destabilize the health care system and seriously disrupt equity of health care. Health professionals and the Ministry of Health generally support these goals and are moving forward with implementation (Phillips and Pearson, 1994b: 130).

SUMMARY AND CONCLUSIONS

As the most populous nation in the world, the manner in which China meets health care needs is of great interest. The vast majority of the population (estimated at 80 percent) resides in rural regions. A system for providing basic health care was developed in the 1960s, with major responsibility given to village leaders and so-called "barefoot doctors" who were minimally trained to promote good health practices and serve community needs. This approach lost favor and has been largely dismantled, to be partially replaced by modern medical practitioners.

China has clearly made great strides in raising health care standards, diminishing infant mortality, increasing longevity, and professionalizing health care. The free market has been allowed to flourish. Health care and other social services have been greatly decentralized and have become the responsibility of provinces, counties, municipalities, townships, villages, and economic enterprises.

Health care has shifted heavily toward the Western scientific model in which nearly all physicians are now trained in modern medical schools, although with varying levels of knowledge and skill. Traditional medicine has been retained and is widely practiced throughout the country, often mixed with modern medicine. Traditional and modern pharmaceuticals absorb a very high proportion of health care resources (near 50 per-

cent) and represent a major economic enterprise supporting domestic consumption and
export to eighty countries.

Health care in rural areas has moved
quickly toward a private enterprise fee-for-service approach. Urban residents are largely
provided with health services through their
places of work, but even here private practitioners are active. Although the country has
never had a centralized national health service of the type common in other communist
countries, the government took an active role
in supporting public health efforts. The central government continues to support health
promotion but no longer provides significant
national financing or insurance protection
for the great majority of the population not
directly employed in government service.

The shift from government ownership and
management of economic enterprises to
greater emphasis on private enterprise is
thus having a profound effect on health care.
Private health insurance schemes are being
organized throughout the country. Physicians are encouraged to enter private fee-for-
service practice. As a consequence of these
changes, there appears to be some reduction
in the comprehensiveness of public health
and prevention activities, but no published
evidence indicates that health status has suffered greatly. It is possible that enterprising
providers and community health leaders can
reconstruct a relatively comprehensive and
universal private health care system.

REFERENCES

BECKER, SHERRI LZES (1990). Critical Care in China, *Focus on Critical Care—AACN*, 17 (6): 440–444.

BRAND, IAN (1992). Problems of Hospital Management in China, *Australian Health Review*, 15 (1): 101–105.

BRAND, IAN, and LIU JUNTIAN (1992). The Beijing Health Administrative Staff Training Center, *Australian Health Review*, 15 (1): 105–106.

BUTLER, WILLIAM T., and STEVEN J. RUMA (1990). China's Quest for Management of Academic Medicine, *Academic Medicine*, 65 (8): 497–501.

BUXIONG, WANG (1990). The Basic Knowledge Indispensable for a Qualified Acupuncture Doctor, *Journal of Traditional Chinese Medicine*, 10 (1): 6–8.

CAI, WEI MIN, HENG SHAN TAN, SHU SEN LING, and MARY H. H. CHANDLER (1994). Clinical Pharmacy Practice in Urban China, *American Journal of Hospital Pharmacy*, 51 (5): 695–696.

CHEN, XIA-MING, TEH-WEI HU, and ZIHUA LIN (1993). The Rise and Decline of the Cooperative Medical System in China, *International Journal of Health Services*, 23 (4): 731–742.

CHUNG-TUNG, LIU (1991). From San Gu Liu Po to "Caring Scholar": The Chinese Nurse in Perspective, *International Journal of Nursing Studies*, 28 (4): 315–324.

COCKERHAM, WILLIAM C. (1995). *Medical Sociology*, 6th ed. Englewood Cliffs, N.J.: Prentice Hall.

CRETIN, SHAN, NAIHUA DUAN, ALBERT P. WILLIAMS, JR., XINGYUAN GU, and YUANQIU SHI (1990). Modeling the Effect of Insurance on Health Expenditures in the People's Republic of China, *Health Services Research*, 25 (4): 667–685.

DE-XIAN, CAO (1990). Medical Informatics in China, *Chinese Medical Journal*, 103 (2): 95–100.

DING, Z. (1990). The Development of Prehospital Emergency Medical Services (PEMS) in China, *Archives of Emergency Medicine*, 7 (2): 61–64.

Europa World Yearbook 1995 (1995). London: Europa Publications, Ltd.

FOX, STEVEN (1994). Blue Cross Over China? A Glimpse at Health Care Financing Reform in the Countryside, *China Exchange News*, 22 (2): 1–4.

GAY, JANICE TEMPLETON, JUANZETTA SHEW FLOWERS, and KUEI-SHEN TU (1990). Women's Health Care in China: An American Travelers' View, *Health Care for Women International*, 11 (1): 65–74.

GUPTA, S. (1991). Child Health and Care Services in China, *Indian Pediatrics*, 28 (12): 1509–1512.

HEQUIN, YAN, and ZHANG MINGDAO (1990). Mental Health Services in Shanghai, *Hospital and Community Psychiatry*, 41 (1): 81–83.

HU, TEH-WEI, (1984). Health Services in the People's Republic of China, in Marshall W. Raffel (ed.), *Comparative Health Systems*. University Park: Pennsylvania State University Press.

HU, TEH-WEI, and YING-YING MENG (1991). Medical Technology Transfer in Major Chinese Medical Schools, *International Journal of Technology Assessment in Health Care*, 7 (4): 553–560.

JIA-ZHEN, HUA (1994). Current Status of Maternal Health Care in China, *Chinese Medical Journal*, 107 (5): 388–390.

JUNSHI, C., T. C. CAMPBELL, L. JUAYAO, and R. PETO (1990). *Diet, Life-Style, and Mortality in China: A Study of the Characteristics of 65 Chinese Counties*. Ithaca, N.Y.: Cornell University Press.

LEE, M.-C., E. Y. T. YEN, and M.-C. CHOU (1993). The Development of General Practice in China, *Family Practice—An International Journal*, 10 (3): 292–299.

LIBERMAN, ROBERT PAUL (1994). Treatment and Rehabilitation of the Seriously Mentally Ill in China: Impressions of a Society in Transition, *American Journal of Orthopsychiatry*, 64 (1): 68–77.

LIU, GORDON, XINGSZHU LIU, and QINGYUE MENG (1994). Privatization of the Medical Market in Socialist China: A Historical Approach, *Health Policy*, 27: 157–174.

LIU, XINGZU, and JUNLE WANG (1991). An Introduction to China's Health Care System, *Journal of Public Health Policy*, 126 (2): 104–116.

LUO, KAILIN, and DONGSHAN YU (1994). Enterprise-Based Sheltered Workshops in Nanjing, *British Journal of Psychiatry*, 165 (Sup. 24): 89–95.

MORALES-MANN, ERLINDA T., and SHU LIN JIANG (1993). Applicability of Orem's Conceptual Framework: A Cross-Cultural Point of View, *Journal of Advanced Nursing*, 18 (5): 737–741.

MOSCOVICH, LIANNE (1991). First and Lasting Impressions During a Visit to a Chinese Hospital, *Canadian Journal of Infection Control*, 6 (4): 95–96.

PEARSON, VERONICA (1992). Community and Culture: A Chinese Model of Community Care for the Mentally Ill, *International Journal of Social Psychiatry*, 38 (3): 163–178.

PHILLIPS, MICHAEL R., and VERONICA PEARSON (1994a). Rehabilitation Interventions in Rural Communities, *British Journal of Psychiatry*, 165 (Sup. 24): 103–106.

PHILLIPS, MICHAEL R., and VERONICA PEARSON (1994b). Future Opportunities and Challenges for the Development of Psychiatric Rehabilitation in China, *British Journal of Psychiatry*, 165 (Sup. 24): 128–142.

RICHMOND, CAROLINE (1991). China Is Now Moving Towards the Western Way of Death, *Canadian Medical Association Journal*, 145 (6): 707–708.

ROEMER, MILTON (1991). *National Health Systems of the World: The Countries*, Vol. I. New York: Oxford University Press.

ROSENTHAL, MARILYNN M. (1992). Modernization and Health Care in the People's Republic of China: The Period of Transition, in Marilynn M. Rosenthal and Marcel Frenkel (eds.), *Health Care Systems and Their Patients: An International Perspective*. Boulder, Col.: Westview Press, pp. 293–315.

SHI, LEIYU (1993a). Family Financial and Household Support Exchange Between Generations: A Survey of Chinese Rural Elderly, *The Gerontologist*, 33 (4): 468–480.

SHI, LEIYU (1993b). Health Care in China: A Rural-Urban Comparison After the Reforms, *Bulletin of the World Health Organization*, 71 (6): 723–736.

SIDEL, VICTOR W. (1993). New Lessons from China: Equity and Economics in Rural Health Care, *American Journal of Public Health*, 83 (12): 1665–1666.

SLOMAN, GRAEME (1990). Prevention and Treatment of Heart Disease in China, *Medical Journal of Australia*, 153 (5): 289–290.

STILLMAN, PAULA L., and WILLIAM D. SAWYER (1992). A New Program to Enhance the Teaching and Assessment of Clinical Skills in the People's Republic of China, *Academic Medicine*, 67 (8): 495–499.

TU, MINGHUA, XIULONG XIA, and TSUNG O. CHENG (1994). One Three-Year Medical School in China: A Reform in Chinese Medical Education, *Academic Medicine*, 69 (5): 346–348.

UMLAND, BERTHOLD, ROBERT WATERMAN, WILLIAM WIESE, STEWARD DUBAN, STEWART MENNIN, and ARTHUR KAUFMAN (1992). Learning from a Rural Physician Program in China, *Academic Medicine*, 67 (5): 307–309.

VARTIAINEN, ERKKI, DU DIANJUN, JAMES S. MARKS, HEIKKI KORHONEN, GENG GUANYI, GUO ZE-YU, JEFFREY P. KOPLAN, PIRJO PIETINEN, WE GUANG-LIN, DAVID WILLIAMSON, and AULIKKI NISSINEN (1991). Mortality, Cardiovascular Risk Factors, and Diet in China, Finland, and the United States, *Public Health Reports*, 106 (1): 41–46.

WANG, CUN (1993). The Important Role of International Exchange in the Development of Medical Informatics in Developing Countries: A Report from China, *Medical Informatics*, 18 (1): 1–10.

WEISS, GREGORY L., and LYNNE E. LONNQUIST (1994). *The Sociology of Health, Healing, and Illness*. Englewood Cliffs, N.J.: Prentice Hall.

XIANGDONG, MENG, and ROBERT W. BLUM (1990). School Health Services in the People's Republic of China, *Journal of School Health*, 60 (10): 483–486.

XINGYUAN, GU, GERALD BLOOM, TANG SHENGLAN, ZHU YINGYA, ZHOU SHOUQI, and CHEN XINGBAO (1993). Financing Health Care in Rural China: Preliminary Report of a Nationwide Study, *Social Science and Medicine*, 36 (4): 385–391.

XINGZHU, LIU, and CAO HUAIJIE (1992). China's Cooperative Medical System: Its Historical Transformations and the Trend of Development, *Journal of Public Health Policy*, 13 (4): 501–511.

YANG, YAOFANG, and LONGLU ZHANG (1991). Feasibility of Problem-Based Learning in Jiujiang Medical College: Why Not Try It?, *Medical Education*, 25: 34–37.

ZHANG, MINGYUAN, HEQIN YAN, and MICHAEL R. PHILLIPS (1994). Community-Based Psychiatric Rehabilitation in Shanghai, *British Journal of Psychiatry*, 165 (Supp. 24): 70–79.

ZHI-KUAN, ZHANG (1994). A Major Reform in Hospital Management System in China: Grading and Assessment, *Chinese Medical Journal*, 107 (4): 243–247.

15

MEXICO

Modernizing Structure and Expanded Rural Services

Mexico

- ✪ National Capital
- Leon ● City
- Internaional Boundary
- State (estado) Boundary
- *Jalisco* State (estado) Name

0 ————— Miles ————— 300

Key to states in
central Mexico

1 Aguascalientes
2 Guanajuato
3 Queretaro
4 Hidalgo
5 Mexico
6 Distrito Federal
7 Morelos
8 Tlaxcala

Mexico is a nation of profound contrasts. Parts of major cities are as modern as anywhere in the world, whereas some rural regions and smaller cities are very traditional. Many rural communities are inhabited largely by Indians who follow native cultural practices. Industrialized centers are usually surrounded by relatively poor neighborhoods consisting largely of migrants from rural communities (Frenk, 1990: 70).

Rural poverty has contributed to migration to the cities in recent decades. This process has drawn many of the better-educated younger people from the villages and has placed major population pressures on urban centers. Mexico City has become the largest metropolitan area in the world (Frenk, 1987: 23).

Health care in larger Mexican cities is readily accessible and relatively modern but is less well developed in lower-income urban areas and rural regions. Nonetheless, advancements in the 1970s and 1980s were sufficient to provide health care facilities in 71 percent of the small communities of less than 2,500 population. Many are served by temporary physicians who are performing 1 year of required rural service after medical school. Other physicians go to rural locations because they cannot find work in the cities; in 1990 more than 25 percent of physicians in major cities were either unemployed or underemployed (Frenk, 1990: 69; Roemer, 1991: 345; Sherraden, 1995: 122). Special features of Mexican health care are summarized in Table 15-1.

DEMOGRAPHIC CHARACTERISTICS

Mexico has a rapidly growing and relatively young population of about 90 million (in 1993), which is about 60 percent urban and 40 percent rural. Population growth has been rapid, making it difficult for education and social services to increase quickly enough to meet demand. Nonetheless, economic growth and modernization have raised incomes and produced a sizable mid-

Table 15-1 Characteristics of Mexican Health Care

- The federal Social Security system operates one relatively high-quality health care system for private enterprise and government employees, and the Ministry of Health operates a second lower-quality system for other citizens.
- A somewhat segregated three-track pattern of funding exists, with
  (1) private insurance or private pay for the relatively affluent (roughly 3.6 million people)
  (2) Social Security programs with high access and quality for urban workers, civil servants, and professionals (roughly 48 million)
  (3) Ministry of Health programs providing lower access and quality, with less funding, for the self-employed or small enterprises—in urban and rural communities (roughly 29 million)
- Well-trained physicians and high-technology medical facilities are concentrated in the national and state capital cities and regional centers, whereas smaller cities and villages have access to less prepared providers and much less technology.
- Physicians do not have a powerful national organization to represent their interests and generally have modest influence on the health care system.
- Improvement in longevity, infant mortality, and primary health services has been significant since 1970.

dle class in most large cities (Sherraden, 1995: 123).

Mortality rates have continuously declined in the last 50 years; life expectancy increased from 37 years in 1930 to 70 in 1991 (66 for males and 72.1 for females). Infant mortality dropped from 80 per 1,000 in 1965 to 35 in 1991. However, improvements have been much more significant in urban areas than in rural regions or slums of large cities (Frenk, 1990: 144; Cockerham, 1995: 329).

Approximately 95,400 villages have fewer than 2,500 people each, often in relatively isolated regions with minimal transportation and other infrastructure. Rural Mexican children under five are twice as likely to be malnourished as urban children. Potable water remains unavailable in many communities, although this situation has improved substantially in the 1970s and 1980s (Stebbins, 1986: 112).

The prevalence of health problems has shifted from a high incidence of infectious disease in the 1960s to a rapid increase in chronic diseases in the 1980s—as longevity increases and the population ages. For example, the leading causes of mortality in 1963 were influenza, pneumonia, childhood diseases, and diarrhea. By 1980, these had been replaced by heart disease, cancer, and accidents (Soberon, Frenk, and Sepulveda, 1986: 674).

HISTORICAL PERSPECTIVE

The first record of medical education was in 1587 under the leadership of medical missionaries. The first formal medical school was founded in 1790. Modern health care developed very slowly, however, until the twentieth century when Mexico's emergence as an industrial nation began (Frenk, 1987: 20; 1990: 145).

The Revolutionary Period: 1910–1941

The Mexican constitution of 1917 was a product of a major social revolution beginning in 1910 and established federal responsibility for health care. The revolution resulted in major land redistribution and the creation of rural *ejidos* or land-owning communities—which had formerly been part of large private estates (*latifundias*). Rural Cooperative Medical Services were initiated in many *ejidos* staffed primarily by minimally trained health aides (Roemer, 1991: 345).

A further social revolution was initiated in the mid-1930s under President Lazaro Cardenas; the government took over many industries, including petroleum and railroads, which had been under foreign ownership. This precipitated the evolution of *Servicio Social*, a mandatory 1-year period of service by physicians in rural communities which continues to the present (Sherraden, 1995: 126).

National Insurance and New Delivery Programs: 1942–1972

New medical services were initially designed to serve workers in the new government enterprises. A 1942 law established the Institute of Social Security as the responsible federal agency. The state and federal governments established relatively modern health centers and hospitals in many parts of the country. All salaried workers in private industries around Mexico's urban centers were covered by Social Security health insurance. The self-employed, small-business employees, domestic workers, and part-time employees were excluded (Roemer, 1991: 346).

Salaried agricultural workers were added in 1954, but the vast majority of small farmers and indigenous Indians were not. A law enacted in 1960 added Social Security coverage for all government employees, but under a different Social Security administrative structure and with more generous benefits. The armed forces and Pemex, the national petroleum monopoly, were also added. Approximately, 45 percent of the population was eventually covered by these programs. Thus by 1973 most urban workers in the private sector had been added to the system (Roemer, 1991: 346; Cockerham, 1995: 328).

Oversupply of Physicians and Expansion of Health Care: 1973–1981

Social Solidarity was created in 1973 as a consolidation of rural health programs. It was the precursor for IMSS (Mexican Social Security Institute) Solidarity, which greatly expanded rural services in the 1970s and 1980s (Sherraden, 1995: 130).

The supply of health professionals also expanded rapidly after 1973, as did the population. Student strikes, to which the government acquiesced, led to an open-enrollment policy for medical students. Enrollment nearly doubled in a single year. Eighteen new medical schools were established in as many states during the next 5 years; 59 institutions had been created by 1982—considerably more than were needed. Enrollment reached 93,365 in 1980. Quality varied widely and led to very mixed results for graduates. Only one in four graduates was able to find immediate employment. Despite the surplus of physicians in urban areas, rural communities continued to have difficulty recruiting a sufficient number of practitioners (Frenk, 1987: 21; 1990: 78).

Partially in response to the World Health Organization's declaration of 1977, "Health For All by the Year 2000," the health care system gained another acronym in 1977, COPLAMAR (General Coordination of the Plan for Depressed Zones and Marginal Groups), a special program created by President Lopez Portillo for rural development. The IMSS was made responsible for extending rural health programs to a wider group of rural people. The program was given relatively few resources, but did a careful job of documenting the problems and issues. Oil exports led to a high level of government revenues, which meant the addition of a wide range of other services, including pensions, day-care centers for working mothers, and community recreation facilities for families (Sherraden, 1995: 132).

Primary health care was emphasized as a means of increasing access to all members of the population. More than 3,000 rural medical centers and 61 hospitals were established in a 4-year period after 1979, enhancing service to some 11 million people. More than 250 urban health centers were added to serve another 4 million. The COPLAMAR program was thus a widespread rural development project including food subsidies, new schools, water systems, roads, and home improvements, as well as health care (Frenk, 1990: 79; Roemer, 1991: 346; Sherraden, 1991: 257).

Participation in preventive health care was one of the requirements for recipients of these new health services. This could include involvement in immunization efforts, construction of family latrines, construction of floors in houses, pest eradication, and health education. Community leaders were required to participate in organized health care plan-

ning. Apparently, this requirement met with considerable success in many communities, although the requirement was relaxed if local leaders and citizens strongly resisted; health care was not denied to communities that failed to undertake voluntary preventive activities (Sherraden, 1991: 258).

The new rural facilities were often staffed only by *pasantes*, the new medical graduates required under *Servicio Social* to fulfill 1 year of service. However, the growth of population made it difficult to meet needs in all regions of the country (Roemer, 1991: 346).

Economic Crisis and Health Care Reform: 1982 Onward

A catastrophe struck public services when world oil prices collapsed in 1982, leading to a major crisis. The peso was devalued by 600 percent and the country was unable to meet foreign debt payments.

The inadequacy of services was examined by a commission appointed in 1980. The report, *Toward a National Health System,* included a series of recommendations to reform the system. This led to a constitutional amendment making protection of health a "social right." A General Health Law of 1984 assigned major reform responsibilities to the new Ministry of Health. Primary goals were to conduct strategic planning, implement and finance health-related research and development, improve financial management, and develop quality of care standards. The Ministry was also to have close involvement in national health insurance programs (Soberon et al., 1986: 675).

Other goals of the 1984 law were to assure that (1) services were decentralized; (2) administration was modernized; (3) communities were involved in planning services; and (4) integration of the various administrative units was initiated. The federal health budget allocated to the states increased from 40 percent in 1982 to 63 percent in 1986; the states increased allocations to health care by 250 percent. However, the Social Security part of health care remained independent of Ministry control (Soberon et al., 1986: 675; Roemer, 1991: 347).

A further disaster occurred in 1985 when a major earthquake hit Mexico City and surrounding areas, severely damaging or destroying many health care facilities. The area near the epicenter contained the largest concentration of secondary and tertiary care facilities in the country. More than 4,000 hospital beds were destroyed and some 900 patients, physicians, nurses, students, and other health care workers were killed (Soberon et al., 1986: 673–677).

This could have easily led to a major cutback in resources for health care. However, the government decided to continue emphasis on primary care and social services reform as the most important government priority. Health services were considered a highly important element in developing a more egalitarian society. The foundation had thus been laid for a more universal, coordinated, and accessible health care system. As of 1985, the effort to better serve rural citizens had resulted in a network of 3,246 new rural clinics and a substantial increase in the number of rural hospitals. More than 13 million additional citizens had access to basic primary care services. Special emphasis was given to indigenous and peasant communities. Health services were aimed particularly at preventing or treating respiratory, gastrointestinal, and parasitic infections characteristic of impoverished rural communities. Emphasis was also given to expansion of general family medicine, provision of maternal and child health care, immunization against contagious diseases, control of chronic and degenerative diseases, and family planning (Sherraden and Wallace, 1992: 1433).

Beginning in 1988, President Salinas de Gortari personally emphasized health and traveled the country encouraging new programs. IMSS-COPLAMAR was converted to IMSS Solidaridad as a symbol of government commitment to the people. Between 1989 and 1992, 1,000 primary care clinics and

seven new regional hospitals were constructed, (Frenk, 1990: 155–156).

A surplus of physicians continued and a decision was made to begin lowering access to specialized medical school training. At about the same time, an effort was undertaken (in the late 1980s) to create greater equivalence in services and salaries of physicians and other professionals serving in each segment of the health care system (Soberon et al., 1986: 673–675; Frenk, 1990: 155–156).

The health care system has thus advanced considerably, despite the obstructions of economic problems and natural disasters. Nonetheless, the poorest communities, especially in the southern states of the country, remain underserved.

CULTURAL FACTORS

The culture has a rich and distinctive artistic and architectural heritage that blends indigenous and European traditions and values. A Roman Catholic religious orientation predominates.

Historically, leaders of the middle and upper classes have not demonstrated great concern about the well-being of the indigenous populations. Traditional *curanderos* (healers) are widely accessible and are the primary source of health advice for many native villagers (Stebbins, 1986: 112–114; Hunt, 1994: 844).

A fatalistic belief system is based in part on a religious viewpoint that accepts unavoidable suffering and death. The political system is viewed as corrupt and disinterested in serving the public, and therefore not helpful. This means that consumer criticism of the health care system is most often limited if not absent (Ponce de Leon and Ponce de Leon, 1993: 49).

POLITICAL INFLUENCES

Mexico has been governed by a single political party (PRI, or the Institutional Revolutionary Party) since the 1930s after the presidency of Cardenas. The party is dominated by urban labor and elite interests. Although efforts at greater democratization have been underway, particularly at the state level during the 1980s and early 1990s, the health care system and the Institute of Social Security have been closely identified with the PRI as a political entity and have to some extent been instruments of government policy. Polarization against government has led to open rebellion of large groups of citizens in the southern state of Chiapas amid great unhappiness with the central government in other regions of the country (Frenk, 1990: 148).

Although there are thirty-one states (plus the Federal District of Mexico City), the national government has generally maintained relatively centralized control over most public services. Health officers responsible for services in each state are appointed at the federal level and are responsible directly to the Minister of Health. Each state has an elected governor and legislature, both of which have limited health care responsibilities. Each state is further divided into regions, averaging eight major subdivisions per state. Each jurisdiction has a health officer appointed by state health officials. Physicians with public health training usually occupy these positions on a part-time basis. Local jurisdictions are further divided into municipalities or rural villages served by one or more health centers (Roemer, 1991: 347).

The centralized political structure has generally meant that very little meaningful participation in health care planning or management occurs at the local level, despite decentralization attempts in the 1980s. Local participation is verbally encouraged by the government, but there appears to be relatively little room for real innovation or initiative (Frenk and Gonzalez-Block, 1992: 35).

SOCIAL ORGANIZATION OF HEALTH CARE

The federal Ministry of Health has overall responsibility as the organizing enterprise for Mexico City and the thirty-one states. The Ministry directs health planning, health promotion, development of quality of care standards, and finances health-related research. It also has close involvement in one of the major government insurance programs. However, the Social Security part of health care is in a separate Ministry and remains somewhat independent of Ministry of Health control (Roemer, 1991: 348).

Several coordinating mechanisms have been developed to increase integration of the various health care provider organizations. A centralized program for purchase and dispensing of drugs was created as an efficiency measure. Councils for Health Coordination have been initiated at the state level to coordinate health care provision and health professional education programs. Twelve state health departments were selected for an experimental decentralization effort and have assumed increasing responsibility for health care, with relatively close federal supervision and funding through the Ministry of Health. Service delivery, staffing, and facility design are standardized, and generally must operate according to national guidelines (Roemer, 1991: 348–349; Sherraden and Wallace, 1992: 1438).

Public Health

A concerted national effort has been undertaken to promote health and prevent disease, through public nutrition programs, water system development, sewage control, and other systematic efforts. A program of infectious disease control has been underway for many years under federal auspices, as noted earlier. Tuberculosis control, cancer detection, diarrhea control, and other such measures have been undertaken. This responsibility has been delegated to the state level in the twelve states targeted for decentralization (Roemer, 1991: 348; Cockerham, 1995: 329).

Restaurant and food inspections, water supply sanitation, and other basic sanitary regulations fall within the Ministry of Health responsibilities. The Ministry of Urban Ecology has responsibility for solid waste management (Roemer, 1991: 350).

Physicians

Primary care is provided through four principal organizational mechanisms (Frenk, 1990: 145):

1. Private fee-for-service practitioners
2. Social Security system clinics
3. Federal clinics
4. National specialized institutes

Private practice serves only a small segment of the more privileged population (5 to 7 percent), but absorbs a high proportion of health resources. Payments are made largely out of pocket, because private medical insurance is not widely available. Social Security clinics serve those insured through that system (about 47 percent). Federal clinics under the Ministry of Health operate outreach programs for low-income citizens in urban and rural areas who are not covered by the Social Security system (about 45 percent of the population). In addition, ten National Institutes of Health units within the Ministry are responsible for research and development in health care but also provide direct tertiary health services to the noninsured population. The primary health system is thus segregated based on income, occupation, and location (Frenk, 1990: 146; Cockerham, 1995: 328).

Most physicians employed in public health administrative activities also engage in private practice on a part-time basis. The extent of this practice is difficult to measure because careful records of physician activity are not kept by the federal government or physician organizations. It is not entirely clear how many physicians are in active practice or are administrators of health programs (Roemer, 1991: 348).

Community health centers. Local health centers are usually staffed by a physician, one or more nurses, other allied health professionals, and clerical support personnel. Indigenous health workers are trained as assistants to administer injections of various kinds, provide first aid, and perform other needed tasks. Outreach workers are trained to provide rudimentary services in the communities and organize preventive health projects. A pharmacy is often located on the premises to dispense drugs. Clinic staff attempt to develop working relationships with traditional practitioners such as *curanderos*, midwives, and herbalists. In addition, special health centers in the community, usually staffed by one or more nurses, provide preventive services for mothers and children (Roemer, 1991: 347; Sherraden and Wallace, 1992: 1435).

Physicians have gone to rural regions in considerable numbers, but rewards are not sufficient to keep them there. Most serve their required time and return to the city. This applies as well to trained nurses and other paraprofessionals (Sherraden and Wallace, 1992: 1440).

Physician organization. Physicians in Mexico do not have a powerful national organization to represent their specific interests. An organizational effort in the 1960s led to an Alliance of Mexican Physicians, which threatened strikes to secure higher pay. The government refused to negotiate with the group and eventually repressed the movement and its leaders. This has been a major political disadvantage for physicians who must now express their interests though unions of health workers that include the full range of health professions. Health care professionals are largely dominated by the Ministry of Health and the PRI political organization (Frenk, 1990: 150).

Medical education. Mexico had fifty-nine medical schools in 1982 as noted earlier. The number was down to 28 by 1993 as a consequence of resource shortages, physician surplus, and poor quality of many institutions. The primary emphasis has been on training of specialists, with relatively little attention to family practice. Although primary health care has been emphasized in the national programs described earlier, medical education has not changed accordingly (Irigoyen-Coria and Gomez-Clavelina, 1994: 162).

A survey undertaken in 1986 indicated a physician underemployment rate of 22 percent and an unemployment level of 7 percent in urban areas. Underemployment refers to the situation in which trained physicians work at tasks such as nursing care or administrative roles that are well below their level of training. This was particularly a problem for graduates of the less prestigious medical schools, for whom the underemployment rate was 47 percent. Primary care physicians tend to be unemployed or underemployed at a higher rate than specialists, despite rural shortages (Frenk, 1985: 321; 1990: 149; Roemer, 1991: 349).

Medical school training is based on modern concepts imported from the United States and Western Europe. Students generally complete 4 years of course work and clinical training and 1 year of hospital internship, followed by 1 year of "social service" in public clinics. These young physicians often do not have access to a level of modern technology to fully implement procedures learned in their training. This is especially a problem in the more remote and less modern cities and communities. Because students are trained largely for specialized, scientific, and hospital-based medicine, they also have trouble adapting to the primary care needs of rural communities (Frenk, 1990: 150; Frenk et al., 1991: 26; Hunt, 1994: 843).

Residency opportunities are relatively limited. Specialized residency training is therefore not possible for many new graduates. The competition is intense for the available slots each year. Entry of new students has been restricted since 1983 when there were 14,100 graduates—far more than needed to fill the open positions. The limitations are based on the recommendations of an Inter-Institutional Commission for Education and

Health (involving the Ministries of Health and Education and medical school administrators). The Commission is responsible for coordination of education for all health professionals, and also coordinates allocation of research-and-development resources for pharmaceuticals, medical equipment, and other medical technology (Frenk, 1987: 21; 1990: 150).

Women have been entering medicine at an increasing rate. Female physicians also tend to be unemployed or underemployed at a much higher rate than men. Most are family practitioners, whereas men dominate the specialties (Frenk et al., 1991: 27–28).

Training for physicians in public health administration has been provided at some level since 1922, through programs now supported by the Ministry of Health. Five university schools of public health have been established in outlying states, primarily to train physicians responsible for federal, state, and local public health programs (Roemer, 1991: 348).

Traditional Medicine and Midwives

A study by the Social Security Institute in 1984 indicated there were four times more traditional healers in rural areas than there were physicians. Roughly 40 percent of them were midwives who delivered most babies. Midwifery is quite diverse, with five general types (Bortin, 1993: 170):

1. Untrained traditional village woman with ancestral roots and on-the-job learning
2. Untrained urban midwife, who responds to requests in communities surrounding large cities
3. Trained, with 2 to 4 weeks of formal instruction
4. Foreign-trained
5. Fully trained nurse-midwives

By far the largest number fall in the first category. They are part of the local community and culture. Trained midwives, on the other hand, are more likely to use modern medical practices. Estimates in 1987 suggested that 80 percent of all births in Mexico are under the care of the first three classifications. Foreign-trained and nurse-midwives have more advanced preparation but are less likely to work in traditional communities (Bortin, 1993: 171).

Traditional healers generally subscribe to the "hot-cold" or *naturaleza* (nature–based) concept, which defines all health conditions as either hot or cold. Pregnancy is viewed as a "hot" condition, which reverts to "cold" after birth. Traditional baths and massage are used for therapy. Herbal treatments are also common.

The health care system is attempting to incorporate the traditional healers in appropriate roles. Additional training is available to traditional midwives. Despite the inadequacies of both traditional *curanderos* and midwifery, these practitioners fill health care gaps in rural communities that modern medicine does not yet satisfy. They play a much larger role in Mexico than in most other countries (Bortin, 1993: 177).

Hospitals

The early hospitals in Mexico were operated by the Roman Catholic church as charity institutions (*beneficiencias*). After the revolution of 1910, most were taken over by the government. Some became teaching facilities for medical schools. They were originally intended to serve the poor and indigent; many continue to fulfill that role (Roemer, 1975: 93).

Social Security hospitals are much more modern and provide higher-quality care than public hospitals serving the uninsured and indigent population. Physicians are handicapped in the poorer facilities because patients cannot afford the treatments or medications that may be most appropriate for their condition (Hunt, 1994: 847).

The larger government hospitals are generally distributed in each state to serve a population of about 100,000, although the most advanced and high-technology institutions are located only in the very largest cities.

Staffing usually includes four basic specialties: internal medicine, surgery, obstetrics/gynecology, and pediatrics (as well as general practice). States usually have immediate management responsibility under the general oversight of the Ministry of Health (Roemer, 1991: 348).

Occupancy rates of hospitals are generally less than 50 percent, indicating a surplus of hospital beds. On the other hand, in areas of health services shortages, such as border areas with the United States, public hospital occupancy may approach 100 percent. In these locations, physicians are also often in short supply and overworked. Facilities serving the low-income population at little or no charge are the busiest, notably in the border city of Juarez (Roberts, 1991: 12; Roemer, 1991: 350).

The Ministry of Health has recently assumed responsibility for all medical emergency services. Municipal governments of larger cities have generally operated their own ambulances and emergency clinics (Roemer, 1991: 350).

Medical technology is fully available in the most modern hospitals of the larger cities and in regional medical centers in most states. This includes advanced imaging, intensive care, and the latest surgical equipment. However, smaller cities and rural communities have access to only minimal technology. Some advanced medical technology has been provided by U.S. companies with investments in Mexico. For example, imaging technology in several industrial locations has been financed and donated to hospitals through collaborative efforts between U.S. and Mexican companies (Burns, 1993: 8).

ECONOMIC CHARACTERISTICS AND ISSUES

Mexico continues to be categorized as a "developing nation" by the United Nations because of the relatively low per capita income ($3,750 in 1993) and modest overall level of economic development, despite major progress in recent decades. Approximately 6 percent of GDP was spent for health care in 1990, although this declined to 4 percent by 1994—still a significantly greater investment than in earlier years (Irigoyen-Coria and Gomez-Clavelina, 1994: 163; Cockerham, 1995: 329).

The economy is the thirteenth largest in the world and improved steadily between 1910 and 1973. After a brief interlude until 1976, rapid growth resumed until 1982 when another setback occurred, as noted earlier. Once again recovery proceeded until the currency collapse in 1994. The setbacks in each case led to cutbacks in resources available for health care as well as other services—although deliberate government policy allowed funds for the Social Security system and medical education to continue increasing (Frenk, 1990: 144–150; Roemer, 1991: 351).

The Financing System

Roughly 47 percent of the population is covered by the two major government insurance schemes: Social Security and the Institute for Government Workers. The remaining 53 percent have access only through Ministry of Health programs or through private payment. About 21 percent secure some form of public care under Health and Welfare programs; another 15 percent are served by the "marginal families program" or other programs for low-income people. About 7 percent pay directly for private care. Approximately 12 percent are without any form of direct access to regularly available modern medical care, although Ministry of Health programs are supposed to serve them. It should be noted that estimates of coverage vary considerably depending on the source and timing of data (Cockerham, 1995: 328). The various sources of health care financing are summarized in Table 15-2 (Roemer, 1991: 346).

The Institute for Social Security program is by far the most adequately funded, absorb-

Table 15-2 Major Sources of Health Care Financing

Program	Approximate Percentage of Population Covered
Institute of Social Security	39
Institute for Government Workers	8
Health and Welfare Secretariat	21
Marginal Families Program	15
Other federal programs	2
Private insurance or private pay	7
Uninsured	12

Sources: Based on data from Roemer, 1991: 346; Cockerham, 1995: 328.

ing 62 percent of the resources to cover 39 percent of citizens. Expenditures per capita are three times higher for those covered under this program as compared to those covered by the Health and Welfare Secretariat or Marginal Families Program (Frenk, 1990; 146; Roemer, 1991: 347).

Payment of physicians. Approximately 75 percent of physicians are on salaries within one of the federally sponsored health care programs, plus what they earn in private practice. The remaining 25 percent are private fee-for-service practitioners. The average salary income for primary care was $7,000 in 1994, but surgeons could earn an average of $90,000 (Irigoyen-Coria and Gomez-Clavelina, 1994: 163; Cockerham, 1995: 329).

Funding of community health centers. Essentially all costs for health centers are paid through one of the major government programs noted earlier. These resources were cut back significantly in the economic downturn periods, creating a great deal of uncertainty among health professionals. The Inter-American Development Bank has provided support for construction of new health centers and health houses in rural areas but does not provide ongoing support. New funds also became available in the late 1980s through the National Solidarity Program (Roemer, 1991: 348).

Payment for Hospitals

The federal government pays about 79 percent of hospital costs through the various programs noted earlier; the twelve states included in the decentralization scheme contributed 21 percent within those states in 1986. The Inter-American Development Bank provided considerable hospital construction funding, through both grants and loans, particularly in rural areas (Roemer, 1991: 348).

PROBLEMS AND REFORMS

Despite efforts over many years to increase resources to meet health care needs in rural and traditional communities, much remains to be achieved. The periodic economic crises have interrupted these efforts, and discouraged local communities. Preventive efforts to overcome malnutrition, poor housing, environmental hazards, alcoholism, and drug abuse have been inadequately funded and supported. Services at the state and local level remain fragmented and inefficient. For example, the border communities of northern Mexico are poorly served as are a high proportion of the *colonias* surrounding the larger cities. Many individuals and families cross the border into neighboring U.S. states in search of medical care for which they often cannot pay (Sherraden and Wallace, 1992: 1439; Albrecht, 1994: 41).

The Social Security System has achieved major advances in services for those individuals covered. But, the concentration of resources and responsibility with this agency has not been conducive to community-based care and involvement of local citizens or officials in management. Coordination of services has been difficult because of the power and influence of this one agency, which has traditionally been closely aligned with the dominant PRI political party (Frenk and Gonzalez-Block, 1992: 35).

An effort was made to deal with this problem through actions taken in the mid-1980s to involve the Social Security Institute in delivering Ministry of Health programs to the rural poor. States and local governments were to help manage the services. However, Social Security constituents felt threatened and opposed the decentralization efforts (Frenk and Gonzalez-Block, 1992: 37).

The highest priority for health care development in the 1990s is to provide additional services to the rapidly expanding, urban, lower-income population. This group is not able to secure adequate access to either traditional or modern medicine. They live in housing conditions that are sometimes much worse than in the rural villages from which many of them came (Cockerham, 1995: 330).

SUMMARY AND CONCLUSIONS

Mexico has a long history of efforts to provide expanded access to health care, and has achieved considerable success in urban areas. Major progress has been made in lowering infant mortality and increasing life expectancy. However, many of the rural regions of the country remain very poor and do not yet have access to modern services. Similarly, the communities surrounding large cities inhabited largely by poor rural migrants also remain underserved.

The Ministry of Health and the Social Security System have the experience and organizational structure to effectively offer primary care and hospitalization. A surplus of physicians provide flexibility in the system for recruiting needed providers. A widespread traditional health care system in both rural villages and urban fringe communities provides a potential network of supplementary providers who might be further trained.

There is thus clear potential for developing a more universal and comprehensive system. The basic infrastructure is in place and a sufficient number of well-trained health care professionals are available. Had it not been for several major national crises in recent decades, more of the population might have been reached. The basic obstacles to completing the system appear to be lack of political will and a certain prejudice by the more affluent population against the rural and indigenous population that remains unserved.

REFERENCES

ALBRECHT, LAURA J. (1994). Medical Frontier, *Texas Medicine*, 90 (9): 34–43.

BORTIN, SYLVIA (1993). Interviews with Mexican Midwives, *Journal of Nurse-Midwifery*, 38 (3): 170–177.

BURNS, JOHN (1993). Firm Expands to Open Center in Mexico City, *Modern Healthcare*, 23 (32): 8.

COCKERHAM, WILLIAM C. (1995). *Medical Sociology*, 6th ed. Englewood Cliffs, N.J.: Prentice Hall.

FRENK, JULIO (1985). Career Preferences Under Conditions of Medical Underemployment, *Medical Care*, 23 (4): 320–332.

FRENK, JULIO (1987). Mexico Faces the Challenge, *World Health* (April): 20–23.

FRENK, JULIO (1990). The Political Economy of Medical Underemployment in Mexico: Corporatism, Economic Crisis and Reform, *Health Policy*, 15: 143–162.

FRENK, JULIO, JAVIER ALAGON, GUSTAVO NIGENDA, ALEJANDRO MUÑOZ-DEL RIO, CECILIA ROBLEDO, LUIS A. VAQUEZ-SEGOVIA, and CATALIN RAMIREZ-CUADRA (1991). Patterns of Medical Employment: A Survey of Imbalances in Urban Mexico, *American Journal of Public Health*, 81 (1): 23–29.

FRENK, JULIO, and MIGUEL A. GONZALEZ-BLOCK (1992). Primary Care and Reform of Health Systems: A Framework for the Analysis of Latin American Experiences, *Health Services Management Research*, 5 (1): 32–43.

HUNT, LINDA M. (1994). Practicing Oncology in Provincial Mexico: A Narrative Analysis, *Social Science and Medicine*, 38 (6): 843–853.

IRIGOYEN-CORIA, ARNULFO, and FRANCISCO JAVIER F. GOMEZ-CLAVELINA (1994). Can Family Medicine Survive in Mexico? *Family Practice*, 11 (2): 162–163.

PONCE DE LEON, SAMUEL, and SERGIO PONCE DE LEON (1993). Quality of Medical Care in Latin America: Do It Yourself Versus Caveat Emptor. Is There Really a Choice?, *Clinical Performance and Quality Health Care*, 1 (1): 49–50.

ROBERTS, MARGARET (1991). One Flag, Many Worlds, *HealthTexas*, 46 (10): 10–13.

ROEMER, MILTON I. (1991). *Health of Nations: The Countries*, Vol. I. New York: Oxford University Press.

SHERRADEN, MARGARET SHERRARD (1991). Policy Impacts of Community Participation: Health Services in Rural Mexico, *Human Organization*, 50 (3): 256–263.

SHERRADEN, MARGARET SHERRARD (1995). Development of Health Policy and Services for Rural Mexico, in Eugene B. Gallagher and Janardan Subedi (eds.), *Global Perspectives on Health Care*. Englewood Cliffs, N.J.: Prentice Hall, pp. 122–140.

SHERRADEN, MARGARET SHERRARD, and STEVEN P. WALLACE (1992). Innovation in Primary Care: Community Health Services in Mexico and the United States, *Social Science and Medicine*, 35 (12): 1433–1443.

SOBERON, GUILLERMO, JULIO FRENK, and JAIME SEPULVEDA (1986). The Health Care Reform in Mexico: Before and After the 1985 Earthquakes, *American Journal of Public Health*, 76 (6): 673–680.

STEBBINS, KENYON R. (1986). Politics, Economics, and Health Services in Rural Oaxaca, Mexico, *Human Organization*, 45 (2): 112–119.

16

Organizational Variations and Reforms

National health care systems come in many organizational variations, as the preceding chapters indicate. Yet, certain patterns emerge. Much of the diversity arises from the following major factors:

Locus of responsibility for health policy, funding, and health services delivery

- Centralized government
- Mixture of centralized and local government
- Decentralized control

Organization and focus of specific services

- Public health services: widespread availability with comprehensive services vs. more modest accessibility
- Primary or ambulatory care: role of physicians, nurses, and other professionals in providing basic services
- Hospital services: outpatient, inpatient, specialized secondary and tertiary care
- Pharmaceuticals: mode of delivery and extent of use
- Medical technology and information systems: widespread or limited
- Mental health care: delivery mode, complete or less complete services

- Long-term care and other special elderly health services: delivery mode, widely available or limited

Context of reforms

- Citizen attitudes
- Politics of social equity
- Geographical and income disparities
- Integration of services
- Access and quality
- Cost-control priorities
- Assessing outcomes

LOCATION OF RESPONSIBILITY FOR HEALTH CARE

Major organizational types range on a continuum from low government responsibility, funding, and involvement in delivery, to highly centralized government control, funding, and operation. The degree and nature of government involvement are clear differentiating features among countries. All countries rely on government for major public health activities. However, the mix of public and private roles in prevention, diagnosis, and treatment of illness has at least four identifiable but very fluid patterns, as summarized in Table 16-1. The "X" designation identifies the closest association with each type. Those countries in a clear state of transition are identified with a "T" in the category toward which they appear to be moving.

Summary of Each Major Type

Type I. The *centralized planning and management,* or fully socialized, type was implemented by the former USSR in the 1930s and was characteristic of other communist countries except China. All major decisions were made at the central government level. Funding was from a central government fund. Services were owned and managed by various levels of government. Individual providers and citizens had little freedom of choice or control over services.

Type II. The mixed public/private *national health service* type was established by the United Kingdom in the 1940s and is also characteristic of Sweden and other Scandinavian countries. The central government plans and manages the health care system, but many specific functions are decentralized to lower levels of government. Providers are somewhat independent but are closely supervised by some level of government; citizens must generally seek health care through a limited selection of providers at the local level.

Type III. The *mixed public/private social insurance* type was initiated by Germany in the 1880s and is also characteristic of several other countries, especially in Europe and Japan. The government assumes responsibility for planning and oversight to assure that all citizens have access to health care. Quasi-government social insurance provides financ-

Table 16-1 Health System Types Based on Centralization of Control, Funding, and Management

General Types:	I	II	III	IV
Country	Centralized Government Control, Funding, Management	←—————→ Mixed Public/Private		Decentralized, Private Control, Funding, Management
		Government Sponsors		
		Health Service	*Social Insurance*	
United States			T ←———	X
Japan			X	X
Canada			X	X
Germany			X	X
The Netherlands			X ——→	T
France			X	
United Kingdom		X ——→	T ——→	T
Sweden		X		
Czech Republic	X ——→		T ——→	T
Hungary	X ——→		T ——→	T
Russia	X ——→		T ——→	T
China		X	X ——→	T
Mexico		X ——→	T ——→	T

X indicates primary type; T indicates the direction of recent movement.

Sources: Based in part on Field, 1989: 7; Glaser, 1993: 696; Vienonen and Wlodarczyk, 1993: 166; Kirkman-Liff, 1994: 6.

ing. Services are delivered privately by independent practitioners and voluntary organizations.

Type IV. The *generally decentralized*, or pluralistic, type characterized the United States at least until the passage of Medicare and Medicaid in 1965. Government is minimally involved in direct operation or management but has a major role in sponsoring, financing, and regulating health care for specific social subgroups such as the elderly, low income, military services and veterans. Otherwise, financing is private as is service delivery. Planning and management are largely initiated by private for-profit businesses and voluntary organizations. Individual and corporate providers have a large measure of freedom to determine how services are to be offered. Citizens have considerable choice about providers and form of private insurance. Only modest effort is made, largely by individual states, to assure access to everyone.

There are no entirely *pure* types, given the recent tendency toward reform and convergence. The most striking feature of the current reforms is the shift toward decentralization and privatization. The United States is the only country in which the reform movement has recently been toward greater emphasis on social insurance as a replacement for the private system. The changes have occurred selectively at the state level and are justified as necessary to increase insurance coverage and general access for the large number of lower-income and younger citizens who have no health insurance.

The formerly centralized countries are nearly all shifting toward more flexible and consumer-responsive systems—in part as a consequence of the change to democratic governments but also because available evidence strongly suggests major health *outcome* inadequacies in the form of high morbidity, declining life expectancy, and high infant mortality. The centralized approach is judged by current governments to have been ineffective.

It is noteworthy that the countries at the most decentralized and centralized extremes appear to be moving toward the middle, converging toward a mixed public/private system. All of the countries continue to rely on government for a major policy role in establishing the rules for health care delivery even when management and delivery of services are decentralized.

ORGANIZATION AND FOCUS OF POLICIES AND SERVICES

Each country has a distinct method of reaching (or *failing* to reach) consistent national health care policies. The United States has had great difficulty in reaching consensus in part because no clear mechanism has existed for organizing and managing the policy process. Other countries have done better. For example, Germany and the Netherlands have national health care councils with responsibility for developing policy and with representation from insurance organizations, employers, employees, physicians, hospitals, and government. The councils provide a forum for negotiations among all the major parties. The process is slow but seems to have been generally effective. The "national health board" proposed in the Clinton health plan would have had a similar function had it been approved (Kirkman-Liff, 1994: 38).

The Important Role of Public Health

It is evident in every country that public health measures, such as immunizations, maternal and child health programs, improved sanitation, and enhanced environmental conditions, have a profound effect on health outcomes. Those countries that have strongly emphasized public health, even with less investment in curative health care, have succeeded in improving outcome measures such as infant mortality, longevity, lower death rates, and generally improved health status. Table 16-2 displays public health

Table 16-2   Expenditures, Relative Priority of Public Health, and Health
Outcomes

Country	Public Health Spending per Capita (1988) (U.S. Dollars)	High ($750+) Moderate ($500+) Low ($500 or less)	Health Status Outcome
United States	989	High	Modest
Canada	1,262	High	High
Japan	756	High	High
Sweden	1,225	High	High
The Netherlands	829	High	High
Germany	887	High	High
France	935	High	High
United Kingdom	727	Moderate	High
Czech Republic	} Less than $500	Low	Low
Hungary		Low	Low
Russia		Low	Low
China		Low	Moderate
Mexico		Low	Low

Source. Public health spending data are based on Babazono and Hillman, 1994:
377.

expenditures and tentatively identifies the countries with the most developed and fully functioning public health care systems.

Estimated health outcomes and public health spending are positively related. Those countries with lower expenditures generally have lower life expectancies and higher infant mortality (Babazono and Hillman, 1994: 377).

Japan and China provide useful illustrations. Despite relatively modest government investments in formal health *care* systems, longevity and infant mortality outcomes are very positive in Japan and relatively good in China, probably as a direct consequence of widespread public health measures (Vagero and Illsley, 1992: 229).

Prenatal and postbirth care.   All of the countries listed in the upper section of Table 16-2 except for the United States have a very strong emphasis on prenatal and maternal care for all income groups. This clearly helps prevent infant mortality and extends life expectancy. Pregnant women receive public prenatal care regardless of income or insurance coverage. Complications during pregnancy are usually covered by health insur-

ance. In most cases, mothers receive financial assistance or some level of income continuation during and immediately after a child is born. Japan, Canada, the Netherlands, and Sweden have comprehensive preventive maternal and child health care as an integral part of public health programs, which is certainly part of the explanation for the low infant mortality rates (also see Fig. 2-6, Chapter 2) (Chaulk, 1994: 11).

Midwives provide a high proportion of prenatal care in several of these countries, notably Sweden, the United Kingdom, Japan, and France. Obstetricians are responsible in each case for any abnormal and problematic deliveries. Postbirth care is provided at home by visiting nurses or health aides in these countries as well as in Germany, the Czech Republic, and Hungary (Chaulk, 1994: 12).

Child   health.   Comprehensive   child health programs are considered a part of the public health responsibility in most of the countries (in the United States, such services are sporadic) in the upper section of Table 16-2, often extending through preschool, elementary school, and high school. The service usually includes

- All routine childhood immunizations
- Screening for metabolic diseases
- Hearing, vision, and speech screening
- Special services for children with disabilities

Public or school health centers are staffed by trained nurses and physicians. France and Japan have particularly noteworthy programs, either within the schools or in child health centers located throughout the country. Sweden has a strong dental health program for children. United Kingdom general practitioners not only provide child health care, but receive a bonus for high immunization rates. A home visiting service in several of the countries, staffed by nurses, offers preventive services in the home for children with special problems. The nurses visit newborns and assist mothers with appropriate care (Chaulk, 1994: 13).

The immunization rates for children under age 2 for diphtheria, whooping cough, and tetanus (DPT), polio, and measles-mumps-rubella are 80 to 95 percent in most of these countries (see Figure 2-2). The U.S. rate was only 57 percent in the 1980s, but has risen to 72 percent for polio, 82 percent for measles, and 83 percent for DPT in the early 1990s (Chaulk, 1994: 13–14).

Primary Care: Benefit Packages

Public social insurance coverage has many common features in the Western European countries and Canada, including the following (Glaser, 1993: 703):

- Nearly all citizens are covered.
- All citizens are treated equally; the elderly and low-income populations are not excluded because of required co-payments.
- A defined benefit package is available to all families.
- Employers and employees are required to help finance insurance through payroll taxes or insurance is funded through other forms of public taxation.
- Participation and payment conditions are defined by the national government, for physicians, hospitals, and other providers.

- Participation conditions for private insurance carriers are specified by state, provincial, or federal law.
- The methods for submitting claims, reimbursing providers, and other procedural rules are defined nationally or at the state or province level.

The Czech Republic and Hungary are basing their new national systems on these same basic principles. The United States continues to rely on private indemnity insurance for provision of comparable benefits to much of the population. However, increased costs and competition are forcing indemnity insurers to exercise control over providers through formal managed care arrangements and rigorous utilization review (Organization for Economic Cooperation and Development, 1992: 141).

Problems in provision of universal benefits. Private insurance is characterized by several features that make provision of universal care difficult (Organization for Economic Cooperation and Development, 1992: 15):

- All citizens are not equally able to afford insurance to guarantee health care. Some form of income redistribution or publicly provided access is essential to assure care to lower-income individuals and families.
- Private insurance systems will generally attempt to exclude unhealthy people or small groups to lower costs and increase predictability. Costs can be estimated for large groups with known health characteristics, even though health care needs are unpredictable for the individual or family.
- Many individuals and families have insufficient knowledge of how to appropriately access and use private primary care and thus have relatively little control over their options.
- Providers with greater knowledge and resources (physicians and health care organizations) must intervene to represent the consumer in decisions about the nature and level of health care required for particular problems.

This combination of factors is part of the rationale for introducing public subsidies or guarantees of insurance for those parts of the population that do not have the characteristics or capacity to use private insurance.

Freedom of choice for primary care. Freedom of choice for primary care is widely available in some countries, but is severely restricted in others. Considerable evidence has been generated through cross-national surveys that patient satisfaction with health care is directly related to freedom of practitioner choice, especially at the primary care level. Table 16-3 summarizes degree of choice for primary care, specialists, and hospitals.

Freedom of choice has increased recently (early 1990s) in many countries, notably in Sweden, China, the Czech Republic, and Hungary, where physicians had previously been assigned groups of patients in identified geographic areas. Russia has been slower to adopt greater choice, although laws requiring greater freedom are in place. As noted earlier, steps have recently been taken to increase consumer choice and decrease the government's primary care role in many countries of Western Europe as well. Patients have relatively free choice of both primary care and specialist physicians in Germany,

Table 16-3 Freedom of Choice for Ambulatory, Specialty, and Hospital Care

Country	Primary Physician	Choice of Specialists	Choice of Hospital
United States	Partial*	Partial*	Partial*
Canada	Yes	Yes	No
Japan	Yes	Yes	Yes
Germany	Yes	No	Yes
France	Yes	Yes	Yes
The Netherlands	Yes	No	Yes
Sweden	Yes	No	Yes
United Kingdom	Yes	Yes	Yes
Czech Republic	Yes	Yes	Yes
Hungary	Yes	Yes	Yes
Russia	Partial	No	No
China	Yes	No	No
Mexico	No	No	No

* Choices exist under fee-for-service indemnity insurance, but are limited under managed care.

Source: Based on Organization for Economic Cooperation and Development, 1994: 26, and previous chapters.

France, Japan, the United Kingdom, and Canada, as well as in the Czech Republic and Hungary (Organization for Economic Cooperation and Development, 1994: 26).

The United States, on the other hand, is moving rapidly toward greater use of managed competition and somewhat less freedom. The change is justified as a cost-saving measure, but has the potential for severely restricting choice. Many managed care plans limit choice of physicians, specialists, and hospitals. Health maintenance organizations employ their own physicians and specialists, and usually either operate their own hospitals or contract with specific hospitals for inpatient care (Organization for Economic Cooperation and Development, 1994: 26–46).

Variations in physician-practice patterns. The intensity of contact with physicians varies widely between countries. Japan and Germany appear to have a much higher primary care use rate than most other countries. This seems clearly a matter of cultural inclination rather than greater need for health care (Sandier, 1989: 37).

Most countries have a surplus of specialists and a shortage of primary care providers. Access to specialists and hospitals is often easier than to primary care practitioners. Unfortunately, specific data that distinguish between access to primary care and specialist care are not available for most countries. It seems reasonably clear nonetheless that density and distribution of primary care providers is a more important indicator of access to health care than the overall number of physicians (see Figure 2-2, Chapter 2) (Organization for Economic Cooperation and Development, 1994: 41).

Payment systems and use rates. Although no clear evidence exists of a relationship between the number of physicians or hospital beds and health outcomes, a direct relationship exists between the nature of payment systems and use of services. Fee-for-service payment of physicians is directly associated with more consultation time and higher costs per patient visit (United States,

Canada, Germany, and France). Capitation or salaried physician payment is associated with fewer consultations and less cost per patient (the Netherlands, United Kingdom, and Sweden). Japan appears to be an exception with frequent physician visits and lower costs (Organization for Economic Cooperation and Development, 1992: 133).

However, some evidence indicates that patients in the fee-for-service countries tend to receive more skilled, prompt, and personal treatment than is the case where physicians are salaried or capitated. Similarly, levels of satisfaction indicated by consumers in random sample surveys suggest that fee-for-service countries (with the exception of the United States) tend to be more satisfied with their health care than consumers in countries where physicians are salaried or capitated. This evidence may be part of the basis for the new democracies (Czech Republic and Hungary in particular) to adopt the fee-for-service system, while diminishing the role of salaried physician services (Organization for Economic Cooperation and Development, 1992: 133).

Impact of universal insurance coverage. Universal coverage as it exists in Europe, Canada, and Japan results in somewhat greater use of health care services, but at a lower cost per case. For example, both Canada and Germany demonstrate higher use of physicians (6.6 contacts per year in Canada and 11.5 in Germany), compared to the United States (5.3), and greater use of inpatient beds (1,468 per 10,000 population in Canada, 2,237 in Germany, and 910 in the United States). However, physician costs per person per year in 1990 were considerably lower in Canada ($241) and Germany ($251), compared to the United States ($414), as were hospital costs. This pattern holds true for other European countries and Japan as well (Weil, 1994b: 47).

Nurses in Ambulatory and Hospital Care

Despite efforts by nurses organizations to increase the status and rewards, the profession remains of relatively low status in most countries, with modest rewards. The situation has improved substantially in the United States, Sweden, and to some degree in Canada, where the prestige and pay for nurses have risen in recent years. But the same cannot be said for most other countries where shortages are evident. Exhausting schedules, poor hospital working environments, inadequate legal protection, as well as relatively low pay, provide *disincentives* to nursing careers, especially in hospitals. No country has fully solved this problem for a profession so vital to health care (Soberon, 1987: 44).

However, increased involvement of nurses in ambulatory care, home health care, and independent practice in a number of countries has improved both status and pay for a significant proportion of nurses. These changes have been slow to evolve in most countries, in part because of the dominance of physicians, but also because of limited political power of nurses and shortages of health care resources.

Pharmacists and Pharmaceutical Care

The great increase in use, and higher costs, of pharmaceuticals has become a major issue in most countries. Pharmacists are key players in the quest for more helpful and cost-effective medications. As the number of alternative drugs increase, it has become more difficult for physicians in any country to keep abreast of new products and their proper use. The pharmacist is the logical supporting expert, and has become a close consultant to physicians in the "pharmaceutical care" of patients.

Pharmacology and toxicology have become major fields of study in most economically advanced countries. These sciences provide direct support to better understanding and improvement of pharmaceuticals, and are basic to the effective role of pharmacists in helping physicians to improve patient care while avoiding adverse drug reactions. Pharmacists in many countries are advancing their professionalism through higher levels of advanced education. The Doctor of Pharmacy is becoming the entry-level university degree for the pharmacy field in some countries.

The varying use and contribution of pharmaceuticals. Tremendous variation in the use and costs of pharmaceuticals is evident from one country to another. One explanation seems to be cultural inclination, in the form of physician and patient preferences, rather than evidence of health outcome differences. Pharmaceutical development has proceeded swiftly in many countries, contributing significantly to improved results from medical treatment. Greater use is thus in part a result of better products that can be prescribed for a wider range of worthwhile treatments (Organization for Economic Cooperation and Development, 1994: 41).

Administrative Organization and Management

The use of professional administration techniques varies widely among countries. Administration tends to be dominated by physicians in several countries (Japan, China, Hungary, the Czech Republic, and Russia) who usually have very little modern management training. Other countries rely on professional administrators (United States, Canada, Germany, Sweden, the Netherlands, and the United Kingdom) who have specialized training in administration and who compete with physicians for responsibility in health care institutions.

The need for increased managerial skills in health care has been widely recognized in those countries without advanced training programs. Efforts are underway to improve the situation in Russia, China, the Czech Republic, and Hungary (World Health Organization, 1989: 201).

European countries, Canada, and Japan tend to *macromanage* health care, whereas the United States *micromanages*. Macromanagement has allowed those countries to avoid the major cost shifting from insured patients to the uninsured that occurs in the United States, while also achieving economies in the administration of insurance and in general management (Weil, 1994b: 44).

Other Health Professional Fields

Dental services are part of national health care plans in most countries except Canada and the United States. Dentists usually bill insurance plans within a set fee schedule that limits their payments. Prevention is emphasized by requiring that patients see a primary care dentist before specialized services can be used. Dental care for children is provided with no required co-payments, whereas adults are required to pay some part of the fee. Funding tends to be constrained for reconstructive and other specialized services (Weissman, 1993: 44–46).

A wide array of other health professions make major contributions to health care, but as with dentists, are not discussed here or in previous chapters in any detail largely because of very limited comparative information. These include but are not limited to physician assistants, physical therapists, chiropractors, occupational therapists, speech and audiology therapy, dietitians, social workers, clinical psychologists, medical records administrators, orthotics and prosthetics specialists, and dental technologists (Boyce, 1993: 202).

All of these groups are becoming increasingly professionalized as they achieve higher levels of training and skill. Their professional organizations are also gaining influence in the larger health care arena in many countries as they learn how to take advantage of organization action to gain professional and political power (Boyce, 1993: 202).

Changing Health Professional Education Needs

Many countries are moving toward

- Greater focus on training health professionals in public health, health promotion, and prevention, as a vehicle for lowering health care costs

- Greater emphasis on training of primary care physicians, while continuing to emphasize specialty training
- Improving and professionalizing nursing to improve competence, status, and pay
- Upgrading training for other support personnel in the use and application of technology

Medical education is under examination in nearly all countries—because of its high cost and "overproduction" of graduates. For example, the oversupply problem in Germany has reached the point that only about 10 percent of graduates in ambulatory care were able to enter practice in their first year after graduation during the early 1990s (Jones, 1993: 59).

The Czech Republic, Hungary, and China have increased the level of training for physicians, emphasizing primary and community-based care. Community-based training is also increasing in the United States, Western European countries, and Canada—to help alleviate the maldistribution of primary care and specialist physicians as well as other health professionals (World Health Organization, 1989: 211).

Remote rural areas are usually short of providers whereas urban areas have surpluses. Similar maldistribution of trained professionals exists for several categories of health personnel. For example, nurses are in short supply in both rural and urban areas of Eastern and Central Europe. This is becoming less the case in the United States, which has particularly emphasized nurses training in recent decades. The decline in hospital inpatient care has greatly diminished the demand for hospital nurses, whereas increased emphasis on managed care and home health care has increased the demand for nurse-practitioners (World Health Organization, 1989: 217).

The Changing Roles of Hospitals, Physicians, and Outpatient Care

Outpatient care is increasingly emphasized in most countries. Inpatient care is diminishing as improved surgical and rehabilitation methods enable patients to be mobile much more quickly. The distinction between hospital inpatient and outpatient practice by physicians continues to be much more pronounced in Europe and Japan than in North America. Salaried hospital-based specialists are fully responsible for inpatient care, often duplicating diagnostic work already performed by the ambulatory physician. The high cost of this tradition is gradually causing the distinction to break down in most countries as outpatient surgery and services increase.

Despite the noted changes, hospitals continue to serve as major providers of inpatient and outpatient care in all countries. They serve as the primary "workshop" for specialty physicians and the primary employer of nurses in every country. They also continue to be the high-technology and specialty centers, as well as the single highest-cost part of health care.

Institutional and individual information systems. Modern health administration increasingly emphasizes use of computerized management information systems—which include detailed data on costs, uses of resources, formalized quality and outcome measures, patient records, billing data, and other information that can help to determine effectiveness and productivity of the institution. It is now possible to create community health information networks that enable data to be shared among institutions, thus increasing access to commonly needed information while lowering paper transactions (Kirkman-Liff, 1994: 26).

Several countries (France, Canada, Germany, and the United States, for example) are implementing "smart card" technology that places patient data on a plastic card encoded with a memory chip. The card can be used to replace paper files for medical records and insurance identification, as well as for other data about patients. Such technology will not only decrease paper flow, but can also increase the accuracy and completeness of information (Kirkman-Liff, 1994: 9).

Medical informatics is becoming a major international subfield, providing support for electronic communication and networking, and for development of databases on diagnosis, patient records, accounting data, education, outcome measures, and other applications. The new technology makes information readily accessible and usable for research and other analytical purposes, while increasing health care access, improving quality of diagnosis and treatment, and lowering the cost of services. Electronic mail and data transmission can greatly decrease the isolation of physicians and other professionals working in remote areas. The very nature of advanced information technology facilitates cross-national diffusion of innovations (O'Reilly, 1994: 1173).

Special Services for the Expanding Elderly Populations

The organization and development of services for the elderly are changing quickly in most countries. This is clearly an example of the value of comparative analysis; there is great potential for learning from the creative solutions of countries with the most experience, such as Sweden, Germany, and other nations with high proportions of the elderly who seem to be doing well.

The elderly in most countries have full access to health care with minimal co-payment requirements. The United States is the major exception. Despite availability of Medicare, older people must pay a premium for Part B services (primary and physician), must pay for most of the cost of pharmaceuticals, and must either buy insurance for long-term care, be prepared to pay the costs, or go on Medicaid. The more affluent elderly purchase some form of "medigap" insurance to cover such costs. Premiums are substantial, especially for long-term-care insurance.

A recent study in five nations (Canada, Germany, Japan, the United Kingdom, and the United States) indicated that only the elderly in the United States worry about the costs of health care. Nonetheless, older

Americans tend to be more satisfied with their lives (61 percent) than in any other country; the proportion in Canada is 58 percent, while only 28 percent of older Japanese are satisfied (Modern Maturity, 1993: 10).

Current national policy in most countries gives priority to ambulatory rather than institutional care for the elderly. In the Netherlands, for example, roughly 9.3 percent of the over-65 population live in institutional care settings (6.7 percent in homes for the elderly and 2.4 percent in nursing homes). The government is attempting to replace much of the institutional care with less costly private home care whenever possible, through increases in home help as well as other outreach programs. Sweden is pursuing the same policy.

However, growth in the oldest age categories is requiring continued investment in institutional care in all countries for the increasing proportion of elderly over age 80. Predictable demographic changes in all countries will certainly cause an increased demand for health services despite evidence of a generally healthier older population (van den Berg Jeths and Thorslund, 1994: 6–10).

Variations in Mental Health Care

Severely ill mental patients are the primary target for mental health care systems in most countries—usually in mental hospital settings. However, because mental hospitals are expensive, and often inhumane, "deinstitutionalization" has become a primary objective in Europe and North America. A complementary emphasis on community mental health services attempts to assist the deinstitutionalized or noninstitutional patient (Bachrach, 1994: 3).

The successes of such efforts remain to be fully examined, but some consequences are clear: deinstitutionalization in the United States and Canada has led to a high incidence of homelessness for individuals who cannot function well enough to secure employment and who have no alternative to an institutional home. Medicaid has become the only health insurance option in the United States for individuals who have no reliable source of income and no access to adequate public community mental health services. In Canada and some Western European countries, deinstitutionalization has apparently been more successful, in part because universal health insurance has provided greater access and continuity of care. However, outcomes have not been adequately measured to clearly indicate effectiveness of results (Bachrach, 1994: 5).

Mental illness and treatment are not understood to the same degree as physical health care in most countries. Nor is it generally recognized that mental health problems are often the direct cause for physical health complaints. Many primary care visits to physicians have a mental illness origin, rather than a physical cause. However, primary care physicians as a rule are not well trained in mental health and do not particularly like dealing with mental health problems. Most patients who have a mental disorder diagnosis are referred to a mental health specialist. The initial contact is billed as a cost to the physical health care budget (Kirkman-Liff, 1994: 30).

Each country has its own unique mechanism for dealing (or failing to deal) with mental health problems. The capitated payment systems in the Netherlands, United Kingdom, and in U.S. health maintenance organizations appear to have the most comprehensive and least costly approaches. Clients with indications of mental illness are interviewed by a social worker trained in mental health who refers to a psychiatrist or psychologist if needed. Lack of understanding or appreciation for mental health services means they are often the first component of health care to suffer when funds are cut or constrained (Kirkman-Liff, 1994: 30).

THE PERVASIVENESS OF REFORM

Reforms are generated in most instances by public dissatisfaction and by health professionals who communicate their feelings to the policy makers.

Citizen and Physician Attitudes Toward Health Care

Surveys reveal a high level of public discontent with the current mode of health care delivery, although satisfaction levels are considerably higher in Western Europe, Canada, and Japan than in the United States (comparable data are not available for other countries). The preference for change is highest in the United States, with significant dissatisfaction in each country. Each type of health care system is perceived by consumers to have deficiencies (see Figure 2-5) (Becher, 1993: 37).

Recent surveys reveal that dissatisfaction levels of physicians are much higher in the United States than in other countries. For example, physicians in Germany and Canada are much less concerned than in the United States about their ability to obtain needed services for their patients. A very high proportion of U.S. physicians express concern that some patients cannot afford the care they need. However, both Canadian and German physicians had greater concerns about delays in access to hospitalization and shortages or unavailable services (Blendon et al., 1993: 196).

In part because of dissatisfaction, health care leaders in each country are searching through the experience of other countries in a quest for better solutions. Exchanges of information, through scientific literature, international conferences, and direct cross-national consultation, are leading to a common body of information about health care systems. This process has been characterized as "simultaneous reform," and is likely to cause further convergence in the structures and delivery systems. Health care institutions thus may become more and more similar (Kirkman-Liff, 1994: 4).

Changes in Political Organization and Social Equity

The explanation for differences in national health programs rests in part on the national sense of ethical and social responsibility. The cultures of European countries and Canada emphasize an ideology of "social solidarity" manifested in a commitment to provision of equitable health services for all the members of the population. In the United States, on the other hand, the sense of ethical responsibility leads to "charity care" at the local level through voluntary services by physicians, hospitals, nurses, and other health professionals. The attempt to assure that no one is completely deprived of care is left to voluntary actions of individuals and groups at the national, state, and local level.

Commitment to social equity in health care appears directly related to completeness of other forms of public welfare. The countries with a tradition of active worker-oriented political parties and labor unions generally have more developed welfare systems, including health care. "Liberal" political parties have been generally supportive of such programs in Western Europe and North America. The most developed, universal, and comprehensive health care programs are in these regions.

The consequences of ideology. Communist countries also had a strong commitment to social welfare and health care. This was clearly subordinated however, to the quest for industrialization and military power. The communist political leadership generally disregarded health care needs in favor of industrial development priorities. Information on problematic health conditions was also suppressed. Industrial workers were rewarded financially and given higher status than physicians and other health care workers (Vagero and Illsley, 1992: 231).

The consequences were severe. Health status deteriorated and life expectancy declined (particularly for men) in most East European nations and former Soviet republics. Environmental conditions worsened, and incidence of cancer, heart disease, alcoholism, major industrial accidents, and other destructive conditions increased. Some emphasis on child health and prevention remained in place, but could not fully counter the negative environmental and health care conditions. Despite the democratization of many of these countries, it will take some time to overcome the problems accumulated over several decades (Vagero and Illsley, 1992: 226).

The free-market ideology in the United States also has consequences. Formal government health care guarantees are sporadic and incomplete within national programs and among states. Special public programs have been implemented for the most obviously needy and ill-served groups such as the elderly (Medicare) and those poor citizens who meet specified criteria (Medicaid). However, there is inconsistency in meeting the public need. Political leaders regularly change the rules and occasionally withdraw resources that were earlier supposed to serve as reliable safety nets (Cook and Lampe, 1993: 11).

Overcoming geographical disparities. Social equity in health has not been fully achieved in any country, although some societies have certainly done much better than others. Most countries have some degree of regional inequity. Rural regions are less adequately served than urban areas, although this disparity has been considerably reduced in recent decades. Particularly wide differences continue to exist, within the United States, China, Russia, Japan, and Mexico (Illsley, 1990: 230–231).

Most countries are characterized by concentrations of physicians and other health professionals in major urban centers. The problem is less pronounced in the smaller and more densely settled countries of Western Europe, where distances between rural regions and urban centers are small. Some countries such as Sweden have been quite successful in overcoming this problem by establishing publicly supported health centers in remote rural regions. The United States has partially solved the problem through subsidizing public clinics. Practitioners are offered incentives through a National Health Service Corps (Organization for Economic Cooperation and Development, 1994: 16).

Integration of Services

Integration and coordination of services form a major thrust of reform in most countries. The continuity of health care is expanded through deliberate administrative coordination of providers to achieve improved patient services. Shared financial risk and responsibility are viewed as key elements in achieving the needed changes. Integration can involve combinations of several forms (Kirkman-Liff, 1994: 13–14):

- Greater collaboration among primary care and specialist providers
- Transforming the primary care physician into a gatekeeper to specialist and hospital services
- Ambulatory and inpatient care can be linked in the form of ambulatory surgery, postinpatient home care services, and other actions providing for greater continuity of care
- Control of costs by close management of patient care and providers

Health maintenance organizations in the United States, the general practitioner fundholder/gatekeeper systems in the United Kingdom, and the emerging gatekeeper concept in the Netherlands are clear examples of integration. The new design for health care in the Czech Republic and Hungary attempts to achieve the same general kind of integration. Unnecessary referrals to specialists are minimized through greater attention to primary care. The consequences of change are illustrated in the Netherlands by the fact that 55 percent of surgeries were ambulatory in 1992, compared with only 5 percent in 1988 (Kirkman-Liff, 1994: 15).

In the fundholder/gatekeeper approach of the United Kingdom, productivity-based payments are made to primary care physician groups who have professional and financial responsibility for a group of patients. Costs of diagnoses, drugs, specialist referrals, and hospitalization are charged against their practice budgets. Surpluses are allocated to the physicians responsible for patient management as a reward for careful use of resources and referrals. Comprehensive management information systems are crucial to the success of these integrated systems (Kirkman-Liff, 1994: 15).

The United States has experimented with several types of integration in recent years through a wide variety of categorical government programs, new regulations, and private entrepreneurial developments. The complexity of integration has required deep understanding of programs and options, giving a competitive advantage to those organizations with major resources to invest in staff who can interpret and act on the rules.

Health maintenance organizations, preferred provider organizations, multi-institutional chains, and other large complex organizations have had the advantage over small provider groups and individual institutions. These large organizations have created a variety of new organization forms with potential international relevance—some of which have been adopted as part of "managed competition" by the conservative government of the United Kingdom, and more selectively in Sweden and the Netherlands as well as in other countries (Tuohy, 1994: 252).

The Role of Rationing

Rationing is viewed as a primary method to control volume and costs of services in many countries, but the methods vary widely—as summarized by country in Table 16-4. Types of rationing include (Taylor, 1993: 26):

- Limitations on the introduction or dissemination of *technology* (Technology)
- Restrictions on the choice of *treatment and procedures* used (Treatment)
- Restrictions on the distribution of *accessible* places for health care (Access)
- Limitations in the choice of *primary care provider or hospital* (PCPH Choice)
- Restrictions on the *point in time* care is available or received (Time Point)
- Limitations on the *benefits* received in terms of insurance coverage, cost to be paid, or quality of the service (Benefits)

Table 16-4 Estimated Incidence of Rationing

Country	Technology	Treatment	Access	PCPH Choice	Time Point	Benefits
United States	X	X	X	X		X
Canada	X	X	X	X	X	X
Japan		X				
Germany.	X	X				X
France	X			X		
The Netherlands	X			X		
Sweden	X	X			X	
United Kingdom	X	X		X	X	
Czech Republic	X	X				X
Hungary	X	X				X
Russia	X	X				X
China	X			X	X	X
Mexico	X	X	X	X		X

Source: Constructed by the authors based on data in country chapters.

The tendency to formally or informally ration through any of these actions is a consequence as much of cultural preferences as cost control. For example, physicians in Japan have a very strong inclination to undertake diagnostic tests, but a very low preference for surgical interventions. Consequently, CT scanners and MRI technology are widely available, but organ transplants are very limited and might be considered rationed. By contrast, Canada severely limits the availability of CT scanners and MRI technology, but has a high incidence of organ transplants (relatively speaking). Global budgeting as it exists in most countries other than the United States has a tendency to limit access to technology and many forms of surgical treatment (Taylor, 1993: 27).

There are shortages in the United States because of limited funding for certain services. Kidney dialysis, for example, is underfunded by Medicare, Medicaid, and many forms of insurance, leading to considerably poorer outcomes than in Europe and Japan. Mortality of dialysis patients in Japan is one-third the U.S. rate. This occurs in part because U.S. physicians and hospitals do not secure adequate reimbursement for treatment of dialysis under Medicare or from most other insurance programs (Carlson, 1993: 28).

Research on Health Outcomes as the Basis for Reform.

The causes of good health status and positive outcomes from treatment are very complex and not easily explained by the nature of the health care system. As noted earlier, public health prevention activities and environmental conditions play a major role, as do diet, exercise, mental disorder, and physical stress. Failure to fully attend to all the causes of ill health has led to a high incidence of cancer, heart disease, alcoholism, mental illness, and other ailments that diminish overall population health status despite an otherwise progressive health care system. The economic prosperity of countries, or communities, clearly does not fully explain health conditions (Vagero and Illsley, 1992: 228).

Research budgets to increase understanding of health outcomes are very constrained in Russia, China, the Czech Republic, and Hungary, whereas greater resources and personnel are available in Western Europe and North America. Consequently, the flow of knowledge and technology tends to be from those countries with major research enterprises toward those nations with less investment in knowledge creation (World Health Organization, 1989: 220).

Outcomes assessment. Outcomes assessment, as a specific tool for measuring the condition of individual patients and as a basis for comparison among providers, communities, and countries, has been given major emphasis in recent years. Several measurement categories are used, including (Ware, 1992: 15):

- General health status
- Physical functioning and well-being
- Mental functioning and well-being
- Social functioning as a contributor to family and community
- Health-related quality of life
- General health satisfaction

Each of these general categories can be subdivided and measured for each patient with diagnostic instruments designed for that purpose.

These measures establish the condition of patients based on formal signs, symptoms, and laboratory tests. Measures can be designed to reflect how patients are coping with their physical and mental conditions. The information can be entered into computerized information systems and summarized by disease category, by institution or provider setting, and eventually at community, region, state, national and international levels so that outcomes can be compared. This kind of data would provide a much better basis for comparisons among countries than is currently possible (Greenfield, 1990: 6–10).

INTERNATIONAL ORGANIZATIONS AND HEALTH CARE

The World Health Organization and the World Bank have been actively promoting and supporting improvements in health care. In 1990, EUROHEALTH was established as a specific program to help countries move toward the realization of health goals particularly in the newly independent states of the former USSR and the countries of Central and Eastern Europe. Priority in allocation of resources is for emergency needs such as vaccines, pharmaceuticals, and medical equipment. The needs continue to greatly exceed available resources, but nonetheless the World Health Organization is attempting to provide basic information and encourage cooperation and knowledge sharing as well as limited financial support to the newly emerging countries (Danzon and Litvinov, 1993: 155).

Very positive developments have occurred in Central Europe (the Czech Republic and Hungary) with strong support and resources from the European Community and the Organization for Economic Cooperation and Development. Rapid social and economic development in these countries resulted in major improvements in health status during the early 1990s (Vagero and Illsley, 1992: 226).

SUMMARY AND CONCLUSIONS

The comparisons discussed here indicate clearly the continuing diversity in health care systems. Reforms tend to accelerate when knowledge is applied based on the experience of other countries. Much of the change is a direct result of systematic adoption or adaptation of practices already proven workable in one or more of the economically advanced countries. This emphasizes the value of information sharing, which contributes to convergence in health care systems, especially evident in the emerging democracies of Central and Eastern Europe.

Managed competition has become a formal vehicle in many countries for both cutting costs and improving health care efficiency. Reliance on government to plan and manage the details of health care is no longer generally acceptable. Rather, a combination of private enterprise delivery, publicly sponsored or regulated health insurance, and regulated prices or budgets is emerging as the "model" that seems to work best and toward which the convergence is directed.

REFERENCES

BABAZONO, B., and L. HILLMAN (1994). A Comparison of International Health Outcomes and Health Care Spending, *International Journal of Technology Assessment in Health Care*, 10 (3): 376–381.

BACHRACH, LEONA L. (1994). Deinstitutionalization and Service Priorities in Canada and the United States, *New Directions for Mental Health Services*, 61 (Spring): 3–9.

BECHER, GUNTER (1993). European Health Issues, *Employee Benefits Bulletin*, 18 (1): 34–41.

BLENDON, ROBERT J., KAREN DONELAN, ROBERT LEITMAN, ARNOLD EPSTEIN, JOEL C. CANTOR, ALAN B. COHEN, IAN MORRISON, THOMAS MOLONEY, and CHRISTIAN KOECK (1993). Health Reform Lessons Learned from Physicians in Three Nations, *Health Affairs (Millwood)*, 12 (3): 194–203.

BOYCE, ROSALIE A. (1993). Internal Market Reforms of Health Care Systems and the Allied Health Professions: An International Perspective, *International Journal of Health Planning and Management*, 8 (July–September): 201–217.

CARLSON, ROBERT H. KOLFF, HOSÉ (1993). Compare Mortality between Europe, Japan, and the U.S., *Nephrology News & Issues*, 7 (11): 28–30.

CHAULK, C. PATRICK (1994). Preventive Health Care in Six Countries: Models for Reform, *Health Care Financing Review*, 15 (4): 7–19.

COOK, R. J., and L. G. LAMPE (1993). Macroethical Responsibilities of Societies of Gynaecologists and Obstetricians, *Acta Medica Hungarica*, 49 (1–2): 1–16.

DANZON, MARC, and SERGUEL K. LITVINOV (1993). EURO-HEALTH Programme, *World Health Statistical Quarterly*, 46 (3): 153–157.

FIELD, MARK G. (ed.) (1989). *Success and Crisis in National Health Care Systems: A Comparative Approach.* New York: Routledge.

GLASER, WILLIAM A. (1993). Universal Health Insurance That Really Works: Foreign Lessons for the United States, *Journal of Health Politics, Policy and Law*, 18 (3): 695–722.

GREENFIELD, SHELDON (1990). What's Next for Outcomes Assessment, *The Internist* (January): 6–10.

ILLSLEY, RAYMOND (1990). Comparative Review of Sources, Methodology, and Knowledge, *Social Science and Medicine*, 31 (3): 229–236.

JONES, FREDERIC G. (1993). Study Tour Examines Health Care Systems in Germany, Holland—Part II: The German System, *Physician Executive*, 19 (5): 58–62.

KIRKMAN-LIFF, BRADFORD L. (1994). Management Without Frontiers: Health System Convergence Leads to Health Care Management Convergence, *Frontiers of Health Services Management*, 11 (1): 3–48.

MODERN MATURITY (1993). Only Americans Fear Costs of Health Care, *Modern Maturity* (October-November): 10.

O'REILLY, MICHAEL (1994). Health Care Begins to Merge with the Information Highway, *Canadian Medical Association Journal*, 151 (8): 1173–1176.

ORGANIZATION FOR ECONOMIC COOPERATION AND DEVELOPMENT (1992). *The Reform of Health Care: A Comparative Analysis of Seven Countries.* Paris: OECD.

ORGANIZATION FOR ECONOMIC COOPERATION AND DEVELOPMENT (1994). *The Reform of Health Care Systems.* Paris: OECD.

SANDIER, SIMONE (1989). Health Services Utilization and Physician Income Trends, *Health Care Financing Review* (Annual Sup.): 33–48.

SOBERON, G. (1987). An Overview of Country Studies, in Z. Bankowski and T. Fulap (eds.), *Health Manpower Out of Balance: Conflicts and Prospects*, Highlights of a conference in Acapulco. Mexico City: Secretary of Health.

TAYLOR, ROGER S. (1993). Rationing Health Care in Other Countries, *Employee Benefit Research Institute Issue Brief*, 136 (April): 23–34.

TUOHY, CAROLYN (1994). Response to the Clinton Proposal: A Comparative Perspective, *Journal of Health Politics, Policy and Law*, 19 (1): 249–254.

VAGERO, D., and R. ILLSLEY (1992). Inequality, Health and Policy in East and West Europe, *International Journal of Health Sciences*, 3 (3–4): 225–239.

VAN DEN BERG JETHS, ANNEKE, and MATS THORSLUND (1994). Will Resources for Elder Care Be Scarce?, *Hastings Center Report*, 24 (5): 6–10.

VIENONEN, MIKKO A., and W. CEZARY WLODARCZYK (1993). Health Care Reforms on the European Scene: Evolution, Revolution, and Seesaw?, *World Health Statistical Quarterly*, 46 (3): 166–169.

WARE, JOHN E., Jr. (1992). Measures for a New Era of Health Assessment, in Anita L. Steward and John E. Ware, Jr. (eds.), *Measuring Functioning and Well-Being: Medical Outcomes Study Approach.* Durham, N.C.: Duke University Press.

WEIL, THOMAS P. (1994a). A Cost Comparison of Canadian and U.S. Hospital Pharmacy Departments, *Hospital Pharmacy*, 29 (1): 15–23.

WEIL, THOMAS (1994b). American Macromanaged Health Care System, *Health Services Management Research*, 7 (1): 43–55.

WEISSMAN, P. (1993). Foreign Reform, *Journal of the American Dental Association*, 124 (9): 44–46.

WORLD HEALTH ORGANIZATION (1989). Development of Health Systems, *World Health Statistics Quarterly*, 42 (4): 201–227.

17

Economic Organization of Health Care: Comparative Perspectives

Changes in the means of financing health care are underway in every country. The reasons are manifold. Aging populations are adding to expenditures. Advancements in technology have particularly important implications for service costs. Consumers are demanding more access to high-technology services. Profound economic stresses arise from expanding services, leading to a continuing effort in all countries to exercise control over the growth of the health care industry. Very few countries (only Sweden and the United Kingdom among the industrialized countries discussed here) have managed to contain or lower the proportion of GDP expended for health care—although Russia has spent less because of pronounced economic decline. Fortunately, there has been a significant lowering of the *rate* of growth in the last 10 years compared to the 1960s and 1970s in each country (Pfaff, 1990: 2; Organization for Economic Cooperation and Development, 1994: 39).*

Most nations are thus struggling to identify the form of economic organization for health care that will not only control costs but also provide the financing base for an acceptable level of quality and service. The primary economic considerations include

- Extent and content of the benefits package
- Sources of health care financing
- Level of payments to providers
- National and regional expenditure limitations
- Methods for controlling cost increases

BASIC HEALTH CARE BENEFITS

All countries except the United States and China require a nationally defined basic package of benefits. Nearly all medical bills for ambulatory care, hospital care, and medical goods are totally or partially covered, as summarized in Table 17-1. Coverage of pharmaceuticals varies widely.

---

*The growth rate depends in part on the method of measurement. For example, *purchasing power parities*—international price indices that compare the prices of the same set of goods across countries—can be used to

compare per capita spending for health care. When such conversions are used, *per capita* spending increased even more in the 1970s and 1980s than earlier estimated, although overall spending leveled off (Pfaff, 1990: 5–7).

Table 17-1   Primary Benefits Provided Through Public Health
Insurance or Direct Services (1990)

| | Services Paid | | |
Country	Primary Care	Hospitals	Income Replacement While Ill
United States	Partial	Partial	Partial
Canada	Full	Full	Partial
Germany	Largely	Largely	Partial
Sweden	Full	Full	Partial
Japan	Largely	Largely	Partial
The Netherlands	Largely	Largely	Partial
France	Largely	Largely	Partial
United Kingdom	Full	Full	Partial
Czech Republic	Full	Full	Partial
Hungary	Full	Full	Partial
Russia	Full	Full	None
China	Partial	Partial	None
Mexico	Partial	Partial	Partial

Sources: Based on Organization for Economic Cooperation and
Development, 1992, 1994; Becher, 1993: 36.

Although many countries have not
required significant payment by patients, the
situation is changing rapidly as costs increase. Co-payments or premiums are becoming more common as a means of lowering public costs or as incentives to discourage
overuse of health care resources.

The greatest costs in all countries are for
hospitalization benefits, followed by primary
care. Drugs are the highest cost item in
China and are substantial in several other
countries. Income replacement during illness is one of the highest cost items in Sweden because a high proportion of missed
income is paid from health insurance funds.

FORMS OF HEALTH CARE FINANCING

Financing the basic benefits is achieved primarily by levying payroll taxes on employers
and employees or by directly taxing all citizens
via income tax or various forms of sales taxes.
Supplemental private insurance is available in
most European countries and Canada to cover
costs not paid through publicly mandated
insurance. The predominant financing alter-

natives include (Organization for Economic
Cooperation and Development, 1992: 7):

- *Voluntary private (indemnity) insurance.* Premiums
are paid to for-profit or nonprofit insurance
companies. Reimbursement is usually directly to
providers and occasionally to patients who must
pay providers. No direct link exists between
insurers and providers. This option has historically been the predominant pattern in the
United States and as a source of supplementary
insurance in several countries.

- *Private insurance contracts.* These contracts are
between insurers and providers to cover designated groups of individuals. When employers
provide insurance to employees, this is the primary pattern. It is commonplace in the United
States; is the basis for supplementary insurance
in Germany, the United Kingdom, and France;
and is evolving in the Czech Republic and Hungary. A variation of this form operates in China
for public employees.

- *Managed care contracts.* These contracts are
between insurers and individuals, public organizations, or businesses. Insurers own and manage
health care programs and develop an integrated
health care system for groups of subscribing
individuals or for employers who have purchased this form of insurance for employees. A

designated group of benefits is provided for a specific fee (capitated rate per insured person). The typical examples are health maintenance organizations or preferred provider organizations in the United States. The method is used experimentally in Ontario, Canada, and is under examination in a few other countries.

- *Compulsory public insurance.* Payroll taxes are collected by the government from employers, or general income taxes are levied on citizens, and are paid into insurance funds that negotiate contracts with providers. Reimbursement goes directly to providers and patients do not always know the actual costs. This is the typical pattern in Germany, the Netherlands and France, and is emerging as the primary pattern in the Czech Republic and Hungary.

- *Compulsory public health care.* Payroll or income taxes are collected to support public ownership and management of health care services through an integrated system. This has been the typical pattern in the United Kingdom, Sweden, the Czech Republic, Hungary, and Russia, but is now changing in all of these countries.

- *Out-of-pocket payment to providers.* The consumer must pay for services as they are received. This remains typical in the United States for the uninsured population, as a supplement for the insured or for affluent families that choose not to purchase insurance. It is accompanied by so-called "charity care" provided without compensation by physicians and hospitals for the uninsured patients. The rural uninsured population of China must pay out of pocket, although low-cost insurance is emerging in more affluent rural areas.

Problems with Each Option

None of these alternatives has been sufficiently successful to form an ideal "model" for widespread international adoption. Each has certain drawbacks (Organization for Economic Cooperation and Development, 1992: 7):

- The voluntary options and private insurance contracts tend not to fully insure populations, and wide discrepancy is evident in access to health care. Forms of voluntary insurance represent less than 15 percent of health expenditures in any country except the United States.

- The managed care or managed competition option restricts choice of providers and severely limits patient and provider decisions about care options.

- The compulsory public insurance forms are characterized by detailed government regulation and limitations on provider payments as government attempts to control cost.

- The compulsory public ownership and management of services are criticized for management inefficiencies, impersonal treatment of consumers by physicians and other health professionals, poor outcomes, and public dissatisfaction.

- Out-of-pocket costs can be very high for the uninsured and can be substantial for partially insured patients in cases of major illness, sometimes resulting in poverty or bankruptcy.

The compulsory public insurance approach is the most widely used. It is different from private insurance systems in several important respects (Yakoboski, Ratner, and Gross, 1994):

- Insurers (sickness funds in Germany and other European countries) are subject to detailed regulation, and may be considered "quasi-public" even though they function independently of government. Medicare, Medicaid, and veterans benefits for special needs groups in the United States are in certain respects comparable to public insurance in other countries.

- Insurers are required to provide minimum benefit packages and to cover all citizens in their jurisdiction. Membership in the public system is compulsory in most countries unless incomes are above a defined minimum in which case private insurance may be purchased as an alternative.

- Most countries with public systems have moved toward nationwide controls on primary care prices, global budgets for hospitals, and firm limitations on insurance payments for pharmaceuticals. These controls force insurance units and providers to negotiate prices—which tend not to be entirely uniform within or between countries.

Relationship Between Public Payment and Cost

There appears to be little relationship between the type of health care coverage

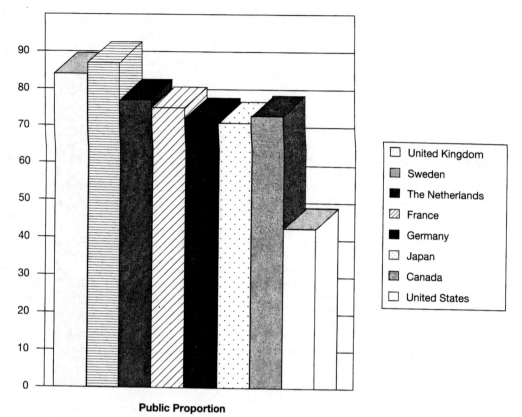

Public Proportion

Figure 17-1. Public proportion of health care costs (1994).

Sources: Based on data from Wolfe and Moran, 1993: 55; Hakansson, 1994: 108; Weil, 1994a; 47; Organization for Economic Cooperation and Development, 1994: 37–38; Memmott, 1995: 4B; National Center for Health Statistics, 1995: 220.

and per capita health care costs. Per capita costs are more a function of per capita income in each country, as indicated in Figure 2-1, Chapter 2. Figure 17-1 summarizes the proportion of health expenditures covered through public resources for eight countries.

Despite the high levels of universal coverage in most countries, only 70 to 85 percent of health care expenditures are paid through public sources. In the United States, the proportion reached about 43 percent in 1994. Remaining costs are paid by individuals through out-of-pocket payment or through purchase of supplementary private insurance. Much of this extra cost in each country is for pharmaceuticals, which

are rarely covered in full by insurance (Organization for Economic Cooperation and Development, 1994: 49).

The public insurance systems in Europe (for example, Germany and the Netherlands) were somewhat more costly with an average of 8.7 percent of GDP in 1992, as compared to the direct health care provision systems (for example, United Kingdom and Sweden) that used an average of about 7.5 percent of GDP. There was considerable cost divergence as indicated in Figure 2-1 (Hakansson, 1994: 105).

Required contributions by employers and employees vary considerably, as displayed in Table 17-2. This is indicative of the variation in sources of financing. The payroll tax cov-

Table 17-2 Required per Person Payroll Deductions (1992)

Country	Employer (% of Salary)	Employee	Total
France	12.8	6.8	19.6
Germany (average)	6.5	6.5	13.0
The Netherlands (average)	4.0	1.2	5.2
Sweden	7.8		7.8

Source: Based on data from Becher, 1993: 37.

ers only part of the package of benefits in some countries, while other taxes cover the balance.

The cost of disability benefits is included in the employer/employee contribution in France, Germany, and Sweden (Becher, 1993: 37).

Growth of Private Insurance

Several countries have begun to cut back on the comprehensiveness of public health insurance coverage—because of high costs—with private insurance plans encouraged as an alternative. New forms of private insurance plans are now expanding in the Netherlands, the United Kingdom, China, the Czech Republic, and Hungary, and have become part of employee compensation packages—especially for the larger private companies. A very high proportion of companies offer supplemental private insurance in France, the United Kingdom, and the Netherlands. The practice is less commonplace in Germany and Sweden—in part because of more complete public insurance programs (Becher, 1993: 40).

Employer-provided supplementary insurance is very popular in those countries where publicly provided benefits are viewed as inadequate or incomplete (United Kingdom, France, and the Netherlands), whereas in other countries with better benefits, or where restrictions on private coverage are the norm (Canada), employer insurance is much less common. Some of the employer plans allow employees to continue their private coverage into retirement, but usually at personal expense (Becher, 1993: 40).

In a few countries, private insurance replaces public insurance for the higher-income population (Germany and the Netherlands, for example). Higher-income and healthier individuals or families who purchase private insurance effectively increase average costs to the sickness companies that serve the lower-income, sicker, and older individuals. The private funds are able to offer greater benefits at lower cost. Physicians and hospitals are reimbursed at higher rates, thus creating certain inequities and resentments among sickness fund participants (Wolfe and Moran, 1993: 62).

Private insurance usually offers greater convenience for the beneficiaries—such as private hospital rooms, shorter waits for surgery or other procedures, and long-term care. Table 17-3 summarizes employer-provided supplementary insurance for managers available in several countries (Wolfe and Moran, 1993: 62).

Supplementary Insurance for the Elderly Population

Although most countries provide special benefits to the elderly (without requiring them to pay costs commensurate with the actual expense), the situation is changing as the numbers of elderly increase and financing becomes tighter. The United States levies taxes on Social Security recipients with higher incomes. The European countries require all of the elderly to pay taxes on Social Security benefits, but their health care benefits are generally more accessible and complete (Glaser, 1993: 707).

PAYMENTS TO PROVIDERS

Primary Care Payment

Primary methods for paying primary care physicians include salaries, capitation for

Table 17-3   Availability of Employer-Provided Private Medical Plans (1993)

Country	Medical Plan for Three Management Levels (% of Firms)		
	Top Management	Middle Management	Other Management Employees
United States*	0–100	0–100	0–100
France	77	74	68
Germany	10	8	8
The Netherlands	69	67	60
Sweden	22	11	8
United Kingdom	90	81	67

*Nearly all firms in the United States with 100 or more employees provide full employee insurance, whereas very small employers tend not to offer insurance at all.

Source: Becher, 1993: 40; through a survey by the Wyatt Company.

each patient served, and traditional fee for service, as illustrated in Table 17-4.

As noted in earlier chapters, none of these systems of payment is ideal. The *fee for service* payment method is the dominant mode in most countries. However, this kind of payment often encourages overuse of services because providers earn more if they increase what they offer or require of patients. "Supplier-induced demand" is the term used by economists to characterize this result. It leads almost invariably to increased overall cost of services. This problem is among the reasons for continued increasing costs in the United States, Canada, Germany, and France. Deliberate caps on fees were instituted in the latter three countries to help solve the problem. A shift toward capitation through managed care has been developed as the major counter-strategy in the United States, along with the Resource-Based Relative-Value Scale used in Medicare to define and limit physician charges (Organization for Economic Cooperation aand Development, 1994: 47).

The cost of fee-for-service medicine varies considerably between countries. Furthermore, each type of insurance has a different payment method. In the United States, Medicaid generally pays the lowest rate, followed by Medicare and managed care plans; private indemnity insurance has traditionally paid the highest rate and has subsidized the lower-paying plans (Sandier, 1989: 34).

Salaried physicians and other health professionals have been the predominant mode in socialized systems. Because there is little incentive to please patients, salaried staff are sometimes accused of inefficiency and discourtesy. However, many of the most competent and hard-working specialists are on salary and would certainly reject such accusations. The Czech Republic, Hungary, Russia, and China are shifting toward fee-for-service for primary care in an attempt to overcome poor quality of service—by increasing physician accountability to patients. Sweden is adding a fee per visit to the salaries of physicians as an attempt to increase physician interest in satisfying patients (Organization for Economic Cooperation and Development, 1994: 47).

Capitation is increasingly used to pay for primary care. Because the fee is the same regardless of service delivered, physicians paid by capitation may have a tendency to refer patients for specialty care as a means of lowering the time required for primary care. However, managed care plans in the United States offer subsidies in some cases as a reward for *not* referring to specialists or hospitals. The United Kingdom has had long experience with capitation under the National Health Service and is currently attempting to change the incentive system by adding a small fee for service to encourage more attention to efficiency and to discour-

Table 17-4   Method of Payment for Primary Care

Country	Mode of Payment	Additional Charges Allowed
United States	Fee for service (primarily)	Extra billing allowed*
	Capitation (HMOs)	No extra billing
	Salary (HMOs, public clinics)	No extra billing
Canada	Fee for service (primarily)	None
	Salary (CHCs)†	
Sweden	Salary	$6–9
	Fee for service	
France	Fee for service	25%, including extra billing
Germany	Fee for service	None
The Netherlands	Fee for service	Upper-income patients
	Capitation	None for lower income
Japan	Fee for service	10% for employed
		20% for dependents
		30% for self-employed
		Patient "gifts"
United Kingdom	Capitation	None
	Salary	
China	Salary	Patient "gifts"
	Fee for service	Varies
Russia	Salary	Patient "gifts"
	Fee for service	
Czech Republic	Salary	Patient "gifts"
	Fee for service	
Hungary	Salary	Patient "gifts"
	Fee for service	
Mexico	Salary	None
	Fee for service	Varies

*Extra billing refers to the practice of collecting the insurance payment, and then billing the patient for additional costs over the allowed amount.
†CHCs: Community Health Centers primarily in Ontario and Quebec.

Sources: Based on data from Organization for Economic Cooperation and Development, 1992; 1994: 43.

age unnecessary referrals (Organization for Economic Cooperation and Development, 1994: 46–47).

Physician Incomes

Japanese physicians have the highest total gross incomes, followed in rough order by the United States, Sweden, Germany, the Netherlands, Canada, France, the United Kingdom, the Central European countries, Mexico, Russia, and China. The ratio of physician income to general per capita income in a country is highest in Japan (about 7.5 times the average wage), Germany (4.5), the United States (3.9), Canada (3.8), and France (2.5), and is the lowest in the Central European countries and Russia. This ratio has been decreasing in most countries (except Japan) during the recent 20-year period. The average income (adjusted for inflation) of physicians has stabilized in most countries, although it has continued to rise into the 1990s in the United States (Sandier, 1989: 41–42).

Specialist physicians are nearly always paid considerably more than general practitioners or primary care specialists. This results in part because specialists tend to use the highest levels of medical technology, which generates higher returns per patient than the more modestly priced diagnostic and treatment technology used by primary care specialists (Sandier, 1989: 42).

Generally, physicians have much greater earning potential in those countries where fee for service is the primary mode of payment, as in Japan, the United States, Germany, and Canada. In the United Kingdom, China, Russia, the Czech Republic, and Hungary, where either capitation or salaries are the basis for physician payment, incomes tend to be considerably lower. Nonetheless, economic level of the country, average income levels of the general population, degree of intervention by insurance organizations, and level of available medical technology appear to be more influential as income determinants for physicians than the specific method of payment (Sandier, 1989: 41).

Undercompensation or overcompensation of physicians. Gift giving by patients is commonplace in several countries, often as an illegal "under-the-table" payment for special service or treatment. This practice evolved in countries where physicians are poorly paid and have lesser status (Russia, China, the Czech Republic, and Hungary). But it is widely and legally practiced in Japan as well, where physicians generally have higher incomes (Wolfe and Moran, 1993: 61).

Canada, Germany, and other European countries impose caps on fees through negotiation with physician organizations. The intent is to lower costs and at the same time diminish provider-induced demand. A fee-control system was initiated in the United States in 1992 for Medicare physicians (the *Resource-Based Relative-Value Scale* or *RBRVS*), as noted earlier. The scale attempts to put a value on services based upon the resources used (Organization for Economic Cooperation and Development, 1994: 47).

Thus, a process of adjustment is underway as each country tries to improve the payment system while also lowering costs of physician services. Recent research evidence suggests these measures have had some short-term success in Germany but are only partially effective in long-term efforts to control costs (Yakoboski et al., 1994: 32–33).

The differential between various forms of payment has been very upsetting for many physicians in the United States. For example, Medicaid paid an average of only 40 to 50 percent as much as private commercial insurance in 1994. Medicare paid approximately 80 percent. Managed care HMOs and PPOs paid 70 to 80 percent of private insurance rates. Because many physicians have patients in many, or all, of these arrangements, a complex and high-cost record-keeping and billing system is required. Because the amount of payment is often uncertain and slow, a cash-flow problem sometimes results. This is much less of a problem in countries with universal health insurance and single or few payers (Galvin, 1993: 22–23).

The "fundholding physician" system. The United Kingdom has introduced the practice of "fundholding physicians," in which general practitioners (usually in group practice) are given a block of funds for each patient that they collectively use for serving a population of patients. Savings achieved through efficient care may be used for improving services and purchasing specialized services as needed. The idea is to encourage practitioner gatekeepers to carefully select specialized services for patients based on price and quality. Greater efficiency, less waiting time, higher patient satisfaction, and greater practitioner innovation in service delivery seem to result (Organization for Economic Cooperation and Development, 1994: 48).

Paying Hospitals

Hospitals receive payment for patient services directly from public insurance funds in most countries, either on a per diem basis or in the form of a block grant. Global budgets have been instituted in several countries as the principal method of allocating hospital resources. Capital investment in new facilities or equipment is decided by state, provincial, or national governments in most of Europe and Canada. Projected national and regional needs serve as the basis for decisions.

This contrasts with the United States and Japan, where hospitals have traditionally been part public and part private. Most hospitals are therefore subject to the expectations of private-practice physicians—who generally want the latest technology and equipment readily available. Hospitals in the United States borrow funds from banks or through the bond market for capital investment and gradually cover the costs through rate increases. This leads directly to increases in health care costs. An attempt was made to limit such investment in the 1970s through a "certificate-of-need" permit process. However, hospitals were generally able to circumvent the restrictions through persuasion and political influence. The situation is changing dramatically in the mid-1990s as cost cutting is increasingly emphasized (Glaser, 1991: 389).

Hospitals in most Western European countries do not suffer from the same kind of financing problems that impact the United States. For example, because of universal insurance coverage and a greater emphasis on preventive maternal and child care, hospitals in the other countries do not have the high incidence of patients with critical maternal and neonatal conditions characteristic of many U.S. hospitals. American hospitals also have a higher incidence of patients suffering from gunshot wounds and accidents, which are much less prevalent in other countries (Glaser, 1991: 391).

This is among the reasons that hospitals in Western European countries and Canada are generally able to function efficiently with a much lower staffing level than U.S. hospitals. Global budgeting has had the effect of forcing them to become more efficient. For example, despite an average length of stay nearly 50 percent longer in Canada, hospitals had a $2,720 lower average cost per discharged patient than the United States in 1990. Hospital expenditures per capita were 47 percent lower (Weil, 1994a: 15).

It should be noted that considerable progress has been made in lowering costs during the early 1990s in the United States and other countries. As the United States shifts toward managed care and managed competition and European countries shift to more competitive systems (all of which tend to emphasize health care methods that minimize hospitalization) per capita cost increases have been moderating—although overall expenditures continue to grow in most countries (Glaser, 1991: 394).

THE BASIS FOR GROWING EXPENDITURES

Several major factors have led to expenditure increases, as summarized in Table 17-5. Gen-

Table 17-5 Contributing Factors to Higher Expenditures

- Expansion of health insurance benefits and increased coverage for the elderly and other special population groups
- Demographic change, particularly growth in the numbers of elderly in all countries
- Greater numbers of health professionals credentialed through the health professions education process, coupled with higher fees or wages for physicians, nurses, and other professionals. Equity gains for women in the health professions has had considerable impact in the United States and Canada
- Continuing introduction of new and more expensive technologies and procedures
- Growth in high-cost hospital beds and services, including new outpatient services
- General growth in intensity of resources used per patient, for cancer, heart disease, AIDS, and chronic health problems
- Overall growth in per capita income that enables individuals and governments to demand more health care
- General price inflation, as well as inflation specific to health care

Source: Based on Pfaff, 1990: 7–8.

erally, per capita expenditure is closely related to the proportion of total GDP spent for health care in each country. As incomes rise, per capita spending rises and GDP increases. However, as Figure 17-2 indicates the proportion of GDP going to health care has risen in all countries but Sweden during the 5-year period between 1989 and 1994,

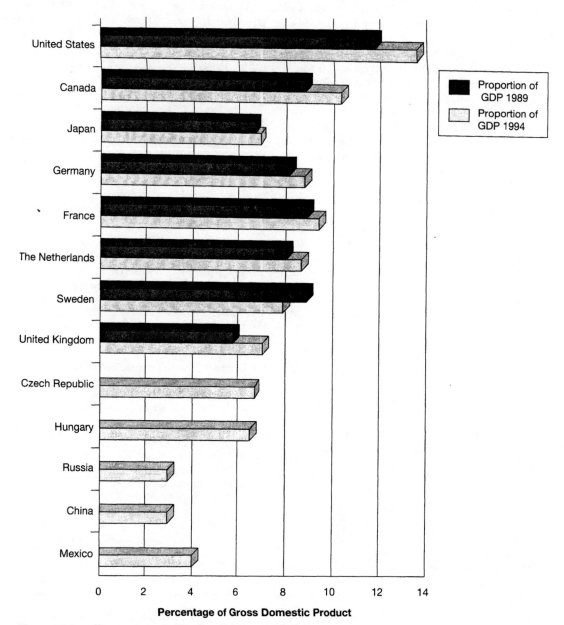

Percentage of Gross Domestic Product

Figure 17-2.   Changes in spending from 1989 to 1994.

Sources: Based on data from Organization for Economic Cooperation and Development, 1994: 38; Weil, 1994a; 47; National Center for Health Statistics, 1995: 220.

but with substantial variation between countries in the *rate* of increase.

The proportion of GDP growth for health care is particularly notable in the United States and Canada, but significant growth also occurred in Germany, France, the Netherlands, and the United Kingdom. Hospital care is among the major expenditure differences among European, Canadian, Japanese, and U.S. health systems. For example, the average operating expense per day for 1990 in Canada was $353; in Germany, $215; and in the United States, $901 (Weil, 1994a: 51).

The following key differences between countries are notable (Kirkman-Liff, 1994: 38; Weil, 1994a: 51):

- There is a higher intensity of high-cost technology in the United States. Surgery costs twice as much in the United States ($6,535 in 1990) as compared to Canada ($3,815) and Germany ($2,972).
- There is a greater intensity of nursing care in the United States, with 5.5 employees per bed as compared to 3.3 in Canada and 1.4 in Germany.
- European and Canadian hospitals generally do not perform as many high-cost procedures.

Yet, there appears to be little evidence of poorer outcomes.

Administrative Costs

There is evidence of substantial differences between countries in administrative costs. Estimates of actual costs vary widely, depending on the basis for comparison, but it seems clear that the multiple-payer U.S. system is the most expensive with 24 percent or more of health care costs going to administration. The single-payer systems in the United Kingdom, Canada, and Eastern Europe are the least expensive at 3 to 10 percent—depending on whether costs of tax collection are included. The European sickness fund systems cost about 4.5 percent for administration. Administrative costs are thus critical components of total costs and cost increases (Davis, 1994: 16).

Implications of Increasing Health Expenditures

There appears to be little evidence that universal coverage and comprehensive benefits necessarily increase costs. On the contrary, those countries with universal coverage and comprehensive benefits have generally been most successful at controlling costs—possibly because of greater political determination. As noted earlier, the most significant contributors to the expenditure growth rate appear to be increases in the number of beds and technology in hospitals and growth in number of physicians—the two highest cost sectors of health care. The proportion of elderly in the population also contributes, but modestly compared to the other growth factors (Pfaff, 1990: 15).

Cost control in health care has major implications for other sectors of economic activity. A higher proportion of GDP going to health care means less is available for education, housing, welfare, transportation, and other valued activities. There is already evidence at the state level in the United States that the proportion of state budgets going for education has diminished as the costs of Medicaid increase. The infrastructure (highways, roads, and services of other kinds) has been suffering from lack of maintenance in many states because of funding shortages (Yakoboski et al., 1994: 31).

SUMMARY OF COST-CONTROL STRATEGIES

Cost control has been the major focus of reform strategies in most countries. The several types of controls discussed in earlier chapters, and in use within one or more countries, include the following:

- Establishing *budget limitations* ("global budgets") for all health care programs, or in specific sectors such as hospitals, ambulatory care, or pharmaceuticals ("sectoral" global budgets).

- *Negotiating or imposing fee limitations* ("fee caps") for primary care physicians, specialists, and hospital per diem costs.

- *Capitation by imposing an average health care budget for each consumer.* Management of patient costs becomes the responsibility of primary care gatekeepers or "managed care" plans. Fixed-price contracts are negotiated for specialist and hospital services.

- *Shifting more costs to consumers,* through deductibles, co-payments, or allowing for supplementary private insurance for noncovered services.

- Other forms of *rationing* by limiting the availability of technology for primary care and hospital use, or limiting patient access to some uses of technology and other high-cost services.

National or Global Health Care Budgets

Nationalized or socialized health care programs (largely current or former communist systems, except for the United Kingdom) have for many years imposed relatively strict limitations on health care costs by constraining investment in health care facilities, limiting health professional salaries, limiting technology, and using other budget-constraining methods. The countries with relatively centralized and government-funded health care systems, such as Sweden, the United Kingdom, Russia, and China have had difficulty with such controls in part because of health cost inflation (which has always exceeded the overall rate of economic growth), the increasing costs of technology, and the aging of populations (Wolfe and Moran, 1993: 63).

Other countries, such as France and the United Kingdom, establish an overall national hospital budget that provides the basis for individual public hospital budgets. Rates of annual increase are set nationally and applied to all hospitals—with adjustments for volume, degree of needed specialization or technology, and other local factors. More decentralized countries, such as Germany, the Netherlands, and Canada, encourage state or provincial flexibility by allowing discretion in negotiating per diem rates for hospital services and physician fee rates

within an overall budget framework. They have not had a specific national cap on spending. Global budgeting for hospitals in most countries applies only to expenditures by some level of government for government-owned and -operated facilities. Germany, the Netherlands, and France have also initiated global budgeting on nongovernment facilities (Wolfe and Moran, 1993: 71).

Global budgeting obviously puts strong pressure on managers to economize. Each institution is required to file records of utilization and spending as part of new budget proposals for the succeeding year. Rate regulators or sickness-fund staff (depending on the country) examine the record, compare with peer institutions, and recommend cuts where they determine budgets are too high. After some negotiation between hospital officials and regulators, a budget is approved that is deemed to be appropriate. Estimates suggest the annual savings under hospital global budgets reach an average of about 13 percent in OECD countries (Glaser, 1993: 711).

Global budgets for other health care sectors such as ambulatory care, mental health care, and long-term care are also underway in Germany, the Netherlands, the United Kingdom, and Canada. Capital expenditures are nearly always controlled by public or government entities. Global budget limitations usually mean specific controls on growth of high-technology diagnostic and surgical facilities (Organization for Economic Cooperation and Development, 1992: 141; Wolfe and Moran, 1993: 63; Kirkman-Liff, 1994: 8). Table 17-6 summarizes global budgeting.

The United States adopted the Diagnosis-Related Groups (DRG) approach in which payments to hospitals are based on the estimated costs for treatment of categories of disease or illness diagnoses. The DRG system has had the effect of decreasing the length of stay, or shifting patients to outpatient treatment, and thus lowers the rate of increase in costs of hospitalization. The savings have been demonstrated for Medicare patients. The concept has been

Table 17-6   Global Budgeting

Country	Sector	Type of Expenditure	Procedure to Set Budget
United States	Medicare Hospital	Price per diagnosis-related group	Set by health care financing administration in consultation with physicians/hospitals
Canada	Physicians	Fees	Negotiation between province and physician organizations
	Hospitals	Operating costs	Negotiation between province and hospital
France	Public Hospitals	Operating costs Capital debt service	Negotiation involving insurance fund, government agency, and hospital
Germany	Physicians	Fees for ambulatory care	Negotiation between sickness funds and physician organizations
The Netherlands	Physicians	Fees for ambulatory care	Negotiation between sickness funds and physician organizations on income and volume "cap"
Sweden	Hospitals	Operating costs	Negotiation between county and hospital
United Kingdom	Physician and hospital	Operating and capital costs	Established by Ministry of Health
Russia	National health care budget	All services operated by government	Recommended by Ministry of Health and approved by legislature
China	National health care budget	All services operated by government	Established by Ministry of Health with party approval
Czech Republic	Public health care budget	Supplementary to emerging national insurance system	Recommended by Ministry of Health and approved by legislature
Hungary	Public health care budget	Supplementary to new national insurance system	Recommended by Ministry of Health and approved by legislature
Mexico	Health care budget	Service prices Capital investment	Set by Ministry of Health and Social Security units

Source: Based in part on Wolfe and Moran, 1993: 64–65.

sufficiently successful that an adaptation has been used by selected hospitals in Sweden and other countries (Organization for Economic Cooperation and Development, 1994: 46).

Several countries are attempting to increase equity in allocation of limited health resources by deliberately dispersing health care funds on the basis of population distribution. For example, in the United Kingdom and Sweden, funds are allocated from the federal level to various parts of the countries based on population (Organization for Economic Cooperation and Development, 1994: 45).

Limitations on Fees or Prices

Imposition of specific price or fee controls is used in many countries as a primary cost-control mechanism. Germany, Canada, and the Netherlands, for example, have successfully placed limits on physician expenditures—through negotiation of rates among insuring organizations and physician groups. However, these efforts often fall short of targets because of increases in the numbers of physicians and increases in individual physician work load (Wolfe and Moran, 1993: 63).

Price controls generally tend to hold down prices only temporarily unless the fee schedules become a permanent and ongoing part of the system, as is the case of Germany and some countries where they are used. Price controls also have a tendency to distort supply and demand, leading to shortages and inefficient allocation of resources. Moreover, physicians attempt to increase their income by providing more services (induced demand), although providers are not generally able to increase volume enough to regain more than about half of the revenue lost through controls (White, 1994: 8).

Problems are associated with any form of price constraint. A large bureaucracy must be created to administer the controls. Potentially higher administrative costs are therefore created, although this may be less of a problem in health care than in nonhealth care markets because of the relatively limited number of payers in most countries. In fact, there is evidence from Canada and Germany that fee schedules may lower administrative costs if accompanied by only a few payers (White, 1994: 9).

Overall, the evidence from recent studies indicates that budget caps and targets have been effective in holding down prices since 1986 in the German ambulatory care sector, relative to growth in the remainder of the economy. However, the evidence on quality of care impacts accompanying budget limitations has not been documented (Yakoboski et al., 1994: 36).

Despite the distortions and incentive problems, limitations on fees and prices for providers and pharmaceuticals continue to be a primary cost-control strategy for many countries.

Controls on Use and Prices of Pharmaceuticals

The cost of pharmaceuticals is a major factor in those countries with high consumption—such as Japan, France, Germany, and China. Most countries attempt to control drug prices to some degree. Limits have in some cases been placed on use of high-cost drugs through "positive" and "negative" lists. A *positive* list specifies which drugs can be prescribed and paid for through public health insurance. A *negative* list specifies which drugs the insurance will not pay for. Table 17-7 summarizes these policies for several countries (Organization for Economic Cooperation and Development, 1994: 25).

Controls on drug costs are imposed through so-called reference pricing in a number of countries, notably Germany and the Netherlands. This method establishes a price for approved drugs that limits what the public insurance schemes will pay. Anything over the reference price must be paid out of pocket by the consumer. The problem with this approach is the risk of discouraging pharmaceutical companies from developing new drugs because of very limited profit potential (Organization for Economic Cooperation and Development, 1994: 47).

The European Community has urged European governments to require generic prescribing and pricing of drugs as a mechanism for encouraging competition between drug companies. Governments are also encouraged to require patient payment of a percentage of drug costs to increase understanding of the true costs and to stimulate

Table 17-7   Price Controls, Positive Lists, and Negative Lists for Pharmaceuticals

Country	Price Controls	Positive List	Negative List
United States	Some insurers	No	No
Canada	Province discretion	Yes	Yes
Japan	Yes	Yes	No
Germany	Yes	No	No
France	Yes	No	No
The Netherlands	Yes	Yes	No
Sweden	Yes	Yes	No
United Kingdom	Yes	Yes	Yes
Czech Republic	Yes	Yes	No
Hungary	Yes		
Russia	Yes		
China	Yes	} No Data Available {	
Mexico	Yes		

Source: Based on and expanded from Organization for Economic Cooperation and Development, 1994: 25.

shopping for the best priced products. Competition is viewed in this context as more effective than price controls (Lewis, 1993: 1043).

However, generating sufficient competition in the face of constant efforts by domestic pharmaceutical companies to increase profits is a difficult and challenging problem. Greater dependence on competition between competing international companies may be a better strategy than relying on price controls with the potential by-product of disincentives for research and development of new products.

Capitation

Capitation has been in effect in the United Kingdom for many years and continues to be the basic method of payment to general practitioners—with the "fundholding" changes noted earlier. The capitation system has been adopted for managed care in the United States and is rapidly becoming the predominant system in health care markets throughout the country. Experiments with capitation are also underway in a number of other countries. It clearly achieves cost control, but also imposes limits on freedom of choice for both health practitioners and consumers.

Cost Shifting to Consumers

Patient charges are usually intended to lower national health care costs while increasing the cost consciousness of consumers. The most notable negative feature is the potential inequity of such charges for lower-income individuals who will be less inclined to seek health care if a significant out-of-pocket cost is required. Nonetheless, required consumer contributions are increasing in most countries (Organization for Economic Cooperation and Development, 1992: 139; Kirkman-Liff, 1994: 10).

Available evidence indicates that increasing the direct cost to consumers somewhat reduces the demand for health care. Other evidence suggests that shifting costs to consumers through required co-payments or cost sharing does not achieve significant overall cost control, but simply changes how costs are paid (Pfaff, 1990: 21–23).

France and Japan have highly complex cost-sharing requirements. In France, out-of-pocket expenditures amount to approximately 17 percent of health care costs—but are largely covered by supplemental private insurance. In Japan, the patient costs range between 10 and 30 percent, depending on (1) the insurance program covering the patient, (2) whether the patient is a dependent, and (3) where treatment occurs. A cap on required co-payments limits the monthly costs for any individual (Wolfe and Moran, 1993: 60; Organization for Economic Cooperation and Development, 1994: 15).

Extra private insurance often covers the cost of deductibles or user charges, special additional benefits (such as private hospital rooms), or other services not included in the public benefit package. China and the Central European countries are developing this alternative to supplement their other insurance schemes (Kirkman-Liff, 1994: 10).

As noted earlier, supplemental insurance for Medicare beneficiaries in the United States has become increasingly necessary. Out-of-pocket costs to Medicare recipients had risen to 17.1 percent of their after-tax income in 1993, up from only 10.6 percent in 1961 before Medicare was implemented (Hackler, 1993: 5).

Increased user charges have recently been imposed in Sweden, the United Kingdom, and the United States for specialist services—as a mechanism for discouraging inappropriate use when lower-cost primary care would suffice for nonlife-threatening health care problems (Ham, 1994: 25).

The Role of Increased Market Competition

Although several countries are moving toward greater market competition as a primary vehicle for containing costs and improving quality, the evidence in the United States suggests that the market system is not particularly effective at cost control. Much of health care at the community level is minimally competitive and in fact competition operates to increase expenditures for expensive technology and services (Organization for Economic Cooperation and Development, 1994: 39).

In the 1995 period after the failure of nationally sponsored health care reform under the Clinton Administration, insurance rates were rising rapidly in many states. Managed care appears to have a short-term beneficial effect but may be insufficient to control the inflationary effects of all of the cost pressures noted earlier and the inclination of insuring organizations to collectively raise prices.

SUMMARY AND CONCLUSIONS

Most countries have a well-established package of health benefits required by government mandate and available to all citizens. The content of the benefits varies considerably and is shrinking somewhat as a consequence of cost controls. The forms of financing are also shifting as reforms are implemented to improve methods for providing universal insurance at lower cost.

The changes are largely away from direct government control and financing through taxes, at one extreme, and from dependence on private insurance or out-of-pocket payment, at the other extreme. A middle ground is emerging in which governments guarantee coverage for the disadvantaged, but employers and the more affluent are expected to pay directly for insurance. It seems very clear that the polar extremes do not work effectively in providing widely accessible and high-quality health care.

However, no ideal middle-ground formula has yet been created that effectively balances government and private involvement. Some countries are moving toward greater competition between providers as the economic balancing solution, and others are moving toward greater central control through global budgeting and fee caps. Each country has a somewhat unique approach to controlling costs while attempting to sustain access to high-technology and quality care.

The political determination of governments to contain costs—through the imposition of specific measures such as global budgets on hospitals, caps on physician fees, control of drug costs, and efforts to increase administrative efficiency—has been somewhat effective. However, government efforts seem invariably to be somewhat clumsy and may be even more inadequate than free-market competition. The continued existence of a "safety net" for most citizens is an advantage in the countries where governments have actively created universal insurance while deliberately controlling costs. Nonetheless, the safety net seems to be diminishing in the free-market situation as well as in centralized, government-control situations (Organization for Economic Cooperation and Development, 1994: 40).

Some form of explicit or implicit rationing is used everywhere as a principal method for containing costs. U.S. cultural values are antagonistic to explicit rationing, but implicit rationing is clearly a major consequence when large numbers of citizens are uninsured or have limited coverage. Given the recent effort to limit Medicare and Medicaid expenditures, coupled with higher insurance costs, projections indicate an even larger proportion of citizens will have limited coverage or no insurance. The European countries and Canada seem to have done better than the United States at creating an economic basis for health care that sustains the elderly and low-income populations. It is not yet clear how these issues will be managed in Central and Eastern Europe where the resources for health care remain much less adequate than in the more advanced countries (Taylor, 1993: 23).

REFERENCES

BECHER, GUNTER (1993). European Health Issues, *Employee Benefits Journal*, 18 (1): 34–41.

DAVIS, W. GRAYBURN (1994). Is the American Health Care Delivery System Ready for Change? *Physician Executive*, 20 (2): 15–17.

GALVIN, ROBERT S. (1993). Physician Payment in Canada, Germany, and the United States, *Physician Executive*, 19 (3): 22–28.

GLASER, WILLIAM A. (1991). Paying the Hospital: American Problems and Foreign Solutions, *International Journal of Health Services*, 21 (3): 389–399.

GLASER, WILLIAM A. (1993). Universal Health Insurance That Really Works: Foreign Lessons for the United States, *Journal of Health Politics, Policy and Law*, 18 (3): 695–722.

HACKLER, CHRIS (1993). Health Care Reform in the United States, *Health Care Analysis*, 1: 5–13.

HAKANSSON, STEFAN (1994). New Ways of Financing and Organizing Health Care in Sweden, *International Journal of Health Planning and Management*, 9 (1): 103–124.

HAM, CHRIS, SUE ATKINSON, PETER GLUCKMAN, and RON KERR (1994). Why Travel Broadens the Mind, *Health Services Journal*, 104 (S406): 24–25.

KIRKMAN-LIFF, BRADFORD L. (1994). Management Without Frontiers: Health System Convergence Leads to Health Care Management Convergence, *Frontiers of Health Services Research*, 11 (1): 3–48.

LEWIS, SARA (1993). EC Prescribing Policy, *The Lancet*, 342 (October 23): 1042–1043.

MEMMOTT, MARK (1995). Redefining the Wealth of Nations, *USA Today*, September 18, p. 4B.

NATIONAL CENTER FOR HEALTH STATISTICS (1995). *Health United States, 1994.* Hyattsville, Md.: U.S. Public Health Service.

ORGANIZATION FOR ECONOMIC COOPERATION AND DEVELOPMENT (1992). *The Reform of Health Care: A Comparative Analysis of Seven OECD Countries.* Paris: OECD.

ORGANIZATION FOR ECONOMIC COOPERATION AND DEVELOPMENT (1994). *The Reform of Health Care Systems.* Paris: OECD.

PFAFF, MARTIN (1990). Differences in Health Care Spending Across Countries: Statistical Evidence, *Journal of Health Politics, Policy and Law*, 15 (1): 1–28.

SANDIER, SIMONE (1989). Health Services Utilization and Physician Income Trends, *Health Care Financing Review* (Annual Sup.): 33–47.

TAYLOR, ROGER S. (1993). Rationing Health Care in Other Countries, *Employee Benefit Research Institute Issue Brief*, 136 (April): 23–34.

WEIL, THOMAS P. (1994a). An American Macromanaged Health Care System?, *Health Services Management Review*, 7 (1): 43–55.

WEIL, THOMAS P. (1994b). A Cost Comparison of Canadian and U.S. Hospital Pharmacy Departments, *Hospital Pharmacy*, 29 (1): 15–23.

WHITE, JOE (1994). Paying the Right Price, *The Brookings Report*, 12 (2): 6–11.

WOLFE, PATRICE R., and DONALD W. MORAN (1993). Global Budgeting in OECD Countries, *Health Care Financing Review*, 14 (3): 55–76.

YAKOBOSKI, PAUL J., JONATHAN RATNER, and DAVID J. GROSS (1994). The Effectivenss of Budget Targets and Caps in the German Ambulatory Care Sector, *Benefits Quarterly*, 10 (3): 31–37.

18

Expectations for Reform: A Glimpse at the Future

Countries around the world obviously share many common problems, despite their overall diversity. Attempts at resolution of the major issues have led to a series of reforms, some common and some unique to one or two countries, as previous chapters have indicated.

THE DIRECTION OF REFORMS

Although outcomes remain somewhat unpredictable, a number of definite trends are discernible (Schneider et al., 1992: 51):

- A commitment to improvement in public health as the primary vehicle for improving population health status
- Diminishing commitment to paying the high costs of inpatient hospital care when other alternatives will serve as well or better in sustaining health
- A focus on primary care as the least cost and most effective alternative for dealing with acute and chronic health problems
- An advancing commitment to equalization of access through a "safety net" or foundation of benefits available to everyone regardless of income

- Improving cost effectiveness and overall cost containment to avoid undue investment in health care at the expense of other national and international priorities
- Increasing information flow between countries and an international sharing of ideas about organization, insurance, cost-effective technologies, other cost-saving devices, and specific modes of health care delivery

The Public Health Priority

Major public health problems in many countries—arising from pollution, environmental contamination, and specific diseases such as AIDS—have increased consciousness that investments in this realm will have the most profound long-term health benefits to citizens. The realization has been strongly affected by the clear evidence in Central and Eastern Europe that failure to attend to these issues can have disastrous consequences for life expectancy and specific classes of illness. At the same time, there is clear evidence that investment in preventive health measures for women, children, working adults, and the elderly pays off in greater life expectancy and lower infant mortality.

Governments in the most successful countries take firm responsibility for the necessary infrastructure and ongoing investments. Those countries with poorer results clearly give less emphasis to public sector environmental health and widespread preventive activity. The most gains can be made at the least cost from investments in public health (Vagero and Illsley, 1992: 232–237).

The evidence suggests that private fee-for-service health providers are unlikely to emphasize public health to the desirable degree because profit accrues more for treating illness than preventing it. However, some organizational innovations such as health maintenance organizations and physician "fundholders" appear to have much greater incentives to prevent illness than private fee-for-service medicine in general. Keeping people healthy in these cases lowers costs and increases provider income potential.

Unfortunately, public health work offers less status and lower pay for professionals in most countries than personal health care activities. This means that public health advocates have difficulty garnering the resources and developing the programs to undertake the needed programs. The problems faced by the World Health Organization in financing and supporting the public health program, "Health For All 2000," illustrates the point on an international scale. Deliberate efforts must be made to overcome this problem if this priority is to be successful.

Primary Care

Primary care is of next importance but was clearly losing ground in most countries to specialized care until recently. Only a few countries (Sweden, Canada, the United Kingdom, and the Netherlands) have managed to maintain a reasonable balance. There is now clear evidence that comprehensive primary care has great potential to control the entry of patients to more expensive secondary and tertiary care, and is considerably less costly.

The political power of specialized hospitals and physicians continues to mean that the bulk of resources go to the high-technology health centers and surplus hospital beds in many countries. It is extraordinarily difficult to shift resources with any speed away from these locations and priorities toward greater primary care emphasis. Nonetheless, this is clearly the trend in Eastern and Central Europe as well as in Western Europe and North America.

Declining Emphasis on Inpatient Hospitalization

The primary care trend is supported by the need to cut costs and the clear indication that outpatient care can serve a high proportion of patients better than inpatient care. The length of inpatient care has also declined significantly because of improved surgical techniques and other treatment methods. Expansion of home health care means that many inpatients can be transferred home and cared for quite adequately at lower cost by family, well-trained nurses, and support personnel.

Entire hospitals are being abandoned in some countries (notably Canada) or converted to long-term care for the expanding dependent elderly population. In other cases, hospitals are shifting radically toward managed care through creation of their own insurance programs, through discounted contracts with managed care organizations for inpatient services, and through physician hospital organizations. Staff cuts have been widespread and drastic as institutions respond to declining numbers of patients. Surpluses of specialized physicians and other health professionals are noteworthy in several countries (for example, Germany, Canada, and the United States) partially as a consequence of this trend.

Equalization of Access

A strong case can be made that a more equal distribution of health care and health resources contributes to greater overall health status of the population. Several countries have demonstrated that a healthy population appears to be more productive (notably Sweden, the Netherlands, and Japan). There is also strong evidence that the highest per capita costs are associated with

- Lower-income individuals who do not have access to good public health services or primary health care and contract acute problems that might have been prevented
- The older population who contract chronic diseases that demand constant and expensive care, much of which also could have been minimized or avoided with adequate public health and primary care at younger ages.

The combination of improved primary care, coupled with better public health for deprived and elderly populations, thus has the potential to improve overall health status and lower health care costs over the long term. The countries with the best health status outcome indicators have come closest to realizing these goals.

Improved Cost Effectiveness

Cost effectiveness appears to be associated with greater investments in public health and primary care, decreased hospitalization, and equalization of access to care. Increasing cost effectiveness requires major realignment in allocation of resources, with less money going to expensive hospitals and other tertiary care centers, and more money going to prevention, basic primary care, and equalization. The political will to make these changes has proceeded farther in some countries than others.

Leaders are being forced to consider realignments if they are to exercise restraint in the growth of health care costs as expenditures approach or exceed 10 percent of GDP. They are faced with demands from consumers, on the one hand, for increased access and quality, and a need to ration the investment of resources, on the other. All countries are faced with further major decisions to achieve greater cost effectiveness if

the constant pressures to increase services and investments in technology are to be constrained (Organization for Economic Cooperation and Development, 1992: 147).

The Czech Republic, Hungary, Russia, and China were all low investors in health care until recently, and all have deliberately chosen to shift toward a competitive and partially private primary health care system. Each is drawing elements of experience from the Western European, Japanese, and American models—despite the evidence of cost pressures associated with fee-for-service medicine and consumer freedom of choice. They clearly find the cost effectiveness of mixed public/private models more appealing than the centralized public system that failed them in the past.

Information Flow and Internationalization of Health Care

Information technology has permitted and encouraged the international exchange of ideas and experience—allowing concepts that appear to work well in one country to be quickly adopted or adapted for use in another country. The concepts of "managed competition," "integrated delivery systems," and "diagnosis-related groups" as pricing or delivery mechanisms are examples of ideas that are being widely considered and applied in many countries. Health professionals—especially managers—are being encouraged by their organizations to secure foreign experience or exposure.

The evidence is mounting that advanced information systems are critical for efficient management, including monitoring health status and specific outcomes, measuring costs, determining satisfaction of consumers, and assessing general performance of the health care system. Adequate information is a key to the operation of integrated health systems, but also for establishing local and national health policy.

Information systems using risk-adjusted indices of patient outcomes have been used as a technique for measuring and comparing differences in treatments and application of technologies in two or more countries. Experimental controls are used to correct for sickness of patients when treatment or technology is applied—to avoid biasing results. The goal is to further improve quality of care through use of careful measurement of outcomes from various treatment and technology alternatives under varying conditions (DesHarnais and Simpson, 1992: 14).

There is general agreement that we can learn much from the experience of each other through use of electronic mail, facsimile (FAX) document exchange, the Internet, internationally shared databases, and other high-speed methods of communication as tools that facilitate exchange of experience. Health care is increasingly provided by large organizations that attempt to integrate policy, management, and delivery systems by using these advanced communication methods (Hunt, 1994: 51).

MAJOR REFORM ALTERNATIVES

The priorities noted earlier have been translated into reform efforts of various types as vehicles for moving toward one or more major changes. Several market concepts are among the methods in process of wide implementation or consideration (Kirkman-Liff, 1994: 11):

- Competition among insurers and providers
- Vertical or horizontal integration of services
- Development of advanced management and administrative knowledge and skills
- Privatization of services

Encouraging Greater Competition

Several nations with former centralized national health insurance systems now see advantages in competitive health care markets for increasing the efficiency and responsiveness of health care providers. Competition is of course a basic concept that has not always worked well for providing widespread

access and equity in the "free-market" system.

Competition with some level of government management has the potential to generate higher levels of quality, service, and cost control. As noted earlier, a variety of experiments with new forms of competition are underway, often in the form of deliberate efforts to provide greater choice of both insurers and providers. Examples include (Kirkman-Liff, 1994: 12)

- Managed competition
- Generating greater competition among insurers
- Separation of purchaser and provider

Managed competition. Several manifestations of managed competition are available. In the usual situation, physician and hospital provider groups secure contracts with private or public insurance organizations and are offered financial incentives to improve efficiency and quality. Competition takes place between providers who attempt to attract groups of patients with costs paid through capitated fees. Provider groups earn greater income if they are able to attract large numbers of patients and manage their care so as to provide high quality at a cost below the capitated fee (Kirkman-Liff, 1994: 12).

Early evidence suggests that managed competition results in greater provider productivity, reduced waiting times, and lower use of hospitals. Efficiencies are achieved by diminishing the excess capacity of hospitals through greater outpatient service and less inpatient care. Downsizing and decreased staffing are important outcomes, with consequent lower costs. Productivity is increased and wasted time for health professionals is diminished. Work load tends to rise for primary care providers and specialists (Ham et al., 1994: 24).

These features serve as part of the rationale for major increases in managed care in the United States. Projections indicate that numbers of patients served via this mode will rise rapidly over the next several years (Vincenzino, 1994: 32).

Another form of managed competition is practiced in Canada and Germany, where patient choice is limited to selecting between physicians or hospitals at given prices paid by provincial insurance or sickness funds. Physicians and hospitals compete for patients at fixed rates, although access to alternative hospitals without considerable travel often limits patient choice (Kirkman-Liff, 1994: 13).

Competition between insurers. Several countries are now encouraging competing insurance alternatives for the express purpose of creating innovations and efficiencies in the market as they seek customers. These experiments are based in part on the experience of managed care systems described earlier. Multiple insurance systems, on the other hand, are often criticized because they add extra layers of expensive administrative cost. The long-term effect on costs is not yet clear (Organization for Economic Cooperation and Development, 1994: 48).

Deliberately limiting insurance to a "single insurer and payer" has the advantage of greater payment efficiency while providing equitable treatment of all citizens. The disadvantage is lack of significant competition, which may have the effect over time of actually increasing costs. Innovations may not occur and alternative services or optional insurance may be severely limited (Organization for Economic Cooperation and Development, 1994: 48).

Separation of purchaser and provider. National health service systems in Sweden, the United Kingdom, the Czech Republic, and Hungary have traditionally merged provider and insurance in a single operating unit under government auspices, with consequent inefficiencies, quality problems, and impersonal treatment. The current changes separate "purchasers" from "providers." Government purchasing units (insurers) contract with physicians and hospitals (providers) for services at a negotiated rate (Vagero and Illsley, 1992: 230).

The physician as "fundholder" in the United Kingdom (discussed earlier) is an example. The insuring organizations allocate blocks of captitated funds to physician groups who provide primary care services to their patient lists. They manage services for patients by *buying* secondary and tertiary care on their behalf. The physician groups with substantial patient lists are able to bargain for better rates and may use any savings achieved to enhance their practices and incomes. However, patient choice is severely limited under this arrangement (Ham et al., 1994: 24).

Incentives for greater efficiency are achieved because capitated funds follow the patient to hospitals. Hospitals are reimbursed on a case-by-case basis and compete for patients by negotiating lower costs per patient. One of the outcomes of this practice has been shorter lengths of stay in hospitals (Ham et al., 1994: 25).

Integrated Networks

Greater formal interaction among primary care groups, hospital providers, mental health providers, and insurers or purchasers is considered advantageous from an efficiency perspective. These relationships need to be formally developed in many countries where primary care, public health, and specialized care are sharply separated. Mutual advantage and more effective competition in the health care marketplace can be achieved if linkages are formalized and enhanced by common information systems. Such systems can provide shared data about the population served, specific patient information, clinical procedures, financial inputs, and outcomes. Formal contracts tie institutions together and define the specific role of each partner in the network (Kirkman-Liff, 1994: 40).

Consumers, health professionals, and purchasers of care (insurers) can each play a major role. Effective management of the relationships in an integrated network is not always an easy task for senior managers or physicians who have been accustomed to maintaining primary control of the health care institutions. A new way of thinking and managing is required.

Management and Administration

The health problems of Eastern and Central Europe have been heavily attributed to centralized and unresponsive governments as well as very limited investment in health care. However, another major factor has clearly been the relative absence of modern management knowledge and processes. Managerial incompetence was evident at all levels, in part because personnel were selected on the basis of ideology and political connections rather than training and expertise. Improvement in managerial competence is among the highest priorities in the Czech Republic, Hungary, and Russia as they attempt to reform both public health systems and personal health care. Progress is already clearly evident in the Czech Republic and Hungary (Vagero and Illsley, 1992: 235).

Privatization

Privatization of insurance programs and health care delivery has become a primary reform strategy in several countries where publicly provided health care has been the norm—notably in the former communist nations of Central Europe and Eastern Europe as well as in China. The goal is to add quality and efficiency incentives, organizational innovation, competition, greater pluralism, and higher income potential for providers. The new private nonprofit insurance structures are coupled with private for-profit primary care providers in an effort to greatly increase the quality of services to consumers. Early results suggest much greater effectiveness than under the former centralized system, but at considerably higher cost.

THE CONVERGENCE OF HEALTH SYSTEMS

At the same time that the United States is moving toward some of the practices of European countries, and away from unrestrained free enterprise in health care, several other countries are experimenting with U.S. organizational innovations—such as DRGs and managed care. The United States is moving away from the case-based per diem method of hospital payment, and several European countries are adopting variations of this method as devices to increase competition and quality. In Europe, the movement is away from the integrated publicly sponsored health service approach toward multiple-payer contract insurance. The movement in the United States is toward greater integration (Organization for Economic Cooperation and Development, 1994: 50).

Several other signs of exchange and convergence are emerging:

- Greater management responsibility is delegated by national authorities to nongovernment entities in many countries, such as private for-profit or nonprofit insurers, groups of ambulatory care providers, and regional hospital organizations; governments are less inclined to be directly involved in management.

- A basic guaranteed package of benefits is provided to all citizens, but provision of benefits is through a pluralistic choice of providers. Supplemental benefits packages can be purchased privately to cover deductibles, co-payments, and additional services.

- Capitation as the method of payment for providers is replacing both fee for service and salaries in some countries, and a controlled form of fee for service continues to be viewed as desirable for purposes of quality care, provider incentives, and patient satisfaction—especially in countries shifting away from the centralized government health system.

- Payment to hospitals is increasingly on the basis of contracts with insurers, and is undertaken prospectively under capitation formulas; global budgets for hospitals have become the norm in many countries.

- Competition is increasing for patients among insurers, among providers, and between integrated insuring and providing organizations.

- Formal quality improvement and assurance procedures are becoming central to management and serve as the tools for measuring patient and organizational outcomes.

- Integrated management information systems are used to identify, measure, and control the flow of external information, patient records, financial data, and outcomes, while also serving as a link to insurers and other health care units in the community, region, and nationally. "Smart cards" containing patient data are used to identify, condense, and process patient information.
- Self-regulation of prices and expenditures through negotiation among the major stakeholders is becoming commonplace.

The newly decentralized, government-sponsored, health care systems in the former communist countries are each moving toward these patterns, although resource shortages have limited the speed with which changes are actually made (Vienonen and Wlodarczyk, 1993: 168).

MAJOR ISSUES FOR THE FUTURE

Despite the innovative efforts described earlier, perfected national organization, funding, and delivery mechanisms for health care remain elusive. The reforms remain incomplete. Moderation of health care cost increases has not been universally successful. Costs remain out of control in many countries.

Other continuing major issues include

- The degree of choice and freedom from constraint that should be reserved for both providers and patients
- The proper balance of government role vs. private responsibility in health care
- Assessment of the appropriate role, intensity, and cost of medical technology
- The proportion of health care costs that should be borne by the patient
- The proportion of individual and national income that should be allocated to health care
- The appropriate emphasis on quality of care, as opposed to cost control
- The level of appropriate control on entry of new physicians and other professionals as well as degree of specialized training that should be required

- The appropriate level of compensation for health professionals given their roles and costs
- The proportion of health resources that should be allocated to the older members of the population

Rapid aging of populations is possibly the greatest health care challenge in the developed countries. The very success of public health measures to increase longevity and decrease infant mortality, accompanied by lower birthrates, now means that larger proportions of citizens will be older, dependent, and in need of both Social Security support and health care. Fortunately, the health status of older people is improving, enabling them to provide much more of their own support into advanced age. The age of retirement, level of social support, and health care to be provided will be a continuing subject of ethical concern and political debate in all countries (Jazwiecki and Schwab, 1989: 366).

The European nations—particularly Sweden, Germany, France, and the United Kingdom—have the most advanced experience with this issue, because their populations are already considerably older on average than in North America or Asia. In all cases, they have developed universal health care systems, home health care, and other community services for the elderly that supplement family responsibility. Some medical procedures have been restricted for older people in the United Kingdom (Jazwiecki and Schwab, 1989: 368).

Serious Problems

A number of other serious problems can be noted (Mooney, 1988: 1):

- A growing gap between what citizens want and what the health care system can provide, given financial constraints
- The frustration for health professionals imposed by increased emphasis on consumer sovereignty in demanding personal attention and quality from the health care system

- The demand by health policy makers for an emphasis on greater consumer responsibility, in the form of co-payments, deductibles, and supplemental premiums
- Tension between available technology and ability of societies to pay for it
- Pursuit of both cost controls and maintenance of quality standards, with likely conflict between these worthy goals
- Struggle within and among the health professions over their respective roles, autonomy, and incomes, as available funds and employment opportunities are constrained
- Implications of inadequate benefits and required purchase of private insurance plans to fill the gaps in public coverage; premiums may or may not be affordable to employers as a means of gaining competitive advantage in the hiring of high-quality employees
- The shortcomings of managed competition as it replaces other insurance, including the uncertainties of a managed care environment that has not yet proven to be substantially more effective than other delivery formats for long-term cost control or as a satisfier of consumer needs

The resolution of these issues will take extensive experimentation and research over the ensuing years.

The discussion here focuses only on those nations at the relatively more advanced end of the economic development continuum. The problems of these advanced countries are modest compared to most countries, where even the minimal public health and primary care institutions are weak or missing. Major issues of access, cost, and quality are nonetheless common to most countries. The demand for services keeps rising as information is shared across international boundaries.

Increasing expectations among citizens, health professionals, and political leadership, for an expanded degree of access, a higher level of technology, and greater quality of care, are likely to be continuing issues in advanced countries and will certainly be characteristic of developing nations as well. The solutions noted here may be useful to policy makers in the less advanced nations—despite the wide disparity of development levels. The sharing of experience should be helpful as a means of avoiding some of the errors experienced in the advanced nations.

REFERENCES

DESHARNAIS, SUSAN I., and KIT N. SIMPSON (1992). Indices for Monitoring Hospital Outcomes in Developed Countries, *Health Policy*, 21: 1–15.

HAM, CHRIS, SUE ATKINSON, PETER GLUCKMAN, and RON KERR (1994). Why Travel Broadens the Mind, *Health Services Journal*, 104 (S406): 24–25.

HUNT, ROGER S. (1994). Health Care Management in the Global Village, *Frontiers of Health Services Management*, 11 (1): 50–52.

JAZWIECKI, TOM, and TERESA SCHWAB (1989). Conclusions, in Teresa Schwab (ed.), *Caring for an Aging World: International Models for Long-Term Care, Financing, and Delivery*. New York: McGraw-Hill, pp. 366–375.

KIRKMAN-LIFF, BRADFORD L. (1994). Management Without Frontiers: Health System Convergence Leads to Health Care Management Convergence, *Frontiers of Health Services Management*, 11 (1): 3–48.

ORGANIZATION FOR ECONOMIC COOPERATION AND DEVELOPMENT (1992). *The Reform of Health Care: A Comparative Analysis of Seven OECD Countries*. Paris: OECD.

ORGANIZATION FOR ECONOMIC COOPERATION AND DEVELOPMENT (1994). *The Reform of Health Care Systems: A Review of Seventeen OECD Countries*. Paris: OECD.

SCHNEIDER, MARKUS, RUDOLF K.-H. DENNERLEIN, AYNUR KOSE, and LEA SCHOLTES (1992). *Health Care in the EC Member States*. Amsterdam: Elsevier.

VAGERO, D., and R. ILLSLEY (1992). Inequality, Health and Policy in East and West Europe, *International Journal of Health Sciences*, 3 (3–4): 225–239.

VIENONEN, MIKKO A., and W. CEZARY WLODARCZYK (1993). Health Care Reforms on the European Scene: Evolution, Revolution, or Seesaw, *World Health Statistical Quarterly*, 46 (3): 166–169.

VINCENZINO, JOSEPH V. (1994). Developments in Health Care Costs—An Update, *Statistical Bulletin* (Metropolitan Insurance Company), 75 (1): 30–35.